ANTIQUITY

A World History

ANTIQUITY

A World History

FIRST EDITION

by Frank E. Smitha

M. THOMAS BELL PUBLISHING
LEXINGTON, KENTUCKY

M. Thomas Bell Publishing
P.O. Box 608 Cynthiana, KY 41031
mtbp33@yahoo.com

First published in print in 1999 by M. Thomas Bell Publishing.

Library of Congres Cataloging-in-Publication Data
Smitha, Frank E.
Antiquity, a World History
Library of Congress Catalog Card Number: 98-88782
ISBN 0-9669955-0-3 pbk.

Printed in the United States of America by McNaughton & Gunn Inc.

Contents

List of Text Maps

ANTIQUITY

A World History

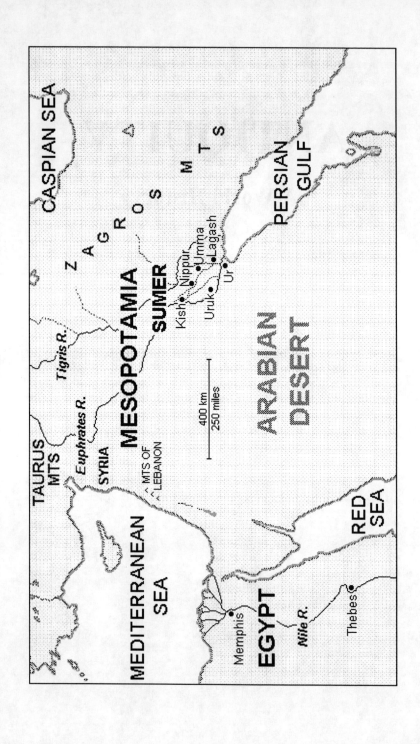

CHAPTER 1

GENESIS IN SUMER

SUMERIANS AND THEIR GODS

Sumerian writing is the oldest writing that archaeologists have discovered. The Sumerians wrote poetically, describing events as the work of their gods, and they wrote to please their gods. Their writing influenced those who came to Mesopotamia after them, and it influenced the people of Canaan and the Hebrews.

The Sumerians moved into Mesopotamia around 4000 BC, perhaps from the vicinity of the Caspian Sea. They found a people archaeologists call Ubaidians, who were living in villages, farming and using canals for irrigation, near where the Tigris and Euphrates rivers emptied into the Persian Gulf – an area that came to be known as Sumer. And they found in Sumer a people who spoke a Semitic language who had moved in among the Ubaidians.

By 3800 BC the Sumerians supplanted the Ubaidians and Semites, and the Sumerians were working toward their civilization. Sumerians cooperated with each other in building better canals for irrigating crops and for transporting crops by boat to village centers. They improved their roads, over which their donkeys trod, some of their donkeys pulling wheeled carts. The Sumerians grew in number, the increase in population the key element in creating what we call civilization – a word derived from an ancient word for *city*.

At least twelve cities arose among the Sumerians. Among them were Ur, Uruk, Kish and Lagash – Ur, for example, becoming a city of about 24,000 people. In the center of each city was a temple that housed the city's gods, and around each city were fields of grain, orchards of date palms, and land for herding. Besides planting and harvesting crops, some Sumerians hunted, fished, or raised livestock. In addition to an increase in population, civilization was also about variety, and enough food was produced to support people who worked at other occupations – such as the priesthood, pottery making, weaving, carpentry and smithing. There were also traders, and the Sumerians developed an extensive commerce by land and sea. They built seaworthy ships, and they imported from afar items made from the wood, stone, tin and copper not found nearby.

A Belief in Spirits

Like people who were not yet civilized, the Sumerians saw movement around them as the magic of spirits, magic being the only explanation they had for how things worked. These spirits were their gods, and with many spirits around, the Sumerians believed in many gods – gods that had human like emotions. The Sumerians believed that the sun, moon and stars were gods. They believed in a goddess of the reeds that grew around them and in a goddess of the beer that they distilled.

Sumerians believed that crops grew because of a male god mating with his goddess wife. They saw the hot and dry months of summer, when their meadows and fields turned brown, as a time of death of these gods. When their fields bloomed again in the autumn, they believed their gods were resurrected. They marked this as the beginning of their year, which they celebrated at their temples with music and singing.

The Sumerians could dig into the earth and within a few feet find water. They believed that the earth was a great disk floating on the sea. They called the sea Nammu, and they believed that Nammu was without a beginning in time. They believed that Nammu had created the fish they saw and the birds, wild pigs and other creatures that appeared on the marshy wet lands – a story of creation around two millennium before the Hebrews would put their own story of the creation into writing.

The Sumerians believed that Nammu created heaven and earth, heaven splitting from earth as being the male god, *An,* and the earth being a goddess called *Ki.* They believed that Ki and An had produced a son called Enlil, who was atmosphere, wind and storm. The Sumerians believed that Enlil separated the day from night and that he had opened an invisible shell and let waters fall from the sky. They believed that with his mother, Ki, Enlil set the stage for the creation of plants, humans and other creatures, that he made seeds grow, that he shaped humanity from clay and imbued it, as it states in Genesis 2:7, with "the breath of life."

The Sumerians believed that humanity had been created to serve the gods, and they served their gods with sacrificial offerings and supplications. They believed that the gods controlled the past and the future, that whatever skills they possessed their gods had revealed to them, and they believed that their gods provided them with all they needed to know. They had no vision of their civilization as having developed by their own efforts against worldly conditions. They had no vision of technological or social progress, and they saw no need of knowledge to aspire to beyond what they already knew.

Nevertheless, Sumerian priests altered the stories that they told. They let human invention intrude into their religious life and created a new twist to old tales, serving that which would be common with religious belief for millennia to come: change. But, consistent with their tradition, they failed to acknowledge this as a human induced change of any sort. They gave no thought to a change in their story meaning that they had failed to get it right the first time. New ideas were simply revelations from the gods. The Sumerians did not recognize interpretation. They saw no need for rules of reason. No evidence remains in their writings of their respecting doubt or that they understood any benefit from suspended judgment. These, along with a distinction between spirit and matter, would come in a later age, beginning with self-examination, attempts at analyzing matter, and attempts at an all encompassing consistency called philosophy, and they would be served by the rise of science and a belief in change and progress.

The priests did believe in axioms. A part of the change they had made in their religion was working their stories about their gods into axioms. Sometime around 2500 BC, Enlil became the greatest of the gods and the god who punished people and watched over their safety and well being. Like the gods of other ancient peoples, Enlil was a god who dwelled somewhere. He was a god of place, and that place was the city was Nippur, a sacred city believed to have been inhabited at first only by divine beings.

By around 2500 BC, the Sumerians were individualistic enough to believe in personal gods – gods with whom individuals had a covenant. Individuals no longer prayed just for the community. Sumerian society was dominated by males, and Sumerian scholars claimed that the head of every family – a male – and every other adult male had his personal god. Men hoped that their god would intercede for them in the assembly of gods and provide them with a long life and good health. In exchange, they glorified their god with prayers, supplications and sacrifices while continuing to worship the other gods in the Sumerian pantheon of gods.

A Belief in Sin

Believing that the gods had given them all they had, the Sumerians saw the intentions of their gods as good, and believing that their gods had great powers and controlled their world, the Sumerians needed an explanation for their hardships and misfortunes. The obvious explanation was that their hardships and misfortunes were the result of human deeds that displeased the gods – in a word, sin. They believed that when someone displeased the gods, these gods let demons punish the offender with sickness, disease or environmental disasters.

The Sumerians experienced infrequent rains that sometimes created disastrous floods, and they believed that these floods were punishments created by a demon god that lived in the depths of the Gulf of Persia. And to explain the misfortunes and suffering of infants, the Sumerians believed that sin was inborn, that never was a child born without sin. Therefore, wrote a Sumerian, when one suffered it was best not to curse the gods but to glorify them, to appeal to them, and to wait patiently for their deliverance.

Conflicts Among the Gods

In giving their gods human characteristics, the Sumerians projected onto their gods the conflicts they found among themselves. Sumerian priests wrote of a dispute between the god of cattle, Lahar, and his sister Ashnan, the goddess of grain. Like some other gods, these gods were vain and wished to be praised. Each of the two sibling gods extolled his and her own achievements and belittled the achievements of the other.

The Sumerians saw another dispute between the minor gods Emesh (summer) and his brother Enten (winter). Each of these brothers had specific duties in creation – like Cain the farmer and Able the herdsmen. The god Enlil put Emesh in charge of producing trees, building houses, temples, cities and other tasks. Enlil put Enten in charge of causing ewes to give birth to lambs, goats to give birth to kids, birds to build nests, fish to lay their eggs and trees to bear fruit. And the brothers quarreled violently as Emesh challenged Enten's claim to be the farmer god.

A dispute existed also between the god Enki and a mother goddess, Ninhursag – perhaps originally the earth goddess Ki. Ninhursag made eight plants sprout in a divine garden, plants created from three generations of goddesses fathered by Enki. These goddesses were described as having been born "without pain or travail." Then trouble came as Enki ate the plants that Ninhursag had grown. Ninhursag responded with rage, and she pronounced a curse of death on Enki, and Enki's health began to fail. Eight parts of Enki's body – one for each of the eight plants that he ate – became diseased, one of which was his rib. The goddess Ninhursag then disappeared so as not let sympathy for Enki change her mind about her sentence of death upon him. But she finally relented and returned to heal Enki. She created eight healing deities – eight more goddesses – one for each of Enki's ailing body parts. And the goddess who healed Enki's rib was Nin-ti, a name that in Sumerian meant "lady of the rib," which describes a character who was to appear in a different role in Hebrew writings centuries later, a character to be called Eve.

Writing

The Ubaidians may have introduced the Sumerians to the rudiments of writing and recorded numerical calculation, but the Sumerians believed that the gods had given them these skills. And writing appears to have spread among the Sumerians with the rise in trade, with the need to calculate and to keep records of supplies and goods exchanged. The Sumerians wrote arithmetic based on units of ten – the number of fingers on both hands. Concerned about their star-gods, they mapped the stars and divided a circle into units of sixty, from which our own system of numbers, and seconds and minutes, are derived. The Sumerians wrote by pressing picture representations into wet clay with a pen, and they dried the clay to form tablets. Instead of developing their writing all at once, as one might expect with divine revelation, they developed their writing across centuries. They streamlined their pictures into symbols called ideograms. Then they added symbols for spoken sounds – phonetic letters – which had the advantage of representing ideas with fewer symbols than ideograms.

PROPERTY, POWER AND POLITICS

Early in Sumerian civilization, eighty to ninety percent of those who farmed did so on land they considered theirs rather than communal property. Here too the Sumerians were expressing a trend that was common among others. Another individual effort was commerce, and with a growth in commerce the Sumerians had begun using money, which made individual wealth more easily measured and stored. Commerce required initiative, imagination, an ability to get along with people and luck, and, of course, some merchants were more successful than were others. Farming took stamina, strength, good health, good luck and organization. And some farmers were more successful than were other farmers.

Those farmers who failed to harvest enough to keep themselves in food and seed borrowed from those who had wealth in surplus. Those who borrowed hoped that their next harvest would give them the surplus they needed to repay their loan. But if the next harvest were also inadequate, to meet their obligations they might be forced to surrender their lands to the lender or to work for him. When Sumerians lost their land, they or their descendants might become sharecroppers: working the lands of successful landowners in exchange for giving the landowners a good portion of the crops they grew.

Accompanying divisions in wealth was a division in power, and power among the Sumerians passed to an elite. Sumerian priests had once worked the fields alongside others, but now they were separated from commoners. A corporation run by priests became the greatest landowners among the Sumerians. The priests hired the poor to work their land and claimed that land was really owned by the gods. Priests had become skilled as scribes, and in some cities they sat with the city's council of elders. These councils wielded great influence, sometimes in conflict with a city's king.

Common Sumerians remained illiterate and without power, while kings, once elected by common people, became monarchs. The monarchs were viewed as agents of and responsible to the gods. Governments drafted common people to work on community projects, and common people were obliged to pay taxes to the government in the form of a percentage of their crops, which the city could either sell or use to feed its soldiers and others it supported. And priests told commoners that their drudgery was necessary to allow the gods their just leisure.

Men Dominate Women

Physically stronger than women, men could rule women by brute force, and in societies where men were the warriors, it was they who got together and made the decisions. Among the Sumerians, this domination was sanctioned and collectivized into law. In Sumerian society it had become accepted that females were under the control of males. If a husband died, the widow came under the control of her former husband's father or brother, or if she had a grown son under his control. A woman in Sumer had no recourse or protection under the law. A woman's only power, if she had any, was the influence of her personality within her family.

Education

Early in Sumerian civilization, schooling was associated with the priesthood and took place in temples. But this changed, and an education apart from the temples arose for the children of affluent families, who paid for this education – and with men dominating women, most if not all students were males. The students were obliged to work hard at their studies, from sun up to sun down. Not believing in change, there was no probing into the potentials of humankind or study of the humanities. Their study was "practical" – rote learning of complex grammar and practice at writing. Students were encouraged with praise while their inadequacies and failures were punished with lashes from a stick or cane.

War and Slavery

As Sumerian cities grew in population and expanded, the virgin swamps that had insulated city from city disappeared. And, like other peoples, the Sumerians were inclined to empathize more with those closer to themselves and inclined to see their own interests more clearly than those distant from them. Sumerians from different cities were unable or unwilling to resolve their conflicts over land and the availability of water, and wars between Sumerian cities erupted – wars they saw as between their gods.

Eventually, the Sumerians made slaves of other Sumerians they had captured in their wars with each other, but originally they acquired their slaves from peoples beyond Sumer. The Sumerian name for a female slave was mountain girl, and a male slave was called mountain man. The Sumerians used their slaves mainly as domestics and concubines. And they justified their slavery as would others: that their gods had given them victory over an inferior people.

Wars with distant people were fueled by the greed and ambitions of kings. The Sumerians described this in a poetic tale of conflict between the king of Uruk and the distant town of Arrata, a tale written by a Sumerian some five hundred years after the event, a tale of which only fragments remain. Here was reporting as it would be for more than three thousand years, as it would be with Homer and his Iliad, the sacred writings of Hindus and with the Old Testament, with gods in command and not disapproving of war.

Among the Sumerian cities was an impulse to be supreme, and, around 2800 BC, Kish had become the first of the cities to dominate the whole of Sumer. Then Kish's supremacy was challenged by the city of Lagash, which launched a bloody conquest against its Sumerian neighbors and extended its power beyond Sumerian lands. A bas-relief sculpture uncovered by archaeologists depicts a king of Lagash celebrating his victory over the city of Umma, the king's soldiers, with helmets, shields and pikes, standing shoulder to shoulder and line behind line over the corpses of their defeated enemy.

Dissent

The variety of populous, civilized life produced differing opinions, and dissent – something authoritarians would never be able to extinguish. Sumerians complained. One wrote that he was a "thoroughbred steed" but drawing a cart carrying "reeds and stubble." Another complained in writing of the stupidity in one city taking enemy lands and then the enemy coming and taking its lands. Rather than docility, people in the city of Lagash instigated history's first recorded revolt. This came after Lagash's rulers had increased local taxes and restricted personal freedoms. Lagash's bureaucrats had grown in wealth. And the people of Lagash resented this enough that they overthrew their king and brought to power a god-fearing ruler named Urukagina, who eliminated excessive taxation and rid the city of usurers, thieves and murderers – the first known reforms.

PARADISE, THE FALL OF
HUMANKIND AND A GREAT FLOOD

Clinging to their belief in the goodness and power of their gods and wondering about their sin and the toil and strife with which they lived, the Sumerians imagined a past in which people lived in a god-created paradise. This was expressed in the same poetic tale that described the conflict between the king of Uruk and the distant town of Arrata – the earliest known description in writing of a paradise and the fall of humankind. The poem describes a period when there were no creatures that threatened people – no snakes, scorpions, hyenas, or lions – a period in which humans knew no terror. There was no confusion among various peoples speaking different languages, with everyone praising the god Enlil in one language. Then, according to the poem, something happened that enraged the god Enki (the god of wisdom and water who had organized the earth in accordance with a general plan laid down by Enlil). The clay tablet on which the poem was written is damaged at this point, but the tablet indicates that Enki found some sort of inappropriate behavior among humans. Enki decided to put an end to the golden age, and in the place of the golden age came conflict, wars and a confusion of languages.

On another clay tablet, surviving fragments of a poem describe the gods as having decided that humans were evil and the gods as having created a flood "to destroy the seed of humanity," a flood that raged for seven days and seven nights. The tablet describes a huge boat commanded by a king named Ziusudra, who was preserving vegetation and the seed of humankind. His boat was "tossed about by the windstorms on the great waters." When the storm subsided, the god Utu – the sun – came forward and shed light on heaven and earth. The good king Ziusudra opened a window on the boat and let in light from Utu. Then Ziusudra prostrated himself before Utu and sacrificed an ox and a sheep for the god.

CHAPTER 2

AFRICA AND EGYPT, TO 1750 B.C.

EARLY AGRICULTURE AND HERDING

Between 9000 and 4000 BC, northern Africa and the Sahara were grass and woodland with an abundance of rainfall, rivers, lakes, fish and other aquatic life. Anthropologists speculate that from North Africa's Mediterranean coast, people migrated into the Sahara and that people migrated into the Sahara from the south. There communities raised sheep and goats, as people did along the Mediterranean coast. And communities of people fished in the lakes and rivers of the region, using intricately made bone harpoons and fishing hooks, some using nets with weights and other tools for harvesting aquatic creatures. Living a settled life, people began using pottery and growing food, using stone and wooden tools. To the east, along the upper Nile, including what was to be Nubia, people by 6000 BC were growing sorghum and millet and a wheat believed to be of African origin. And by 4000 BC, people in the middle of the Sahara region were raising cattle. Then around 3500 BC the climate of North Africa began to dry, perhaps in part because of overgrazing – wetness needing vegetation as well as vegetation needing water. The Sahara started to change from grass and woodland to desert.

Anthropologists speculate that some people fled the drying to the northern Nile River, taking with them their cultivation of wheat, barley, flax, various vegetables and their goats and sheep. And perhaps some people in western Sahara retreated southward to wetter land, taking with them their pigs, sheep, goats, cattle and knowledge of farming. In the Ethiopian highlands, herding and farming appeared, people there growing a cereal crop called tef and starchy stalks called *enset*. Remaining in the Sahara region were sparse populations of dark-skinned people and also a blue-eyed people called Berbers, the Berbers occupying territory near the Mediterranean Sea. Those who had migrated to the northern Nile were related to the Berbers, or at least the languages of the two people were related – a language classified as *Afro-Asian*. And scholars speculate that the Afro-Asian dialect had origins with people who had come to Africa from the eastern side of the Red Sea.

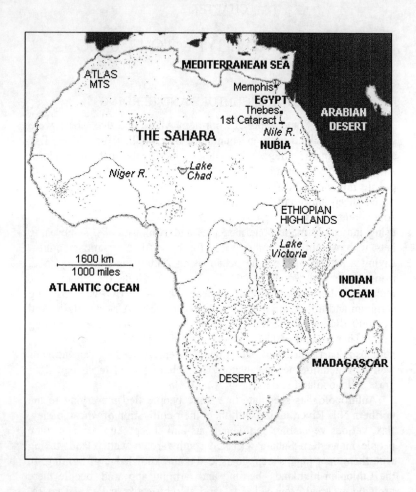

Meanwhile, in Africa south of the desert region many had begun small-scale farming and raising cattle. Those living in the continent's equatorial forests continued to rely almost exclusively on their hunting and gathering, which provided them with all they needed. It would be want and deprivation elsewhere that would mother new ways of doing things, and these people saw no reason to hack clearings to grow food that was already sufficient for their few numbers.

South of the Sahara, the raising of cattle was at first limited to regions without the blood sucking tsetse fly, which could spread disease fatal to both cattle and people. It took many generations for people to build immunities to local diseases, which kept migrant communities from growing in the moist valleys and thickly wooded regions where the tsetse fly thrived. In some other parts of Africa where inadequate rain or other conditions discouraged farming, people continued to gather food that grew wild. Using exquisitely handcrafted spears, bows and arrows, animal snares and poisons, they hunted small game. And with food supply limited, the populations of these various areas remained sparse, unlike what was developing along the northern Nile.

CIVILIZATION ARISES IN EGYPT

The waters of the Nile came from annual rains in the tropics to the south of Egypt. The Nile rose in early July, and in October it receded, leaving little water and a layer of black, fertile soil – inspiring people there to call the area the Black Land. Where the soil retained enough moisture, people could grow crops. But for farming to thrive along the Nile, a system of controlling its waters was necessary. To increase their ability to plant, people along the Nile trapped waters when the river rose, and they lined their water basins with clay to prevent the water from sinking into the soil – so there would be water to use when the river dried again. From sometime around 3500 BC the Egyptians began building a system of dikes and sluices, and around this time Egypt began growing food in greater abundance than elsewhere in Africa. They grew wheat, barley, beans, lettuce, peas, radishes, onions, olives, dates and figs, and they raised cattle, sheep, goats and pigs. The construction would continue for more than a millennium so that by 2000 BC both sides of the Nile would be a checkerboard of water basins, sluices and canals, with water being drawn from basins upstream whenever water was insufficient downstream.

As desert, Egypt had no violent storms. Egypt had no great floods – nor myth of a great flood. Nor did the Egyptians have the problem with accumulation of salt which periodically ruined Sumerian farms. And living in a desert, Egyptians had little to fear from wild animals. People along the Nile worked with more cheer and confidence than did the people in Sumer. The abundance of food along the Nile allowed a rise in population greater than elsewhere in Africa, and, along the Nile, small villages with rectangular houses of dried mud grew into towns. The abundance of food and population growth needed for civilization had occurred along the Nile. As in Sumer, enough food was produced to support a variety of non-farmers: traders, merchants, craftsmen, priests, scribes and soldiers. And having the same basic nature as the people of Sumer, people held land as personal property. Some farmers were most successful than others and grew richer. Class divisions arose, as did local governments. Irrigation systems and grain storage had to be maintained, property divisions had to be maintained and disputes mitigated. Large landowners formed aristocracies and allied themselves with kings, or chose who would be king, while most people remained small farmers and were expected to give a share of their crops to their king as taxes and to give free labor for community projects.

War and Peace in Egypt

As among the Sumerians, communities came into conflict and warred against each other. Local kings vied with each other for wider power and control. And by 3200 BC, people along the northern 600 miles (960 kilometers) of the Nile had amalgamated into a northern and a southern kingdom. The two kingdoms remained antagonistic toward each other, and in what was most likely a series of wars across generations during the 2900s, one of the kingdoms conquered the other. The conquering king, according to legend, was Menes – the first king of all Egypt.

With the unification of Egypt came a new era of peace and security along the Nile. Along with unity, peace was served too by natural barriers against wandering tribes: the Mediterranean Sea in the north, vast deserts to the east and west, and a great mountain range to the south. Peace benefited Egypt's economy. Egypt's new dynasty of kings provided work for an increasing number of craftsmen. Carpentry increased, aided by the use of copper tools. Brick and stone of fine quality were drawn from nearby quarries and used in building.

Egypt's trade expanded. Tradesmen went north by sea along the coast of the eastern Mediterranean, to the Mountains of Lebanon, from which they imported timber. They traveled south along the Red Sea to the coast just east of the Ethiopian Highlands, south to the coast of eastern-most Africa, and to the southern coast of the Arabian peninsula. They found ivory, rare animals, sweets and the incense that they were to burn in their temples. They traveled south along the Nile into Nubia, and there they acquired more incense and ivory, ebony, animal skins, and boomerangs. And, on at least one occasion, they found a pygmy from the Congo basin, whose appearance entertained the court of Egypt's king.

Contact with other peoples brought one of human history's most recurring developments: the adopting of ideas and techniques. From Mesopotamia, the Egyptians acquired the use of bronze, shipbuilding techniques and artistic motifs. The Egyptians learned to write – not gradually and starting with pictographs as the Sumerians had. Instead, they started writing suddenly, with script that had a Sumerian structure. But with time, Egypt's script became distinctively Egyptian.

EGYPTIAN RELIGION AND AUTOCRACY

Egyptian kings (*pharaohs* in Egyptian) put members of their immediate or extended families in charge of their government's central administration. The kings functioned as makers of law, as chiefs of justice and as supreme priest. And they passed their power and property to their sons. A distance had developed between the kings and common people, and official priests prohibited common people from using rituals that were believed suitable only for the king. And commoners were not recognized as having an afterlife like the king and his associates.

Much of Egyptian writing was religious in nature and concerned with the king's religion, and both the religion of the king and that of the masses had much in common with humanity's earliest religions. The workings of nature were explained as the magic of the gods and as secrets kept by the gods. Seeing spirit as will and the world as working by magic, the Egyptians believed that spirits could permeate anything. They believed that spirits moved in and out of objects and people, that sickness and dreams, being unwilled, were invasions by spirits. And, like the Sumerians, the Egyptians believed that the gods gave order to the world.

Like the religion of the Sumerians, Egyptian religion was built on descriptions of the world created from imagination, passed down from generation to generation and acquiring the authority of tradition. These myths were literal explanations as to how things came to be. Rationalizing myths into abstract poetic symbols would come millennia later. Like the Sumerians, the Egyptians had no idea as to what was distinctly matter and what was distinctly spirit. Also like the Sumerians, the Egyptians had a creation mythology. The religion of the kings and commoners described the world as having begun in watery chaos and the sun as a god having risen from this chaos. The Egyptians believed that while having risen to a mountain top, their sun-god gave form to the universe and created other gods and all living things. They saw their sun god rising each day in the east, descending in the west and disappearing under the world. They saw this descent as a daily death for their sun god, and they saw their sun god as born again each morning as it rose again in the east.

Before Egypt was unified, various communities along the Nile had different names for their sun god. Then, conquest and unification of Egypt brought unification in religion. An aggressive priesthood from the center of power, at the city of Memphis, spread worship of the sun god called *Re* across the whole of Egypt. The various gods belonging to various shrines along the Nile were joined into a single pantheon of gods with whom the kings of Egypt associated themselves.

From claiming that they ruled Egypt in behalf of the gods, Egypt's kings began to claim that they had been born by the gods, that they were the son or the incarnation of Re. Among the Egyptians the belief spread that their kings were immaculately conceived. The kings believed that as members of the family of the gods they had to keep their bloodline untainted, and, to protect the purity of their blood, kings married their sons to their daughters.

Life after Death

The Egyptians mummified their kings, believing that so long as a king's body survived – and so long as his spirit was fed by offerings of food – his spirit would survive and he would continue in his watch over their safety. A king's organs were preserved in jars, his heart believed to be the center of his being. And not knowing what the king's brain was for, the Egyptians threw it away.

The Egyptians saw death as one's spirit moving to a world that the living could not see, to the underworld where the sun went after it set, a place where the social order was the same as in life, with commoners remaining commoners and aristocrats and kings remaining aristocrats and kings. People believed that while their dead king was in the underworld he remained with his body, and to provide their dead king's body a grand place to reside they built great burial chambers of limestone and granite. The king's burial chamber was decorated with artistic depictions of his happier moments so he could cling to that which pleased him. And into the burial chamber the Egyptians put artifacts that they believed would migrate in spiritual form with the king to the underworld.

Egyptians who had little fear of the gods robbed the king's tombs of its treasures, and after this was discovered the burial chambers of kings were put into great pyramids, which allowed more space to hide the king's tomb. One pyramid was the labor of as many as ten thousand workers on the scene at any one time: craftsmen, engineers and common laborers. Smaller pyramids were built for the king's officials and overseers. Believing that the universe had been created from the

top of a mountain shaped like a pyramid, the Egyptians believed that
from the peak of the pyramid the spirit of the king would begin its
climb up to a unity with the god Re. They believed that the king's spirit
would accompany Re on his daily journey across the sky and into the
underworld.

The Osiris Legend

Like Sumerian religion, Egyptian religion changed. New ideas were
added to old ideas – despite instances of disharmony. One new twist in
Egyptian religion was the Osiris myth. Osiris was a local god from
southern Egypt who developed into one of Egypt's more important
gods. By 2400 BC, Egyptians believed that when the pharaoh died he
became the god Osiris. Osiris was seen as the spirit of a real former
king, a king who had been murdered by a jealous brother. The brother
of the god Osiris was Seth, who was said to have sliced Osiris' body
into parts and to have thrown them into the Nile. It was said that Osiris'
queen, Isis, grieved and collected the pieces of her husband's body for
a proper burial so that his spirit could live among the dead. She invoked
the magic of the gods and put her husband's body together again. And,
together again, Osiris became ruler of the spirits in the underworld as
he had been among those who lived above ground.

The Egyptians believed that as god and ruler of the underworld,
Osiris exercised expanded magical powers, that he granted all new life,
including the sprouting of vegetation. They believed that Osiris made
the annual flooding of the Nile, and they believed that all people had
been cannibals until Osiris taught humanity how to make agricultural
tools and to grow crops. They came to view Osiris as a god of nature, a
god of imperishable life. His evil brother Seth became a god of sterility
whom the Egyptians associated with the sandy, barren desert east and
west of the Nile. Osiris, the Egyptians believed, passed into one's body
when one ate his creation: vegetables – which may have helped
Egyptian mothers in feeding their children. Isis became the Egyptian
ideal of womanhood. Egyptians believed that it was she who gave
women their techniques in grinding grain and weaving cloth, and that it
was she who gave to humanity the concept of marriage. And Isis was a
model for women mourning the death of their husbands.

Mixed into the Osiris myth was the falcon god, Horace – the son of
Osiris and Isis. Because falcons sometimes flew so high that Egyptians
lost sight of them, the Egyptians came to think of falcons as lords of the
sky associated with their sun god. According to the Osiris legend, Isis
sent Horace to avenge the death of Osiris. And Horace became the
avenger of all evils.

Other Gods

The Egyptians also believed in a god called Thoth, who was the moon, a god of learning and the inventor of writing, all languages and social order. Thoth was believed to have a wife, the goddess Ma'at, who embodied truth and justice. And the Egyptians believed that one was living in accordance with Ma'at when one did no harm to other people or to cattle.

The Egyptians believed in a goddess of war that had the form of a lioness – in keeping with their belief that war was part of a natural order. They saw cats as like this lioness and therefore as gods, and, because the cats were gods, the Egyptians mummified them. They saw crocodiles as threatening and therefore as embodiments of a demon god. But because crocodiles appeared on sandbanks of the Nile when the river declined, the Egyptians associated this god also with the return of land.

Like many other ancient peoples, the Egyptians believed in the godliness of bulls. Bulls were respected for their physical power, and the Egyptians believed that a bull's presence renewed the fertility of their fields. The Egyptians chose one bull as a god to represent all bulls. Women stripped naked before this bull in hope of ensuring their ability to bear children. Like other peoples, the Egyptians saw their gods as revealing knowledge in small portions, and the Egyptians asked questions of their bull god by taking the bull down a path lined with opposing propositions written on pots. They perceived the bull as choosing between the propositions according to which side it swayed its head. And when the god bull died, the Egyptians mummified its body, and a new bull was chosen as its replacement.

Spirit and Healing

An examination of Egyptian bones and mummies reveals that the ancient Egyptians suffered from arthritis, pneumonia, pleurisy, kidney stones, gallstones, appendicitis and broken bones. The Egyptians also experienced terrible epidemics, including small pox and tuberculosis. They suffered from various waterborne parasitic worms, and they probably suffered from many other illnesses that are known today. The Egyptians saw disease as the work of the demon goddess Sekhmet, and they saw their gods Re, Thoth and Isis as important healing gods. To treat their maladies, especially at the king's court, the Egyptians had physicians and dentists. They had specialists in gynecology and veterinary medicine. They treated internal illnesses, eye and skin diseases, and they used emetics and bandages. They chanted incantations while one of various medicines was applied: beer, woman's milk mixed with oil and salts, goat's milk with honey, oils or other plant and animal substances. And they tried exorcisms to remove from one's body whatever evil spirit was creating the illness.

POLITICAL CHANGE

Egypt's politics, like its religion, changed. Local authorities who had been appointed by ministers at the king's court were allowed to bequeath their positions to their sons. Their descendants became hereditary nobles, and they believed that their positions were part of the god-given order. The new hereditary nobles wished to be united with Osiris after death, as was the king. And if the opportunity presented itself – if a king were weak or lazy – some nobles ruled their domains without interference from the king.

Family feuds among royalty and problems involving the succession of kings, led to the demise of many Egyptian dynasties. When the eighth dynasty collapsed around 2130 BC, local nobles took control over what had been units of the king's army stationed in their area, and they began to rule on their own. Kings remained at least in name, but for two centuries no king ruled over the whole of Egypt, and common people suffered under the control of the local nobles. This happened at the peak of one of North Africa's drier periods, and perhaps a period of low flooding of the Nile, and there was widespread famine. Unable to express their wills by voting, common Egyptians expressed their wills as had the people of Lagash: they rebelled. Anarchy swept over Egypt. Peasants seized property and servants overpowered their masters and made their masters servants. It was written that the high born were full of lamentations and the poor full of joy. And taking advantage of the anarchy, people from Nubia (called Cush by the Egyptians) came north and settled in Egypt, as did mercenaries from elsewhere.

The uprisings were disorganized, as rebellions usually are. Rebellions in different areas failed to unite with each other, and eventually nobles with armies suppressed the uprisings. Amid the warring, the same tendency that brought unity to Egypt a thousand years before brought unity to Egypt again. One ruler (from Thebes) spread his power over the whole of Egypt. Shortly thereafter (around 1900 BC) a king, to be known as Amenemhet I, usurped power at Thebes. He began a new dynasty – the twelfth. And his rule was to be different from that of pharaohs of previous dynasties.

The new king had learned from the past. He believed that it was his duty to promote justice – as embodied in the goddess Ma'at. The worship of Ma'at now included a belief that during the social upheavals the gods had abandoned Egypt and that it had been prophesied that a king would come and end the injustice. And it was believed that the prophecy had been fulfilled. The king was aware that poor people and nobles expected their king to be more concerned with their welfare than had kings centuries before, that they expected a system of justice that redressed mistreatment. The king and his ministers were more concerned than were previous kings about protecting common people from exploitation. The king opened positions in government to people of ability from outside his family.

Nobles were allowed to retain some of their powers, and they received recognition of the place in the afterlife that they had wanted. Commoners were also recognized as having an afterlife, and it was now believed that commoners would meet Osiris when they died, and that Osiris, working with Ma'at, would judge people entering the underworld. The Egyptians now believed that before one entered the underworld, his or her sins were put onto scales of justice. An ostrich feather represented Ma'at, and if an individuals sins outweighed the ostrich feather he was rejected. Commoners saw their sins as weighing little, for most of them expected an eternal afterlife of paradise in pleasant labor, maintaining their earthy status amid kindly gods.

Peace and stability had returned to Egypt. The trade that had fallen away during the upheavals returned, and the kings of the Twelfth Dynasty, from around 1900 to 1750 BC, helped Egypt's trade and economy rise to new heights. But not all Egyptians were content. Hopes had been raised, and some Egyptians expressed disappointment. More than a thousand years before the prophets of the Old Testament, an Egyptian priest wrote a denunciation of the rich for what he saw as their injustice to the poor. He wrote that the poor still had no power to save themselves from the abuse of those who were younger and stronger than they. Another Egyptian, Amenemope, wrote a book of thirty chapters that objected to how society was structured. He wrote that people should earn their bread by their own labors, that they should be content with little, should tolerate the weaknesses of others, should forgive others their transgressions and should rely on their gods for serenity.

CHAPTER 3

NEW SOCIETIES IN WEST ASIA

INVADERS AGAINST SINNERS

In Mesopotamia, just north of the Sumerians, a Semitic people had settled. And pushing on the Sumerians, a dynasty of Semitic kings came to rule the city of Kish. There, around 2400 BC, a former cup-bearer to one of these kings overthrew the ruling dynasty. With good military tactics that included holding and fighting from high ground, he extended his rule. He defeated the Sumerian king of Nippur, where the Sumerian god Enlil was believed to dwell. He claimed that his victories were given to him by Enlil. And he became known as Sargon the Great.

Sargon established his capital near Kish, at a city called Agade – which has never been located by archaeologists. Sargon's kingdom became known as Akkad – derived from the name Agade. His warriors were an aristocracy that lived off the taxes collected from conquered farmers and artisans. And his empire became commercial, with fortresses at strategic points along its trade routes. These were times in West Asia when bronze weapons had replaced those of stone, and supplying an army with bronze weapons required control over trade routes that gave access to the tin and copper from which bronze is made. Perhaps responding to this need for tin and copper, Sargon extended his empire northwest into Syria, and some scholars speculate that he crossed the Taurus Mountains and extended his empire into the center of Asia Minor. He placed governors throughout his empire to rule in his name. He built himself a library of thousands of clay tablets. And to help unite his empire he built an efficient system of roads and a postal service.

Sargon passed power to his son, creating a new dynasty of kings. Around 2150 BC, during the rule of Sargon's grandson, Naramsin, a wave of nomads called Gutians, from the east, overran Agade and Sumer. Why Naramsin was unable to defeat the invaders is unknown. His empire may have been weakened by drought and famine or by plague. But like the Sumerians, the people of Agade saw adversity as the work of displeased gods, and they interpreted the Gutian invasion

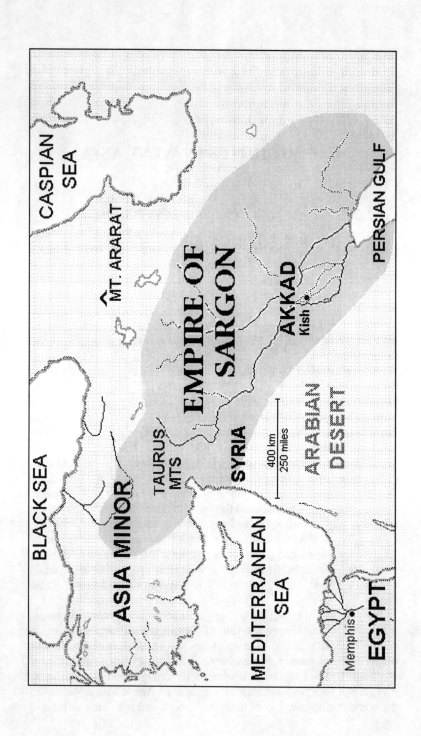

as the result of their goddess Inanna having left their city because of Naramsin's sins.

After only a hundred years, Sargon's empire became a memory, but Sargon remained as a legend. It was said that Sargon's mother had abandoned him in a cradle of reeds, that she had placed the cradle on one of Mesopotamia's great rivers and that Sargon had been found and adopted by Sumerians – a story similar to one which would emerge centuries later about a man called Moses.

Revival and Demise of the Sumerians

After the fall of Sargon's empire, war erupted between the Sumerians and Gutians, and the Sumerians exterminated or evicted the Gutians. Sumerian civilization revived, including rule in the city of Ur by a king called Ur-Nammu, who, around the year 2050, created the first known code of laws. Ur-Nammu created retribution and punishment in the form of fines, superseding the justice of an eye for an eye and tooth for a tooth. He was described as having removed the "grabbers" of the citizen's oxen, sheep and donkeys, as having established laws that guarded an orphan or widow from anyone who might wish to exploit them, and as having guarded the poor from the rich.

The Sumerian renaissance lasted until about 1950 BC, when Sumer was attacked by Elamites from the Zagros Mountains, just east of Mesopotamia. And Sumer was attacked by a Semitic-speaking people from Syria who became known as *Amorites* (a word meaning *westerner*). The Amorites sacked and burned Sumerian cities. And Sumerians wrote lamentations, complaining that the blood of their people filled holes in their grounds like hot bronze in a mold. They wrote of bodies dissolving like fat in the sun and their cities covered with a shroud of smoke. What weakness if any among the Sumerians prevented them from successfully defending themselves remains unknown. But the Sumerian writers of lamentations saw their demise as the result of their gods having abandoned them like migrating birds.

The Amorites overran much of Sumer and settled along the Euphrates River just north of Sumer, where they founded the city of Babylon, and the Amorites settled to the north, along the Tigris River, in an area that included the city of Ashur. A Sumerian had described the Amorites as nomadic: as a people knowing no submission and having no house in their lifetime. The Book of Genesis in the Old Testament describes an Amorite as the grandson of Noah and the son of Ham and describes them as living between "the river of Egypt" and the Euphrates (Genesis 10:16 and 15:18-21). And in the Old Testament, Amos describes the Amorites as being as tall as cedar trees (Amos 2:9).

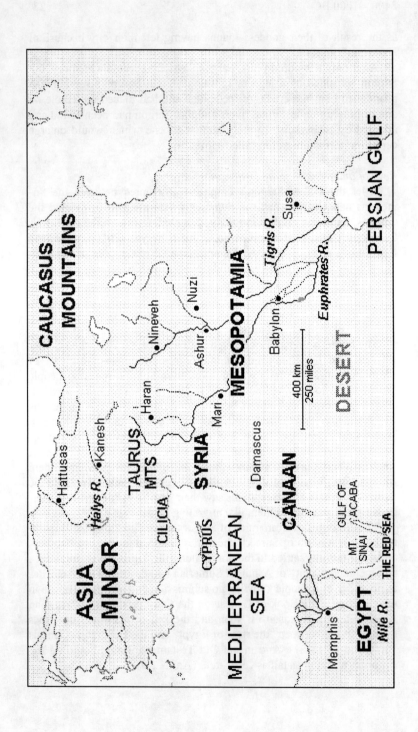

Assyria, Babylon and Marduk's Punishment

With the passing of generations, Amorites adopted some of the culture of those they overran, and Sumerian culture lived on. The Amorites fought off new waves of migrating peoples, and they increased their skills in the art of combat. Amorites spread through more of Mesopotamia. They joined in the trade that remained among Mesopotamian cities, and they extended their trade into Asia Minor, exchanging woolen cloth and tin for gold, silver and copper. Amorite merchants created colonies to their west, in parts of southern Asia Minor. The center of this empire was the city of Ashur, and Ashur was the center of a kingdom that was to become known as Assyria.

In the 1800s BC, an Amorite king at Babylon, Hammurabi, sent his armies out and conquered other kingdoms, cutting down his enemies, as he put it, "like dolls of clay." Hammurabi overran Assyria and conquered Ashur. He established his authority from the Persian Gulf to the city of Haran. Like Sargon, he built a new network of roads, he created a postal system, and he delegated power to governors, who were to rule conquered territories in his name.

Babylon was a city where trade routes crossed, and, under Hammurabi, Babylon became a bronze-age city of commerce and agriculture. It was a city with skilled artisans, architects, bricklayers and businessmen, with an efficient secular administration and a chain of command. The city was at the hub of an intricate network of canals. It was surrounded by great fields of barley, melons, fruit trees and the wheat the Babylonians used in making unleavened, pancake-like bread. From their barley, the Babylonians made beer. They sheared wool from their flocks of sheep. And they imported wood from Lebanon and metals from Persia.

Like other emperors, Hammurabi operated a protection game, offering towns he captured the security of his superior military might in exchange for their obedience and tribute: payment in taxes. He believed that by conquering far and wide he had put an end to war among established powers, and he wanted to protect his subjects from the terror of nomads.

Like king Urukagina of Lagash and the pharaoh Amenemhet and others, Hammurabi wished to promote what he saw as welfare and justice for his subjects. He saw that contracts between people had to be witnessed and ratified, that deeds of partnerships had to be maintained, that properties had to be registered and wills written. Hammurabi established laws that protected landholders from the landless. He regulated the treatment of women and slaves. He made a doctor liable if the doctor made his patient worse. Under his laws, an architect might be executed if his negligence resulted in the collapse of a house he had designed.

Like other rulers among the civilized, Hammurabi saw some people as more worthy than others. His laws divided his subjects into three classes: the nobles, who owned much land; the merchants and ordinary farmers; and the slaves. All classes were to be protected from what he believed was unnecessary abuse, but punishments were to differ according to one's class. If a noble destroyed the eye of another noble he had his own eye put out, or if he broke the bone of another noble he had one of his own bones broken, but if he broke the bone of a common person or destroyed that person's eye he only had to pay a fine.

Hammurabi claimed that he received his laws from Babylon's chief god, Marduk – a god acquired from the Sumerians. And according to Hammurabi's scribes, the people of Babylon saw events as directed by the gods and saw Hammurabi as wise and as having created a world of order and justice under Marduk.

Seeing their god Marduk as a god of justice, the Babylonians believed that Marduk punished people for lack of respect for his and Hammurabi's laws. And during the reign of Hammurabi's son, around 1800 BC, the Babylonians believed that such a punishment had arrived in the form of an invasion by those called Kassites, from the mountainous region just east of Mesopotamia – the first people known to have entered Mesopotamia on horseback. It was more than a thousand years before Hebrew prophets, as described in the Old Testament, would see their god of justice, Yahweh, as sending the Assyrians to punish the people of Israel.[*]

Whether drought or plague or something else weakened the Babylonians, preventing them from defeating the Kassites, is unknown. Hammurabi's son led an army that was able to drive the Kassites away, but the Kassites returned and were able to overrun Babylon, in the eyes of the Babylonians inflicting Marduk's punishment. Hammurabi's descendants continued to rule in Babylon, but with reduced power and perhaps only locally. Babylon declined as a great power, and other kings in and around Mesopotamia began a new competition for resources and trade routes.

HYKSOS INTO EGYPT, AND HITTITES AND HURRIANS INTO MESOPOTAMIA

Improved transport with the horse had made Egypt more vulnerable to the kind of invasions that had been taking place in Mesopotamia. Numerous migrants and traders had begun moving through Canaan to Egypt. In the mid-1700s, a literate people with a Semitic language

---

[*] Assyria overran Israel in the eighth century BC.

moved through Canaan, took control of some cities there, and then conquered northern Egypt. It is not known who they were, except that the Egyptians called them Hyksos (hyk khwsht), which identifies them only as foreigners. Like the Kassites, the Hyksos had horses, and they had lightweight chariots. They introduced Egyptians to the wheel and to new weapons of war. They introduced the Egyptians to new musical instruments, new techniques in making bronze and pottery, new animals, new kinds of crops, and they introduced the Egyptians to new gods.

Meanwhile, by the year 2000, an illiterate, warlike, Indo-European people called Hittites had migrated on foot southward into Asia Minor, where they overran and conquered tribal, bronze-age farming communities. Like Sargon's warriors, the conquering Hittites made themselves an aristocratic warrior elite living off the labors of those they had conquered. And like Sargon and others they saw their victories as willed by their gods and as proof of the righteousness of their conquests. Like others, the Hittites made deities of their dead kings, but they saw their living kings as human and expected them to obey their laws. Their neighbors considered them sexually lax. But the Hittites were less brutal than some: they disliked the mutilations of human bodies that they saw among other peoples, and they were less inclined to punish people by killing them.

From those they overran the Hittites learned how to make bronze. And sometime after the coming of the Kassites to Mesopotamia, the Hittites acquired horses and chariots. With horses and light chariots, the well trained, highly disciplined Hittites launched a new conquest of neighboring peoples in Asia Minor. A horse pulling a man on a lightweight chariot was faster than a horse carrying a man on its back, and the Hittites were able to move rapidly, sometimes under the cover of darkness, and spring surprise assaults upon their adversaries. The Hittite king, Mursilis I, forced a loose federation of city-states into the first Hittite empire. A Hittite army crossed the Taurus Mountains into Mesopotamia, and, in 1593, they sacked Babylon, ending the dynasty that had been created there by Hammurabi. But Babylon was too distant for the Hittites to rule – 1200 miles from their capital at Hattusas – and the Hittites withdrew from Babylon.

The Hittites remained the leading power north of Egypt until 1590, when the Hittite king, Mursilis, was assassinated by his brother-in-law. More palace intrigues and a murderous struggles for power followed, among Hittite princes, priests, nobles, regents and ambitious widows. It was to be a recurring development at other royal palaces in the world, and for the Hittites it brought what it would often bring to other ruling families: decline in power.

After the Hittite invasion of Mesopotamia, an Indo-Iranian people called Hurrians, from the Zagros Mountains, poured into Mesopotamia and overran the Assyrians. The Hurrians settled down, gradually adopted civilized ways, and became dominant in such cities as Mari, on the upper Euphrates, and Nuzi, which became a thriving commercial center. Then came another wave of Kassites, who occupied Babylon and briefly overran other parts of Mesopotamia. Kassite warriors settled down, adopted Mesopotamian culture and made themselves warrior-aristocrats. A few of them became rulers of great estates, from which they dominated surrounding territory. And from this elite came Babylon's new kings.

STORIES OF THE CREATION, FLOOD AND MORTALITY

The Sumerians had vanished as an identifiable people, but they left behind their myths. The Assyrians adopted and altered Sumerian stories, and they preserved the Sumerian language much as Christians were to preserve Latin. The Babylonians translated Sumerian religious writings, and these Babylonian translations influenced the Hurrians and Hittites. And after the Kassites conquered Babylon they came to accept Babylon's literature as sacred.

The Babylonians compiled separate Sumerian descriptions of the creation of the universe into a new version that was to become known as the *Enuma Elish*. The Enuma Elish begins by describing heaven and earth as already existing but with these places not yet having meaning because the gods had not yet given them names. According to the *Enuma Elish*, the world began with the salt waters and the fresh waters not yet separated, and with the fertile marshlands not yet having appeared. The *Enuma Elish* describes creation as birth: a godly male in the form of fresh waters, called Apsu, mated with a goddess in the form of salt waters, called Tiamat, and the goddess Tiamat gave birth to a variety of gods and to the earth and all things upon it. The gods born of Tiamat grew and multiplied and became rivals of one another. Eventually the gods born of Tiamat chose one of their number as king of the universe. This was Marduk, the god of light, who could perform miracles. According to the *Enuma Elish* the other gods called out to Marduk, declaring: "Say but to destroy or create and it shall be."

Marduk, as king among the gods, did what kings did on earth: he went forth and battled his enemies – demon gods. According to the *Enuma Elish*, in pursuing these demon gods, Marduk created the winds from the north, south, east and west so that his enemy might not escape him. Then in victory he surveyed the heavens and added to Tiamat's creations. He created the firmament and stars. He designated the zones of constellations of stars and thereby created the year. He made the moon shine, and he created vegetation. Then, seeing wars among other gods, and knowing that the defeated served the victorious, Marduk decided to create humankind. No god, he decided, should be a servant. Instead, it would be the place of humans to serve the gods.

Gilgamesh and the Flood

The Gilgamesh epic poem originated with stories that Sumerians had written as separate tales. During the centuries around the year 2000 these tales were put together as one poem. The tale survived among the peoples of Mesopotamia, and, after Hammurabi, new versions were written, most notably by the Assyrians.

Centuries after the fall of the Sumerians, a Mesopotamian scribe listed a Gilgamesh as the fifth king of Uruk, as a king who ruled after a great flood had inundated the region around Uruk. It was common among ancients to view kings who had died as gods, and Gilgamesh was described as part god, but mostly man.

The story of Gilgamesh addressed the mystery of why men had to die while gods lived forever, and it was a story about human audacity and willfulness against the wills of the gods. The story begins with a barbarian named Enkidu coming out of the wilderness. Enkidu was Gilgamesh's opposite: Enkidu had been living in the untamed wilds and was happy living with the animals he had befriended; Gilgamesh lived among people in the sophisticated city and because of his willfulness was estranged from the people he ruled.

From Uruk, Gilgamesh sent a temple prostitute to seduce Enkidu, and Enkidu lost his innocence – vaguely similar to Eve giving Adam the apple of knowledge, which in this instance was explicitly carnal. The prostitute gave Enkidu bread fit for a god and wine fit for royalty, and she introduced him to Gilgamesh. Enkidu and Gilgamesh became friends and attempted great feats together, including the killing of a god in the form of a bull, a god who was the bringer of droughts to their valley. The great mother goddess, Ishtar – a goddess seen in the heavens as the planet Venus – thought that in killing the bull, Gilgamesh and his friend had exercised too much willfulness and that as punishment either the barbarian or Gilgamesh had to die. It was Enkidu who died, and following his death Gilgamesh was heartbroken and lost himself by wandering from town to town.

Gilgamesh wondered why people had to die, and he decided to seek the answer from the keepers of such mysteries: the gods. He crossed the waters of death to the end of the world in search of a man who had been made into a god: Utnapishtim. He found Utnapishtim, and Utnapishtim told him there was no permanence. He told Gilgamesh about the god Enlil, a god of air, storms and floods, a god who had wished to destroy all of humankind in a great flood. He told Gilgamesh of other, kinder gods who had told him to tear down his house and to build a ship, to abandon his possessions, to save his life and to take into his ship his family and the seed of all living things.

Utnapishtim told Gilgamesh of a terrible rain that came, so terrible that the gods fled. He told about his floating in his ship upon the waters and seeing in the distance a mountain called Nizir. Utnapishtim said that when the waters subsided he found silence and mud, that people outside his ship had turned to clay, and he said that his ship became stuck against Mount Nizir. He told Gilgamesh that he sent forth a dove, and that having found no place to rest, the dove returned. He told Gilgamesh that he then sent forth a swallow and then a raven. And he said that when the raven saw that the waters had abated, it ate and cawed and flew away.

Utnapishtim told Gilgamesh that on his ship he poured tea as a libation for the gods and as thanks for his deliverance, and he said that in smelling the tea's sweet aroma the gods gathered around. He said that among these gods was Enlil and that Enlil was enraged at finding that humankind had survived his flood. Utnapishtim told Gilgamesh that the other gods scolded Enlil for attempting to destroy humankind without the help of the great god Ea, the god of earth and water, who alone understood all things. The god Enlil, according to Utnapishtim, then became repentant and went aboard Utnapishtim's ship. Enlil took Utnapishtim and his wife by their hands and made gods of them, and he brought them to dwell where Gilgamesh now found them.

Utnapishtim then told Gilgamesh the secret of eternal life: the story about a plant that when eaten in old age gives one youth. Utnapishtim gave Gilgamesh such a plant, and Gilgamesh began his return to Uruk. During his journey, Gilgamesh stopped to bathe in a pool of cool water, and he put his plant aside. And while he was bathing a serpent caught the scent of his plant, found it, grabbed it and raced away, shedding its skin in rejuvenation as it went. Gilgamesh felt shattered by the loss of the plant. He returned to Uruk and there, like other people, he had to face old age and eventual death.

A NEW ERA OF WARS, MIGRATIONS, IRON, CULTURAL BLENDING AND POLUTION

More than a century after the Hyksos invaded Egypt, protracted struggles between the Egyptians and the Hyksos resulted in the Egyptian pharaoh, Ahmose, uniting Egypt and driving the Hyksos across the Red Sea. Egypt's elite was wounded in pride by what had been the Hyksos conquest, and Ahmose's successor, Thutmose I, pursued the

Hyksos through Canaan and into Syria, the Egyptians supporting themselves by booty as they went. The Egyptians believed they were on a holy crusade and that they were protected by their gods. Thutmose expanded Egypt's empire southward into Nubia, and he boasted that he had made Egypt superior to every other land.

Egypt's advance in Syria was halted by the Hurrians. In the mid-1400s, Egypt allied itself with the Hittites while they continued to clash with the Hurrians. Egypt gained wealth from booty but failed to push the Hurrians out of Syria. Eventually the Egyptian, Thutmose III, negotiated peace with the Hurrians. Two successive Hurrian kings married their daughters to the Egyptian kings Thutmose IV and Amenhotep III.

The Hurrians weakened themselves with internal conflicts, and the Hittites – who had regained their strength – warred with the Hurrians and weakened them more, which helped Assyrians in northeastern Mesopotamia free themselves from Hurrian domination. Having experienced oppression under the Hurrians, the Assyrians were motivated to build a great military machine, led by their horse-breeding and landed nobility. The Assyrian king, Ashur the Great, who ruled from 1365 to 1330, married his daughter to a Babylonian, and he invaded Babylon after Kassite nobles there murdered his grandchild. Ashur's successors continued Assyria's war against the Babylonians and the Hurrians, and by around 1300 the Assyrians controlled all of Mesopotamia.

In the mid-1300s, Egypt withdrew from Syria and Canaan, as the pharaoh Amenhotep IV – also known as Akhenaten – tried to force his subjects to worship the god Aton, whom he believed was the god of the universe. After 1300 BC, the pharaoh Ramses I and his son Seti I revived Egyptian imperialism. Seti went with his army into Canaan and re-established Egypt's imperial administration there. Then he clashed with the Hittites over control of Syria. During the reign of Seti's son and successor, Ramses II, the Hittites pushed south and retook the city of Kadesh, seventy-five miles north of Damascus. Ramses II tried to retake Kadesh but failed, and a war between Ramses and the Hittites dragged on until the 21st year of Ramses' reign, when the Hittites saw a growing danger from other enemies. Then Ramses and the Hittites signed a treaty that they called an "everlasting peace." Egypt was to control lands as far north as Lebanon, and the Hittites were to control lands north of there. The Hittites gave Ramses a Hittite bride, and Ramses returned to Egypt, where he explained his exploits in Syria as a great victory – for he was supposed to be divine and incapable of failure. To celebrate his victory and create symbols of his glory, Ramses ordered the creation of great buildings and monuments across Egypt.

While the Egyptians had been reestablishing their empire, tribal peoples from Central Asia had been moving westward with their herds, running from droughts. They pushed on other tribal peoples, and around 1200 BC these tribal peoples pushed into Asia Minor. Around this time, the Hittites suffered from a plague that greatly reduced their population and made them vulnerable to attack. The Hittite capital, Hattusas, was overrun and was burned to the ground, and the Hittite empire collapsed. The heart of Hittite territory became occupied by an illiterate people called Phrygians, while people in Cilicia and Syria held onto their Hittite culture and identity. Migrants overran the island of Cyprus and other copper producing areas. The invasions disrupted trade in West Asia and the Eastern Mediterranean region, and bronze production declined. People sought a substitute for bronze and started producing more iron, which required a higher temperature and a greater sophistication in smelting.

Nomads called Chaldeans pushed against the Babylonians and against the Assyrians. A camel breeding, Bedouin people called Aramaeans, from northern Arabia, marauded their way across Mesopotamia. The Chaldeans settled near what had been Sumer. The Aramaeans settled around the upper Euphrates River and in Syria and established numerous city-kingdoms. Assyria became exhausted from warring against the invaders. Its trade fell, but it held onto much of Mesopotamia and to territory as far as the Caucasus Mountains. With the passing of generations, some Aramaeans maintained their nomadic ways and became the foremost traders in West Asia. Their language spread, and in the coming centuries Aramaic would be the most widely spoken language in West Asia – the language resorted to for diplomacy and business, and a language spoken by those called Hebrews.

Centuries of migrations into Mesopotamia had resulted in genetic and cultural blending. Sumerians had integrated with Semites. Hittite queens had Hurrian names. Kassites had integrated with the Amorites, and Aramaeans assimilated and intermarried with various peoples. At least one Aramaean married Assyrian royalty and, around 1050 BC another Aramaean became king of Babylon. Cities in Mesopotamia, Syria and Canaan – especially port cities – had become cosmopolitan. And in much of Mesopotamia, Syria and Canaan an ethnic tolerance had developed.

The people of different areas in Mesopotamia had come to worship gods that were similar in character and sometimes in name. The goddess Ishtar was worshiped in various cities, but with different characteristics in different cities. The Sumerian god Enlil was also worshiped among various peoples in Mesopotamia. Enlil was looked upon as the force behind hurricanes and floods, and being the creator of floods he was viewed as the god of punishment. It was to Enlil that the righteous prayed in attempts to inflict punishments on those they thought to be sinners. Another god worshiped across Mesopotamian was the god Ea, who, as described in the Gilgamesh epic, was a god of knowing, understanding and wisdom. Mesopotamians also believed in a sun god, commonly called Shamash, who was the giver of light and life. They saw Shamash as a giver of justice and as able to see wickedness and evil in people.

Mesopotamians continued to believe that not fearing the gods was the greatest of human errors. They believed in discovering what they had done wrong in the eyes of the gods so that they could make amends. Someone suffering from an ailment might ask himself whether he had alienated a son from his father or a father from his son, or a daughter from her mother or a mother from her daughter, or a brother from brother, or a friend from a friend. He might ask whether he had offended his father or mother, sister or brother, or a god or goddess. He might ask whether he had used false scales or had moved a boundary stone to a false location. He might consider whether he had approached his neighbor's wife, carried off his neighbor's clothes, told lies or whether his heart had been untrue. To avoid wrongdoing, one scribe suggested charity: responding with kindness to "an evil doer," or providing an enemy with justice, or honoring and clothing one who begs for alms.

Meanwhile, Mesopotamians living in villages and towns faced the problem of rubbish, sewage and contaminated water. Royal families and some others among the wealthy had indoor lavatories, but most others in villages and within town walls used nearby fields or orchards as their lavatory. Most towns or cities had no rubbish collection. Refuse was often merely thrown into the streets, where pigs, dogs and rats were free to scavenge. Often corpses were buried in very shallow graves. And with rains and a waterlogged ground, sewage and refuse washed into local rivers and contaminated water supplies. The result was typhus and other epidemics, which spread and lasted for years, while people saw disease as the result of sin or the work of demon-gods or someone's witchcraft.

In addition to appealing to the gods, Mesopotamians saw remedy to illness in sprinkling cleansing water upon the sick. Coincidences led them to believe a variety of specious remedies and things to avoid. In Babylon, the sick were left in the street so that any passerby might advise them. There and other places in Mesopotamia, priests attempted to foretell the course of a disease by examining the livers of sacrificed animals.

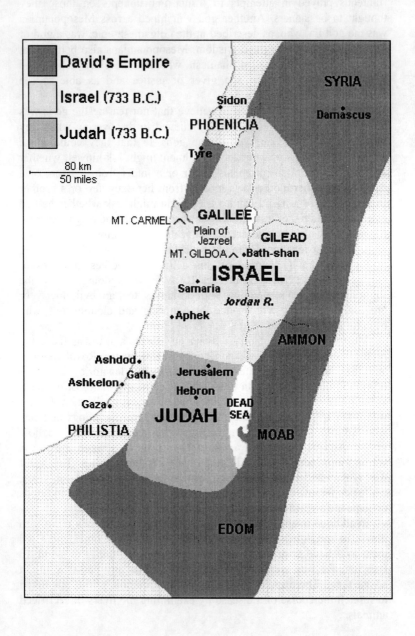

CHAPTER 4

THE HEBREWS BETWEEN ASSYRIA AND EGYPT

INTO THE LAND OF CANAAN

The source that introduces us to people called Hebrews is the Book of Genesis in the Old Testament, Genesis 14:13 describing a man called Abraham as a Hebrew. Genesis describes Abraham as the son Terah and the brother of Nahor and Haran, a family that dwelled at Ur, in the land of the Chaldeans. According to Genesis, Terah took his family to Haran, where he died. And from Haran, Abraham migrated with his family into Canaan. Some believe this was toward the end of the 2000s BC, long before the Chaldeans established themselves in Sumer. Some others speculate that Abraham's migration from Haran came much later than 2000 BC.

The term Hebrew perhaps originated with the word *Hiberu* found in writings sent to Egypt by the small independent states that Egypt left behind when it withdrew from Canaan in the 1300s. These states were disturbed by the arrival of nomadic tribes that came in waves across generations. "Hiberu" meant *outsider* and probably referred to a great variety of migrants.

The Hebrews appear to have been semi-nomadic herders of sheep and goats and occasional farmers, without knowledge of metal working, sophisticated craftsmanship or a written language. Like other nomadic herders, they were tent dwellers – as Abraham is described in Genesis 13:3. As was common among herders, the Hebrews had a masculine god of the sky and weather. The Hebrews organized themselves around their extended families, and Hebrew families were combined into kinship groups governed by a council of elders that left the head of a family with a sense of self-rule. These heads of families were males with absolute authority over their wives and children, and they were the priests for their families, each family having its own sacred images.

Typical of pastoral peoples, Hebrews saw vengeance as necessary for justice – an eye for an eye and a tooth for a tooth. And they believed in collective guilt: that an entire tribe or family was responsible for the acts of one of its members – a view that was to color their picture of divine acts of vengeance. Like other peoples, the Hebrews saw their god of the sky as concerned with them rather than as a god for all peoples. Genesis 15:18 describes their god as making a covenant with Abraham, saying:

> To your descendants I have given this land, from the
> river of Egypt as far as the great river, the river
> Euphrates.

Like other pastoral peoples, the Hebrews had a portable, sacred box, which they called the Ark of the Covenant, described in the Old Testament as about 3 by 2 feet, with poles along its sides. And, like other peoples, they carried their sacred box into battle, believing that it would be bring divine intervention and victory.

Like others, the Hebrews believed that a ritual killing of an animal sent the animal as a gift to the invisible world of the gods. Some people also sacrificed humans to their gods. According to chapter 22 of Genesis, Abraham was at least familiar with human sacrifice and he was tested by the Lord's command that he make an offering of his son Isaac.

The Land of Canaan

Canaan before the arrival of the Hebrews was a thinly populated land with relatively prosperous agricultural communities. In Canaan lived Phoenicians and Amorites, both of whom have been called Canaanites. The Amorites lived primarily in the hilly regions west of the Dead Sea and east of the Jordan River. As latecomers to Canaan, the Hebrews settled in the more sparsely populated and less fertile hills east of the coastal plains, and some settled in the dry plains of Galilee.

Some Hebrews lived in tight communities led by priests or military chieftains, and others lived in Canaanite towns, including an Amorite town that was to be known as Jerusalem. Some Hebrews learned agriculture from the Canaanites. Some learned to become tradesmen, and they became involved with the caravans that carried spices, ointments and resin across Canaan. Others remained with the tradition of herding and wandered with their flocks to and from desert watering places. During the dry seasons some of these herdsmen migrated south to the greener pastures of Egypt's Nile Delta and then returned when pastures near home turned green again. Some Hebrews wandered into Egypt and stayed, and there they were despised for their foreign ways.

Moses, Exodus from Egypt, and the Ten Commandments

When the pharaoh Ramses II returned from Syria with his treaty of "everlasting peace," he put slaves to work on his creation of great buildings and monuments to celebrate what he claimed was his victory.

Art work from this period depicts a tall and threatening Ramses holding a Semite, an Asian and a black man by their hair – three slaves feeling the sternness of Ramses' rule.

The Old Testament's Book of Exodus describes an unnamed pharaoh ordering the slaughter of all male Hebrew infants, and it describes a Hebrew woman trying to save her infant son, Moses, by putting him adrift on the Nile in a tiny boat of reeds caulked with tar pitch. The legend of Moses is the heart of Judaism – Moses being to Judaism what Siddartha Gautama is to Buddhism and what Jesus Christ is to Christianity.

According to legend, rather than the infant Moses being found by one of a multitude of common people who walked about the banks of the Nile, he was found by none other than the pharaoh's daughter – the stuff of legend or myth, but suitable for those who believe in miracles. The pharaoh's daughter recognized the infant as a Hebrew, and the princess was allowed to adopt Moses, despite Egyptians believing that Hebrews were an inferior people. The Old Testament suggests more improbable transformation in royal family values by describing the grown Moses as having acquired an identity as a Hebrew, although having been reared by the pharaoh's family from infancy.

The Book of Exodus describes Moses as flying into a rage when coming upon an overseer mistreating another Hebrew. Moses killed the overseer, and although Moses was a member of Egypt's ruling family he found it necessary to flee into the desert. There he joined the family of Bedouin people called Midianites. The head of the family was a priest, and Moses married the priest's daughter. One day the god of his father-in-law spoke to Moses from a burning bush that did not suffer the effects of fire, and the god described himself to Moses as the god of Abraham. It was then, according to the Book of Exodus, that the Hebrews acquired the god called Yahweh, to be translated in the Middle Ages as *Jehovah.*[*]

According to the Book of Exodus, rather than use his magic directly and immediately to free the Hebrews in Egypt, Yahweh instructed Moses to return there. Moses did so, and there he converted Hebrews to the worship of "the Lord" and convinced them to flee with him from Egypt. Yahweh chose to punish not only Egypt's pharaoh, who alone had the power to hold or release the Hebrews, he punished Egyptians far and wide, including all of the first-born there. Such was justice in the eyes of people who believed in collective guilt.

---

[*] Jehovah: the J was pronounced as if it were Y and the V as if it were W. Yahweh was written by the Hebrews as YWHW. Yahweh was often referred to in the Old Testament as *the Lord* because it was believed that His name was too awesome to be mentioned respectfully.

And Yahweh is described as adding misery to the Egyptians in much the same manner that the goddess Innana punished Sumer for having been raped while she slept. Innana had sent three plagues against Sumer. Yahweh cast down upon the Egyptians plagues of frogs, insects, boils, hail, locusts and a disease that killed their cattle.

To aid the escape of Moses and his fellow Hebrews, Yahweh opened the Red Sea to let the Hebrews pass. Then he closed it again, drowning the pharaoh and all his soldiers. This event was not corroborated by any mention in the extensive records kept by the Egyptians and known to modern historians. Nor has any mention of Moses in Egyptian writing has been found. Nor has there been found any mention of any great event involving plagues and other sufferings as described in the Old Testament – with those wishing to believe the Old Testament account of Moses arguing that Egyptian royalty would not have wanted to admit any defeat associated with the Hebrews.

Three months after leaving Egypt, Moses and his followers camped at the foot of Mount Sinai. Moses climbed the mountain, and Yahweh told him that if he and his followers obeyed Him they would be His "own possession among all the peoples." Yahweh told Moses that he would appear again in three days. And three days later, with Mount Sinai rumbling and smoking as if about to erupt, with thunder and lightening from the sky above and trumpets blaring, Yahweh descended onto Mount Sinai and beckoned Moses to ascend the mountain. In agreement with the belief common in West Asia that nearness to the gods was the privilege of a few, Yahweh told Moses to let the priests come "near the Lord" to consecrate themselves. But he said that the others should not "break through to the Lord to gaze" because it would cause many to perish. Moses assured Yahweh. Then Yahweh delivered his Ten Commandments and numerous other laws.

According to the Old Testament (Exodus 20:1-17), Yahweh commanded that Moses and his followers have no other gods, worship no idol "or any likeness of what is in heaven above or on the earth beneath or in the water under the earth." He commanded that they should not take His name in vain, that they should keep the Sabbath holy, that they honor their father and mother, not murder one another, nor commit adultery, steal, bear false witness, and not covet their neighbor's possessions, including wives and servants.

According to the Old Testament's First Book of Kings, 6:1, Moses and his fellow Hebrews fled from Egypt 480 years before Solomon was to begin building his temple in Jerusalem. This would have placed the exodus from Egypt in 1446, around a century and a half before the rule of Ramses and during a time of no major building in Egypt. The Book of Exodus describes Moses as having come across the small kingdoms of Edom and Moab, which archaeologists believe came into being after

1300. Those believing that the Old Testament is without error cling to 1446 as the year of the exodus. Others estimate that it was under Ramses' successor, Merneptah, that the Hebrews might have managed to flee *en masse* from Egypt – Merneptah having ruled from around 1224 to 1211. The mass exodus of Hebrew slaves might have occurred when Merneptah withdrew his troops from his frontier facing Canaan in preparation for a war developing on his frontier with the kingdom on his western border.

THE RISE OF ISRAEL

The great migrations that pushed against the Assyrians and overran Asia Minor and the Hittites around 1200 BC also pushed on some seafaring people from the region around the Aegean Sea. These people – described as "Sea People" by the Egyptians – threatened Egypt during the reign of pharaoh Merneptah while he was warring with the kingdom on Egypt's western border. Egypt under Merneptah drove off these Sea People. Then around 1177 BC, in the eighth year of the reign of Merneptah's successor, Ramses III, more raids came by the sea, and Ramses III repelled the invaders, and he boasted of re-establishing Egyptian rule through Canaan as far north as the Plain of Jezreel. But by the time of pharaoh Ramses XI, who ruled from around 1100 to 1085, the Egyptian domination of Canaan had again ended, and along the southern coast of Canaan, in such towns as Ashkelon, Ashdod, Gath and Gaza, were the sea peoples who had been driven away from Egypt. They were to become known as Philistines, from which the word *Palestine* is derived.

The Philistines were literate people with a language that had been spoken in Crete, Cyprus, and the southwestern portion of Asia Minor called Caria. And the script of this language echoed the script of the Mycenaean Greeks, whose civilization was among those disrupted by the great migrations of around 1200 BC. Some have speculated that the Philistines were Greeks fleeing from the invasions that ended Mycenaean civilization. In Canaan, the Philistines mixed and probably intermarried with the Canaanites. They adopted the Canaanite language. They melded their religion with Canaanite religion and gave to their gods the names of Canaanite gods.

Two of these gods were *Ba'al* and *El*. El was described on Canaanite tablets as the creator, the majestic father and the king of gods and men. Ba'al was his son and a god of life and fertility, in continual combat with the god Mot, a god of death and sterility. Ba'al was a god of the mountains, where rainstorms began. He rode the clouds. And worshipers of Ba'al saw him dying when the dry season came and vegetation disappeared, and they saw him as resurrected during the rainy season, when vegetation reappeared.

In their coastal cities, the Philistines maintained some cohesion as a people, while the Hebrews remained scattered in the inland hills. The Hebrews were resisting occasional attacks by camel riding nomads from the east. Then the Philistines attempted to expand against them. The Philistines forced the Hebrew tribe of Dan to leave their home in the foothills and to move to the north.

A legendary leader from the tribe of Dan who fought the Philistines is described in the Old Testament as Samson. The Book of Judges 16:17 describes Samson as a Nazirite. The Nazirites according to some scholars were originally a Canaanite fertility cult. Now they were a movement of holy men who worshiped Yahweh. Chapter 6 of the Book of Numbers describes the Nazirites as engaged in ecstatic frenzies and abstained from wine, strong drink and cutting their hair. The Nazirites were zealous, and if they were strong enough they were inclined to take the lead in combating people they detested – and they detested the Philistines for having refused circumcision.

As described in the Old Testament, Samson was both a leader in the fight against the Philistines and had a weakness for Philistine women. The Book of Judges describes Samson as burning Philistine crops and killing a thousand Philistines in a place called Ramathlehi, which means with "the hill of the jawbone." Judges 15:17 describes this as the place Samson killed Philistines with the jawbone of a donkey. According to the Samson legend, the Philistine woman Delilah learned from Samson that he was a Nazirite and that if his hair was cut he would lose his strength. As Samson slept, Delilah cut his hair. Here was a lesson for Yahweh worshipers about the dangers of foreign women.

Having lost his strength, the Philistines overpowered Samson and gouged out his eyes. They took Samson to Gaza, bound him in chains and put him to work "as a grinder." There his hair grew back. And when the "the lords of the Philistines" assembled they had Samson brought to them so they could look upon him with amusement. Watching from the roof of the building were about 3,000 Philistine men and women. The Philistines put Samson between two pillars. Samson, according to the legend, pushed on the pillars, bringing the roof down, killing himself and all the Philistines in and on the building.

Samuel, Saul, and the Rise of David

The Hebrews disrupted Philistine caravans bringing goods from the desert, and the Philistines established military outposts between their cities and hills occupied by the Hebrews. Around the year 1050, the Hebrews combined their forces for the first time and confronted an army of Philistines near the Philistine outpost at Aphek – the Philistines with iron weapons and horse drawn chariots, the Hebrews riding into battle on donkeys. As described in 1 Samuel 4:2, the Hebrews lost the battle. Hebrew elders wondered why Yahweh had allowed this, and they sent for the Ark of the Covenant so, the elders said, it would "deliver us from the power of our enemies." The ark came to the camp of the Hebrews, but it failed as the Hebrews were defeated again. The Philistines captured the Ark of the Covenant and took it with them to their city, Ashdod. But, according to the Old Testament, this angered the Lord and he "ravaged and smote" the Philistines of Ashdod and its territories "with tumors."

After the Hebrews had lost two battles, another Nazirite rose as leader among them. This was Samuel – a holy man, an oracle and a soothsayer. Samuel's military units managed to remain outside Philistine control. Samuel, perhaps at the urging of Hebrew elders, arranged the making of a monarch for the Hebrews: a warrior king to better unite the Hebrews. The monarch they chose was Saul, who had been a leader in politics and religion. Saul's kingship was a common form of rule and the kind of kingship that the Canaanites had, but for the Hebrews it was a new institution.

The First Book of Samuel, 9:15, described Saul as the Lord's choice. And in Chapter 10 of the First Book of Samuel, Saul is described as one of Yahweh's prophets. Saul appears to have been close to the Canaanite religion. He named one of his sons Eshbaal (meaning Ba'al exists) and another son he had named Meribaal (meaning Ba'al rewards). Also, one of Saul's Benjamite clansmen was Bealiah (which meant Yahweh is Ba'al).

Saul successfully engaged the Philistines in at least three battles, which were followed by the Philistines withdrawing their garrisons from around Hebrew territory. With Saul was a former shepherd boy named David, who was attached to Saul's court as a musician and shield bearer. A Philistine named Goliath challenged Saul's army, and Goliath, according to 1 Samuel 17:4, was six cubits (nine feet) tall. David alone was unafraid of Goliath. He took up the challenge and slew Goliath. David rose in standing as a warrior and in further warfare, exceeding that of Saul. As reported in 1 Samuel 18:6,7:

> When David returned from killing the Philistines...the women came out of all the cities of Israel, singing and dancing, to meet King Saul, with tambourines, with joy and with musical instruments. And the women sang as they played and said: "Saul has killed thousands. And David tens of thousands."

According to the Old Testament, King Saul was jealous of David and tried to kill him, and David fled from Saul and his agents to a cave in the "southern wilderness," near Hebron. There, David gathered around him a band of adventurers and debtors. Already he was married to Saul's daughter, and now he took another wife – the daughter of a local, wealthy herdsman – that gained him more local support. And for more advantage, David allied himself with the Philistine king of Gath, Achish.

At a battle beside Mount Gilboa, overlooking the Plain of Jezreel, the Philistines apparently lured Saul and his army down from the high ground, and the Philistines, with their chariots, horsemen and Canaanite allies, overwhelmed Saul's forces. Three of Saul's soldier sons were killed, and rather than be taken prisoner, Saul fell on his sword. When the Philistines found Saul, they cut off his head and posted it for display in the temple of their god, Dagon. They fastened his body to the wall at the town of Beth-shan. And the Philistines took possession of the greater part of Canaan.

Saul was succeeded by his fourth son, Eshbaal, who ruled over territory that had been greatly reduced in size by the Philistines. War between the forces of David and those of Eshbaal ended with Eshbaal dead and David anointed priest-king in place of Eshbaal. From Hebron, David and his army ventured out to make his rule over Israel a reality. David captured the Amorite town of Jerusalem and various other towns.

When the Philistines heard that David had been anointed king of Israel, they turned against him. War broke out between the Philistines and David, and David triumphed against the Philistines, succeeding where Saul had failed. By force of arms, David expanded his rule – while the great powers of Assyria and Egypt were too preoccupied to challenge his expansion. He conquered Edom, which extended south to the Red Sea, David gaining its mines of copper and iron. He conquered Moab, rich with cattle. He conquered Ammon, and he conquered north into Syria, to Damascus and beyond to the Euphrates River – which was the border of the Assyrian Empire. And, like other conquerors, as David conquered he took booty and demanded tribute.

David's Rule, and Tolerance in Yahweh Worship

Like conquerors before him, David appealed for support among his subjects by claiming to be the agent of his god. He called himself the son of Yahweh. He acquired the trappings of a great potentate. His subjects prostrated themselves in his presence. He ruled in great splendor, including a great harem. In addition to Saul's daughter and the wife he took while at Hebron, David took wives from his conquered territories, ostensibly to help link his empire. And, enjoying his power, he took what women suited his fancy, including Bathsheba, the wife of a local neo-Hittite.* And soon Bathsheba was to be the mother of David's son: a child to be named Solomon.

In the Old Testament, David's rule is described as inspired by Yahweh. And David is described as bringing to Jerusalem the Ark of the Covenant and proclaiming his intention to build in Jerusalem a temple to house the ark. But like many Hebrews, David had been influenced by the religion of the Canaanites. He gave one of his sons, Beeliada, a Canaanite name. David kept in his house images of gods other than Yahweh. His "leaping and capering before the Lord" with music accompaniment, as described in chapter six of the Second Book of Samuel, was a Canaanite practice. No evidence exits that David knew of the Ten Commandments given to Moses.

Doing service at David's court were a variety of peoples, including Philistines, people from Crete and neo-Hittites. And beyond the royal court more genetic blending was taking place. However much the Hebrews were already a mix of peoples, they were becoming more of a mix. During David's rule and after, non-Hebrews, among them the Amorites, were absorbed by the Hebrews. And – like the Ubaidians and Sumerians – the Amorites were to vanish as an identifiable people.

David created what was to be called a golden age for the Hebrews. His rule benefited from the wealth taken from conquered peoples, and Israel benefited as had Egypt and Hammurabi's Babylon from a peace created by conquest. But it was a golden age that had, like other civilizations, antagonisms between rich and poor. David taxed his subjects and forced them to labor for the state. And David's subjects rebelled. According to the Old Testament, his discontented subjects were led by his own son, Absalom. The Second Book of Samuel describes a messenger reporting to David that the "hearts of the men of Israel" are with Absalom. But David crushed the rebellion, and with it the life of Absalom.

King Solomon

After David's death in 965, two of his sons, Solomon and Adonijah, vied with each other to succeed him. Solomon emerged as the victor, and he had Adonijah executed on the pretext that Adonijah had demanded a woman from David's harem. It was a kind of sibling rivalry common with monarchies.

Like David, Solomon benefited from an era of peace and prosperity. He enjoyed alliances with his Egyptian and Phoenician neighbors. He encouraged trade and built a merchant fleet that he harbored at the Gulf of Acaba at the northeast end of the Red Sea. He acquired copper mines and built refineries for smelting metals. His ships brought goods from

---

* Neo-Hittite: someone having Hittite culture after the Hittites and their empire vanished.

afar, and commerce passed through his kingdom from south, north, east and west.

Solomon thought he should live as splendidly as the great king of Assyria, and to create many luxurious palaces for himself he imported the skilled craftsmen that he could not find among his subjects. According to the Old Testament, Solomon, like his father, had many wives, as many as seven hundred, including princesses from other kingdoms given to Solomon as gifts to promote good relations. And he had four hundred horses.

A priest-king like his father, Solomon, according to the Old Testament, led sacrifices to the god Yahweh. To give Yahweh a home and to put Yahweh worship under his domination, Solomon had the temple constructed that his father had intended to build, a temple to be described in the Old Testament as "the House of the Lord." The temple was built on property on a hill north of Jerusalem that David had purchased, property that the Amorites had used as a huge threshing floor. The temple's design resembled the temples of other religions. It was decorated with sculptures and other works of art, and in the inner sanctum of the temple was the Ark of the Covenant.

It was still a time of religious toleration among the Hebrews, and Solomon had temples built for his wives who worshiped other gods. To run his own temple in his behalf, he appointed a high priest named Zadok, the court priest who had performed religious duties for David. And Zadok became the first of a hereditary priesthood that would last for centuries to come.

This was an age in which kings acted as a judge in their community, and the Old Testament describes Solomon as a judge who was wise. The First Book of Kings, 4:29, reads:

> Now God gave Solomon wisdom and a very great
> discernment and breadth of mind, like the sand that is
> on the seashore.

The Old Testament also finds fault with Solomon, fault with his love of luxury, his marrying pagans and his turning to idolatry. These later writings would describe Solomon as having enslaved his subjects. Solomon forced his subjects to work four months of every year on his projects, and, late in his reign, many of his subjects became displeased enough that they rebelled against him, as had the people of Israel against David. And like David, Solomon crushed the uprisings, while two of Solomon's vassal nations – an Aramaean kingdom around Damascus, and Edom – took advantage of the uprisings and broke from Solomon's rule.

WRITING GENESIS

Some Hebrews had learned the Canaanite language, and some of them adopted the writing of the Canaanites. This was a Phoenician language, which included words of Sumerian origin. The language that the Hebrews adopted was in later times to be called Hebrew. And in taking the Canaanite language as their own, Hebrew scribes acquired some of its poetry, and they may have borrowed from the Mesopotamian stories written in that language. The *cherubim*, or angels, mentioned in Genesis, Ezekiel, 2 Samuel and elsewhere in Hebrew sacred writings were known to the Canaanites. Some of what was to find its way into The Book of Proverbs matched Canaanite literature. The obligation of a man to marry the childless widow of a dead brother had been a part of the law of the Hurrians, who had influenced the Canaanites. The story in the Book of Genesis of Rachel stealing the gods of her father is similar to Hurrian custom. The Hebrew version of the story of the great flood that covered the earth had the ark grounding on Mount Ararat as did the Hurrian version of that story.

The earliest known works by worshipers of Yahweh are the Book of Jashar and the Song of Deborah – believed to have been written no sooner than the 1100s. Some believe that the Song of Deborah may have been a part of the Book of Jashar. The Book of Jashar vanished but is referred to in the Book of Joshua 10:13. The earliest Hebrew writing that archaeologists can actually date comes after 1000 BC, around the time that David acquired power. This archaeological find looks like a child's exercise in creating a calendar, the so-called *Gezer* Calendar, written on stone, an exercise that suggests that by now an elite among the Hebrews had acquired writing and was passing it to their children. This was writing that used a phonetic alphabet that had been used by the Phoenicians and Aramaeans.

In work that remains controversial, scholars have separated authors whose work appears in the Old Testament – a separation according to writing style, modes of thinking, and use of names. Four writing styles have been suggested by scholars: the Elohist, Deuteronomist, Yahwist and Priestly. Regarding different modes of thought, one writer who contributed to the Old Testament described the Israelites as calling their god Yahweh from the time of Noah, and another contributor described Yahweh as becoming known to the Hebrews when he revealed himself to Moses. The Book of Genesis also has conflicting descriptions suggesting more than one author.[*]

---

[*] In the description of the Creation that runs from the beginning of Genesis to Genesis 2:4, grass, herbs and trees were created before man, on the third day, man was created on the sixth day, and Yahweh created woman at the time that

The Creation described in the Book of Genesis is similar to the Creation described in the *Enuma Elish*: the world as a watery chaos, light coming before there were bodies that gave off light, and the heavens and earth becoming separated. The Creation described in Genesis is a poetic account that today is read as symbolism. But read literally the description of creation is compatible with the way people viewed the universe at the time that Genesis was written, when there was no awareness of hydrogen atoms trillions of years before the earth was formed; when the earth was seen as disk-like; when light and darkness were seen as different matters rather than darkness being merely the absence of light; and when rain was believed to come from waters above the atmosphere that were held back by an invisible shield.

The Book of Genesis describes Yahweh as having created man (Adam) "in His own image" and Yahweh as having planted "a garden paradise eastward in Eden," a place including the Tigris and Euphrates Rivers. Man was to be free to choose, but his choice was limited: he could eat freely from any tree in the garden except the tree of knowledge, and if he ate of the tree of knowledge he would die.

According to the Book of Genesis, Yahweh then decided that man needed a helper, and Yahweh caused a deep sleep to fall upon Adam. He took one of the man's ribs and fashioned from it a woman (Eve). "He took her to Adam, and Adam called her *woman*." Genesis describes a serpent tempting Eve to eat of the forbidden "fruit." Serpents were a part of Canaanite and Aramaean religion and perhaps found their way into the oral tradition from which the Hebrews borrowed.

The woman gave some of the forbidden fruit to the man, and, because of this disobedience, Adam and Eve became ashamed of their nakedness and hid from Yahweh's sight. Yahweh responded to their disobedience with vengeance. Women thereafter were to give birth in pain. Women were to be ruled over by their husbands. Humans would need to work to eat, and humans were to be denied the everlasting life that Yahweh enjoyed. "For you are dust," he told the man and woman, "and to dust you shall return."

Humans from then on were to suffer from aging. With the short lives that human would lead, the ability to correct mistakes and mend relationships would be limited, and power would go to those with little accumulated experience and wisdom. By condemning humanity to an early and inevitable death, God was helping to create the very foolishness he would be said to despise.

In a one-page story in Genesis, Eve gives birth to a son called Cain and then another son called Abel. It is a story remotely similar to the Sumerian story about the conflict between the gods Emesh (summer)

---

he created man. The account of the Creation that appears from Genesis 2:5 to 3:24, man is created before plant life and woman is created later.

and his brother Enten (winter). Cain became a farmer and Abel a herdsman. God liked Abel's offerings but not Cain's. Cain was angry. God asked why and told Cain he should master his anger. Instead, the jealous Cain murdered his brother. God cursed Cain, made him a failure at farming, put a mark on him and made him a vagrant and wanderer. Cain thought his punishment was too much of a burden to bear. He feared that alone (without his clan to protect him) he could be killed with impunity. God promised Cain that whoever killed him vengeance would be taken on him sevenfold. How much comfort this gave Cain cannot be known. But rather than remain a wanderer, Cain settled in the land of Nod, east of Eden, took a wife and started a family. Cain's son was called Enoch, and, according to Genesis, Enoch built a city by the same name.

According to the Book of Genesis, Yahweh saw wickedness among the descendants of Adam and Eve and decided to "blot out man" from the face of the earth. But God finally discovered a righteous man called Noah and changed his mind. He chose to save Noah and his family and to use Noah to save other creatures that he had caused to dwell upon the earth. Like Utnapishtim, Noah obeyed his god and built a boat. In that boat, Noah, his family and other creatures of the earth, survived a great flood. And like the gods who were attracted to Utnapishtim's boat, God smelled a soothing aroma – the aroma of Noah's "burnt offerings."

After the flood, Yahweh made his covenant with Noah, Noah's descendants multiplied, and all humanity spoke the same language. Then, as if the flood and Noah's righteousness were in vain, evil again appeared among humankind. According to Genesis, one of Yahweh's early disappointments was the descendants of Noah attempting to build a city in Mesopotamia with a tower that would reach to heaven – the Tower of Babel.* Yahweh disapproved of this project and brought the project to an end by causing them to speak different languages, making it impossible for them to understand each other. And he scattered humankind "over the face of the whole earth."

PROPHETS AND A DIVIDED ISRAEL

Around 922 BC, Solomon died of old age, and with his death his son and successor, Rehoboam, confronted the people of Israel. According to the Old Testament, the people said to Rehoboam: "Lighten the heavy burden which your father put upon us and we will

---

* The Sumerians built their temples on platforms, one platform on top of another, some temples reaching higher than others, apparently to reach nearer to heaven. These temples have been called ziggurats.

serve you." Rehoboam responded by asking the crowd to return in three days. And when the crowd did so, Rehoboam said to them:

> My little finger is thicker than my father's loins. Whereas my father loaded you with a heavy yoke, I will add to your yoke. My father disciplined you with whips, but I will discipline you with scorpions. (1 kings 12:11)

Rehoboam's subjects to the north of Jerusalem rebelled, and the rebellion turned into a bloody civil war. The leader of the revolt was a man called Jeroboam. Under his leadership, the north became an independent state, maintaining the name Israel. The state to the south, which included Jerusalem, was smaller and less commercially advanced, and it became known as Judah.

Jeroboam was no revolutionary. He ruled Israel as a divine king and represented his rule as a return to the House of David. Under Jeroboam, Israel's economy grew. So too did its bureaucracy, the debt of peasants and herdsmen, and the number of people losing their land and selling themselves into slavery.

Jeroboam was a conventional monarch, and like Solomon and other Hebrews of his time he found no fault in worshiping a variety of gods. Believing that gods dwelled in places, Jeroboam saw Yahweh as representing not Israel but the kingdom of Judah. Feeling threatened by the rule of Rehoboam from Jerusalem, he saw loyalty to the priests and god of the temple in Jerusalem as a threat to his rule, and Jeroboam set up shrines for worshiping gods other than Yahweh, gods that included those described in the Old Testament as "the Golden Calves."

Ahab and the Prophet Elijah

Following Jeroboam's death in 901, Israel suffered from drought and an economic depression. With these came bitterness, intensified social unrest, a search for scapegoats and the rise to prominence of a man called Elijah. Elijah was a new kind of Hebrew prophet. Earlier prophets had been advisors to, or supporters of, Israel's monarchy. Elijah was hostile to that monarchy.

Described in the First Book of Kings, Elijah was from a rural, cattle-raising region in Gilead, east of the Jordan River. The agricultural ways of the Canaanites were foreign to him. He preferred the rustic simplicity of Gilead to the cosmopolitanism that he found in Israel's cities. And, according to the Old Testament, he disliked injustice. Elijah was outspoken and acquired a following among Israel's rural people. He protested against land tenure and the enslavement of the poor by the rich. He called for worship of Yahweh and opposed worship of Ba'al.

Ba'al was worshiped by Israel's new king, Ahab and his wife Jezebel, and Ba'al worship was extensive among the wealthy and cosmopolitan of Israel. According to 1 Kings 18:1, Yahweh told Elijah that if he, Elijah, confronted king Ahab, he, Yahweh, would bring relief from the drought by making rain. When Elijah presented himself before Ahab, Ahab recognized him as the "troubler of Israel." Elijah replied that it was not he who troubled Israel but Ahab, because Ahab had "forsaken the commandments of the Lord" and had "followed the Ba'als." Elijah challenged Ahab to arrange a gathering on Mount Carmel, and Ahab, according to the Old Testament, did so.

Mount Carmel was where Ba'al ritual dances were staged, and there Elijah is reported to have spoken to the people of Israel and to have challenged them to make a choice between the supremacy of Yahweh and the gods of the Canaanites. The drought had reflected badly on Ba'al, a god of fertility. The miracles performed by Elijah were impressive. Elijah convinced the crowd, and excited by the new support he had gained, Elijah called upon the crowd to "seize the prophets of Ba'al," and he and those who followed him went on a murderous rampage. According to 1 Kings 18:40, they took the priests of Ba'al "down to the brook of Kishon and slew them there." Then Elijah fled into the wilderness to escape from the agents of Queen Jezebel, who was angry over the murders of her Ba'al priests.

King Ahab and Allies Defeat the Assyrians

Assyria was re-establishing control in places in Mesopotamia, and Assyria's king and his warrior nobles yearned to win for themselves glory, gold, silver, copper, iron and whatever else they could plunder. They made raids westward, and they conquered Aramaean kingdoms in northern Syria. They headed south toward the Aramaic city of Damascus. King Ahab of Israel allied his nation with the Phoenicians and with Damascus against the Assyrians. In 853, in a great battle at QarQar, in Syria, this alliance, with a reported 10,000 infantrymen and 2,000 horse drawn chariots, defeated and stopped the Assyrians.

But after their victory, the allies quarreled, and Israel and Damascus fought another one of their wars, Israel allying itself on this occasion with Judah. King Ahab died in battle against Damascus. And, with its former enemies divided, Assyria began making new threats in the direction of Israel.

Elisha and the Bloody Rise of King Jehu

After Ahab died in battle, one of his generals, Jehu, wished to succeed him. In the often bloody business of succession, Jehu enlisted the support of the god Yahweh and Elijah's movement, now led by Elijah's companion, Elisha. According to the Second Book of Kings,

Jehu and Elisha murdered more priests of Ba'al. They burned the temple of Ba'al worship and converted it to a latrine. They murdered the remaining members of the Ahab family, including Jezebel, who is said to have been thrown from a window, run over by Jehu's chariot and left to be torn apart by dogs. And Jehu murdered others he saw as possible rivals.

In 842, Jehu became king of Israel, and during his reign economic conditions improved and hatreds subsided. The movement begun by Elijah faded, and Jehu lost interest in Yahweh worship and began worshiping other gods, as expressed in the Second Book of Kings (10:31-32), where it was written that Jehu "...did not depart from the sins of Jeroboam."

The Prophet Amos

According to the Old Testament, the prophets Elijah and Elisha were followed a century later by the prophet Amos, a sheep farmer and dresser of figs from the rural village of Tekoa, ten miles south of Jerusalem. Amos had gone north into Israel and taken with him his worship of Yahweh. He too disliked the cosmopolitanism and luxury he found in Israel. According to the Old Testament he condemned those "who oppress the poor" and "crush the needy." He spoke against the restoration of Ba'al worship, he called on people to seek salvation in the worship of Yahweh, and (in Amos 4:2) he warned that days were coming "when they will take you away with meat hooks, and the last of you with fish hooks." Amos complained that evil was not a failure of worshiping the right way but a failure of living correctly, and he quoted Yahweh as saying "I reject your festivals" and "let justice roll down like waters and righteousness like an overflowing stream."

The prophecies of Amos would serve those who needed to explain the destruction of Israel. According to the Old Testament, Amos declared that Yahweh had to destroy Israel because its people would not repent. Moved by Amos' denunciations against Israel, a priest reported Amos for conspiring against Israel's king, Jeroboam II. Amos tried to defend himself by claiming that he was only a simple herdsman and grower of figs. But many in Israel saw him as a nuisance, and Amos felt compelled to flee back to Judah.

THE ASSYRIANS THROUGH ISRAEL TO EGYPT

Assyria's trade had expanded, which, with the spoils of war brought to Assyria more wealth than any other state. Former capitals of neighboring kings were now the capitals of Assyria's provinces. The Aramaeans had been absorbed into its culture. Assyria's cities had absorbed many displaced persons and had become large, metropolitan centers. Its people, and its princes, remained a religious people, believing like others that disasters were caused by displeasing the gods. Assyrian women were veiled – except for prostitutes, slave-women and unmarried priestesses, whom the law forbade to wear veils in public. Abortion was considered immoral and a crime against the state. A woman who willfully caused a miscarriage was impaled on a stake and left unburied. "Unnatural" sexual acts were forbidden and severely punished.

The Assyrians Advance to Gilead and Galilee

Jeroboam II died in 746. His son and successor, Zechariah ruled Israel six months. Zechariah was assassinated, and then Israel weakened itself with civil war, and this weakness made expanding southward more attractive for Assyria.

In 745, a military coup in Assyria brought to power a general who made himself king and called himself Tiglath-pileser III. He decided to expand the realm of Assyria's god, Assur, and to win for himself more wealth. He created a new, permanent army, largely of well-trained and disciplined mercenaries – an army unmatched in West Asia and North Africa. They had iron weapons, siege machines that could break down city walls, and they had archers on horseback who could move fast in hilly terrain.

Tiglath-pileser defeated tribes that had been menacing the Assyrians and other civilized communities. Waging total war, he extended Assyrian rule across Syria, expelling the Urartians and conquering Syria's Aramaean city-states, including King Ahab's old ally, Damascus. He destroyed cities, robbed and often deported whole populations, resettling them elsewhere in order to disunite them and put an end to their consciousness as a nation.

The Assyrians Overrun Israel

Remoteness from others was a blessing that had been denied the Israelites. The area that had been accessible to the Hebrews was easily accessible to the Assyrians. In 733, Tiglath-pileser's army conquered Gilead and Galilee. Bending to the realities of power, Israel recognized Assyria's domination and paid Assyria tribute. Assyria replaced the king of Israel with someone of their choosing: Hoshea. Then, Hoshea rebelled against paying tribute to Assyria. Hoshea sent messengers to Egypt, hoping to win the alliance with Egypt. The worried kings of Tyre and Sidon also sought an alliance with Egypt. But before Hoshea could create any meaningful alliance, Assyria attacked.

Looking back on these events, writers of the Old Testament needed an explanation as to why the nation of Israel was destroyed – and why Israel was denied God's "lifting the weak to confound the strong." The

Old Testament describes another prophet, Hosea, as declaring Israel's government godless in its putting trust in armies, fortifications and alliances rather than in repentance and in the goodness of Yahweh. And the Old Testament describes the prophet Hosea as declaring the coming of Assyria's army to be Yahweh's punishment. Hosea described Yahweh as saying "Because of the wickedness of their deeds I will drive them out of my house. I will love them no more." According to Hosea no matter how much an individual Israelite loved Yahweh he too would suffer Yahweh's wrath. And the claim of Yahweh's collective punishment would prove fitting, for the Assyrians would not discriminate between those Israelis who worshiped Yahweh fervently and those who did not.

Some Israelis fled before the invaders. For three years the Assyrians besieged Israel's capital, Samaria. In 721, under a new king, Sharru-kin (called Sargon in the Old Testament), Assyria conquered Samaria. Then it conquered the whole of Israel. To keep the conquered from regaining power, and, as the Assyrians had done with other nations it conquered, it deported and dispersed large numbers of people. The Assyrians took 27,000 Israelis away as slaves. And Israel as a nation vanished.

The Assyrians Overrun Judah and Egypt

According to the Old Testament, another Hebrew prophet who addressed the issue of Assyrian aggression was Isaiah – a nobleman from Jerusalem. Isaiah joined the prophet Hosea in opposing alliances. He saw wisdom in pacifism rather than relying on arms. He believed that what mattered above all else was devotion to Yahweh. Like Hosea, Isaiah saw the Assyrians, in their drive through Israel, as the agents of Yahweh.

But the king of the Assyrians pushed his army beyond Israel and into Judah. The Assyrians laid waste to Judah's countryside and gathered before the walls of Jerusalem. They threatened to destroy Jerusalem unless the Hebrews paid a ransom. The Hebrews paid, and the Assyrians spared the city.

According to Isaiah, the Assyrians as agents of Yahweh had suddenly come to an end. Isaiah quoted Yahweh as saying "I will save Jerusalem for my own sake and for my servant David's sake" (Isaiah 37:35). According to the Second Book of Kings, 19:36, Yahweh intervened against the Assyrians, sending an angel during the night into their camp and slaying 185,000 Assyrian soldiers in their sleep.

The impact of such a loss would have reversed Assyrian gains, but no description of events in Assyrian writings compatible with such an event has been found. And rather than suffering a reversal, the Assyrians were able to continue their rule over Judah. The great

Assyrian army continued its victorious march southward. They occupied Lower Egypt in 676, introducing iron to the region, and a few years later they sacked the city of Thebes. A weakened Egypt, meanwhile, had been invaded by Nubia. A Nubian had become pharaoh. The Assyrians defeated the Nubian pharaoh, and the Nubians withdrew to their homeland.

By 640 BC, Assyria had extended its rule south along the Tigris and Euphrates rivers to the Persian Gulf, and they had extended their empire northeast into mountainous territory and south into Arabia. Assyria had created a great empire: all of Mesopotamia, Egypt beyond Thebes, Cyprus, Syria, and beyond Kanesh in Asia Minor. They believed that they were enjoying the blessings of their great god, Assur. Isaiah, meanwhile, seeing the horror of war, wished to leave his people with a hope of better things to come. He spoke of the day when Yahweh would create a new world, a world in which the wolf would lie down with the lamb, when men would beat their swords into plowshares and their spears into pruning hooks, and nations would not lift up swords again other nations, and people would learn of war no more.

A Decline in Yahweh Worship

In the lands that the Assyrians conquered they established, for a short while, the same kind of peace that Hammurabi had created in Mesopotamia and that the pharaoh Menes had created in Egypt. The Assyrians built roads, which helped West Asia become more integrated economically and helped trade and industry to flourish. And Assyria and its empire prospered.

In Judah, the Hebrew king from about 692 BC, Manasseh, ruled as Assyria's puppet. He gave his support to the god Assur, whose image he placed at the entrance to the temple that Solomon had built for Yahweh. He allowed pagan priests in the "House of the Lord" alongside the priests of Yahweh. Scribes whose writing would find their way into the Old Testament described Manasseh as erecting altars for Ba'al worship, practicing witchcraft, using divination and mediums. They claimed that Manasseh had "seduced" the people of Judah "to do evil more than the nations whom the Lord destroyed before the sons of Israel."

Some in Judah were dismayed at Yahweh's toleration of the success of the wicked and the subjugation of the righteous. Many in Judah saw Yahweh as having abandoned them, or they lost faith in Yahweh's ability to do anything for their benefit. Merchants in Judah abandoned their identities as Hebrews and adopted foreign dress. Manasseh enjoyed more than fifty years of rule, while Judah benefited from peace and from the rise in commerce that had come with Assyrian domination.

CHAPTER 5

INDIA, HINDUISM, AND RELIGIOUS REBELLION

THE LOST CIVILIZATION OF MOHENJO-DARO

Sometime around 6000 BC a nomadic herding people settled into villages in the mountainous region just west of the Indus River. There they grew barley and wheat using sickles with flint blades, and they lived in small houses built with adobe bricks. After 5000 BC their climate changed, bringing more rainfall, and apparently they were able to grow more food, for they grew in population. They began domesticating sheep, goats and cows and then water buffalo. Then after 4000 BC they began to trade beads and shells with distant areas in central Asia and areas west of the Kyber Pass. And they began using bronze and working metals.

The climate changed again, bringing still more rainfall, and on the nearby plains, through which ran the Indus River, grew jungles inhabited by crocodiles, rhinoceros, tigers, buffalo and elephants. By around 2600, a civilization as grand as that in Mesopotamia and Egypt had arisen on the Indus Plain and surrounding areas, and by 2300 this civilization was trading with Mesopotamia. Seventy or more cities had been built, some of them upon buried old towns. There were cities from the foothills of the Himalayan Mountains to Malwan in the south. There was the city of Alamgirpur in the east and Sutkagen Dor by the Arabian Sea in the west.

One of these cities was Mohenjo-Daro, on the Indus river some 250 miles north of the Arabian Sea, and another city was Harappa, 350 miles to the north on a tributary river, the Ravi. Each of these two cities had populations as high as around 40,000. Each was constructed with manufactured, standardized, baked bricks. Shops lined the main streets of Mohenjo-Daro and Harappa, and each city had a grand marketplace. Some houses were spacious and with a large enclosed yard. Each house was connected to a covered drainage system that was more sanitary than what had been created in West Asia. And Mohenjo-Daro had a building with an underground furnace (a hypocaust) and dressing rooms, suggesting bathing was done in heated pools, as in modern day Hindu temples.

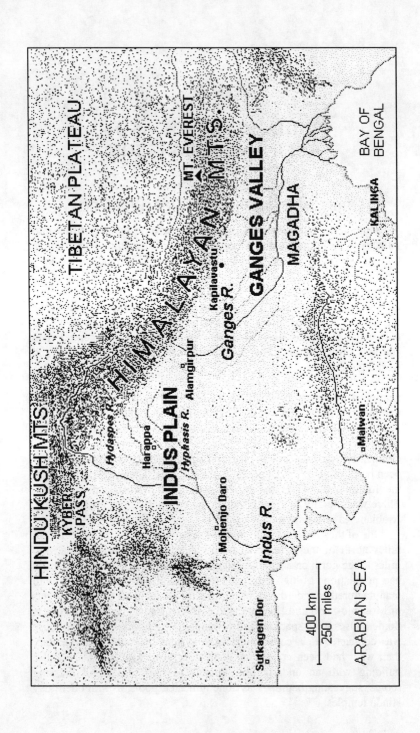

The people of Mohenjo-Daro and Harappa shared a sophisticated system of weights and measures, using an arithmetic with decimals, and they had a written language that was partly phonetic and partly ideographic. They spun cotton and wove it into cloth. They mass-produced pottery with fine geometric designs as decoration, and they made figurines sensitively depicting their attitudes. They grew wheat, rice, mustard and sesame seeds, dates and cotton. And they had dogs, cats, camels, sheep, pigs, goats, water buffaloes, elephants and chickens.

Being agricultural, the people of Mohenjo-Daro and Harappa had religions that focused on fertility, on the earth as a giver of life. They had a fertility goddess, whose naked image as a figurine sat in a niche in the wall of their homes. Like the Egyptians they also had a bull god. They worshiped tree gods, and they had a god with three heads and an erect phallus, which they associated with fertility. Like some others, including the Egyptians, they buried objects with their dead. And they had taboos, especially about cleanliness.

The Disappearance of Mohenjo-Daro Civilization

Between the years 1800 and 1700 BC, civilization on the Indus Plain all but vanished. What befell these people is unknown. One suspected cause is a shift in the Indus River. Another is that people dammed the water along the lower portion of the Indus River without realizing the consequences: temporary but ruinous flooding up river, flooding that would explain the thick layers of silt thirty feet above the level of the river at the site of Mohenjo-Daro. Another suspected cause is a decline in rainfall and an accompanying decline in the abundance of food – or an insufficient military strength and will to secure food supplies from distant areas.

Whatever the causes, people abandoned the cities in search of food. Later, a few people resettled in some of the abandoned cities, in what archaeologists call a "squatter period." Then the squatters disappeared. Knowledge of the Mohenjo-Daro civilization died – until archaeologists discovered the civilization in the twentieth century.

ARYANS AND THE ORIGINS OF THE HINDUISM

If rainfall declined in the Indus region between 1800 and 1700 BC, around 1500 BC it increased again, making the Indus Plain better able to support life. It was between 1500 and 1200 that an illiterate, pastoral people migrated from the steppe lands of central Russia through what is now Afghanistan, through the Kyber Pass and onto the sparsely populated Indus Plain. These migrants were to be called Aryans and classified as Indo-Europeans, their speech having been related to all modern European languages except Basque, Finnish and Hungarian.

The Aryans came to the Indus Plain on horseback and oxcart, in waves separated perhaps by decades or longer. Like other pastoral peoples, they were warriors. They had two-wheeled chariots like the Hyksos, and coming through the mountains and the Kyber Pass they had the precious wheels of their chariots packed away on their carts.

The Aryans were familiar with prowling and hunting with bow and arrow. They enjoyed chariot racing, gambling and fighting. Like other pastoral peoples, men dominated the women. Like the pastoral Hebrews, each family was ruled by an authoritarian male. And each Aryan tribe was ruled by a king called a *raja*, who felt obliged to consult with tribal councils.

Gods, Creation and Human Mortality

Like other pastoral people, the Aryan invaders were storytellers. They brought with them to the Indus region their centuries old sacred hymns, myths and oral history – stories that expressed desire to please their gods. Like the Hebrews, the Aryans who invaded India had a father god of the heaven, sky and atmosphere: Dyaus Pitar (sky father). They had a male god of thunder and rain called Indra, who was a god also of that other awesome disturbance: war. Indra was also called the "breaker of forts." And he was what the Aryan men thought a man should be: a warrior with courage, strength and energy who enjoyed drinking and making war.

The Aryans had a god of fire called Agni. To the Aryans, Agni was fire, and they believed that Agni hungrily devoured the animals that they had sacrificed in their rituals of burning. These sacrifices were performed by priests to obtain from their gods the gifts of children, success in war, wealth, health, longevity, food, drink or anything else that contributed to their happiness.

The Aryans enjoyed singing around their campfires, and they had a hymn about creation. Like many other creation myths, theirs described the world as beginning with the kind of creation they understood: birth. They believed that their father god, Dyaus Pitar, the embodiment of sky, had mated with his own daughter, the goddess that was earth. A later Aryan version of the Creation reads:

> In the beginning was nothing, neither heaven nor earth nor space in between. Then Non-being became spirit and said: "Let me be!" He warmed himself, and from this was born fire. He warmed himself further, and from this was born light.

The Aryans had a story that described humanity as having been created with virtue and everlasting life. According to this story, the gods were concerned that humanity would become gods like themselves, and to guard against this the gods plotted humanity's downfall. The gods talked Dyaus Pitar into creating a woman who lusted after sensual pleasures and who aroused sexual desires in men. According to this story, the world had become overcrowded because humankind lived forever like the gods. So Dyaus Pitar decided to make humankind mortal, and he created the goddess Death – not a goddess who ruled over death, but death itself. This creation of mortality for humankind pleased the gods, for it left them separate and of a higher rank than humans.

According to this story, Dyaus Pitar proclaimed that he did not create the goddess Death from anger. And the goddess Death was at first reluctant to carry out the task assigned her, but she finally did so, while weeping. Her tears were diseases that brought death at an appropriate time. To create more death, the goddess Death created desire and anger in people – emotions that led to their killing each other.

Settlement, Conquest and Autocracy

With the passing of generations, the waves of Aryan tribes that had come to the Indus Plain spread out across the region. They warred against local, non-Aryan people, and they settled in areas that provided them with pasture for their animals. They grouped in villages and built homes of bamboo or light wood – homes without statues or art. They began growing crops. Their environment supplied them with all they needed, but, responding to their traditions, and perhaps impulses, the different Aryan tribes warred against each other – wars that might begin with the stealing of cattle. The word for obtaining cattle, *gosati*, became synonymous with making war. And their warring grew in scale, including a war between what was said to be ten kings.

Gradually, Aryan tribal kings were changing from elected leaders to autocratic rulers. Aryan kings had begun associating their power with the powers of their gods rather than the voices of their fellow tribesmen. They had begun allying themselves with priests. And, as in West Asia, kings were acquiring divinity. By taxing their subjects, these kings could create an army that was theirs rather than an instru-ment of the tribe. And these kings allied themselves with the horse owning warrior-aristocracy to which they often belonged.

A Migration East

In the decades around 1000 BC came a shortage of rainfall, and, running from drought, Aryan tribes trekked eastward along the foot of the Himalayan mountains, where jungles were less dense and rivers easier to cross. They entered the plains of the Ganges Valley. And some Aryan priests wandered ahead of their tribe and tried to evangelize among the peoples they came upon. They found these people with a more egalitarian organization than they had, and they despised them for not having kings as autocratic as theirs.

By now, the Aryans had iron tools and weapons, iron having spread eastward through Persia. And with their superior weaponry and self-confidence, the Aryans fought those who resisted their advance, the Aryans believing that their gods were on their side and that resistance from local peoples was inspired by demons. Gradually the Aryans spread over much of the Ganges Valley, clearing land for themselves by calling on their god of fire, Agni.

Some Aryans migrated south along the western coast of the Indian continent, and some Aryans went down the eastern coast, to an area called Kalinga. A few Aryans went as far south as the island described in Hindu literature as *Lanka*. And some Aryan priests went as missionaries to southern India, where they found a dark-skinned people called Dravidians. Occasionally the missionaries felt mistreated. They sought the aide of their king, and their king's warrior nobles came south to their rescue. But southern India remained independent of Aryan rule.

The Beginnings of Caste

With the Aryans settling alongside local peoples, a complex hierarchy of classes developed that would be called *caste*. One class was the priests, called *Brahmins*, and their entire families. Another was the warrior-aristocrats, the *Kshatriyas*, whose job it was to practice constantly at combat. Neither the Brahmins nor the Kshatriyas conceded superiority to the other, but they agreed that the other classes were lower than they. The first of these lower classes were the *Vaishas* and their families: Aryans who tended cattle and served the Brahmins and Kshatriyas in others ways. The lowest class was the conquered, darker, non-Aryans who were servants for the Aryans and called *Shudras*. The Aryans made these four classifications a part of their mythology. The four groups, it was claimed, came from the body of the god Prajapati, the Brahmins from the god's mouth, the warriors from the god's arms, the tenders of cattle from his legs, and the Shudras from his feet.

This class system was less rigid than it would be centuries later. People from different classes could dine together. A man not from a Brahmin family could still become a priest and therefore a Brahmin. And although marriage within one's own class was preferred, there was no absolute restriction against marrying people from a different class.

Brahmins married women from a lower caste whom they found attractive, but this was a male prerogative. A girl from a Brahmin family was allowed to marry only someone also from a Brahmin family.

Urbanization, Trade and War

By around 700 or 600 BC, the migrations of the Aryans had ended, and with their new successes in agriculture the Aryans increased in number, and they began to create cities. Aryan traders, merchants, landlords appeared, as did money lending. Aryans began trading with Arabia and the great empire of the Assyrians. In the 600s, India began trading with China, the Malay peninsula and the islands of what are now Indonesia and the Philippines. By 600 BC, numerous cities had arisen in northern India – cities with fortifications, moats and ramparts in response to the dangers of war. In northern India along the Ganges River, sixteen different kingdoms had emerged.

A Blending of Pastoral and Agricultural Religion

Like the mix between the agricultural religion of the Canaanites and the pastoral religion of the Hebrews, in India a mix developed between the pastoral religion of the Aryans and the local religions of the conquered. This mix came with Aryan males marrying non-Aryan females, and it came with some among the conquered accepting the religion of their conquerors – much as those in the Americas the 1500s AD would accept the religion of their Christian conquerors. In India this blend of Aryan and local religions became known as Hinduism, a word derived from the Aryan word *Sindu*, the name the Aryans gave to the Indus River. The Hindu religion ranged from veneration of traditional Aryan gods by urban intellectuals to the worship of a diversity of local, rural, agricultural deities.

Hindu Scripture and Sin

Around the same time that writing spread to the Hebrews, it appeared among the Aryans in India. Some Brahmins considered it a sacrilege to change from communicating their religion orally. But a sufficient number of Brahmins supported the innovation, and they put traditional Aryan stories into writing, in what became known as the *Vedas* – *Veda* meaning wisdom. The Vedas became wisdom literature, a literature that would be considered an infallible source of timeless, revealed truth.

The most important of the Vedas was the *Rig* Veda, which consisted of hymns or devotional incantations of 10,562 written lines in ten books. Another Veda, the *Yajur* Veda, focused less on devotional incantations and more on sacrificial procedures as a means of pleasing the gods. A third Veda, the *Sama* Veda, was mainly concerned with the god Indra. Indra was now seen as the god that had created the cosmos, the ruler of the atmosphere, and the god of thunderbolts and rain – Dyaus Pitar having diminished in importance. Also mentioned in the *Sama* Veda were other gods of the sky and atmosphere: Varuna, guardian of the cosmic order; Agni, the god of fire; and Surya, the sun. A fourth Veda, the *Atharya* Veda, was a collection of 730 hymns, totaling six thousand stanzas, containing prescriptions for prayer, rituals for curing diseases, expiations against evils, protection against enemies and sorcerers, and prescriptions for creating charms for love, health, prosperity, influence, and a long life.

Among the Vedas were descriptions of funeral rites that included cremation, and there were descriptions of lengthy and solemn rituals for marriage. The Vedas implied that humanity is basically good, and in marked contrast to views in West Asia, sin was viewed not as bad judgement but as a force from outside oneself – an invader. The Vedas saw evil as the work of demons that might take the form of a human or some other creature, which could be removed by the prayers and rituals of priests.

Diversity and the Upanishads

The religion of the Aryans continued to change. The Vedas, like other writings, had to be interpreted, and among the Hindus arose diversity in interpretations. Diversity in opinion was becoming a normal part of civilization, the result of a rise in population and freedom from tribal isolation and conformity. And diversity in opinion among the Aryans included skepticism. One Brahmin had the genius to see that there were truths not yet known, and he advocated doubt and recorded his insights in a late contribution to the Rig Veda, writing that some priests had an unwarranted certainty in belief and were blind men leading the blind.

Some Hindu intellectuals became less interested in the monotonous routines of the ritual sacrifices of Hindu worship and more interested in probing Hinduism's relations between self and the universe and how one could attain religious bliss. These new interests were expressed in writings that were to be collected into what would be called the *Upanishads*, a collection of as many as two hundred books written across two centuries.

The Upanishads consisted of attempts to describe truth through poetry and analogy. Some contributors made points drawn from observed fact, and some merely recorded their intuitions and asked the reader to accept their insights on faith. Some contributors to the Upanishads repeated beliefs already expressed in the Vedas, such as every living thing having a spirit, or soul, and spirits being able to migrate in and out of things. They wrote of death as the passing of one's spirit into other beings, and death as a rebirth, with souls returning to earth within another human or some other creature – reincarnation. Where a soul went, they wrote, depended upon how well a person had behaved in his previous life. Good actions led to a soul being bound to a higher form of life and the soul of the doer of evil found its way to a lower form of life.

Some contributors to the Upanishads pleaded that one's fate could be altered only by learning – like a born-again Christian who transforms himself by acquiring a knowledge of God. In the Upanishads this was expressed in the claim that rather than rejoice in externals known through the senses, people should turn their thoughts inward in a quest for self-realization and knowledge about themselves. They claimed that material or sensual pleasure should not be ultimate goals, that what people really want lies more deeply, that God is within us and that the wise seek the joys of the infinite, the joy that comes with separating the self from the body and freeing oneself from the clutches of birth and death.

It was written in the Upanishads that there are two kinds of knowledge. One kind was called *lower* knowledge, which was described as knowledge about the existence of a god, knowledge of rituals and the knowledge that one acquires through one's senses about the material world. This *lower* knowledge was described as standing in the way of the other kind of knowledge: *higher* knowledge. This *higher* knowledge was described as impossible to explain, like trying to explain warmth to someone who knows only cold. *Higher* knowledge was described as a personal experience that touched one's soul. It was claimed that written instructions might help guide one toward acquiring this knowledge but that in this acquisition emotions had to dominate.

This view of knowledge did not acknowledge a limited ability to know so much as it did a limited ability to teach. Some contributors to the Upanishads wrote that all they could do was stimulate thinking in others that would lead these others to acquire wisdom on their own. They described this search as an adventure on behalf of the human spirit. One contributor to the Upanishads wrote:

> Into blind darkness enter they who worship igno-
> rance; into darkness greater than that enter they who
> delight in knowledge.

Additional contributions to the Upanishads made this search for higher knowledge an attempt at awareness of an underlying, universal unity. Assumptions were made about universal consciousness. Various writings described different unifying forces: Vishvkarman, the Great Soul; the god Hiranyagargha, who established the earth and sky; Brahmanaspate the Lord of Prayer, who also produced the world; and Aditi, the mother of gods.

In these later contributions to the Upanishads the search for unity led to the question of how many gods exist – unity suggesting a single, all encompassing god. One contribution described a youth asking a learned man how many gods there are. The learned man named three hundred and three. "Yes," responded the youth, "but how many are there really?" The learned man narrowed their number to thirty-three. "Yes," responded the youth, "but how many are there really?" And finally the learned man said there was only one god.

One contributor to the Upanishads wrote that a person had to realize the god in himself before he could realize the god of the cosmos, and he claimed that realizing the god in oneself is recognizing oneself in all others.

Another view in the Upanishads held that everything is unified but that there is a world of the senses, which is illusion, that God is a maker of this illusion, and that there is the world of the spirit and mental realization. This view held that to grasp reality and reach one's goal of harmony with the cosmos one must turn from the illusion of materiality to the world of mental realization.

A contrary view in the Upanishads combined the material and spiritual worlds more closely. Instead of turning from materiality, this view claimed that one helped oneself understand the unity of the universe by gaining knowledge about materiality, including the origins of the universe. One writer of this persuasion speculated that the world had begun as water, that the earth is water solidified, that every solid is basically water and that water and God are one. Another contributor to the Upanishads saw reality and God as fire.

One contributor to the Upanishads described God as mystery, and another contributor claimed that in the beginning there was nothingness, that the world was created from nothingness and would eventually return to nothingness. Another writer described God as having existed before all else. He wrote that in the beginning God was alone, that he looked around and saw nothing, and, being lonely, he divided himself into male and female, and that these two aspects of God then mated and brought into creation all living things.

Epic Literature – the Ramayana and Mahabharata

Eventually, Hindus followed the impulse that had appeared among the Sumerians and others and they wrote poetic stories that focused on the power of the gods. These Hindu stories were written to create ideals for people to follow. The better known of these are poems called the Ramayana and the Mahabharata.

The Ramayana is believed to have been written by a Brahmin named Valmiki, a man whose style of poetry was new and was to be copied thereafter. The Ramayana appeared perhaps as early as 500 BC. It describes an earlier period when Aryans were expanding their influence over the Dravidians in southern India. It describes missionary endeavors supported by military power and the Aryan strategy of divide and conquer. In its seven books and 24,000 verses the Ramayana praises the heroism and virtues of the Aryan warrior-princes: the Kshatriyas. The Ramayana has as its main hero a prince called Rama, whose life the Ramayana describes from birth to death – Ramayana meaning the story of Rama. Rama and his brothers are depicted as embodying the ideals of Aryan culture: men of loyalty and honor, faithful and dutiful sons, affectionate brothers and loving husbands, men who speak the truth, who are stern, who persevere but are ready and willing to make sacrifices for the sake of virtue against the evils of greed, lust and deceit.

The Mahabharata, meaning Great India, might also have first appeared by 500 BC, give or take a century or so. Across centuries, priestly writers and editors with different attitudes in different centuries were to add to the work, and the Mahabharata emerged three times its original size. The Mahabharata was divided into eighteen books of verses interspersed with passages of prose. It attempted to describe the period in which Aryan tribes in northern India were uniting into kingdoms and when these kingdoms were fighting to create empire. The work attempted to be an encyclopedia about points of morality. One of its heroes is Krishna, described as a royal personage descended from the gods – an eighth incarnation of the god Vishnu. The Mahabharata's heroes are described as yearning for power but, like the heroes of the Ramayana, as devoted to truth and as having a strong sense of duty and affection for their parents.

The Materialists

Intellectual unrest continued in India through the 500s. A few writers in India challenged Hinduism by proclaiming that the universe was essentially inanimate and functioned other than by the magic of gods. They claimed that when a person dies he dissolves back into primary elements, that after death there is neither pain nor pleasure, that there is no afterlife or reincarnation, that soul and god are only words and that Hindu sacrifices accomplish nothing.

The materialist point of view found its way into the Upanishads, and Brahmin authorities responded by removing the offending entries, and they destroyed other materialist writings. No writings expressing the materialist point of view were to survive. They were to be known only through those who argued against them.

Spirituality without Mental Struggle
During the 500s, an alternative grew to spiritual attainment through the attainment of knowledge as advocated in the Upanishads. Many seeking spiritual fulfillment were uninterested in metaphysical complexities. They continued to worship gods such as Indra and Agni but they also found satisfaction in devotion to gods that were parental figures, gods with whom they could have a personal relationship – like Christians who believed in God the father and had their personal relationship with Jesus Christ. In the northwest of India, people worshiped a personal god called Shiva, a god who embodied a reconciliation between the extremes of passionate eroticism and ascetic renunciation, and between frenzy and serenity. Shiva was believed to dwell in the Himalayas, to have a benevolent goddess counterpart called Pavati, and to have many brides and numerous children.

Some Hindus turned from the complexities of the Upanishads to a more simple spiritual benefit by way of good behavior, which they claimed was more important than whatever god one worshiped. This good behavior included proper eating, restrictions on drinking, keeping oneself in godly cleanliness, performing one's duties and behaving in a manner appropriate with one's class and stage in life – all described as good for one's soul.

In the latter half of the 500s came growth in another effort at spirituality through proper behavior: asceticism. These were times of insecurity and misery, and a greater number of young men were giving up on the material world and searching for eternal bliss. Orthodox Brahmins attempted to keep in check the loss of youthful manpower to asceticism, and they tried to confine asceticism to men beyond middle age. To this end they invented four stages in life regarding duties of a Hindu: the celibate religious student; the married Hindu, including priests; the forest hermit, who was older than the students; and the elderly wandering ascetic.

THE JAINS AND BUDDHISTS

In the far northeast, Brahmins performed as teachers and gave instruction to local, non-Aryan elites who had not been completely Hinduized. These elites were accustomed to deference from local people, and they were offended by the posturing, pride and arrogance of the Brahmins. They resisted the claims of Brahmins to higher rank and superior knowledge. Some among them opposed the bloodletting of Hinduism's animal sacrifices. Some of them thought the Brahmins too involved in ceremonial formalities and ritual and saw the Brahmin's view of gods and salvation as strange. With this dissent against orthodox Hinduism, a variety of men with visions appeared who tried to create followings. These new sect leaders denied the authority of the Vedas, and each developed a code of conduct and claimed to have found the secret of eternal bliss. Local merchants who were gaining in wealth and influence threw their support to one or another of the religious rebels in their area. Sect leaders wandered across the northeast, sometimes with large bands of followers. They entered communities to engage in disputations with rival sects and orthodox Brahmins, disputations that were welcomed entertainment for local people.

The Jains

The most successful of the new sects were those that attempted to provide relief from orthodox Hinduism's failure to alleviate human suffering. One such sect was the *Jains* – from the Sanskrit verb *ji,* meaning to conquer. The Jains sought relief from suffering by conquest over one's own passions and senses. This, the Jains believed, gave one purity of soul. According to legend, the Jains were led by Nataputta Vardhamana, the son of a royal governor from the Magadha region. Nataputta Vardhamana gave up his princely status for a life of asceticism and became known as Mahavira (Great Souled One). Legend describes Mahavira beginning as a reformer, as not seeking to overthrow the Hindu caste system or the worship of Hindu gods but wishing to do something about the misery that he saw. Legend describes him as having sympathy not only for people but also for the animals that the Brahmins sacrificed.

Mahavira appealed to people who wanted religion without the metaphysical speculations that most people found too vague and complex. He rejected the idea of everything connected into oneness: the doctrine of the universal soul included in the Upanishads. In its place he indulged in some metaphysics of his own, describing a reality that includes differentiation among things as well as associations. He envisioned a dualistic reality, a world with both conscious and unconscious elements, a world that is both spirit and material.

Mahavira became popular among the urban middle class and women in northeastern India. Jainist legend describes his following at the time of his death as 359,000 women and 159,000 men, including full-time devotees numbering 36,000 nuns and 14,000 monks.

After Mahavira's death his followers held onto the view that plants and insects, as well animals, had consciousness. It was not yet understood that life included microorganisms and viruses, or that fleas and other insects carried diseases, and the Jains believed that the destruction of any life, including that of insects, was evil. Maintaining Hinduism's belief in reincarnation, they held that by refraining from killing they could liberate their soul from the cycle of births and deaths. Jains monks swept the path in front of them to avoid crushing insects, and they strained their water believing that this prevented them from consuming any living organisms. Lay persons were less persistent, believing that it was enough that they not *intentionally* kill.

Jain lay persons took the following vows: never to intentionally destroy a living thing; never to speak falsehoods; never to steal; to always be faithful in marriage; to always be chaste outside of marriage; to possess no more money or other things than one had set for oneself as sufficient (a practical restriction that varied with how wealthy one was); to travel no farther than the limits that one had set for oneself; to think no evil thoughts about others; to sit in meditation as often as one had planned; to spend time as a temporary monk or nun; and to support the nuns and monks with contributions.

The Buddhists

Another who led a religious movement to relieve suffering was a prince named Siddhartha Gautama, to be known as the Buddha (Great Teacher). Siddhartha was born into the Sakya tribe at the foot of the Himalayan Mountains north of the Ganges Valley, in a small city, Kapilavastu, in what is now southern Nepal. He is reported to have seen his native city overrun and its people butchered. The Sakya tribe was under Aryan suzerainty and had retained independence in exchange for tribute paid to Aryan overlords. The Sakya tribe had aristocrats and commoners, and according to legend, Siddhartha was a prince.

According to legend, Siddhartha was sheltered in his youth from the ugliness and poverty around him, but when he was twenty-nine – around 534 BC – he decided to become a wanderer. Apparently, Siddhartha withdrew from a world that was inhospitable to conquered royalty such as he, while he remained disturbed and fascinated by the Aryan civilization that had overrun his state and its traditions. The legend created by his followers describes Siddhartha as becoming a wanderer in order to learn about human existence. He became an ascetic and abused his body by hardly eating. Failing in his quest to understand human existence, and for spiritual satisfaction, Siddhartha began eating better, and he began devising what he believed were his own solutions to human misery.

Siddhartha agreed with the view expressed in the Upanishads that the cause of human misery was humanity itself, but he was determined not to fall into what he saw as the error of those who sought salvation in idle speculations. He refused to question or discuss whether the cosmos is finite or infinite, whether there is life after death or other metaphysical questions, on the grounds that these sidetrack people from doing something practical about the misery of their existence. Siddhartha decided that human misery came with people looking for permanence where there was no permanence and with people clinging to objects of desire that were transitory. He saw relief in self-control over one's appetites and ambitions. He concluded that it was not wrong to desire good food and drink, fine clothes, or sexual satisfaction but that it was eventually destructive psychologically to persist in these appetites. He believed that giving up hope for that which one cannot have was a means to peace of mind.

According to legend, Siddhartha became a master of the tenets and practices of other sects, and many of his disciples were recruited after hearing him debate with religious rivals in gatherings that were then popular entertainment in towns across the Ganges Valley. Siddhartha preached no warnings of torments for evil deeds. Instead he preached the attaining of serenity, or nirvana, through self-discipline. He outlined numerous rules for attaining this personal salvation. The first was proper understanding, by which he meant realizing that there is nothing essentially permanent, that there is only change – a radical departure from orthodox Hinduism. His next rule was proper attitude, by which he meant not wanting the impossible and accepting the inevitable. His third rule was proper speech, which he believed important because words preceded actions. Proper actions, was his fourth rule, Siddhartha seeing proper actions as important in creating a righteousness about oneself that engendered serenity. His fifth rule was to do no injury to other living things. This included refraining from theft, lying, sexual immorality, and drinking liquors which engendered slothfulness. Siddhartha's additional rules reinforced his first five rules and included having a proper vocation, making proper efforts, exercising proper reflection, and partaking in proper meditation.

Like Mahavira (the founder of the Jains), Siddhartha rejected the authority of the Vedas and rejected animal sacrifices, and he rejected the claims of the Brahmins that they were superior. Siddhartha claimed that people should not expect assistance from any source other than themselves, that one could not lean on gods or other spiritual agents, that each person must work out his own salvation, that people had will and could not escape choice by choosing to follow the advice and assistance of others, that people should be their own lamps and their own salvation and take refuge in nothing outside of themselves. But Siddhartha did not ask his followers to give up their Hindu gods, and Indra, Brahma, Shiva and Vishnu would be worshiped by his followers for centuries to come.

Siddhartha created an order of monks, with whom he met during the rainy season for strategy sessions and teaching. The monks and nuns did not regard themselves as apart from lay followers or apart from the world. They saw themselves as promoters of the welfare and happiness not just of themselves but of the many.

Like Mahavira, Siddhartha did not preach against the caste system, which outside his movement was widely viewed as an essential ingredient in family values and necessary for social order. But he opened his movement to all classes and eventually to females, and within his movement everyone was released from caste restrictions.

Siddhartha Gautama died in 483 at the age of eighty. And according to legend, a council of five hundred Buddhist monks met at the city of Rajagriha, concerned about preserving Siddhartha's teachings. They had reason for worry: diversity in belief would soon appear among Buddhists as it had among the Jains and the rest of civilized humanity.

Soon splits among the Buddhists occurred over a variety of issues, some as small as whether one should drink buttermilk after dinner. A split arose among the Buddhists as some older members wanted to limit membership in the Buddhist movement to the ascetic monks and nuns. Other Buddhists wanted a broader movement, one that included those not ready to discipline themselves or to withdraw from the normal routines of life as did the monks and nuns – a split between purists and inclusionists that would appear among other religious movements.

CHAPTER 6

THE RISE OF CHINA

SHANG CIVILIZATION

Through mountains and the Wei River Valley, a stone-age people migrated eastward to a thickly wooded North China Plain, along the Yellow River (Hwang Ho in Chinese). Hunting, fishing and gathering food remained important to these people, but where they were free of forest and had access to water they began growing millet. Farming came as early as 5500 BC, and in addition to farming they raised dogs, pigs, sheep and goats. They had spinning wheels, and they knitted and wove fibers. They had pottery that they decorated with art. They built one-room homes dug into the earth, with roofs of clay or thatch – pit homes grouped in villages.

Flooding along the Yellow River was worse than to the south, where farming had also developed – in the Hupei basin along the Yangtze River and along the coastal plain by Hangchou Bay. People along the Yellow River had to work harder at flood control and irrigation, and perhaps this greater challenge stimulated a greater effort at organization than among the growers in the south – which may have contributed to civilization appearing along the Yellow River earlier than it did to the south.

Civilization along the Yellow River came as it did elsewhere: with food abundant enough to allow a substantial growth in population. Across centuries, migrations into the North China Plain may have continued. And where people were producing more food than they needed to survive, warriors had the incentive not only to plunder but also to conquer. And conquering kings arose on the North China Plain as they did in West Asia.

The first dynasty of kings belonging to the civilization along the Yellow River has been described as that of the Hsia family – whose rule is thought to have begun around 2200 BC. But the first dynasty of which there is historical evidence is that of the Shang family, who are thought to have begun their rule around 1750 BC. The Shang clan came out of the Wei River Valley. By force, the Shang unified people along

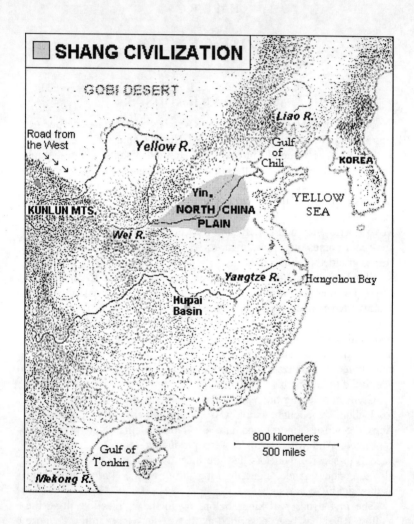

SHANG CIVILIZATION

GOBI DESERT

Road from
the West

Yellow R.

Liao R.

Gulf
of
Chili

KOREA

KUNLUN MTS.

Yin.
NORTH CHINA
PLAIN

Wei R.

YELLOW
SEA

Yangtze R.

Hangchou Bay

Hupai
Basin

Gulf of
Tonkin

Mekong R.

800 kilometers
500 miles

the North China Plain, building an empire in much the same way as other conquerors: by leaving behind a garrison force to police local people, by turning a local king into a subservient ally free to manage local matters, and by taxing the conquered.

Class and Economy during the Shang Dynasty
Around 1384 BC, the Shangs moved their capital to Yin. By now, alongside Shang kings were nobles and aristocrats. As a regular pastime, the Shang kings and nobles hunted in organized game drives. Kings and aristocrats had splendid homes with walls of pounded earth or earthen bricks while common people continued to live in the pit homes of earlier times. A Shang king was chief priest, and he had an administrative bureaucracy, with councilors, lesser priests and diviners. As with other warring civilizations, slaves were held, the slaves laboring at growing crops. And women in Shang civilization were subservient to men, with aristocratic women enjoying a greater freedom and equality than common women.

During the Shang dynasty, the civilization along the Yellow River had canals for irrigating crops. Communities had drains that ran water out of town. They made beer from Millet. They extended their trading and used money in the form of cowry shells. Shang merchants traded in salt, iron, copper, tin, lead and antimony, some of which had to be imported from far away. As early as the 1300s a bronze casting industry had developed. This was later than the rise of bronze casting in Europe and West Asia, but it had become the most advanced in the world.

Writing and Religion under the Shang
It was around 1300 BC that the first known writing appeared in Shang civilization – writing that developed more than three thousand characters, partly pictorial and partly phonetic. These writing were done on plate-like portions of the bones of cattle or deer, on sea shells and turtle shells and perhaps on wood. These writings were inscriptions concerned with predicting the future. By applying a pointed, heated rod to a bone or shell, the item cracked, and to which characters on the item the crack traveled gave answers for various questions: what the weather was going to be like, whether there would be flood, a successful or failed harvest, or when might be the best time for hunting or fishing, questions about illness, or whether one should make a journey.

The people of Shang civilization appear to have had the same religious impulses as others. They saw nature as numerous gods using magic, gods called *kuei-shen*, a word for ghost or spirit. They had a god they thought produced rain. They had a god of thunder and a god for each mountain, river and forest. They had a mother god of the sun, a moon goddess, and a god of the wind. Like others who worked the soil, they had a fertility god. They believed in a master god who had a palace in the center of heaven and who rewarded people for being virtuous. And they depicted their gods as having faces that were more Asiatic and Western.

Like priests in West Asia, the priests of Shang civilization made sacrifices to their gods, attempting to bribe them, believing that the gods could exercise either benevolent or malevolent magic. The frequency of floods and other calamities led the people of Shang civilization to believe that some gods were good and others demonic. And they believed in an evil god who led travelers astray and devoured people.

The people of Shang civilization believed in an invisible heaven that people went to when they died. Shang kings told their subjects that heaven was where the ancestors of Shang kings dwelled. Aristocrats also believed they had ancestors in heaven. Concerned with their status, aristocrats boasted about their ancestral roots. They kept records of their family tree, and they saw their ancestors as going back to gods who often took the form of animals – gods who became family symbols like the totems that were to be familiar in the Americas. The common people, on the other hand, had no surnames and no pedigree and did not participate in ancestor worship.

Aristocrats believed that humans had a spirit that was created at conception. They believed that this spirit both continued to reside in one's body after death and ascended to the invisible world where the spirits and dead dwelled. Aristocrats believed that in this invisible world their ancestors resided in the court of the gods and had powers to help guide and assist their living descendants. Aristocrats saw their ancestors as needing nourishment. At grave sites they offered food and wine to their deceased family and ancestors – a ritual that males alone were allowed to perform, adding to the preference for the birth of a male into a family. They believed that if offerings to the dead were discontinued, the spirits of the dead would become lost and starving ghosts who, in revenge, would do evil. When an aristocrat wanted a special favor from an ancestor, he supplemented the offerings by sacrificing animals. And like Abraham, the Shang knew of human sacrifice. If a king wanted a special favor from the gods, he might sacrifice a human.

Shang Violence and Splendor

To the east, north and south of Shang civilization were those the Shang saw as barbarians, including those along the Yangtze River. Shang kings sent out armies to repulse invaders, and the Shang kings went beyond their domains to plunder, and to capture foreign peoples needed for sacrifice to their gods. Uncovered tombs of kings from the

Shang period indicate that they could put into the field as many as three to five thousand soldiers. Found buried with the kings were their personal ornaments and spears with bronze blades and the remains of what had been bows and arrows. Buried with the kings were also horses and chariots for transporting soldiers to battle. And buried with the kings were his charioteers, dogs, servants and people in groups of ten – people who had been ceremonially beheaded with bronze axes.

CHOU* KINGS REPLACE THE SHANG

Around 1000 BC, Shang rule was threatened from forces outside and within its empire. To the west of Shang civilization, in the Wei River Valley, lived a rugged, pastoral people called Chou who led an alliance that included other tribal peoples neighboring Shang civilization. While the Shang king, Chou-hsin, was occupied by a war against tribal people to his southeast, rebellions broke out among people that Shang monarchs before him had conquered. The Chou and their allies saw the Shang king's troubles as an opportunity to move against him, and they overpowered him at the battle of Mu-ye and had him beheaded.

A dynasty of Chou kings began ruling what had been Shang civilization. They claimed that all lands belonged to heaven, that they were the sons of heaven and therefore that all lands and all people were their subjects. Seeing the lands they had conquered as too vast for one man to dominate, the Chou kings divided these lands into regions and assigned someone to rule each region in their name, choosing for this position a close family member, a trusted member of their clan, or the chief of a tribe that had been allied with them against the Shang.

Each local ruler had at his disposal all the lands around him. He had his own militia. And from the Chou kings the local rulers received gifts such as chariots, bronze weapons, servants and animals. The local rulers received the title of lord (kung). Local rulers passed their positions to their sons, their titles of lord becoming hereditary. And to control their areas better, the lords made sub-lords of those who had dominated the common people before they arrived.

---

*A note on pronunciation:

Ch is pronounced as is the s in *pleasure*. Ch' is pronounced as is the ch in *choose*. The ou in Chou and other words is pronounced as is the word *oh*. As does the Encylopaedia Britannica, this book uses the Wade-Giles rather than the more recent Pinyan spelling of Chinese.

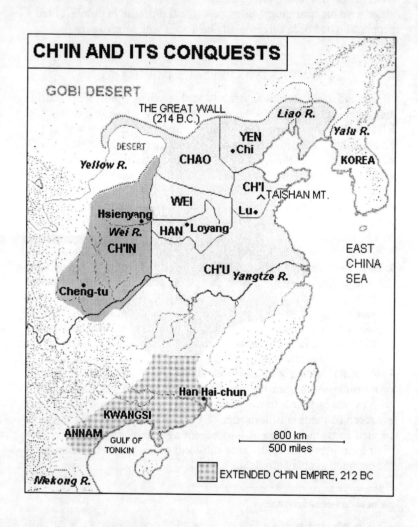

CH'IN AND ITS CONQUESTS

GOBI DESERT

THE GREAT WALL
(214 B.C.)

Liao R.

Yalu R.

YEN
• Chi

DESERT

CHAO

KOREA

Yellow R.

CH'I

WEI

TAISHAN MT.

Hsienyang

Lu

Wei R.

HAN • Loyang

CH'IN

EAST
CHINA
SEA

CH'U Yangtze R.

Cheng-tu

Han Hai-chun

KWANGSI

ANNAM

GULF OF
TONKIN

800 km
500 miles

Mekong R.

EXTENDED CH'IN EMPIRE, 212 BC

A hierarchy of status and obligations emerged among families and within families, with older brothers ranking higher than younger brothers, with rules of succession as to which male would head their families. If a married aristocrat became infatuated with another woman, rather than drive his wife from his home he could bring the other oman into the family as a concubine, where she would rank beneath his wife.

Religion under the Chou Kings

Chou kings told those they had conquered that they, the Chou, had ousted the ancestors of Shang kings from heaven and that heaven was occupied by their supreme god, a god they called "The Lord on High," who, they said, had commanded the downfall of the Shang kings. Like emperors in West Asia, Chou kings claimed that they ruled by divine right. They claimed that they represented on earth the "Lord on High" and that it was their position to mediate between the Lord and heaven, to perform the appropriate sacrifices and to maintain a proper relationship between heaven and their subjects. They claimed that any opposition to their rule was opposition to the will of heaven.

It was from the Chou kings that local lords received the right to act as a priest: to perform sacrifices, to have certain hymns sung and certain dances performed, the right to propitiate the gods of local mountains, streams and of the soil and crops. Meanwhile, local aristocrats continued to keep track of their ancestral heritage. They married with religious rites and sanctions while common folk continued to have no such marriages, no surnames or recorded ancestors. They merely lived together and were recognized as a couple by their neighbors.

As in India and West Asia, with time came a mixing of the religions of the conqueror and conquered. Chou rulers admitted into their pantheon of gods some of the gods of Shang civilization. The worship of various gods from the Shang period continued, including gods of grain, rain and agriculture – one whom was believed to have had a virgin birth. Among these gods was a god of the Yellow River who had the body of a fish but the face of a man.

In Chou civilization, people continued their attempt to appease the gods by giving them gifts. Those who could afford it sacrificed cattle, sheep, pigs or horses. The sacrificing of humans diminished from what it had been under the Shang kings, but Chou kings had their wives or friends join them in the grave, and each year a young woman was offered as a bride to the river god. This latter sacrifice began with sorceresses choosing the most attractive woman they could find. They dressed the girl in satin, silk and jewelry and put her on a nuptial bed on a raft. They floated the raft down river. The raft sank and the girl drowned, gone as a gift to the invisible world of the river god.

The Chou Dynasty Loses Power

After more than two hundred years of rule, the Chou dynasty began to decline in power. According to legend, a Chou king named Yu-wang appointed the son of his concubine as his heir, rather than the son of his wife. This angered the queen, and she and her father allied themselves with a nearby nomadic tribe called the Ch'uan-jung. Yu-wang is described as having wasted his energies on pleasures and as having neglected the defense of his realm, and in 771 BC the Ch'uan-jung tribesmen overran the capital city in the Wei Valley (near what in the coming centuries would be the city of Hsienyang. They killed the king, and then, with friendly wishes, they sent the queen, her father and the queen's son away to a new capital, Loyang, and the queen's son become the next Chou king.

Local lords across the Chou empire responded to the Ch'uan-jung victory over Yu-wang by making themselves powers in their own right, and the new Chou king and his successors were unable to recover their power over these local lords. The new Chou kings lost the revenues that previous Chou kings had received from the provinces, and they survived on the taxes they received from those who worked their personal, nearby lands. The Chou kings continued to issue edicts and to conduct religious ceremonies that according to custom they alone were allowed to perform, and they maintained at their court numerous officials and many priests, but they now ruled the Chou empire in name only.

WARS, CONFUCIANISTS, MO-TZU,
TAOISTS, AND LEGALISTS

With the demise in power of the Chou kings came wars between the local lords. Each local lord had his own army. Each jealously adhered to the formalities that symbolized his status, and each created his own court of law. Some local lords pursued vendettas against a neighboring lord, or one raided another lord's land in search of loot. Lords entered into alliances with each other, sometimes through marriage. They made treaties and exchanged goods. But for some lords war was a sport – better than a good hunt. Often wars were fought as a gentleman's acti-vity, with battlefield courtesy such as letting an opponent cross a river and form ranks before attacking. They believed that heaven disap-proved of extreme measures and that a ruthless victor might suffer from the displeasure of the gods.

The Confucius Legend

Exercising what they believed was their religious authority, the Chou kings maintained a collection of scholarly specialists on morality, festivals and sacrifices. And local lords imitated the Chou kings and attracted scholars to their courts to conduct their sacrifices and funerals and to teach their children. A new age of scholarship had appeared, and among the scholars was a man named K'ung-fu-tzu (Master K'ung), a name that in the seventeenth century AD in Europe was to be Latinized to *Confucius*.

The earliest biography on Confucius was written four hundred years after his death, and those writing about him most likely portrayed him without any details that had become disagreeable. The earliest copy of the writings of Confucius that are available to modern scholars date back only to the fourth century AD, seven centuries after Confucius lived – plenty of time for followers copying his work to edit it to suit changing times and attitudes. These writings purported to have been by Confucius are called *The Analects*, which describe requisites for being a good person, a good ruler and a good follower.

According to legend, Confucius was born in 551 BC, in a principality called Lu, about 150 miles west of the Yellow Sea – an area in which Shang culture remained strong. Confucius is said to have lost his father when he was three and to have studied in his early youth. Some have claimed that he may have been the illegitimate son of a nobleman and a concubine, for, rather than work in the fields and remain illiterate as common boys did, he went to work for the local ruler, managing stables and keeping books for granaries. After marrying at nineteen, he completed studies that earned him the title of scholar. As a scholar he was a master of ritual, music, archery, charioteering, calligraphy and arithmetic and he had some familiarity with poetry and history.

Confucius lived after people around him had begun using iron tools. The use of iron had brought a higher productivity in agriculture, a greater rise in population, more urban growth, improvements in transportation and trade, coinage and new wealth. This loosened social stratification and may have led Confucius and others to see society as having become chaotic and in moral decline. Some scholars saw the world as hopelessly askew and became recluses. But, according to legend, rather than become a recluse, Confucius decided to change society through education. He is described as having opened a school for those he thought were potential leaders and as having taught any male willing to learn. Confucius is described as a teacher who conversed rather than lectured. He is described as the first among the Chinese to support himself by teaching – by charging tuition. According to legend, Confucius also became active in politics, advocating government for the happiness of the common people rather than the pleasure of their rulers, and he advocated a reduction of taxes, the mitigation of severe punishments and the avoidance of wars.

Confucius is described by his biographers as advocating the restoration and renovation of the institutions of the first of the Chou kings. He is described as blaming the ills of his day on leaders neglecting old Chou rituals or performing these rituals incorrectly. Controversy exists over whether Confucius actually revered the early rule of the Chou kings or merely pretended such reverence in order to make his views more palatable to contemporaries – a subterfuge that would have contradicted sayings attributed to Confucius about honesty, sincerity and straight-forwardness.

By the time of Confucius, the founder of the Chou dynasty, Hou-chi, was described as having been born by a virgin. Confucius may not have believed this, but he is described as believing the claim of Chou kings that their rule was a mandate from heaven. Confucius is described as seeing events as a morality play directed from heaven, as believing that Shang kings had lost the mandate of heaven through a decline in their virtue and especially through the wickedness of their last ruler, Chou-hsin. To the Confucianists the Chou leaders who overthrew Chou-hsin were great heroes. According to the followers of Confucius, he believed that early Chou rule was a golden age, a time of order, reason and virtue, and that Chou kings lost their power by having failed to exercise virtue.

Confucius is described as believing that a return to the golden age of the early Chou kings could be accomplished by the return of rule that was similarly ethical and wise. Apparently, Confucius believed that a king had to earn this mandate from heaven. According to his followers, Confucius saw the Lord of Heaven not as a tyrant but as the embodiment of a system of laws. He believed that kings should conduct themselves in accordance with these laws, including observing established ceremonies and offering all sacrifices in accordance with the proper rites. He believed that the king should set a moral example for commoners and that commoners should conduct themselves in accordance with the laws of heaven and remain obedient to the rule of the king. Confucius is described as believing that people should respect and obey their parents as well as the king who ruled over them. The state, he believed, was an extension of the family, a collection of families. He believed that a family should be ruled by the eldest adult male, and that families should be led by the superior family of the emperor. In this regard, Confucius was a man of his time: he placed his hope for humanity in the sincerity of the ruler rather than in checks and balances in government and the watchful eye of the public.

The right course, believed Confucius, was for a king to behave like a king and a son to behave like a son. He created what he called *categories* and held that a king who did not behave as a king was not a king, and a son who did not behave as a son was not a son. According to Confucius, obedience was the prime ingredient of the authentic individual. To maintain harmony, believed Confucius, people should not wander from what is authentic.

Confucius is described as believing in class distinctions – what he called social categories. He not only supported the religious values of the elite, he supported their good manners, and he dissociated himself from the religion that had become identified with the common people: shamanism, witchcraft and sorcery. Although he favored the elevation of males according to their learning and superior moral qualities, he appears to have failed to see that equal opportunity was not possible in an autocratic society dominated by aristocrats.

When Confucius was around fifty, he served as a minister of public works and as a minister of justice, but his support for Chou kingship could not have set well with the ruler of Lu – who owed his power to independence from Chou rule. And the moral posturing of Confucius might have alienated him from those around the local ruler – advisors and servants of various sorts who often wished to entice the ruler with sensual pleasures.

Confucius was disappointed that his views were not taken seriously and put into practice. He left politics in disgust and went on a decade of dangerous travels through various states. When he was sixty-seven, he responded to an invitation from some of his disciples to return to Lu, and there he taught five more years. Then he died viewing the world as askew, his optimism from earlier years having gone unrewarded.

Mo-tzu – Rival to Confucius

After Confucius' death, his teachings were overshadowed by the scholar Mo-tzu (Master Mo), who was born nine years after Confucius died. Like Confucius, he was trained in classical literature. Mo-tzu saw the Confucianists of his time as pretentious and selfish aristocrats – further evidence that Confucius did not support equality or democracy. He condemned Confucian preoccupation with religious ritual, and he ridiculed Confucianists for putting family and class above the welfare of common people.

Unlike Confucius and his followers, Mo-tzu believed that all men were equal before the lord of the heavens. He believed that the powers of heaven acted on the world and exercised a love for all humankind. He spoke of the value of the labor of common folks, and he advocated promoting people to positions of power solely on the strength of their abilities and virtues.

In place of Confucianism's dutiful love for the father of a family, Mo-tzu supported a wider devotion: he urged people to follow heaven and reciprocate or duplicate heaven's love with their own love for all. He claimed that members of the aristocracy should love commoners and that commoners should love members of the aristocracy. Unlike the haughty Confucianists, who would lecture for only those who treated them with what they thought was proper respect, Mo-tzu and his followers would lecture anyone willing to listen.

But in some ways, Mo-tzu was also a man of his time. He supported monarchical rule – support for democracy in China during his time being considered his time to be criminal. He saw evil as having originated in individualism in pre-civilized society, an individualism in which everyone had his or her own standard of what was right or wrong. Drawing from this misconception of pre-civilized society, he believed that heaven had overridden individualism by creating civilization and by giving power to the most worthy of persons, the king – rather than the king's power being derived from common people. It was a king's duty, claimed Mo-tzu, to unify the standards of morality according to heaven. He believed that rulers might deviate from the wishes of heaven but that it was the duty of people to adhere to heaven's standards by exercising reason.

Disorders, Mo-tzu believed, came from men of power understanding only trifles and not matters of great importance, most importantly heaven's universal love. Disasters such as hurricanes and torrential rains he explained as heaven's punishment for people deviating from these standards. He believed that heaven manifested its love for humankind by providing humans with their material needs.

As Mo-tzu pondered and taught, trade and the money economy had been expanding, and Mo-tzu wanted the blessings of material benefits extended among common people – especially food, clothing and housing. He saw as waste those activities that did not contribute to the creation of these. He found fault with aristocrats spending enormous sums on their weddings and funerals. He condemned luxury, music, extravagant entertainment, frivolity, heavily ornamented coffins and embroidered shrouds. And in his opposition to waste, he opposed war.

Mo-tzu lived in a time of many wars. He witnessed lords sending their armies into weaker states, devastating crops, slaughtering cattle, burning towns and temples, killing civilians and dragging people away to be made slaves. He spoke against lords who already had much but who sought what little some other lord might have. He said that killing people in great numbers should not make one a hero. He tried mediating between rulers at war with each other. It was military aggression that he opposed, and, rather than losing himself in a utopian pacifism, he created an army of well-trained, highly disciplined warriors which he offered to local rulers defending themselves against aggression.

Mencius Defends Confucianism

Among the contributors to an intellectual vitality among the people on the North China Plain was a Confucian scholar named Meng-tzu, who lived from 372 to 289 – whose name would be Latinized to *Mencius*. Confucianists would call Mencius the Second Sage. Mencius attempted to defend Confucianism against the teachings of Mo-tzu. Whereas Mo-tzu had worn the simplest and most unpretentious clothing and otherwise appeared humble, Mencius rode around in style in a carriage. Mencius claimed that like Mo-tzu he was for adequate living conditions, and he agreed that such conditions were needed for morality to prevail, but he attacked Mo-tzu's belief in universal love. Mencius claimed that people must give love in varying amounts to different people. He accused Mo-tzu of having failed to give sufficient importance to loving one's parents and of wishing to abolish fatherhood. He argued that a good king was needed to assure that the people were properly fed and clothed, and he argued that a king was needed to spare people the horrors of war.

Mencius defended Confucianism against another critic, Yang-chu, accusing him of failing to recognize the need of a king, and he said that to fail to recognize the primacy of a father and a sovereign "is to be a bird or beast." He claimed that the substance of being human was serving one's parents and that "the basis of righteousness" was obeying one's elder brothers. In advocating heaven's harmony through the virtue of kings and the obedience of common people, Mencius argued that people overall were essentially good but that anarchy made them evil and that people had to be encouraged to be good. And while he wished to find a ruler who would put his teachings into practice, local rulers faced with increased competition and warfare were not inclined to listen with much patience to his lectures about essential goodness.

The Taoist Alternative

An alternative to both Confucius and Mo-tzu appeared that would eventually become the second most influential school of thought among the Chinese. This was Taoism, whose founder is believed to have been Lao-tzu. During the life of Mencius, China's literate minority was reading a book now believed to have been written by Lao-tzu.

Lao-tzu saw nature as paradoxical and essentially indescribable. He claimed that people should forget trying to acquire truth. Knowledge, he çlaimed, merely contributed to discontent and unhappiness. According to legend he declared:

> Banish sageliness, discard wisdom, and the people will benefit a hundredfold.

Early Taoism rejected Confucianism's striving for virtue, its belief in social reform, ritual and governmental regulation. Lao-tzu advocated withdrawal from social strife, and he expected society to continue being driven by greed and a lust for power. His early followers scoffed at Confucianist veneration of early Chou kings. They saw futility in lecturing a king on doing right. They saw lectures on morality as attempts to parade one's own excellence. Lao-tzu is believed to have written that humanity should discard words such as *duty, humanity, benevolence* and *righteousness*. Only during disorders, he claimed, did people hear talk of "loyal servants." These words, he claimed, were the flip side of strife, and strife should be avoided.

The second man of Taoism has been described as Chuang-tzu, a contemporary of Mencius. Chuang-tzu is said to have been a minor official who dropped out to become a teacher. He advocated liberating oneself from narrow mindedness – by accepting Taoism. In accord with Lao-tzu's opinions, he described Confucianism's professing values as an artifice. In the place of such values he proposed that people focus their attention on and submit to nature. Nature, he claimed, was primary.

While Mencius wrote of duty and decency, the wisdom of monarchical rule and of anarchy returning people to beastliness, the Taoists insisted that all social organization was ruinous. The Taoists claimed that more laws created more robbers and thieves, that more government created more greed and ambition. They claimed that the best rulers would be those who converted to Taoism, gave up luxurious living and warfare and who just left people alone.

The Taoists saw military leaders as murderers who built their reputations on the bodies of thousands of innocent people. They claimed that a military hero was to be pitied because he was unaware of his guilt and ignorance. Like the Buddhists, early Taoists sought salvation for themselves through a pursuit of serenity. Like many others, they believed in harmony. He who did not fight, they believed, would live in peace, and he who did not strain after success would suffer no failure.

One of their paradoxical expressions claimed that "he who does nothing accomplishes everything." In this, like Mo-tzu, they believed that one should refrain from devoting oneself to the pursuit of material gains or fame, that one should live modestly, that luxury bred envy and envy bred strife. And they believed that to help end strife and greed, profits should be banished.

Against Confucianist and Mo-tzu's moralizing, the Taoists believed in acting on impulse, such as eating when one is hungry and sleeping when one is tired. This, they believed, left them in "perfect harmony" with their original nature. The realization that much that was conflict originated with impulse – from infants fighting over toys to adults fighting over territory – eluded them.

The Taoists sought harmony between themselves and heaven by joyfully surrendering to the will of heaven. In this, they believed, they could achieve a happiness unaffected by change and death. They favored moving to a quiet, sparsely populated area where one could contemplate the beauties of nature. If evil came one's way – as with the arrival of a murderous army – they believed in remaining passive, and if this brought death so be it, because death was inevitable.

Hsun-tzu Revisionist Confucian and Anti-Taoist

A couple of generations after Mencius, a Confucian scholar appeared whose name was Hsun-tzu. He lived from 315 to 236, and like Mencius, he was to be looked upon as a great contributor to Confucianism. As a Confucian he believed in education, activism, class hierarchies and accessing heaven's powers through religious rites, but he believed that earlier Confucianists had erred in believing that the order and virtues of the early Chou dynasty could be re-established. He called on Confucianists to give up what he saw as their excessive idealization of the past.

Hsun-tzu revised the Confucian view of human psychology. He argued against the view of Mencius that all men were born with a nature that was essentially good. He put himself more in accord with what would be the view of modern psychology: that goodness was a product of socialization – what Hsun-tzu called learning. Hsun-tzu believed that one should ask not whether humanity was basically good but what was the source of people doing evil. Befitting his Confucianism, and contrary to Taoism, he concluded that evil was the work of impulse, that impulses had to be controlled and that this was accomplished by reason. Correct behavior, he believed, came from the teachings of the sages and could therefore be learned by striving. Believing in reason over impulse, Hsun-tzu attacked those religious practices that he thought were unreasonable, including fortune telling. He also opposed the Taoist claim that people should submit to nature, arguing that the destiny of humankind was decided to a degree at least by humans themselves. He saw recourse to the ills of his time not in the skepticism and withdrawal of the Taoists but in leaders of society understanding and discriminating between wise and foolish policies. This ability to discriminate, he believed, was what distinguished humanity from beasts.

The Legalists

Among those who believed in an activism shunned by the Taoists were scholars who would be called *Legalists*. These scholars saw themselves as realists. They saw Confucian worship of the past as a waste of time and Mencius' theory about the goodness of humanity as misguided. The Legalists saw goodness as people cooperating with authority. They believed that to keep people from deviating from this cooperation, authority had to threaten punishment. Society, they believed, had to be organized by the state. They accepted as a fact of life that power was in the hands of autocratic monarchs, and they approved, seeing power in the hands of a single rational ruler and his ministers as better than someone wielding power as a product of conflict and compromise.

Seeing rivalries between various states as a fact of life, the Legalists believed in strengthening the state. They believed a society benefited from military strength, and some among them advocated expansion as a means of strengthening their state. To strengthen the state they also believed frugality, and some among them believed in a devotion to agriculture and restrictions on commerce. And, seeing Confucian teachings and other rival theories as unessential and divisive, they favored restricting these.

Developments Despite the Taoists and Confucianists

During the rise of Taoism and the time of wars between the various petty states there was a pursuit of knowledge that rivaled Taoism's belief in withdrawal, impulse and banishment of sageliness, and there were developments unrelated to what Confucianists were advocating – developments in mathematics, physics, technology and the economy. Someone discovered the relationship between radius and circumference. Someone else re-invented what a Greek named Pythagoras had discovered about the sides of a right-angled triangle, and someone invented quadratic equations and formulas for measuring prisms, cones, and cylinders. Astronomy was being studied in the belief that the heavens affected human affairs, and, pursuing this, someone discovered how to calculate the distance between the sun and the earth. Using the principles of hydraulic engineering, intricate irrigation works and numerous dams and dikes were constructed that were to function into modern times. New canals and roads were built. Crop production had increased. And with this came the usual increase in populations and growth in the size of towns.

But science in the North China Plain remained a matter of private learning and not widely, or publicly, taught. Many, including the Confucianists, still believed that it was the gods that made things work. And technological progress remained hampered by secrecy. New techniques most often remained a trade secret among a family's males, kept from the women so it would not spread to another family through marriage.

THE KINGDOM OF CH'IN CREATES CHINA

During the lifetime of Mencius and the Taoist Chuang-tzu, a Legalist named Shang Yang became chief minister to the local ruler of Ch'in. Ch'in was a principality in the Wei River Valley, where the Ch'uan-jung had overrun the Chou king in 771. Ch'in was one of the smaller of the seventeen or so states that made up Chou civilization, and it was seen by peoples of the others states as inferior, as semi-barbaric, because of the many Tibetan and Turkish people that it had absorbed. Ch'in retained the martial spirit and vigor of nomadic herdsmen, and Ch'in was a thoroughfare for trade between Chou civilization and the tribal lands in Central Asia, a trade that had been contributing to Ch'in's wealth.

As chief minister, Shang Yang began organizing Ch'in according to Legalist tenets. He convinced the ruler of Ch'in to apply law to all his subjects. With this, he sought to reward people for good service and merit rather than give favor according to kinship. He rewarded battlefield heroism. He had none of Confucianism disdain for commerce and instead encouraged trade and work. He encouraged the making of cloth for export. He threatened with slavery any able-bodied man who was not engaged in a useful occupation. And he encouraged immigration: he asked educated and talented persons from other principalities to move to Ch'in, and he offered farming people from other principalities a piece of virgin lands and promised that they would be exempt from military service.

Many came to Ch'in, increasing Ch'in's manpower and food production and strengthening its military. The size of an army had become more significant – armies no longer being mainly adventuresome aristocrats. With commoners flooding into the army of Ch'in, the ruler of Ch'in was able to reduce the power of his warrior-aristocrats and nobles. In one revolutionary sweep the ruler of Ch'in divided his principality into counties and had these counties administered by appointed officials rather than by nobles – while the divisive power of nobles in other states in Chou civilization was being eliminated only gradually.

Ch'in Conquers

When the ruler of Ch'in died, Shang Yang was left without protection at court. Jealous and power hungry persons within the court had Shang Yang executed, but the wealth and power of the principality of Ch'in lived on. And Ch'in started winning great battles. In 314 BC – twenty-four years after the death of Shang Yang – Ch'in won a great military victory over nomads to its north. In 311, Ch'in expanded southward against more nomadic people, and there it founded the city of Cheng-tu. By now, other states had expanded: Yen against so-called barbarians east of the Liao River, and Ch'u south of the Yangtze River. War and conquest had reduced the number of states to eleven. Ch'in joined a coalition of four other states against Ch'i, which the allies of Ch'in feared the most. Ch'i was traditionally expansionist and hegemonic, well organized, densely populated relative to most other states, high in food production and had grown wealthy also from trade in iron and other metals. To their detriment, the allies of Ch'in viewed Ch'in as semi-barbaric and therefore weaker and less of a threat than Ch'i.

In 256, Ch'i absorbed Lu, and Ch'in expanded into territory that belonged to the Chou family – an area containing about thirty thousand people and thirty-six villages. A Chou prince counterattacked, trying to claim the Chou throne for himself, and Ch'in's army defeated him. The Chou had come to an end at the sharp end of a sword.

In 246 BC, Cheng, the thirteen-year-old son of the ruler of Ch'in, succeeded his father. After sixteen years of rule, Cheng embarked upon the conquest of the remaining states that had been a part of Chou civilization. Armies of hundreds of thousands were involved on both sides. Ch'in defeated one state after another: Han in the year 230, Chao in 228; Wei in 225, the large but more sparsely populated and less tightly knit Ch'u in 223, Yen in 222 and the powerful state of Ch'i in 221. Occasionally, to eliminate possible military opposition, the armies of Ch'in slaughtered all enemy males of military age.

Cheng became ruler of all that had been Chou civilization. He took the title *First Sovereign Emperor*, Shih Huang-ti, and he went to a sacred mountain, Tai Shan, where, it would be said, he received the mandate from heaven to rule the entire world. In accordance with this mandate, Shih Huang-ti expanded the frontiers of what had been Chou civilization – southward to Nan-Hai-chun (now Canton) and to Kwang-si, creating what would thereafter be considered China. And he pushed into Annam, or northern Vietnam – an area the Chinese would hold only temporarily. Shih Huang-ti had become the great father of China.

Shih Huang-ti, the Oppressor

Many of those whom Shih Huang-ti conquered obeyed him from fear rather than seeing him as their legitimate ruler or as having heaven's mandate, and some in various areas continued to fight his rule. To further secure his rule, Shih Huang-ti tried collecting weapons from all those not in his armies. He saw danger in what people thought, and in 213 BC his agents began confiscating books he thought were dangerous: all books other than those thought practical subjects, such as agriculture, forestry, herbal medicine and divination. The confiscated books were burned, except for one copy of each, which were to be kept from the public in the state's private library. Among the burned books were the centuries old writings of Confucius and books by his followers. Future generations of Confucianists would see Shih Huang-ti as evil, and they would accuse him of having buried alive hundreds of scholars.

Across China, Shih Huang-ti took powers away from the local nobles – as had been done in Ch'in the century before – ending feudalism. In the place of the nobles he divided China into thirty-six administrative units, each staffed by people appointed by and responsible to his administration, and he gave his administration the exclusive rights to tax and mint coins. And from the provinces to his capital, Hsienyang, moved 120,000 noble families.

Shih Huang-ti was hardworking, setting daily quotas of administrative tasks for himself and not resting until he had completed them, and he was good about consulting with his ministers. Shih Huang-ti standardized Chinese script, weights and measures, and laws. Across China he spread the right of people to buy and sell land – which increased his revenues from taxation. He built magnificent public buildings in his capital and great palaces for himself. He built a vast system of highways to interconnect his empire, and he began expanding irrigation canals. And he drafted several hundred workers to begin connecting the old walls along the northern frontier into a single system fortified by watchtowers – called the Great Wall.

Embittered aristocrats and oppressed intellectuals hated Shih Huang-ti, and he was hated as a conqueror and hated because of his heavy taxation, his harsh legal code and his having worked common people hard on his building projects. And fearing assassination, Shi Huang-ti had secret passages throughout his great palace and slept in a different palace apartment each night. It was not the serene life sought ˙ by the Taoists, and the Confucianists must have seen him as an immoral usurper. But he was a man of religion, and he worried about the sexual morality of his subjects, believing that behavior displeasing the gods would adversely affect the well-being of his kingdom.

Succession and Turmoil

Shih Huang-ti liked touring his capital city incognito at night, and he liked to travel through his empire, to cities, mountains, rivers, lakes and to the shores of the sea. It was said that when a strong wind impeded his crossing a river, he sent three thousand prisoners to deforest a nearby mountain that was believed to be the home of a goddess who had created the wind.

In 210, at the age of forty-nine, Shih Huang-ti, became sick while on one of his journeys, and he died. His death was followed by an attempt by palace eunuchs to hold onto influence. They murdered some of Shih Huang-ti's top aids, withheld news of Shih Huang-ti's death and sent a forged note to Shih Huang-ti's son and heir apparent, ordering him to commit suicide, which he did. Then they elevated to the throne a younger son of Shih Huang-ti, a boy whom they hoped to control.

Some in areas recently conquered by Shih Huang-ti saw in Shih Huang-ti's death an opportunity to break from Ch'in rule, and some intellectuals came out against the rule of Shih Huang-ti's younger son. Peasants decided it was an opportune time to express their displeasure with imperial authority, the result largely of their having suffered too much forced labor on Shih Huang-ti's many construction projects. Some commoners began killing local officials. Among common people there arose local leaders who led them in rebellion. And in an attempt to regain their former powers, noble families began organizing their own gangs of armed men.

Early during the chaos, a middle-aged rebel leader and former Ch'in policeman named Liu Chi gathered an increasingly large army under him. He allied himself with a more powerful rebel, a noble named Hsiang Yu, who was organizing military operations against Ch'in rule and hoping to re-establish the privileges of his family. Respecting the power of Liu Chi's force, Hsiang Yu made him prince of the district of Han.

Shih Huang-ti had claimed that his dynasty would last 10,000 generations, but the rebellion was too great for his son and the eunuchs around him, and in 206 BC an army under Liu Chi defeated the Ch'in army and entered the capital city: Hsienyang. All members of the royal family were slaughtered, including the boy-emperor. Hsienyang was burned to the ground, and the state library that contained the only copy of various forbidden books burned with it. The centuries old writings of

Confucius and others would have to be recreated from memory and imagination.

With the Ch'in emperor defeated, Liu Chi and Hsiang Yu warred against each other. Hsiang Yu was a brilliant general and a colorful leader, but he relied too much on ruthlessness as a means of winning obedience. He slaughtered defeated troops, and in taking cities he looted and seized attractive women. Liu Chi was colorless but he made an effort to conciliate and convert those he defeated. He was a more attractive leader, and he surrounded himself with bright and sound thinkers. Contrary to the views of the Legalists, more than coercion was contributing to success in creating order. Liu Chi defeated Hsiang Yu, and in the year 202, having established military supremacy, he made himself emperor of all China. The era of Chinese history called the *Han* had begun.

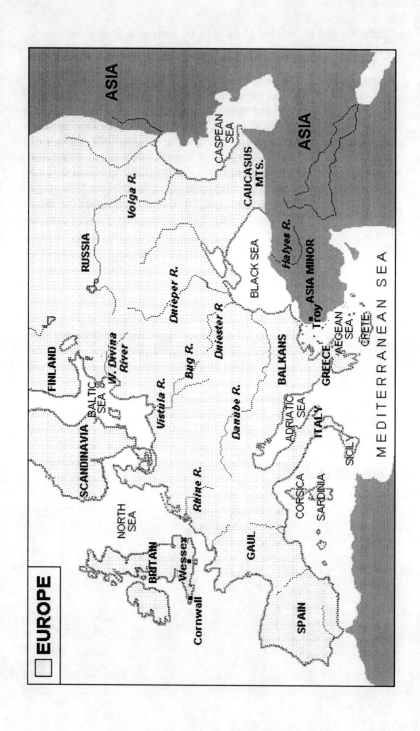

CHAPTER 7

EUROPE, GREECE, AND PHILOSOPHY

AGRICULTURE IN EUROPE

Civilization came to Europeans later than it did to people in West Asia, North Africa, India and China. And as elsewhere, civilization in Europe was preceded by agriculture and the raising of animals. These appeared in sunny Greece as early as 6000 BC, around the time that people there built stone walls around their villages, presumably to protect themselves from wild animals and marauding outsiders. In the coming thousand years, farming spread from Greece into the colder southern Balkans. Then between 5000 and 4000 BC it spread up the Danube River into central Europe, along the Rhine River, the Netherlands, Gaul and finally into what is now Switzerland. During these times, Europeans used digging sticks and hoes made of wood. They had stone axes with a sharpened and polished edge, and they had stone knives for reaping their crops. They used ornamented pottery. And where wood was plentiful they built log homes – as large as thirty by forty meters.

By 4000 BC, Europeans were using a wooden plow, and, sometime after 4000, farming spread to people around the Vistula River and into Scandinavia, while in Finland those people to be known as Finns hunted seals and bred pigs. Farming spread to Britain as people with farming skills crossed the English Channel in boats probably made of skins and wood. And, sometime between 4000 and 3000 BC, farming spread along the Dnieper, Bug and Dniester rivers.

Humanity likes to tinker, and, like others, the Europeans did much of this. To make it easier for their oxen to transport their loads, they hitched the oxen to carts with solid wooden wheels. They began weaving and embroidering. They made skis for hunting during winter. In southern Britain, southern Scandinavia and in what is now Russia, people built mine shafts to follow seams of flint. They used fire to loosen the flint and shovels made from the shoulder blades of cattle. And along the western coast of Spain they built great stone monuments to their dead, a practice that soon spread to Scandinavia.

In Europe, copper had been picked from the ground and used as jewelry. The Europeans shaped the copper by pounding it cold. Then someone discovered that heating copper made it more malleable. Working with metals had begun in southeastern Europe as early as around 4600 BC – almost a thousand years before it reached Asia Minor. Around 3300 BC, flint tools were still widely used in Europe – while copper, silver and lead were being smelted in Spain. But soon the working of copper spread through much of Europe. Copper workers made plaques, wires, copper punches, axe and adze heads, pins, and jewelry such as spiral armbands. They crafted copper and gold to adorn their religious idols and as offerings to their gods. Those working copper sought to maintain a supply of the ore, and after the year 3000 prospectors looking for copper ore were combing Europe and creating copper mines.

Europe remained less densely populated than West Asia and Egypt, but a great migration into Europe began as Warrior-herding peoples from farther east moved into Eastern Europe searching for pasture for their animals. Sometime after 3000 BC, an Indo-European people called Balts – including Lithuanians – and a Finnic people called Estonians settled along the Baltic Sea, near the West Dvina River. From Asia came more Indo-Europeans, who would be called Slavs, who settled around the Vistula, Bug and Dnieper rivers. Between 2900 and 2700 BC, came more Indo-Europeans, who settled in and around what are now Belgium and the Netherlands, near where the Rhine River runs into the sea. They brought to Western Europe a new kind of husbandry of animals, and they brought individual burial as opposed to the group burials practiced by Europeans before them.

Around 2500 BC, small communities of metal working tradesmen from Spain began a peaceful migration in Europe. They are called Bell Beakers after their pottery, and they too buried their dead individually. Europe was rich in the deposits of tin needed for making bronze, and the Bell Beakers exploited local sources of copper and tin. The Bell Beakers began trading in bronze, in addition to gold, amber and perhaps furs. By around 2000, Bell Beakers had traveled as far as what is now Czech Republic in central Europe, as far as Corsica, Sicily and North Africa, and they had entered Britain as far north as what is now Scotland.

In Britain, the Bell Beakers started the monument to be known as Stonehenge, and they played a major role in the birth of early bronze age Wessex culture of southern Britain – where people grew barely, wheat and raised sheep and cattle. Wessex became a prosperous area that benefited from the commercial talents of its chiefs, who acted as middlemen in trade with Cornwall, Ireland, Central Europe and the

Balkans. And with the rise in population and prosperity from trade, Wessex began to take on the characteristics of civilization, including distinction between aristocrats and commoners.

THE MYCENAE GREEKS, MINOANS, AND A DARK AGE

Between the years 2300 and 2000, Indo-Europeans moved south into Greece, and in the southern portion of Greece they conquered and made themselves an aristocracy over those who had migrated there many centuries before. These latest migrants are known as the Mycenae Greeks, who had gods similar to other Indo-Europeans, including a father god of the sky, Zeus, whom they believed held power over the entire world.

The Mycenae Greeks came into contact with sea-going tradesmen, the Minoans of Crete, an island one hundred miles south of Greece. Minoan civilization was about as old as Egypt's. It was a commercial society with people differing greatly in wealth, with rule by the wealthy and a government with a well-organized bureaucracy. Workmen in Crete produced fine vases, sheet metal, tweezers, stonework and other artifacts. Wealthy Minoans lived in palaces with plastered walls, which they decorated with art – palaces that show the influence of Hittites and Mesopotamians.

From the Minoans, the Mycenae Greeks acquired their alphabet and learned to write – the first Europeans other than the Minoans known to do so. From the Minoans, they also learned seafaring, shipbuilding and other crafts. And as land suitable for agriculture was scarce in mountainous Greece, some Mycenae Greeks took to the sea, becoming pirates and trading in slaves and other goods.

Sometime around 1400, after an earthquake on Crete had perhaps weakened the Minoans, Mycenae aristocrats, clinging to their warrior heritage, invaded and conquered Crete. Also they went east and colonized the island of Cyprus. They established themselves on islands such as Ceos, Melos, Paros, Delos, Naxos, Rhodes and Cos. They settled on the shores of Asia Minor. They sought trade in spices, tin, copper and amber and maintained a luxurious way of life that included objects laid with imported gold. They journeyed as far as Italy, the Black Sea, and up the Danube River into central Europe. Looking for loot or perhaps land, they raided the city of Troy – a wealthy, metal working, trading center in western Asia Minor near the straits that led to the Black Sea.

A Dark Age Descends upon Greece

Around 1200 BC, Dorian Greeks – who had been living just north of Greece and spoke a dialect different from the Mycenae Greeks – began the first of their invasions into the Greek peninsula. They bypassed some areas but overran much of the Mycenae civilization that had spread into the central part of the Greek mainland. They looted and destroyed palaces and sent people fleeing: some eastward to Asia Minor, some southeast to nearby islands and to Cyprus.

In the mid-1100s, after decades of respite, came more Dorian invasions. In Ithaca, an island off the western coast of Greece, Mycenae Greeks made common cause with the native people and were able to maintain a semblance of their way of life. So too were some others in Greece. The city of Athens and cities in Euboea survived, but the Dorians pushed countless Greeks to a new exodus. Legend tells of a well-organized expedition from Athens to the island of Lesbos off the coast of Asia Minor. Other migrants from Greece fled to Asia Minor and mixed with local peoples, and western Asia Minor became a mixture of peoples speaking a variety of Greek dialects.

Mycenae Greeks fled to Crete, and soon the Dorians overran that island, as people were fleeing from there to Cyprus. The Dorians moved eastward to the southwest shores of Asia Minor, island hopping by way of Melos, Thera and Rhodes. On the coast of Asia Minor they destroyed Miletus and other cities, and some Mycenae Greeks migrated from the coast of Asia Minor farther inland.

The Dorian invasions destroyed the prosperity and cohesion of Greece. There was a sharp drop in agricultural production and in population. Greek cities became villages, and writing declined and was lost. Trade between Greece and elsewhere disappeared as the Dorian Greeks had no desire for contact with foreign peoples, believing that beyond them lived only strange people and monsters.

A NEW GREEK CIVILIZATION

Between the years 1000 and 800, people on the Greek mainland and Greeks in Asia Minor became more settled and grew in number. By 750, a continuing growth in population and trade resulted in an amalgamation of villages and the rise of many small city-states. By the 700s, along the coast of Asia Minor numerous Greek city-states were thriving, such as Smyrna, Ephesus and Miletus. On the Peloponnesian peninsula in southern Greece were the city-states of Argos, Olympia, Corinth and Sparta. And on the peninsula of Attica the city of Athens governed an area of more than a thousand square miles.

Wealthy farmers had begun growing crops that would sell abroad: mainly wine and olive oil. The Greeks increased their trade in timber and grain, which they moved across local seas. Trade increased between the Greeks and the island of Cyprus, and the Greeks established trading contacts at harbors on the coast of northern Syria, contacts that again introduced Greeks to writing.

Many landless Greeks were hired to make pottery, furniture and other wares, and some employers accumulated much wealth. An industry arose in the forging of iron – Greece lacking the necessary tin to forge bronze. The use of iron spread among the Greeks, and iron tools increased productivity in both agriculture and manufacturing. With the increase in productivity and prosperity, the population of the Greeks soared. With more people and limited land, young Greeks began migrating elsewhere. Greeks established colonies in southern Italy at Cumae, just west of what would in Roman times be Neapolis (Naples), and Croton. On the island of Sicily they established colonies at Syracuse and Messana. And they established colonies on the coast of what is now Libya and on the southern coast of the Black Sea.

Greek Scripture: Homer's Epic Poem on the Trojan War
Homer was a Greek poet who lived on the coast of Asia Minor. Sometime before 700 BC he wrote an epic poem called the *Iliad*, a story that had been passed from generation to generation by those who told stories from memory, a story about war between the Mycenae Greeks and the city of Troy. Homer's *Iliad* played on conflicts of will – mainly among the gods. Like the Sumerian scribes, those who wrote the Old Testament, and those in India who wrote the Ramayana and Mahabharata, Homer described events as governed by the gods, and for centuries to come the Greeks would view his works as divinely inspired. For the Greeks, Homer's works would become a reference for religious thought. The Greeks would study Homer like Jews would study the Talmud and Christians their New Testament.

In Homer's *Iliad* the father god of the Greeks, Zeus, prefers love to war, but, while he is distracted with lovemaking, lesser gods create war. Foremost among these lesser gods is the troublesome goddess of love, Aphrodite, who creates a love affair between the mortals Helen of Troy and a Greek aristocrat named Paris.

Homer and his readers perceived the Trojan War as taking place in a great age of heroes – a time when aristocrats led armies and accepted raiding and plundering as normal activity. Homer's work extolled soldierly honor and duty, the obligation of revenge, pride, class privilege, military prowess and glory. The *Iliad* also extolled emotional control over surrender to rage. It extolled individualism, and it depicted human life as precious.

Homer described mortals as making decisions, but also he described them as committing acts they did not intend, acts originating in emotion as if emotion rather than reason led men to follow the dictates of the gods. Homer described dreams as religious messages, such as those sent by Zeus to the Greek king Agamemnon. And Homer's *Iliad* described religious rituals that included cremation – which allowed a warrior's remains to be transported home for ceremonial entombment.

The Poet Hesiod, the Myth of Prometheus, and a Flood

Another Greek poet who wrote before 700 was Hesiod – also from the coast of Asia Minor. Many Greeks were attracted to his ideas, and after many generations the Greeks viewed his writings as divinely inspired, like the works of Homer.

Hesiod speculated and worked popular religious myths into what he thought was an improved view of the reality of the gods. He believed that the Greeks were descended from a golden race that lived in idle luxury in the distant past, before Zeus was lord, when Zeus' father was king, and Hesiod sought to account for the golden race's demise and successive declines in civilization.

To explain the fall, Hesiod reworked an old myth about the god Prometheus – a tale reverently believed by the Greeks. Like the Hindu god Agne, Prometheus was a god of fire, a god interested in the welfare of humans and a god who taught humanity their arts and crafts. Hesiod described Prometheus as stealing fire from the heavens and giving it to mankind. This theft angered Zeus, and he had Prometheus chained to a rock on a mountain in the Caucasus, where an eagle or vulture tore at his liver each day, Zeus causing the liver of Prometheus to grow anew each night in preparation for the next day's torture.

To punish mankind for accepting fire stolen from the heavens, Zeus was said to have sent them a curse in the form of woman. Here was the Greek version of man's fall was the creation of women. The woman's name was Pandora, and Zeus sent her with a magic box that he forbade her to open. But after she had been on earth awhile she grew curious and opened the box, and out came the earthly plagues and misfortunes that forever after harmed humankind. Pandora hurriedly put the lid back on the box, but all that remained inside was hope.

Eventually, Zeus became angry enough with conditions on earth that he summoned other gods to a conference at his heavenly palace. To arrive at Zeus' palace, the gods traveled across the Milky Way, and there with Zeus they decided to destroy humankind and to provide the earth with a new race of mortals worthier of life and more reverent to them. Zeus feared that the destruction of humankind by fire might set heaven itself aflame, so he called for assistance from a god of the sea, and humankind was instead swept away by a great flood.

Greece's Gods versus the Worship of Yahweh
The Greeks of these times acquired a vision of the world different from those who worshiped Yahweh. For centuries to come, the Hebrew worshipers of Yahweh would see the universe as guided by divine purpose, and they would hope for divine intervention that would deliver them from their suffering. Those who worshiped the gods of Homer and Hesiod looked for no such intervention. They perceived the universe not as guided by a single divine will but as a chaotic conflict of divine wills. They saw their gods as experiencing the same blessings and misfortunes experienced by humans. They viewed their gods not only as vain in their desire for reverence from humans but as generally imperfect and as negligent and playful.

Like others, the Greeks believed that gods rather than men made laws, and they wished to obey these laws in order to please their gods. But the Greeks did not claim their gods as wise as much as the priests of Yahweh claimed that Yahweh was the source of wisdom. The gods of the Greeks, for example, were incestuous, while the Greeks abhorred incest. And seeing their gods as more human and with faults of their own, they tended more to look for wisdom within themselves. The priests of Yahweh wanted people to focus on their sins and sufferings and tended to dislike hedonism while looking forward to a blissful, uneventful, heavenly perfection. The religion of the Greeks, on the other hand, glorified the ups and downs of life, which led to their greater appreciation of grace and life for its own sake.

The Greeks saw Zeus as a god of the sky, the god of thunder and lightening and all other aspects of the weather. They saw Zeus as the lord of the heavens, the father of other gods and of humankind. They saw Zeus as *their* god and concerned primarily with them – attributing to themselves a greater importance than other peoples. Unlike the worshipers of Yahweh, they did not see their father-god as jealous and with chronic concerns about the wrongdoing of his people. But they did see him as a god who became angry, and they respected him and feared his thunderbolts.

The Greeks had a goddess called Athena, who was said to have sprung from the forehead of Zeus. She was a goddess of war and peace, of wisdom and a patron of arts and crafts. The Greeks also believed in a god called Eros, a god of love (from whom the word *erotic* is derived), a god whom the Romans would call Cupid. The Greeks had a goddess of love and beauty named Aphrodite, who would also be called Venus.

They believed that Aphrodite had a sweet smile and bathed in sweet smelling flowers, that she was a goddess of fertility, that plants bloomed after having been touched by her feet and that she made gardens grow and animals multiply. They believed that Aphrodite's ability to exude love and desire stole the wits even from the wise.

Another Greek god was Adonis, a god the Greeks acquired from Syria or the Phoenicians sometime around the time of Homer or Hesiod. Greek myth described Adonis as a beautiful youth with whom both the goddesses Aphrodite and Persephone fell in love. Persephone was the daughter of Zeus and a goddess of fertility in competition with Aphrodite. She presided over Hades, the place where the spirits of the dead resided. According to the myth of Adonis, Persephone, wanting Adonis, held him captive in Hades, and Aphrodite, also wanting Adonis, freed him from Hades and Persephone's captivity. Then, while hunting, Adonis was killed by a wild boar, which sent him back to Hades and Persephone. Aphrodite bitterly mourned his death and pleaded with Zeus to restore Adonis to her. Zeus decided to be impartial between the desires of Persephone and Aphrodite, and he decreed that Adonis would spend his winter months with Persephone – an annual death – and his summer months with Aphrodite – an annual resurrection. These deaths and resurrections coincided with the seasonal cycles and the growth of crops. Adonis had become a fertility god. Every year, Greeks celebrated Adonis' death and resurrection, often with wailing and the beating of one's own breast with one's fists.

One of the important gods among the Greeks was Apollo, believed to be the son of Zeus. Apollo was a god of foreign origin who changed across the centuries. Since the time of Homer, Apollo was seen as a god of life, light, knowledge and laws, a god who made men aware of their guilt, and a god of healing. For some, Apollo was a god of crops and herds. He became established at Delphi and was to be seen as a god of communion, music, poetry and dance. At Delphi, he was served by an oracle, a woman over fifty, who took hallucinogenic drugs in the form of leaves, which she chewed. People, including statesmen, came as pilgrims to Delphi from various parts of Greece to ask questions of the oracle, questions such as whether they should marry, whether their spouse was unfaithful, whether their city should go to war. The oracle would utter unintelligible messages that a priest would interpret and pass to the pilgrim in the form of riddles rather than answers that were specific and clear, leaving the pilgrim himself the task of interpretation.

Wars, Aristocracy, and the Olympics

Like the Sumerians, Egyptians and others, the Greeks of different cities were slow in seeking compromise and mutual understanding.

And, without the kind of political unity that the pharaohs had created in Egypt or that Hammurabi had created in Mesopotamia, wars erupted frequently between the Greek city-states – over water, trade and other matters. Their wars portended a disastrous future for the Greeks, but for the time being those who fought these wars were mostly landowning farmers – aristocrats – who could not stay long from their fields, so their wars were shorter and less damaging that would be the wars of later times.

Aristocrats and the wealthy among the Greeks ate better than did ordinary Greeks, who lived on a few figs, olives and coarse bread. The aristocrats and rich lived in fine houses, wore fine, embroidered robes and gold trinkets. They had trimmed beards and perfumed hair. Traditionally aristocrats were the warriors, and they had finely smithed armor. It had been aristocratic youth alone who were given schooling, which was mainly military training: horsemanship, chariot racing, foot racing, the long-jump, throwing a discus and javelin, wrestling and boxing. Instruction included indoctrination about the ideal noble warrior. Choral music, dancing and playing the lyre were added to the curriculum in an attempt to instill in aristocratic youth the refinement that was supposed to be a part of their superiority. Then poetry reading was added to their curriculum, to celebrate further their superiority and to set themselves apart from common Greeks, who remained illiterate.

A sense of religious community had developed among Greece's aristocrats, and, beginning in 776, aristocrats from various city-states held mid-summer religious festivals at Olympia, on the Peloponnesian peninsula. Greeks believed Olympia to be the center of the world and the home of the gods, and Olympia was a place of sanctuary and worship. And, for these religious festivals at Olympia, participating cities would put aside their differences and postpone their wars.

The festival at Olympia took place in a stadium that held around twenty thousand spectators. It opened with as many as a hundred oxen sacrificed to Zeus. Participants prayed and were judged for their moral suitability. The festival exalted the warrior tradition of the aristocrats and their god-given right of supremacy over common folk. Participants competed in athletic competitions, sang, played music, danced, read their poetry and competed in oratory.

Conflict and the Rise of Republics

Living in a city, a Greek king had a good view of his subjects, and his subjects had a good view of their king, and those unhappy with their king, including aristocrats and others of wealth, could murmur together and gain strength and courage from their numbers. In the 700s were numerous risings against monarchical rule led by men from the community's aristocratic and wealthy families. Many kings were deposed and replaced by oligarchies: rule by a clique of wealthy men. Then sometime after the year 675, in commercially developed cities such as Argos, Sicyon, Corinth, Mytilene, Samos, Naxos, Miletus, and Megara, rebellions arose against these oligarchic governments. These rebellions were led by men of commerce who often promised rule for society as a whole rather than for the wealthy, and they were joined by peasants grasping the opportunity to strike against those local aristocrats who dominated them. But the leaders of these rebellions did not believe in democracy. Few people did. Instead they established tyrannies: popular but despotic rule backed by a clique of their followers. As men with knowledge about economic matters, they often improved the economic lives of the ordinary citizens of communities, which helped them maintain popular support.

The Worship of Dionysus

The political upheavals of the 600s enhanced a longing for security among the Greeks. Some among the Greeks found relief in a new religious cult that promoted everlasting life and community. The new cult was believed to have been founded by a priest and poet named Orpheus, who was from Thrace. The new cult worshiped a god called Dionysus, a god of fertility and vegetation. The movement's practices and outlook were partly a reversion to pre-civilized communal worship. Like the religious rites of the pre-civilized, the worshipers of Dionysus had to be initiated. The cult of Dionysus, like other cults, worshiped together and ate and danced together.

The Dionysus cult held a special attraction for women, who broke away from domination by males and abandoned their families. Cult members believed that people could touch the greatness of the supernatural through their emotions. They hiked to hilltops at night, carrying torches, and there they danced wildly and worked themselves into self-abandon. Rumors spread among males who opposed to women dancing together, and they imagined sexual activity and the eating of raw meat, and claims were made that the dances culminated in sexual as well as spiritual ecstasy – similar to fertility rites.

Men and women members of the Dionysian movement traveled about Greece claiming personal intimacy with the gods and proclaiming Dionysus a son of Zeus. Some of them made their living by making prophesies and by performing what they believed were ritual purifications and spiritual healings. They told their listeners of a paradise that could be theirs. They told their listeners that they should be aware of the divine origins of their soul and that through the ecstasy of the movement's rituals they could let their souls escape from the prison of their body. They claimed that their movement's rituals and purification rites would liberate their souls from prevailing evils. They preached that by following the movement's strict rules of conduct, including living ascetically and not eating animal meat, they could achieve eternal blessedness. They spoke of their being judged after death according to their deeds during life. And they warned people that they would receive either the reward of eternal bliss or they would suffer punishment in Hades.

Men of wealth, power and influence in Greece feared that the worship of Dionysus might become so widespread that it would disrupt the peace and order upon which they depended. But the spread of the worship of Dionysus proved to have limits, as many Greeks wished to hold onto the gods they had grown up with and as many believed more in reason than in letting their emotions lead them to the acceptance of promises of eternal bliss.

SPARTA AND ATHENS

Sparta was a collection of villages and agricultural lands on the Peloponnesian peninsula, inland from the sea and surrounded by mountains, about a hundred miles south of Athens. It was a city-state ruled by Dorian Greeks who had conquered local farmers called Helots. The Spartans had made themselves a ruling aristocracy over the Helots, who outnumbered the Spartans seven to one. The Helots apparently had suffered the consequences of military weakness, the peoples of farming communities such as theirs having been traditionally less warlike than pastoral, nomadic peoples.

Sparta's economy was almost entirely agriculture, with only a few craftsmen and tradesmen. Spartans saw themselves as warriors and looked upon trade and commerce as beneath their dignity. Each Spartan family had an allotment of land and managed the Helots that came with the property, and they took half of what the Helots produced. With land divided equally among the Spartans and the Spartans not allowed to sell their land, no great disparity in wealth arose among them, and without a disparity in wealth, kingship did not become the property of a single family. Nor could there be an oligarchy of the rich. Instead, among the Spartans, as among the pre-civilized, rule remained with popularly selected kings.

Without a division in wealth among the Spartans, there was greater stability among them than with the peoples of other Greek cities. But the enslavement of the Helots was a source of trouble, and occasionally the Helots revolted, which the Spartans suppressed with bloody reprisals. To guard against plots among the Helots, the Spartans created a secret police, and Spartans were free to kill a Helot if they merely regarded him with suspicion.

Being greatly outnumbered by the Helots, as well as needing to defend themselves from outsiders, the Spartans saw their ability to wage war as paramount in preserving their way of life. And, having the Helots to labor for them, the Spartans were able to devote a good portion of their lives to training for warfare. Being a warrior was a job of glamour in Sparta, and young men hoped for the drama of military action. From the age of seven the Spartans reared their sons as warriors, putting them in barracks and giving them rigorous physical training – until the sons were thirty. Respecting strength, discipline and equality among themselves, the Spartans forbade themselves luxuries, including possessing wealth in the form of silver or gold. And for the sake of an efficient army, education and marriage were also regulated.

Sparta's concern for strength and discipline extended to women. Not understanding genetics, the Spartans believed that females who became physically strong through exercise passed these acquired characteristics biologically to their children. So to breed a physically strong and healthy nation, girls and young women were trained in gymnastics, and Sparta's females enjoyed a status uncommon elsewhere in Greece.

Also to maintain their success and way of life, the Spartans forbade any among them to travel abroad or to receive visitations by outsiders. Sparta was a closed society, void of the stimulations of travel that had contributed to the creativity found in other Greek cities. Philosophy and critical literature would not develop in Sparta as it would elsewhere among the Greeks, but the Spartans did enjoy music and choral poetry, and every year they held a grand festival of poetry in honor of the god Apollo.

Athens, from Prosperity to Social Crisis

Athens was a city on the water's edge, and unlike Sparta it was a city of maritime trade and commerce, but devoted mainly to agriculture. By the 600s the city ruled an area of about 25 by 50 miles. With enough land for distribution among its people, the Athenians prospered. They had no need for additional lands and launched no wars of conquests. And they enjoyed peace as well as prosperity.

Like most other cities in the 600s, Athens was ruled by an oligarchy. Power within Athens and its surrounding countryside was distributed among local families of wealth, each of which ruled over the common people in its locality. Such families provided these people the kind of protection that the Sicilian Mafia in modern times provided people in its community.

With Athens' success in agriculture came a rise in its population, and with this came trouble in farming. An old law that a father's estate was to be divided among all his sons resulted in lands being divided into smaller and smaller plots. Land became scarce, and people began plowing land that was only marginally arable. Over plowing increased soil exhaustion. Those who owned and worked small plots of land were at times obliged to borrow money to tide themselves over until their next successful harvest. Money was scarce and was lent at ruinous interest rates. Across Attica small farms became covered with stones on which mortgage bonds were written. The failure of a borrower to continue his payments left the lender – often an aristocrat – with a choice: leaving the borrower a free man and taking a sixth of what he produced or selling him into slavery. Increasingly, to avoid slavery small farmers were working the lands of others and giving up a sixth of their crop. And increasingly, lenders were selling borrowers as slaves abroad.

Another source of trouble in Athens was its numerous slaves who were foreigners or the descendants of foreigners. A third of the people of Athens were slaves. And with an abundant supply of slave labor, landless freemen could be hired to work in fields or small shops at very low wages. City jobs were also occupied by slaves. People of wealth and the city saw themselves as benefiting from slavery. And those with wealth felt no responsibility for those who had grown poor.

Solon Attempts to Implement God's Justice

In 621 BC, while unrest was rising among the poor of Athens, the leader of Athens' ruling oligarchy was Dracon (from which the word *draconian* is derived). Dracon had existing laws put into writing. He made a legal distinction between intentionally killing someone and accidental homicide. He asserted state power in intervening in blood-feuds. And for almost everything that the ruling elite considered a crime he devised one penalty: death. Not only were rebellion and murder punished by death, so too were idleness and the stealing of vegetables and fruit.

If Dracon's laws could have been enforced effectively and allowed to work long enough, they might have ended rebellion by killing most of Athens' malcontents. But, before this could happen, unrest among common Athenians grew rather than abated, and, fearing revolution, the elite decided to try appeasing the unrest through reform. In the year 594, the elite chose as their leader a fellow aristocrat named Solon. Solon was one of only a few aristocrats in Athens who were interested in philosophy, and he was religiously devout. He believed in the innate superiority of his own class, but he also believed in a justice that was decreed by Zeus for all Athenian citizens.

Solon described Athens as having fallen into "base slavery." Under Solon, slavery was to continue, but he put restrictions on it. Solon prohibited enslavement of the poor and rescued many Athenians who had been sold and sent abroad. He forbade Athenians to sell their children into slavery – except for girls who had committed fornication before marriage. And he made a master responsible for protecting his slaves and liable for his slave's actions.

Solon wished to protect the poor from the rich and the rich from the poor, and using dictatorial powers given him by fellow aristocrats he overturned Dracon's death penalties, except for murder. To preserve the justice of Zeus he increased state intervention in society. He had the state give relief to the poor. He canceled mortgages. He passed a law against debt-bondage. He put an end to tenant farming by returning farms to those who had lost them through debt. And he limited the size of land that any one person could own.

Solon left the aristocracy with much of their land. He also left the aristocracy with top government jobs and seats on ruling bodies. Under his laws, only those whose lands produced a certain amount could hold office. But Solon took a step in the direction of democracy: the Athenian citizen would be given a voice in an assembly. Solon also gave common people a greater role in Athens' system of justice: positions on the city's courts. Judges were chosen by lot so that the poorest people would have their turn sitting with the panel of judges that decided cases. And Solon maintained a check on judges by allowing them to be accused of wrongdoing after their service as judges had ended.

Solon reduced the penalty for idleness to a small fine. He enacted laws to care for widows and orphans. Under Solon it was illegal to strike another person, and parents could be punished for mistreating their children. Under Solon it was illegal to slander others, to use abusive language or to engage in other forms of offensive conduct. Solon outlawed pimping and male prostitution, and he had the city remove the dead from its streets.

Solon's Failure and the Rise of the Tyrant Pisistratus

Solon's laws eased the sufferings of the poor and saved others from slipping into degradation. But Athens continued to be overpopulated in relation to the availability of land and the productivity of its agriculture, and common Athenian citizens continued to suffer from or to feel threatened by hunger and poverty. Hoping that a rising economy would, as the saying goes, raise all boats, Solon encouraged trade. After this failed to end economic hardship and unrest, Solon hoped to create a spirit of cooperation among the common people by launching military campaigns and building empire. With this, Solon instituted another intrusion by the state into the lives of people: the conscription of males from the ages of eighteen to sixty for military service.

The inability of common people to change government through elections left violence as the likely means of change, and when Solon's military aggressions resulted in defeat, unrest at home brought the violent uprising that the elite had long feared – after Solon and his aristocratic allies had ruled for thirty-four years. The uprising was led by a man named Pisistratus, an enterprising aristocrat whom the ruling elite of Athens had driven into exile. While abroad, Pisistratus had gained wealth in mining and timber ventures. With his own wealth he had hired an army. And in 560 BC, with this army and other men who joined him, he marched toward Athens and defeated a force that the ruling elite of Athens had sent out against him.

Pisistratus took power by having his army occupy the hill over-looking Athens, where remains of the Parthenon now stand. He had become popular among the Athenians, but to consolidate his power his army disarmed the populace. For added security, his army took as hostages the sons of leading families, while the head of some families fled into exile. But he left their property unconfiscated, just as the former rulers had left his property unconfiscated after driving him into exile.

Pisistratus tolerated no political party or policy except his own, but he sought continued support from the common people of Athens. Like Solon, Pisistratus increased state involvement in social matters. He sponsored religious festivals and public games. He went further than Solon's reforms by taxing everyone equally, and he moved to protect the common farmer from those with wealth by providing them with the loans they might need between good harvests. With an aggressive foreign policy he supported trade and industry, and he helped trade by building roads. He improved the city's means of obtaining fresh water. He beautified the city by sponsoring sculpture for public places and by improving the city's temples. His policies and interventions gave Athenians full employment and brought renewed prosperity, giving Pisistratus success where Solon had failed.

Athenian Women and the Family

The Athenians had been living in communities of related families. And, as when Athens had a king, its ruler tried to arbitrate conflicts between families. But it was left to each family to protect its members and to punish others for shedding the blood of one of its members. If one were without a family, one might be killed with impunity. It was the duty of the head of an Athenian family to administer justice in behalf of the family, to enforce morality within his family and to see to it that his women and children were clothed.

Unlike the Hebrews and others, an Athenian could have only one wife. But he could have a concubine living within his family – whose children were not recognized as legitimate and not given citizenship. Wives were valued as the bearers of children with citizenship status. As among the Hebrews, it was believed that females should be virgins at marriage and faithful after marriage.* And while the male was not required to be faithful to his wife, law demanded that a husband divorce an unfaithful wife and return her dowry.

In Athens, women were without independent status. They could own no property except their clothes, jewelry and slaves, and they could enter into only minor market transactions. As members of farming families, women had helped in the fields, but with city-dwelling had come the practice of protecting women from public view and confining them to their homes. In such homes, women had their own quarters, and they dined together in a room apart from the men. A man committed an outrage if he entered a house where women might be present without his having been invited by the master of the house.

Women were expected to be accompanied if they left their house. They were expected to be under the protection of a guardian at all times: their father or a close male relative if they were unmarried, their husband if they were married, their son or a close male relative if they were widowed. The only women free of these controls were prostitutes or those few others who worked in public, which was a sign that the woman was living in poverty or that she was not an Athenian citizen.

A TRIUMPH IN IDEAS

With people having become exposed to different ideas through contacts with other societies, and people having become free of the pressures of tribal conformity, in Greece, as in India, ideas came in great variety. Among the Greeks, variety in interpretation produced philosophy. As in India, philosophy was pursued by those who were

---

* Some scholars speculate that originally there was no marriage and that a female having given birth was an attraction in that it proved her fertility. Some believe that the demand for virginity arose with the rise of ownership of land and the passing of land from father to son, and a father wanting to know if a child is really his. On the other hand, primitive pangs of jealously along with brute power of males over females may also have been involved if not the major source of the demand.

free from having to labor through each day at menial tasks. It was the preoccupation of only a few – mainly aristocrats.

Philosophy came after writing had been around for a while. Among the Greeks it came with a view of the world not void of gods but with a view of nature apart from the will and magic of gods. Philosophy among the Greeks began between the years 640 and 546 BC, in the city of Miletus, the richest and most powerful Greek city on the coast of Asia Minor. Miletus was on the edge of interacting cultures: Greek, Mesopotamian and Egyptian. Its people traveled, giving them an awareness of conflicting ideas, which encouraged thinking and logic. Here too was an independence of thought that was part of an effort toward individual excellence that had been encouraged among aristocrats as justification for their privileges.

The earliest known of these philosophers is Thales – a man of wealth, leisure and energy. He went to Egypt and saw there the use of simple and practical geometry in land surveying. He was interested in the nature of things and worked this geometry into a set of new mathematic principles. He became an engineer, and it is said that for king Croesus of Lydia he made the river Halys passable by diverting its waters. Thales was also interested in heavenly bodies. In his travels he might have come into contact with the astronomical data that Babylonians had accumulated across the centuries, but he also made his own observations of the stars, and he predicted a solar eclipse.

Like others of his time, Thales was unconcerned with that ingredient of scientific proof called verification, and he believed in gods. But, as an engineer who manipulated material realities he thought the material world was understandable rather than merely secretive magic, and this led him to speculate about its basic nature. He believed with his contemporaries that the world was flat and rested on a great body of water. He saw that water was necessary to live and that it was everywhere. He theorized that the world was in essence water and that it had originally been in the form of water – as if without moisture everything would become dust and nothingness.

Anaximander

Thales was mentor to a younger generation of aristocratic thinkers, and among his disciples was Anaximander, also of Miletus, who lived from around 611 to around 547. Anaximander rejected Thales' belief in a world derived from one substance. He thought that because the universe was vast and complex it might consist of a great variety of basic elements. Also, Anaximander adopted the Egyptian belief in endlessness. Infinity and eternity are difficult if not impossible to visualize or conceptualize, but Anaximander at least grasped it as an idea, an idea that rivaled that which he rejected: that something could be created out of nothing. This led him to speculate that the universe was boundless and everlasting. He speculated that there were countless other worlds beyond the world known to humanity. And he surmised that change came from inanimate forces interacting with each other rather than by the whims of gods performing magic.

Like Thales, Anaximander dabbled in mathematics and made contributions to geometry. He is believed to have introduced the Greeks to the sundial. Like Thales, his interest in the world led him to travel, and his travels led him to make a contribution to geography. He was the first to map what the Greeks knew of the world, and in an effort to see the heavens clearly and rationally, Anaximander attempted to map the distribution of celestial bodies. He theorized that the earth was at rest in the center of space. Anaximander speculated that early in its history the earth was covered with water, as indicated by signs of marine fossils[*] across the plains and mountains of West Asia. He theorized that if the first creatures on earth were of the sea, humanity must have evolved from such creatures.

Pythagoras and the Origins of Western Theology

Pythagoras lived from around 582 to 507 and was another remarkable thinker from Asia Minor. From Asia Minor he had migrated to Croton, a Greek city in Italy. He believed in the magic of the gods, was influenced by the cult that worshiped the god Dionysus, and he believed in Zeus, Apollo and other Greek gods and in the old and common notion of the transmigration of souls. He believed that the dust one can see aimlessly floating about in sunlight was pulled about by a spirit. But he also believed in self-examination, and he was interested in astronomy and mathematics and wished to apply observation and reason toward understanding the universe and its gods. He wished to combine his ideas on religion, astronomy and mathematics into a coherent view that would create a way of life beneficial to others.

Pythagoras and his followers advanced astronomy by examining the movements of celestial bodies. They observed the shadow of the earth on the moon, and they made some calculations and concluded that the earth was a sphere. They also concluded that the earth was one of a group of planets. They blended these observations with Greek religion, concluding that the sun reflected light from a great fire at the center of the universe, which they called the throne of Zeus, around which, they believed, all else revolved.

---

[*] Marine fossils on mountains were, of course, the result of lands rising from the sea rather than sea rising to the mountains.

Pythagoras advanced geometry from practical measurements to new geometric theorems. He found harmony in geometry and arithmetic, and in the harmonics of sound he found mathematics – that the tone of a vibrating string depends upon its length. He concluded that mathematical harmony was a part of the perfection of the heavens. Like the Sumerians and others, he believed that the heavens moved but were essentially unchanging, as permanent as the realities of mathematics. He believed that the universe and mathematics were in essence idea created by the gods. He believed that mathematics held the universe together and that its harmony created a kinship between the gods and humankind. Seeing reality as idea and unchanging, Pythagoras described the changes one saw on earth as an illusion. He described knowledge through sense perception as faulty compared to the reason that allowed one to grasp unchanging mathematical principles.

Having given mathematics a divine significance, Pythagoras searched for signs of divinity within numbers. With much theorizing he found what he was looking for. For example, the first number greater than 1 that could be the square of two other numbers is the number 4, and mixing this with his belief about justice as a work of the gods he concluded that the number 4 contained the divinity of justice.

Pythagoras created a religious sect organized around strict religious rules. Believing that souls migrated after death into the bodies of other beings, he saw the possibility of an animal containing a human-like soul, and therefore he saw eating animals as cannibalism and as an abomination. He and his followers became vegetarians. But they forbade the eating of beans, which they thought harmful to the soul.

In his later years, according to his followers, Pythagoras searched for the significance of his own brilliance and concluded that he was semi-divine. After his death, some of his followers described him as having been capable of miracles. Some claimed that he was the son of Apollo. But whatever he was, he had created a school of philosophy that would influence other Greek philosophers and rival the views of those who believed in the validity of sense perception.

Xenophanes

When the Persians extended their empire to Greek areas in Asia Minor in the mid-500s, a Greek named Xenophanes chose to flee rather than live under Persian rule. He became a philosopher and a wanderer from city to city, attended by a slave. He was disgusted with the Greeks for their feeble resistance against the Persians, and his disgust spread to a rejection of religion. He favored what he thought was reason rather than being guided in outlook by emotions or mere tradition. He objected to mysticism and to divine revelations. He rejected the revered poet

Hesiod, and he denounced Pythagoras. He described the priests of the Dionysus movement as impostors. He described the gods of Homer as morally bankrupt. All they had taught men, he said, is theft, adultery and mutual deceit. He ridiculed seeing gods as human-like and said that if oxen, horses or lions had hands to make images of their gods, they would fashion them in their own image. He pointed out that Thracians represented their god as Thracian and that Black Africans saw their gods as black.

Xenophanes constructed a philosophy of his own, knowing that he was going beyond humanity's ability to know. He speculated that the earth stretched infinitely in all directions, that the earth was infinitely deep and that air extended infinitely upwards. He imagined a god as a central force in the universe but not human like in shape, thought or emotions: a god that was everywhere and everything, a god that was the whole universe. And his belief that god is nature and nature is god left him open to the charge that he believed in no god at all.

Heraclitus

Xenophanes influenced a Greek named Heraclitus, who lived between 535 and 475 BC. Heraclitus was from Ephesus, another city on the coast of Asia Minor. Like Xenophanes, the views of Heraclitus conflicted with those of Pythagoras. Unlike Pythagoras, Heraclitus believed in a continuum between the world of change visible in materiality on earth and the world of the heavens. Heraclitus believed that the universe consisted of motion, that everything was in a state of change – as in the comment attributed to him that one never steps in the same river twice. And change, Heraclitus believed, made yearning for permanence in God and immortality futile.

Like Xenophanes, Heraclitus despised traditional views about the universe and religion. He was an elitist, believing in government by aristocrats, and he intended his writings to be read only by a worthy minority. But like Thales, Pythagoras and others he continued to believe in a supreme god who presided over the universe, a god that was the prime mover behind all things. Fire had been held in awe by the ancients and had been seen as a spiritual force, and in fire Heraclitus also saw soul or spirit. Humans, he concluded, are flames while things are processes.

Names, he is reported to have said, encourage us to look at the world in a fragmentary way and to obscure the whole. And he tried to construct a view of the whole according to what seemed reasonable or fit together – on coherence rather than a construction of proven facts. A part of this whole was his belief that conflict was inherent in nature rather then the work of the gods. He believed that it was conflict that produced change, in the physical world and in human society, that conflict created development and decay. He believed that the ever-presence of conflict made wars inevitable and that humans were unable to harmonize their differences through reason. Heraclitus was not a utopian, but he did believe that clarity about oneself led to appropriate behavior toward others and that the search for enlightenment could lead to a sound mind and virtue. And he believed in compromise. In seeing conflict as natural, he introduced the idea of objectivity into questions of justice, the idea that in some cases justice might best be served by superimposing compromise upon conflicting interests.

CHAPTER 8

BABYLON, PERSIA AND JUDAISM

BREAKUP OF ASSYRIA'S EMPIRE
AND ASCENT OF THE MOSES LEGEND

Assyria's great empire lasted no longer than the empires of the late nineteenth and early twentieth centuries: about seventy-five years. Its demise came with Assyria's kings warring incessantly against the petty kingdoms that they attempted to control. In 705 they stopped an invasion from the northeast by an Indo-European people called Cimmerians. They spent themselves in expanding into Egypt and in quelling the rebellions of Egyptian princes. The Cimmerian menace increased, and more rebellions occurred within the empire. Assyria was burdened by more military campaigns and by the expense of maintaining its army. Soldiers had to be paid. Massive numbers of horses had to be cared for and fed. Siege engines had to be moved against rebellious cities. In 655 BC, Egypt was able to break away from Assyrian rule. The Assyrian army had trained the Chaldean military leaders when they were loyal subjects, but then the Chaldeans joined the Egyptians in rebellion.

The Assyrians were also weakened by conflicts over succession, by coups and civil war. During these conflicts, cities in Canaan broke away from Assyrian control. Phoenicia began ignoring Assyrian directives. Other petty kingdoms joined the rebellion against Assyria. And, in 623, the well led Chaldean army drove north from around Sumer and expelled the Assyrians from Babylon.

With the independence of Egypt and Babylon, and a weakened Assyria, the new king of Judah, Josiah – the grandson of Manasseh – declared Judah independent. The hereditary Yahweh priesthood, which had suffered a loss of status during Assyrian domination, seized independence as an opportunity to advance its cause. With the support of Josiah and the zeal of the newly liberated, they moved against the foreign religious cults that had gained ascent during Assyria's domination.

The Yahweh priesthood claimed to have found in a secret archive within Solomon's temple a scroll signed by Moses – a document to become known as the Book of the Covenant. Why a work of such importance as Moses' scroll was lost or misplaced and forgotten for the two hundred years since the building of Solomon's temple, remains a mystery. King Josiah treated the scroll as genuine. He supported the Yahwist priests, and he complained that previous generations had not listened to Yahweh. Now began an official intolerance that had not been the policy of kings David, Solomon, Jeroboam, Ahab, Jehu and Manasseh. According to the Old Testament, King Josiah, accompanied by a great crowd, went to Solomon's temple and there made a covenant with Yahweh. Josiah ordered all objects of worship that were not Yahwist taken from Solomon's temple, and these were burned in a field outside Jerusalem.

The high priest of Yahwism ordered lesser priests to Jerusalem, and he issued a new code that forbade all subjects of Josiah to practice religious rituals of "foreign" origin. According to the Old Testament, the code's proscriptions included religious ordeals of passing through fire. It included practicing witchcraft, sorcery, using omens, worshiping images of gods in wood or stone, and it included a prohibition against orgiastic fertility festivals – festivals held in the spring and autumn that were accompanied by mass drunkenness and religious frenzy. The new code forbade all religious worship outside of Solomon's temple. Temples outside of Jerusalem were rendered unusable. The new code forbade human sacrifices. According to the Second Book of Kings, Josiah defiled a place called the "Tropheth," a word meaning drums, which had been beaten loudly to drown out the screams of sons and daughters being burned to death in sacrificial offerings. And the new code forbade the sacred prostitution that had been attached to temples, including the homosexual prostitution that was a part of Ba'al fertility worship.

The penalty for adhering to any of the newly forbidden practices was death, and death was the punishment too for the priests of rival religions. According to the Second Book of Kings 23:20, king Josiah led the assault:

> And all the priests of the high places who were there
> he slaughtered on the altars and burned human bones
> on them.

Those who had been indulging in the now forbidden religious practices were great in number, and their religious practices had become habits not easily surrendered. And rather than try to force people to completely eradicate all of their old habits, the priests gave Josiah's subjects a new meaning to various rituals that could fit with Yahweh worship. In the place of human sacrifices, animal sacrifices were to be performed. Instead of fertility festivals, they would engage in festivals that demonstrated their gratitude and devotion to Yahweh. The most important of these festivals, the spring festival, became the Passover – a commemoration of the exodus from Egypt led by Moses.

BABYLON AND THE JEWISH CAPTIVES

Between Mesopotamia and the Caspian Sea, tribes of an Indo-European people called Medes had become united under a single king. A later king of the Medes, Cyaxares, reorganized his army and attempted to expand westward against the Assyrians. He allied his army with the Chaldeans, who were now in control of Babylon and Sumer. The Medes and Chaldeans attacked and together defeated the Assyrians, overrunning Assyria's capital, Nineveh, in 612. Nineveh's walls were broken by the siege engines that Assyria had introduced centuries before. A community that had existed for more than two thousand years was obliterated. Those who escaped from Nineveh took refuge in Haran, and they fought on, but Assyria's remaining forces were defeated in 609. And such a terrible revenge was taken on the Assyrians that two hundred years later the area would still be sparely populated.

The Medes conquered as far as the Halys River and the Black Sea in Asia Minor, to the border of a new kingdom called Lydia. The Chaldeans conquered as far as Cilicia and the Taurus Mountains. Meanwhile, with the demise of Assyria a revitalized Egypt felt free to move into Palestine, as it had after it had expelled the Hyksos. And when King Josiah heard that an Egyptian army was coming, he went south with an army to do battle against them, believing that Yahweh would protect him. But, in battle, Josiah was promptly killed.

A contributor to the Old Testament's Second Book of Chronicles was to claim that Yahweh had failed his faithful servant Josiah because Josiah had neglected to listen to Egypt's pharaoh proclaim that Egypt was moving, with Yahweh's help, not against Judah but against others. But the Egyptians took control of Judah as Josiah had feared. The Egyptians carried Josiah's son and designated heir, Jehoahaz, back to Egypt. They placed on Judah's throne, as their puppet, his brother, Jehoiakim. Disaster was still seen as the result of displeasing the gods, and the Old Testament (2 Kings 23:29) describes Jehoahaz as it does other Jewish victims: as having done evil in the eyes of the Lord.

The Chaldeans Overrun Judah

The Hebrews continued to suffer the misfortune of living on a bridge of land between great, imperial powers. The Chaldeans saw Egypt as a rival to be reckoned with. Their army went against the

Egyptians in Syria. They drove the Egyptians back to Egypt, and in 598 they extended their conquests to Judah. Judah was captive once again.

Eleven years later the people of Jerusalem rebelled against Chaldean rule, and the Chaldeans responded by burning Jerusalem, tearing down its walls, destroying Solomon's temple and strengthening their position there by sending Judah's royalty, priests and skilled workmen into exile. The Chaldeans rounded up about forty thousand from Judah as captives, including political leaders and high priests. And the Chaldeans took them to their capital, Babylon, while some from Judah fled into Egypt, some fled eastward into Arabia, and some went north into Chaldean controlled Mesopotamia.

Again, many Hebrews saw Yahweh as having abandoned them. Some Hebrews believed that the god of the Chaldeans, Marduk, had defeated Yahweh. Contributors to the Old Testament would describe Judah's loss of independence as more of Yahweh's punishment for his people's failings. The Old Testament would describe another prophet, Jeremiah, as having warned the people of Judah about their failure to obey Yahweh and of their failure to achieve economic and social justice.

Jewish Captives See Yahweh as the One and Only God

The Hebrews who fled from Judah and went to Mesopotamia were allowed to settle where they wished and to take up whatever occupation they chose. These Hebrews found in Mesopotamia a prosperity that the priests of Yahweh had claimed Yahweh would provide them in Judah. Some of these exiles became farmers. Some prospered as merchants, rent collectors, contractors or bankers. Some among them adopted local names, converted to the worship of local gods and were content to remain in Mesopotamia permanently.

Those who were taken from Judah to Babylon as captives were also allowed to live according to their customs, including a freedom to practice their worship of Yahweh. These captives found Babylon a magnificent city compared to what they had known in Jerusalem. Like some rural, religious people in modern times who went to a big city, they found Babylon filled with wickedness and temptation, and in combating these temptations they clung desperately to their worship of Yahweh. Believing like others that gods dwelled in places, the captives in Babylon asked themselves how they could "sing the Lord's song in a foreign land?" (Psalms 137:4) They wondered whether Yahweh had accompanied them to Babylon. And some among them claimed that they could feel Yahweh's presence among them.

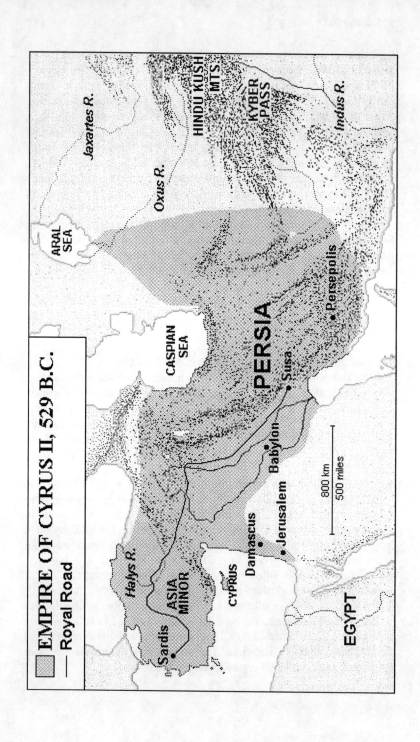

EMPIRE OF CYRUS II, 529 B.C.
— Royal Road

Jaxartes R.

HINDU KUSH MTS.

KYBER PASS

Indus R.

Oxus R.

ARAL SEA

PERSIA

Persepolis

CASPIAN SEA

Susa

Babylon

800 km
500 miles

Jerusalem

Damascus

Halys R.

CYPRUS

ASIA MINOR

Sardis

EGYPT

Prior to their exile, worshipers of Yahweh had seen him as one of many gods. The Old Testament's Book of Deuteronomy, 10:17, describes Yahweh as saying to Moses: "For the Lord your God is the God of gods." The worshipers of Yahweh had seen Yahweh as other peoples saw their god: as territorial, as ruling from a place. But now, in Babylon, those who worshiped Yahweh heard derision spoken against him, and they responded defensively. Was not Yahweh, they asked, the god who had formed and made the earth? They reasoned that Yahweh was not only their god but a great god. They concluded that rival gods were false and that Yahweh was the only god. A late entry in the Book of Isaiah, amid descriptions of the captives in Babylon, would state the issue of Yahweh and other gods differently than is expressed in Deuteronomy: "There is no other god besides me...," it reads. "There is none but me." (Isaiah 45:21.)

Awaiting Deliverance

The captive worshipers of Yahweh found community and consolation in regular meetings that differed from what they had known in Judah. There was no temple and no altar at which they could worship Yahweh, and their worship gave new emphasis to prayer, fasts, confession, and study. Believing that their exile was punishment for their sins, they hoped that their faith and dedication to Yahweh would win for them Yahweh's forgiveness. They prayed for redemption and for Yahweh to allow them to return to Judah and to restore their homeland to its former greatness. They prayed for a king – a word that in Hebrew translates to *messiah*. Conquest, despite its violence, was still the source of glory, and the captive worshipers of Yahweh prayed not for a meek or suffering messiah but a man of strength like David, preferably someone descended from David

PERSIA, ZOROASTRIANISM AND THE JEWS

Alongside the Mede people, south of the Caspian Sea, was another Indo-European people: the Persians. The Persians had arrived from Central Asia sometime before 800 BC, and they had come under the rule of the Medes. To weaken the Medes, the Chaldeans supported a Persian rebellion. A Persian prince, to be known as Cyrus II, led the rebellion, and some in the Mede army joined his rebellion. Cyrus and his army deposed the Mede king, and Cyrus united the Persians and Medes under his rule.

With Cyrus the Chaldeans got more than they had bargained for: Cyrus was an able administrator and military leader; he consolidated his power over tribes in central Persia; and then he started building a greater empire. He moved his army of cavalry and light infantry into

Asia Minor, and there, in 547, he overthrew King Croesus of Lydia, who had ruled all of Asia Minor west of the Halys River. Cyrus acquired Croesus' great riches, and in name he acquired all of Croesus' empire. The Greek cities on the western coast of Asia Minor submitted peacefully to Cyrus' rule. But in the more rugged terrain in southwestern Asia Minor, Cyrus' generals had rebellions to crush.

Cyrus began his attempt to rule the Greeks of Asia Minor benevolently, taking annual tribute from them while leaving them to their religion and customs. He connected his empire by a royal road that stretched from the Greek city of Sardis in western Asia Minor to Susa, a road with post stations one day's ride apart, with riders covering as many as 1600 miles in a week. For six years Cyrus embarked on more expeditions, his army conquering eastward from central Persia. And, with his occupation of the trade route between Europe and the Far East, Cyrus' empire prospered economically.

Persia Expands and Releases the Jewish Captives

Cyrus' army was strengthened by warriors he had gained from newly conquered peoples, and he turned his greater army southward against the Chaldeans. He claimed that Babylon's god, Marduk, had been awaiting a righteous ruler and that Marduk had called upon him, Cyrus, to become ruler of the world. The Old Testament gives a different interpretation of these events. It describes Cyrus as Yahweh's agent and claims that Cyrus was stirred by Yahweh into taking revenge against Babylon's wickedness and that Yahweh had "taken Cyrus by the right hand." (Isaiah 45:1.)

In October 539, Babylon fell to Cyrus without a struggle. According to the Old Testament, the captive worshipers of Yahweh expected Cyrus to wreak Yahweh's vengeance upon the wicked Babylonians. But Cyrus failed to punish Babylon, and the disappointed Yahwist captive's found Cyrus honoring Babylon's gods and treating Yahweh as just minor god of some distant place.

With his conquest of Babylon, Cyrus acquired rule of the Chaldean Empire, and kings who had been vassals of the Chaldean king came and paid homage to him. A king of kings, Cyrus now ruled as far as Egypt. He saw himself as the benefactor of all those he ruled, and he permitted a captive named Zerubbabel – a descendant of one of Judah's former kings – to lead forty thousand or so Jewish captives back to their homeland.

Some among the returning exiles believed that Yahweh had promised them good things to come, but in Jerusalem they found impoverishment, foreigners and few worshipers of Yahweh. Nearly half a century had passed since the massive exiles from Jerusalem, and

Zerubbabel found people in Jerusalem unwilling to accept his authority and resenting the intrusions of those returning from captivity. Those who returned to Jerusalem began rebuilding Solomon's temple. They laid a foundation for the new temple, but two years after their release from Babylon, the hostility of local people and Yahweh's failure to intervene on their behalf led them to abandon the project.

Cambyses and Darius The Great

In conquering Babylon, Cyrus acquired control over a vast trading network: through Canaan, Arabia to the Red Sea, Egypt and Africa. And Cyrus – now in his sixties – sought additional territory eastward. In 529 he led his army across the Jaxartes River at the foot of the Hindu Kush mountains. There a queen called Tomyris, told him to rule his own people and to bear the sight of her ruling her's. During this expedition, Cyrus died, and his son, Cambyses, succeeded him.

Cambyses tried to win glory to his name by conquering new territory, and after four years of preparation he conquered a portion of Egypt, bringing an end forever to the rule of the pharaohs. And Cambyses absorbed the island of Cyprus, which surrendered to him voluntarily. While in Egypt, Cambyses scoffed at Egypt's religion. His Persian religion opposed the worship of idols, and, to cure the Egyptians of what he saw as their superstitions, he had their idols burned. Cambyses is said to have killed with his dagger the bull representing the Egyptian god Apis and to have opened royal Egyptian tombs.

Cambyses' stay in Egypt was disrupted by news of an attempted usurpation of his power in Persia. He had been away three years, and when he returned to Persia he found insufficient support against a formidable opposition. His death was reported as a suicide. And the Egyptians saw his death as the revenge of their gods

The rising against Cambyses was led by Darius, an able soldier and a member of Cyrus' extended family – the Achaemenids. Darius had allied himself with some other aristocrats. A son of Cyrus – an heir to the throne – had been killed, and Darius claimed that it was Cambyses who had killed him. Darius presented himself as having thwarted a take over by someone impersonating the murdered son, and he claimed that as a member of Cyrus' family he was restoring legitimate rule. Not everyone accepted Darius' claims, and in many places Darius had to combat uprisings and competing claims to the throne and to win recognition by force of arms. Succeeding at this, Darius turned his attention to expanding the empire he had acquired. Stating that his god had chosen him as king of the entire world, Darius extended Persian rule in Egypt and beyond into what is now Libya. And in 517 BC, attracted by tribal divisions and wars in India, he extended Persian rule through the Kyber Pass to the Indus River. Darius made his capital Persepolis, in the south of Persia. He built highways, maintained postal service across his empire and encouraged commerce. He built a canal 150 feet wide, linking the Red Sea and the Nile. He reformed the empire's money and revised its administration, dividing the empire into twenty provinces, called *satrapies*.

Darius carried with him a portrait of his beloved wife, Artystone. He respected the religions of the various peoples he ruled, and he wished for and won the good will of people across his empire. Inspired by the tradition of law that he found in Babylon, he codified what he believed were just laws for his empire, and he wanted the various peoples he ruled to have local laws that pertained to their own customs.

Religion and Other Customs among the Persians

Under the Achaemenid dynasty, before Darius, temples had appeared for the first time in Persia. Related to the Aryans who had invaded India, or a least having a language closely related to the Aryans, the Persians had gods similar to those found in the sacred Hindu Vedas. Having mixed with the Medes, among the Persians a Mede priesthood called the Magi had come to dominate their religion. The major god of the Medes was Zurvan, a god of time and destiny. Another god of the Persians was Mazda, whom Darius adopted in an effort to unify his empire. And in western Persia the god Mithra and goddess Anahita were also worshiped.

The Persians buried their dead above ground, their faith holding that a corpse defiled the earth. As a religious people they saw virtue in modest eating, in having only one meal a day and nothing to drink but water. They valued cleanliness and associated a lack of cleanliness with the devil and his diseases. Severe penalties were given those thought to have spread disease by their uncleanness. And concern with the evils of the Devil led to stern laws against what the Persians saw as sinful sexuality, including masturbation, promiscuity and prostitution.

Etiquette was important to the Persians. Persians holding superior positions in society offered their cheeks to be kissed by those of a lower status, while equals embraced each other and kissed on the lips. The Persians thought it unbecoming to eat or drink anything in the street, or to spit, and like the Japanese today they thought it rude to blow one's nose around others. And in this age of travel and contacts among people, Persians were described by others as a hospitable, generous, warm hearted, open, and honest in speech.

In keeping with their concern for others, Persian punishments for crimes were severe. The punishment for manslaughter was ninety strokes with a horsewhip. Capital crimes included treason, rape, sodomy, cremating or burying the dead, murder, accidentally sitting on the king's throne, invading the king's privacy or approaching one of his concubines. Death was administered by poisoning, stabbing, crucifixion, hanging, stoning, burying one up to his head, smothering one in hot ashes, crushing one's head between huge stones or other methods of serving Mazda in his battle against the Devil.

Thus Spake Zarathustra
According to legend, Zoroastrianism had origins in a prophet named Zoroaster, also called Zarathustra, who appeared sometime after the Persians had arrived in Iran. It was said that when Zarathustra was born his laugh scattered the evil spirits that had been hanging around him as they did around all people. Legend claims that Zarathustra grew up with a love of wisdom and righteousness. It was said that when he was thirty he immersed himself in water during a spring religious festival and when he emerged in a state of purity he had a vision of a shining being who introduced himself as *Good Purpose*. According to the legend, Good Purpose took Zarathustra up a mountain to the great god, Mazda. And Zarathustra came down off the mountain with a message that he wished to preach to all humanity.

Legend describes Zarathustra as having had a vision of Mazda as all wise and the source of all justice and goodness, from which all other divine supporters of goodness emanated. Zarathustra perceived wickedness and cruelty as residing in Mazda's adversary: the Devil. Here, according to Zarathustra, was the answer to why righteous people suffered.

According to Zarathustra, when Mazda and the Devil first met, Mazda created life and the Devil created its opposite: death. According to Zarathustra, thereafter a struggle took place between Mazda and the Devil. Zarathustra described Mazda's goodness and creation of life as the force of light, and he described the Devil as the ruler of darkness, including the world of hell under the earth. Zarathustra described the Devil as the leader of all the evil spirits that hovered in the air, tempting people to commit crime and sin. He described the Devil as creating not only darkness but winter, ants, locusts, vermin, serpents, sin, sodomy, menstruation and the other plagues of life that had ruined the paradise into which Mazda had placed the first humans.

According to Zarathustra, in the great battle between Mazda and the Devil, people were responsible for their thoughts, and, in choosing between right and wrong, people became their own saviors. Zarathustra called people to a rigid discipline to support Mazda's goodness, and he claimed that in this struggle between right and wrong, every man, woman and child had a guardian angel that was under Mazda's leadership – an angel that helped them achieve virtue.

According to legend, people ridiculed Zarathustra and persecuted him. But then a king was converted to Zarathustra's teachings, and the religion of Zarathustra spread. When this happened is unknown, for none of the Persian kings mentioned Zoroaster in their inscriptions nor mentioned supernatural beings that were unique to Zoroastrianism, and the early Zoroastrians left no records. Long after Zarathustra, Zoroastrians priests declared writing unfit for Zarathustra's holy words. But the Zoroastrian priesthood did leave a legend of Zarathustra's death. Zarathustra, they said, was consumed by a flash of lightening.

The Optimism of the Zoroastrians

Zoroastrians did not see evil as inherent in nature or inherent in the human body. They saw nature as good because of the power of their god Mazda, whom they thought stronger than the Devil and omnipotent except for the temporary battle he was facing with the Devil. Zoroastrians were optimistic, believing that Mazda's triumph was assured. They believed that the birth of Zarathustra had been the beginning of a final epoch that was to last three thousand years – ending perhaps around the year AD 2000. They believed that Mazda's message would be carried throughout the world, that the foolish followers of the Devil's lies would dwell in darkness and misery, that the final epoch would end with the pronouncement of a Last Judgement and the utter destruction of the Devil and all his forces of evil. They believed that with this ending would come a great resurrection of all good souls beginning life anew, and all good people (the followers of Truth) would cross the bridge into Mazda's kingdom, free of decay, old age and death.

JUDAH – THE NEW JEWISH STATE

Judah was fifty miles at its widest point and one hundred miles long: a small land within the great Persian empire. A Persian governor in Judah allowed Zerubbabel and his Yahweh priesthood subordinate authority over Judah's internal affairs. One member of this priesthood, Jehozadek, spoke around 520 BC of the people of Judah having harvested little, not having enough food to satisfy their hunger nor enough clothing for warmth (Haggai 1:6). He blamed this on their own errancy, and he called for a renewed effort at rebuilding Solomon's temple, which he believed would strengthen them spiritually.

After permission was received from Darius, work on the temple began, and it was finished in 516. It was a meager structure compared to the temple Solomon had built, but the temple's opening ceremony was grand. It included the sacrifice of one hundred bulls, two hundred rams, four hundred lambs and twelve male goats – paid for by Darius. (Ezra 6:17.)

As is written of Cyrus in the Book of Isaiah, 44:28 and 45:1, the Yahweh priesthood looked kindly upon Persia's kings. For Cyrus had freed the Hebrew captives and Cyrus and his successors had protected them from the aggressions of others and allowed them to worship their own god. Moreover, both the Yahweh priesthood and the Persians believed in one supreme god, and both stressed morality and a strict adherence to a code of laws.

Persian officials and their families were stationed in Judah, Persian officials and their families were stationed in Judah, and in Judah were colonies of Persian merchants. With them in Judah were Persian temples and priests. And with the good feelings of Yahwists toward the Persians, Yahwists might have been open to receiving religious ideas from the Persians. Not known to have been a part of Yahweh worship before the coming of the Persians were hierarchies of angels, demons in conflict, Satan as an independent and evil force rather than an agent of Yahweh, reward and punishment after death, the immortality of the soul, the coming of a final judgement ending in a fiery ordeal and resurrection of the dead. It appears that the aristocratic Yahwist priesthood – the Sadducees – resisted these changes to Yahwist belief and that commoners accepted them – ideas to be championed by those to be known as Pharisees.

Satan and the Book of Job

In the sacred writings of the Yahwists, Satan had never been a ruler over evil. In the Old Testament's Book of Numbers, Satan is described as an angel – from the Greek word *angelos*, a messenger, a bringer of unexpected obstacles. Instead of a ruler over evil, this Satan is described as sent by God to obstruct wrongful activity. This Satan appears again as an agent of Yahweh in the Old Testament's Book of Job. Job's disasters are described as Satan testing his devotion to Yahweh, a test to see if he would blame and curse Yahweh. In the Book of Job, Satan appears as one of Yahweh's obedient servants, an angel messenger and a member of Yahweh's royal court with whom Yahweh agrees that Job is to be tested.

The story of Job attempts to resolve the problem of Yahweh being well meaning and powerful while those loyal to him suffer. Job is described as a wealthy man, with "7,000 sheep, 3,000 camels, 500 yokes of oxen and 500 female donkeys," the kind of man whom the prophet Amos might have despised. But the Book of Job describes him as a good man: devout and fearing Yahweh. Job is advised by a friend that the innocent do not perish and that the upright are not destroyed, that whoever sows trouble harvests it. The message for Job is to be patient, that if he endures his suffering Yahweh will do right by him. Job endures and is faithful to Yahweh, and Yahweh restores his good fortunes.

The Book of Esther

Because of its account of the rule of Xerxes (from 486 to 465 BC), the Book of Esther appears to have been written sometime after the early 400s, perhaps as late as the 100s BC. In the Book of Esther, the Persian monarch, Ahasuerus, dumps his queen, Vashti, and marries Esther, a young Jewish woman. Esther's cousin and foster-father, Mordecai, warns the Persian monarch that a plot is afoot against his royal life. A Persian grand vizier, Haman, who opposes Mordecai, convinces the monarch to decree death against Mordecai and other Jews in his empire, selected by lot, on a certain date. The queen, Esther, intervenes, and the Grand Vizier is instead executed – hanged – and Mordecai is made grand vizier in his place. On the day that Jews were to be executed, they defend themselves and slay as many as seventy-five thousand.

This day became a holiday for the Jews, celebrated during successive days and called the Feast of Lots. There is in the Book of Esther nothing about the worship of Yahweh. Among Persian writings no record of any queen named Esther or a Persian minister named Mordecai or Haman have been found. Esther is an Aramaic name for the goddess Ishtar. Mordecai means worshiper of Marduk. The story of Esther resembles an ancient Persian story about the shrewdness of Harem queens. The description in the Book of Esther of the parade through the streets dressed in royal robes, the mock combat and other happenings are similar to the Persian celebration of the New Year. This celebration had mock combat between one team representing the old year and other team representing the New Year, with the old year being hanged in effigy. Apparently, Jews also took part in this New Year celebration, and eventually the story of Esther was invented to explain the celebration and to turn it into a Jewish celebration – much as Christians were to change pagan holidays into Christian holidays.

Artaxerxes and Ezra

Darius spent his later years at his palace enjoying his expanded harem, which had women of various races. In 486, at the age of sixty-four, he fell ill and died, and he was succeeded by his son Xerxes, who ruled for twenty-one years. Under Xerxes, some women at court acquired great influence, and jealousies surrounded Xerxes. A eunuch commander of the guard conspired with others and assassinated Xerxes and Xerxes' first son. The conspirators put on the throne another of Xerxes' sons: an eighteen-year-old named Artaxerxes – the son of a foreign woman from the royal harem. Artaxerxes asserted his authority and had the eunuch commander executed. And Artaxerxes ruled over the vast Persian empire for forty-two years.

Like Darius, Artaxerxes was interested in the peoples of his empire remaining orderly under their local laws and religion. He appointed as Judah's new governor a Yahwist scholar and priest named Ezra, who had been living in Babylon, and he instructed Ezra to appoint magistrates and judges who would keep Judah in the laws of its god, Yahweh.

According to the Old Testament, Ezra and a following of eighteen hundred males moved to Judah. And what Ezra found must have been far from what he had expected, for when he arrived he tore at his hair, his beard, his garment, his robe, and he sat down appalled. He found that the Hebrews of Judah had not separated themselves from other peoples and that they had been practicing "abominations."

Ezra wanted to separate the worshipers of Yahweh from foreign influences and to advance their identity as a community of worshipers of Yahweh. He called the people of Jerusalem to assemble, and he told the assembly that new demands would be put upon them. Judah was to become a Yahwist state and its people to be considered one people. Ezra ordered foreign women expelled from the community. He commanded that no one could marry any of the foreign women and that any man who had already married such a woman must expel her from his house.

Already the people of Judah were a mix of peoples. Solomon himself had been the son of a woman described as a Hittite: Bathsheba. Nevertheless, Ezra was concerned with the racial purity of the Yahwist priesthood, and he purged from the priesthood those who could not prove that they were descended from purely Hebrew families. But rather than attempt to extend his stricture on racial purity, he made observance of Yahwist practices the deciding issue whether one belonged to the Jewish community – beginning what would eventually be Judaism's racial tolerance. Judaism is a word derived from the word *Judah*, and the heart of Judaism was to be the worship of Yahweh, the Moses legend and adherence to Yahweh's laws as described in the Moses legend.

Judah's New Laws

Ezra's laws were Yahweh's laws, just as Hammurabi's laws were Marduk's laws. And Ezra's laws included the traditional eye for an eye and a tooth for a tooth. But the custom of an entire family being considered guilty for the act of any one of its members was discarded in favor of individual responsibility: the father was to continue to have supreme authority within the family, but a father would not be punished for the sins of a son, or a son for the sins of the father.

Marriage was strictly regulated as before. Fathers were to arrange the marriages of their sons and daughters without their consent. Marriage was recognized as the basis of a family, and marital promises were supported by the harshest of measures: if an engaged woman copulated with another man, both she and the man were to be stoned to death; if a married man or a married woman committed adultery they were to be stoned to death – unless the man copulated with a slave, in which case he was merely beaten. (Leviticus 19:20.)

If a father found his son stubborn, rebellious and disobedient, he could take him to the city elders, and then the son could be stoned to death. In a dispute that went to court, the man judged wicked would be whipped, but no more than forty times. If a man had two wives and one was loved and the other unloved and the unloved one gave birth to the first son, that son would remain favored as the first son. If a neighbor need help with his stray oxen, sheep or donkeys, one should help him. And one should not move a neighbor's boundary marker.

The Jewish priesthood expected people to look after their health by following Judaic law. Touching the dead or touching persons having certain types of ailments was prohibited. To clean a leper, one was obliged to sacrifice a male lamb to Yahweh and to sprinkle the patient with the blood of a bird mixed with running water.

In the Old Testament's Book of Leviticus, Yahweh is described as giving laws to Moses that rejected Canaanite ways. Moses is described as prohibiting the wearing of garments made of both linen and wool or garments with tassels, as was custom among the Canaanites. And it was written that one should not eat pork or any animal that did not both chew its cud and have cloven feet. Pork had been the major source of meat among the Canaanites, who, having been a settled people could raise pigs. The nomadic Hebrews had raised sheep and goats, which, unlike pigs, could be herded over long distances. And, with pork having been a food eaten by the detested Canaanites and not traditional among Hebrews, it had been described as unclean, although there is no evidence that the Canaanites suffered from eating their pigs anymore than the Hebrews suffered from eating their sheep or goats.

The Five Books of Moses

Apparently by the time that Ezra was in Judah, the first five books of the Old Testament were assembled: Genesis, Exodus, Leviticus, Numbers and Deuteronomy. These books were declared to have been written by Moses himself, inspired by God. In Hebrew they were called the Torah of Moses. They appear to have been assembled with national unity in mind, as a compilation of the history of the Jewish people, with a clear distinction between the people favored by Yahweh and the outsiders detested by Ezra. Included were writings on genealogies and the priestly matters and legalities that were concerns during the time of Ezra. Not included among the books were those writings that supported one group or another rather than the Jewish nation as a whole, writings that were later to be described as *apocrypha* (hidden things) and *pseudepigrapha* (falsely attributed writings).

Wisdom and the Book of Proverbs

Among the sacred writings of the Hebrews were The Proverbs. Legend held that Solomon was its author, but some Biblical scholars believe that Proverbs may have been written after the year 400 BC. Proverbs begins with the statement that "The fear of the Lord is the beginning of knowledge." From there, Proverbs advises its readers to avoid being enticed by greed into joining with others in thievery and mugging. Do not envy sinners, it states. "Drink water from your own well. Pay your debts, and fear the Lord." By fearing the Lord, it claims, one acquires security and wisdom. Integrity, it states, brings security, and hatred and arrogance stir up strife. Be kind and true, Proverbs admonishes. "Trust the Lord with all your heart." If you honor the Lord "your barns will be filled with plenty, and your vats will overflow with new wine." Do not weary yourself to gain wealth. Wisdom and a good name are better than silver and gold. Do not boast about tomorrow. Do not slander a slave to his master. Be good to your neighbors. Smell good for the sake of others. Do not be enticed by an absent neighbor's wife. Do not associate with one given to anger. And wives, do not be idle, and be happy in your work.

The Jews Await a Great King

The prosperity that the followers of Yahweh had expected continued to elude them. In and around Jerusalem poverty continued, and famine appeared. As described in the Book of Nehemiah, 5:1-5, the poor protested:

> We are mortgaging our fields, our vineyards, and our houses that we might get grain because of the famine.... We have borrowed money for the king's

tax on our fields and our vineyards. And now our
flesh is like the flesh of our brothers, our children like
their children. Yet behold, we are forcing our sons
and our daughters to be slaves. And some of our
daughters are forced into bondage already, and we
are helpless because our fields and vineyards belong
to others.

The priests who governed Judah after Ezra attempted economic and
social reforms. As described in the Book of Deuteronomy, usury within
the community of Hebrews was prohibited, but usury against non-
Hebrews was allowed. As a part of these reforms, every seventh year
debts were to be abolished. And every seventh year, fellow Jews who
had been enslaved were to be set free – while the slavery of others was
to remain. And adversity and hardship continued among the Jews.
Suffering Jews continued to look nostalgically to the glorious days of
King David. And they looked forward to Yahweh bringing them
another great king – a messiah – like David.

CHAPTER 9

THE GREEKS IN TRIUMPH AND FUTILITY

ATHENS, DEMOCRACY AND HUMANISM

The tyrant Pisistratus died in 527 and was succeeded by two sons who ruled jointly. In 514, a young aristocrat opposed to popular rule assassinated one of the sons, and some aristocrats attempted but failed to assassinate the surviving son, Hippias. Hippias retaliated, and some aristocrats went into exile. The priest at the principal shrine of the god Apollo, at Delphi, encouraged the exiled aristocrats by suggesting that Apollo was on their side. A leading aristocratic family from Athens, the Alcmaeonidaens, won the support of Sparta, and to do the will of Apollo, Sparta, in 510, sent an army that defeated Hippias and sent him fleeing to Persia.

Sparta's army put into power an oligarchy of Athenian aristocrats, but most Athenians did not want a return to the subservience and dependence on local powerful families that existed before the rule of Pisistratus. The oligarchy found itself unable to rule, and, in 508, a clique of progressive members of the upper classes united with commoners and led a popular resurgence that brought them to power.

The most prominent leader of the resurgence was Cleisthenes, who wished to govern in a way that brought more unity among the Athenians. Across recent generations immigration had made Athens a mix of people unrelated by blood, and Cleisthenes extended to many immigrants, and to some slaves, the same rights that Athenian citizens had. He drew up a constitution for Athens that divided Athenians into ten "tribes" based not on blood relations but on where people lived. Each tribe had its own military unit, shrine, priest and assembly. Any member of a tribe could participate in the election of local and state officials, and each tribe sent fifty representatives for one year of service to a city assembly. This was democratic government – unlike any other government among the civilized.

The popularity of Cleisthenes' reforms brought new enthusiasm among Athenians for their government and city. This and Cleisthenes' new military organization made Athens stronger militarily, and its strength was soon tested. In 506, Sparta and its Peloponnesian allies invaded Attica hoping to crush the democracy in Athens, which

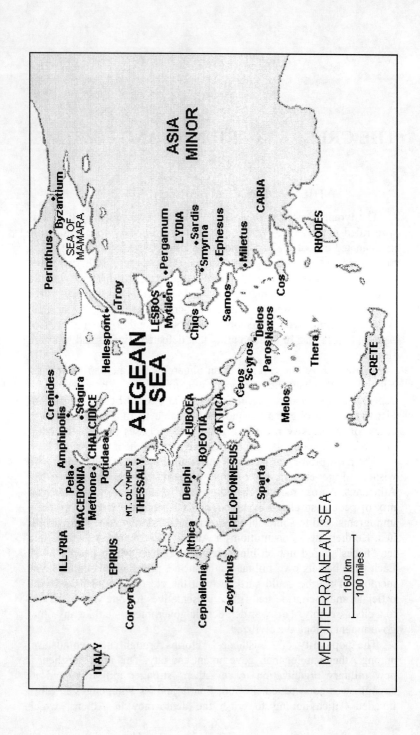

ILLYRIA

EPIRUS

ITALY

Corcyra

Cephallenia

Zacyrithus

Ithica

MACEDONIA
Pela
Amphipolis
Crenides
Methone
Potidaea
CHALCIDICE
Stagira

MT. OLYMPUS
THESSALY

Delphi
BOEOTIA
EUBOEA
ATTICA

Sparta
PELOPONNESUS

AEGEAN
SEA

Hellespoint

Troy

Perinthus
Byzantium
SEA OF
MAMARA

LESBOS
Mytilene
Pergamum
LYDIA
Sardis
Smyrna
Ephesus
Miletus
CARIA

Chios

Samos

Ceos
Scyros
Paros
Delos
Naxos
Melos

Thera

Cos

RHODES

ASIA
MINOR

CRETE

MEDITERRANEAN SEA

160 km
100 miles

Spartans saw as a defiance of religious tradition. The new politics and morale won over tradition, with Athens defeating the invaders and the invaders withdrawing. And to stave off any future aggressions from Sparta and its allies, Athens made an alliance with Persia.

Education in Athens

In Athens, physical training and education was extended to the male children of common families, and it became commonly accepted that boys of commoners should be able to read and write. Schooling was inexpensive because teachers were paid little. Boys started school at the age of seven, and for many it continued for only three or four years, while some others continued until they were eighteen.

In addition to reading and writing, the boys studied literature and grammar. They learned poetry by heart, especially the works of Homer, which was believed to contain messages of morality. Prose authors were not studied, nor were mathematics and technical subjects. Education in music declined in importance from what it had been centuries before, but school included choral singing, dancing and the playing of musical instruments. Physical education emphasized individual efforts rather than team sports. As before, education in Athens – and elsewhere in Greece – fostered loyalty to the group. It fostered pride in Athens and pride in being Greek as opposed to being "barbarian."

Humanist Literature

In Athens and some other Greek cities, dramas and writings appeared that focused on the human condition. The spirit that contributed to other Greek achievements helped the Greeks create an easy, lucid poetry about shared pleasures, love and other feelings. Some innovative writers went beyond simple divisions of good versus evil people and dramatized human complexity and weakness, including the flaws in exemplary heroes. They wrote dramas that contained insights that modern psychology would build upon and refer to: narcissism, the Oedipus complex, phobias and manias. In 535, an Athenian, Thespis, introduced acting to choral music and recitation. In the 400s, two of the greatest Athenian playwrights were Euripides and Aristophanes. The Athenian, Aeshylus, wrote a number of plays: *The Suppliants, The Persians, The Seven against Thebes, Prometheus Bound, Agamemnon, Choephoroe,* and *Eumenides.* An Athenian named Sophocles – who lived from around 497 to 405 BC – wrote plays entitled *Oedipus Rex, Philoctetes, Women of Trachis, Electra, Oedipus at Colonus, Antigone* and *Ajax.* These were pursuits that prophets of the Old Testament

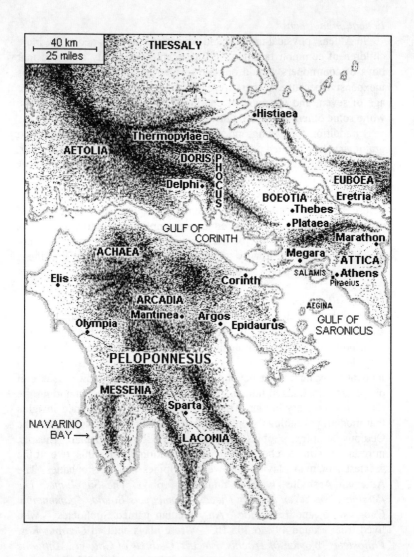

would have seen as frivolous distractions, as in the complaint of Isaiah that "...they do not pay attention to the deeds of the Lord." (Isaiah 5:12) It was a celebration of humanity – a humanism – that would appear centuries later in Europe's renaissance and influence Shakespeare and other great dramatists of the future.

The Limitations of Democracy in Athens

Democracy brought Athenians greater contentment and political stability, but slaves and women remained without a voice in political affairs, and of the forty thousand adult males free to participate in deciding issues, less than a sixth did so. Also, Athens lacked a professional, responsible, civil service. The functioning of governmental offices remained the special knowledge of a few ambitious politicians who used this knowledge to gain or maintain power and influence. Politics and the judiciary in Athens remained under the influence of people of wealth. Venal judges presided at courts of law marked by corruption and perjury. Common people did not have the leisure to serve their city as officials or as members of juries. Not until after 460, when Athens acquired wealth from empire, would people be paid to participate in jury duty or paid to serve as one of the five hundred city council members – pay that would enable common people to leave their work for such activities.

Athens was an intellectual center, but only a few there were interested in advancing their worldly knowledge, and these were mostly young men of leisure from wealthy families. Self-interest remained stronger than community interest, and in the city's market place one could see poverty, slave drivers, loud peddlers and those who cheated their customers.

Some wealthy Athenians grumbled about the vulgarity of democratic politics. Among them was the playwright Aristophanes, who disliked seeing men attempt to create a following by promising rewards and playing on superstitions. Some men of wealth felt exploited for the sake of what they saw as the ignorant, disorderly mob. And some found democratic government too slow in making judgments and getting things done.

HERODOTUS, THE FATHER
OF JOURNALISM AND HISTORY

Before Herodotus, events were described in imaginative poems often by priests who wished to put their god or gods in the best light. Herodotus – a Greek from Asia Minor – also believed that gods intervened in human affairs, and he believed in oracles and that dreams were sent by the gods, but he tried to add discipline to his work and to describe what people had done and why they had done it. Before Herodotus, the past was seen in legend and myth, without a sense of measured time. Herodotus wrote about events that he placed in linear time. He wrote that his purpose was to describe the deeds of people so that these deeds would not be forgotten by posterity. Unlike priestly writers, he admitted that his work was subjective, in other words that his work remained within the limits of his own ability to interpret.

Living in an age of travel, diversity and exploration, Herodotus was motivated in part by his curiosity. He attempted to describe and explain what he thought was interesting. Running from Persian authority, he traveled for seventeen years, to Egypt, the Black Sea, through Greece and to Italy and Sicily. He described the places and people he had seen – descriptions that would be of great value to modern historians. He saw the pyramids and wondered about them. He speculated about the causes of the regular flooding of the Nile. Drawing from folk tales, Herodotus tried to describe Cyrus II historically, a modern source on Cyrus more detailed than that recorded in the Old Testament.

Herodotus' open-mindedness about the cultures of the people he visited may have been helped by the mix of cultures of his home city, Halicarnassus, which was a mix of Greek and Carian peoples. It was an open-mindedness that led Greeks less open-minded than he to accuse him of being a "barbarian-lover."

Herodotus' methodology was less precise than that of some modern journalists and historians, but during his travels he tried to verify a story by listening to a variety of people. His chronology was vague, and sometimes he failed to describe conflicting political forces, but unlike the storytellers who preceded him he sought accuracy and discernment between fact and fiction. And he tried to do more than just tell a story: he tried to analyze.

In modern times Herodotus would be called the father of history – from the Greek word *Historia*, meaning research or investigation. Herodotus was the first known to have described war analytically. This was the war between the Persians and cities in Greece. People around him quickly turned what they had heard of the war into inaccuracies and exaggerations – into legends – and inadvertently Herodotus included such distortions into his work. But he tried to be objective: he wrote of the war without undue adulation of his fellow Greeks, whom he favored, or undue vilification of the Persians.

WAR AGAINST PERSIA AND
ORIGINS OF THE PELOPONNESIAN WAR

The empire of the Persian Achaemenid dynasty extended to Thrace and Chalcidice – Darius the Great having led an expedition along the northern coast of the Aegean Sea in 513 BC. As for Darius' rule among the Greeks in Asia Minor, it was generally tolerant of local customs, it provided its subjects protection from attacks from wandering warrior tribes, and it offered its subjects peace, good communications and a stable coinage. But in 499, a desire for self-rule among the Greeks of Asia Minor helped fuel a rebellion against the Persians.

Athens and the city of a Eretria, about thirty miles north of Athens, supported the uprising. By 494, the Persians crushed the rebellion, destroying Miletus, sacking and burning other towns and taking select Greek boys and girls back to Persia. Then, believing that his god-given right to rule should not have been challenged, Darius set out to punish Athens and others who had supported the uprising. He hoped to extend his rule down the Greek peninsula, and many Greeks opposed to democracy, including some Athenians, favored submission to the Persians. They saw Persia as a champion of authoritarian rule and expected that Persian rule would include freedom of worship and allow local self-government as it had in Asia Minor.

Those who supported democracy favored resisting the Persians. So too did many Greeks who made their living in industry and trade, these Greeks fearing that the Persians would give trading favors to rivals such as the Phoenicians – who were subjects of Darius. And the Spartans feared the Persians, believing that if the Persians came to the Greek mainland they would try to eliminate them as a military power.

In the year 490, the Persian fleet sailed across the Aegean Sea and landed a force of many thousand soldiers near Marathon, twenty-six miles by road north of Athens. Athens responded by sending troops to Marathon, and it sent a fast runner to Sparta with the news of the Persian landing. Sparta announced that it would join Athens against the Persians. But remaining faithful to their gods, the Spartans waited for the passing of a full moon, and the Athenians had to confront the Persians without them.

The Greek city of Plataea, faithful to a new alliance with Athens, fought with the Athenians at Marathon, and there a highly motivated force of about 10,000 Greeks, in phalanx formations, defeated a much greater number of Persian cavalry and archers. More than six thousand Persians died, and around two hundred Greeks.

The Spartans arrived after the battle had ended, and they returned home praising the Athenians. Greeks far and wide, including the

Athenians, were inspired by their victory over the great Persian Empire, and they held a religious festival at Delphi as thanksgiving to the gods for the victory at Marathon. And there the oracle of Apollo praised Athens as an eagle "for all time."

Soon it was said that the god Pan had given the Athenians their victory by his causing panic among the Persians. It was said that Pan had done so after having seen a slack in devotion to him among the Athenians, Pan wanting to regain their devotion – a tactic different from Yahweh's reaction to the lack of devotion he had found among his Hebrews, and one that apparently worked better.

Persia Tries Again

After Darius died in 486, his son and successor, Xerxes, intended to carry out his father's plan to invade the Greek mainland again. Xerxes failed to appreciate adequately the costs that would be incurred by such an expansion, or the burdens of maintaining an empire that would be farther reaching. He had trouble enough with the empire as it was: his plans for invading Greece had to be delayed so he could crush more rebellions, again by the Egyptians, and by the Babylonians – rebellions that had been encouraged by the death of his father, Darius. But Xerxes believed in the power of his god, Mazda.

Athens, Sparta and some other Greek city-states expected the return of the Persians. And they did as so many others had done before them: they set aside their differences and formed a military alliance. Their alliance was called the Hellenic League and was led by Sparta, still seen as the greatest military power among them. Member cities sent representatives to league congresses, the first of which was held in 481. This congress ended the small wars that were taking place among member cities. And at these congresses, oaths were taken that were supposed to bind the city-states to each other permanently.

Xerxes assembled the greatest military force ever, and in the year 480 he launched his invasion, marching his armies along the coast of Macedonia and down into Greece, while keeping these armies supplied by his navy. Sparta and Thebes sent armies to meet the invaders at Thermopylae – thirty miles northwest of Thebes and eighty-five miles northwest of Athens. There they held the Persians at a narrow pass while the league's navy, mostly Athenian, engaged Persian naval forces offshore. Herodotus described the storm that wrecked much of the Persian fleet as an intervention by Zeus, but, inexplicably, Zeus appeared uninterested in helping the Greek cause on land. A traitor among the Greeks showed the Persian foot soldiers a way around the pass at Thermopylae, and the Persians attacked the Greeks from behind. The Thebans surrendered while the Spartans fought and died to the last man. The main force of Persians swarmed through the pass toward Athens. Persia's army overran Attica and Athens, while Athenians fled to the islands of Salamis, near their port, and Aegina, tens miles to the southwest. The Athenian navy placed itself between Xerxes' force and the Athenian refugees on the island of Salamis, and it rallied support from numerous coastal Greek cities. Near Salamis, the Athenian navy and its allies won a great naval battle, destroying the Persian fleet – the waters said to be covered with Persian wreckage and blood. With much of the Persia army dependent on ships for supplies, it was forced to march out of Greece and back to Asia Minor. But peace was not declared, and Persia and the Greeks remained at war.

From Unity to Division among the Greeks

During their war against Persia, a spirit of unity and brotherhood had arisen among those Greek cities opposed to the Persians, a unity served by their common language, common customs and common religious beliefs. But federation among their cities was far from their minds, and the spirit of unity among the Greeks proved superficial as those of different cities drifted back to seeing themselves as different from each other.

Unity between Athens and Sparta cracked as Sparta became fearful of Athens. Sparta was alarmed over Athenian insistence on rebuilding fortifications that the Persians had destroyed, including protection of its harbor at Piraeus, which to the Spartans indicated that Athens aimed at an independent military strength. Sparta was annoyed at Athens taking command of naval operations at the straits to the Black Sea, a place of greater interest to Athens because of the grain it imported through those straits. And differences arose between Sparta and Athens over the question of continuing their war against Persia. The Athenians were interested in trade with the Greek cities still ruled by Persia, and they wanted to continue the war in order to liberate their fellow Greeks from Persian rule. Sparta had no interest in trading with those Greek cities, nor interest in democracy. Moreover, the Spartans were concerned about the many men they had already lost in battle, and they feared that their Helot slaves might take advantage of this loss and and further military losses and revolt. So Sparta was ready to let Persia continue its rule over other Greek cities.

Sparta and its allies on the Peloponnesian peninsula withdrew from the war, leaving Athens as the most influential among those cities continuing the war. Athens created a new league of states – a voluntary association called the Delian League. Member states agreed to donate money, ships and crewmen to the war effort and to police the Aegean

Sea, and they sent representatives to assemblies where league policies and goals were to be decided.

Athens Creates an Empire

Recent successes by Athens and its rise to prominence increased the pride of the Athenians, and some Athenians, including its leader, Pericles, saw the greatness of Athens as rooted in its political power. Athens arrogated to itself the role of policeman within its alliance. According to the Athenian journalist Thucydides, the Athenians were heavy handed in pressuring allies who were "neither accustomed nor willing to undertake protracted toil." Athens forced back into its alliance a city that had broken its oath to remain in the league. It suppressed petty wars within the league and intervened in disputes within member cities, favoring those who supported democracy (to the chagrin of Athenian aristocrats) while those in other cities who supported aristocratic rule tended to look to Sparta for leadership.

The Athenians were creating an empire. Seeing themselves as superior to other Greeks, some Athenians argued that empire was the natural order of things, that if they did not have the strength to dominate others they would soon be dominated. Some saw empire as a remedy to over-population. Some landless Athenians favored the confiscation of lands abroad as an opportunity to become landowners. Some wealthy Athenians saw in imperialism an opportunity to gain more land. Those Athenians making money from trade supported empire believing that it would benefit them commercially. Some believed that imperialism would provide them jobs, such as jobs on ships that policed the seas, and jobs on the docks that serviced those ships. Some supported empire also because it appeared to guarantee supplies of grain. Many Athenians saw benefit in their city receiving tribute from those city-states that Athens dominated, taxes they would otherwise have to pay. And Pericles, seeing democracy as popular, believed that with his support for democracy and democracy's spread would come an increase in the popularity of Athens' power.

Athens forced its rule on the island of Scyros (seventy-five miles to its southeast), and Athenians claimed authority there on the grounds of the discovery in Scyros of the bones of a mythical king of Athens who was said to have migrated there during the Dorian invasions. And claiming that during the Dorian invasions Athenians populated the western coast of Asia Minor, Athenian propaganda portrayed Athens as the mother of cities there. These cities, according to the Athenian imperialists, owed Athens religious homage – as was customary between a mother city and its offspring. These Athenians claimed that their goddess Demeter, a goddess of harvest and fertility, had given grain to humanity and that Athens therefore was a benefactor of humanity and was justified in ruling others.

The Little Peloponnesian War and the End of War against Persia
In 464, an earthquake leveled most of Sparta's dwellings and killed around 20,000. The Spartans believed that the earthquake was the work of the earthshaking god Poseiden and that Poseiden had been offended by a recent violation of his sanctuary, from which some Helots had been dragged away and executed. Following the earthquake, the Helots revolted, encouraged perhaps by their belief that the god Poseiden was sympathetic with their cause. They attacked what was left of Sparta, and they were joined in their rebellion by nearby enemies of Sparta who sought advantage from Sparta's sudden tragedy. The Spartans managed to contain the revolt, which lasted into 462, while it had only ineffective support from Athens, which was still nominally its ally.

In 462, Athens concluded an alliance with Argos, and with Thessaly (north of Thermopylae). And Sparta found these alliances offensive – as it did Athens' meager support. An ally of Sparta, Corinth, was also displeased with Athens. Corinth was a maritime commercial power fifty miles west of Athens. It had colonies, and it feared Athens as a rival. Corinth was in conflict with the city of Megara, which lay between Corinth and Athens. Megara was unhappy over Corinthian encroachments on its territory, and when Athens accepted Megara into its league, the Corinthians responded with enmity for Athens. The alliance between Megara and Athens gave Athens a naval base in the Gulf of Corinth, just west of Megara. The Corinthians disliked this intrusion into the waters near their city. The navy of Sparta's Peloponnesian League was dominated by ships from Corinth, and it came to blows with the Athenian navy in the Gulf of Saronicus.

Meanwhile, Athens and its league had won additional naval victories against Persia, and Persia had withdrawn from all Greek territories in Asia Minor. It seemed that the war against Persia might be over, but Athens continued hostilities against Persia. It helped Cyprus rid itself of Persian rule. Then the potentate of Libya, who was fomenting rebellion in Egypt against Persian rule, invited the Greek fleet to help the Egyptians. Athens saw this as an opportunity to win more control of foreign trade, to gain much needed grain from the region of the Nile and to establish a naval station on Egypt's coast. The Athenian navy and marines invaded Egypt. Believing that Athens was too involved in Egypt to defend Megara effectively, Corinth invaded Megara's territory, but a small force of Athenian infantry drove the Corinthians back.

Then Sparta, having recovered to a degree from the Helot revolt, felt able to send a force north to Boeotia. It sent a force to revive the Boeotian League in order to check growing Athenian power and to give support to the little state of Doris, which had been attacked by an ally of Athens: Phocis. Athens and its ally Thessaly sent troops against the Spartans, and in the clash that followed, in 457, both Sparta and Athens suffered heavy losses. And the wounded Spartans returned to Sparta, ravaging Megara's territory on their way home.

With Spartan forces gone, Athens was able to assert its power in Boeotia. Athens acquired control over the whole of Boeotia except for the city of Thebes, and even at Thebes it was able to set up a democracy, driving from power oligarchs who had been allied with Sparta. Athens sent a naval expedition around the Peloponnesian peninsula, attacking the Peloponnesian alliance in places, and it gained Achaea (in the northwest of Peloponnesus) to its alliance – which put Athens at the height of its power.

Another Attempt at Peace

In 454 – six years after the Athenians had invaded Egypt – the Persian emperor, Artaxerxes, with help from his Phoenician navy, drove the Athenians out of Egypt. Athens lost its hoped for grain from Egypt, and in the years of 451 and 450 Athenians suffered from famine. Wearied by its continuing war against Persia and believing that it could not wage war against both Persia and members of the Peloponnesian League, Athens invited members of the Peloponnesian League and other Greek states to send representatives to Athens for a congress to discuss matters of common interest, such as the restoration of temples burned by the Persians, the payment of offerings due the gods for their delivering Greece from the Persians, and common measures for clearing the seas of piracy. Sparta was reluctant to acknowledge Athenian supremacy in the Aegean Sea, and Sparta and its allies feared that membership in any congress with Athens would lead to their domination by Athens. Sparta opposed attending a congress with Athens, and the congress failed.

With the failure of this congress, Pericles prepared for more war against Sparta and its league. He increased taxation (tribute) from Athens' league of cities – much more than was necessary to cover the costs of providing these subject-allies with protection. He launched a program to tighten control over them, and he ordered them to send representatives to the annual religious festival of the Greater Dionysia. He began a civic building and restoration program in Athens that gave relief to the unemployed and boosted Athenian morale. Then Pericles made peace with Persia, leaving the Greek cities on Cyprus to deal with an attempt by Persia's Phoenician navy to exterminate Greek civilization there.

Drift and Decision for War

On-again, off-again wars among the Greeks continued. Phocis sought control of Delphi. Sparta sent a force north to expel the Phocians. The Phocis was allied with Athens, and Athens restored Phocian rule at Delphi. Athens also intervened in Boeotia, where, after misgovernment by democrats, an oligarchy had come to power again in Thebes. Thebes had become a refuge for oligarchs from elsewhere in Boeotia. A rebellion against Athenian power broke out in northern Boeotia, and a Boeotian force defeated an Athenian force of a thousand Athenian volunteers, led by men who had mistakenly believed that their small force could subdue the rebellion.

In 446, cities in Euboea joined the revolt against Athenian domination. Pericles was worried about the example that rebellion would set for others in the Athenian Empire, and with an army and navy he went to Euboea to crush the rebellion. Megara had become unhappy with the Athenian bullying, and it took advantage of Athens' troubles by joining the rebellion. Pericles withdrew from Euboea to fight Megara. An army from the Peloponnesian League, under a Spartan king, Pleistoanax, responded by invading Attica, but after laying waste to some countryside it withdrew. Then Pericles and an army of five thousand infantrymen supported by fifty ships returned to Euboea. They subdued all of that island and established a settlement with all but the city of Histiaea, whose inhabitants they drove away, Athens taking the territory for itself.

During the coming winter, Athens suffered again from famine, and Pericles led Athens in peace overtures to Sparta. Still fearing its Helots, Sparta agreed to a settlement with Athens – a treaty that was supposed to be good for thirty years. Athens agreed to recognize Sparta's superiority on land, to return to Megara its ports and to withdraw control of all inland territories that it controlled, including Achaea. And Sparta agreed to recognize Athenian power among the islands and along the coasts of the Aegean Sea.

Before the end of 444, Athens was running out of money, and revenues from its subject-allies that otherwise would have paid for naval services Athens used in finishing its building projects, including the completion of its temple, the Parthenon, on the acropolis in Athens. In 441, Samos (off the coast of Asia Minor) tried to secede from the Athenian alliance. Samos appealed for help from Sparta and the Persians, but Sparta remained passive and Persia remained fearful of the Athenian navy. By 339 the Athenian navy was able to blockade

Samos and starve it into submission. Samos surrendered its navy. Its defensive walls were torn down. It was forced to pay Athens reparations with money and land. Its oligarchs were exiled and replaced by democrats. And none of this was viewed by Sparta as a violation of its treaty with Athens.

Next came a conflict between Corinth and its colony at Corcyra, an island and city off the northwestern coast of Greece. Corcyra was challenging Corinth's trade monopoly in northwestern Greece and was hampering Corinth's trade with Sicily and southern Italy. Corcyra rebelled against Corinth, and in 435 the navies of Corinth and Corcyra battled each other near Corcyra, and Corinth lost fifteen ships and some prisoners to Corcyra. Corcyra sold some of the Corinthians into slavery, and Corinth began organizing a bigger attack against Corcyra. To protect itself, Corcyra appealed to Athens, and Athens allowed itself to become involved in the conflict by accepting Corcyra as an ally.

The Corinthians again sailed for Corcyra, with a larger force than before, but victory was snatched from them as the great Athenian fleet appeared. Hatred for Athens among the Corinthians rose to a new high. The Corinthians had advocated peace during the conflict between Athens and Samos, but now it wished Sparta at the Peloponnesian League to go to war against Athens. Sparta saw the alliance between Athens and Corcyra as no violation of its thirty-year peace agreement with Athens, but another conflict between Athens and one its subject-allies helped Corinth in its advocacy of war against Athens. Cities in Chalcidice disliked the extension of Athenian power into their area, and they were ready to support Corinth against Athens. Athens saw revolt coming in one of its subject-ally cities in Chalcidice -- Potidaea -- and, to prevent the spread of revolt, Athens demanded that Potidaea dismantle its defensive walls and give to Athens some Potidaeans as hostages. Instead of giving in to the demands of Athens, Potidaea sought support from Corinth and the Peloponnesian League. Corinth joined Potidaea and some cities in Chalcidice and Boeotia joined the revolt against Athens. All of Sparta's allies that had grievances against Athens were aroused. Corinth again appealed to Sparta, suggesting that if Sparta would not fight for its allies then its allies would seek leadership elsewhere. A meeting of the Peloponnesian League was called, and Sparta sent someone to consult with Apollo at Delphi.

Total War

In Boeotia, Thebes desired a solid front against Athens, and it sent a delegation and a small force to its neighboring city, Plataea, which was allied with Athens. The Thebans strode through Plataea and shouted their summons that the people of Plataea declare their support for

Boeotia. The Plataeans reacted with hostility, including throwing tiles onto the Thebans from their roof tops. The Thebans took refuge in a building and then surrendered. The Plataeans held the Thebans as hostages against a perceived threat from Thebes. A greater force from Thebes arrived at Plataea's walls and withdrew after the Plataeans assured them that the hostages they held would be spared. Soon the Plataeans let their hatred and fear of Thebes overrule good judgement and they killed their hostages, defeating the purpose of hostage taking and assuring the arrival of another, greater force from Thebes. Many Plataeans fled to Athens for safety, and Athens sent troops to Plataea. To the enemies of Athens, events at Plataea were a signal for war. They saw the thirty-year peace agreement between Sparta and Athens as violated and as having ended. Sparta, meanwhile, was encouraged by the Oracle at Delphi, who stated that Apollo was on its side, that if Sparta made war with all its might it would win.

The year was 431 BC, described by some as the end of Greece's Golden Age. Sparta and its allies invaded Attica, announcing that they were fighting against Athenian imperialism for their independence and for the liberty of Greeks. The great Peloponnesian war had begun. The common people of Athens joyously welcomed the news. They blamed the war entirely on Sparta and its Peloponnesian allies. They called for revenge and looked forward to the elimination of the Peloponnesian League as an obstacle to the destiny of Athens. They were either unaware or unconcerned with how long a major war against Sparta and its league would take, or that the goodwill of people throughout Greece was in balance on the side of Sparta and its allies.

Some aristocrats in Athens saw the enthusiasm for war among the crowds as misplaced. They had been offended by the zeal with which common Athenians had supported extensions of their city's power, by the harshness with which Athens applied its power abroad, by their city's use of alliance funds for its own benefit, and they had been unenthusiastic about attempts by their city to extend democracy to other cities. Among the aristocrats who were critical of their city was the journalist Thucydides. Thucydides was also a democrat. He was willing to fight for Athens, but he thought his city had been too inflexible in foreign affairs and too reluctant to admit mistakes.

War had come because people believed in empire, because people feared being dominated by others and because the Athenians did not fear war enough that they would try harder to avoid it. The war was to be a lesson in the benefits of caution over optimism and self-confidence, in the benefits of restraint and modesty in pursuing one's interests and the benefits of cooperation and compromise – lessons that would often be ignored.

THE GREAT PELOPONNESIAN WAR – PHASE ONE

Pericles wished to fight where his city had the advantage: on and from the sea. So he let Sparta and its allies advance into Attica. People in Attica abandoned their vineyards and farms and fled to the safety behind the great stone walls of Athens. Those with property exposed to the ravages of the enemy were offended by Pericles' strategy. And sound though it was, Pericles' strategy offended the Athenian multitude. Most Athenians favored direct and immediate attacks. Sparta's army was reluctant to try to breach the walls that protected Athens, and when that first year of fighting ended, Sparta withdrew from around Athens, having accomplished nothing more than some harassment, destruction of property and having killed many people. Athens now had many dead to bury, and Pericles, in his funeral oration, addressed the benefits versus costs of the war by flattering those who had gathered to pay their respects to the dead. He praised their ancestors and fathers for their efforts at having made Athens great and claimed that those who had died had done so for a glorious cause.

The following year, 430, plague made an appearance in Athens – probably arriving from a ship carrying grain – a plague made worse by the overcrowding that had come with people entering the city from the countryside. Again the public found fault with Pericles, and they removed him from office. In 427-26 the plague appeared again, and one-quarter to one-third of the city's population died, including Pericles.

Cleon and Diodotus Debate Genocide

The war intensified the passions of the Athenians, and their passions influenced their choice of a new leader, a man named Cleon, a merchant tanner by trade who was more excitable than had been Pericles and whose desire for vengeance matched theirs. Thucydides described Cleon as a demagogue. In two of his plays (*The Acharnians* and *The Knights*), Aristophanes depicted Cleon as a demagogue and a rogue. Aristophanes ridiculed the Athenian public's enthusiasm for empire. He called for an end to the war, and giving voice to his dislike for democracy he expressed his wish that leaders of Athens be chosen by less excitable, more moderate-minded men.

A member of the Athenian's league and the richest Greek island in the Aegean Sea, Lesbos, rebelled against Athenian domination. The city of Mytilene, on Lesbos, led the revolt, and Athens sent its navy against Mytilene. While the Athenian navy held Mytilene under siege, in the Athenian assembly Cleon argued that Mytilene should be destroyed and its inhabitants put to death. Pity, sentiment and indulgence, he said, were fatal to an empire, and brutal measures were necessary because of the tenacity and malice of their enemies. Punish Mytilene, he advised, or give up your empire and live in the danger of weakness that would accompany this. A member of the assembly, Diodotus, argued against him, claiming that haste and passion were the two things most opposed to good counsel. Haste, he said, usually goes hand in hand with folly and passion usually with a coarseness and narrowness of mind. He described the brutal measures advocated by Cleon as terrorism that would not prevent other subject states from rebelling but would encourage them if they did rebel to fight to the bitter end. In a close vote the assembly chose to spare Mytilene's population. Athenian marines conquered Mytilene, and instead of slaughtering the city's inhabitants they tore down the city's walls and confiscated its navy. Athens also confiscated Mytilene lands on the shores of mainland Asia Minor, and Athens opened Mytilene to settlement by Athenians. And, as Cleon proposed, Athens had the leaders of the Mytilene's revolt executed.

The War into Its Tenth Year
The city of Plataea fared worse than Mytilene. The Thebans returned, joined by an army from Sparta. They besieged Plataea for almost two years before they were finally able to overrun the city, and they took vengeance for Plataea having killed its Theban hostages. The Theban army slaughtered all citizens of Plataea who could not prove that they had supported Sparta and its allies.

As the war continued, Athens encouraged Sparta's Helots to revolt, while Sparta encouraged slaves in Athens to run away. Many slaves in Athens did. And to increase opposition against Athens, Sparta encouraged aristocrats wherever it could, and in Corcyra aristocrats attempted to seize power. They burst into a meeting of the city council and assassinated sixty democrats. Democrats fought back and won the upper hand. A fleet of Athenians ships arrived, scaring away ships from the Peloponnesian League, and as the Athenian ships lay offshore the democrats slaughtered the coup leaders and their supporters.

Meanwhile, the Athenian navy had been blocking the Peloponnesian peninsula, while Sparta continued to exercise its superiority on land. In 425, six years into the war, Sparta again invaded Attica. The Athenian navy made a more effective move: it subdued a fleet of enemy ships at Navarino Bay on the southwest coast of Peloponnesus, and the Athenians cut off a battalion of Spartans there. Feeling pressured by this setback, Sparta promised Athens peace and requested an armistice – without having consulted its allies. Cleon rejected Sparta's offer. He wanted to wait for Sparta's unconditional surrender and to press what he saw as his city's advantage. The Athenians took 292 Spartan captives back to Athens as hostages and warned Sparta that they would kill these hostages if Sparta again invaded Attica.

Believing that it had neutralized Sparta, Athens attempted a large-scale assault by land against Sparta's Boeotian allies, led by Thebes. It was the only major use of land forces by Athens in the war, and the Boeotians defeated them. Seeing this as a sign of Athenian weakness, cities in Chalcidice turned against Athens. They resented an increase in tribute demanded by Athens, and they were inspired by agents from Sparta. Feeling desperate, Cleon convinced an assembly to allow him to lead a force against the rebellion. In Chalcidice, Cleon defeated some of the rebellions, but on the way to the city of Amphipolis his bravado failed him. He was killed and his army defeated.

Athens and Sparta Form an Alliance

Athens was now financially exhausted. Replacing Cleon as the Athenian leader was a more moderate man, a military commander, Nicias, who was willing to end the war. Sparta wanted its hostages back, and it was concerned about its deteriorating position vis-a-vis other cities in Peloponnesus, including the nearby city, Argos – a neutral power and a democracy. A treaty between Sparta and Argos was soon to end, and Sparta feared that Argos might then join sides with Athens.

In 421, Sparta agreed with Athens to end the fighting, an agreement that included a return of prisoners and captured lands. The war between Athens and Sparta seemed to have ended. In Athens rejoicing erupted, inspired by weariness of war. The Athenian playwright Euripides, who had also wearied of the war, wrote with enthusiasm in one of his plays: "Down with my spear! Let it be covered with spider webs!"

Allies of Sparta, namely Megara, Corinth and Elis, refused to sign the peace treaty. This alarmed Sparta. Desperately wanting peace, Sparta offered Athens an alliance in addition to peace, Sparta pledging that it would be an ally of Athens for fifty years. Athens accepted, and the two city-states pledged to defend each other, including Athens helping Sparta should the Helots revolt.

INTERLUDE

Technically, Megara, Elis and Corinth remained at war with Athens. And Corinth, which had a small empire of its own, was still competing with Athens for advantages in empire. While Sparta and Athens tried to remain at peace with each other, tensions and sporadic fighting among others continued. Athens employed force against cities that rebelled against its rule, and it retaliated against rebellion in Scione by killing all of that city's adult males and making slaves of its women and children. As Diodotus had argued in his debate against Cleon, such action brought no advantage to Athens. Other cities that wished to be free of Athenian rule responded to Athenian cruelty at Scione with a greater determination to win their independence.

Sparta Recovers

Within two years of having made peace, Sparta felt it had recovered from war. With Athenian imperialism creating tensions and Athens interfering in Peloponnesian affairs, Sparta feared that its alliance with Athens might break down, and it renewed its ties with Corinth, Megara and Elis. Athens asked Sparta to sever its ties with these cities and Sparta refused.

In 418, Athens and Sparta went to the assistance of Peloponnesian cities at war with each other, Sparta on one side and Athens on the other, and the armies of Sparta and Athens came to blows. It was the largest land battle since the beginning of the Peloponnesian war – while officially Sparta and Athens were still at peace with each other. The Spartans won easily. Some Athenians belatedly realized the wisdom of Pericles' strategy of not fighting on land, and the Spartans felt a renewed sense of military superiority and enjoyed a new prestige across Greece. In Argos, supporters of Sparta overthrew democrats who had allied Argos with Athens, and they allied Argos with Sparta. And Sparta concluded agreements with other cities in Peloponnesian, which called for the exclusion of Athens from Peloponnesian affairs.

Massacre at Melos

In an effort to advance its empire, Athens, in 416, confronted the neutral island of Melos, and to officials of Melos it argued that Melos should join its empire. Athens claimed that it wished to do what was best both for itself and for Melos. It argued that Melos would benefit from Athenian strength, that Athens was strong and Melos weak and that it was a law of the gods that the stronger rule over those who were weaker. The people of Melos responded by asking Sparta for support. Athens attacked Melos in the spirit expressed in the Book of Samuel (15:18), where its states: "Go and utterly destroy the sinners ... and fight against them until they are exterminated." The Athenians slaughtered all the adult males of Melos and they enslaved its women and children.

Again, as Diodotus had claimed in his argument against Cleon, such an act brought no benefit to Athens. Other neutral states saw that to be neutral was to invite annihilation, and this encouraged them to join

Sparta and its allies. Athens was losing the most crucial battle: for hearts and minds.

The same year that Athens attacked Melos, the Athenian playwright Euripides presented his play, *The Trojan Women*, in which he warned against the war lust that he believed had taken hold of this fellow Athenians. "How blind you are," he wrote, "who lay waste to cities, cast down temples and defile graves, yourselves soon to die."

The Great Athenian Naval Expedition to Sicily

In western Sicily, the city-states of Selinus and Segesta went to war against each other. Selinus had the support of Syracuse. Segesta looked around for help and sent a request to Athens for an alliance. Athenian trade was booming again and Athenians believed their city had recovered financially. The population of Athens had started growing again, and it had many slaves, but it still had no sure source of the grain, and some among the Athenians saw remedy in the acquisition of grain from across the Mediterranean Sea to the west, in the region of Sicily and southern Italy. The Athenian assembly saw the request from Segesta as an opportunity to extend their city's power and influence to that part of the world, so the Athenian assembly voted to send a force to Sicily.

Aristophanes was to satirize the expedition in his play *The Birds*, portraying it as a project by crooks, profiteers and fiddling bureaucrats. Another who opposed the expedition was one of the three men designated as its commander, who consulted with various seers and diviners who prophesied its doom. And supporters of the expedition hired rival oracles who predicted a glorious triumph.

At night an anonymous group opposed to the expedition went around Athens defacing the busts of Hermes – the god of travelers. The next day, Athenians were alarmed that the defacements might have been the beginnings of a conspiracy to overthrow their democratic constitution and that it might be a bad omen for the expedition. Government agents searched for and executed men they thought to be subversives, and some men fled the persecutions and went abroad.

In June, 415, the expedition sailed from Athens: more than one hundred ships carrying 27,800 combatants, including around five thousand infantry and some cavalry from allied cities, and an additional ten thousand service personnel. The expedition approached Sicily in late summer. Its main objective was Syracuse – the wealthiest and most powerful Greek city in the western Mediterranean. Believing that Syracuse was on the verge of being taken over by democrats, the Athenians were optimistic that they could win Syracuse to its side with just a little pressure.

The expedition established itself on land and in the protected waters around Syracuse, and slowly it began to encircle and blockade the city. It won allies among some cities in Sicily, who supplied the expedition with stores of food. Sparta feared that if Athens succeeded in Sicily, Athens would overshadow Carthage in the western Mediterranean and would become more of a threat. Responding to a request from Syracuse, Sparta and Corinth sent aid, including an able military commander from Sparta, Gylippus, who took charge of Syracuse's defense. Gylippus led a force that broke through the Athenian's blockade and rallied the city's defenders – while the Athenian expedi-tion bungled opportunities.

THE PELOPONNESIAN WAR – PHASE TWO

In the spring of 413, Sparta and its allies overran Attica, destroying crops, animals and mines. Twenty thousand slaves in Attica, mostly men who had worked Attica's mines, deserted to the side of the Spartans. In the fall, news reached Athens that, two months before, the expedition's great fleet had suffered a disastrous defeat in the bay just off Syracuse. Many Athenians had lost sons in the expedition, and the citizens of Athens grieved and feared for their city and themselves. Hoped for supplies of timber and grain were lost, with timber and grain still scarce and money being in short supply.

News of the Athenians loss in Sicily encouraged Persia to regain control of Asia Minor, and Persia began sending envoys to Sparta in hope of gaining Sparta's assent and cooperation. Athenian losses also encouraged members of its empire to revolt against its rule. From Euboea, Lesbos and Chios went messages to Sparta's King, Agis, stating that they would revolt against Athens as soon as a Peloponnesian fleet appeared off their coasts. Sparta promised the Persians recognition of their control over Greek cities in Asia Minor in exchange for funds for building ships and for hiring men to row these ships, and Sparta sought naval reinforcements from Syracuse. While Athens was building ships to replace what they had lost at Syracuse, Sparta was hoping to build a navy that could neutralize the power of Athens at sea.

Sparta sent ships and troops to the eastern side of the Aegean Sea, and there in the winter of 413/412 the revolts against Athenian rule began. Lesbos and the city of Miletus signed a treaty with both Sparta and Persia – while Persia was reasserting itself as an arbiter in the region and demanding tributes from local rulers.

For Athens, defeat abroad led to turmoil at home. In 411, while the Athenian navy was in the eastern Aegean, a group in Athens opposed to democracy launched a coup and set up an oligarchy called the Four

Hundred. They created a constitution based on nostalgia for ancestral custom, and they began a rule of terror and totalitarianism. The Athenian fleet would have liked to return to Athens to drive the Four Hundred from power, but they believed they were needed where they were to defend the empire. The Four Hundred sought help from those with whom they shared a disdain for democracy: the Spartans. But before help could arrive from Sparta, the Four Hundred were driven from power by those who called themselves the Five Thousand, and the following year democracy returned to Athens.

The playwright Aristophanes, as frustrated as ever by his fellow Athenians, had by now written his play *Lysistrata* about women withholding sex from their husbands until they stopped making war. But the war was winding down. With Persian financial resources behind them and a new fleet, Sparta and its allies won a series of military successes, including a great victory over the Athenian main fleet. This left Athens surrounded by enemy forces on land and sea and cut off from sources of food. Through the winter of 405-04 Athens starved. The following spring – twenty-seven years after the war had first begun – Athens surrendered. The Great Peloponnesian War had finally ended.

SPARTA TURNS VICTORY INTO DEFEAT

Sparta had been promising to protect the liberty of those threatened by Athens and to restore liberty to those states that had been "enslaved" by Athens. It celebrated its victory over Athens as the dawn of liberty for Greece. But the Spartans were not suited for the task of leadership and liberty for all of Greece. Like the Athenians before the war, they believed in rule by force rather than cooperation. Like many Athenians, they believed that the strong should dominate those who are weaker and that victors should dominate the vanquished. The Spartans had not considered the role of hearts and minds in the defeat of Athens.

At the war's end, from among Sparta's allies came calls for killing Athenian adult males and enslaving its women and children, as Athens had done to others. But Sparta spared the Athenians, claiming that it was doing so because of the good service Athens had provided the cities of Greece generations before in combating Persia's invasions. But Sparta had another motive for sparing Athens: they feared that a destroyed Athens would add to the growth in influence of Thebes, just north of Athens. Sparta put hope in a new, anti-democratic oligarchy in Athens, and the new oligarchy in Athens executed some fifteen hundred fellow Athenians whom they considered dangerous. They also executed resident aliens whose wealth they wished to confiscate. And about five hundred democrats fled Athens and became the nucleus of a resistance group based in Thebes. In various cities, Sparta left a military force backing local aristocratic oligarchies. Violence erupted against these oligarchies. And in 403 BC, while Sparta busied itself in putting down these rebellions, in Athens a coalition of moderate conservatives and democrats overthrew the oligarchy there and took power.

Sparta's Efforts to 379 BC

Sparta found itself fighting numerous little wars, and from 395 to 386 it fought against a coalition that included Boeotia, Corinth, Argos and Athens. Then Greeks under Persian rule in Asia Minor rebelled again, and they asked Sparta to act on its claim as the defender of liberty for Greeks. The Spartans had honored their promise to Persia and had recognized Persia's power over the Greeks in Asia Minor. But now, Sparta tried to redeem itself as the defender of all Greeks, and it went to war against Persia.

Sparta was discovering the disadvantages of being policeman and the supreme defender of Greek liberty. Military actions were weakening it. Persia defeated Sparta's fleet, which ended Sparta's naval superiority among the Greeks. And to the alarm of Sparta and the Persians, Athens – a quarter-century after the end of the Peloponnesian war – was rebuilding its navy. In 379, Athens was able to help Theban exiles liberate their city from an oppressive, pro-Spartan oligarchy.

Sparta Is Defeated

Ultimately, security for Sparta lay not in its physical might but in support it had, however passive, among other cities. But, like Athens around the time of the Peloponnesian war, Sparta had been generating a lot of animosity toward itself, not only by interfering in local politics by supporting aristocratic oligarchies but also by collecting tribute with methods more brutal than had Athens.

In response to the threat of the coalition that was forming against it, Sparta made peace again with Persia, which offended many Greeks. With the Greeks responding to new realities and forgetting the Peloponnesian war, Athens was able to create a maritime confederacy that included most of its former allies. Thebes built its own federation among neighboring cities in Boeotia. And Thebes and Athens fought skirmishes against Sparta.

Sparta, Athens and Thebes attempted negotiations to settle their differences, but the negotiations collapsed over Thebes' insistence on recognition of her federation. In 371, believing that it was defending its dominant position in Greece, Sparta moved against Thebes by invading

Boeotia in force. Sparta had already lost its dominance in Greece, and now the Thebans defeated Sparta's army, destroying the myth that Sparta's army was invincible. Greeks far and wide now recognized that Sparta's domination of Greece had ended. New coalitions were formed. Thebes was the strongest military power, and, to put a check of Theban power, Athens joined a coalition with the humbled Sparta and Elis, Achaea and Mantinea.

Sparta's Transformation and Greece's Economic Decline

The way of life that Sparta had hoped to maintain by devoting itself to militarism now came to an end. Sparta had exhausted itself. It had lost much in manpower, and many Spartans had lost their enthusiasm for war. Outside their own city, the Spartans had been less inhibited and often corrupt and avaricious. The travel that accompanied military and diplomatic operations had made many Spartans more interested in leisure and other pleasures. With a change in values, land in Sparta had begun being bought and sold, two-fifths of the landowners being women – the survivors of war. Trade between Sparta and the outside world had increased, with some Spartans accumulating luxuries. The acquisition of money promoted inequalities among the Spartans. Some were declining into poverty and becoming malcontents. And those who were still wealthy with land feared that these malcontents might make common cause with the Helots.

Meanwhile, despite all of the war, the birth rate in Greece began to rise again, adding to the chaos. There was a loss in Greece's ability to export manufactured goods to pay for the greater need to import food to feed the rising population. A ruinous shift in the balance of trade developed against Greece's cities. These conditions gave rise again to numerous Greeks looking for places to emigrate. Desperate young men sold themselves as mercenary soldiers to almost any power. With all of the heroism, sacrifice, speech about glory and communications with the gods, the Greeks had failed to elevate themselves in their well-being.

CHAPTER 10

IDEAS, FROM ANAXAGORAS
TO ARISTOTLE

ANAXAGORAS

Anaxagoras is the first known scientist. He had been born a Persian subject in Asia Minor, around 500 BC, and he was in the first of a wave of Greek intellectuals who migrated to Athens. There he pursued his interest in philosophy and in investigating materiality. He observed and tested hypotheses – a step up from merely applying one's imagination to what one heard, read and saw. He lectured students – among them Socrates. Anaxagoras gave laboratory demonstrations and conducted experiments. He wrote theories on physics. Having learned about meteorites he described the sun and moon as fiery stones, and he attempted to describe the eclipses of the sun and moon. Anaxagoras discovered that air tends to rise above solids, and he described air as a gas, which he saw as consisting of material particles too small to be visible. He believed in infinity, and he speculated that matter too small to see is infinitely numerous and infinitesimally small, and he called these particles *atoms*.

In pondering connections in nature, Anaxagoras concluded that much is a mixture containing opposites, like tiny specks of black in what might look from a distance to be white. Sounding somewhat like Heraclitus, he claimed that opposites clinging together bring change, and he added that variation arises because of differences in preponderance.

Anaxagoras believed in both an inanimate materiality and in a spiritual substance: he was a dualist. He called his spiritual substance *Nous* and described it as an eternal intelligence that gave order to the world of atoms. In this view of how the world worked he joined Xenophanes and Heraclitus in challenging Greece's Homeric religion.

Athens had conservatives who disliked Anaxagoras' view of the cosmos. They associated impiety toward the city's gods with disloyalty toward the city. Among them were city officials who managed the city's religious festivals and made sacrifices to the gods before each official action. They had a tradition of punishing those they thought guilty of impiety. These city officials disliked Anaxagoras not only for his views on religion but for his having once sympathized with Persia. Anaxagoras was a friend of Pericles, who had been one of his students. But being a friend of Pericles was no protection from the courts of Athens. Before the beginning of the Great Peloponnesian war, the city fathers sought to protect their city from disloyalty, and they forbid the teaching of Anaxagoras' opinions and outlawed the teachings of others on astronomy and meteorology. They drove both Anaxagoras and the musician Damonides into exile, and Anaxagoras returned to Asia Minor, where he taught until he died in 428.

PROTAGORAS AND OTHER SOPHISTS

Among the Greeks the worship of Homer's gods dominated, but secularism had developed in education – while among most other civilized people education remained the function of priests. Among the Greeks, teachers called Sophists had appeared who were willing to fill the demand among youths for instruction on becoming a lawyer or success in politics. These youths wanted training in rhetoric: in the forceful presentation of a point of view. The Sophists also taught grammar, mathematics, physics, political philosophy and literary analysis. They had been influenced by philosophers such as Anaxagoras, and they tended to see humanity as a part of nature. Many among them questioned myths about the gods, and many of them believed that morality was learning how to get along with others rather than a matter of pleasing the gods. Some among them spread Heraclitus' ideas about conflict and the inevitability of wars, and some claimed that right lay with whichever people were stronger militarily, while other Sophists advocated peace, tolerance and understanding.

Outstanding among the Sophists was Protagoras from Thrace, who moved to Athens in 445. Like Anaxagoras he became a friend of Pericles. Drawing from his travels, Protagoras took positions about foreign peoples that were more advanced than most others of his time: he spoke of peoples from different areas of the world as sharing a common humanity. He claimed that by criticizing tradition and eliminating customs derived from "barbarian times" people could create better societies. Like many other Sophists, Protagoras believed in democracy. In the place of the rule of gods and their representatives, he advocated laws made by and for people. He lectured that people became good citizens not by obedience to authority but by learning what is just and right. Believing that people were dependent on what they learned and on their own will, he claimed that "Man is the measure of all things."

Like Anaxagoras, Protagoras believed in acquiring truth through sense perception. But, limited by the age in which he lived, he was not much of a psychologist or epistemologist: he failed to distinguish between perception and knowledge, as if knowledge does not require organizing the impressions one gathers through one's senses. During the Great Peloponnesian War, Athenian city officials restricted what could be taught, and Protagoras defied the repression. At the home of the famous poet and playwright Euripides he read aloud from his book and claimed that gods were the figments of people's imaginations. City officials accused him of impiety and put him on trial, and they put many others on trial. In a drive against atheism and against other thoughts they considered dangerous, city officials had books burned – the first known official book burning. Then Protagoras was sent into exile, and he was lost at sea.

THUCYDIDES: JOURNALIST AND HISTORIAN

Thucydides – twenty-five years younger than the Greek historian Herodotus – surpassed Herodotus in recording events with precision and impartiality. Thucydides was more concentrated in his writing than was Herodotus. There were no writings that Thucydides could draw from about actual events among the Greeks in previous centuries, and Thucydides believed that serious study of events could be concerned only with the present or immediate past. Some would call Thucydides the first real journalist and historian. Thucydides was an Athenian from a wealthy family, educated in rhetoric, and he had studied philosophy under Anaxagoras. Thucydides believed that people acted according to self-interest and social circumstances rather than by divine guidance. He practiced journalism with a skeptical mind, giving importance to conflict between peoples. He was obsessed with methodology. He tried to clarify issues with lengthy descriptions. And, in expressing complex ideas, he molded the Greek language into more mature forms.

Thucydides saw both strengths and weaknesses in Athenian democracy and in Sparta's society, but he favored the democracy of Athens – and he favored unity among the classes. He was a moderate democrat who complained that people too often put revenge above agreements that would benefit all. He pleaded for cooperation among Greeks and favored an increase in inter-state obligations.

He was twenty-nine when the Great Peloponnesian War broke out in 431 BC. He was made a general. And, in 424, he was ordered to relieve the city of Amphipolis, which was under siege by the Spartans. He blundered, was recalled, was put on trial, and he was exiled until the end of the war. Meanwhile, he continued to make a record of the course of the war, creating his masterpiece, *The History of the Peloponnesian War*. His purpose, he claimed, was not to win applause but to benefit posterity. He hoped that an accurate portrayal of events would help people avoid mistakes of the past.

HIPPOCRATES: THE FATHER OF MEDICINE

During the Great Peloponnesian War, some continued to advance human awareness. Among them was Hippocrates, who lived from 460 to 377. Hippocrates was the son of a priest-physician from the Greek island of Cos. Forty years younger than Anaxagoras, but, armed with the philosophy of Anaxagoras, Hippocrates revolted against the medicine tied to religious dogma, medicine that attempted to cure by use of charms, amulets and incantations. He believed that diseases are subject to nature's laws. He wanted health care to be built upon observation. He sought to improve diagnoses by examining symptoms. Seeing the human body as influenced by materiality as opposed to spirit, he advocated principles of public health, including building a patient's strength by a good diet and by hygiene. And recognizing the damage that could be done through acting on ignorance – as in faith healing and dependence on religious ritual – his first rule was *do no harm*.

DEMOCRITUS

Another who was forty years younger than Anaxagoras was Democritus, a Greek from Thrace. Democritus added to Anaxagoras' view of gas as matter too small to be visible. He constructed his theory of atoms while pondering the problem of density. An apple, he reasoned, can be divided with a knife because it has air in it. Borrowing from Anaxagoras, he labeled as an atom that which had no air, that which was too dense to be cut, that which was the smallest and most dense of matter. Democritus theorized that atoms collide and combine with each other and that in combining they create visible substance. Like Heraclitus, he believed that some things are developing and other things decaying. He believed that heavenly bodies sometimes collide with each other and that the Milky Way consists of unresolved stars.

Unlike those influenced by Pythagoras, Democritus believed that a word is a conventional label – rather than the perfect embodiment of a god-created idea or substance. Unlike Pythagoras, Democritus believed that sense perception is not just illusion. He believed that humans were capable of an awareness of matters outside themselves. And looking at the relationship between the human body and the human mind, he decided that human flesh, bones and bodily fluids were are elements found elsewhere in nature, that the human brain is functioning matter, that people are matter organized in a way that allows them awareness and self-directed movement.

SOCRATES

What we know about Socrates is what his contemporaries – mainly his student Plato – wrote about him. Early in the Peloponnesian War, when Socrates was in his late thirties, he was an Athenian infantryman, and he fought in a few of the minor battles that Athens fought on land. He was recognized for his courage in battle and for his ability to stand hardships such heat and cold, hunger and thirst. After his service in the military he devoted his life to truth, beauty and justice – in a world he found filled with wrongdoing, confusion and ugliness. He studied the art of debate and became a master at cross-examination and irony. He became a teacher, mainly of the sons of aristocrats, and without asking for money. But like the Sophists he questioned assumptions about religion and ethics.

Socrates took oracles seriously, but he did not worship the traditional gods of the Greeks – the gods of Homer. Like Xenophanes, he believed that these gods were no guides for morality. Instead of the chaos created by the conflicting passions of these gods, Socrates believed that the universe was guided by a god with a sense of purpose – the god of Anaxagoras. He believed this god was the source of human consciousness and morality. And he heard an inner voice that he believed was God's.

Socrates' main interest was ethics. Believing in goodness created by God, he believed that people needed to match that goodness. Socrates believed that knowledge and obedience to truth improved one's soul and diminished the ungodliness of wrongdoing, confusion and ugliness. To help people gain knowledge and improve their soul he tried to expose their ignorance and mistaken reasoning – often starting with the question whether they understood what they were talking about.

In the market place, where Socrates often argued, he must have annoyed many people with his persistent and seemingly pointless questioning. To many of those in his city of Athens, he was a foolish babbler. The Athenian playwright Aristophanes made Socrates a subject in his play *The Clouds*. In this play, a philosopher's meeting place burned, which the audience was supposed to enjoy and to care little if Socrates burned with it.

Socrates' view that no one knowingly did wrong, that evil, trouble and pain were the creations merely of ignorance, was part of the naïveté about human psychology that dominated his time. Like others he believed that truth was absolute rather than gained through approximation. But it is said that Socrates contributed to philosophy by his searching for truth through questioning and uncovering contradictions and by his championing moral responsibility. And Socrates may have had a gigantic influence in his passing to his student Plato the concept of God as mind and spirit and all encompassing.

Socrates is not known to have been politically active. He is not known to have spoken in favor or against the murderous Spartan supported oligarchy that took power at the end of the Peloponnesian War, and he is not known to have spoken in favor of or against the pro-democracy regime of moderate conservatives and democrats that replaced that oligarchy. But perhaps because Socrates had associated with many of the aristocrats who had supported the oligarchy, or because many of his students had been against democracy, some members of the pro-democracy regime held him suspect. Some members of the pro-democracy regime believed that Socrates was hostile to them and that Socrates believed they were immoral. These were times, moreover, when people had been made nervous by civil strife and bloodshed and by attacks on traditional beliefs. Believing that Socrates was a danger to their democratic regime, leaders of the regime had him arrested. They believed in the traditional gods of Athens, and they charged him with not believing the gods of the state, with introducing new gods and with corrupting young people with his talk.

In court, Socrates admitted that he did not believe in the gods of the state. He told the court that the views he was accused of holding were those of Anaxagoras. He said that he had not intentionally corrupted Athenians, and he told the court that rather than prosecute him the honorable jurors should tell him what course of thought was correct. The court was not amused. It found Socrates guilty, and it suggested a sentence of death. If Socrates had requested a reasonable lesser sentence, as was the custom in Athens, he would have given the court an opportunity to reduce his sentence. Instead, he shocked the court with his hostile announcement that instead of being sentenced he should be praised as a public benefactor. So the death sentence stood.

According to Plato, Socrates announced that he honored and loved the men of Athens and that he would never abandon philosophy. As ordered by the court, Socrates drank the poison hemlock and died. Then, because of the public hostility that remained against those perceived as supporters of oligarchy and as enemies of the pro-democratic regime, friends of Socrates and others who felt endangered fled into exile.

PLATO

Plato was among those who fled Athens following Socrates' death. He was twenty-seven then and perhaps among those Athenians who blamed democracy for having created the Peloponnesian War. At least he saw democracy as having contributed to Athens' defeat, and he was among those who wished for a government wiser and smarter than that which had arisen from the Athenian multitude.

Like Socrates, Plato was dissatisfied with the world that had unfolded around him, but rather than see remedy only in individuals improving themselves, as Socrates seemingly did, Plato saw remedy in new institutions – in a new social order. He searched his imagination for an ideal society, one strong enough to win wars, a society able to provide a livelihood for its people, a society free of what he saw as the self-serving individualism and commercialism of Athens, a society unified by a harmony of interests.

Plato's Republic

Plato perceived the ideal society as a city-state of no more than 20,000 people, ruled by an elite. He wanted something better than the kind of rule that had existed among the Spartans and societies with aristocracies, and looking into the past, Plato saw that societies led by aristocrats could degenerate and that some aristocrats were unfit for leadership. So he decided on a ruling elite made up of men of learning, men who could pass their status to their sons but who would lose that status if their peers decided that they were unfit, and men who would admit to their ranks only those who had developed into sound philosophers. Plato's republic removed the weaknesses of rule by inheritance and the weakness of leadership chosen by the multitude. Like Solon and others, Plato thought of justice as harmony emanating from godliness. He believed that philosophers who understood the harmony of all parts of the universe were closest to God and that only they were capable of creating a harmonious and just society. These philosophers, he believed, would agree and get along with each other with equal harmony rather than break into hostile factions.

Plato believed that his ruling elite had to be free from labor so they could specialize in philosophy, and his utopia had a second class and third class. The second class were the warriors, who were to be free from ordinary labors so they could train to become as highly skilled in combat as possible – as with Sparta's warriors before Sparta's demise. And the third class was to those who labored.

Plato wished his ruler-philosophers to be unconcerned with possessions. He wished that they be interested in harmony and justice only.

The best men, he believed, serve society out of devotion rather than for pay. Therefore, he believed, the ruling elite should share rather than compete for possessions.

As for women, Plato believed they were equal to men in many ways, that they had philosophic capacities and were capable of virtue, that a mentally accomplished female was superior to a mentally incompetent male. He approved of the greater respect and freedom for women that he had seen among the Spartans. He thought it best that men rule, but he believed that women should be free rather than possessed by men. He believed that the harmony that was essential to his utopia would best be served by his ruler-philosophers and their women associates and children living as one large family, the men and women coupling freely with whomever they pleased.

Idea, God and Love

Plato followed his teacher Socrates in devotion to philosophy, and like Socrates he was concerned with godly perfection, but unlike Socrates he attempted to express a coherent view of reality. Plato rejected the views of Heraclitus that reality was a process, and he rejected Heraclitus' belief in evolution. Plato rejected the atomism of Democritus, Anaxagoras and others. He believed in the same absolute truth that Socrates believed in. Like Pythagoras, he believed in perfection and saw perfection in mathematics. He believed in perfect reason and that the mind was located in the head because the head was round and roundness was the perfect shape and therefore the appropriate place for reason. As had Pythagoras, Plato looked to the heavens and speculated in astronomy. Unaware of asteroids, other chaos and the imperfect shapes of solar bodies that modern astronomers would know of, he believed that the perfection he and Pythagoras saw in mathematics existed in the heavens. He believed that the heavens consisted of perfect spheres and circles. Like Pythagoras, he made harmony fundamental to his philosophy. He sought what Pythagoras had described as the permanence that lay behind the flux and chaos of appearances, and he saw abstractions as real and permanent and the changing world known through the senses as illusion – a view of the senses that could be found in Hinduism. In his *Vision of Er the Pamphylian*, Plato displayed familiarity with Hindu doctrines.

Plato likened the world of the senses to that of a prisoner in a cave, with a fire behind the prisoner and the prisoner seeing only his shadow cast on the cave's wall. It was a poetic analogy that said something about the difficulty of obtaining truth through the senses, but it missed the significance of sense-experience: Plato's prisoner was chained and merely perceiving, not interacting, weighing, correcting, learning and adjusting his approximations of reality as people were capable of doing in the real world of sense experience, and as did science.

Rather than being concerned with the mechanics of work and manipulation that would help give rise to science, Plato remained concerned with the world of spirit and the perfection of the heavens. According to Plato, a person as a material being develops and dies while his soul remains eternal. He believed that a person's soul had its rational side and its irrational side, that on one side was mind and the ability to reason and on the other side was desire – what some would call impulse. Plato believed that a person served his or her soul by denying oneself the bodily desires of the material world. He believed that the part of the soul that was mind survived death while desire did not.

Plato believed that wise people loved beauty in the abstract more than they loved specific, material things. He believed in love that begins as a lowly specific and perhaps as a carnal and amorous experience that a good person turns into spirituality, through thought, by comprehending it as an abstraction. As an abstraction, he believed, a lowly experience could be elevated to a pure form of beauty, to perfection – to an ideal. At this level, he believed, love and beauty motivated one to beneficent deeds.

Believing in harmony, Plato, like Socrates, disliked Homer's description of gods engaging in deceptions, quarrels, adultery and violence. According to Plato, Zeus was absolute, eternal, infinite and harmonious. He believed that Zeus was the ultimate source of all idea, that Zeus embodied universal mind, in other words that Zeus was ultimate soul. Seeing philosophy as the highest of pursuits, he believed that one should approach Zeus through reason and the grasping of the harmony and perfection of abstractions. Melding philosophy and religion – as had Pythagoras – Plato believed that the highest activity of an individual was to contemplate the beauty of Zeus and the immortality of his own soul.

Plato's Republic Lost

Plato recognized that philosophers were unpopular and that his utopia would never be achieved by the force of popular will. He foresaw too that philosophers would not and could not band together and overpower established authority. So, like Confucius, the best he could hope for was someone who already had power implementing his political ideas. Not until late in his life did he come close to finding such a ruler. A close friend, Dion, had become advisor to the young king, Dionysius II, of Syracuse. Dion invited Plato to tutor Dionysius, but a few months after Plato's arrival the king sent Dion into exile. Plato lost what influence he had over Dionysius, and he returned to

Athens. Dion then gathered mercenaries and overthrew Dionysius. But Dion's rule was unpopular, and soon Dion was assassinated, ending Plato's hope that Dion would make Plato's utopia a reality.

Late in his life, Plato added to his ideas about his ideal society. He believed that it should be official doctrine in his utopia that the three classes – philosophers, warriors, and workers – had been created by Zeus. Plato's search for perfection was accompanied by the usual companion of such a search: illiberality. He decided that for the sake of order, citizens should be obliged to believe in Zeus. He decided that the reading of certain kinds of literature should be forbidden – among them the works of Homer and stories that depicted virtuous people as unhappy or villains as happy. He declared that religious cults that attempted salvation of the soul should be outlawed because their attempts at salvation implied that wrongdoing could be absolved through ritual. He thought his utopia should control the kind of music people listened to in order to prevent corruption. He believed that to help prevent the spread of corruption, dissidents – including atheists – should be imprisoned. These dissidents, he believed, should be reformed by persuasion, and if they proved incorrigible they should be executed.

ARISTOTLE

Aristotle was the son of a Greek doctor who served the king of Macedonia – a land just north of Greece. Supported by his father, Aristotle at eighteen went to Athens to study under Plato, and he remained at Plato's academy for twenty years – until Plato's death in 347.

Aristotle began as an ardent supporter of Plato's philosophy, but he modified that support. He attempted to systematize what he saw as best among the philosophers who preceded him and to bridge their contradictory beliefs. Like other philosophers, he believed in intellectual progress through effort rather than revelation from the gods. He believed in reason and the spirituality of the heavens as did Plato, but he also believed in observation of the material world and not relying on commonplace opinion. Many, for example, still assumed that rivers flowed from some great pool of water hidden from humanity's view, and he advised such people to climb mountains and observe that rivers began as small streams in high places.

Aristotle became a collector of facts, and he believed in exact classifications – when classification was still largely ignored. He made his classifications according to common sense, finding consistent attributes that ignore insignificant differences (humans, for example, having common attributes that allow them to be classified as humans while differing in minor attributes such as height). Aristotle divided things into classes and sub-classes and made contributions in biology, botany, and embryology.

Aristotle's theory of motion was limited by the time in which he lived. With others he believed that the earth was the center of the universe, and what modern people understand as gravity he saw as objects having a will to rush to this center. He believed that the natural state of all bodies was rest, that all bodies tended to return to rest and needed a mover to keep them in motion. For Aristotle this mover was Zeus. Not until the late 1600s AD would anyone advocate inertia as a law of motion. Unaware of gravity as an ever-present force, Aristotle held that everything moved in a straight line until something intervened to deflect it or to stop it, and that the object then fell to earth. Speed, he believed, was governed by the resistance through which an object had to travel, water slowing a body down more than air. He believed that if there were no resistance, a body would move from place to place in an instant, but he also believed that there was no such thing as a complete void, or vacuum. God Himself, he stated, could not make one.

Aristotle combined his study of the world, his classifications, with his work in logic and theology. He was burdensome in his discourse and would be among the hardest philosophers to read, but in the breadth of his interests and the great amount of work he did in classification, Aristotle would become the most influential philosopher in the coming two thousand years.

Aristotle's Logic

In ancient times, Aristotle became recognized as the foremost authority on logic, and he would be recognized as such during the Middle Ages. He began his study of logic as lessons on how to succeed in the kind of debates found in Plato's writings. He built his logic on the rejection of contradiction, and he drew from the law in geometry with which Pythagoras had worked: the simple, common sense theorem which holds that if two items are alike and a third is similar to one, it is similar to the other. In other words, if humans can be described as mortal and Socrates can be classified as human, then Socrates could also be described as mortal.

Aristotle recognized that the consistency on which his logic rested depended upon properly distinguishing between classes and subclasses – as in "Socrates is ugly and Socrates is Greek, therefore all Greeks are ugly." And Aristotle recognized that logic cannot take one from a false premise to a valid conclusion.* But Aristotle did not fully appreciate the extent to which premises might consist of hidden, often unexamined complexities. Using Aristotle's logic, people would build with confidence from premises to a great variety of conflicting conclusions. Aristotle himself used his logic to arrive at conclusions about which he had no knowledge, such as: because the eye disconnected from the body does not see, it is not the eye itself that sees but the soul. Aristotle's logic was deductive. It conflicted with science, which made generalities from observed particulars (facts) – in other words, induction. But Aristotle made a contribution to humanity's effort to think more clearly and to examine presumptions and contradictions.

Classification and Theology

In working with classifications, Aristotle rejected Plato's view of abstractions. Plato viewed abstractions as real, or, as Aristotle put it, as *having substance*. Contrary to Plato, Aristotle associated substance with specific forms and saw abstractions as the creation of imagination dependent upon specifics.

Aristotle classified reality into three types of substance: SUBSTANCE-TYPE ONE was earthly matter – that which could be both seen and felt. Similar to Plato, he thought of earthly reality as a lower order, a world of imperfection, a world of decay and impermanence. Concerned with classifying the difference between what is basic and what was not, Aristotle reduced this earthly substance to four basic ingredients: air, earth, fire and water. Believing that these elements were things-in-themselves and irreducible, he rejected the atomic theory of Anaxagoras and Democritus. SUBSTANCE-TYPE TWO consisted of the visible heavenly bodies: the moon, planets, sun and stars. As did Plato, Aristotle saw these as moving and eternal, as orderly, unchanging and perfect in form. And he judged these heavenly bodies as an order superior to earthly substance. SUBSTANCE-TYPE THREE Aristotle deduced from his view of the heavens. This substance was the invisible world of spirit – Anaxagoras' *Nous*, which can be translated as *soul*. In not understanding inertia Aristotle assumed that the moon, planets, sun and stars needed a force to move them. Everything, he reasoned, must have a cause. Soul, on the other hand, according to Aristotle, was that which was not moved by some external force. Soul was the mover. Like Plato, Aristotle saw soul as embodying reason. Soul, he believed, moved itself with a sense of purpose. The cause of motion of all things, he concluded, is Divine Will.

---

* Some discoveries are stimulated by falsehoods, and from a falsehood one might accidentally stumble to some truth, with intermittent logic, but this has nothing to do with the consistency that is the basis of Aristotelian logic.

Aristotle believed that soul descended from the perfection of heaven to earth in the form of life. Classifying life into different levels, he saw plants as having the lowest level of soul, animals other than humans as having a higher level of soul, and humans, because of their capacity for reason, possessing a greater soul. More than Plato, Aristotle saw soul (or mind and reason) as having a connection with the human body. In his work *De Anima*, Aristotle connected body and mind – the first work in psychology grounded in biology. He believed that one's body developed earlier than one's soul, and one's appetites developed earlier than one's ability to reason. He held that one's body should be trained for the sake of one's soul and one's appetites harnessed for the sake of reason. He saw imagination as a by-product of sensation. He saw memory as a combination of imagination and accumulated sense experience.

Aristotle saw soul as moving one's mind and body, but unlike Plato he believed that a person's soul did not survive death in individualistic form. He believed that with the death of an individual, soul remained as a collective, transcendent force. But, like the Deists of the 17th and 18th centuries, Aristotle's god was not an interventionist. His god was The Source. His god was the unmoved mover of the universe – the eternal inaugurator of motion. He did not see God as the creator of the universe. Instead, he clung to his belief in eternity. He could not bring himself to believe in something created out of nothing.

Happiness and the Golden Mean

Aristotle concerned himself with what was right and wrong in everyday life. He believed that people pursued self-fulfillment, or happiness. He believed that people should search for happiness in the divine and in the material world. And not surprising for a philosopher, he believed that the greatest happiness and self-benefit and the greatest virtue came with the pursuit of theoretical wisdom. Like the Hindus, Socrates and Plato, he believed that the pursuit of knowledge moved one closer to the harmony of God.

Happiness, Aristotle believed, could be achieved by choosing a *golden mean* between extremes. This was a recognition that humanity functions within a range of possibilities and limited conditions and that it functions best at a point of balance within these ranges. For example, humanity needs sunshine, but people can have too much sunshine and too little rain, which would ruin their crops. Aristotle believed in the kind of moderation advocated in *The Analects* by Confucius. For example, he advocated moderation over the extremes of gluttony and self-deprivation, and he chose courage over the extremes of rashness and cowardice. Aristotle believed in moderating one's passions. He compared a man in a state of passion to a man asleep, drunk or insane.

Aristotle applied his Golden Mean to economic and social order and to the relationship between the state and the individual, but he could not, of course, apply it to those matters that had no median, such as choosing between honoring and ignoring one's contracts, between commitment and being uncommitted, or between loyalty and disloyalty.

Aristotle on Politics

Harmony was central to Aristotle's theory of politics, as it had been with Plato. Aristotle saw that humans were social creatures, that social participation was inescapable, that no one was immune from the rules of a community, in other words that no citizen belonged just to himself, that everyone was a member of the state.

Aristotle saw politics as the manner in which people govern their relations with each other and that people, therefore, were political creatures. He believed that the welfare of a community contributed to the well-being of its individual members, and, drawing again from classification, he put the city-state above the family and individuals, claiming that the whole must necessarily be prior to the part. He saw the state as necessary in creating harmony – by promoting balance, moderation and protecting the individual from abuse. But he was for a balance between the powers of the state and the rights of individuals, claiming that the state should not be so powerful or all encompassing that it fails to offer a good amount of liberty to its individual citizens – which put him at odds with Plato's totalitarianism.

Much of Aristotle's political writing was a retort to Plato's republic. He believed that Plato's communism – the elite holding everything in common – was impossible. He wrote that property owned in common received less attention that property owned by an individual. Men, he wrote, care most for their private possessions.

In addition to opposing communism, Aristotle opposed excessive wealth. Responding to the strife between Greece's rich and poor, Aristotle applied his *golden mean* and advocated a balance between great wealth and poverty. To this end he favored the creation of a strong middle class and government assistance to the poor, with everyone having the right to property but no one accumulating more than was needed for what he called "intelligent living."

It was Aristotle who made the first effort at political science. His interest in data led him to gather information on 158 Greek and foreign cities. But his conclusions were hardly scientific. From his data he concluded that the best form of government was rule by an elite. Like Plato he believed that rule should go to the wise, that rule to the wise is the best way of creating harmony and that democracy was unsuitable because of the lack of wisdom among common people. He did not consider that democracy gave power to an intelligence drawn from the broadest spectrum of experiences or that with democracy and a developed middle class his moderation could prevail.

But Aristotle's elite differed from Plato's. Aristotle abandoned the notion of a permanent aristocracy. The best rulers, he believed, were people who had first learned to be good subjects. There was, he wrote, nothing degrading about obedience when obedience is directed toward good ends. When men are young, he suggested, they should be warriors. They should not rule until they are older. And they should be priests when they are older still – past an active life.

Aristotle linked social harmony with ethics. He saw virtue in honesty, in keeping one's promises, in abiding by one's contracts and in paying one's debts. He believed that refinement and education made one a better person, a better citizen, and made people more suited for rule.

He saw weakness in Sparta having trained only for military prowess. This narrow focus, he believed, made Sparta an unsuitable leader in the years following its victory in the Great Peloponnesian war and had contributed to its failure.

According to Aristotle the state should follow the same morality that applies to individuals. He believed that the state should be a moral agent. But he believed that a superior people should rule over an inferior people, just as it was better that tame animals be ruled by humans rather than allowed to run wild. The superior people, according to Aristotle, were the Greeks. Greeks, he believed had the high spirit of "the northern races" and the intelligence of "the eastern races," and as a result they had a higher civilization than others.

Here was Aristotle's rationale for slavery. In his ideal society the tillers of soil would be barbarian serfs or slaves rather than citizens. He wrote that Greeks should not be slaves but that they should be slave owners. Here he got his classes and sub-classes mixed, believing that justice was served by any dull-minded Greek being master to the brightest foreigner. In supporting slavery Aristotle was a man of his times and millennia to come – while his quest for social harmony remained incompatible with the coercions of slavery.

Events, meanwhile, were moving beyond Aristotle's notions about the supremacy of the city-state, as cities were beginning to be incorporated into nation-states.

CHAPTER 11

ALEXANDER CHANGES THE WORLD

MACEDONIA AND PHILIP II

Since the mid-500s BC, Macedonia's kings had been absorbing Greek culture and technical skills. Macedonia was just north of Greece, and its people worshiped the same gods as the Greeks and spoke a dialect of Greek. It was a dialect that was difficult for the Greeks to understand, and Greeks saw the Macedonians as uncouth barbarians and made jokes about them. The Greeks looked upon the murderous dynastic intrigues that had marked Macedonia's recent history as tribal antics, and often dynastic disputes in Macedonia had provided Athens or Thebes with an excuse to intervene there. But events in the latter part of the 300s were to upset the attitude of Greeks toward Macedonia. Instead of Greeks dominating Macedonia, Macedonians would dominate Greece.

In 359 BC, the Macedonian king, Perdiccas III, was killed fighting an invasion by the Illyrians. His infant son succeeded him, and Perdiccas' twenty-two year-old brother, Philip, was made the infant's regent. Thebes and Athens backed pretenders to Macedonia's throne and Paeonian tribesmen continued to raid Macedonia from the north. Philip pushed aside his infant nephew. Perhaps he had the child murdered. Then he made himself king, taking the title Philip II.

Ruling from the city of Pella, Philip needed a few months to strengthen his army. He bought time by bribing the Illyrians and the Paeonians. And he bought time too by appeasing Athens, ceding to Athens the city of Amphipolis. In 358, with his strengthened army, he invaded Paeonia. Then he led his army against the Illyrians, killing seven thousand in one battle and reversing the defeat of the year before. That year he transferred Macedonians to his kingdom's northern plain, splitting hostile groups and defining the frontier against the Illyrians. The following year he helped stabilize his western frontier by marrying the daughter of king Neoptolemus of Epirus: Olympias.

Philip Builds a Nation-State

Philip claimed to be descended from Greeks of the Peloponnesian city of Argos, where Homer's king Agamemnon was said to have ruled – a city from which, it was also said, some Greek aristocrats in the 600s had emigrated to Macedonia. Philip championed Greek ways. He saw Athens as the center of Greek civilization. In his home he spoke the dialect of Greek common among the Greeks. Soon he was to have his son, Alexander, taught to play the lyre, to recite and to debate, and he was to provide Alexander with no less a tutor than the great Aristotle. Ambassadors from Athens would tell Philip that he was "thoroughly Greek." They would praise him as a drinker and praise him for his memory and for his ability as a speaker.

Philip was determined to strengthen the country and to unite it into a nation. He saw that Macedonia could become a great power, and he saw opportunity in the divisions and quarrels among the Greek city-states. He knew that Macedonia had much in natural and human resources. Macedonia was developing agriculturally. Unlike many Greek states to the south, Macedonia was economically self-sufficient. It had timber. It had great mines on its northwestern and eastern frontiers. Its plains were abundant with fruit, sheep and cattle. It had grass pastures for horses. Philip encouraged trade, which provided him with more revenues. Macedonians were hard working, hard fighting and unaccustomed to the soft living and luxuries that many in Greece enjoyed. And Macedonia had a great abundance of unquestioning, obedient men who lived for war.

The nobility in Macedonia had been a source of division, and Philip mitigated this by elevating to the nobility some men who supported him. Also, he created a service for teenagers as Royal Pages, which helped foster the spirit of national identity among them and their parents. But Philip's greatest instrument of unity was his army. It was a national army, professional and highly disciplined. He trained it constantly and kept it permanently mobilized, rewarding talent with promotions and bonuses. It was an army with an elite cavalry, with men superior in horsemanship to those in Greece. It had siege weapons, and it had a new formation called the phalanx: rows of soldiers packed closely together, unweighted by body armor and carrying pikes fifteen feet in length – longer than those carried by Greek soldiers.

Feeling sufficiently strong vis-a-vis Athens, in 357 Philip took back Amphipolis, a gateway to Thrace. And Athens, with its powerful navy, failed to win back Amphipolis or to prevent further expansion by Philip. In 356, Philip took the Thracian city of Crenides and renamed it Philippi, a city from which he began controlling neighboring gold mines.

Greek cities invited Philip to join them as an ally in their quarrels with other Greek cities. And, skilled at diplomacy as well as at war, Philip made alliances. He deceived those he planned to swallow and fought when he had to. In 353, Philip took the city of Methone on the coast just south of Pella. He advanced south of Mount Olympus. In 352 he began dominating cities in Thessaly. In 350, he absorbed the city of Stagira, just south of Amphipolis, and within two years he had all of Chalcidice.

These successes gave Philip more land with which to support horses, more men for his armies and more revenues. He had gained more land to give to nobles as rewards for their loyalty, and the nobles, impressed by Philip's military successes, were now firmer in their recognition of his authority. Philip's military successes made common Macedonians feel more secure. It lifted their optimism and morale and brought him more enthusiastic support.

In 342, Philip installed his brother on the throne of Epirus. He left his sixteen-year-old son, Alexander, in charge of Macedonia and led his army eastward into Thrace, reaching the city of Perinthus in 340. Philip's army laid siege to Perinthus and Byzantium, and Alexander led a force that defeated a rebellion by the Maedi people of Thrace. Then Philip backed away from his sieges against Perinthus and Byzantium. He had decided that he did not want to provoke Athens by threatening its trade route into and out of the Black Sea.

Philip Dominates Greece

Sparta was the weakened city described in Chapter Nine, and the Greeks remained weakened by their divisions and wars. By now, Philip's kingdom was the dominant power in a league with Greek cities. Athens and Thebes were at war against each other over control of the sacred site at Delphi, and late in the year 339 Philip took advantage of this war by moving his army into central Greece. Thebes and Athens became alarmed and put aside their warring to join forces against Philip and his Greek allies. The following year, Philip defeated Thebes and Athens, which gave Philip domination over all of Greece's mainland cities except Sparta. Alexander, now eighteen, had contribut-ed to these victories by having commanded the left-wing of Philip's army, Alexander having proved himself a courageous and resourceful commander. Philip garrisoned Macedonian soldiers in Thebes and stripped the city of its power in Boeotia. He offered Athens an alliance with favorable terms that Athens was glad to accept.

Having failed at unity among themselves, the cities of mainland Greece had become united by Macedonia. Philip held autocratic author-ity over his league of Greek cities. He created a federal constitution and a council of representatives for his league, and he made the city of

Corinth the meeting place where these representatives would settle issues that arose among them. He held all the member states responsible for contributing to order within the League: for defense against brigandage, against piracy and against trouble from those seeking a redistribution of wealth or abolition of debts. The League's politics were to be conservative, the new trend toward unity bringing an end to the trend toward reform and democracy that had begun with Solon more than two hundred years earlier.

Philip Moves against a Weakened Persia

Since the death of Persia's king Artaxerxes I in 425, Persia had been suffering from incompetent monarchs. There were the usual palace conflicts that developed in monarchies: jealousies within the royal family, corruption, palace and harem intrigues and regicide. Darius II, who ruled to 404, had been unpopular and had spent much time quelling revolts. Under Artaxerxes II, the subject peoples of the Persian Empire had become restless. His son, Artaxerxes III, massacred his brother's family and gained the throne in 358 BC, and he ruled by terror until he was poisoned in 338 by one of his eunuch ministers.

Meanwhile, money that poured into Persia's royal treasury from tributes and taxes had been hoarded rather than spent, which resulted in economic stagnation. Also, Persia's aristocracy – the backbone of its military – had been growing soft. Their moderation in eating and drinking had given way to eating as a preoccupation, with meals lasting from noon to night. They had grown accustomed to being waited on by numerous slave-servants.

Philip was aware of Persia's weakness. He saw opportunity to punish the Persians for their ruinous attacks on Hellenic sanctuaries the century before. Also he wished to free Greek cities in Asia Minor from Persian domination, to extend his league's naval power (which was mainly Athenian), to extend his league's commerce, and to settle people deep in Asia Minor as a buffer against Persia. Philip's league declared war and commissioned Philip to lead their armies against Persia. In the spring of 336, Philip sent an advance party of several thousand into Asia Minor, which overthrew various dictators favored by Persia, and a few Greek cities in Asia Minor joined Philip's league. But before Philip's great invasion of Asia Minor, personal problems intervened. Philip had divorced Alexander's mother, Olympias, and married a younger woman. Olympias and Philip attended the marriage celebration of their daughter, and there one of Philip's former close companions, who now had a bitter grudge against him, leaped upon him and murdered him. When the assassin ran to a horse to escape, he was killed by Philip's bodyguards, and it would never be known whether the assassination was the work of this lone individual or of a conspiracy. Philip's generals supported Alexander as Philip's successor, and Alexander restored his mother as queen of Macedonia. Soon Olympias was to execute the young woman Philip had recently married, Cleopatra, and the daughter Cleopatra had had by Philip. Alexander held an inquiry into who might have conspired with the assassin, which concluded with the announcement that the assassination was the work of Persian agents.

ALEXANDER FROM ASIA MINOR TO EGYPT

Philip's passing created hope for freedom among some Greeks. And in 335, Thebans heard and believed a rumor that Alexander had also died. They revolted and trapped a Macedonian garrison in their city's citadel. Alexander led an army to Thebes, and in street fighting he overpowered the Thebans. He scattered the Thebans and sold many into slavery. All other Greek resistance to Macedonian domination suddenly ceased, and Alexander returned to pursuing his father's plan to liberate the Greeks in Asia Minor.

In 334, less than two years after the assassination of Philip, Alexander started his army eastward toward Asia Minor. It was an army of nearly forty thousand Macedonians, Greeks, and Balkan troops, accompanied by secretaries, scientists and philosophers. Security on the homefront was supplied by Greece's navy, an army of 12,000 infantry and 1,500 cavalry, a militia in Macedonia, and troops elsewhere within the alliance who could be called up in an emergency – all under the command of Alexander's most trusted general: the aging Antipater.

Alexander had inherited an efficient military machine, and he had learned lessons in good military strategy and diplomacy. Moreover, among kings he was exceptional: he could plan like a master chess player, and in battle he would be bold and quick in seeing sudden shifts in advantages and disadvantages. He was perhaps foolhardy about his own safety but not toward the safety of his troops, and because of his care and tactics his casualties would be lighter than those of his enemies.

Alexander's opponent was the forty-six year-old Darius III, a refined and intelligent man but without much energy or foresight and a poor military commander. Darius underestimated Alexander's strength, but he sent against him a force three times as large, a force that included able horsemen and 20,000 or so Greek mercenary infantrymen, largely men who had run from Greece with the defeat of their cities by Philip.

Alexander's army crossed into Asia Minor at Hellespont and found Darius' army waiting only a few miles into Asia Minor, on the opposite

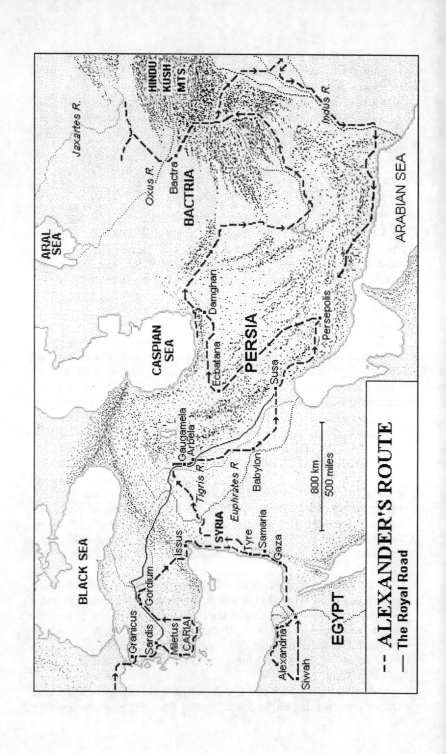

ALEXANDER'S ROUTE
-- Alexander's Route
— The Royal Road

side of the Granicus River. On horseback Alexander led a charge across the river, and he was met by Darius' top ranking officers and combatants. He emerged from this hand to hand combat alive, with most of Darius' leading generals dead. The disorderly ranks of the Persian infantry became easy targets for the long spears and solid ranks of the Macedonians, and the Macedonians cut them to pieces. Darius' Greek mercenaries remained in formation and refused to surrender. Alexander's forces charged, and only around two thousand of the mercenaries survived, to be sent as slaves to work Macedonia's mines.

Winning Hearts and Minds

Alexander was intelligent enough that he avoided hating those thought to be his enemies, and after his first victory over the Persians he honored the dead Persian troops as well as his own, and he paid a special honor to the Persian commander who had come close to killing him. But the historian who accompanied Alexander, Callisthenes (Aristotle's nephew), described Alexander's victory over the Persians as the work of the Greek goddess of revenge, Nemesis – a revenge for Persia's misdeeds against the Greeks more than a century before.

News of Alexander's victory spread fast through the Mediterranean region and West Asia. Greek cities in Asia Minor began setting up democracies and opening their gates to Alexander. And awed by Alexander's success, various cities proclaimed Alexander a divinity. But Miletus and a couple of other cities resisted, and Alexander overpowered them. Alexander was always ready to punish rebellion, as he had against Thebes, but he also wished to win hearts and minds. In the fighting at Miletus he offered a pardon to Greek mercenaries and citizens holding the inner city, and, respecting the courage of the Greek mercenaries there, he offered them service in his own army. In Asia Minor his forces limited their taking of spoils mainly to armor and weapons. They took no more captives to sell as slaves, and Alexander forbade reprisals against civilians.

It had been spring when Alexander invaded Asia Minor, and, by the end of the year, most of the Greek cities on the western coast of Asia Minor were declared free. Cities that had been ruled by Persian satraps were now garrisoned by Macedonians and their Greek allies. These cities were allowed to run their own local affairs, with Alexander unopposed to any inclinations they had toward democracy. Where local people were accustomed to a Persian system of administration, Alexander adopted its use, and he improved the system by dividing what had been the powers of the local Persian governor into three different offices: civil, military and financial.

Aristotle had advised Alexander to turn those non-Greeks he defeated into slaves, but Alexander had begun a policy of winning their respect and cooperation. He brought a Persian commander into his own entourage. And he happily let himself become the adopted son of a princess – soon to be queen – of the non-Greek royal house of Caria, in Asia Minor's southwest.

The Persian Navy is Neutralized

Alexander and his army marched into the middle of Asia Minor in pursuit of Darius, leaving behind them the pacification needed for expanded conquest. They passed the winter of 334-33 at Gordium, and they waited there into the spring for reinforcements and local crops to ripen. Meanwhile, Persia's fleet of three hundred warships and some sixty thousand men sailed for the Aegean Sea from their ports along the Eastern shores of the Mediterranean. By the end of April the fleet had established bases for itself at various islands in the Aegean, and the fleet threatened Alexander's line of communications to Macedonia and the Greek mainland.

Alexander sent money to his homefront commander, Antipater, to strengthen defenses in Greece. Then in June, he left Gordium with an enlarged army. He veered away from the Persian empire's old Royal Road, turning toward Syria, along the way leaving those who surrendered to him in charge of their cities. His march was delayed for two months as he lay sick, perhaps from malaria. Then, in November, at Issus, on the Mediterranean coast just north of Syria, he met and defeated Darius' army again. Darius fled eastward through Mesopotamia, leaving behind his family, his harem and his treasury. Alexander treated Darius' family and harem with tact and courtesy. And, with this victory, Alexander now considered himself king of Asia.

From Issus, Alexander moved southward through Syria, taking one Mediterranean seaport after another. In January 332, he and his army came upon the Phoenician city of Tyre, a naval base and home for many crewmen in Persia's navy, a city of fanatical fighters and a city that was a bitter enemy of surrounding city-states. Alexander began a seven-month siege of Tyre, and against Tyre he used catapults, rams and finally swords. Finally, he resorted to tradition: the many who did not surrender were put to death, and the women and children of Tyre were sold into slavery.

The loss of Tyre broke Persia's naval power. Syrian and Cypriot contingents of Persia's navy deserted. Alexander's Greek navy regained control over the Aegean Sea, and one by one Darius' military forces were compelled to withdraw from the Aegean islands.

Into Egypt

Alexander set his next goal as Egypt. He bypassed Jerusalem, his entourage believing that Judah was an unimportant priest-state run by an ineffectual collection of stargazers. He and his navy confronted the well-fortified Phoenician city of Gaza, which, for Alexander was a gateway to Egypt. At Gaza, as at Tyre, the fighting was bitter. It lasted two months. Gaza's defenders fought to the last man. Alexander sold its women and children into slavery, and he repopulated the city by allowing the settlement there of people from the surrounding area. Then, while supplied by his navy, Alexander and his army marched across the Sinai desert into Egypt. Alexander's reputation had preceded him there. Happy to see the end of Persian rule, Egyptians welcomed him as a liberator. They had little choice, for they no longer had the cohesion nor an army needed to resist him. Egypt's priesthood hailed Alexander as pharaoh – as a king of kings. And, like other pharaohs, he was hailed as a god. He became the guest of Egypt's king, staying at the pharaoh's palace in Memphis. There, Alexander made sacrifices to Egypt's gods, including the bull god Apis.

Early in the year 331, Alexander sailed down the Nile, and he found a place he thought perfect for a city. There he founded Alexandria, soon to be Egypt's new capital – a city that would be populated by people from neighboring villages and towns and by retired Macedonian, Greek and Balkan veterans from Alexander's army. Like a Macedonian city, Alexandria's inhabitants were to be subject to royal edicts but otherwise self-governing, with an assembly and a city council.

Affirmation of Alexander's Birth Having Been Divine

Concerned about his glory and his relationship with the gods, Alexander and a small party with camels crossed the Egyptian desert to an oasis and holy place called Siwah. There the sun god, Amon-Ra, the father of the pharaohs, was believed to dwell. It was common among Greeks to see their own gods in foreign deities, and for some time Greeks and Macedonians had visualized Amon-Ra as another manifestation of Zeus. Alexander and his party traveled in the coolness of twilight and night, and their journey became biblical in its telling. They endured a sandstorm. They crossed an area infested with snakes and became lost, and their water supply was just about finished. Alexander's historian, Callisthenes, was to claim that they were rescued by gods: two crows that flew in front of them to show them the way. According to another account they were led by gods in the form of two talking snakes.

At Siwah, Alexander was welcomed by the local high priest as a great conqueror and as the son of Amon-Ra. Alexander welcomed this proclamation of his divinity. It was Macedonian and Greek tradition that a hero might be the son of a god and yet human. And it was commonly believed that a hero or great conqueror – having a power greater than priests performing their rituals or common folk in prayer –

had to be divine. And when news of Alexander at Siwah reached Alexander's mother, Olympias, it reinforced her view that Alexander's birth had been divine.

ALEXANDER BECOMES KING OF THE PERSIANS

In early 331, Alexander returned to his pursuit of Darius. He marched with his army toward Babylon, where Darius had been organizing a force for a showdown against him, a force that included Indian elephants and chariots armed with scythes. Along the way during the early summer, Alexander conducted a campaign against a rebellion in Samaria. There a group of Jews had captured and burned alive their governor. Samarians surrendered those responsible for the killing, and Alexander had the murderers executed on the spot. Then, as a further lesson against such rebellions, he expelled Samaria's inhabitants. And in their place he invited Macedonians to populate the city.

Moving eastward across Mesopotamia, Alexander came again to the Royal Road, and he turned south toward Susa. On October 1, Darius and his army of a million men arrived on a wide plain along the royal road, by a town called Gaugamela, and the two armies clashed. Commanding his army from his chariot, Darius was slow in correcting weaknesses that developed in troop positions, and he was slow in taking advantages of weaknesses that had developed in the position of Alexander's army. Darius had failed to delegate enough command to subordinates. And when he thought he saw Alexander's army overpowering his army, he fled with his retinue – the second time he deserted men who were dying for him. Darius' poorly led army was massacred.

Leaving behind his chariot, bow and a substantial hoard of coins as a prize for Alexander, Darius fled to Arbela, without destroying river bridges behind him. There he was joined by Bactrian cavalrymen, 2,000 loyal Greek mercenaries and a few of his surviving Royal Guards. From Arbela they pushed east through the Zagros Mountains and then south, dropping down to Ecbatana. Darius' nerve had been broken by his last defeat, but he hoped to gather and re-organize his army. He expressed hope that Alexander and his army would weaken themselves in luxury, idleness and the women they would find to the south, in Babylon, and he wrote nervously to his governors in Bactria and elsewhere in the east, urging them to remain loyal.

Alexander marched southward unimpeded, leaving the Royal Road and traveling along the Tigris River, past great fertile fields of barley and millet, past rows of date palms, man made canals and huge estates, to Babylon. The Persian governor of Babylon surrendered the city to him, and with his army Alexander entered the city in triumph.

The local priesthood made a show of welcoming Alexander, and Alexander in turn displayed his respects. He consulted the local priesthood on the correct worship of the Babylonian god, Marduk. He made animal sacrifices to Marduk. He pleased the priesthood by ordering the restoration of Marduk's statue and the temples that the Persians had long before destroyed as punishment for a revolt. Men of wealth in the area, wishing to make peace with Alexander, gave him great sums of money. For Alexander's soldiers it was time for another rest, and they spent their pay on Babylon's women.

Sparta's Last Hurrah

Sparta still resented Macedonia's occupation of the Peloponnesian peninsula, and Sparta's king, Agis II, was encouraged by a large force of replacement or reinforcement troops leaving Macedonia to join Alexander. Agis II was encouraged also by an uprising against Macedonian rule in Thrace. Agis believed that Alexander had marched too far east to counteract him, and with gold from Persia he hired soldiers from other Greek city-states. He brought the Peloponnesian city of Elis and much of the Peloponnesian districts of Arcadia and Achaea into an open alliance with him, and he launched a war against Macedonian rule in Greece.

Alexander's general in charge of defending the homefront, Antipater, sent an army against the uprising, and Alexander sent his navy to give support to the many Greek cities that preferred Macedonian power to a revival of Spartan power. Alexander also sent a large sum of money home to help finance the war against Sparta. In 331 BC Antipater's army crushed the armies of Sparta and its allies – indicating again that Sparta's days as a great military power had ended.

Alexander Conquers Susa

Alexander pushed farther east – leaving the former governor of Babylon in charge of Babylon's civil affairs and a military force in Babylon under Macedonian charge. In twenty days he and his army traveled two hundred miles and arrived at Susa, the administrative center of the Persian empire. Susa surrendered to Alexander before he entered the city. With this Alexander acquired the city's great treasury, which allowed him to reward his troops generously – his troops not having been allowed the usual form of payment to soldiers: pillage and loot.

In Susa, Alexander sacrificed to the gods in accordance with Macedonian custom. Then he held a festival that included athletic events. Not expecting to meet another great army like the one he fought at Gaugamela, he reorganized his army for guerrilla and siege warfare in mountainous country, dividing it into smaller units of seventy-five to a hundred. And he included in his cavalry some recruits from among the East's good horsemen.

The Conquest of Persia and Death of Darius

In December, 331, Alexander left the Persian governor in charge in Susa, a Macedonian in charge of local troops, and with a refreshed army of about sixty thousand, he fought his way southeastward through mountains. Then he swept through an open plain of woods, canals and estates, toward Persia's capital city, Persepolis. Alexander and his army of sixty thousand entered Persepolis and took control of its palace. They saw themselves as in the heart of enemy territory, with Alexander no longer concerned with winning hearts and minds as he had been in Asia Minor. Alexander seized a wondrous amount of money from the Persian treasury. Then he stooped to the tradition of vengeance. Those in Persepolis were to pay for the misdeeds he believed the Persians had committed some hundred and fifty years before, when Xerxes had invaded Greece. Alexander turned the city over to his troops, who stormed through its streets, slaughtered men, plundered their property and stripped women of their jewelry.

Alexander and his troops spent the remainder of the winter at Persepolis, and there Alexander began thinking that he could not be both the avenger of the wrongs wrought by the Persians and their exalted ruler. But in early spring he allowed vengeance one last great fling, a vengeance perhaps for Xerxes having burned the Athenian Acropolis and the towns and temples of Attica in the year 480. After a night of drinking, Alexander and his army burned Persepolis' great palace of Xerxes.

Alexander and his troops then pushed north along a mountainous course toward the Caspian Sea, to Darius' summer palace, where, according to reports, Darius and Persian troops were encamped. Hearing a report of Alexander's approach, Darius' military, including Greek mercenaries, began escaping in a hard ride eastward. Alexander and five hundred of his toughest men went ahead of the rest of his army. They rode across forty-four miles of desert, and at dawn, near the town of Damghan, they came upon Darius' troops. Alexander had hoped to leave Darius as a subordinate king – similar to the pharaoh he had left in Egypt – with himself as King of Kings. But before Alexander and his men could reach Darius, the leader of Darius' Bactrian cavalry, Bessus, and some accomplices, killed Darius. And moved by the sight of Darius' corpse, Alexander covered it with his cloak.

Alexander Conquers Bactria and Captures Darius' Assassin
Bessus moved eastward with his troops and proclaimed himself Darius' successor. In pursuit, Alexander pushed eastward into Bactria. With reinforcements that arrived from Greece and Macedonia, Alexander fought local rulers and independent tribes whom the Persians had only barely managed to dominate. Alexander inflicted heavy casualties on them. He gained control of the route further east, and he forced local peoples to accept his rule. Hoping to end their marauding ways and to create peace in the area, he encouraged tribal people to adopt a settled way of life and to move into new towns that he founded.

Alexander marched into the Hindu Kush mountains, from whose summit Aristotle believed one would be able to see the end of the world. And, in these mountains, local people showed Alexander the rock where the mythical Prometheus was said to have been chained after he gave the gift of fire to humanity.

Bessus scorched the earth behind him as he fled. Alexander, together with local rulers, managed to capture Bessus, who was brought naked in bonds and a wooden collar to stand before Alexander at the town of Bactra. Alexander asked Bessus why he had killed his king and kinsman. While Bessus tried to justify himself, a herald announced his errors, and Bessus was flogged – a punishment of Macedonian tradition. And in keeping with Persian tradition, Bessus' nose and ears were cut off. Then he was sent to be tried by a Persian court, which had him executed.

Alexander Adopts Eastern Ways
In the vast area of Bactria, Alexander founded more towns. He married a local chieftain's daughter, Roxana, apparently more for good relations with a local ruler than for love. Alexander was still ignoring Aristotle's advice, for he was treating non-Greeks and non-Macedonians as kinsmen, which encouraged local peoples to treat him as a liberator and to join forces with him.

Alexander was concerned about his image among Persians, and to match his court to the expectations of his new subjects and courtiers in the East, he began to discard the Macedonian custom of openness with which he could be addressed. As king of the East he began borrowing from the pomp of the Persian throne, and those who came to see him had to prostrate themselves before him, in recognition of his divinity. This was easily accepted by the Persians and other easterners, but Alexander's troops found it embarrassing and considered it a part of the slavishness and inferiority of eastern people.

Drink and the Burdens of Command

Alexander took more Persians into his ranks, including Darius' brother as one of his companion soldiers. One of Alexander's most trusted commanders, Cleitus, who had saved his life at Granicus, was offended by Macedonians having to petition Persians for an audience with their own king, and he objected to positions of command passing to Persians. While Alexander and his companions were having one of their wine parties, Alexander and Cleitus argued. Alexander tried to strike Cleitus but was held back by others. Alexander called on his trumpeter to sound the call for military help, but the trumpeter refused. Alexander might have thought that Cleitus and those around him were conspiring against him. A bodyguard named Ptolemy pulled Cleitus out of the room. Cleitus returned and Alexander, thinking that Cleitus was attacking, ran him through with a pike and killed him. Then Alexander noticed that Cleitus had not been armed, and he realized that Cleitus had not returned to kill him. For days Alexander lay on his bed filled with remorse and taking no food. Then he recovered and made a sacrifice to appease the god of wine, Dionysus.

Into India and back to Susa

After two years in Bactria, the king of an area by the Indus River – which had been a part of the Persian Empire – declared himself an ally of Alexander and requested Alexander's help against a rival kingdom. In the summer of 327, Alexander and his army started a 400-mile journey to India, arriving there in the spring of 326. By the Hydaspes River, Alexander's army of 16,000 confronted the force of the rival king – an army of 34,200 men, with elephants, chariots and cavalry and archers. Typical of his other battles, Alexander avoided a center confrontation by taking the initiative. He attacked the enemy's flank, compelling the enemy to rearrange his forces, and he took advantage of the enemy's confusion and imbalance. Alexander lost 990 men. The other side lost 2,180 and the battle.

Alexander hoped to advance to the Ganges River and make it his eastern border, but after a march of a hundred miles his troops refused to go farther east. With his Macedonians troops Alexander was still a leader by persuasion, as warrior-kings were traditionally. Unable to persuade them to continue, and seeing what he thought were unfavorable omens, he and his men returned to the Hydaspes River and began their return to Susa. They journeyed south along the Hydaspes to the Indus River and down the Indus to the Arabian Sea. Some of Alexander's entourage boarded ships, and Alexander and the others began a murderous march of fifteen hundred miles through mountainous and dry terrain to Persepolis, then another three hundred miles to Susa – a journey that began in September, 325, and ended in the spring of 324.

PLANS, DEATH AND MYTH

During Alexander's absence some of his local governors had acted in accord with tradition: they had lusted after more power, recruited private armies and abused local peoples. Alexander and his army remained the dominant power, and Alexander listened to charges against the errant governors, and he had most of them executed. Then he continued his policy of integrating his forces with local people. He encouraged his Macedonian officers to take native wives. He set an example by taking two more wives for himself. One of them, Stateira, was a daughter of Darius, which added legitimacy to Alexander's claim of kingship over the Persians.

Some ten thousand of Alexander's soldiers are said to have married local women. These soldiers received generous dowries, and they were demobilized and sent back to Macedonia and Greece. Their wives and children stayed in the east, where the children were to be maintained and educated in Macedonian ways, at state expense, and to be handed over to their fathers when they had reached adulthood.

Alexander replaced the demobilized soldiers with Persian troops, which outraged some of his remaining veterans. But Alexander was undeterred. With new troops that arrived from Macedonia, Alexander created an integrated force, with Macedonians in the front rank, carrying pikes, and Persians in rows behind them, with swords and javelins. It was a force with greater mobility than before – and a creation that was to be adopted by the Roman Republic.

More Reforms, Plans and Death

In 323, Alexander returned to Babylon, which he planned to make the capital of his great new empire. He saw himself as creating the kind of government Aristotle thought best: rule by a benevolent, philosopher-king. He hoped to create a new loyalty across the lands he had conquered: a feeling among his subjects that they belonged to a world outside their town or city. He prayed for a new cooperation and brotherhood across his empire. He looked for his empire to be strengthened by a common culture, Hellenism, including the Greek language. His Persian cadets were to have instruction in Greek literature, and his other eastern subjects were to be encouraged to become like the Greeks and Macedonians.

Alexander hoped that commerce would help tie his empire together. He decided to exploit new commercial possibilities and to make Babylon the center of an enhanced world commerce. Already his warring had created a new demand for iron, his conquest of Persian treasury had put more money into circulation, and his conquests had broken down trade barriers. Already he had stimulated economic activity by building new ports and by founding new cities and seventy urban Greek military colonies in the conquered territories. Now Alexander began planning for the building of docks along the Euphrates at Babylon and for the clearing and dredging of the Euphrates to its mouth at the Persian Gulf. He planned to colonize the eastern shore of the Persian Gulf and to have Arabia circumnavigated and explored.

Alexander wished to unite the world under his rule and was laying plans to extend his conquests to Sicily and Italy. But fortuities exercise an influence on great events as they do on small, and in 323, at the age of thirty-two, Alexander died – possibly from malaria. How different the world might have been had the gods seen fit to reveal to humanity their secrets as to what caused diseases!

Alexander and Myth

By his conquests, Alexander had changed the world. But what had not changed was the inclination to create myth. Even while Alexander lived, his court historian, Callisthenes, had written of an incident in which the sea had retreated from before Alexander's path. Now mythmakers colored their image of Alexander as they pleased. Some others described Alexander as having had godly powers. But Persian priests demonized Alexander. They were jealous of foreign creeds and, reeling from the damage that Alexander had done to the prestige of their religion, they began a legend that described him as one of the worst sinners in history, as having slain many Persian teachers and lawyers and as having quenched many sacred fires. Some others in Persia would describe Alexander as a member of Persia's royal family – the Achaemenids. In Egypt, Alexander would become known as the son of the last pharaoh, Nectanebus. Arabs would come to know him as Iskander and would tell fanciful stories about him. And in Ethiopia, Christians would describe his father, Philip, as a Christian martyr, and they would describe Alexander as an ascetic saint.

CHAPTER 12

HELLENISTIC CIVILIZATION
– AN ALMOST MODERN WORLD

ALEXANDER'S EMPIRE DISINTEGRATES

An unreliable account of Alexander as he neared death describes him as offering rule to his generals. Another account describes him as putting the hand of one of his generals, Perdiccas, with the hand of his wife Roxana and naming Perdiccas as his heir. Perdiccas apparently did not wed Roxana – who was pregnant with Alexander's child. Perdiccas did favor making this child Alexander's heir, if the child was to be a son. To some Macedonians, however, it was unthinkable that their king should be the son of a "barbarian" Asian woman. This was the beginning of the break-up of Alexander's empire and the spilling of much more blood. It was another failure in succession that plagued monarchies through all of antiquity. It was a failure that would leave the Hellenistic civilization that followed Alexander weak and vulnerable to a power that was rising in the west: Rome.

Those opposed to Roxana's child as Alexander's heir favored Alexander's half brother, Philip III, a simpleminded and illegitimate son of Philip II and one of Philip's mistresses. When Roxana gave birth to Alexander's son, Alexander IV, the different opinions about who should succeed Alexander intensified, and civil war appeared imminent. But war was averted by a compromise in which it was agreed that Philip III and Alexander IV would reign jointly while each was supervised by a general.

In Epirus, Alexander's mother, Olympias, supported her grandchild, Alexander IV, and was hostile toward Philip III. With Perdiccas also favoring her grandson, she sought an alliance with Perdiccas and offered Perdiccas marriage to her daughter – Alexander's full sister.

Another actor in this grand drama was Alexander's general and former bodyguard, Ptolemy, who was at the head of a significant number of Alexander's former troops. Conveniently for his ambitions, he believed that he and his fellow generals would be unable to keep Alexander's empire unified, and he proposed that they divide the empire among themselves. Less than a year after Alexander died, Ptolemy murdered the man Alexander had put in charge of Egypt:

Cleomenes. And in the place of Cleomenes, Ptolemy, with his army, took power in Egypt.

Alexander's generals and governors made a show of their devotion to Alexander's memory, and, except for Ptolemy, they spoke of the need to keep the empire unified. But between them came rivalry: The aged Antipater and those Alexander had assigned to govern various parts of his empire resented and feared Perdiccas' power. And Antipater, who governed Macedonia and Greece, joined with two other generals, Antigonus and Craterus, and prepared for war against Perdiccas. Power rivalry was again manifesting itself as one of the bigger sins of all time.

War erupted first over Alexander's bones, which Ptolemy is reported to have buried in the Egyptian city of Memphis. Perdiccas went with an army into Egypt against Ptolemy, but when Perdiccas needlessly lost many of his troops crossing the Nile it angered his troops, and they mutinied. A group of Perdiccas' officers assassinated him in his tent. And with the elimination of Perdiccas, the remaining generals agreed that Antipater be regent to both Alexander's son and to Philip III. A military officer named Seleucus – who had led the mutiny against Perdiccas – was chosen to govern Babylon, and Antigonus was chosen Commander-in-Chief of what had been Alexander's army in the east.

Antigonus Fails to Unite the Empire

Antigonus took command of the most powerful naval forces in the Aegean, and in eastern Asia Minor (Cappadocia) he warred against and executed the man Alexander had assigned there as governor. Meanwhile, in 319, Antipater died of natural causes. His son, Cassander, replaced him as the ruling general in Macedonia and Greece, and the hostility between Olympias and Antipater became a feud between her and Cassander. Olympias had raised an army and claimed rule over Macedonia. Philip III, aware that Olympias opposed his sharing rule with her grandson, allied himself with Cassander. Feeling threatened by this, Olympias had Philip III, his wife and a hundred friends of Cassander executed. Cassander then marched from Greece into Macedonia with his army. He won battles there against Olympias' armies. He had Olympias executed, and he put Roxana and Alexander IV under guard.

It was Antigonus who controlled Alexander's great treasury in West Asia, and he hoped that by asserting his power he could unite Alexander's empire. Fearing his power, the other generals united against him just as they and Antigonus had against Perdiccas. Seleucus fled from Babylon to Egypt and allied himself with Ptolemy; Cassander also allied himself with Ptolemy; as did a Macedonian general named Lysimachus who governed Thrace. In 315, with mercenaries of many nationalities, Antigonus and Ptolemy fought each other, and Antigonus forced Ptolemy out of Syria. Then Antigonus cited Cassander for crimes against Olympias and sent his troops to Greece, while in 313 Antigonus' son, Demetrius, fought and lost to Ptolemy at Gaza. In 312, Ptolemy moved against Antigonus by sending Seleucus with a small army back to Babylon. In 311, Cassander had Alexander IV executed. The struggle between Antigonus and the alliance of Seleucus, Ptolemy, Cassander and Lysimachus continued for ten years. In 301, the alliance against Antigonus triumphed. Antigonus lost the battle of Ipsus in Asia Minor and his life. Seleucus emerged as nominal ruler of territory from Syria to Bactria. Lysimachus ruled Thrace, and in name he became ruler of Asia Minor. Cassander continued to rule in Macedonia and much of Greece. And Ptolemy formally declared Egypt as his independent kingdom. Their remaining enemy, Antigonus' son, Demetrius, was left with command of a powerful Greek navy and the support of only a few island cities in the Aegean Sea. He thought of himself as carrying on his father's struggle to unify Alexander's empire, but reasonable hope for unification had come to an end.

The New Monarchies
    The new rulers over what had been Alexander's empire drew from the Alexander legend and made themselves monarchs in the Macedonian tradition. They sought support in religion, pretending that their bloody wars were the will of the gods. And, as had Alexander, they claimed themselves divine. In Egypt, Ptolemy claimed that he was descended from Heracles and Dionysus. In Syria, Seleucus claimed lineage that extended back to the god Apollo, and he claimed that his rule was under the special protection of both Apollo and Zeus. Zeus, he claimed, resided at a temple in his capital city, Antioch, and Apollo resided in a temple at Daphne, just outside Antioch. Ptolemy attempted to appeal to the glory of Egypt's ancient past and portrayed himself as a new pharaoh, but he staffed his administration with Greeks rather than Egyptians, and many Egyptians continued to view his rule as foreign.
    Drawing from the Alexander legend, the upstart monarchs attempted to have a striking personal appearance. They wore headbands similar to the one Alexander had worn, which became a symbol of monarchy, and they continued Alexander's use of the title "king." In meeting visitors, these ex-soldiers postured haughtily, while visitors were obliged to gesture submission, respect and deference.

More Wars, a Celtic Invasion, and New Boundaries and Dynasties
    Alexander's prestige had rested on his military conquests, and the new monarchs believed that their military prowess was a part of their

prestige. They would fight one another for territory and make war a way of life in their time. Armies as large as sixty to eighty thousand would go into battle – to be thought the maximum size for armies as late as the eighteenth century.

Cassander apparently died of an illness, and his enemy Demetrius extended his rule in Greece, Demetrius taking power in Athens and starving the city into surrender. By 294, after more warring, he won control over Macedonia and named himself its king. But in 288, Seleucus and Lysimachus drove him out. In 285 Demetrius surrendered to Seleucus, and he died two years later.

Friction developed between Lysimachus and Seleucus over who would succeed Demetrius as king of Macedonia. Seleucus proclaimed himself king of Macedonia, but Lysimachus extended his rule there, and Seleucus invaded Lysimachus' territory in Asia Minor. In 281, Seleucus defeated Lysimachus at a battle in which Lysimachus died. And this left Greece and Macedonia open to a series of wars and power struggles.

Celts to the northwest of Greece and Macedonia heard of the anarchy in Greece and Macedonia, and they had heard stories of gold and silver offerings to Greek gods in temples there. They invaded, and in Macedonia they defeated, captured and executed a newly crowned king. In Greece they burned and looted as they went. They invaded Thrace and Asia Minor. Seleucus' son, Antiochus I – the first successor in a long line of Seleucid kings – was unable or unwilling to send a force against them, and cities in Asia Minor had to defend themselves as best they could. Antigonus II – Demetrius' son and the grandson of the once heroic Macedonian general, Antigonus I – rallied a force against the Celts and drove them from Thrace and Macedonia.

Antiochus ruled from Syria. He had given up hope of ruling Macedonia, and he befriended Antigonus II, taking support where he could find it. Not having the power base in Macedonia and Greece that Alexander had, and not having Alexander's reputation, Antiochus' hold on what had been Alexander's empire to Bactria was tenuous at best. He allowed some Celts to settle in central Asia Minor. But he lost control over western and northwestern Asia Minor, where Pergamum, with financial help from Ptolemy II, won its independence and detached neighboring cities. Ptolemy II sent troops into Asia Minor and took the coastal city of Eupheus, while the Seleucid dynasty also lost a large part of Cappadocia in eastern Asia Minor.

The East Fragments and is Invaded by the Parthians

The region in southwestern Persia called Persis (which included the city of Persepolis) had become an independent collection of tribal monarchies that remembered the glorious past of the Persian emperors

Darius the Great and Artaxerxes. Bactria was ruled by a governor whom the Seleucids ignored. Territories east of Bactria were conquered by India's first great empire, under Chandragupta. And the Seleucids did little if anything to stop the migrations into northern Persia by a people called Parthians, whom the Seleucids saw as no significant threat. From steppe lands east of the Caspian Sea, the Parthians were settling down in northern Persia and absorbing Persian culture. They founded their own towns, and around the year 250 BC a Parthian chief founded a Persian-style hereditary monarchy called the Arsacids. Then in 246, the governor of Bactria formally declared Bactria's independence, and he allied Bactria with the empire of Chandragupta's Buddhist grandson: Asoka.

Drawing mainly from Greek and Macedonian support, the Seleucids continued to control Syria, Mesopotamia, Palestine and parts of Persia. Colonies that Alexander had founded in Persia and Bactria remained Greek islands in a sea of eastern peoples. And in these colonies, Greek and Macedonian ways were being diluted by the taking of Asian women as wives.

COMMERCE AND ATTITUDE

Power rivalries, war and authoritarian rule left the world much as it had been before Alexander, but in some other respects the world had changed. The trade and commerce that Alexander stimulated continued to expand. This expansion was stimulated by arms production, by the building of new roads that connected distant places, by the creation of a common currency, and by Greek as the common language of business from the border of India to as far west as what is now the French port city of Marseilles.

Trade was changing the world more than was religion. With an increase in trade came expanded mining, manufacturing and ship building. Freight carrying ships were built much larger, as much as five tons, using methods of construction first applied to warships. Egypt's port city of Alexandria became a center of imports and manufacturing. The Egyptians and Phoenicians produced and traded cotton cloth, and the Egyptians produced silk, paper, glass, jewelry, cosmetics, salt, wine and beer. In West Asia, large workshops appeared alongside the small family stores that were common there. The manufacture of woolens increased in West Asia, along with asphalt, petroleum, carpets, perfumes, bleach and pain relieving drugs.

Across what had been Alexander's empire, some privately owned businesses grew into large enterprises. With the increase in circulation of money, credit became more sophisticated. Money-changing grew into banking. Private banks began making loans. The use of checks appeared, and people could deposit their savings for safekeeping and collect interest, which was around ten to twelve percent annually. Many aristocrats – traditionally landowners – gave up their contempt for trade and enterprise and enthusiastically joined in the money making.

The Spread of Hellenism

With Alexander's conquests also came significant cultural change. In West Asia and North Africa, well-to-do tradesmen, intellectuals and aristocrats who were neither Greek or Macedonian, including those who were Jews, had begun developing an interest in things Greek – to the annoyance of those who believed that the old ways were best. From Marseilles to India, Greek became the language of intellectuals and tradesmen. The Greek gymnasium became popular. It was a place for bathing and physical exercise – without clothes for the sake of freedom of movement in their exercises. The gymnasium was also a place for training in grammar, rhetoric and poetry. And those who passed through training at the gymnasium acquired a status similar to a modern college degree.

The increase in trade and travel enhanced an awareness of distant places. An increase in Persians, Greeks, Syrians, Jews and others migrating from city to city and from the countryside to cities cut these people off from their old tribal ties and increased their individualism. So too did the increase in commerce. A new cosmopolitanism was on the rise, and the possibility of a new sense of brotherhood, as had arisen between the Greeks and Macedonians who had fought shoulder to shoulder under Alexander.

Among city governments came a greater desire for cooperation with other cities, such as offering other cities freedom from import and export duties to encourage trade. Cities began offering other cities exchanges of citizenship. This occurred first between Athens and Rhodes, then between the Peloponnesian cities of Messene and Phigalea, the island of Paros and Allagria, between Pergamum and Temnos, Miletus and others. Conflicts that previously might have erupted into war were now more inclined to be arbitrated, with the arbiters most often being a commission from a third city. Common legal formalities appeared among various cities, and in place of trial by local juries an inter-city system developed in which commissions came from other cities to hear cases and settle lawsuits that would otherwise have been subject to local prejudices, politics and passions.

From Greek cities as far west as Italy and through West Asia and North Africa, a new interest in science, art and literature was stimulated. These interests remained largely unrestricted by those rulers who succeeded Alexander, not because they were libertarians but because they saw little threat in it to their rule. Some people read seriously, and many, including wives of the wealthy, read escapist works about what they believed were the good-old-days: a rural life that was idealized, with shepherds, shepherdesses, wooded valleys and true love. Libraries collected serious works and grew in number. Pergamum had a great library. Alexandria's library became the most famous. It accumulated as many as four hundred thousand scrolls and several thousand original works and copies, and it had a scientific museum that attracted people from far and wide. The academy that Plato had founded still flourished, and Athens remained a famous center of philosophy, but Pergamum and Alexandria rose to eclipse Athens as an intellectual and commercial centers.

Advances in Knowledge

In Hellenistic times the observation of facts was becoming widely recognized as important, and science became the pursuit of professionals divorced from philosophy and metaphysics. There were education and training for various professions such as engineering, medicine and other sciences. In medicine, corpses were dissected and studied. Doctors discovered the difference between motor nerves and sensory nerves, and for various parts of the body they created names that would still be used in modern times. Specialists advanced the study of plants and herbs, and manuals were written on agriculture and farm management. In mathematics, Euclid contributed to geometry by creating a system of proofs based on deduction. Stimulated by what had been Alexander's expedition into Asia, map making and a study of geography improved. Pytheas of Marseilles voyaged up the coast of Britain to Norway or Jutland and became the first Greek to hear of the Arctic Sea. One mapmaker, Eratosthenese, described the world as round and gave a reasonably exact figure for its circumference.

Philosophers and common folk continued to believe that the sun revolved around the earth, that the earth was at the center of the movement of heavenly bodies, but some Hellenized astronomers began challenging these views. Astronomers calculated the movements of the sun, moon and planets with greater accuracy. Heraclides of Pontu discovered that the planets Venus and Mercury revolved around the sun. Then Aristarchus of Samos concluded that the sun was much larger than the earth, that the earth revolved around the sun and that the distance to the stars was enormous compared to the diameter of the earth's orbit around the sun. And other astronomers confirmed his views.

In the field of mechanics, Aristotle's school made advances in understanding levers, balances and wedges. In the mid 200s a Greek from Syracuse named Archimedes worked on the relative densities of

bodies and the theoretical principles of levers. He invented the ratio *pi*.*
And he invented numerous mechanical contrivances, including
machines used in war.

Formal Schooling

The professions that required education belonged mainly to the sons
of the wealthy. But a part of Hellenism was education for the poor as
well as the rich. In the more progressive, Hellenized cities of West Asia
and North Africa, elementary schools for the children of common folk
were established. Children learned reading, writing and arithmetic.
They memorized lessons about the glories of Greek culture, and they
were taught "civilized" behavior. And, as in Greece centuries before,
educators saw physical punishment as their only recourse against
inadequate effort by their pupils.

In western Asia Minor an elementary school education was
provided for girls and boys. The girls ended school at a younger age
than did boys, who continued their education if their fathers cared to
pay for it. But some women did acquire higher education, and a few
became philosophers. In the 200's, women poets began to reappear.
Aristodama of Smyrna toured Greece giving recitals and receiving
many honors. A woman named Hestiaea acquired a reputation as a
scholar, and women were painting.

TURMOIL IN RELIGION

From Greece through West Asia, a growing interest in knowledge
brought turmoil in religion. Before Alexander, religions tended to be
local, tribal or national. After Alexander, religions knew no frontiers.
Religion continued to be influenced by historical circumstance. Religions traveled from city to city with the new migrants. Numerous
eastern cults spread westward as far as Greece. In Greece the rise of
individualism and a diminishing identity with the old Olympian gods
was accompanied by some people adopting astrology** and some
people adopting asceticism and rejecting worldly society. Some Greeks
adopted doctrines preoccupied with repentance, salvation, resurrection
and life after death. Many often spoke of a goddess named *Fortune*.
Across Greece and West Asia a few among the Hellenized responded to

---

* Pi is the ratio of the circumference of a circle to its diameter.

** Astrology had come from Babylonian priests centuries earlier, and now
Babylonian astronomers rejected it, as did the Epicureans and Stoic
philosophers discussed at the close of this chapter. A leading Stoic named
Carneades (214-129 BC) asked why men whom the stars had fated to die at
different times die in the same shipwreck.

the new individualism and cosmopolitanism by abandoning religion. Some others decided that all the gods worshiped across the world were really Zeus, that Zeus was the universal god. Some worshiped new gods, such as the healing god called Asclepius, which appeared in such cities as Epidaurus in Peloponnesia, the island city of Cos, and in Pergamum. Greeks spread the worship of Dionysus as far east as the Indus Valley, and some eastern peoples had begun worshiping Dionysus by another name, including some Hebrews outside of Judah who worshiped Dionysus under the name of Sabazios.

The Hellenized in Syria adopted the god Hadad, who was described in the Old Testament as Rimmon. And Hadad was another god whom some called Zeus. In Syria a local stone goddess whom the Persians had transformed into a goddess called Ahahita, now, in Hellenistic times, became the goddess Atargatis and Hadad's consort. She was both a Greek goddess and Syria's greatest of goddesses, and people came from all over Asia to be purified in her sacred pool of water.

The Spread of Isis Worship from Egypt

In Egypt, Ptolemy attempted to bring Egyptians closer to his Hellenized followers by creating a new religious cult that drew from Egyptian mythology. He gave the Egyptian god Osiris a new temple in the Egyptian quarter of Alexandria and a new name, Serapis. Serapis was described as a member of a trinity of gods that included Isis, the mother of all and the cleanser of sins. Rounding out the trinity was the son of Isis and Serapis: Harpocrates.

Priests, clad in white, initiated people into Ptolemy's cult by baptism – submerging them in the Nile or sacred water from the Nile – which was believed to remove one's sins, a conversion that often evoked considerable emotion. The daily routine of the priests of this faith included their leading ceremonies with the singing of hymns and sprinkling sacred water. Members of the cult believed that they would be judged after death, and they hoped that with death they would pass into an everlasting life.

To many native Egyptians this attempt by the Ptolemies to create a new religion from Egyptian mythology appeared as a lack of faith in their own gods, and most Egyptians rejected the new cult. But some Greek women in Egypt found in the worship of Isis an appeal that other fertility goddesses, virgin goddess warriors, and Aphrodite lacked. Like most women, Isis was a mother and a bearer of children. Like other women, Isis had suffered. And, most importantly, Isis offered them understanding. To women Isis was a friend, and to them she was the glory of womanhood. She was said to have ordained that women should be loved by men, that she invented the marriage contract and ordained that women should bear children and that children should love their parents. Isis' unique qualities helped spread worship of her and Serapis through the Aegean, to Italy and the Western Mediterranean. And in centuries to come some of Isis' statues would serve as images of the Madonna.

Scholarship by the Zoroastrian Priesthood
Alexander's conquest of Persia and Persia's subsequent rule by the Seleucid dynasty diminished the power and influence of the Zoroastrian priesthood, and in their new isolation, Zoroastrian priests devoted themselves to scholarship. Foremost was their wish to date their prophet, Zarathustra. With Zoroastrianism having adhered to oral history rather than writing, the priests had no Zoroastrian writings to research. Instead they researched through writings of the Babylonians, believing that events about something as important as their prophet would surely have been recorded by the scribes of Babylon. They found a vague reference to a great event having taken place in Persian history in 539 BC. This was the conquest of Babylon by Darius. But the Zoroastrian scholar/priests chose to interpret this great event as the time when Zarathustra received his revelation from the God Mazda – another instance of priestly writing interpreting events as they wished.

HELLENISM AND THE JEWS

In the middle of the transformations from Marseilles to India were the Jews. Contact between them and the peoples around them had increased, beginning with the military colonies Alexander had established at Samaria and Gaza and the Greek bureaucrats and soldiers who filled Palestine. Alexander's successors, Perdiccas, Antigonus and the Ptolemies, also established cities in Palestine, and their armies frequently passed back and forth across the land, including Judah – called Judaea by those speaking Greek. Some Jews were taken as slaves. Some of Judaea's young men joined the invading armies as mercenaries, and Jews became military colonists for various kings – mainly for Ptolemy. After Judaea came under the rule of Ptolemy, many Jews emigrated to Egypt, especially to Alexandria. Some other Jews migrated along the Mediterranean and Black Seas and settled in Asia Minor.

Cultural Diffusions and Preservations
Ptolemy interfered in Judaea's affairs more than had the Persians. His tax collectors were more prevalent, but he allowed the Jews the freedom of worship and the same autonomy that they had enjoyed under the Persians. Judaea's Jews continued to be governed by their High Priest and Council of Elders, and most Jews continued to worship Yahweh.

Many Jews, especially in rural areas, were among those in West Asia who preferred their old ways. It was from them that a revolt against Hellenism would come in the following century. Nevertheless, for the time being, many Jewish merchants, aristocrats and intellectuals came to admire Greek education, Greek schools and libraries. Some of them found lofty ideals in Greek philosophy, significance in Greek logic, and beauty in Greek art. Many Jews were attracted by the excitement of Greek athletic games and tournaments, and in Jerusalem a Greek-style amphitheater and gymnasium were built. Many Jews adopted Greek dress. Jews with Greek names – including Alexander – became common. Many Jews who traveled had a Hebrew name for use within their community and a Greek name for contacts with others. And Jews began using Greek style grave inscriptions.

Influenced by Hellenism, Jews began giving titles and honors to women. Some among them tolerated the mixed marriages that Ezra had forbidden. Some Hellenized Jews abandoned circumcision, restrictions on foods and other laws that their Hellenized neighbors thought barbaric. A few Hellenized Jews decided that people everywhere worshiped the same god under different names and that religions could therefore be united. Some others decided that Yahweh was not just the god of the Jews but the god of the whole world. Some of these Jews wanted to convert non-Jews to their god. And in places outside Judaea, where Jews and gentiles spoke Greek, some curious gentiles came to Jewish synagogues, listened, and were converted to Judaism.

Some Jewish writers in Egypt wished to instill in their fellow Jews a pride in their Jewish heritage, to counter the feelings of cultural inferiority that many felt. Near the end of the 200s, a Jewish scribe named Demetrius wrote a work describing Judaean kings, and he tried to prove that all of Jacob's many children could have been born within seven years. Other Jewish writers attempted to describe Jewish culture as the oldest in the world and the Jews as teachers of other peoples rather than having been influenced by others.

Greek was the language of educated Jews, and Greek translations of the Zoroastrianism of the Persians made Zoroastrian ideas more accessible to literate Jews. But Aramaic remained the language of most Jews – in Judaea and Mesopotamia – and an effort was made to preserve Hebrew as the main language of literature and religious gatherings, while Jewish scribes writing in Hebrew adopted Greek literary forms in their religious writings. And scholars believe that in these adoptions, Jewish scribes borrowed concepts that were not commonly known to Jews before the rise of Hellenistic society, including concepts borrowed from Plato's *Book of Wisdom* and Aristotle's *Testament of the Twelve Patriarchs*.

The Septuagint

Perhaps because most literate Jews could no longer read Hebrew and perhaps it was to correct this that Jewish scribes in Alexandria were put to work translating into Greek the *Five Books of Moses*. The finished product became known as the *Septuagint*. Demonstrating their conviction that the Septuagint was the final word on Jewish history, the high priests in charge of the work proclaimed a curse upon any changes that might be made to it. And into modern times it would be Judaic doctrine that seventy-two translators had worked independently of each other on the translation and had produced exactly the same result, word for word – a miracle in keeping with the belief that the books were the works of divine intervention.

The Septuagint was written in a Greek that was in places difficult for Greeks and others to understand, and because Jews from different areas used words differently and interpreted what they read differently, when the Septuagint was distributed to Jews outside of Alexandria it created confusion. For the sake of clarification, different Jewish communities ignored the curse that had been put on making changes to the Septuagint, and they inserted new words to fit local meaning. With the passing of decades, the Septuagint was reproduced by hand and more changes were made. Then other writings were imperfectly translated into Greek and added to the Septuagint: Isaiah, Jeremiah, Ezekiel, Kings, Judges, Psalms, Ecclesiastes, and Daniel. The last book of the Old Testament, the Book of Esther, would be translated into Greek around 77 BC. It would be from the Septuagint that various other translations would be made: an old Latin translation, Coptic, Ethiopian, Armenian, Georgian, Slavonic, Jerome's Latin Vulgate and others that led to the King James version, commissioned in England in AD 1604.

The Book of Ecclesiastes

The author of the Old Testament's Book of Ecclesiastes called himself "the preacher." And he claimed to be a "son of David," an expression used commonly to describe oneself as a Jew rather than as an actual son of David. But in modern times some people would believe Ecclesiastes was written by Solomon, despite it being unlikely that Solomon old age he would have turned his view of the world upside down and written about futility and the evils of oppression. Some others estimate that Ecclesiastes was written several hundred years after Solomon: around 200 BC.

The Preacher began Ecclesiastes by writing:

> Vanity of Vanities! All is vanity... All things are
> wearisome... The eye is not satisfied with seeing. Nor
> is the ear filled with hearing.

The Preacher was not as optimistic as the writer of the Book of Proverbs, where it was written that if one honors the Lord "your barns will be filled with plenty, and your vats will overflow with new wine." The Preacher denied that people could apply themselves and better their lot. He suggested that there was no hope in this world. "That which has been," he wrote, "is that which will be." (Ecclesiastes 1:9) He held that knowledge was futile: "What is crooked," he wrote, "cannot be straightened, and what is lacking cannot be counted... in much wisdom there is much grief, and increasing knowledge results in increasing pain." (Ecclesiastes 1:15-18)

The Preacher described himself as having built houses for himself, as having planted vineyards, gardens and fruit trees and as having made parks for himself. He claimed that he had collected silver, gold, slaves and many concubines, and that all this had been in vain. Then he got to the heart of his message, a message that made it more likely that his writing would be included with the other writings that were scripture: Without Yahweh, he wrote, all is in vain, "For who can eat and who can have enjoyment without Him?" The Preacher described Yahweh as having power over everything. "There is nothing to add to it and there is nothing to take from it," he wrote. "That which will be has already been, for God seeks what has passed by." (Ecclesiastes 3:14-15)

Some Jews had been asking why unrighteous people were enjoying success while some who devoutly worshiped Yahweh were suffering hardship and deprivation. The Preacher had an answer for them: he wrote that in a world controlled by God there was wickedness because God was testing people "in order for them to see that they are but beasts." "All go to the same place," he wrote, and "all came from the dust and all return to the dust." (Ecclesiastes 3:18-20)

In Chapter 4, Verse 2, the Preacher congratulates the dead, whom he claimed were better off than the living. "But better off than both of them," he writes, "is the one who has never existed, who has never seen the evil activity that is done under the sun."

In Chapter 5, Verse 10 the Preacher denounces the incentives that make free enterprise work. "He who loves money," he writes, "will not be satisfied with money, nor he who loves abundance with its income." Expressing a disbelief in rewards, he writes:

"The race is not to the swift, and the battle is not to the warriors, and neither is bread to the wise nor wealth to the discerning, nor favor to men of ability." (Ecclesiastes 9:11)

In Chapter 8, Verse 2 the Preacher delivers an old, conservative message, which must have pleased the priestly authorities: he calls on his readers to obey their rulers, to "Keep the command of the king, because of the oath before God." Then, in Verse 5, he made an incongruently optimistic comment: "He who keeps a royal command experiences no trouble, for a wise heart knows the proper time and procedure." Toward the end of his message, the Preacher contradicts what he wrote about the blessing of being dead or never having been born. Life, he claims is worth living: "Surely," he writes, "a live dog is better than a dead lion." "Go then," he continues. "Eat your bread in happiness, and drink your wine with a cheerful heart; for God has already approved your works." (Ecclesiastes 9:7) "Enjoy life with the woman whom you love all the days of your fleeting life which He has given to you under the sun, for this is your reward in life, and in your toil in which you have labored under the sun." (Ecclesiastes 9:9). Then, in his next verse, the Preacher advises to do what "your hand finds to do" and to do it "with all your might." Yet he claims (in 9:12), that man is "like fish caught in a net or birds trapped in a snare."

OVERPOPULATION, MISERY
AND DREAMS OF REVOLUTION

In some cities, Alexander had favored the common people against local nobles, who were potential competitors with him for power. In some cities, he had backed the creation of councils to tackle local issues. And the monarchs who followed Alexander also supported popular participation in local government. But, with the passing of time, participation in local government by common people declined. The gap between the rich and poor widened. And local power and influence gravitated toward men of wealth.

City governments called on local men of wealth to help their city, and in prosperous times such merchants contributed to the construction of temples, gymnasiums, schools and other city buildings and to the construction of bridges, closed sewers and other civic projects. They paid for city festivals and ceremonial sacrifices to the gods, for banquets for local people, free meals for the hungry, and prizes for school children. They patronized the arts, and they contributed to city beautification that included a proliferation of fountains and statues. Many of the statues were of these patrons, to honor their services. Being free from the daily labors that burdened poorer folk, men of wealth had the time to serve as diplomats. And, in times of war, they contributed to supplying armies with war material.

While assemblies elected by the common citizenry continued to meet and pass decrees, real power passed into the hands of these men of wealth – as happened in Athens, where the courts, which had been controlled by common citizens, came under the control of wealthy magistrates. And as a result of their rise in influence, these men of wealth began paying less in taxes than did common people.

The Miserable

Aside from the misery and insecurity created by continuous warfare, there was in Hellenistic times a misery that was economic in its origins. The wealthy could afford an abundance of luxury goods, but for the multitude there was deprivation. The population was small compared to modern times, but not small relative to the amount of food being produced. In Greece and through the Middle East a bad harvest still meant famine. In Greece hunger prevailed because the area was not exporting enough in minerals or manufactured goods to exchange for food. Greece was still dependent upon imports to keep people fed. And in the place of exports in goods, men were exporting themselves as soldiers.

Across Greece and West Asia, migration from the countryside to the cities created urban slums and overcrowding. With new supplies of slaves and an abundance of freemen looking for work came a drop in the wages, often while the price of food was rising. An abundance of slaves offered no incentives for creating devices that would replace muscle and sweat, and those who labored were physically burdened beyond their ability to stay fit.

Many people in normal times were barely able to survive, and often they became dependent on relief in the form of free grain. From the landless in the countryside came calls for land redistribution, and small landowners called for relief from their debts. The landless in the towns and cities had no trade organizations or labor movement to enhance their power. Strikes were not tolerated by those who had power and influence, and strikes were almost impossible where there was slavery.

Mining was an especially hard occupation. Egypt's gold and quicksilver mines were worked by slaves, criminals and prisoners of war, including women, elderly men and children. Young men hacked the quartz loose. Older men broke the quartz into fragments. Children dragged the quartz to the grinders, powered by women who like others worked without rest, walking in circles and pushing levers that rotated a shaft. According to the Greek writer Agatharchides, relief came only with death, which these miners welcomed.

More Utopian Dreams

As it was in Athens before Solon's reforms, many who were wealthy feared revolt by those who were miserable, and from a few who empathized with the miserable came dreams of a better society. Some dreamed of a "brotherhood of man." In dreaming about a better world, some looked back to what they thought was an unspoiled past, to what they imagined were virtuous barbarians living according to nature. Some put into writing their ideas about a harmonious society. A writer named Iambulus designed a society without slavery and other class differences, a society in which people would be equal, sharing what they produced and taking turns in doing menial work. This, of course, meant that people had to be equal politically, and Iambulus saw his utopia as a democracy. And he saw people in his utopia acquiring equality also in wisdom, and relating to each other with love.

A Failed Revolution and a Growing Unity in Macedonia

The most serious attempt at changing society came with hate and violence. In 279 BC, a man named Apollondorus rode a wave of discontent that gave him power in the Macedonian port city of Cassanderia (formerly Potidaea). His followers vented their anger on the wealthy with physical violence, and they confiscated wealth and property. Apollondorus established a communist dictatorship, and, with money taken from the rich, he hired an army of mercenaries to defend the revolution. To have succeeded, the revolution would have had to grow in power by spreading to other cities. Instead, after a few months, forces directed by the king of Macedonia, Antigonus II, who had been busy uniting Macedonia under his rule, overran Cassanderia and stop the revolution.

Failed Reforms in Sparta

Sparta remained like many other cities. Among the Spartans debt had increased. A few people had bought up lands and had combined them into plantations. Sparta had no middle class as a buffer between rich and poor. As elsewhere in Greece, many landless Spartan men sold themselves abroad as mercenary soldiers, and by the mid-200s, with citizenship tied to the ownership of property, seven hundred Spartans were fully enfranchised.

Sparta still had two kings, Agis IV and Leonidas. Agis proposed reforms. To increase the number of landowners and enfranchise more Spartans he proposed the cancellation of debts and a redistribution of lands into small units. Those with large holdings united behind Leonidas. Wishing to avoid civil war, Agis went into exile, where, in 241, he was murdered. Thirteen years later, Leonidas' son and heir, Cleomenes III, led a Spartan army in war alongside other Greek cities opposing Macedonia's attempt to renew hegemony in Greece. Concerned with military strength, Cleomenes decided that returning to the institutions of old Sparta would bring Sparta added military strength. When he returned with his army from one of his battles, he ousted Sparta's second king and installed one of his brothers in that position. Then he embarked upon his revolution. He stayed the same regarding the Helots, but for others he abolished debts, he nationalized the land, dividing it into 4,000 lots for Spartans and 15,000 lots for those who had come to live in villages surrounding Sparta. He created a new constitution for returning to the old Sparta, and his reforms allowed Sparta's army to grow in size and morale.

Cleomenes encouraged reformers elsewhere in Greece. Across Greece, men of wealth and land responded with fear. They opposed reforms more than they did Macedonian hegemony, and they sought help from Macedonia. War erupted between Sparta and cities led by those resisting reforms. Cleomenes allied Sparta with other Peloponnesian cities. But the Macedonians annihilated Sparta's army, and for the first time a foreign army entered Sparta in triumph. Cleomenes fled to Egypt, and there he again took up what he saw as the cause of social justice. In Alexandria, he tried to raise a revolt, but he failed and took his own life.

HELLENISTIC PHILOSOPHIES:
A SEARCH FOR A WAY OF LIFE

Some people in Hellenistic society adhered to the school of philosophy called Cynicism, a school of thought some other philosophers saw as hardly worthy of the name of philosophy. The founder of Cynicism was Antisthenes, who was about forty when he watched Athens go down to defeat in the Great Peloponnesian War. He was a former student of Socrates, and he had witnessed Socrates' execution. Like Plato, Antisthenes was disgusted with the world around him. He had grown tired of what he saw as the worthless quibbling of refined philosophy. Believing in his own intuitive ability to discern between truth and falsehood, he saw no importance in a structured theory of knowledge as a foundation for truth. He saw himself as a teacher, and he left the company of other philosophers and preached to common people in market places, speaking to people there in a manner he thought they could understand and that he thought was common sense. Antisthenes told people that virtue demanded withdrawal from involvement with a world that was immoral and corrupt.

Antisthenes' best known disciple was Diogenes. Diogenes was disgusted by his father's profession: money changing. He rejected living a life of chasing after wealth. He found virtue in having few or no possessions, in simplicity and in modest wants. He rejected fame and honor. Nevertheless, his demonstrations of asceticism were so novel to his fellow Greeks that it attracted great attention, and as decades passed many Greeks came to think of him as an extraordinarily wise man. In his old age his fame was enough that Alexander visited him and asked if there was any favor he wished, and Diogenes, the story goes, replied that he wanted only that Alexander stand out of his sunlight.

A few other people in Hellenistic times adopted the thinking and style of Antisthenes and Diogenes. They wandered from place to place, and at town squares they discussed social conventions and simple virtues. It was from among these Cynics that the word *cosmopolitan* was coined, a word used to signify that they belonged to no state. They advocated salvation from worry and conflict by what some in modern times would call dropping out. They were entertaining to listen to, but Cynicism would forever remain a small and barely influential movement. For most people the call to drop out made no sense: they were already barely able to feed and clothe themselves and their families. As with Buddhist monks and others who devoted themselves entirely to spiritual matters, only a few could go about without working, living off what was provided by those who labored in the fields or at other occupations. For most who had to struggle to get by the Cynics were as much the intellectual babblers that Antisthenes thought other philosophers to be.

The Epicureans

Another philosophy that focused on how one should live was Epicureanism. Like the Cynics, they believed it best to purge oneself of the appetite for power or fortune, and they favored withdrawal from the corruptions of society. Nevertheless, they wished to keep the wealth and possessions that helped make life pleasant, and most Epicureans were people of wealth.

Epicurus was from an Athenian family from the island of Samos. He went to Athens at the age of eighteen to confirm his Athenian citizenship – the year before Alexander died. Later he took up residence in the city of Mytilene, and there, at the age of thirty, he acquired recognition as a philosopher.

Epicurus was influenced by the materialism of Democritus. He believed that all reality is matter. A soul, he said, is warm breath – atoms that after death dissolve with our bodies. He believed that humanity created its destiny without interference from capricious spirits. He claimed that it was frightening to be at the mercy of gods and demons and that religion created unnecessary terrors and fears. But he escaped from the unpopularity of atheism by speaking of gods as if they were materiality, as if they were products of nature rather than nature's creators. The gods, claimed Epicurus, should be worshiped with neither fear nor hope. Do not fear death, he said, for death is but eternal sleep and the dead feel no pain or torment.

Epicurus addressed the ultimate question about life by claiming that life was worth living. He saw reason for living in the pleasures of contemplation, the sights of physical beauty, attachments to others, a sunny day, music and physical well-being – all that which can be enjoyed by those free from continuous drudgery and who have an adequate respect for the marvels of nature and awareness. Epicurus believed that the driving force of life is the avoidance of pain. He believed that the essence of virtue is avoiding inflicting pain upon others – quite different from the view of Elijah and Elisha, who saw beneficence in their assaults on rival priests. Epicurus believed that the avoidance of pain for oneself and for others should take precedence over the pursuit of pleasure. He believed that by applying self-control as one pursued pleasure one could avoid the painful consequences that can accompany such pursuits. He believed that pleasure should be adjusted to equilibrium in one's body and mind, that an excessive devotion to the gratification of appetites produced misery rather than happiness and should therefore be avoided.

In addition to believing in possessions, Epicurus and his followers differed from the Cynics in their belief in community. Epicurus was political insofar as he saw that it was in the best interest of society that people carry out agreements that promote fellowship. This implied a contractual form of government. But Epicurus and his followers did not advocate group action for social change. They saw political struggle as creating a distress that should be avoided. They advocated civic tranquility and a search for peace of mind. They advocated living unnoticed, abstaining from public life and from making enemies, the kind of approach to politics that suited living under authoritarian rule, an approach that suited those who lived comfortably and enjoyed tending their rose gardens.

Unlike the Cynics, the Epicureans were interested in theories of knowledge – epistemology – and they believed that knowledge about the nature of things helped one discover the best way to live. In their disputes with other philosophers, Epicureans questioned various methods of arriving at truth. They recognized that Aristotle's logic was limited by its use of redundancies, and in place of Aristotle's logic they advocated a search for truth through a process of confirmation and disconfirmation. For example, when a person far away whom you think you might know comes closer and closer, you confirm or reject that it is he – which is what scientists were to do as microscopes and telescopes advanced their ability to perceive.

Epicureanism, like agnosticism and atheism in modern times, appealed to that minority of people who preferred cold rationality to comforting beliefs in divine intervention and everlasting life. But Epicureanism also appealed to those who claimed to believe in God. Epicureanism was to be the avowed philosophy of Thomas Jefferson, who must have found Epicureanism compatible with the Deism popular in his day, which also placed God outside of human affairs. Jefferson was to describe Epicureanism as the most rational philosophical system of the ancients. And his Epicureanism was to find expression in his contribution to the American Declaration of Independence, in its phrase "pursuit of happiness."

The Stoics – Precursors to Christianity

The Stoics clung to the traditional view of godly intervention in human affairs. They believed in a god that was a supreme being and a divine fire, from which came all that exists in heaven and earth, a god called by many names: Zeus, Providence, Nature. They sought to explain various gods as being one god. They attempted to explain the myths of various religions as allegories representing universal truths – despite these myths having been invented without the use of abstract symbolism.

The founder of Stoicism was Zeno, who was seven years younger than Epicurus. On a business trip from his native Cyprus, Zeno arrived in Athens at the age of twenty-two, ten years after the death of Alexander, and there he became involved in philosophical debates and stayed. Zeno was influenced by the dissatisfactions expressed by Cynics, but rather than seeking withdrawal he dreamed of change. In the place of separate, independent states he dreamed of one great nation under a set of divine laws that everyone consented to, a nation in which all were bound together by love. He embraced the notion of brotherhood of man that came with Alexander's attempt to unite a great variety of people into a single empire. He believed that God was the father to all and that all men were therefore brothers. In his belief in a society held together by love, Zeno borrowed from Plato's and Aristotle's teachings that the universe was in essence a manifestation of godly reason and that all men had a soul – a divine spark – that eventually returned to divine eternity.

Like Plato and Aristotle, Zeno and his followers advocated reason and harmony. Ethics was central to Zeno's philosophy, and central to his ethics was his belief that people had to choose between God's purpose and error. He believed that rulers and humble alike should be the servants of God's plan. And seeing life as planned by God, Stoics believed in facing all circumstances with resignation. They believed that one should accept and compose oneself for whatever came one's way – as would Christian martyrs.

At the heart of Zeno's philosophy was a phrase to be heard among Christians: "Thy will be done." They believed that God worked in mysterious ways, that humanity was able to see only a tiny portion of God's plan. They explained the existence of evil within this master plan as God exercising people for virtue – as if God were conspiring with evil rather than evil and virtue being separate, as believed by the Zoroastrians.

Addressing the question of will, Zeno and his fellow Stoics stated that freedom came not from the power to choose, it came from the power to imagine. They saw freedom as a state of mind. An individual, they believed, could be free whatever his circumstances, including imprisonment, if he contemplated God. For the Stoics, poverty and slavery affected only the body, and what affected only the body was a matter of lesser importance than that of attitude. The poorest slave, they held, could be a king in his own soul.

Some Stoics actively opposed slavery, and some opposed the power of the wealthy, while others were advisors to kings and saw monarchs as noble servants and as a part of the Divine Plan. Most Stoics believed that the violence that would be involved in overthrowing existing institutions would be worse than existing injustices, and some of them believed that society would improve if people would only obey their rulers. And, in keeping with their belief in the brotherhood of man, some favored change through reason and agreement – as if conflicting interests and conflicting views could be overcome by education or collective revelation.

Believing in people serving God's master plan, Zeno and the Stoics rejected the claim of Epicureans that one's purpose in life should be to seek happiness. They rejected the Epicurean belief that the search for happiness was a basic human drive. The Stoics claimed that humanity's basic drive was survival – as if even the most miserable people would not want more than mere survival.

The Stoics believed that self-discipline was the starting point of virtue and necessary in their contemplation of God. As had Plato, the Stoics saw reason as godly. And, like other philosophers before them, they saw passion as detrimental to reason and as ungodly. In seeing God as great, the Stoics believed that people exercised virtue by freeing themselves from conceit, by adhering to a humility that would better open them to follow what God had destined for them. This included being indifferent to worldly success, rank or status – as advocated by the Cynics.

Believing in reason, the Stoics drew from Aristotle and studied his logic. They saw logic as a means of arriving at fundamental truths and as a means of defending their views against rivals such as the Epicureans. They devised a formal logic of their own which, like Aristotle's, took them from evident facts to the certainty of the existence of their god, Zeus.

Like Plato, the Stoics tended to be utopian. Borrowing a title from Plato, Zeno in his own book entitled *The Republic* described his own utopia: a world state of people joined voluntarily under a common, divine law, free from sexual jealousy and family rivalries. In his utopia there would be no need for courts of law, and love and sharing would make money unnecessary. Zeno's utopia, like Plato's, would always remain just utopia – while in the coming centuries Zeno's Stoicism would spread. Like Buddhism it would provide its adherents with some comfort, but it would do little in alleviating the disharmonies in the world that were responsible for humanity's miseries.

The Skeptics

Already in the 200s BC, variety in ideas had become a well-established part of civilization, and now among the Hellenized, where freedom to speak ideas was great, one more school of philosophy was bound to emerge. This was Skepticism.

The founder of Skepticism was Pyrrhon, who, while campaigning as a soldier with Alexander, became familiar with Zoroastrian priests in Persia and Hindu ascetics in India. Having come into contact with a great variety of conflicting beliefs, he was aware of humanity's substantial capacity for erroneous thought, and he saw contrary belief as a source of trouble in the world. While in his thirties, Pyrrhon established himself as a teacher in the city of Elis, in the northwest of Peloponnesia. Nothing is known of any writing he may have left, but he is known to have taught that equally valid arguments can be made on both sides of any question. He taught that there is no way to be absolutely sure which of any alternative points of view is correct and therefore that it is best to draw no conclusions about the nature of things. Consequently, he believed, one should live according to one's circumstances, desires and however the world appears to oneself. He believed that what mattered was living well and living unperturbed.

The imperturbability that Pyrrhon believed in he failed to gain for himself. He made a lot of money teaching his doctrine of Skepticism, and rather than being content to see others take up his cause he spent much time attacking a philosopher named Arcesilaus, whom he believed had copied his ideas and was endangering his source of wealth.*

Some who followed Pyrrhon in championing Skepticism did so by examining and exposing inconsistencies and contradictions within various beliefs. They examined the logic of Aristotle and the Stoics and concluded that people could not deduce their way to certain truths from self-evident premises. They also examined materialism, and like Plato, Hindus and others they concluded that the senses were unreliable and an invalid source of knowledge.

Like others in their age, Pyrrhon and other Skeptics saw knowledge as absolute: that an idea was either wholly true or not true at all. They failed to grasp that knowledge of any subject consisted of a mix of generalizations and specifics sometimes ably and sometimes less ably

---

* Arcesilaus revived Plato's academy and left it devoted to Skepticism and the refutation of Stoicism.

connected into one idea. They failed to see that people could grasp realities partially while being in partial error. They failed to grasp the validity of knowledge as approximation: that some ideas are more accurate than others. Pyrrhon and the Skeptics had not yet achieved a scientific point of view, in other words that it was useful to choose between rival hypotheses and that hypotheses should be based on verifiable generalizations drawn from sense perceptions.

The skeptics rejected conclusions but not judgements. Judgements had to be made in finding how to live well or right. They were left with judgements based on intuition, guess or faith. Skepticism became the philosophy of some priests and some others who found justification for believing in their god or gods as insurance against damnation.

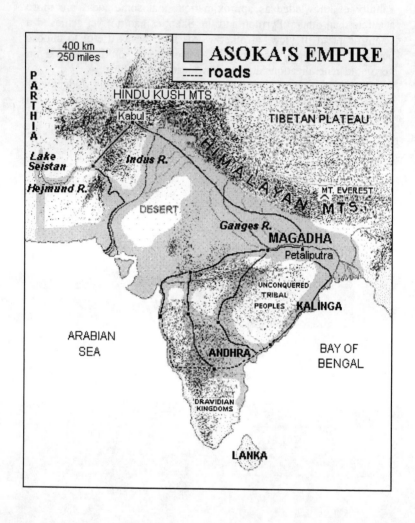

400 km
250 miles

☐ ASOKA'S EMPIRE
---- roads

PARTHIA

HINDU KUSH MTS
Kabul

TIBETAN PLATEAU

Lake
Seistan

Indus R.

HIMALAYAN

Hejmund R.

DESERT

MT. EVEREST
MTS.

Ganges R.

MAGADHA

Petaliputra

UNCONQUERED
TRIBAL
PEOPLES

KALINGA

ARABIAN
SEA

ANDHRA

BAY OF
BENGAL

DRAVIDIAN
KINGDOMS

LANKA

CHAPTER 13

EMPIRE, FRAGMENTATION
AND SALVATION IN INDIA

CHANDRAGUPTA – EMPEROR AND MARTYR

Shortly after the passing of Alexander, India's first great empire arose, ruled by Chandragupta Maurya. According to legend, Chandragupta Maurya was the son of a herdsman, and when he was a young man he met Alexander the Great. Days later, according to legend, Chandragupta was awakened by a lion gently licking his body – an omen that he would become royalty.

Chandragupta is described in legend as following the advice of his adoptive father, Kautilya, a Hindu priest (a Brahmin), also described as a materialist, and as gathering a following among soldiers and the public. Kautilya is said to have been Chandragupta's counselor and advisor and to have kept Chandragupta's youthful impulses in check. He is said to have been learned in medicine, Hellenism and Zoroastrianism. And it is said that he guided Chandragupta in a bloody war that began two years after Alexander left India and culminated with Chandragupta overthrowing the Nanda dynasty that had been ruling the state of Magadha.

Kautilya became Chandragupta's Prime Minister and the genius behind the throne. Legend describes Kautilya as the author of a book entitled *Arthasastra*, which some have compared with Machiavelli's book, *The Prince*. The book *Arthasastra* appears to have been written during the time of Chandragupta but with writings added centuries later. *Arthasastra* means science of property and material success, and in the book this success includes political and diplomatic strategy aimed at uniting India. It has a flavor to it similar to the Legalism that rivaled Confucianism and Taoism in China. The book advises a king to control his subjects, especially his ministers, and the Brahmins, wealthy merchants and his beautiful women. And to help in this, according to the author, the king should employ an army of various artful persons as spies who keep watch at all levels of society. *Arthasastra* advises a king to be energetic, ever wakeful, to make himself accessible to his subjects, and to guard against six enemies: anger, greed, lust, exuberance, hauteur and vanity. But foremost is the book's advocacy of military expansion. In *Arthasastra* it is claimed that aggrandizement is human nature, that a power superior in strength to another power should launch a war against that power, and that war keeps a nation's blood circulation regular.

After Chandragupta's acquisition of Magadha, Kautilya was aware that in northwestern India were tribal republics and monarchies that had been weakened by war against Alexander. Moreover, Alexander had demonstrated that a disciplined and strong force could conquer the region. And it appeared that an India united by a great conqueror was the best defense against a recurring foreign intrusion. Chandragupta, in accordance with the views of Kautilya, sent an army of infantry, cavalry, many chariots and elephants into northwestern India, extending his rule there and beyond, into the Hindu Kush. The first Seleucid king, Seleucus I, attempted to recover lands taken by Chandragupta. But in 305, Chandragupta turned back Seleucus' drive. Seleucus was forced to settle with Chandragupta. Chandragupta held onto his conquests, and then he conquered northward from Magadha, into the Himalayas and the whole of northern India.

Life in and around Chandragupta's Capital

Chandragupta's capital was Pataliputra, a city nine by two miles surrounded by walls of timber, 570 towers, a moat 900 feet wide and thirty feet deep, and drawbridges. The city's streets were laid in geometric order, along which were three-story wooden buildings, marketplaces, inns and gambling houses. And the city had a track for horse racing.

Pataliputra's wealthy had homes that were sumptuously furnished, well-carpeted, surrounded by gardens, fruit trees and ornamental ponds. They enjoyed festivals, gambling, horsemanship, hunting game, archery, and swimming competitions. They attended private parties on each other's terraces. Pataliputra's leisure and merchant classes were literate. The city had a university for its elite, where Brahmins taught grammar, rhetoric, economics and politics. Pataliputra also had trade guilds and schools that taught crafts and technical subjects.

An ambassador to Chandragupta, Megasthenes, from the Hellenistic west, described people under Chandragupta as skilled in the arts, as having an abundance of nourishing food, with thievery among them rare and people in general leaving their houses and property unguarded. He described them as uncomplicated in their manners, never drinking wine except at sacrifices, and as seldom going to court against one another.

According to Megasthenes, some upper class women received an education and some were recognized as accomplished in the arts, but ordinarily Brahmins did not wish to educate their wives, believing that knowledge and learning were not for females. Megasthenes described a deterioration in the position of women accompanied by a rise in honor bestowed upon courtesans. He described a drop in the age at which females could be married, hopefully guaranteeing a husband a virgin. A man of twenty-four might marry a girl as young as eight, or a man of thirty might marry a twelve-year-old – marriages that were to be consummated when the bride matured.

Chandragupta as Autocrat, Sensualist and Martyr
All land around the capital belonged to Chandragupta, which he "rented" for a quarter or sometimes a half of what was produced on them. And he made those peasants working his fields exempt from service in his military or other obligations to the state.

Chandragupta divided his empire into districts, which were administered by his closest relatives and most trusted generals. Civil servants ruled various departments such as trade, taxation, mining, roads, and irrigation canals. Chandragupta's government held trade monopolies, which it preserved by discouraging competition from private traders. His government owned slaughter-houses, gambling halls, mines, shipbuilding operations, armament factories and spinning and weaving operations. His government oversaw the standardization of weights, measures and coinage. It controlled prices and trade, including trade in liquor and prostitution. It obliged drinking places to have couches, scents, water and other amenities, and drinking places and "public houses" were not to be near each other.

Chandragupta feared revenge and assassins. Against these possibilities he had a network of secret spies. He expected authorities in various districts to know all comings and goings. People who were considered dangerous to his rule might disappear without a trace. He had food tasters to avoid being poisoned, and somewhat like Shih Huang-ti he never slept in the same bed two nights in succession.

Eliciting confessions by torture remained a normal method in police work. Punishment depended on class: Brahmin's were not tortured, but upon conviction of a crime they could be branded, exiled or sent to work in the mines. The low incidence of thievery described by Megasthenes might have been a result of the punishment for such a crime. Common people were executed for theft, damaging property of the king, breaking into someone's home, evading taxes, injuring an artisan working for the state and many other crimes. Failure to meet a contract could lead to a fine if not a harsher penalty, as could incompetence in various forms of work, from washing clothes to treating the ill.

Toward the end of his more than twenty years of rule, Chandragupta surrounded himself with dancing-girls and courtesans –

women who also worked as housemaids, cooks, garland makers, shampooers and who fanned Chandragupta or held an umbrella for him. He seldom left his palace, except for an occasional festival. But he remained a man of religion and concerned about his subjects. According to legend he was converted to Jainism by a sage who had predicted a twelve-year drought. With the drought came famine in place of the affluence described by Megasthenes. In an effort to combat the drought, Chandragupta, in 301 BC, abdicated in favor of his favorite son, Bindusara, and he withdrew with the Jainist sage to a religious retreat in India's southwest. There, according to legend, while appealing to God for relief from the drought, he fasted to death.

THE BUDDHIST EMPEROR, ASOKA

Chandragupta's son, Bindusara, ruled for twenty-five years. He warred occasionally, reinforcing his authority within India, and he acquired the title "Slayer of Enemies." Then in 273, he was succeeded by his son Asoka, who in his first eight years of rule did what was expected of him: he looked after the affairs of state and extended Maurya rule where he could. Around 260 Asoka fought great battles and imposed his rule on people southward along the eastern coast of India – an area called Kalinga.

The sufferings created by the war disturbed Asoka. He found relief in Buddhism and became an emperor at least a little different in values from his father, grandfather and others. He became a Buddhist lay member and went on a 256-day pilgrimage to Buddhist holy places in northern India. Buddhism benefited from an association with state power that Hinduism had enjoyed – and that Christianity would enjoy under Constantine the Great.

Like Jeroboam and other devout kings, Asoka was no revolutionary. Rather than India changing fundamentally, Buddhism was in the process of changing. In the years to come, Asoka mixed his Buddhism with material concerns that served the Buddha's original desire to see suffering among people mitigated: Asoka dug wells, constructed irrigation canals and roads, built rest houses along roads, built hospitals, planted public gardens and grew medicinal herbs. But Asoka kept his empire much the same as it had been before his conversion, just as the Roman Empire remained fundamentally unchanged after Constantine converted to Christianity. Asoka maintained his army, and he maintained the secret police and network of spies that he had inherited as a part of his extensive and powerful bureaucracy. He kept his hold over Kalinga, and he did not allow the thousands of people abducted from Kalinga to return there. He announced his intention to "look kindly" upon all his subjects, as was common among kings, and he offered the people of Kalinga a victor's conciliation, erecting a monument in Kalinga which read:

All men are my children, and I, the king, forgive
what can be forgiven.

Asoka converted his foreign policy from expansionism to that of coexistence and peace with his neighbors – which fit with his interest in consolidating the empire he already had and avoiding the additional conquests that would make more, or too much, to administer. In keeping with his Buddhism he announced that he was determined to ensure the safety, peace of mind and happiness of all "animate beings" in his realm. He announced that he would now strive only for conquest in matters of the human spirit and the spread of "right conduct" among people. And he warned other powers that he was not only compassionate but also powerful.

Asoka's wish for peace was not disturbed by famines or natural disasters that might have brought rebellion. Nor did his rule suffer from the onslaught of any great migration. And during his reign, no neighboring kings tried to take some of his territory – perhaps because these kings were accustomed to fearing the Mauryan monarchs and thinking them strong.

The resulting peace helped extend economic prosperity. Asoka relaxed the harsher laws of his grandfather, Chandragupta. He gave up the kingly pastime of hunting game, and in its place he went on religious pilgrimages. He began supporting philanthropies. He proselytized for Buddhism, advocating non-violence, vegetarianism, charity and tenderness to all living things.

Asoka had edicts cut into rocks and pillars at strategic locations throughout his empire, edicts to communicate to passers-by the way of compassion, edicts such as "listen to your father and mother," and "be generous with your friends and relatives." In his edicts he spread hope in the survival of the soul after death and in good behavior leading to heavenly salvation. And in keeping with the change that was taking place in Buddhism, in at least one of his edicts Asoka described Siddhartha Gautama not merely as the teacher that Siddhartha had thought of himself but as "the Lord Buddha."

Asoka called upon his subjects to desist from eating meat and attending illicit and immoral meetings. He ordered his local agents of various ranks, including governors, to tour their jurisdictions regularly to witness that rules of right conduct were being followed. He commanded the public to recite his edicts on certain days of the year. Some of his subjects may have been annoyed over having to recite his edicts. And such compulsions never had or would change people permanently. But for the time being Asoka's patronage of Buddhism gave it more respect, and in his empire Buddhism spread, more people became vegetarian, and perhaps there was some increase in compassion toward others.

Asoka avoided jealousy toward Buddhism's rivals in India: the Hindus and Jains. There would be no murder of priests of rival religions. Asoka worshiped no jealous god. Instead, he pleaded for tolerance. Mindful of the close ties between Buddhism and Hinduism he claimed that the Brahmin's creed deserved respect, and he included Brahmins among his officials.

Not all Brahmins returned Asoka's kindness. They were displeased with Asoka's campaign against their sacrificial slaughtering of living creatures. But Asoka's opposition to such sacrifices did please many among India's peasantry, whose flocks had long been plundered by local rulers seeking animals for their sacrifices.

Asoka's Failure

Asoka sent missionaries to the kingdoms of southern India, to parts of Kashmir in the northwest, to Persia, Egypt and Greece, but as Christians were to learn, old habits are not easily broken. Buddhism outside his kingdom took root only on the island of Lanka. Work, taxation, class relations, government bureaucracy and village politics changed little, all of which – like Asoka's authority – were considered the natural order of things. Whether the prostitution that had existed during Chandragupta's time ended is unknown – probably not. In religion, old habits continued among Buddhists, as they looked to Brahmins to conduct those rites associated with births, marriages and deaths. Conflicts remained outside and within Buddhism, and Asoka attempted to resolve differences among the Buddhists – as the Christian emperor Constantine would among the Christians – but conflicts among the Buddhists would remain and grow.

In the final years of his reign, Asoka withdrew from public life, and in 232 BC – after thirty-seven years of rule – he died. His heirs saw his empire begin to split apart, including the breaking away of Kalinga. Why this happened is unknown. Buddhist writings suggest that decay had come before Asoka's death. Perhaps more decay came with the happenstance of few competent heirs. Some scholars attribute the decline of the Mauryan dynasty to economic pressures: revenues from taxing agriculture and trade that were inadequate in maintaining the large military and army of bureaucrats that the Mauryas maintained. Trade had not yet developed enough yet to bring much in revenues from taxation. Perhaps palace politics reduced the ability of Asoka's heirs to govern and encouraged local rulers to assert their independence. Perhaps Asoka's heirs inherited from Asoka a pacifism that played a role in this. Whatever the cause or causes, Asoka's heirs allowed regions to reassert their independence, and the Mauryan empire came to an end – as empires do.

A NOT-SO-DARK AGE

In 185 BC, the rule of the Mauryan family ended when an army commander-in-chief, Pushyamitra, murdered the last Mauryan kings during a parade of his troops. Pushyamitra's rise to power has been described, perhaps inaccurately, as a reaction by Brahmins to the Buddhism of the Mauryan family. Nevertheless, the influence of state power on religion continued, with Pushyamitra supporting orthodox Brahminism and appointing Brahmins to state offices. And, with Pushyamitra's rule, animal sacrifices returned that had been prohibited under Asoka and his heirs. Other matters outlawed by the Maurya's also returned, including musical festivals and dances.

Then came another phenomenon common across the span of ancient civilization: invasion, or the migration of warrior peoples. Perhaps the collapse of the Mauryan Empire signaled to outsiders that India was now vulnerable – much as division after Alexander's death had brought an assault by Celts. The first of the great invasions began roughly two years after Pushyamitra took power. The king of Bactria, Demetrius, followed the footsteps of Alexander through the Kyber Pass and extended his power into northwest India, where he began what was to become a series of wars between the Greeks and Indians.

The Greeks brought with them a better coin, improving the coins used in India, which contributed to regional and inter-regional trade. They brought with them ideas in astronomy, architecture and art that spread through India, and with the new art came new depictions of Hindu gods and a new image of the Buddha that would spread through the East.

Between the years 155 and 130, a Greek named Menander (known to Indians as Milinda) ruled in India's northwest. Menander tried to extend his rule eastward. He captured Mathurak, and he threatened Magadha's capital, Pataliputra. But he failed and returned to his kingdom in the northwest.

Like Asoka, Menander converted to Buddhism. This conversion may have facilitated the passage of Buddhist ideas west to Bactria and from Bactria farther west. The Greeks in India helped in spreading ideas westward. The road between Bactria and India had become a bridge to and from the west. To India's northwest came ideas from Zoroastrianism, and in India arose the belief in a savior who at the end of time would lead the forces of light and goodness in a final victory against of the forces of darkness and evil.

MAHAYANA BUDDHISM: SAINTS AND A LOVING GOD

Buddhism had developed within a predominately Hindu society, and just as Christianity was to cling to a Judaism in its religion, Buddhism clung to the Hindu beliefs in karma and in reincarnations: in one's past life determining the karma of his next life. Buddhists believed that life was an illusion and that there was no permanent existence of self in the form of the soul. The aim of an individual, according to Buddhist doctrine, should be to escape from oneself, from the cycles of births and pains of the material world. Buddhists believed that one could do this by living an exemplary moral life, by becoming pure in word, deed and thought and by respecting one's superiors and animal life, and that one then became blended with the universal spirit and acquired nirvana.

A difference remained between the religious habits of Buddhist monks and Buddhist laymen. A tightly organized fraternity of ordained monks, the Sangha, dominated the Buddhist movement. They had opted for a strict morality: remaining celibate, ingesting no intoxicants, not eating after noon, not singing or dancing or attending any entertainments, not using scents or wearing ornaments, not sleeping on a raised bed, and not receiving money or valuable objects. Buddhist laymen, on the other hand, were allowed a more normal life, including having children, eating dinner, enjoying entertainments and intoxicants – a partaking in those appetites that Siddhartha had thought one should not persist in.

Invasions by the Scythians and Kushans

The great changes in Buddhism came when India and other parts of Asia were still in turmoil. Pushed upon by a Chinese resurgence, those whom the Chinese called Hsiung-nu pushed on the Indo-European speaking tribes whom the Chinese called the Yüeh Chih – a people also called Kushans. The Kushans pushed on Scythians, who left their homeland in Central Asia and pushed into an area southeast of the Caspian Sea, an area to become known as Parthia. From 141 to 128 BC the Scythians were able to push into lush, agricultural Bactria, against the Greeks there, who were weakened by warfare. Soon thereafter, the Kushans invaded Bactria. Then around 50 BC, the Parthian empire, which had replaced the Seleucids in Persia, invaded northwestern India. And also invading India were the Scythians from Bactria.

The last of the Greek kings in India, Hermaeus, tried unsuccessfully to defend his rule from these attacks. In northwestern India, Greeks, Scythians and Parthians fought into the first century AD, and the Scythians extended their rule into north-central India and south along

India's western coast, to the Gulf of Cambay. They ended Greek rule in India but maintained the Indo-Greek culture, some of which they had acquired in Bactria. In India, the Scythians became known as Sakas. Like other conquerors, the Sakas kept the local royalty as their subordinates. And Saka rulers became known as Satraps or Viceroys. In AD 48, another tribe of Kushans left Bactria and pushed into northwest India. A Kushan named Kanishka. He became the second successor to the Kushan king who first invaded India. And he became the greatest of the Kushan kings. He expanded his rule from Bactria to the center of the Ganges valley and south along the Indus River to the Arabian Sea, absorbing lesser kings and making them sub-rulers, as did the Sakas.

Kanishka and the New Buddhism
Like tribal people before them – and like the Germans who would invade the Roman Empire – Kanishka and the Kushans adopted aspects of the civilization they had conquered. Kanishka's empire prospered economically, and it is said that Kanishka's wealth and wisdom attracted to his court merchants, artists, poets and musicians from all over Asia. Like other barbarian rules, Kanishka found Buddhism more accessible than Hinduism. Kanishka converted to Buddhism, becoming another Buddhist king who believed in empire. Buddhists would rank Kanishka with Asoka and Menander as a great king. And Kanishka would remain attached to warfare for the remainder of his life, his Buddhism like the Christianity of some people centuries later: an ideal separate from the struggle over power.

Kanishka was eclectic in religion. He appears also to have been inclined toward the Persian cult of Mithras, to Zoroastrianism, and to have also worshiped Greek and Hindu deities. Buddhism dominated in the cities of Kanishka's empire and in Kanishka's court, while through his empire Brahmin families maintained orthodox Hinduism.

Kanishka is said to have converted to Buddhism a Brahmin who was attempting to reconcile Hinduism and Buddhism. Kanishka convened a Buddhist council in Kashmir – much as the emperor Constantine would call a council of Christians – in hope of resolving conflict in religious ideas. It is said that this council gave rise to a new Buddhism: Mahayana Buddhism, Mahayana meaning the Great Vehicle. The Buddhism elsewhere in India, mainly in the southern half, was called Hinayana, the Little Vehicle.

The Buddha becomes a Compassionate and Loving Savior
Change, or drift, in religious belief, had taken place at least since the Sumarians, and now Buddhism was becoming a full-blown religion. The Buddha, Siddhartha Gautama, was elevated from a teacher to a

god, possessing, as gods do, miraculous powers. Siddhartha as God was said to be the latest of a series of his incarnations.

Mahayana Buddhists became concerned with grasping even for nirvana, and they advocated acquiring nirvana by focusing on an infinitesimal present that was too brief to grasp. They believed that this allowed one freedom from self-concern, which, in turn, allowed one's energies to flow outward in a love for all beings.

Hinayanists believed that one could be saved only by oneself, while the Mahayanists believed that a devotee could help save others through love. It became a Mahayanist ideal to emulate the Buddha and to sacrifice one's own effort at accomplishing nirvana in order to help others find their nirvana. Following this ideal, the most devoted among the Mahayanists acquired what was seen as saintliness. Among the Mahayanists arose many saints, called Bodhisattvas, whom the faithful worshiped. It was at Kanishka's capital, Peshawar, that the first images of the Buddha and the Bodhisattvas have been found, marking a difference between Hinayana and Mahayana Buddhism.

While the Hinayanists continued to advocate salvation by achieving fulfillment of the rigid demands listed by Siddhartha, the Mahayanists permitted people salvation merely by their efforts, however lax – a matter of the heart as would develop within Christianity. This had a greater appeal than offered by the Hinayanists, and it was Mahayana Buddhism that became the most popular, spreading to hundreds of millions in Asia.

TRADE, PROSPERITY AND CULTURAL DIFFUSIONS

The centuries of invasions were dark times for much of India, but not so for its more remote southern part peopled by Dravidians. Unlike other Dark Ages, during the period of invasions into India much of its roads and ports were maintained. Southern India benefited from expanded economic and cultural contacts with the world outside India and an expanded trade with West Asia and the Roman Empire. The south had become the most prosperous part of India. Leaving southern ports were ivory, onyx, cotton goods, silks, pepper and other spices, and from the Roman empire the Indians imported tin, lead, antimony and wine.

Indian ships sailed south to Lanka and then east to Southeast Asian ports, where Indian merchants sold cotton cloth, ivory, brass wear, monkeys, parrots and elephants to Chinese merchants, who transported their goods by sea to China. From these Southeast Asian ports, Indian merchants acquired spices that they traded elsewhere. Trade between India and China passed also across Central Asia by camel caravan, across what would become known as the great northern silk route,

China sending musk, raw and woven silk, tung oil and amber westward into India.

The Indians established colonies along their trade routes. They created settlements along the coastal lands of Burma, settled in what is now Cambodia and in the Malay peninsula and spread their culture among the Malays, Mons and Khmers, in places such as Bali, Sumatra, Java and the Philippines. Their colonies became states, ruled by descendants of the original Indian settlers. In Cambodia, Hindu settlers blended with the Khmers.

The increase in India's trade led to the rise of bankers and financiers among the Indians, and these men of wealth gave support to monarchies and landlords short on cash. Families in banking and commerce extended their enterprises into as many urban centers as they could, in India and abroad. The increase in trade brought a rise in intellectual activity among the Indians – as it had among the Greeks. Science and the arts flourished, stimulated too by ideas that the Greeks brought from Bactria, while Indian ideas went abroad with its trade.

HINDUISM, SCRIPTURE AND KRISHNA

Like Buddhism, Hinduism was also changing. From the tribal, outdoor, fire and blood sacrifices that had been a part of the Vedic worship of the Aryan invaders more than a thousand years before, Hinduism was shifting to a worship of gods residing within temples and gods concerned with individuals. Elaborate rituals in beautiful temples had a popular appeal. Vishnu, an old Vedic sun god, was transformed into a savior of humankind, and Vishnu gradually emerged as one of Hinduism's two great gods.

The other great god was Shiva. Shiva had origins among non-Aryans. Shiva was hailed in several myths as the supreme god, a god of death and destruction, a god who was thought to dwell in the Himalayas. He was a god of many attributes: a god of art, especially dancing, a god represented as having five heads and three eyes, and one of his representations was half-male and half-female, signifying a unity within creation.

Hinduism was becoming a religion that warmed the heart rather than stimulated the mind as the Upanishads had. But a new, formal logic had also made its way into Hindu writings, with only minor variations in method from Aristotle's syllogism. And there was the rise of yoga in Hinduism, developed by a man named Patanjali, who built upon references in Hindu scriptures to physical and sensual means of attaining independence of one's soul. Patanjali believed that knowledge was not enough in working toward salvation. The exercises he developed wee intended to help attain a concentration of mind and self-control. These exercises included religious observance, regulation of breathing and restraint of the senses.

The Mahabharata and a New Holy Book, the Bhagavad Gita

New contributions to Hinduism's epic poem, the Mahabharata gave greater focus to the gods Vishnu and Shiva. A story incorporated into the Mahabharata became known as the Bhagavad Gita (the Lord's Song), composed perhaps as early as 200 BC. The Bhagavad Gita became Hinduism's most popular scriptures and into modern times it would be read by many for daily reference – a work that Mahatma Ghandi would describe as an infallible guide to conduct.

In the Bhagavad Gita, Vishnu acquired a new incarnation: Krishna. Krishna was originally a non-Aryan god in northwestern India. In the old Mahabharata he was a secondary hero, a god who had appeared as a human. But in the Bhagavad Gita, Krishna became the Supreme Deity in human form. The Bhagavad Gita is an account of the origins, course and aftermath of a great war between royalty. It is the human imagination at work justifying matters as they are – rather than inspiring social change. In the Bhagavad Gita a dialogue takes place between a prince, Arjuna, and the charioteer alongside him as the two ride into battle at the head of Arjuna's army. The charioteer is really Krishna in disguise. Arjuna sees that his opponents ahead of him are his relatives. He drops his bow and announces that he will not give the signal to begin the battle. He asks whether power is so important that he should fight his own kinsmen, and he states that the pain of killing his kinsmen would be too much, that it would be better to die than to kill just for power and its glory. Krishna is like the god of war of former times: Indira. He gives Arjuna a formula for accepting deaths in war, a Hindu version close to the claim that those who die in battle will go to paradise. He tells Arjuna that bodies are not really people, that people are souls and that when the body is killed the soul lives on, that the soul is never born and never dies. Krishna reminds Arjuna that he is a warrior and that to turn from battle is to reject his karma, in other words his duty or place in life. He states that Arjuna should make war because it is his destiny to do so. He states that it is best to fulfill one's destiny with complete detachment because detachment leads to liberation and allows one to see the irrelevance of one's work.

To give weight to his argument, Krishna reveals to Arjuna that he is not just his charioteer, that he is the god Krishna – a claim that Arjuna accepts. Some readers of the Bhagavad Gita interpret this to mean that Arjuna does not need to step from his chariot to find God and that humanity does not need to search for the divine: that God is with a person and for a person.

Krishna became the most loved of the Hindu gods, a god viewed as a teacher, a personal god much like Yahweh, a god who not only believed in war but a god of love who gave those who worshiped Him a gift of grace. A loving god could be found here and there in the old Vedic hymns of the Aryans, but this new focus on a loving god and the satisfaction it brought to the people of India was a challenge to Hindu priests, for it offered salvation without the need for ritual sacrifices. It also offered salvation without withdrawal from the world of material possessions – without becoming a monk.

In the Bhagavad Gita (1:41), Krishna says:

> Give me your heart. Love me and worship me
> always. Bow to me only, and you will find me. This
> I promise.

Arjuna expresses his support for family values, and he is a defender of tradition. He complains of lawlessness corrupting women, and when women are corrupted, he says, a mixing of caste ensues. The Gita (2.22) describes Hinduism's belief in reincarnation:

> As leaving aside worn-out garments, man takes new
> ones. So, leaving aside a worn-out body, to a new
> one goes the soul.

According to Krishna, as expressed in the Bhagavad Gita (2:37), one could accumulate possessions and not lose blessedness so long as one remained indifferent about success and failure. According to Krishna, if one died in battle he went to heaven, or if he conquered he would "enjoy the earth." So, according to Krishna, one should go into battle with "a firm resolve." Attitude was of the utmost importance. "Let not the fruits of action be thy motive, nor be thy attachment to inaction." In attitude, seek a religious refuge. One can attain salvation so long as one restrains one's passions in whatever one does. One should be fearless, steadfast generous and patient. One should be compassionate toward other creatures. One should be without greed, hypocrisy, arrogance, overweening pride, wrath or harshness in speech. One should "study the Holy Word, austerities and uprightness." (16:1-2)

Hinduism and the Law Code of Manu

The uncertainties of the era of invasions may have inspired a new book of laws, called the Law Code of Manu. These were books that combined Hinduism with law – a sacred law much as law was among the Jews and Zoroastrians – and laws that kings and commoners alike were thought obliged to follow. The Law Code of Manu drew from the Vedas, where Manu was described as the world's first king, as the father of the human race and the one who had received the god

Brahma's plans. Manu, according to the Vedas, was the first who described the universe and the first who sacrificed to the gods. And the Law Code of Manu included Manu's story about the creation of the universe, and it attempted to bring together, in the form of maxims, Brahma's commandments regarding ritual, custom, caste and other institutions.

The Law Code of Manu expressed the values of India's Hindu priesthood. It claimed that authoritarian rule and class privilege were best for everyone. Among Manu's commandments, expressed in the Law Code, was that one should give no pain to any creature. Such behavior would, according to the Law Code, allow one to gather spiritual merit that stayed with one after death. Another commandment held that in childhood a female had to be subject to the authority of her father. When she married she was to be under the authority of her husband. She was to remain cheerful, clever in the management of her household affairs, careful in using utensils, economical in spending, and to do nothing independent of male authority. As a widow or in old age she was to be under the authority of her sons. According to the Law Code, if a female sought to separate herself from her father, husband or son, she made her family, or her father's family, contemptible.

The Law Code of Manu declared that rulers were obliged to be considerate in judging and punishing their subjects. It claimed that punishment kept the world in order, that punishment properly applied kept all people happy, but applied without consideration it destroyed everything. The Law Code of Manu claimed that without punishment, inferior people would "take the place" of their superiors, that the castes would be corrupted by intermixture, that "all barriers" would fall and "men would rage against each other."

CHAPTER 14

THE RISE AND FALL OF HAN CHINA

NEW MONARCHS, CONFUCIANISM AND PROSPERITY

In 202 BC, Liu Chi, the former policemen from a peasant family, defeated his brilliant but more ruthless rival, Hsiang Yu, and became emperor. He began his rule having to fight numerous small wars, some against former allies, and he faced a powerful confederation of tribes on China's northern border, led by a Turkish speaking people called the Hsiung-nu. The Hsiung-nu were nomadic herders with supplementary agriculture and some slaves. And, like other nomads, they had a warrior tradition. The Hsiung-nu had been making raids into China. Liu Chi believed that he was not yet strong enough to defeat the Hsiung-nu, so he made a treaty with them, bribing them with food and clothing in exchange for their agreeing to no longer raid, and he gave the king of the Hsiung-nu a woman in marriage whom he claimed was a Chinese princess.

Liu Chi began building a new capital, at Ch'ang-an, which was to become the grandest city in the world. And more than had the early Chou kings, Liu Chi wanted centralized management of his empire, and for this he needed an army of civil servants. But first he needed to consolidate his power. Believing that the Ch'in dynasty had fallen because of division within the Ch'in family, Liu Chi installed his brothers, uncles and cousins as regional princes. He sought the continued support of local warlords that had been a part of his coalition in winning power, and those who had served him as generals or as chancellors he made lesser nobles. Where local Ch'in administrators proved loyal to him, he left them in place. Noble families that were friendly to him he restored to their lands. Liu Chi was obviously no revolutionary, but he sought the support too of the peasantry. He lowered their taxes and the taxes of others. In places he protected peasants from former nobles trying to retrieve lands they had lost. He made amends to the peasants by not working them as hard as had Shih Huang-ti. And the peasants believed that because he had been one of them that he would continue to govern in their interest.

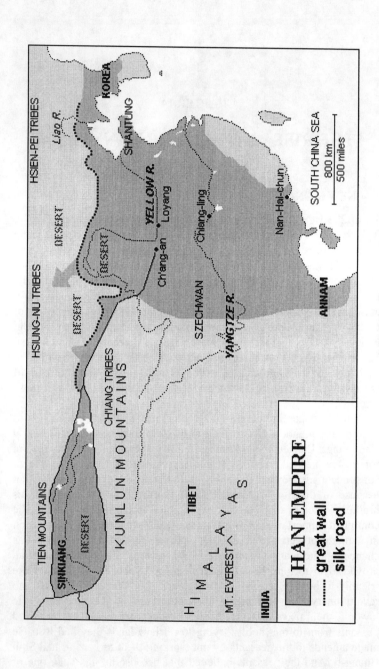

The Beginning of China's Gentry

Drawing on his peasant origins, Liu Chi demonstrated his disdain for scholars by urinating into the hat of a court scholar, but in trying to govern he came to see benefit in scholars, and he made peace with them. Many scholars were Confucianists, and, although Liu Chi continued outlawing denunciations of the Legalist point of view, he began treating the Confucianists with a greater tolerance.

At first, Liu Chi and his aides tried filling civil service positions with their civil war comrades, but they discovered this was unsatisfactory. Having little faith in the innate abilities of soldiers as administrators, Liu Chi rejected military men for these positions. Previous dynasties had placed successful merchants in the civil service, but with Liu Chi and his aides having peasant backgrounds they distrusted merchants. Instead, they turned to men from wealthy landowning families – mostly families that had grown wealthy in recent generations. This gave rise to a new class in China: the gentry – a class different from the nobility. This new class was to send its most able sons into careers in government and let its less able sons run the farm. And with a new interest in opportune marriages, the new class began according its females more respect.

Emperor Wen Begins a New Age

Liu Chi died in 195 BC, at the age of sixty, and in death he was given the honorific name Kao-tzu. Power remained with Liu Chi's wife, the Dowager Empress Lu. She removed members of Liu Chi's family from positions of power, and she replaced them with members of the family from which she came. After five years of rule she died, and Liu Chi's relatives moved to take back their families dominance, and they killed every member of her side of the family. A son of Liu Chi born to a concubine remained as the logical heir. Carrying the Liu family name, he continued what became known as the Han dynasty, and he became known as Wen-ti: Emperor Wen.

As luck would have it, Wen-ti was a wise ruler, known for his regard for the interests of his subjects. When famines occurred, Wen-ti provided famine relief. He provided pensions for the aged. He freed many slaves, and he abolished China's cruelest methods of executions. During his reign, economics was seriously studied, and Wen-ti gave China's economy serious consideration. He helped the economy by reducing restrictions on copper mining, by spending money frugally and by reducing taxes that had been imposed on the peasantry. Under Wen-ti, China enjoyed internal peace and unprecedented prosperity. With this came magnificent art that would dazzle people in modern times. And with prosperity, the population of China began to increase. People pushed into and began clearing and cultivating new lands.

The gentry benefited from the economic boom, and many of them moved to the city. The gentry wished to be thought of as gentlemen like the nobles. And, with time to read, they became interested in the old scholarship. With a renaissance in scholarship, attempts were made to recreate the books that had been burned. Attracted to Confucianism's respect for authority and proper behavior, gentry intellectuals became predominately Confucian. Wen-ti promoted Confucian scholars to his government's highest offices. He became the first emperor openly to adopt Confucian teachings – Confucius' dream of such an emperor finally having been realized.

WU-TI (EMPEROR WU) AND DECLINE

In 156 BC the son of Wen-ti, Ching-ti, succeeded his father as emperor. He ruled sixteen years and attempted to extend his family's domination over noble families. War between these nobles and Ching-ti ended in a compromise: the nobles keeping some of their privileges and powers but no longer permitted to appoint ministers for their fiefs.

Around the year 140 BC, Ching-ti was succeeded by his son, Wu-ti, a bright and spirited sixteen-year-old who enjoyed risking his life hunting big game. Wu-ti began his rule with a hands-off approach to commerce and economic opportunity, which allowed the growth of the economy's private sector. He kept his civil servants under tight control and treated the smallest protest from any quarter as disloyalty. He ended Ching-ti's compromise with the nobility, warred against China's most defiant princes, and at the local level he gave more authority to his representatives and civil servants.

Wu-ti altered laws of inheritance. Instead of a family's land remaining under the eldest son, he gave all the sons of a family an equal share of their father's land, which did much to break great estates into smaller units. And in 138, Wu-ti sent China's first known explorer, Chang Ch'ien, to Parthia, west of Bactria, to establish relations with the Kushan (or Yüeh-chih) people.

Confucianism Becomes Official

In the twentieth year of his rule, Wu-ti made Confucianism China's official political philosophy. Confucianists continued to compete with the philosophy of Legalism, but Confucian ideology became dominant in the civil service. It was knowledge of Confucian ideology that was tested in examinations for China's 130,000 or so civil service positions. These were examinations that were concerned with the content of ancient writings and rules of social grace rather than technical expertise. Theoretically, these examinations were open to all citizens, but in reality they remained open only to those with adequate respectability, which excluded artisans and merchants and others of lesser status than the gentry – a matter that most Confucianists apparently tolerated.

On the job training for civil servants occurred in bureaucracies at the local level, and merit, dear to the hearts of Confucianists, became a consideration during and after a civil servant's apprenticeship. A young man who proved himself able as a clerk might become a manager, and, after proving himself as a manager, he might move up to a position as an advisor in attendance at the emperor's palace or in a high position in the government at a regional capital.

Opening to the West and Wars of Expansion

With economic prosperity, China was better able to wage war. Wu-ti believed he was strong enough that he could stop the payments to the Hsiung-nu begun by Liu Chi. He was concerned that the Hsiung-nu might send an army into northern China's sparsely populated steppe lands or that they might ally themselves with the Tibetans, and he wished to make trade routes for commerce with Central Asia secure from assault. So Wu-ti launched what became a series of campaigns, led by his generals but which earned for Wu-ti recognition as a ruler of vigor and bravery. Wu-ti's drive against the Hsiung-nu was costly in manpower but it pushed most of the Hsiung-nu back from China's northern frontier. Perhaps as many as two million Chinese migrated into the newly conquered territory, Wu-ti creating colonies of soldiers and civilians there. Those Hsiung-nu who stayed behind were converted to farming, drafted for construction labor and employed as farm laborers. And some of them were drafted into China's army, their families forced to remain where they were as hostages to assure against treason.

The war against the Hsiung-nu stimulated exploration farther westward. After a thirteen year absence and ten years of captivity by the Hsiung-nu, the explorer Ch'ang Ch'ien returned to Wu-ti's court and brought with him the first reliable description of Central Asia. Ch'ang Ch'ien and assistants were ordered back to Central Asia, and they gathered information about India and Persia and explored the fertile farmlands of Bactria. Their explorations, and China's success against the Hsiung-nu, brought an exchange of envoys between China and states to the west, and it opened for the Chinese the 4000-mile trade route to the west that would become known as the Silk Road. China began importing a superior breed of horses, and it began growing alfalfa and grapes. Wu-ti learned more about the origins of goods that China was importing, and for added revenues he demanded that neighboring states pay his empire to sell their goods to the Chinese, and he began military campaigns to force them to do so.

Meanwhile, Wu-ti sent his armies north and south. For the sake of control in the northeast, Wu-ti, in 108 BC, conquered an iron-age kingdom in northern Korea equal in many ways to the Chinese states before the unification of China in 221 BC, and a kingdom with many Chinese refugees from the previous century. Wu-ti's armies conquered areas in southern China – including the port town of Nan Hai-chun – areas that had been lost during the civil war that brought the Han dynasty to power. Chinese migrants followed the army. Then, with heavy fighting, Wu-ti's army conquered northern Vietnam, an area the Chinese called Annam, or "pacified south." Here too Chinese migrants came, and some would settle near the Annamite Mountains in the center of Vietnam. The Chinese introduced Vietnam to the water buffalo, metal plows and other bronze tools, and they brought to Annam their written language. The Chinese began to change the people of Annam from slash and burn cultivators into a more settled life. They divided Annam into administrative areas, each area responsible for collecting taxes and supplying soldiers for the central government. But Chinese rule in Annam would remain tenuous, its jungles and mountains giving sanctuary to Vietnamese who would conduct continuous raids and skirmishes against the Chinese.

Economic Decline and Over-population

Wu-ti's wars of expansion and his maintenance of large armies of occupation were a burden on China's economy. The costs of these expansions more than offset the benefits from the increase in trade that followed his conquests. Rather than benefiting China's economic vitality, imports contributed more to the pleasures of the wealthy. The economy suffered too from the influence of government officials who were still Legalist in philosophy. They were hostile to private tradesmen and led a drive for government control of the economy. Under their influence the government levied a new tax on boats and carts and took over trade in China's two most profitable industries: salt and iron.

The same move to larger landholdings that changed Roman agriculture was changing Chinese agriculture, except that in China the number of people in the countryside had been growing. With the size of lands of the wealthy increasing and the population of common peasants also increasing, a shortage of land appeared. Gentry bureaucrats sought a hedge against insecurity by buying land and often taking advantage of their office to do so, and often they were able to make their lands tax exempt. Ordinary peasants were paying a larger share in taxes, resulting in their greater need to borrow money – at usurious rates. Farming productivity declined, and many peasants were evicted or forced to leave farming, making more land available for the gentry.

Some who left farming resorted to banditry, and, to survive, some sold their children into slavery.

Conscription into the military and conscription for labor added to the peasantry's discontent. China's most renowned Confucian scholar, Tung Chung-shu, was morally outraged, and he led the way in expressing concern about the social decay. He complained about the vast extent of lands owned by the wealthy while the poor had no spot to plant their two feet. He complained of those who tilled the land of others having to give fifty percent of the harvests they produced as rent. Tung Chung-shu recognized the disadvantage faced by those farmers who could not afford to buy iron tools, who had to till with wood and to weed with their hands, and he complained that common peasants had to sell their crops when prices were low and then had to borrow money at high interest rates in the spring in order to start sowing. He complained about the thousands put to death every year for banditry.

Tung Chung-shu proposed to Wu-ti a remedy for the economic crisis: reduce the taxes on the poor; reduce the unpaid labor that peasants had to perform for the state; abolish the government's monopoly on salt and iron; and improve the distribution of farm lands by limiting the amount of land that any one family could own. Nothing came of Tung Chung-shu's suggestions. Wu-ti wanted peasants to prosper, but he was often deceived by the gentry bureaucrats who governed at the local level. The drive for reform was being led by a Confucianist, but the Confucianist gentry were not about to rally against their own economic interests. Wu-ti's only substantial response to the economic decline was to levy higher taxes on the wealthy and to send spies around to catch attempts at tax evasion. He did not wish to offend wealthy landowners with land redistribution, believing that he needed their cooperation to finance his military campaigns. Then came another problem, one endemic to monarchy: succession.

Wu-ti's Successors

In 91 BC, as Wu-ti's fifty-four year reign neared its end, around the capital violent warfare erupted over who would succeed Wu-ti. On one side was Wu-ti's empress and his heir apparent, and on the other was the family of one of Wu-ti's mistresses. The two families came close to destroying each other. Then, just before Wu-ti's death, a compromise heir was chosen: an eight-year-old from neither family, who was to be known as Chao-ti. And he was put under the regency of Huo Kuang, a former general.

Huo Kuang sponsored a conference to inquire into the grievances of his emperor's subjects. Invited to the conference were government officials of the Legalist school and worthy representatives of Confucianism. The Legalists argued for maintaining the status quo.

They complained that their economic policies helped maintain China's defenses against the continued hostility of the Hsiung-nu. They complained that the government was protecting the people from the exploitation of traders, and they argued in favor of the government's policy of western expansion on the grounds that it brought the empire horses, camels, fruits and various imported luxuries, such as furs, rugs and precious stones. The Confucianists, on the other hand, saw the grievances of the people as a moral issue. They argued that the Chinese had no business in Central Asia and that China should stay within its borders and live in peace with its neighbors. The Confucianists argued that trade was not a proper activity of government, that government should not compete with private tradesmen, and they complained that the imported goods spoken of by the Legalists found their way into only the houses of the rich.

The debate resulted in little change. Under Huo Kuang's regency, taxes were reduced and peace negotiations began with the Hsiung-nu chieftains. After Chao-ti died in 74 BC, conflict erupted again at the palace. After Chao-ti's successor had been emperor only twenty-seven days Huo Kuang replaced him with someone he thought he could control: Hsuan-ti. Six years later, Huo Kuang died peaceably, but palace rivalry led to charges of treason against his wife, son and many of his relatives and family associates, and they were executed.

With Huo Kuang dead, Hsuan-ti exercised more power. He moved to reduce the corruption that had crept into government, and he tried to provide help in eliminating the suffering among the peasants. But his moves were ineffective and changes under his twenty-eight years of rule were unsubstantial. His heir and son, Yuan-ti, who succeeded him in 48 BC at the age of twenty-seven, was the first of a string of more dysfunctional monarchs. Yuan-ti was a timid intellectual who spent much time with concubines – too numerous for him to know all of them personally. Here, finally, contributing to China's decline, was the kind of moral decay which some would believe instrumental in the decline of states. Yuan-ti left power in the hands of his eunuch secretaries and members of his mother's family. Matters did not improve under Yuan-ti's son, Ch'eng-ti, who became emperor in 32 BC, at nineteen. Ch'eng-ti also had little enthusiasm for governing and was most concerned with personal pleasures, including visiting houses of prostitution at night. During Ch'eng-ti's twenty-seven-year reign he sought guidance from omens, and to satisfy the jealousy of one of his women, he murdered two of his sons born to other women. Then in 6 BC, Ch'eng-ti was succeeded by Ngai-ti, who lived in the company of homosexual boys, one of whom he appointed commander-in-chief of his armies.

TAOIST RESURGENCE AND
CONFUCIANISM'S YIN AND YANG

Again – as with the Greeks and the period of warring states during the Chou dynasty – difficult times in China did not hinder intellectual vitality. Decline had brought disappointment, and with disappointment had come a resurgence in Taoism, while Legalist philosophy continued its hold among some, especially in government. During all of this, Confucianists tried to counter rival schools of thought by forming a more comprehensive view of humanity and the universe. Tung Chung-shu moved Confucianism away from the ethical teachings of Confucius and Mencius and absorbed a variety of ideas beyond the Confucian doctrine of previous centuries. He borrowed from the concept of Yin and Yang – an idea that had arisen to explain all change, physical and social.

Yin and Yang were seen as the two basic opposing forces in the world. Yin was female: the moon, cold, water, earth, nourishment, sustenance, recessives, autumn, winter, et cetera. Yang was male: the sun, fire, heat, heaven, creation, dominance, spring and summer. It was believed that if Yin reached an extreme it was transformed into Yang, and if Yang reached an extreme it was transformed into Yin – a view of the world that would not be found useful when science, with its interest in particulars, flowered centuries later.

Confucianists and others who believed in Yin and Yang believed the world consisted of five basic elements: fire, earth, metal, water and wood. They further tried to make the universe comprehensible by adopting ideas from the Book of Changes, or I-Ching, which saw the universe affected by the arrangement of numbers. They believed that by studying combinations from eight trigrams and sixty-four hexagrams one could uncover any possible activity in nature, similar to Pythagoras' laborious conclusion that the number four contained the divinity of justice.

To round out their view of the universe, Confucianists adopted an explanation of the origins of the universe. They believed that in the beginning all was vague and amorphous, that this was followed by emptiness, and that emptiness produced the universe. They believed that what was clear and light in weight drifted upward to become heaven, and that what was turbid and heavy solidified and became earth. The combined essences of heaven and earth, they believed, became Yin and Yang and a great oneness. They described both heaven and earth as flat and the sun as revolving around the earth.

THE MARTYRDOM OF WANG MANG

With the decline in quality of monarchs following the reign of Wu-ti, some Confucian scholars declared that the Han dynasty had lost its Mandate from Heaven, and this became widely believed. In AD 6 – twelve years after Ngai-ti had ascended the throne – a two-year-old became emperor. Domination of the palace came under the family of the widow of Yuan-ti, and she made her nephew, Wang Mang, regent over the two-year-old Han emperor.

Wang Mang was a Confucianist, and many Confucianists looked to him with hope that China would be ruled again with moral purpose, and some of them looked to him to found a new dynasty. Encouraged by widespread support among Confucianists, in AD 9 Wang Mang declared himself emperor, ending rule by the Han dynasty, and Wang began a struggle for recognition of his legitimacy. He hoped to win support from common people by reforms. Like the Yawhist priesthood during the reign of king Josiah, Wang announced the discovery of some written matter: books written by Confucius, supposedly discovered when Confucius' house had been torn down more than two hundred years before. Not surprisingly, the discovered works of Confucius contained declarations supporting the very kind of reform that Wang sought. Wang defended his policies by quoting from them. He announced that his rule was a restoration of the rule of the early Chou kings – an age that the Confucian scholar Mencius had claimed was supposed to return every five hundred years. It was about one thousand years since the beginning of Chou rule and five hundred years since Confucius had been at the peak of his powers.

Wang claimed that he was doing what the first Chou king or Confucius would have done if they had been in his position. Following what was portrayed as Confucian scripture, he decreed a return to the golden times when every man had his measure of land to till, land that in principle belonged to the state. He declared that a family of less than eight that had more than fifteen acres was obligated to distribute the excess amount of land to the landless. He moved to reduce the tax burden on poor peasants, and he devised a plan to have state banks lend money to whomever needed it at an interest of ten percent a year, in contrast to the thirty percent that was the going rate by private lenders. In order to stabilize the price of grain, he made plans for state granary storage, hoping that this would discourage the wealthy from hoarding grain and profiting from price fluctuations. Wang also delegated a body of officials to regulate the economy and to fix prices every three months, and he decreed that critics of his plan would be drafted into the military.

Wang believed that his subjects would obey his decrees, but again gentry-bureaucrats gave less importance to their Confucianism than to their wealth. They and other owners of good-sized lands failed to cooperate in implementing Wang's reforms. Without newspapers or television, local people remained unaware of the reforms. Wealthy merchants that Wang Mang's government employed to pursue implementation of the reforms succumbed to bribery and proved interested mainly in enriching themselves. Wang needed a broad base of support and a force willing to move against those violating his land reform laws, but he remained timid and wedded to a pacifistic idealism. Rather than Wang mobilizing a peasant army to enforce his reforms, an army of peasants led by the landed rich would mobilize against him.

Famine and Civil War

In AD 11, the Yellow River broke its banks, creating floods from Shantung north to where the river empties into the sea. There had been the usual failure to store enough grain for hard times, and famine followed. And in the year 14 came cannibalism. Believing that his reform program was a failure, Wang withdrew it. But already armed resistance to his rule had arisen. By AD 10, in Shantung province, near the mouth of the Yellow River, Wang faced an organized movement of disciplined bands of peasants called the Red Eyebrows, led by a former brigand chief. In the neighboring province just to the north, another rebellion arose, and rebellion spread across China. In some places, rebel peasants were led by landlords. Some rebel groupings described Wang rule as illegitimate. One of the rebel groupings placed at its head a Han prince: Liu Hsiu.

The failed reforms and peasant unrest were too much for Wang. Peasant armies murdered and plundered, and peasants marched to the capital killing officials as they went. The troops that Wang sent against the rebel armies joined the rebels or went on sprees of plundering, taking what little food they could find. The basic goodness of people that Confucianists had believed in appeared to have vanished. In the year AD 23, a rebel army invaded and burned China's great capital, Ch'ang-an. Its soldiers found Wang Mang in his throne-room reciting from his collection of Confucian writings, and Wang Mang was silenced by a soldier cutting off his head.

DEATH STARTS ANOTHER CYCLE

In the five years following the death of Wang Mang, millions died fighting as rival factions vied with each other for power. The most successful of the rival factions was led by the Han prince (of the royal Lui family): Liu Hsiu. He was popular among his troops and those with whom he had contacts – while in West Asia a man called Jesus was also courting popularity. Liu Hsiu surrounded himself with educated men. His army was the only force that did not loot when capturing towns. His ability to lead helped him win hearts and minds. Liu Hsiu took control of the ruined capital, Ch'ang-an. He proclaimed himself emperor, restoring the Han dynasty, and he moved the capital to Loyang, which he also controlled. For eleven more years he had to combat rivals. He absorbed some bands of Red Eyebrow rebels into his army, and his army killed other Red Eyebrows in great numbers.

What reforms had failed to accomplish had been accomplished by violence: so many had died in the upheaval that land had become available to anyone who wanted it, and with many money lenders among the dead, many more peasants had become free of debt. Liu Hsiu helped the economy by lowering taxes, as much as he thought possible: to a tenth or thirteenth of one's harvest or profits. During his reign of thirty-two years, Liu Hsiu attempted improvements by promoting scholarship and by curtailing the influence of eunuchs and some others around the royal family. He defended China's western and northern borders by launching successful military campaigns on these frontiers, pushing back the Hsiung-nu, enabling him to take control of Sinkiang – now the extreme northwest of China. Also, he tightened China's grip on the area around the Liao River and northern Korea, and he was able to expand control over all that had been China. The restored Han dynasty appeared to have the won back the Mandate of Heaven.

Prosperity Returns

Liu Hsiu was succeeded by his son Ming-ti, who reigned seventeen years, while China's economy continued to recover. Ming-ti supported growth in education, and he lectured on history in the capital's new imperial university – a lecture attended by many thousands. Ming-ti was succeeded by Chang-ti, who ruled from AD 76 to 88, then by Ho-ti, who ruled from 88 to 106. Despite Ho-ti's mediocrity, China continued to enjoy a rising prosperity. The university at Loyang grew to 240 buildings and 30,000 students. The university at Loyang grew to 240 buildings and 30,000 students. China's trade reached a new height. Silk from China was becoming familiar to people as far as the Roman Empire – which was then in its golden age. And in return, China was receiving glass, jade, horses, precious stones, tortoise shell, and fabrics.

With China's prosperity came another attempt at expansion westward. A commander of a Chinese army, Pan Ch'ao, led an army of sixty thousand unopposed to the eastern shores the Caspian Sea. He wished to send an envoy to make contact with the Romans, but the Parthians feared an alliance between Rome and China. Parthians discouraged Pan Ch'ao with tales of danger, and Pan Ch'ao turned back.

PARADISE AND A NEW TAOISM

Having become more aware of the world beyond China, the Chinese heard more rumors about wonderful places. Taoists – who still rejected Chinese civilization as corrupt and who idealized nature and wilderness – helped spread descriptions of far-away places of godliness and paradise. Stories of places of wilderness and paradise appeared at the emperor's court, brought by those who came to demonstrate their magic and to entertain, and the court sometimes responded by sponsoring expeditions to find the wonderful places.

One such story described a paradise along the coast in China's extreme northeast. There the climate was milder than it was inland, and it was said that in this paradise were no diseases, that people never became sick, and that people governed themselves. It was said that in this paradise the young and old had equal rights, that people were gentle and had no quarrels, and that there was no conflict between humanity and nature, that people received what food they needed from a beneficent river, that drinking the water from this river restored one's body to the tautness and smoothness of youth, and that people lived a hundred years.

Another paradise was rumored to be in the distant mountains of Tibet. There, it was said, a Queen mother ruled, and that she had many servants. In this paradise, cool breezes were said to blow – as opposed to the humidity and heat of the summers in China's inland plains and valleys. It was said that in this paradise were hanging gardens, with ponds and a beautiful lake, that waters there gave one immortality, that one could climb a mountain peak and become a spirit with the power to control the wind and rain, and that one could climb another nearby peak and ascend to heaven.

The New Taoism

The Taoists maintained their belief in harmony and solace in nature. They believed in a destiny beyond the disturbing flux of mundane, material life, and they maintained their belief in emotional austerity. A devout Taoist, for example, could still explain his not weeping for his wife who had just died by saying that if he wept for her he would be demonstrating his lack of understanding of destiny. Taoism maintained its paradoxical statements, and it maintained anti-Confucianist notions such as one's sons and daughters are not one's possessions.

Taoism was open to a variety of new ideas, including the search for longevity or eternal life by adopting proper attitude and physical techniques. Some Taoists tried to extend the search for salvation in nature by focusing on the bliss of sexual intercourse, and some Taoist holy men searched for everlasting life though ritual exercises or dietary regimes – an experiment of sorts that failed each time that one of them died. But, rather than accept that everlasting life could not be achieved by a special program, their followers explained the failures as the result of circumstances other than human mortality.

Taoism absorbed practices of magic that had existed in some of China's rural communities. Some Taoists adopted gods that were ridiculed by the gentry and the Confucianists. Contrary to Taoism's original belief in inaction, some Taoists actively sought converts, and some Taoists became activists for social change and initiated political programs. Taoism had had no clearly defined orthodoxy or tightly knit organization of priests, but here and there organizations led by priests were developing. Taoist priests gathered around them followers who believed they had joined an exclusive group that was concerned with their well-being. This annoyed China's authorities – Confucianists and gentry-bureaucrats – who feared that unapproved religious cults might develop into a focal point of opposition to their authority.

Among the Taoist cults was one led by Chang-ling (or Chang Taoling) in the province of Szechwan – mostly basin surrounded by great mountains. He wandered through the countryside promising those who would publicly confess their sins that he would deliver them from illness and misfortune. He claimed that illness was the product of sinful thoughts. Using charms and spells he acquired a reputation as a healer, and the public confessions that he offered gave peasants the feeling that they were cleansing themselves of sin and joining a community.

In the year 142, Chang-ling founded a Taoist church, called "The Way of the Great Masters," moving Taoism from a prescribed way of life to an organized religion. His church also became known as "The Way of the Five Pecks of Rice," five pecks of rice being the annual dues that church members had to pay. Chang-ling promised his followers a long life and immortality, and he earned the gratitude of local common folk by getting done what the emperor's authorities had failed to do: repair roads and bridges, store grain and distribute bread to the starving. Chang-ling had created a local government that rivaled the authority of the emperor.

The Sacred Books of Peace

An idea surfaced in China that society was moving, perhaps willy-nilly, to a heavenly state of peace and equality, and coupled with this idea was the notion of public service, which had survived from the times and influence of Mo-tzu. The concept of public service appeared in a book called *The Spring and Autumn of Lu Pu-wei*, which some consider the start of China's socialist tradition.

These were books that emperors and gentry considered subversive – books that the authorities sometimes confiscated. Some of these books proclaimed that peace and equality would be established by heavenly intervention. These books called on people to be devout and to seek salvation. Some people accepted these books as sacred writings, and at least one book was believed to have been written by someone sent from Heaven. Some of the books were called Books of Higher Peace and contained numerous denunciations of the greed and egoism of emperors, and they announced that society was for common people. One such book, known as the *T'ai-p'ing-ching*, looked forward to arms and armor being thrown away and people living forever in peace.

DECLINE AND FALL OF THE HAN DYNASTY

By the 100s AD, China had caught up with Europe and West Asia in science and technology, and in some ways in these areas it surpassed the West and Near East. Paper was then coming into use in China. China had a water clock with an accuracy that Europeans would be without for more than a thousand years. China had a lunar calendar that would be consulted into the twentieth century. It had a seismograph that had been invented in AD 132 – eight feet wide and made of bronze. The Chinese observed sun spots, which would not be observed by Europeans until Galileo, and they charted 11,520 stars and measured the elliptical orbit of the moon. China had a machine that sowed seeds, and a machine for husking grain. It had water pumps, and unlike Roman civilization it had a wheel barrow. The Chinese had horse collars and stirrups. They were improving their use of herbal medicines and learning more about human anatomy and the diagnosis of physical disorders. They were using minor surgery and acupuncture, and they were aware of the significance of a good diet.

But life continued to be hard for China's common people – its peasants. Too much was still taken from them in taxes. They still had to labor once a month for the emperor. Punishments were still harsh (a poor peasant could be executed for using the central part of a highway, which was reserved for the emperor). And not enough grain was being stored for disasters.

China's prosperity had risen under Ho-ti (85–106), and the court of Ho-ti had become in size and luxury equal to the courts of previous Han emperors. At Ho-ti's court, hundreds of wives and concubines were accompanied by a great many eunuchs to guard them. Under Ho-ti, eunuchs and family consorts had acquired greater influence, with eunuchs having the ear of the emperor.

All Han emperors since AD 76 had become emperors when adolescents, two of them as young as two, and most began their rule with their mothers serving as regents. These women held the title Empress Dowager and remained isolated and dependent upon men – usually their male relatives. As an emperor grew into adulthood, if he rejected his mother's relatives as advisors he usually turned to the only other males with which he had contact – the eunuchs – and he appointed them to high positions as a counter to his mother's influence.

During the reign of Shun-ti (AD 126 to 144), rumor spread among China's peasants that the Han emperors had again lost the Mandate of Heaven. Here and there, peasant rebellions reappeared. The largest among them was a movement called the Yellow Turbans, led by a Taoist faith-healer who fought for improved living conditions. A government army chased the Yellow Turbans into the mountains, and found volumes of what was called the "Book of Pure Guidance of the Great Peace," which described developments in the context of Yin and Yang and used the language of sorcerers. The government forces confiscated the books and denounced its contents as lies.

During the reign of Huan-ti (147 to 167) political decline continued. In 159 the dowager empress died, and eunuchs around Huan-ti, sensing opportunity, moved to eliminate rival political influence by arranging the extermination of the empress's entire clan. Huan-ti became dependent on the eunuchs. He delegated powers to them. They filled governmental positions with their kinsmen. And every official or general they appointed was obliged to pay them in gold.

Huan-ti was succeeded by a twelve-year-old: Ling-ti. This came with the first major clash between the eunuchs and Confucianist gentry-bureaucrats, who favored law and order and good government and looked upon the eunuchs as uneducated. The eunuchs and gentry-bureaucrats clashed over an incident in which a Taoist magician prophesied that a general clemency was forthcoming. The magician had his son murder someone to demonstrate his confidence in the prophecy. The magician's son was a henchman of the eunuchs, and the eunuchs stayed the magician's execution. The governor of the province executed the son anyway. The eunuchs accused the governor of violating an imperial decree and of conspiring with students and scholars to form an illegal alliance against the government. The eunuchs obtained a decree from Ling-ti ordering arrests of the student who had been demonstrating and who had been attempting to deliver petitions to the emperor. And soon, many students died in prison.

In the provinces, respect for the authority of the emperor continued to decline. Local magistrates and governors were losing their authority to local men of wealth who often had influence through bribery with eunuchs at the emperor's court. These local men of wealth were in the habit of hiring armed ruffians to look after their interests. And, with the blessings of anti-gentry eunuchs at court, the generals who were commanding troops in China's provinces were growing more independent.

Another Violent Rising

A Taoist named Chang Chueh, who called himself "The Good Doctor of Great Wisdom," had been moving about in the countryside, offering magical healing, treating all ailments with water and words and calling his method of healing the "Way of the Highest Peace." News of his cures spread. Chang Chueh was also speaking of the Han rulers as having lost the Mandate of Heaven, and he proclaimed their immanent fall. Within ten years, his movement grew to hundreds of thousands – mostly in eastern China but also in the south and west. His movement was divided into districts, with each district led by a "deputy doctor." And his movement also became identified with the Yellow Turbans.

The year of decision for Chang Chueh's movement was 184. The fifth day of the third moon was fixed as the time for a general uprising in Loyang and surrounding regions. But word of these plans was heard at the imperial court, and the authorities picked up local leaders of the revolt and quickly executed them. Chang Chueh changed his plans and called for an immediate uprising, calling on his followers to burn down official residences and to loot the towns. Hundreds of thousands of Yellow Turbans from all corners of the empire began robbing, killing and heading toward the capital.

The eunuchs and intellectual bureaucrats in Loyang forgot their differences in their mutual fear and opposition to the Yellow Turbans. Government forces erected fortifications around Loyang, and governors of provinces were authorized to organize their own armies to combat the rebels. In the countryside, wealthy landowners organized armies to defend themselves. But town after town fell to the Yellow Turbans, with governors and local magistrates fleeing before them to avoid being sacrificed to the rebel's heavenly god. Amid the chaos, the Hsiung-nu began making raids against the Chinese again, and Korean tribal warriors on horseback from the hills drove away Chinese rule.

The militarily disorganized Yellow Turbans were no match against the imperial armies. The Yellow Turbans had been led to believe that their gods had elected them as a force for good, that they were invulnerable and that they did not even need weapons – a view not conducive to an efficient military operation. The Taoist mysticism that had been a part of the movement's creation had become a part of its destruction. Within a year, Chang Chueh's rebellion was defeated. For five years sporadic revolts continued. Eight of China's provinces were devastated. The Yellow Turbans were cut down one after the other by a remorseless military opposition, and peasant supporters of the Yellow Turbans joined a long line of disappointed common people and returned to the business of surviving through work. And they found consolation in their hope of a coming paradise in the world beyond.

The End of Rule from Loyang

Ling-ti died in 188 or 189, at the age of thirty-three, after having ruled nominally for twenty-one years. Real power in China was now divided among military governors, or warlords. A military general, popular figure and half-brother of the Dowager Empress tried to assert leadership at the palace. He schemed against the court eunuchs and their supporters, and to combat them he invited to the capital general Tung Cho and his army from the north, along the Great Wall. But before Tung Cho arrived, murderous fighting broke out at the palace. A eunuch murdered the half-brother, and the half-brother's allies burned the palace and killed every eunuch they could find – or anyone who looked like a eunuch because of lack of beard. More than two thousand eunuchs and supposed eunuchs died.

Soon after, Tung Cho arrived in the capital and put to death the reigning emperor, Shao-ti, and the Empress Dowager. He chose a nine year-old prince as emperor and as a front for his rule. He swaggered about the court with his sword, behaving in a debauched and bestial manner while his troops, many of whom were Hsiung-nu, ran about the capital, pillaging and murdering as they pleased.

Then Tung Cho went off to do battle with rival generals. The child emperor, Hsien-ti, and his following, including an ineffective palace militia, burned Loyang and began a trek westward to Ch'ang-an, taking more than a million civilians with them, most of whom are said to have died of exhaustion and starvation along the way.

Ts'ao Ts'ao and End of the Han

During the war for supremacy among China's generals, Tung Cho's lack of concern for hearts and minds worked against him. His bloodthirstiness and fits of temper alienated his own generals, and in the year 192 they assassinated him and threw his corpse to a mob that hated him.

In AD 196, another general, Ts'ao Ts'ao, found the boy emperor, Hsien-ti. He took control over the boy and declared himself the boy's "imperial minister" and protector of the empire. In the name of Hsien-ti, Ts'ao Ts'ao drafted more men into his army. Ts'ao Ts'ao was a vigorous, bright and able leader – and a poet. His army is said to have numbered as many as a million men. In bloody battles in northern China he defeated warlord after warlord and restored order there. In 208, Ts'ao Ts'ao marched south in an effort to reunify China. The ensuing battle of Chiang-ling, along the Yangtze River, became one of the best known in China's history. In that battle, Ts'ao Ts'ao confronted the allied armies of Liu Pei and Sun Ch'uan, and the alliance defeated him, driving Ts'ao Ts'ao back north.

Liu Pei was a member of the Han royal family, and he was a man with a kindly disposition. He might have united China, but his ally, Sun Ch'uan, broke with him, fearing that if Liu Pei were too successful he would dominate him. Sun Ch'uan conquered Szechwan province, and then he allied himself with Ts'ao Ts'ao, which left three major kingdoms in China: one ruled by Ts'ao Ts'ao, one by Sun Ch'uan and the third by Liu Pei.

The Rise and Fall of an Independent Theocratic State
Meanwhile, along the Yangtze River near Szechwan, a surviving Tao cult had established a theocratic state with its own army. The cult's founder, Chang Lu, traced his teachings back a couple of generations to Chang-ling, the first patriarch of the Taoist church. Like Chang-ling, he performed what were described as miracle healing, and he preached Chang-ling's message of physical and moral well-being, claiming that diseases were punishments for evil deeds and that diseases could be cured by remorse and by ceremonial confessions. Chang Lu established communal, "friendship," meals, and like Chang-ling he established welfare for his community and storage for grain and meat. He encouraged equality. His community offered the travelling homeless a place to stay and a meal. And it offered leniency to criminals.

Another Taoist, Chang Hsiu – no relation to Chang Lu – set up an independent state nearby. Despite their devotion to Taoist ideals, the communities of Chang Lu and Chang Hsiu warred against each other – much as would Christians. And Chang Lu, it is said, killed Chang Hsiu. Soon thereafter, Chang Lu had a more formidable opponent: Ts'ao Ts'ao. Chang Lu surrendered to Ts'ao Ts'ao, who rewarded him with high office and a fiefdom. It is said that Chang Lu died shortly thereafter – in 217. And it came to be legend that twenty-six years after his death he was seen by many witnesses ascending to heaven. The legend held that when his grave was opened in AD 259 his body was found wholly intact, meaning that he had died only in the sense that he had detached from his corpse and had entered paradise.

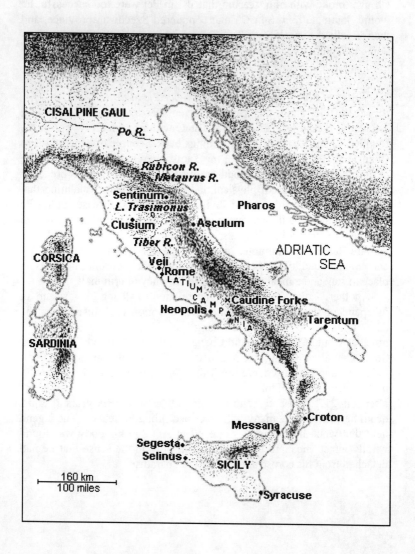

CHAPTER 15

THE RISE OF ROME

FROM LEGEND TO REPUBLIC

Fire awed the early Romans, as it did the Greeks and others. The Romans believed in a goddess of fire called Vesta, and they had a sacred temple of fire tended by four females – the Vestal Virgins – who were selected while they were children and were expected to serve thirty years. During their service they were expected to remain virgins, for the Romans believed that to please the gods, women who were unmarried and not trying to bear children should remain chaste.

A Vestal Virgin was part of the greatest legend among the Romans – the legend about Rome's origins. The legend begins with a Vestal Virgin giving birth to twin boys and claiming that the boys had been fathered miraculously by the god Mars – a god of fertility and later also of war. The Vestal Virgin was the sister of a king. The king believed his sister was lying and that she had violated a sacred law. To put things right with the gods the king had his sister imprisoned, and he had her twins put afloat in a basket on the Tiber River. The two boys, called Romulus and Remus, were expected to drown, but the river receded and the basket carrying the boys came to rest on the river's bank, where a shepherd found them.

Around the time of Jesus Christ, when this legend was still popular among Romans, a Roman historian named Livy tried looking back centuries to determine whether the legend was true. The earliest version that Livy found described the wife of the shepherd who rescued Romulus and Remus. It described her as a she-wolf (a bitch) because of her alleged loose morals. Legends evolve, and by Levy's time the legend held that the boys had been rescued by a real female wolf – a notion that was put into the famous Roman sculpture a wolf nursing the two boys.

According to the legend that Livy studied, Romulus and Remus grew into manhood, and they killed their uncle, the king, in revenge for his having imprisoned their mother and for his having unjustly usurped power from their grandfather. The boys restored their grandfather to the throne, and they founded Rome where they had emerged from the river.

Then Romulus and Remus quarreled – as had Cain and Abel. Romulus killed Remus, and he became Rome's first king. To populate his city, Romulus gathered people from other countries. And, to give his subjects wives, he abducted young unmarried women from a nearby tribe called the Sabines – an incident to be known as "Rape of the Sabine Women." The fathers of the women were outraged, and the Sabines retaliated by attacking the Romans. The abducted Sabine women, now apparently contented wives, intervened in the fighting and brought peace between their husbands and their fathers – a scene that was to be depicted by the famous eighteenth century French painter, David. The legend ends with Romulus, after a long reign, vanishing into a thunderstorm. He had become a god. Then he reappeared, descending from the sky, declaring to those listening that it was the will of heaven that Rome would be the capital of the world, that Romans would cherish the art of war, and that others should realize that they cannot resist the strength of Roman arms.

Rome's Worldly Beginnings

Among the various peoples who migrated southward across the Alps to the warmer climate and rich lands of Italy were Indo-Europeans whose language had evolved into Latin – a language closely related to Celtic. These Latin speaking people settled along fifty miles or so of coastal plains and inland to the mountain range that runs down the Italian peninsula, and they settled among the hills that are now a part of Rome. These were hills whose gentler slopes would support wheat, whose steeper slopes would support olive trees, fruit trees and vineyards. Here, animals could be pastured. And in the marshy land along the coast and farther inland, the Romans drained the stagnant pools of water that they found, making the area more habitable by eliminating malarial mosquitoes.

The legend of Romulus and Remus dated the founding Rome at around 735 BC, but from modern archeology comes evidence that Rome was already a collection of villages around the year 1000. These villages were fifteen miles inland from the sea, along the banks of the then navigable Tiber River. A search of historical records indicates that the Romans were organized around tribal clans. Like other Latins in Italy they tilled small plots of land, pastured cows, pigs and goats and tended flocks of sheep. Like other tribal peoples they had a council of elders, and their chiefs were chosen by clan elders and by the acclamation of their entire people.

Rome under the Etruscans

The Etruscans lived north of the Tiber River, some in cities with paved streets and drainage. They used advanced techniques in mining and agriculture. They borrowed from and traded with cities in Italy that the Greeks had founded. And they traded with central Europe and with others along the coast of North Africa and the Eastern Mediterranean, importing a variety of goods in exchange for the iron and bronze items they made, such as helmets and pails. The Etruscans played music, danced, did acrobatics, and held foot and chariot races. And they were fierce warriors. Various Etruscan kings conquered parts of Italy and held it as empire. And sometime around 600 BC, Etruscan chieftains led an army southward and conquered Rome and areas beyond.

By the time that Etruscans had conquered Rome, the Romans had already been divided between common folk called *plebeians* and aristocrats called *patricians* – modern scholars estimating the patricians to be from ten to five percent of Rome's population. Whether the patricians were descendants of a people who had conquered the Romans before the Etruscans or were Romans who had become an elite is unknown. Most patricians were from the families of successful farmers, but a few were not very wealthy. Like other aristocracies, the patricians based their superiority on their family name, even if the family's success in farming and wealth had declined.

As happened in China and elsewhere, the aristocrats of Rome co-operated with their conquerors while maintaining their higher status and privileges over the *plebeians*. Some patrician families adopted Etruscan names. And patricians held onto priestly positions – which were denied to plebeians.

Rome under the Etruscans resembled a Greek city. Like Greek cities, it had a *senate*: an advisory council of elders who were mainly patricians. Rome's most important temple and meeting place was a building like a Greek acropolis, called the *capitol*. The capitol had a Greek-like public assembly called the *comitia* – where plebeians were a minority and outvoted.

Rome stood at crossroads of major trade routes and was a major center of trade. It had an urban center, approximately one mile wide and four miles long, with paved streets, impressive buildings, and sewers. Under the Etruscans, Roman crafts grew. From the Etruscans the Romans borrowed vase styles and the use of bronze. From the Etruscans they borrowed religious practices, including reading the future by examining the livers of sacrificed animals. From the Etruscans the Romans acquired a twelve-month calendar, and they acquired the use of a personal first name that through Rome was to become the first name and surname commonly used among Europeans. The Romans learned from the Etruscans what Etruscans had learned from the Greeks: the growing of grapes and olives. The Roman alphabet was perhaps an Etruscan adaptation of the Greek alphabet. And from the Etruscans, Rome's aristocracy acquired a familiarity with military organization that included a unit called a *legion*, which warred in phalanx positions like Greek hoplites.

Rome Becomes a Republic

In 509 BC, a group of Roman nobles, who were fed up with their Etruscan king, Tarquin, drove him from Rome and into early retirement. Leading patrician families among the Romans took power and ruled as members of the Senate. Without a king, Rome had become a republic. The Senate, or council of elders, had long been accustomed to watching developments and advising the king at his request, and now the Senate was ready to serve as the supreme organ of government. What the Senate created would develop into a model in some regards for those founding the United States of America.

It was common among the nobility of Greek cities in southern Italy to choose one among them as an executive – a president. And in place of a king, the Senate chose not one but two as executive administrators in order to avoid the unreliability of a single administrator. Each executive was a patrician, and each was called a *consul*. Each was to serve one-year – as among the Greeks – and each was given the power to veto a move by the other.

The selection of the consuls had to be ratified by an assembly of clan leaders (the Comitia Curiata). And, as leaders of the Senate, the consuls decided who would be promoted within the Senate. The consuls could declare an emergency and acquire absolute power for six months. But the consuls' powers were limited in that they could not declare war. War was thought too important to be left to two men. Declaring war would be a prerogative of the Senate. But the consuls would be commanders-in-chief of the military, including the power to have soldiers executed for lack of discipline. And during war, if it was time for elections and both consuls were away on military missions, the Senate could appoint a dictator to preside over the elections.

When there was no war the consuls were occupied with city administration, public finances, and civil and criminal justice. By now, apparently, the crime of murder was no longer dealt with by one's clan but by the state. The consuls could sentence citizens to death, but citizens had the right to appeal such sentences before a special assembly of plebeians.

POLITICAL AND SOCIAL CHANGE

In freeing themselves from Etruscan rule, the Romans lost trade with the Etruscans and with Greek colonies in southern Italy. Imports diminished. Rome's plebeian merchants and craftsmen suffered, and Rome experienced economic depression and grain shortages.

While under Etruscan rule, Rome had been the greatest power among the Latins, and in those times Rome had been resented by the other Latins. Then these Latin neighbors freed themselves from Etruscan rule as had the Romans, and the Latins joined together in a league against Rome. Against Rome they made war over disputed lands, and they made war to free themselves from Rome's hegemony. Troubled by this, Rome abandoned its claim of hegemony in Latium. Rome saw advantage in peace and cooperation, and in 493 Rome joined an alliance with its Latin neighbors as an equal. The alliance treaty held that business contracts between people from different states within the alliance were to be bound by law. And the treaty held that in wars against outsiders, alliance members were to share in commanding armies and in the spoils of war.

The alliance strengthened Rome in the wars that began soon followed. The Etruscans began an attempt to re-impose their rule on the Romans and other Latins. And there were periodic wars across decades against mountain people to the south and central Italy who were increasing in population and attempting to expand. Rome's patricians liked warring, and they tended to be belligerent toward neighboring powers with whom they had no alliance. The patricians were horsemen, and cavalry was their basic fighting unit. Wars gave them prestige and helped them to maintain their claim of leadership over the other Romans. But a development in the art of war was denying the patricians their exclusive right to prestige. The Greeks, Etruscans and now the Romans were using heavily armed infantrymen – men who were commoners. The increased importance of the common man in combat had encouraged democracy in Athens, and now it was increasing the self-confidence of the small-farmer, plebeian soldiers of Rome.

Compromise between Patricians and Plebeians

Economic distress continued among the Romans and exacerbated conflict between patricians and plebeians. Involved in this conflict was the rise of debt slavery among the plebeians. When a debtor was seized for non-payment of his debts, other plebeians, mainly peasant soldiers, might attempt to rescue him by force.

Unrest among the plebeians resulted in the plebeian members of one of Rome's returning armies threatening to found their own city. Rome's farmer-soldiers and farmer veterans demanded a bigger share in the distribution of lands, and they demanded the abolition of veterans' debts. They advocated the creation of an assembly that spoke for their interests and the interests of all of Rome's plebeians. They wanted the plebeians to elect men to preside over this assembly and to keep watch on the Senate and to have the power to veto Senate proposals. And they wanted plebeians to be able to elect a plebeian to one of the Senate's two consul positions.

A strike by plebeians was followed by patricians acknowledging that it was no longer as it had been in the days when aristocrats alone were the warriors. They were willing to compromise. Although the Senate did not give the plebeians exactly what they wanted, it did create military *tribunes*. The tribunes were to be elected by small farmers and by the patricians, and the tribunes could be either plebeians or patricians. The farmer-soldiers were encouraged by this increase in their participation in government. It gave them more of a sense that in war they were fighting for their own interests, and this enhanced their morale and strengthened Rome as a military power.

More Reforms

Having won concessions from the patricians, the plebeians wanted more, and soon they went on strike again, this time demanding freedom from arbitrary punishment and other abuses. The strike stopped work on farms and in shops, and to appease the plebeians the Senate gave tribunes the power to veto any laws passed by the Senate, and the tribunes were to be free from attacks of any kind by the Senate or anyone else. Although officially limited to vetoing laws, the tribunes soon began to initiate legislation, which would become law if it acquired Senate confirmation. And there was a rush of new legislation and laws. Among them, in 471, was a law that created an assembly of plebeians (Comitia Plebus) authorized to meet on special occasions to express their opinions to their tribunes. The tribunes were to preside over and elected by these assemblies, and they were to share authority with the consuls on the field of battle.

By 450, there were incidents of plebeian tribunes serving as military commanders in place of a consul – which might have been the result of the Senate wanting to use men of extraordinary military talent. Also by 450, the number of tribunes had been increased to ten, and another assembly was created: a military assembly (Comitia Centuriata), consisting of both plebeians and patricians. This assembly was presided over by the consuls. It met to consider the names of patricians who would be candidates for the positions of consul, to elect the consuls, to enact legislation, to listen to appeals of those convicted of capital crimes, and to decide whether Rome should go to war.

To relieve the consuls of the duty of taking the census, the office of *censor* was created. There were to be two censors. The census was needed for the collection of taxes and in organizing military duties. The censors learned of the extent of a man's property so that men who could afford it would be obliged to equip themselves with the better and more complete armor of the hoplite warrior. Or, if the census determined that someone could afford the required horse and equipment, he was liable for service as a cavalryman. And plebeian cavalrymen were recognized by the Senate as a new class, called the *Equites*.

To the executive branch of government (the consuls) and the legislative branch (the Senate and assemblies) a third branch of government was created: the judiciary. This had been urged by the plebeians, who wanted laws to apply to them and patricians equally. An officer of the law, called the *Praetor*, was put in charge of the judiciary. He was to be elected annually by the military assembly, and it was hoped that he would exercise judgments independent from politics. But jury duty was to remain exclusively for aristocrats. Only aristocrats had sufficient leisure time for such service, and it was believed that as jurors they would strive to maintain their reputations as men of honor by judging on the evidence presented them.

Putting Law into Writing, and Mixed Marriages

Up to this time Roman laws had been unwritten and connected with religious lore, and the patricians were interpreters of the law, the patricians believing that only they had knowledge of the mysteries of religious lore that was sufficient for proper interpretation. To avoid arbitrary decisions concerning the law, plebeians demanded that laws be put into writing, and this resulted in the creation of what became known as the Twelve Tables, laws written on twelve bronze tablets. Unlike the laws of Moses, these laws were to be open to legislative change. They were laws that adjusted to life, to develop through precedence and experience – a heritage for modern times beyond that derived from Judaism.

One of the earliest adjustments to these laws came with opposition to a law prohibiting marriage between plebeians and patricians. In 442, a tribune introduced legislation against this prohibition. Patricians had been concerned about the purity of their blood, and speaking before the Senate against this legislation, a fundamentalist consul described it as a rebellion against the laws of heaven. He accused the tribune of scheming to obscure or confuse family rank, leaving nothing "pure and uncontaminated." The tribune replied with that which has often been the bane of pretended superiorities: history. He reminded the Senate's patricians of the humble origins of their ancestors, and he claimed that their nobility was not a right of birth or blood but a co-optation. How much this convinced the senators is difficult to determine. But in one respect the law against marriage between plebeians and patricians had become impractical: plebeian families headed by vigorous entrepreneurs had accumulated much wealth. Patricians from poorer families had an interest in marrying into these more wealthy families, and the law against prohibiting marriage between plebeians and patricians was repealed.

The Harshness of Roman Law

A civilized society needed liability laws – liability law having been created by Hammurabi in Babylon a thousand years before Rome's written law and more than a thousand years before Ezra promulgated Judaic law. Roman law concerning liability was harsh, conforming with the belief among Romans in virtue and personal commitment. Punishments for breaking the laws expressed in the Twelve Tables were as follows: anyone guilty of slander was to be clubbed to death; a thief was to be flogged, unless he was a slave, in which case he was to be executed by being thrown off Tarpaian rock on Rome's Capitoline hill; someone convicted of defrauding a client was also to be executed; perjury was also a capital crime; death was the punishment also for a judge who accepted a bribe; or anybody who connived with the enemy or delivered a Roman citizen to an enemy. The sentence of death, however, may have been rarely carried out. At this time in their history, in place of executing someone, the Romans might demolish his house and allow him to go into permanent exile. But Vestal Virgins convicted of being unchaste were usually buried alive.

Roman law recognized the supreme authority of the father within his family. A father could sell his son or daughter into slavery. He could have a rebellious son put to death or, as the Romans put it, sacrificed to the gods. A daughter was her father's property, sold in marriage to whomever he pleased. He could also tell his son whom to marry and when to divorce. Roman law also reflected a Roman harshness toward physical weakness: the dreadfully deformed were quickly put to death shortly after birth, and parents could kill their infant if at least five neighbors consented.

EARLY RELIGION

Like others, Romans saw themselves as a people blessed by their gods and their gods as extending their benevolence only to them. And like others, they had numerous gods – gods representing every force of nature that they perceived. The supreme god of the Romans was Jupiter, a god of sunshine and rain and most importantly Rome's protector. They had a fertility god called Mars, who stirred the plants back to life in spring. And the connection between Mars and land suited another of his occupations: wars were often about possession of land, and Mars was also a god of war.

The Romans had a god called Janus – from which the word *January* derives. Janus was a god of doorways, including the gates at the walls of Rome. Rome's goddess of fire, Vesta, ranked high among the Roman gods, but the largest temple in Rome was for the goddess Venus, the daughter of Jupiter, who was a goddess of vegetation, a bringer of good fortune and victory and the protector of feminine chastity.

Like others, the Romans had acquired much in religion through cultural diffusion, and like others they remained largely unmindful of such origins. It seems that the Romans acquired the gods Jupiter, Juno and Minerva from the Etruscans, and perhaps through the Etruscans the Romans acquired Greek gods. The Roman gods Mercury, Ceres and Diana resembled Greek gods, and the Roman god Hercules *was* a Greek god. With increased contact between Romans and Greeks, the Romans would identify their gods more with Greek gods. And not having much in mythology surrounding their gods, the Romans would adopt Greek mythology to support their gods.

Religion for the Romans was not about their love for gods or of gods who loved them, nor was it about withdrawing from the present and waiting for a happy life in the hereafter. Religion for the Romans was about the here and now and the terrors that the gods could devise. For the Romans, devotion to the gods and pleasing the gods was a duty, an act of patriotism, an act of service and protection for the community. And to serve the gods, the Roman government saw itself as the source of moral as well as legal standards. State priests attempted to appease the gods by carefully performed rituals and offerings. The welfare of the community was seen as affected by such virtues as discipline, soldierly courage, chastity among the women, and frugality, all of which were believed to please the gods. The Romans were afraid of displeasing the gods through some word or deed. And, to protect the community from the anger of the gods, soldiers took religious oaths against thievery. Olive growers took an oath against their conspiring with others to raise prices. Olive pickers took an oath against their stealing olives. And those who handled public money took oaths against stealing. It appeared that religion would keep Rome on the path of virtue.

At the head of Rome's religion was the *Pontifex Maximus*, who, when Rome became a republic, had replaced the Etruscan king in this role. Under the Pontifex Maximus was a college of priests, who were called pontiffs. They were officers of the government in charge of handling Rome's relations with the supernatural. It was their duty to keep the city on good terms with the gods by preserving religious traditions and by making sure that every important act of state was sanctioned by the gods, including relations with foreign communities. Priests were assigned to individual gods, and laws derived from myths governed their actions: the priest of Jupiter was forbidden to walk under an arbor of vines, touch a dead man, eat bread fermented with yeast or to go outside without his cap.

That the state's priests were exclusively patrician had its origins in earlier times – when the aristocracy believed that its interests alone were served by the gods. But common Romans were not about to leave all religion to the state. They saw their relations with their gods as personal. The common Roman saw gods guiding them through all kinds of matters from births to deaths. Each Roman household had its divine protector. And to this god they prayed – much as modern Christians pray while leaving ritual to their priests.

DEFEAT BY THE GAULS AND MORE REFORMS

By the end of the 400s, Rome had grown to about thirty by twenty miles. It had become a respected power through much of Italy, and occasionally it was looked to for help. Around this time, several tribes of Celts – whom the Romans called *Gauls* – ventured southward from their homeland to the Po River Valley in northern Italy. It was an area the Gauls had been familiar with from their trade with the Etruscans who lived there. The Gauls took territory from the Etruscans, and to the surprise of others who thought of the Gauls as restless barbarians, some of the Gauls settled into cereal farming. But several bands of Gauls came farther south and threatened the Etruscan city of Clusium, about a hundred miles north of Rome. Clusium requested help from Rome, and Rome sent three commissioners to Clusium. One commissioner asked the Gauls why they thought they could take lands that belonged to others. The Gauls replied with what might have been a prevalent attitude among those the Romans called barbarians: that the people of Clusium had more land than they needed and that "all things belong to the brave."

The Roman commissioners joined in a skirmish to defend Clusium against the Gauls, and one of the commissioners killed a Gallic chieftain. When the three commissioners returned to Rome the angered Gauls had the arrogance to send representatives to Rome and ask that the three commissioners be turned over to them. Rome refused, and that year – 390 BC – the Gauls headed for Rome to seek revenge.

Eleven miles north of Rome, the Gauls and Roman defenders clashed. The Gauls outnumbered the defenders two to one, and the Gauls shattered Rome's spear carrying phalanx formations. Rome appeared doomed. Many of Rome's defenders fled across the Tiber River to the nearby city of Veii. Some soldiers fled to the countryside. Others rushed through Rome's gates to its citadel, as non-combatants were fleeing the city through these same gates. These gates remained open, and the Gauls poured into the city, where they slaughtered old men, women and children and looted and burned. They attempted an uphill attack on the citadel, but they failed to dislodge the soldiers there.

For seven months the Gauls remained and fought around Rome. Then they gave up and returned north, leaving Rome in ruins. Many Romans wanted to abandon their city and move to the nearby city of Veii. But belief that gods dwelled in places had its impact: a patrician named Camillus made a speech describing such a move as abandoning their temples and their gods. "All things turn out well when we obeyed the gods," he is reported to have said, "and ill when we spurned them." The Romans decided to stay, and they hurriedly rebuilt their city and made its walls more formidable. They began to adopt new military weaponry, dropping the spear in favor of a two-foot long sword, adopting helmets, breastplates and a shield with iron edges. They reorganized their army, putting in the front rank of their battle line not the wealthy soldiers as before but the youngest and strongest. And they defended themselves against attacks by Etruscans and other peoples (the Volscians and Aequians) who sought to take advantage of what they thought was a Rome weakened by the Gauls.

More Political Change

After the invasion of the Gauls, common plebeians fought for relief from economic distress, and the wealthier of the plebeians sought eligibility to run for the position of consul. From 367 through the following eighty years, the Senate approved reform measures, including laws that allowed plebeians to become consuls, praetors, or quaestors – the latter money managers connected to various aspects of government or military campaigns. Bills were passed that, for the sake of greater equality, limited the size of lands that were distributed by the state. Bills were passed that reformed debt payment. And in 326 a law was passed that protected the personal freedom of plebeians by outlawing the age-old practice of debtors being made serfs to their creditors.

It became custom that one consul was to be a plebeian and the other to be a patrician. Another change came with the censor acquiring the power not only to take the census but to fill vacancies that had arisen in the Senate and to remove from the Senate any member he deemed undesirable, and the censor was given charge over state construction of buildings and roads.

THE SAMNITE AND LATIN WARS

While Philip II of Macedonia was expanding his empire, war in Italy erupted again on the plains of Campania, near Neapolis (Naples). People on the plains were invaded by Samnite warrior-herdsmen from nearby hills who wished to use the grasslands of the plains for their animals – lands that the plains people had fenced. Those on the plains sought help from Rome. Roman envoys went to leaders among the hill people for discussions and were rudely treated. War between Rome and the Samnite hill people followed – the First Samnite War. The war lasted two years, ending in 345 with Rome triumphant and the Samnites willing to make peace.

The display of military weakness by the Samnites encouraged Rome's Latin allies to make forays against them. The Samnites asked Rome to control its allies, and Rome called upon the Latins to leave the Samnites alone. Some Latins resented Rome's interference, and some were convinced that Rome intended to dominate all of Latium. Member states within Rome's Latin League demanded equality within the league, and they demanded a sharing in governing Rome itself. What began as Rome's move for peace and stability ended in 340 with Rome going to war against its Latin neighbors and some non-Latin cities. Rome won these wars. It disbanded the Latin League, and it took land from those it defeated and distributed it among its plebeians.

Rather than destroy and disperse those it defeated – as was common in ancient times – Rome treated them with leniency and forgiveness. This leniency, rather than weakening Rome, strengthened it by winning respect and gratitude from its former adversaries. Rome now dominated all the Latins, and it controlled an area from just north of Rome southward almost to Neapolis. This was a heavily populated area for ancient times, and the area was the base from which Rome would spread its power and influence over the whole of Italy.

Rome was consolidating power in Italy as Philip had in Greece, and as was the kingdom of Ch'in in China. Rome used its power and prestige to regulate relations among various Italian cities. It made alliances. It created colonies, giving land in these colonies to common Romans and other Latins, and to the Latins in these colonies it gave full Roman citizenship. The grant of land was accepted with the obligation of military service, the colony serving as Rome's keeper of peace in its area. As in Macedonia, a nation-state was being created. Rome was growing in population. And it was growing in manpower by extending citizenship to cities it trusted – to cities with people who wished to identify with Rome's greatness and were willing to go to war as Romans.

A Second Samnite War

In 327, war broke out again between Samnite hill people and those on Campania's plain. The Samnites established a garrison in Neapolis – a city inhabited by Greeks. Again people of the plain sought Rome's assistance, and again Rome went to war against the Samnites. A Roman and allied force became entrapped at Caudine Forks, and it surrendered. The war stalled for five years. And, as Rome waited for the war to resume, it strengthened its military by increasing recruitment.

In 320 and 319, the Romans returned for revenge against the Samnites and defeated them in what the Roman historian Livy described as one of the greatest events in Roman history. Peace was established between Rome and some Samnite towns. But the war dragged on with other Samnites to 311, when the Samnites were joined by Etruscan cities that had decided to join a showdown against Roman power. The war became a contest for the dominance of much of Italy. Between 311 and 304, the Romans and their allies won a series of victories against both the Etruscans and the Samnites. The Samnites announced that they were ready for peace. For assurance, the Romans demanded inspections, and peace was established between the Romans and Samnites that remained until 298.

A Third Samnite and Pyrrhic Wars

At the turn of the century, the Samnites decided that they had had enough of peace. They wanted to try again to thwart Roman domination of Italy. They organized a coalition that included Etruscans and Gauls, and war began again on the plains near Neapolis. When the Romans saw the Etruscans and Gauls in northern Italy joining the Samnites they were alarmed. The Romans had benefited from a lack of coordination among its enemies, but now Rome faced them all at once.

Some relief came with a victory over the Samnites in the south, but the crucial battle for Italy took place in 295 at Sentinum, a town in Italy's northeast, where more troops were engaged than any previous battle in Italy. At first the Romans gave way before an attack by Gauls in chariots. Then the Romans rallied and crushed the Samnites and Gauls, the Romans benefiting from their self-discipline, the quality of their military legions, and their military leadership.

After Rome's great victory at Sentinum, the war slowly wound down, coming to an end in 282. Rome emerged dominating all of the Italian peninsula except for the Greek cities in Italy's extreme south and the Po valley – the Po valley still being a land occupied by Gauls.

As the war was winding down, the Greek city of Tarentum, on Italy's southern coast, became disturbed by a colony that Rome had established just eighty miles to its north. Tarentum had its own sphere of influence in the south. It had a democratic constitution, the largest naval fleet in Italy, an army of 15,000, and wealth enough to buy a good number of mercenaries. It had ignored an opportunity to join the Etruscans, Gauls and Samnites in their war against Rome, but belatedly it decided to fight Rome. And Tarentum gained the backing of a Macedonian adventurer of high repute named Pyrrhus, who agreed to command the combined troops of Tarentum and other Greek cities in Italy, combined with troops of his own.

Pyrrhus was a former kinsman of Alexander the Great. He had briefly ruled Epirus in 295. In 280, the year Tarentum requested his help, he saw war against Rome as an opportunity to extend Macedonian authority over Italy as Alexander had planned, and he saw an opportunity to win for himself some of the glory that Alexander had won.

Like many other Hellenistic people, Pyrrhus underestimated Rome. In 280, he landed 25,000 troops in Italy, including some 3,000 horsemen, 2,000 archers, and the first elephants brought to Italy. He engaged the Romans in battle at Herclea, using the elephants to drive through Roman lines, creating panic among the Roman soldiers. Pyrrhus won this and more battles against the Romans, but he found Rome's armies more ferocious than those he had faced in the East, and his victories against the Romans came with enormous casualties, giving rise to the expression "Pyrrhic victory."

Pyrrhus tried to win over to his side some of Rome's allies, but without success. Rome's manpower was too much for Pyrrhus, and, by the year 275, Pyrrhus felt defeated. He returned to Greece, where he would be killed in another war, in 272, the same year that Tarentum surrendered to Rome.

Rome treated the defeated Tarentum leniently, allowing Tarentum the same local self-rule it allowed other cities. Tarentum in turn recognized Rome's hegemony in Italy and became another of Rome's allies, while a Roman garrison remained in Tarentum to insure its loyalty. Rome was now undisputed master of the bottom three quarters of the Italian peninsula.

NEW WARS AND BEGINNINGS OF A NEW ERA

The greatest power near Italy was Carthage, 150 miles (240 km) southwest from Sicily, on the coast of North Africa. Carthage was founded around 815 BC by Phoenicians from the city of Tyre. It was a commercial city surrounded by rich farm land, a city with a constitution and ruled by an oligarchy of men of wealth. Carthage dominated the coast of North Africa as far east as Egypt. It dominated the southern coast of Spain and the western half of Sicily. And it dominated the islands of Corsica and Sardinia.

While Rome was expanding on the Italian mainland, it made an agreement with Carthage, acknowledging that Carthage was the dominant power in Sicily. Carthage, in turn, promised Rome that it would stay off the Italian mainland. Rome respected Carthage and abided by its treaty until it ended its war for the domination of Italy. Then an incident arose in Sicily at the small city of Messana just across the channel from the toe of the Italian peninsula.

The incident began with Messana feeling threatened by the Sicilian city of Syracuse. One faction in Messana requested help from Carthage. Another faction, apparently distrusting or disliking Carthage, requested help from Rome. Respecting its treaty with Carthage, Rome's Senate chose not to send help to Messana. But one of Rome's two consuls was eager for action that would give him distinction. He spoke of reluctance to send help to Messana as weakness. With his speech making he aroused the people of Rome, who had been filled with pride over Rome's success in dominating Italy. The Senate gave in to the aroused emotions of the public, and it sent a force to Messana. The world was turning – as it would in the twentieth century – on the ambitions of a rabble-rouser and the passions and vanity of common people.

At Messana the force from Rome came face to face with a force from Carthage. Carthage saw Rome's move as a threat to its interests in Sicily, but it attempted conciliation. Carthage asked that Rome withdraw its troops, but proud Romans called on their city to stand up to Carthage. Some claimed that Carthage's control over the strait between Italy and Sicily was a danger to Rome's security. And, as with the Athenians at the outbreak of the Great Peloponnesian war, there was little reluctance and caution about going to war, including among the civilian farmer-soldiers who would fight the war. With this swagger and willingness to war, a new era was beginning that would lead to empire, and with empire eventually to Christianity.

The First Punic War

Rome took a number of its Italian allies into the war on its side. And shortly into the war, Rome chose goals beyond securing the strait between Italy and Sicily. The contest against Carthage became a war for plunder. Then it became a war for driving Carthage out of Sicily, then a war for all of Sicily. And Rome's enlarged goals would extend the war twenty-three years, to 241 BC.

Across these years, many of those who fought for Carthage were Greek mercenaries, and the unreliability of these men led Carthage to wage war with minimum risks and half measures. Rome was more aggressive. During the war it built its first great navy, which won spectacular victories, first in 260 and then in 241. With Rome as master of the Mediterranean, Carthage decided that the price it had to pay for ending the war was better than the cost of continuing it. Carthage agreed to pay Rome a huge sum of money and to give to Rome the islands of Sicily, Corsica and Sardinia.

Despite the heavy losses in treasure and life that they had suffered, Romans considered the war against Carthage a great victory. Many were pleased by the additional prestige their city had gained. And for many Romans victory confirmed that their city had been called on by the gods for a special destiny.

Rapacity and Rome's Search for Security

The First Punic War helped open the eyes of many Romans to the profits of empire. Also, the war created among the Romans a greater concern for national security, and Rome saw added security in its winning control over Corsica and Sardinia. Failing to see divine purpose in the coming of Roman soldiers, people in Corsica and Sardinia resisted their arrival. Some of the islanders retreated inland, but Roman soldiers with trained dogs hunted them down and carted great numbers of them to Italy for sale as slaves.

Romans were concerned too about security of their northern border. They had heard a prophecy that the Gauls would come south again and overrun their city. City authorities allayed the fears of the public by reviving an old religious ritual. In the city's Forum they publicly buried alive a Gallic man and woman. And Rome sent forces north to secure a barrier against the Gauls, and these forces extended Roman authority across Cisalpine Gaul as far as the Alps.

Next, Rome addressed its concern for security eastward. Italian traders had been calling on Rome to do something about pirates along the coast of Illyricum, on the eastern side of the Adriatic Sea. Rome launched a drive against these pirates, and as a part of this campaign they established friendly relations with numerous small, coastal powers. One of these powers, the island of Pharos, was attempting to expand against its neighbors. Rome made itself the protector of Pharos' neighbors and conquered Pharos – the beginning of Roman intervention east of the Adriatic.

Origins and First Two Years of the Second Punic War

Carthage expanded its enterprises in Spain in compensation for its losses of Sicily, Corsica and Sardinia, and Carthage's success in trade and mining operations in Spain prompted Rome to establish an embassy there. A prosperous Greek colony on the Mediterranean coast in Spain, Saguntum, quarreled with neighboring towns. Lacking friendship with Carthage and desperate for an ally, Saguntum sought help from Rome. Seeing Rome as becoming involved in the dispute, the leader of Carthage, Hannibal, welcomed the opportunity to launch a war of revenge against Rome. More than twenty years had passed since the war between Rome and Carthage, and Hannibal felt that Carthage could now challenge Rome.

While Rome was negotiating with Carthage, Hannibal sent an army against Saguntum, with orders to spare no male of military age.

Saguntum fell, leaving Rome's Senate and the public enraged and regretting that they had not responded in time to help Saguntum. The Romans saw Carthage's attack on Saguntum as a challenge to their prestige, and they matched Hannibal's willingness for war.

The war against Hannibal would be a new kind of war for Rome. Previously, Romans fought only in summer campaigns. Against Hannibal, the number of Romans fighting would increase ten fold and they would fight through the entire year.

Hannibal sent armies to Sicily and Italy by sea. He and a force with cavalry and elephants moved north from Saguntum, across the coast of France, through the Alps and down into the Po valley in northern Italy. For some two and a half years in Italy, Hannibal produced victory after victory, as he and his troops lived off the lands they conquered. But rather than try to win allies among the Italians, he burned and destroyed as he went, and not one Italian city joined him against Rome.

Saturnalia

Hannibal tried to keep himself informed about the Roman leaders sent against him, and occasionally he found weaknesses in these Romans. He took advantage of the untalented consul, Flaminius, who wanted to prove himself to his fellow Romans. Flaminius allowed Hannibal to choose where the battle between them would be fought, and he marched his army into a trap at Lake Trasimenus, where all but the few who were captured were cut down. In the wake of this disaster, Rome introduced a festival to lift the morale of its citizens, a festival for the god of agriculture, Saturn. It began on December 17th. During the festival the courts and schools closed and military operations were suspended so that soldiers could celebrate. It was a time of goodwill and jollity that included visiting people, banquets and the exchanging of gifts. It would become an annual event, called Saturnalia, an official Roman holiday that was the precursor of Christmas.

Defeat at Cannae and Appeals to the Gods

Ever mindful of the importance of morality, some Romans found the reason for their defeats in the anger of the gods over misconduct by the Vestal Virgins. Rome discovered that two of its Vestal Virgins had had sexual relations with a male temple official. Roman authorities had one of the accused Vestal Virgins buried alive, and the other killed herself. Authorities had the accused male official beaten to death. Then Rome sent a representative to the famous oracle in Delphi, in Greece, to inquire what prayers and supplications might atone for the failure among the Vestal Virgins.

Apparently the gods remained dissatisfied. Next came Hannibal's greatest and most brilliant success – at Cannae. Here, in 216 BC, Rome lost five out of every six soldiers it sent to battle. It seemed that Rome was on the verge of defeat, and now some Italian cities, wishing to be on the winning side, opened their gates to Hannibal. In Sicily, Syracuse went over to the side of Carthage. Macedonia's king, Philip V, offered Carthage an alliance.

It was Rome's darkest hour. To counter the gloom, Roman authorities ordered all wailing women indoors and forbade the word peace to be spoken. In another attempt to appease the gods, Rome resorted again to the ancient custom of human sacrifice. Again they buried alive a Gallic man and woman, and a Greek man and woman. In 211, with Hannibal thirty miles from Rome, Roman women appealed to the gods by sweeping the floors of their temples with their hair. It appeared that the gods responded. Hannibal did not attack Rome. Rather than confront the two armies that Rome had placed before him, Hannibal decided to burn the nearby countryside and withdraw to fight elsewhere.

An Appeal to Mother Nature

Six more years of war passed by, and Rome's priesthood added to its concern about the role of the gods by giving attention to the *Sibylline Books*, a work of legend believed to have been written by a woman called Sibyl. It was believed that Apollo had given Sibyl the power of prophesy and that she had prophesied that Rome's enemy would be expelled. Rome's priesthood chose to interpret this as Rome expelling Hannibal if Rome acquired the help of the Great Mother of Gods, Cybele. Cybele was a goddess from Asia Minor who had been adopted by the Greeks and worshiped widely as Mother Nature. Rome's Senate invited the Great Mother goddess to Rome in the form of a stone reputed to have fallen from the heavens – the Black Stone of Pessinus. In 205 BC, with great solemnity and pomp, the stone was transported from Pessinus (a town in central Asia Minor) to Rome, and it was installed in a temple on Rome's Palatine hill.

The Last Five Years of War

The religions of the Romans and the Carthaginians had done little if anything to abate the ferocity of the war. Chivalry and restraint had vanished from both sides. Hannibal continued to destroy Italian lands and to destroy villages that his forces could not hold. To starve Hannibal's forces the Romans scorched the earth in front of Hannibal's advancing army, and they moved people from the countryside to towns. The Romans plundered those towns they believed had befriended Hannibal and beheaded those men they believed had fought on the side of Carthage.

Rome avoided a direct clash with Hannibal in Italy, and it moved its soldiers to Sicily. There, the Roman general Marcellus beheaded two thousand of his troops whom he claimed had been deserters. Other soldiers under his command pillaged Syracuse and destroyed and plundered treasures that had accumulated there for centuries. A soldier in Syracuse came upon the philosopher Archimedes and ran a sword through him.

The contest between Carthage and Rome had become a war of attrition, with Rome gaining the upper hand. Rome benefited from fighting closer to home and having access to more manpower, and it benefited from the egocentricity and short-sighted-ness of Carthage's oligarchs. For a while at least, the oligarch's concern over the security of their positions of power made them fear success by Hannibal. They were reluctant to send him reinforcements. Instead, Hannibal recruited Gauls into his army, which offended the Italians, who remembered that Rome had been a bulwark against the Gauls. Carthage finally sent reinforcements to Hannibal from Spain, but the Romans intercepted them at the Metaurus River in northeastern Italy.

Rome managed to reconquer Sicily. And Rome's navy defeated Carthage's forces in Spain and North Africa, and it cut Hannibal from his supplies. Rome moved the war to North Africa, near Carthage, and Hannibal left Italy to defend home territory. Carthage sued for peace. A council of twenty Roman priests – which governed treaties with foreigners – went to Carthage to present Rome's demands. The priests called on Jupiter to witness that the demands were just. Carthage agreed to reduce its territory to an area that approximates what is now Tunisia, to withdraw from participation in the affairs of Spain, to pay Rome a huge indemnity, and to surrender to Rome all but twenty of its warships. Hannibal's attempt at revenge had failed. In the year 201, after sixteen years of fighting, the war ended, and Hannibal fled, finding refuge with the Seleucid king, Antiochus III.

THE END OF OLD ROME

Rome's second war against Carthage reduced the number of people in the Italian countryside. Men had gone off to war. People had died and people had moved to the cities to escape war. Some people had left the countryside to work in the arms industry, and some went looking for subsistence. In Rome, the migrants enjoyed the festivals and other public entertainment that was created to maintain public morale during the dark days of the war. Newcomers developed a preference for the city over the life of drudgery they had known working on farms. And after the war ended, many veterans from farming families preferred settling in cities, especially Rome, rather than return to the countryside. Cities in Italy became overcrowded, and Rome became the most populous city in Europe and West Asia.

As a result of the war, much farmland in Italy could be bought cheaply. Those with wealth began buying this farmland, some land-owners expanding their holdings and some businessmen from the cities looking for a secure investment and a source of social respectability. With the accelerated trend toward larger farms came a greater use of slaves. More lands in the countryside were transformed into pasture, vineyard, and olive orchards – more suited to Italian soil and climate than was the growing of grain. The richest lands were converted to vineyards and the poorer tracts to olive groves, while ranching was the most profitable for capitalist landowners. Holdings that were a mix of ranching and farming grew to more than three hundred acres, found mostly in southern and central Italy, the area most heavily devastated by the Second Punic War.

Many small farmers found themselves unable to compete with the larger farms and their more numerous slaves. Moreover, a greater importation of grain from Sicily and North Africa brought a drop in grain prices, and many small farmers gave up, sold their farms to the wealthy and joined the migration to the cities. The wars that began with the minor incident at Messana had brought unintended consequences – as wars often do. Many of Rome's small farmers, who had been the backbone of the Roman Republic, had become city-dwellers living off welfare – free bread and circuses.

The Move to Empire

Rome emerged from its second war against Carthage with Spain added to the areas outside Italy that it deemed its possession, and it began what would become a long struggle to conquer Spain's various peoples. Meanwhile, in Greece popular movements had been raising the old demand that land be redistributed and debts be canceled. Men of wealth in Greece – tradesmen, shipbuilders and landed aristocrats – were ready to seek help from Rome against the threat of reform and revolution. Hoping that Rome was interested in peace and stability in their part of the world, representatives from Greece and other states went to Rome and appealed to its Senate for help in local disputes. Rome would now embark upon a new role that would lead to it acquiring the world's greatest empire – an empire to be viewed by many as the work of God.

CHAPTER 16

ROMAN EMPIRE AND DICTATORSHIP

ROME INTERVENES ABROAD

While India was being invaded from Bactria, and while China was at peace and growing in prosperity, Rome was sending armies across the Adriatic Sea to Greece and beyond. In Greece, popular movements had been raising the old demand that land be redistributed and debts canceled, and men of wealth in Greece – tradesmen, shipbuilders and landed aristocrats – sought the help of Rome against the threat of reform or revolution. Some conservative Romans wished that their city avoid entanglements in Greece in order to avoid contacts with fancy philosophies they believed would corrupt their fellow Romans. Some Romans believed that rather than going to Greece it would be best to focus on recovery from the war against Hannibal and other problems in Italy and at home.

Those with rival opinions spoke of Rome's destiny and of its triumphs yet to come. They had become hawkish during the war against Carthage, and they had a heightened concern with security. They wanted the city to use its power to serve what they described as its interests abroad. Among these Romans were a few who sought to advance or acquire military reputations. Some among them believed that Roman military strength backed by their virtues and the power of their gods could improve the world beyond Italy. They saw Rome as more blessed than others and more capable and wise, and they argued for selective intervention beyond Italy as a duty and service to mankind.

Rome against Philip V of Macedonia

An early issue that Rome faced involved the king of Macedonia, Philip V – son of Antigonus II. Philip had been making appeals to the dissatisfied masses in neighboring Greek cities. War broke out between Philip on one side and Rhodes and Pergamum on the other. Greek oligarchs appealed to Rome's Senate, and senators remembered that Philip had sought an alliance with Carthage during Rome's darkest hour. They feared the recent growth of Philip's navy. The senators heard exaggerated reports of Philip's aggressions. They consulted with

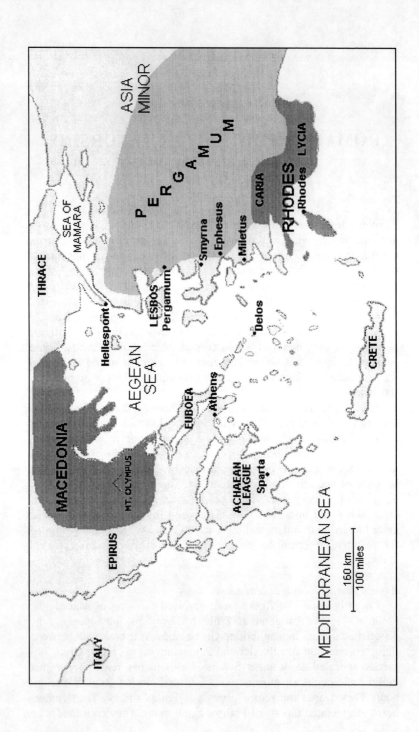

the council of twenty priests who regulated relations with foreigners, and although Philip did not want war with Rome and Rome could have negotiated a settlement with him, the council of priests chose war.

Rome sent an army of volunteers to Greece that was poorly led and poorly disciplined, and for a couple of years Philip pursed a cautious strategy designed to wear-down the military that Rome had sent his way. The war remained mainly between Rome and Philip, Rome allies, including Rhodes and Pergamum, contributing little to the war effort. Rome's navy was vastly superior to Macedonia's, allowing Roman transport across the Adriatic, and Roman and Macedonian land-forces became equal in size. Then at the Battle of Cynoscephalae, in 197 BC, Roman legions outmaneuvered and over-powered Philip's army. Rome drew up a settlement that satisfied their purported purpose in going to war: Philip was to stay out of Greece. Philip agreed to pay war damages. The Romans allowed Philip to stay in power, and Rome's troops returned home.

Some Greeks were impressed by what they saw as Rome's selflessness in protecting order in their part of the world. But some other Greeks were left with unpleasant memories of Roman soldiers looting, or with distaste at having been rescued by what they considered a barbarian power. And Greeks who had feared Philip were upset that Philip was still in power.

Rome against Antiochus III

Trouble then erupted between Rome and Antiochus III. Antiochus had expanded his rule from Syria and Palestine, and he aimed at absorbing Thrace and Asia Minor, believing as a Seleucid that these areas were rightly his. Feeling threatened by Antiochus, Rhodes and Pergamum requested Rome's help. Rome saw Antiochus' expanding empire as a possible rival to its own power, and it remembered that Antiochus had given refuge to Hannibal. Rome asked Antiochus to leave the autonomous cities of Asia Minor alone and to refrain from expanding from Asia Minor into Europe. Antiochus objected to Rome's interference in the east and asked Rome how it would feel if he began intervening in Italian affairs. He spoke of liberating the Greeks from Rome, and with his army he crossed the straits at Hellespont into Europe, a move that was welcomed by some Greek cities opposed to Rome.

Rome allied itself with Rhodes, Pergamum and other Greek cities hostile to Antiochus, and together they defeated Antiochus and his allies in 190. Antiochus agreed to Rome's demand that he withdraw from Asia Minor, and Pergamum gained territory at his expense. Antiochus agreed also that he and his successors would no longer hire

Greeks as soldiers. He agreed to surrender Hannibal, and he agreed to pay a great sum to Rome as tribute.

Giving money to Rome broke Antiochus financially, and in 187, when he tried to recoup his financial losses by sacking a temple in Persia, he was killed. Four years later Hannibal was tracked down by the Romans. But rather than be captured he killed himself.

An Arrogance of Power

Those Greek cities that had allied themselves with Antiochus were forced into an alliance with Rome, and they were made to agree to give no aid to forces hostile to Rome or to allow such forces to cross their territory. Looking at some of the Greek cities that had been friends, Rome resented what it saw as a lack of gratitude. Romans had begun to believe that Greeks were insincere, the Roman leader Cato describing them as speaking from their lips while Romans spoke from their hearts. Romans saw contemporary Greeks as a lesser people than the Greeks of former times, and they believed that rather than just helping the Greeks they were justified in pursuing authority over them.

Roman diplomacy had been growing devious and self-serving. Rome favored oligarchies against democrats, its Senate never having approved of the authority of the masses. And Rome had begun to create borders abroad that served its interests by being ill-defined, borders that kept various powers at odds with each other and desirous of maintaining favor from Rome.

And when the people of Sardinia and Corsica rose against Rome in an attempt to re-establish their independence, Rome sent armies against them. Rome did not wish to tolerate any example of defiance. It crushed the uprisings and made slaves of 80,000 Sardinians, glutting its slave market and making "as cheap as a Sardinian" a common expression among the Romans.

THE HOMEFRONT

After the war against Hannibal, wealthy Romans had begun investing their money abroad, some in mines in Spain and some in vast tracts of land in Sicily and elsewhere, and they turned these lands into slave plantations. Some of them lent money abroad, at high interest rates, and Roman financial operations became greater than that of the Greeks and Near Easterners. The wars in Greece had brought Roman entrepreneurs new wealth from war contracts, Rome spending as much as eighty percent of its budget on its military. There was an increase in fraud, against which the Senate was not always willing to press charges. And those with wealth imported more spices, carpets, perfumes and other luxury goods from the east.

The wars across the Adriatic were a boon also for Romans who volunteered for the military. They brought back money and booty from Greece, which encouraged more Romans to volunteer for military duty. Meanwhile, most freemen who lived in Rome and other Italian cities had no work – most work being done by slaves. Ambition for most of the freemen was limited to getting enough to eat – which for most city folk was boiled wheat or what was becoming a staple diet of baked bread.

Common Romans were packed closely together in rows of jerry-built tenement houses separated by narrow alleyways. People were without protection from fires, and their only heat was the small charcoal brazier they used inside their homes. For a toilet they had a chamber pot. They had to haul their water, which was often polluted. Rome had no theaters or restaurants. Dancing was done only by those thought by others to be insane. Most Romans passed their time on their porches or in the marketplace. There was, however, some makeshift street-corner theater. And the poor were entertained by the occasional circuses and public festivals that included sensational and exciting duels between slaves – paid for by politicians who sought approval from grateful citizens.

Prostitution and thievery flourished. Outcasts from smaller communities migrated to the big cities, especially to Rome, which had no police force. In Rome, feuds and violence between families were frequent, with the participants calling on friends and neighbors for assisance. There were no medical professionals to attend the injured or the ill or to help combat epidemics. Few Romans lived past the age of forty. The poor who died were buried in common pits in the public cemetery on Esquiline Hill. But most Romans continued to enjoy what they believed was the glory of Rome's position in the world.

More Cultural Diffusions

Roman excursions east of the Adriatic had increased their interest in that part of the world, which resulted in many Roman men adopting the Greek habit of shaving. The Romans acquired an interest in Greek athletic games, which in Rome were played for the first time in 186. No Romans participate because the athletes were naked and the Romans saw stripping naked as shameful and as a prelude to vice.

Some wealthy Romans began sending their sons to Greece to finish their schooling, to learn rhetoric – a lawyer's cleverness in oration. The Romans were little interested in Greek literature or other arts, and they were to produce no great plays of their own, or music, or to paint any remarkable pictures. Rome's wealthy families were inclined to leave the adding, reading and music to Hellenized slaves. And they were inclined to reject Hellenist advances in medicine. Most Romans continued to believe that they could get leprosy by passing under a dewy tree. And they continued to seek cures by priestly rituals, including an application of holy water, the "laying on of hands," or by applying salts, herbs, powders, potions, gladiator's blood, human fat or animal dung.

The Romans looked askance at Hellenist advances in astronomy. They saw the idea that the world was round as one of those peculiar, laughable ideas from the east. And they had little interest in Hellenist advances in technology. The Romans kept track of time by the rise and fall of the sun, until they borrowed a water clock from the Greeks, which told time by water dripping from one container into another. The Romans also brought a sundial from Greece, but it took them a hundred years to learn that by having moved the sundial they had to adjust it for the change in latitude.

But Rome's wealthy readily adopted the Greek drinking party and feasting – with the excuse that these were needed to boost morale. In the homes of Rome's wealthy citizens, meals had become elaborate affairs, prepared by professional cooks, served on silver plates, with occasional drinking bouts. Some Romans continued to believe in austerity, which they thought had contributed to Rome's past successes and glory, and some Senate conservatives were concerned about the new extravagances.

No longer was anyone being fined for having too grand a home, but in 182 the Senate passed a law regulating the size of parties. Partying grew, however, with the introduction of a new feast in 173: a celebration at Floralia modeled perhaps after the Greek festival of Aphrodite. The chief attraction at this new Roman festival was dances by prostitutes, dances that ended in a strip tease, which many Romans considered obscene.

The Spread of Religions of Bliss and Salvation

Those who had migrated to the cities found the gods they had worshiped in the countryside no longer significant – gods that had guarded their woods and had made their grasses green. In the cities these folks came into contact with religions that had been imported from the east, religions that had less to do with nature and more to do with bliss, excitement and salvation.

Among these new religions was the worship of the Great Mother, Cybele, the deity that had been imported to save Rome during the war against Hannibal – a worship that involved begging, self-mutilations, eunuch priests and colorful processions. Another imported religion was the Orphic mysteries from Greece, which claimed that the human soul was of divine origin, that human nature was divided between good and evil, and that one's soul could rise above humanity's inherited evil.

Some Romans worshiped Bacchus, the Roman god of wine. Rites of this religion included frenzied, ecstatic trances and self-abandon similar to the worship of Dionysus, the god of wine among the Greeks. Some from Rome's elite families became involved in these gatherings, which were conducted in secrecy. The Senate viewed secret meetings as conspiracies that might foster subversion, and when Rome's Senate finally became aware of the spread of Bacchus worship it became alarmed, outlawed the movement and put to death seven thousand Bacchus devotees.

The Senate also outlawed astrology, seeing this import from the east as subversive. But believing in many gods rather than one jealous god, and remaining confident in Rome's power, state officials saw the worship of most gods as benign, while they continued to foster patriotism by promoting Rome's official gods: the gods that had looked after the welfare of Rome and had made Rome great.

Cato the Elder – Portrait of a Roman Conservative

Marcus Porcius Cato was a much admired Roman patriot, a man who believed in honesty and courage, a respected veteran of the war against Hannibal and a military leader against a 197 BC uprising in Spain. He was a Roman senator, a consul, and then a censor – a position responsible not only for assessing property for taxation and taking the census but also for public morality. While censor he tried to restore what was thought to be the rectitude of the past. He opposed what he saw as a new decadence among the elite. It was he who passed the law limiting the size of private feasting, and he created a tax on high-priced slaves in order to discourage the purchase of attractive young male slaves for use as pages or concubines.

Cato was frugal. He believed in temperance and that luxury corrupted. He lived unostentatiously and ate coarse food, and although he had slaves he did some of his own manual labor. Most of Cato's colleagues saw him as representing the old virtues, the virtues that Cato believed had made Rome superior.

Cato believed that rule was doomed which ignored the collective wisdom of the past. He believed that Rome's republican government was best, that weakness lay in rule by lone kings and tyrants, that it was better to draw from the wisdom of the many, and he believed that Rome benefited from a balance of power between common people and the aristocracy.

Cato disliked the softer manners of the Greeks. He was fluent in Greek but he opposed Greek literature, poetry and art, and he opposed Greek medicine, claiming that it was poisoning Romans. Cato joined other Roman conservatives in fighting against the spread of Greek sophistication. He was influential in deporting from Rome two

Epicureans whom he thought had been sneering at religion, and he played a role in deporting a host of other philosophers and rhetoricians from east of the Adriatic. To keep his children untouched by Greek intellectuality he taught his children himself: Latin grammar, boxing and the history of the great deeds of his forefathers. He wanted to keep Roman youth puritanical. He thought Socrates had been a babbler justly put to death for questioning religious faith and the laws of his city. Rather than all the questions put forth by eastern doubters and philosophers, Cato preferred what he saw as the solid answers provided by Roman tradition.

Cato's solid answers included his belief that by having his wife nurse the infants born to his slaves these infants would grow up loving his own children. Although concerned about love from his slaves, he believed that his slaves should be either working or sleeping, and when his slaves grew too old to work he sold them, which must have been for little money, but it saved him the trouble and the cost of feeding them. Never missing a chance to make a little money, he obliged his male slaves to pay him for sleeping with his female slaves. And after he aged and his wife died he had one of his slave women visit him nightly, Cato apparently believing that her compliance was right in the eyes of Rome's gods.

ROME TAKES MACEDONIA, GREECE
AND DESTROYS CARTHAGE

The eldest son of King Philip V of Macedonia, Perseus, succeeded his father in 179, and by the mid-170s Macedonia had recovered from its defeat by Rome two decades before. Perseus allied himself with Thracian and Illyrian chieftains. He gave refuge to reform-minded exiles and those fleeing debt, and across Greece he became known as a champion of the poor.

King Eumenes of Pergamum continued his father's hostility toward Macedonia, and in 172 he delivered a complaint in person to Rome's Senate and convinced the Senate that Perseus was plotting against Rome. The Senate decided that it was in Rome's interest to destroy Perseus. In the autumn of 172 Rome deceived Perseus by granting him a truce. As planned, Rome spent the winter preparing for war. And early in 171, on the pretext that Perseus had attacked some allies of Rome in the Balkans, the Senate declared war against him.

Greek cities whose rulers feared rebellion and domination by Macedonia joined with Pergamum and Rhodes in an alliance with Rome. Perseus won the sympathy of Greeks who favored the poor and those who saw Rome as a bully, and Perseus won support from a few Greek cities in Boeotia and from the Republic of Epirus, just west of

Macedonia. But, as before, Rome had complete control of the seas, and its troops slightly outnumbered those of Macedonia. Rome's elastic military formations and forged steel swords proved superior to Macedonia's rigid formations of pikemen and its cast iron swords. In one great battle in 168, Rome destroyed Perseus' army, and Perseus died in a Roman prison three years later.

The Republic of Epirus had given Perseus no effective help during the war, but because it had allied itself with Perseus, the Romans attacked its towns and villages and carried away 150,000 people whom they sold into slavery. Rome attempted to eliminate Macedonian kings and to weaken Macedonia by dividing it into four republics. Rome forbade the divided areas to have contacts with each other. It demanded half of what the four republics collected in taxes, and Rome took possession of Macedonia's mines and forests. It was the beginning of Roman annexations east of the Adriatic.

With cooperation from wealthy Greeks, Rome moved to extend its authority over the Greeks. Roman sympathizers among the Greeks gave the Romans reports as to who was anti-Roman, and the Romans deported the denounced people in great number. In helping conservative politicians in one city, Roman soldiers invaded an assembly and murdered five hundred officeholders who had been reported to be anti-Roman. From Perseus' archives, the Romans discovered letters disclosing that he had had secret support from high-ranking officials in the Achaean League of cities in Peloponnesia. In response, the Romans rounded up close to nine hundred Achaean leaders and intellectuals, including the historian Polybius, and shipped them back to Italy, keeping them for a trial that was never held.

Rhodes and Pergamum also suffered. Unhappy with Rhodes and Pergamum for having made a deal with Perseus during the war, Rome let Pergamum's neighbors attack and harass it. And from Rhodes, Rome took Caria, Lycia and the island of Delos. The trade of Rhodes fell as much as eighty-five percent, which benefited Italian competitors. And the sea-going piracy that Rhodes had successfully repressed as a naval power started rising again.

Rome Destroys Carthage and Takes Control of Greece

In 157, Cato, still a senator, visited North Africa and became aware of Carthage's prosperity, and this sparked his belief that Carthage continued to be a menace to Rome. A veteran of the war against Carthage and narrow-minded, Cato still loathed that city. He ended every speech with the words "Carthage must be destroyed."

A neighbor of Carthage, Numidia, took advantage of Rome's hostility to Carthage by making encroachments on Carthaginian territory and then asking Rome for arbitration. Rome failed to act with the impartiality that might have inhibited Numidia from making further encroachments, and after suffering a number of aggressions by Numidia, Carthage lost its patience and retaliated. Rome saw this as a breach of peace by Carthage, and in the year 150 Rome's Senate voted for war against Carthage.

Believing that war against Rome was hopeless, a delegation that Carthage sent to Rome offered Rome surrender in the form of committing Carthage to "the faith of Rome" – a move understood to mean that Rome could take possession of Carthage but that the lives of the people of Carthage would be spared and that they would not be taken as slaves. Rome's Senate responded by granting Carthage self-rule and the right of the city and its people to keep all their possessions on condition that Carthage send to Rome three hundred of its leading citizens as hostages.

Hoping to save their city from destruction and amid much grieving, the Cathaginians sent their leading citizens to Rome as hostages. No longer wedded to its old concept of honor, Rome had already decided to wipe Carthage from the map. Rome demanded that Carthage surrender all its weapons, and Carthage surrendered its weapons, including two hundred thousands suits of mail and two thousand catapults. Rome demanded that the people of Carthage surrender their city and move ten miles inland. Moving back ten miles meant not only leaving behind their homes but also their docks and quays and their ability to carry on their sea-going trade. The people of Carthage preferred war and refused Rome's demands. Rome responded as it had planned, with military operations, which began in the year 149.

Meanwhile, people in what is now Portugal – the Lusitani – were again attempting to free themselves from Roman domination, and so too were peoples in central Spain. Roman legions overwhelmed the Lusitani. Rome offered them peace and land, trapped them, slaughtered 9,000 of them and enslaved 20,000. A new leader arose among the outraged Lusitani and renewed his people's war against the Romans, the Lusitani achieving their first success in the year 147, killing 10,000 Roman soldiers.

One response by Rome to the new trouble in Spain was a change in the New Year. To give one of its generals a longer season for campaigning, the Senate moved the date of the New Year from March 15 to January 1.

While Rome was busy with Spain and Carthage, an adventurer named Andricus, who claimed to be the son of Perseus, defied Rome and reunited Macedonia. Rome sent an army to Macedonia that arrived in 148 and drove out Andricus. By the fall of 147, Rome's legions were in control of the countryside around Carthage. Rome had not yet penetrated Carthage's wall, but the possibility of a united effort against

Rome by Carthage, Macedonia and the Greeks was over. Rome decided that its presence would be needed in Macedonia to keep the Macedonians in line, and it began a permanent rule and military occupation there, Macedonia becoming the first Roman province east of the Adriatic Sea.

By now, of the 900 or so Achaean leaders and intellectuals that had been shipped to Italy some twenty years before, only 200 were still alive. Rome's Senate allowed them to return home, but resentment against Rome remained strong among Greeks of the Achaean League, and this resentment increased when Rome supported Sparta in a war that erupted between Sparta and other members of the Achaean league. Some in the city of Corinth saw the continuing war between Rome and Carthage and the continuing rebellion in Spain as an opportune time to stand against Rome's pretensions of authority over Greek cities. It was a time of economic distress among the Greeks, and a leader from Corinth named Critolaus traveled from town to town in Greece calling for debt reform and opposition to Rome.

Critolaus described the real enemies of the Greeks as those among them who called for conciliation with Rome. In Corinth, moderate opinion was silenced, and in the spring of 146 Critolaus persuaded the Achaean league to declare war against Rome's presence in their part of the world. The city of Thebes, resenting Roman interference in their affairs, allied itself with the Achaean league. Across Greece, patriotic clubs appeared and denounced Rome. Athens and Sparta stayed out of the war, but elsewhere across Greece men eagerly joined Critolaus' army or another army preparing to fight Rome. Slaves were freed and recruited for the fight, and wealthy Greeks who favored Rome were frightened into contributing jewelry and money to the cause.

In the spring of 146, Roman soldiers were finally able to penetrate Carthage's walls. They swarmed into the city and began fighting street by street. First Carthage's harbor area fell to the Romans, then the market area, and finally the citadel in the city-center. Amid suicides and carnage, the Romans demolished and burned the city. They carried off survivors, selling the woman and children into slavery and throwing the men into prison, where they were to perish. Then the Romans spread salt across what had been Carthage's farmlands, and Carthage was no more.

In Greece, Critolaus' army was defeated by the Roman army sent from Macedonia. Later in 146 a force sent from Rome arrived and defeated an army of Greeks at the city of Corinth. To warn others, the Romans slaughtered all the men they found in Corinth. They enslaved the city's women and children, and they shipped Corinth's treasures to Italy and burned the city to the ground. Greek cities hostile to Rome had their walls demolished and their people disarmed. The Romans found Thebes entirely empty of people, its inhabitants having fled to wander through mountains and wilderness. According to the Greek historian Polybius, people everywhere were throwing themselves "down wells and over precipices."

Rome dissolved the Achaean league and had its leaders put to death. Rome's governor to Macedonia became governor also of the entire Greek peninsula. Rome would now allow only internal rule by Greek cities – by wealthy elites. Border disputes would remain, but they would be settled by Roman power. It was the beginning of Rome's permanent presence in the region and of a rule by foreigners that was to last two thousand years.

THE HISTORIAN POLYBIUS

Polybius had fared better than most of the leaders and intellectuals that Rome had taken from Achaea. While a prisoner, he met the head of one of Rome's great families, Scipio Aemilianus. Scipio found Polybius good company and exchanged books with him. He took Polybius with him on military campaigns, and he introduced Polybius to Rome's high society. Polybius remained in Rome after the other captives returned to Greece, and the Scipios became his patrons while he attempted to write the history of Rome to 146 BC – a work that happened to be compatible with the views of his patrons.

Polybius sought to explain how Rome was able to become master over the Greeks. He described the Romans as having moderation, integrity, valor, boldness, discipline and frugality in greater amounts than have other peoples. This, he wrote, enabled Rome to unite and to close ranks when faced with danger. His fellow Greeks, he wrote, were more literate and educated than the Romans but when faced with adversity they had weakened themselves by division and argument.

Polybius described the superiority of Romans as belonging mainly to the aristocrats. Common people, Roman and otherwise, he saw as lightheaded, filled with lawless appetites and inclined toward bursts of anger and fits of temper. He described the recent rebellion of Greece's common people against Rome as insane folly, and he believed that despite its abuses Rome was bestowing upon the Greeks great benefits.

Polybius saw Rome's patriarchal tradition and its religion as serving the cohesion that made Rome successful. Awe of the supernatural, he wrote, helps maintain cohesion. Religion, he wrote, helps to pacify the common man's anarchic temper. And he described Rome's elite and other ruling elites as using religion with this in mind.

Polybius saw Rome's success as partly the result of its willingness to enforce discipline by such punishments as executing a sentry for neglecting his duty or beating a soldier with a cudgel for throwing away his weapon, orbeating a soldier for boasting in order to get a decoration, or for homosexuality. He saw strength in Rome's willingness to punish by decimation – the killing of every tenth man – in any military unit that had displayed cowardice.

Polybius believed that societies went through cycles of growth, decay and fall. And, believing that low birth rates contributed to decline, he warned Rome's aristocracy about their declining numbers. He wrote of the incorruptibility of the Romans but warned them about their new hedonism and the lack of discipline that was creeping into their army. He warned them about the spread of indifference and a growing influence of the mob.

Polybius wrote that Rome's success was in part the result of its superior institutions. How it was that a superior, incorruptible ruling people or their superior institutions might allow decay he did not say. And the quality of leadership and the institutions of his superior people were about to face difficult tests.

SLAVE REVOLTS AND THE GRACCHI MURDERS

With the growing supply of slaves, on some days in Rome thousands of men, women and children might be put on the market, forced to stand naked, a placard around their neck to advertise their qualities, their flesh inspected and felt. For a pretty boy or girl a Roman might have to pay more, but a Sardinian, Gaul or Spaniard cost very little – far less than it cost to breed a slave.

Plantation owners placed male slaves in barracks or housed them in underground dungeons, leaving them separated from their families, which they might never see again. Plantation slaves worked in gangs ordered about by men with lashes. They were chained at night so they could not run away. They could be killed by their master without the master suffering any form of punishment, but, if a slave killed a master, a number of them could be held accountable and any of them put to death.

To appear affluent a Roman family had to have at least ten slaves, and such families had slaves for just about every task. And the power that a master and his family had over their domestic slaves encouraged some slaves to wheedle their way into favor through flattery or sexual favors.

Most Romans saw slavery as a natural part of life, as a result of their being favored by the gods, that defeat and slavery were the fate of inferior peoples. For some Romans slavery was a source of ego enhancement: looking at a creature more wretched than they bolstered their pride, and many Romans made slaves the objects of their ridicule.

Runaway slaves were hunted down, and if they were caught they might be executed. Runaway slaves roamed the countryside, surviving by banditry and making travel dangerous. Slaves sometimes revolted in groups, one of the larger of such revolts coming in 196 BC, a revolt that ended with the Romans executing seven thousand of them. A generation later the Romans crushed another rebellion, involving around four thousand slaves.

In 135 BC, about four hundred slaves in Sicily revolted after being encouraged to do so by a slave priest from Syria named Eunus, who announced the favor of the gods. The slaves massacred most of their masters, sparing only a few who had been most humane to them. This uprising encouraged other slaves in Sicily, and as many as sixty thousand joined the revolt and seized a number of Sicilian towns, and they defeated the first of the armies that Rome sent against them.

Rome Acquires Nominal Rule in Pergamum

In 133, while the slave revolt in Sicily was still alive, Rome acquired its first possession in Asia Minor. This was Pergamum, whose king ruled and received tribute from much of western Asia Minor. Pergamum was a prosperous state, receiving income from state owned, slave powered, textile and parchment workshops and income from cattle raising and agriculture. Pergamum had been allied with Rome and was ruled by an eccentric king named Attalus III. Near death and childless, Attalus willed his kingdom to Rome. It has been surmised that he did so to prevent a relative, Aristonicus, from succeeding him. At the time, the slave unrest had spread east of the Adriatic. And Pergamum was also shaken by a wider social unrest. Perhaps Attalus believed that only Rome would be able to maintain law and order in his empire. At any rate, Attalus died in 133, and Rome accepted Pergamum as its inheritance.

Tiberius Gracchus

It was during the slave revolts of the 130s that Tiberius Gracchus was agitating for reform in Rome. Tiberius Gracchus belonged to a distinguished, noble family. His grandfather had been a consul, military leader and hero. His mother was one of Rome's most cultured women. She had had Tiberius educated. It had been an education that emphasized public duty, the maintenance of godliness and the "divine spark of reason" in men. This was the Stoicism of Tiberius' boyhood tutor, a Greek named Blossius, who remained with Tiberius in adulthood as an advisor.

Tiberius had a reputation as a courageous military leader: he had been a commander in the final war against Carthage and was reputed to have been the first Roman to scale Carthage's wall. In 137 he served with distinction in Spain. And when he returned to Rome he entered politics. He complained bitterly that those who had bore arms for their country enjoyed nothing more than air and light, and he complained that men had fought and many had died to maintain the luxury and wealth of others. He spoke of the restless poor being a threat to political stability, and he expressed his concern that the small farmer, who had been the backbone of the republic, was disappearing. For the safety of all, he said, it was urgent that as many families as possible be restored to the land.

Rome was entering a period of class warfare – the same warfare that had weakened the Greeks. Tiberius won an enthusiastic following among Rome's urban poor. In 133 he was elected by a Plebeian Assembly as one of its ten tribunes. The Senate had gained more power and prestige during the Punic Wars, and the Plebeian Assemblies (Comitias Plebus) had declined in influence. The Romans had emerged from the Punic wars with the widespread understanding that ultimate authority over the military lay with the Senate, that it was the Senate's job to know, advise and guide, and the Senate's job to decide the question of war or peace and other foreign policy matters. But Tiberius' charisma and call for reforms revived the prestige of the Plebeian Assembly and the office of Tribune. Tiberius raised the issue of the right of tribunes to initiate legislation and of Rome's Constitution not having given legislative powers to the Senate.

Senators were unhappy with this sudden questioning of their powers, and they were unhappy too with legislation initiated by Tiberius that called for landless veterans to be settled on public lands that the rich had been using. Tiberius' land reform meant a loss of land among the Senators, but the Senators found another issue to speak to: annoyed with Tiberius' legislation, they complained about what they called his ambition.

The Senate vetoed Tiberius' reforms, and Tiberius moved to override the veto, which the law stated could be done with the backing of all ten of the Plebeian Assembly's tribunes. But a tribune who was a large landowner sided with the Senate. To counter this, Tiberius organized a special election in the Plebeian Assembly that replaced the offending tribune with someone who supported the reforms. The Plebian Assembly then passed into law a modified version of his reform bill, and Tiberius put himself, his brother Gaius and his father-in-law on the board that was to oversee the implementations of the reforms. From the Senate came an anger that Polybius had attributed to the lower classes. The Senate charged that the removal from office of the tribune was a violation of tradition. Tiberius argued that tribunes were sworn to defend the interests of the common people and that by opposing his reforms the tribune in question had broken that trust.

Senators accused Tiberius of attempting to usurp the Senate's prerogatives and accused him of being a dangerous revolutionary with tyrannical ambitions, and they attempted to delay implementation of Tiberius' reforms by refusing to vote for its funding. Contrary to the Senate's authority in controlling finances, Tiberius secured funds from the treasury of Pergamum, which had just been willed to Rome.

After serving his one-year term as a tribune, Tiberius sought a second term, finding precedent for doing so from the previous century. A rumor circulated that Tiberius was seeking dictatorial powers. During Tiberius' campaign for re-election a riot broke out between his supporters and his opponents. News of the riot reached the Senate. One of the Senators – who was also Rome's chief priest, the Pontifex Maximus – quickly gathered a mob that included servants and clients of prominent city leaders. The mob rushed the supporters of Tiberius, clubbing and stoning to death three hundred of them. They found Tiberius, tore his toga from his body, bludgeoned him to death and threw him and the bodies of the other dead men into the Tiber River.

It was the first recorded political murder in Rome in four hundred years. The Senate attempted to legalize the killings: it set up a court that tried surviving supporters of Tiberius, and it posthumously charged Tiberius with having planned an attempt at becoming king. Many Romans viewed the Senators as august and honorable men, and they believed the charges against Tiberius. They reasoned that if Tiberius wanted to become king then he deserved to die. Many others believed the charges against Tiberius were false and that he had died for the common people. The court found some of Tiberius' followers guilty of having supported Tiberius and had them executed. Then, concerned with public opinion, the Senate sent the Pontifex Maximus to the east, ostensibly on business but in fact into exile.

Slave Wars and the Revolt of Aristonicus

The slave revolt that had spread to western Asia Minor was joined by serfs. Aristonicus, perhaps believing himself the rightful heir to the throne in Pergamum, appealed to slaves and serfs and joined forces with them in a common cause against Roman authority. After Tiberius' murder, his old stoic tutor and aide, Blossius, fled from Rome and joined Aristonicus and his movement. Aristonicus warred against Rome's allies in Asia Minor – the rulers of Pontus, neighboring Bithynia and Paphlagonia, and Cappadocia – and he easily defeated them. In Sicily, after three years of struggle, the Romans finally broke the back of the slave uprising there, leaving only mopping up operations to carry out. And Roman legions went to Asia Minor where they defeated Aristonicus and isolated him in a region in Caria. Aristonicus surrendered, and the Romans took him and the treasure of

Pergamum's ruling family to Rome, where Aristonicus was paraded through the streets, thrown into prison and executed by strangulation. The Romans pursued the remnants of Aristonicus' army, which was fighting a guerrilla war. The Romans poisoned the water wells that local people and the guerrillas depended upon, which brought an end to the war and brought Roman control over much of western Asia Minor.

Gaius Gracchus

The reforms of Tiberius Gracchus remained law after his death, and more reforms were made law after the Plebeian Assembly elected his younger brother, Gaius Gracchus, tribune in the years 123 and 122. Gaius Gracchus helped create more colonies for Rome's landless. He sponsored legislation to put people to work building secondary roads. He helped improve conditions within the army and outlawed its recruitment of boys under seventeen. And he increased the capacity of storing grain in Rome, which helped stabilize grain prices.

Enjoying popular support, Gaius successfully challenged the power of the Senate by passing legislation that outlawed proceedings such as those the Senate had used to persecute his brother's supporters. This new law forbade trials with the power of capital punishment that did not have the approval of the Plebeian Assembly.

Hoping to build opposition against the patricians of the Senate, Gaius encouraged the appetite of the class called the equites: families that had made their wealth from government contracts, finance and trade. He gave jury duty to the equites in place of exclusive jury duty by the patricians. He encouraged the equites to have more say in government, which antagonized the Senate.

Gaius sought Roman citizenship for those Italians who had fought with Rome's armies, and he advocated helping the landless among these veterans by founding a colony where Carthage once stood. Among those opposed to giving citizenship to Italian veterans were Roman businessmen, who feared more competition with a lost advantage. Opponents warned Romans that the spread of Roman citizenship would jeopardize their good seats at shows and festivals. They disseminated false rumors about the failure of Gaius' project at Carthage, and they managed to turn enough of Rome's citizens against Gaius that he lost his bid for a third term as tribune.

Taking advantage of a drop in Gaius' popularity, moves were made to repeal some of his and Tiberius' reforms. Gaius rallied his supporters against this, and he gathered bodyguards around himself. A scuffle occurred between his supporters and opponents that left dead the servant of a consul, who was a vociferous enemy of Gaius. The consul used this incident to persuade the Senate to create martial law, which enabled the Senate to create an armed force with which the consul could combat civil unrest.

Knowing they were the targets of the Senate's martial law, Gaius and as many as three thousand of his supporters withdrew to Aventine Hill. The consul's army overran and killed them. A reward had been offered for Gaius' head, and he was decapitated. A soldier, it is said, scooped out the brains and filled the skull with lead and then turned it in for the reward: an equal weight in gold.

MARIUS, SULLA AND DICTATORSHIP

In the North African kingdom of Numidia a prince named Jugurtha became king in an old-fashioned way: he murdered family rivals. And he massacred the male population of a city that resisted his taking power, a massacre that included many Italian and Roman businessmen who had been residing there. Many in Rome saw Jugurtha as having violated Rome's dignity. Roman businessmen concerned with trade and investment in North Africa wanted a full-scale war against Jugurtha, but the Senate did nothing. Then one of Rome's tribunes hinted that Jugurtha had used his great wealth to bribe some senators. And, responding to agitation from this tribune and Rome's citizenry, the Senate, in 112, declared war against Jugurtha.

People in Numidia saw the coming of Roman legions as an invasion, and they swung to the side of Jugurtha. For more than two years the Romans fought a guerrilla war in difficult terrain. A Roman cavalry officer named Gaius Marius rose amid the timid and incompetent aristocratic officers in Numidia. Marius was brave, aggressive, blunt speaking, tough and had disdain for the niceties of the educated elite, which put him in good stead with his soldiers. Marius complained about the way the war was being fought, and letters from soldiers to Rome supported him and his views. Those in Rome with business interests in Numidia were losing money as the war dragged on, and they supported Marius.

While on leave in Rome, Marius decided to run for consul, despite his humble origins. The Military Assembly (Comitia Centuriata) elected him to one of the two consul seats. Moved by Marius' popularity, the Senate voted to transfer command of the armies in Numidia to him. The following year, while Marius was still in Numidia, he won another term as consul – despite a law against a consul serving more than one term in succession and a law against selecting as consul someone away from Rome.

Marius defeated Jugurtha in the year 106, and he returned to Rome, displaying the soon to be executed Jugurtha in his victory parade. By now, Rome was being threatened by tall, blondish, tribes of Cimbri and

Teutons who had been driving from their territory in Jutland and Frisia. Rome had sent armies against them, but these armies were poorly led and fared badly. In one battle the Romans lost as many as 80,000 dead – Rome's greatest defeat since Cannae. These losses left Italy open to a Cimbri and Teuton invasion. Fear and panic swept through Italy, and in Rome frightened people mobbed and stoned senators. The Cimbri knew and respected the power of Rome and went in the direction of Spain, and the Teutons roamed about southern Gaul. The crisis in the north had ended, but fear of the Cimbri and Teutons remained.

In 104, Marius was again elected consul, and he was elected consul the following year and the year after that, while he was preparing an army for war against the Cimbri and Teutons. Before Marius had taken command, only those from families with property had been conscripted into Rome's army, and they were not eager to serve nor as well disciplined as had been Rome's farmer-soldiers of previous centuries. Landless men had joined the army only as baggage handlers. In the war against Jugurtha, poor discipline had become widespread, with the sons of businessmen especially lacking in discipline and motivation. Disturbed by this, Marius rejected conscription and had begun creating an army of Roman and Italian volunteers from among the landless and the urban poor. He motivated his army with pay, booty and the promise of retirement on a piece of land donated by the state, and he improved the training of his recruits, especially with their swords. With longer service, Marius' volunteers had more time to develop their martial skills. Marius gave his army new equipment and new tactics. He standardized the size of each Roman legion to 6,000 men. He created an army with more *esprit de corps*. But it was an army more concerned with themselves as a unit than with the interests of Rome.

In 102 the Romans extended their rule abroad to include Cilicia in the southeastern corner of Asia Minor, which had been a pirate base. And that year Marius and his army went north and crushed both the Teutons and the Cimbri. Coincidentally, Rome's governor to Sicily decided to reduce pressures of slave discontent there by announcing that he would return a few hundred slaves to their homelands. Those who stood to lose slaves protested and persuaded the governor to change his mind. Slaves expecting their freedom responded to their disappointment by revolting, and, as before, other slaves joined in. The new slave revolt overran the whole of Sicily and took Rome two years of bloody fighting to subdue.

More Politics of Violence

Seen as Rome's savior, Marius was elected consul by the Military Assembly in 100 BC for the sixth time. With Marius, common Romans felt that a new era had arrived. A tribune named Saturninus and his praetor friend, Glaucia, wished to revive the reforms of the Gracchi brothers. They were political allies of Marius and supplied him with knowledge of the workings of government that he lacked. They made fiery public speeches, and they wrote a program of reforms for Marius. The program called for Marius' Italian veterans to receive Roman citizenship, and his veterans were to receive lands that had been taken from the Cimbri. Also for Marius' veterans, colonies were to be created in Sicily, Macedonia and Greece. And for people in general, there was to be a reduction in the price of grain.

Marius could not easily oppose these reforms, and he introduced them for legislation. From some opposed to reform came a renewed threat of violence, and Marius countered these threats by calling his veterans into the streets. The Senate vetoed the reforms, and one of the tribunes sided with the senators, preventing the Plebeian Assembly from overriding the veto. But by threatening the Senate with Marius' veterans, Saturninus coerced it into changing its position. The reforms were passed. So too was a law that each senator had to take an oath to support the new legislation or surrender his seat, and only one among the frightened senators refused to acquiesce.

Hatreds remained from the period of the Gracchi brothers two and three decades before, and, given the violence that had been used in the past by those opposed to reform, Saturninus, Glaucia and their backers saw their use of violence as appropriate. Marius and the equites gave Saturninus and Glaucia moral support – the equites having sided with the common people against the patricians. But backers of Saturninus and Glaucia went too far in their use of violence: they murdered a recently elected tribune whom they disliked, then during Glaucia's campaign as Rome's other consul they attacked and killed Glaucia's rival. Bloodshed and chaos frightened the equites, who started going over to the side of the patricians and the Senate. Bolstered by this support, the Senate passed an ultimatum and called on Marius to restore order. Marius was shamed by the killings, and he also sided with the Senate. Using his veterans, he had Saturninus and Glaucia and some of their followers arrested and locked in the Senate house for safekeeping. The place was insufficiently safe. A group hostile to Saturninus and Glaucia tore a hole in its roof and stoned the two men and their followers to death.

The reforms that Saturninus and Glaucia had forced upon the Senate were declared invalid, and many common Romans were left disappointed – disappointed also with Marius. Marius felt humiliated, and to escape from scorn he went on a tour of the empire in the east, hoping that as Rome's most renowned general he might soon again be asked to command its armies. The Senate rejoiced, and in 95 BC it attempted to punish those who had supported Marius' reforms, many of

whom were Marius' Italian veterans. The Senate passed a law that
ordered all non-Roman Italians in Rome to move from the city.

War between Romans and Italians

Italians, meanwhile, were becoming fed up with the Romans taking
advantage of them, as the Romans did in the period of the Gracchi
reforms, when Rome confiscated Italian lands for distribution among
Romans. And they were becoming fed up with the imperious attitudes
of visiting Roman officials, as when the wife of a visiting senior
Roman official had all the men turned out of a bath so she could use it
and then complained that the bath was not clean.

By now, Italians and Romans had the same customs and spoke the
same language. The Italians had fought alongside the Romans in their
imperial wars and against the threat from the Germans. They paid taxes
to Rome and shared the financial burden of Rome's wars but with no
corresponding increase in rewards and without equal protection under
Roman law. A Roman soldier could not be summarily executed by an
officer, but an Italian soldier could. In warfare, Romans got a greater
share of booty, and the Italians were often sent against the tougher
enemies. Now the Italians wanted equality, and they wanted their votes
to count concerning vital issues decided in Rome. They wanted to be
equal partners in what had become a nation.

A Roman senator and tribune, Marcus Livius Drusus II, supported
the Italians, but his effort was frustrated by opposition among Romans
in general and by most senators, who looked with scorn upon anyone
not originally from Rome and not of a Roman noble family. For his
trouble, Drusus was assassinated, and when word of his assassination
spread through Italy it was a signal to Italians that relief from Rome
would not be forthcoming. Various Italian cities increased communications with each other and took steps that to Rome suggested conspira-
torial alliances.

Rome sent officials to Italian cities to spy and to persuade. In the
city of Asculum, a visiting Roman official berated a crowd. The crowd
became enraged and killed him and his aides. Fearing retaliation from
Rome, the crowd closed their city's gates, and they hunted down and
killed all the Romans they could find. Other Italian cities joined
Asculum in an open revolt against Rome. Rome sent its legions against
the rebel cities. A civil war had begun, and in the first year of the war,
Rome moved to prevent more cities from joining the rebellion, and they
did so by extending citizenship to their inhabitants, pretending they
were doing so as a reward for their loyalty. What the Romans had
resisted before the war, they were now offering because of the war.

In 89, the second year of the war, the Romans gained the upper
hand, with Marius having gladly accepted a minor command offered

him by the Senate. A Roman army attacked Asculum, and it was written that only a handful of that city's 60,000 people survived. Anxious to end the war, Rome offered citizenship to those cities that would agree to stop fighting, and many cities accepted, and the war began winding down.

But by now the war had damaged Italy's economy. During the war, debt had become more widespread. Uncertain about the future, financiers had begun refusing more loans and demanding payment. Those Romans angered by the money-lenders had begun a movement against usury. A praetor responded favorably to the movement and invoked an ancient law against usury that had long been ignored. This infuriated financiers, and a gang of men mobbed the praetor and cut his throat, and some who had spoken in favor of the praetor and against usury were lynched.

Sulla against Marius and Rufus

As the war between Rome and the Italians was winding down, wrangling began among Roman politicians as to how the vote should be distributed among Rome's new Italian citizens. A moderate senator and tribune, Sulpicius Rufus, wanted a more equal distribution of voting powers than did conservative senators. Rufus also favored allowing the return of those who had been exiled for siding with the Italians against Rome. And to help curtail the temptation among senators to take bribes, Rufus proposed expelling from the Senate anyone for having debt over a certain amount. Some senators bitterly opposed Rufus, and Rufus gathered around him three thousand bodyguards. Rufus sought support from wealthy businessmen, and, believing that Marius would be of help against the Senate, Rufus supported Marius as commander of an army in the east to counter the expansion of a king named Mithradates.

Mithradates was half-Greek, half-Persian, exceptionally bright, and ruler of Pontus, a kingdom on the coast in northeastern Asia Minor. He had spread his power westward in Asia Minor, to the territory that Rome had taken from Aristonicus – where Roman rule remained unpopular. There Mithradates had inspired a massacre of around 80,000 Romans and Italian residents, many of them businessmen. Then Mithradates sent troops from Asia Minor into Thrace and through Macedonia to Greece, where he inspired more rebellion against Rome.

Instead of choosing Marius to lead the war against Mithradates, the Senate chose one of its two consuls, a man who had become a personal enemy of Marius, Lucius Cornelius Sulla. Sulla was from an impoverished noble family. He had served under Marius in Numidia, and he had become renowned as a general during the war against the Italians. He viewed the political turmoil in Rome of recent years as did most conservatives: not as the creation of patricians reluctant to accept reforms but as the product of anarchical inclinations among common people. The appointment of Sulla instead of Marius disturbed those who favored reforms. Sulla left Rome to take command of the six legions in Italy that had been readied for the war against Mithradates, and those who supported reforms took to the streets to express their frustration. In violation of a sacred prohibition against a military leader marching troops into Rome, Sulla returned with his army. From their roof tops, people threw stones at Sulla's army, and Sulla responded by setting their houses afire. Sulla defeated an army of men that Marius had hastily assembled, and he and his troops overwhelmed others who supported Rufus and Marius. Rufus' severed head was nailed up for public display. Marius and others fled the city, and Sulla had them declared outlaws, which allowed anyone to kill them.

Sulla, Marius and Cinna

Sulla decreed that the Senate would have the power to veto any bill or election it pleased and that tribunes would be unable to initiate legislation. Sulla looked with nostalgia upon his noble ancestry, and he wished a return to what he believed were the principles that had made Rome great. Wishing to establish a legitimate government, Sulla did not run again for consul as Marius had, and in the year 87, the Military Assembly elected one consul who supported Sulla and another consul who was popular among the common people: a man named Cinna. Sulla and his troops were looking forward to going east to combat Mithradates, and before they departed Sulla had Cinna swear that he would not try to subvert the new order.

Soon after Sulla and his troops left for the east, political violence erupted again in Rome. To save himself from conservatives, Cinna fled Rome, and the Senate took away his consulship. Cinna raised an army among Italians, and Marius joined him with a force he had gathered from among his veterans and some local shepherds and runaway slaves. To counter Cinna and Marius, the Senate raised a force, but to no avail. Cinna and Marius marched their armies into Rome and they won control of the city. Marius, almost seventy, sought vengeance for his years of humiliation, and he and Cinna sought to secure their standing against any possible future vengeance. Their troops butchered all supporters of Sulla that they could find. They murdered various senators and nailed their heads up for public display while much of the rest of the Senate fled the city. The violence and disrespect for rule by law that Rome's conservatives had initiated in the days of the Gracchi brothers, Tiberius and Gaius, had come full circle.

Cinna was made consul again, and Marius became the other consul, a consul for the seventh time, as a prophet had told him he would. But the prophesy was apparently only a tease: Marius died after only a month in office. Cinna was left with control of the city, and he enjoyed the support of most the city's plebeians. He repealed Sulla's laws, reduced all debts by seventy-five percent, gave complete equality to Italians, declared Sulla a public enemy, confiscated Sulla's property and persecuted Sulla's family and friends.

Sulla Defeats Mithradates and Returns to Rome

During his war against Mithradates, Sulla was popular with his troops, giving them freedom to plunder and to slay officers who had made themselves unpopular – Sulla wishing his officers to lead rather than command. In 86 (the year that Marius died), Sulla sacked Athens, which had joined Mithradates against Rome. And that year, in a brilliant campaign, Sulla won significant victories against Mithradates. In 85 BC, Mithradates agreed to withdraw from all territories he had conquered, to surrender part of his navy and to pay Rome an indemnity. Sulla restored various kings that Mithradates had deposed. He punished those Greek cities that had been prominent in their support of Mithradates. Then in 84, Sulla began his return to Rome.

In the spring of 83, Sulla and eight legions landed unopposed at the heel of the boot-shaped Italian peninsula. Many of those who had fled from Marius and Cinna flocked to Sulla's ranks. Cinna sent an army east to remove Sulla from his command, but the troops he sent joined forces with Sulla. Cinna sent another force against Sulla, which met Sulla halfway to Rome. Many deserted to Sulla's side. Sulla defeated Cinna's army. Then in 82 Sulla made his assault on Rome. And with the approach of Sulla's army, a mob in Rome slaughtered numerous aristocrats.

Sulla's army overran Rome and conquered it, and it slaughtered 8,000 Romans that it had taken prisoner. Sulla drew up an enemies list: forty insufficiently conservative or insufficiently loyal senators and a list of sixteen hundred members of the equites. He gave rewards to informers who helped round up the enemies. Men were taken by surprise in their homes, in the streets and in temples. Some were killed outright. Some were dragged through the streets, as frightened spectators dared not protest. Sulla had the property of the executed distributed to his soldiers, which inspired some to accuse and attack anyone with property. And Sulla set free the nearly forty thousand slaves of the executed, giving them his name and winning a new source of support and new recruits for repressing and terrorizing those considered enemies of his rule.

Sulla's New Order

Sulla sought to undo the failings of the previous fifty years. He created a new constitution that he believed would restore the republic and traditional order and dignity to Rome. He founded new laws, each supported by a precedent from the old republic. Believing in firm government by leaders of the upper classes, again he gave more power to the Senate. He reduced the powers of the tribunes and the Plebian Assembly. But he gave some of its seats in the Senate to members of the equites, believing that they too should be a part of the ruling elite and that this would put the equites in support of the government rather than with "the mob." He reorganized administration of the provinces. He made it law that one had to hold a lower office before being elected to a higher office. He created term limits, making it law that one had to wait ten years before running for another term for the same office. He made it law that consuls were to be at least 42 years-old. He ended the distribution of free grain among Rome's poor, hoping this would encourage some of them to leave the city. He moved against what he saw as subversive religions, prohibiting what he viewed as magic, the performing of nocturnal rites and witchcraft. Those found guilty of performing these were to be crucified or thrown to wild beasts.

In the year 79, just three years after returning to Rome, Sulla surprised the world by retiring. He was around sixty and believed that peace had been established at home and abroad and that Rome's government was functioning as it had in its glorious past. He thought he had set the world right. In his first year of retirement he hunted and fished, he enjoyed the company of friends, he enjoyed seeing comedy plays he had written preformed on the stage, and he studied philosophy, and like some other bright men he became a believer in Epicureanism. Then, after this one year of peace and contentment, he died, unaware that the Roman republic still lacked that which was essential for peace: the political compromise that Cato had believed in, which could come only with more democratic institutions. Rome's senators did not represent any popular constituency, and the Senate was not obliged to accept initiatives by the Plebeian Assembly.

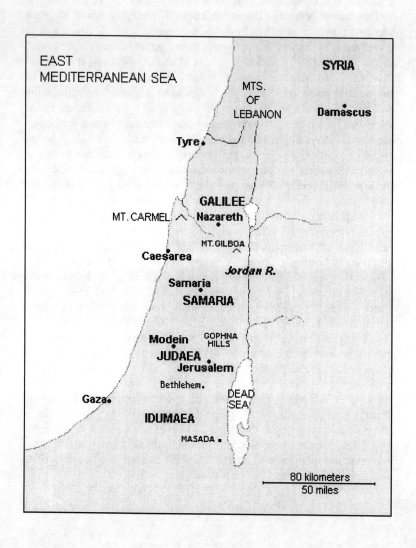

CHAPTER 17

JUDAEA AND CIVIL WAR

REVOLT, INDEPENDENCE AND RELIGIOUS DIVISIONS

Jewish writers continued an attempt to glorify Jewish culture, to defend it as the oldest in the world, to describe the Jews as teachers of other peoples rather than having been influenced by others. Around 150 BC, a writer named Eupolemus wrote that Abraham was one of those who had survived the flood, that it was Abraham who had built Babylon, that Moses was the world's first philosopher, and that Moses had invented letters and had taught the Greeks. Around 100 BC, a Jew named Artapanus wrote a book entitled *On the Jews* in which he asserted that Moses had originated Egyptian civilization and had taught the Egyptians the worship of the bull-god, Apis, and the bird-god, Ibis. Another scribe, named Cleodemus (or Malchus), asserted that two sons of Abraham had joined the mythical Greek hero Heracles (Hercules) on his expedition into Africa and that Heracles had married the daughter of one of the sons.

A few Jews argued that if there were gods, the gods did not care. The devout countered with the claim that Yahweh cared but that he worked in ways that were mysterious to people because mortals were limited in their understanding of Yahweh's labors, and they argued that eventually the righteous would be rewarded and the wicked punished.

Revolt Against Antiochus IV

After his successful war against the Ptolemies of Egypt and before his disastrous war with Rome, the Seleucid monarch Antiochus III, ruling from Syria, had taken control of Palestine and Judaea. He had left Judaea's High Priest and Council of Elders to run Judaea, and he had exempted the temple at Jerusalem from taxation. But after the Romans defeated Antiochus III and forced him to pay tribute, Antiochus burdened the Jews with increased taxes – to as much as a third of all crops harvested.

Many in Judaea had favorable memories of rule by the Ptolemies, and in 175 BC the new Seleucid king, Antiochus IV, suspected that Judaea's High Priest, Onias III, favored Ptolemy VI. Onias was a member of the Zadok family, a dynasty that had ruled as High Priest since the time of King David. Onias was assassinated, and Antiochus IV appointed Onias' brother, Jason, as Judaea's High Priest. And Jason supported the Greek way of life practiced by Antiochus.

It was now that a gymnasium was built in Jerusalem, in which young men performed athletics without the inconvenience of robes. Jerusalem was renamed Antioch – one of many cities so named. Jerusalem's elite – its wealthy and its aristocratic priests – accepted these changes, and common people did not. Then a faction among Jerusalem's cultural elite won support from Antiochus by advocating more Hellenization than Jason was offering. In 172 Jason was replaced as High Priest, and the Zadok family line of High Priests came to and end.

In 171, war between the Seleucids and the Ptolemies erupted again. Antiochus IV invaded Egypt, and while Antiochus was in Egypt, Jason and a group of his supporters moved to regain power. They threw the new High Priest, Menelaus, into prison and slaughtered some of his supporters. To broaden his support, Jason joined forces with an anti-Hellenist movement called the Hasidim. With the Hasidim, Jason created a reign of terror in Jerusalem, and they drove from the city the troops Antiochus had garrisoned there.

While passing through Palestine on his way back to Syria, Antiochus and his troops entered Jerusalem, pulled down Jerusalem's walls, slaughtered Jason's backers and looted the Holy Temple. Jason fled, and Antiochus restored Menelaus as High Priest. Antiochus again had troops garrisoned in Jerusalem, and he fortified Jerusalem's citadel.

As a part of his attempt to unify the different cultures of his empire and to eliminate a source of resistance to his authority, Antiochus ordered the Jews to begin worshiping Zeus, and he commanded that they end circumcision and their celebration of the Sabbath. In exchange, Antiochus offered Jerusalem the right to govern itself in other respects, to mint its own coins, to participate in the Olympic games and other inter-city cultural events, and to join with other cities for mutual defense – that which Antiochus allowed Greek cities that he ruled.

Antiochus wrongly assumed that the worship of Yahweh among the Jews could be transformed into the worship of Zeus as easily as such transformations had been made in his dominions farther east – where Jews worshiped Yahweh under the name of Zeus Sabazions. And he wrongly assumed that the Jews of Judaea would easily accept the notion that all worshiped the same God. In 167 he had the temple in Jerusalem rededicated as a shrine to Zeus. Some Jews, especially among the upper classes, wanted closer ties and more trade with the rest of the Hellenized world, but many, including some of the Hellenized, saw Antiochus' reforms as compulsion to practice idolatry

– something neither the Persians nor the Ptolemies had tried to force upon them.

War, the Maccabees Family and Its Alliance with Rome

Rather than allow time for the Jews to adjust to the change in name of their god to Zeus, a military expedition was sent around Judaea to force compliance with the new laws of worship. The expedition came upon an old priest in the village of Modein who refused to offer a sacrifice to Zeus. The priest, Mattathias, struck down another Jew who was about to do so. To escape punishment, Mattathias, and his five sons – the Maccabees family – went with other Jews into the Gophna Hills. Their rebellion won support from people throughout Judaea. It was supported too by the author of the Book of Daniel – which was written during the time of the Maccabaean war.

The rebellion became partly a civil war and partly a war of national liberation. Its opposition to the rule of Antiochus IV pleased Rome because Rome wished to see Antiochus IV weakened. To strengthen his forces against Antiochus, the leader of the revolt, Judas Maccabaeus, made a treaty with Rome, which made the success of his rebellion more likely.

The Maccabaean rebellion took control of much of Judaea, but because Judas Maccabaeus was not from the kind of aristocratic family that qualified him to be the High Priest, that highest position among the Jews went to a priest and supporter named Alcium. Some among those fighting for independence objected to the appointment, believing that Alcium was insufficiently devout and insufficiently hostile to foreigners and foreign influences, and Alcium had sixty of these critics executed.

In 141 BC, more than twenty-five years into the rebellion (and shortly after Greece lost its independence to Rome) the Jews finally expelled the Seleucid garrison from the citadel in Jerusalem. By now, Antiochus IV, Judas Maccabaeus and other Maccabees had died. The last of the five Maccabaeus brothers, Simon, ruled. With the strength of Rome behind the Maccabees, Judaea won formal independence: a free Jewish state for the first time in more than four centuries. Simon Maccabaeus was chosen by popular assembly as High Priest despite his lack of qualifications by birth. He also took the position of Ethnarch, or *Ruler of the Nation,* announcing that his family would rule only until a true prophet should arise. He created a festival called *Hanukkah* to celebrate both Judaea's independence and the day that his rule began.

Yahweh Worship Splits into Factions

During the Maccabaean rebellion, a small faction claimed that their worship of Yahweh was unadulterated and that worship by other Jews was not. After failing to win the rest of Judaea to their point of view, they left Judaea and went to Damascus, where they hoped to establish a "New Covenant" of repentance. There, they would remain a sect and fade into oblivion.

The Maccabaean war had exacerbated divisions in Yahweh worship, the two most prominent divisions being between those called Pharisees and Sadducees. The Pharisees tended to be men from the lower classes – including craftsmen. They accepted the newer, popular doctrines: the conflict between good and evil spirits, Satan as an independent and evil force, and resurrection. The Sadducees were aristocrats, and among them were the priests who managed Jerusalem's temple. They rejected the new doctrines and saw the Pharisees as contributing to a vulgarization of their religion. Although the Sadducees were the more religiously conservative of the two factions, they were the more Hellenized. According to the Hellenized Jewish historian, Josephus (AD 37-95?), the Sadducees were haughty and harsh in their opinions toward common Jews and were, in turn, disliked by commoners. Supporting the Pharisees rather than the Sadducees, common Jews tended to see the Pharisees as "expounders of scripture" and scholars of Judaic law. And they saw the Pharisees as defenders of religious tradition against Hellenistic influences. This was encouraged by Pharisee insistence on a strict interpretation of Jewish law, including diet and dress, and a strict adherence to ceremony and observance of the Sabbath.

Pharisee concern with religious exactitude led them to encourage readings of portions of the Five Books of Moses every Monday, Thursday and Saturday. This led to the creation of village schools to promote that study, and it contributed to a tradition of reading among the Jews. Under pharisaic influence the synagogue became a university for the Jews, a place where they gathered to learn and read the words of sacred writings from the past, where they read from the Five Books of Moses (The Torah), studied, sang and prayed.

However much they failed to acknowledge it, the Pharisees drew heavily from Hellenism. They were attracted by the student-teacher relationship that had been common in the Hellenistic world but alien to Judaic society. They were impressed by that part of Hellenistic education that tried to develop character in students and that had a high regard for individuality. They were impressed by the Stoic teaching of an inner standard impervious to happenstance and suffering. And the Pharisees were attracted to Hellenistic law-making: Greek-style legislative bodies and scholars helping to create laws rather than laws being the creations of priests. The Pharisees created the *Beth Din ha-Gadol* (Great Legislature) as a lawmaking, law-transmitting and law-confirming body – an institution they did not learn of from scripture. But they saw their legislative body as having its authority in God rather than from a constitution, and they saw the laws created by the legislature as having originated in divine revelation. The Pharisees left interpretations of Judaism's laws open to discussion and scholarly debate. And in debate they invented the cross-examination that was to become a part of modern jurisprudence. They believed that God alone was able to look into the conscience of individuals and measure whether they lived by The Law.

WAR AMONG THE HASMONAEANS
AND LOSS OF INDEPENDENCE TO ROME

The Maccabees family was renamed the Hasmonaeans, and among the Hasmonaeans, as among other ruling families, conflicts developed. In 134, a son-in-law of Simon Maccabaeus, who was military commander of the region around Jericho, assassinated Simon and his two elder sons while they were his guests. A third son, John Hyrcanus escaped the assassination. John was governor of a region in Judaea along the Mediterranean coast and in command of a military force. He took power in Jerusalem, and there he was recognized as Simon's heir and made High Priest.

The Seleucid monarch, Antiochus VII, seeing Judaea weakened by inner turmoil, decided to regain his family's control over Judaea. Judaea fell to his armies. But when Antiochus VII died in 129, John Hyrcanus renewed the treaty between his family and Rome. And fear of Rome left both Antiochus' successor and the Ptolemies of Egypt reluctant to violate Judaea's borders.

With Rome as an ally, John Hyrcanus was able to expand Judaea's frontiers. He destroyed the city of Samaria, having disliked the Hellenized city for what he saw as its heretical form of Yahweh worship and its opposition to the Maccabees revolt. Then, in a series of military campaigns, he won territory that the Jewish state had lost during Nebuchadnessar's invasion some 470 years before. He annexed Idumaea and forced its population to adopt Judaism, including circumcision. He overran and annexed Galilee, and there, where Jesus was to preach a hundred a fifty years later, he forced conversions to Judaism – conquest again to influence belief.

More Civil War

In 104 BC, John Hyrcanus bequeathed rule to his wife and died. Their son, Aristobulus, was High Priest, and Aristobulus had his mother thrown into prison and starved to death, and he became king – the first of Judaea's monarchs to be both king and High Priest. Aristobulus had one brother assassinated and his other brothers jailed.

Then, after less than a year as king, Aristobulus died, and his widow released his brothers from jail and married the eldest of them: Alexander Jonathan. And Alexander Jonathan became king and High Priest.

Alexander Jonathan launched wars in all directions against Judaea's neighbors. Although he was a Pharisee, he allied himself with the aristocratic Sadducees and showed contempt for the Pharisees, and this precipitated an uprising against him and another civil war. The Pharisees hated Alexander so much that they sought an alliance with the Seleucid monarchy in Syria. The Seleucid monarch sent an army of both Syrians and Jews southward to overthrow Alexander, but those Jews who came south deserted and joined Alexander's forces. Alexander crushed the rebellion against him and took revenge against the Pharisees. He had eight hundred of them crucified in the center of Jerusalem and is said to have had the throats cut of their wives and children before their eyes, and to have watched some of the crucifixions from a window while dining among his harem. The executions helped to make Alexander Jonathan unpopular. Independence had proven of little benefit for common Jews, but with the increase in their misery they intensified their hope for the coming a great king – a *messiah* – and a future life in a spiritual kingdom in heaven.

The Ascent of the Herods and Another Civil War
An attempt to improve matters followed Alexander Jonathan's death in 76 BC. He was succeeded by his widow, Salome Alexandra. As queen of Judah she reversed the policies of her late husband and supported the Pharisees, and the Pharisees in turn recognized her right to rule, even though she was not a descendant of David as they believed a monarch should be.

Salome Alexandra died in 67 and her son John became John Hyrcanus II. Three months later, John's brother, Aristobulus II, overthrew him. John sought help from an Arab chieftain named Antipater, who was from nearby Idumaea and the head of a family called the Herods. Seeking an increase in influence in Judaea, Antipater convinced John Hyrcanus II to wage war against Aristobulus II. Another bloody civil war followed. The Hasmonaeans still had an alliance with Rome, and the two brothers sought arbitration there. Rome responded by allowing its army in the east, under the command of Gnaeus Pompey, to intervene. Pompey marched into Jerusalem. The warring brothers remained willing to let Pompey arbitrate their differences, but their followers were not, and Pompey took military action to assert his authority. Supporters of Aristobulus held the ground around Jerusalem's temple, and for three months they held off Pompey and his army. Then Pompey's army broke into the temple, slaying the

Sadducee priests they found there dutifully at prayer. The following year, 63 BC, Rome made Syria and lands south to Egypt, including Judaea, a single Roman province. The homeland of the Jews had lost its independence – not to be regained until AD 1948.

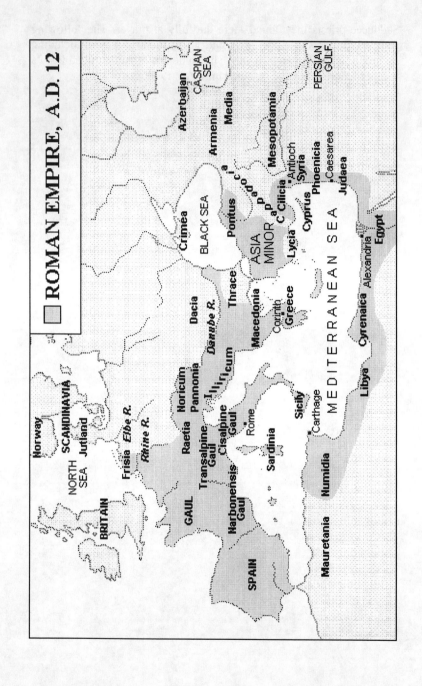

ROMAN EMPIRE, A.D. 12

NORTH SEA
Norway
SCANDINAVIA
Jutland
BRITAIN
Frisia
Elbe R.
Rhine R.
GAUL
Transalpine Gaul
Raetia
Noricum
Pannonia
Illyricum
Narbonensis Gaul
Cisalpine Gaul
Rome
Sardinia
Sicily
Carthage
SPAIN
Mauretania
Numidia
Libya
MEDITERRANEAN SEA
Dacia
Danube R.
Thrace
Macedonia
Corinth
Greece
Crimea
BLACK SEA
Pontus
ASIA MINOR
Cappadocia
Lycia
Cyprus
Cilicia
Phoenicia
Caesarea
Judaea
Antioch
Syria
Mesopotamia
Armenia
Media
Azerbaijan
CASPIAN SEA
PERSIAN GULF
Cyrenaica
Alexandria
Egypt

CHAPTER 18

THE FALL OF ROME'S REPUBLIC

SPARTACUS AND A DECLINE IN SLAVERY

A Roman soldier named Spartacus became an outlaw, perhaps after having deserted. For survival he joined drifters in bandit raids, and he was caught. For punishment, Roman authorities sold him as a slave. He became a prisoner at a training school for gladiator contests in the city of Capua. And there, in 73, he and seventy-seven other prisoners and slaves escaped and seized control of nearby Mount Vesuvius. As before, news of the revolt encouraged other slaves to revolt, and they joined Spartacus on Mount Vesuvius – an army of from fifty to a hundred thousand.

The slaves on Vesuvius were too diverse for any one leader to control. Some wished to go north across the Alps and disperse. Others wished to remain in Italy and plunder. Despite their disorganization they managed to hold off the first Roman legions sent against them, which were incompetently led. Rome sent more legions, led by the talented Marcus Crassus, an ambitious aristocrat with the unostentatious manner traditionally valued among Romans. Crassus was a former slave trainer. He had amassed a great fortune, much of it by buying estates cheaply from Sulla's victims and reselling them later for a big profit. He had acquired political position by lending money to young aristocrats with political ambitions, and he had made money by operating a fire brigade in Rome that would rush to the scene of a fire and buy the property at a bargain price before agreeing to put the fire out.

The slave army broke through Crassus' lines and pushed south to the toe of the Italian peninsula, where it hoped to cross into Sicily. But the slaves were unable to buy passage or commandeer ships, and Rome's legions cornered them. To escape, the slaves scattered. Piecemeal they were defeated and captured, and, to advertise their defeat and lift the morale of Roman citizens, Crassus had them crucified along the road (the Appian Way) between Capua and Rome.

After this latest slave uprising the demand for slaves declined among the Romans, largely from fear of slaves in great numbers. Landowners in Italy began replacing gangs of slaves with what they saw as an easier and less frightening alternative: freemen farming as tenants, the landlords receiving a third or more of their harvests. Slaves would still be used by the Romans, especially in workshops and as domestics. They would work as firemen, torturers for the police, laborers in the military, accountants, and guards for public buildings, but slavery had seen its peak among the Romans. With less warring abroad and a reduced supply of slaves, the price of slaves would rise and the purchase of slaves decline.

EXPANSION, POETS AND THE CATILINE REVOLT

Crassus won prestige by defeating Spartacus, and so too did another general: Gnaeus Pompeius, known to his fellow Romans as Pompey. In the year 70 BC, the Military Assembly elected them as Rome's two consuls, and while consul, Pompey added to his prestige by sweeping away much of the piracy that had begun to cut Italy off from vital food supplies. In Pompey's drive against pirates, Rome established a garrison at Cyrenaica (in eastern Libya), and he made Cyrenaica a Roman province. And with the arrival of a greater supply of grain its price dropped.

Meanwhile, thanks in part to his friendship with Crassus and Pompey, a young aristocrat named Julius Caesar acquired a position as *quaestor* in Spain, a position responsible for government finances. Three years later, in a campaign financed by Crassus, Caesar ran for and won the office in Rome that was responsible for supervising public games. And, with money he had borrowed from Crassus, Caesar spent lavishly on public entertainments, including gladiator contests, which added to his popularity.

Roman Expansion in Asia Minor, Syria and Judaea

After Sulla died, his old enemy Mithridates of Pontus abandoned the agreement he had made with him, and Mithridates began extending his rule again. Rome sent another force against him, drove him from Greece and Macedonia and continued to war with him. The Senate sent Pompey to the East, and it gave him authority to settle all matters there – a move supported by businessmen impatient to defeat Mithridates. Naval squadrons under Pompey went into the Black Sea after Mithridates. Mithridates slipped away to the Crimea, where he began hastily rebuilding his army. Then Pompey went southward into Syria, where Seleucid princes had been feuding. He brought that area under Roman control, and there he learned of Mithridates' death. Mithridates had been too hard on his conscript troops, who had rebelled against him.

It was now that Pompey went into Judaea to put and end to civil war there. The following year, 63 BC, Rome made Syria and Palestine, including Judaea, a Roman province, and it reduced Judaean territory.

In 62, Rome annexed Pontus, leaving Cappadocia the only independent region in Asia Minor, and in 62 Rome took control of the island of Crete.

By now the Parthians, under their Arsacid king, had expanded from southeast of the Caspian Sea and had taken control of Media and much of Mesopotamia. The Seleucids were off the world stage, and only the Ptolemies in Egypt and the Parthian Arcasids remained as rivals of Roman power.

Dissent by Lucretius, Catullus and other Poets

Amid the variety of attitudes among the Romans was that of their distinguished poet, T. Lucretius Carus, who lived from 94 to 55. Lucretius denounced conventional morality and the traditional mythology that he believed supported it. He turned in disgust from the strife he found in Rome, and like Sulla he found solace in Epicurianism. He had the Epicurean's awe for the beauties of nature. He wrote a book entitled *On the Nature of Things (De Rerum Natura),* which described the ideas of Democritus and Epicurus and was to be the source among moderns on Epicurus.

Rome had other poets: young men from wealthy families who were clever with words, who hung out together and delighted in being different. Like the Cynics these poets felt themselves to be outsiders and superior to much that their society was about. One of them, C. Valerius Catullus, was to be considered Rome's greatest lyric poet. Like many brilliant poets he died young, at around thirty. Being self-centered, he and his poet friends wrote mostly about their love-life, their petty jealousies and acts of revenge.

The Revolt of Catiline

Rome now had bakeries and public eating places. But around 320,000 Romans were still dependent on free grain, and widespread discontent among the poor still existed. And, while some aristocrats continued believing in simplicity and frugality, many others wished to keep up with or surpass the affluent in high living.

Like other cities, Rome had no municipal police force, and hired ruffians in the pay of discontented aristocrats ruled the streets. Among these discontented aristocrats was one who was deeply in debt: Lucius Catiline. He was a greedy, ambitious, former soldier who had zealously participated in Sulla's bloody repressions. In 73, Catiline had been prosecuted but acquitted of having fornicated with a Vestal Virgin. Then Catiline had begun climbing the political ladder. He served as Praetor in the year 68. In 67-66 he served as a governor in northern Africa. He wished to run for consul in 65, but he was ineligible because he was being prosecuted for extortion.

Catiline was acquitted, and he ran for consul in 64, but he was defeated. He ran again in 63, and by now he was opportunistically appealing to the discontented to build a popular base. He promised the poor that if he were elected he would abolish all debts. Again he was rejected, and, believing that he had been cheated, he gathered around him a group of hardcore supporters: aristocratic malcontents, unhappy veterans of Sulla's army, some who had lost their property under Sulla, some who had tried but failed at farming, and a various assortment of opportunists. Maintaining the spirit of politics by violence, Cataline plotted a coup. A leading senator, Marcus Cicero, exposed the plot before it was executed, and Cicero succeeded in having the Senate declare martial law. Catiline fled with an army of followers, and on the run they accepted what support they could, taking into their ranks some foolish slaves and proletarians, while few from the Italian countryside joined them – discontent among Italy's peasantry having declined. Soldiers sent by the Senate overpowered Catiline's forces as the latter were fleeing across the mountains into Cisalpine Gaul. Catiline, it has been written, died rushing into battle. Cicero asked life imprisonment for those few conspirators who were apprehended. Instead, the Senate sentenced them to death. The episode with Catiline ended with some seeing Catiline as a martyr for the poor, and at the grave on the hill where he was buried, flowers would be strewn for years to come.

Cicero

For his role in exposing and defeating Catiline, Cicero received from the Senate the title "Father of his Country," a title he was to speak of with pride. Cicero was from a town about seventy miles east of Rome, a town whose inhabitants had been Roman citizens for a century and a half. Snobbish senators from old Roman families saw a man like Cicero as a foreigner. And although Cicero was from a well-to-do family, Rome's elite looked down upon him because they thought his family undistinguished. Cicero's family and several friends had perished in Sulla's first massacre, but Cicero had sided with Sulla, because he believed in law and order, found ordinary people crude, and hated mob violence.

At the age of twenty-six, Cicero had begun his career as a lawyer, and he won a case for a man who was heir to property confiscated during Sulla's terror, a case in which he won fame for himself. Ambitious and talented, he had risen to the rank of senator. Later he was elected consul. He gained wealth by investing in land and tenement houses, and he bought a great house on classy Palatine Hill and eight country houses. He delighted in reading philosophy, and he translated much of it into Latin, becoming a source for the study of these philosophies by Romans and by modern scholars. He respected Greek learning, observing that Greek literature was read world wide.

Cicero saw the Greeks as having thought of every philosophical alternative, and from these philosophical alternatives he sided with the Stoics against the Epicureans, for whom he had contempt. He believed it necessary to persuade Romans that there were gods who governed all things, that these gods were the benefactors of mankind and that the gods judged the character, acts, intentions and the piety of individuals. Concerned with morality of his fellow Romans, he was disgusted by the sight of people, some with pretensions of being cultivated, watching animals tear a weak man to pieces or by the sight of strong men with spears killing what he saw as splendid animals.

Cicero believed that Rome should remain a nation of laws. He believed in Rome's ancient customs and its constitution. He saw as rivals those politicians whose words and actions were designed to please what he called "the mob." He believed that conservatives appealed to the best in Romans, that they appealed to thinking people. He believed that Tiberius Gracchus had been a rebel against Rome's constitution, and he blamed Tiberius for having begun a century of bloodshed.

Early in his career, Cicero had thought that subject peoples were inferior to Romans, but, after the war between Rome and the Italians he changed his mind. After that war, the Stoic belief in universal ties among people was preached on street corners and supported in literary gatherings and philosophical debates. Cicero had come to believe in Stoicism's brotherhood of man, and he saw this brotherhood as compatible with Roman imperialism. Rome, he believed, had created safety, Rome was the light of the world, and the Roman Empire was the work of the gods.

CAESAR CONQUERS, CREATES AND FALLS

Helped by the popularity he won in creating great entertainments, Julius Caesar had been chosen Pontifex Maxiumus. Then in 62 he was chosen Praetor, and in that position he supported Cicero and other conservative Senators against Catiline, but he showed courage by protesting against executing the conspirators without a trial, arguing that such a trial was an ancient right that was supposed to be accorded all citizens. And this increased Caesar's popularity among the common people of Rome.

In 61 BC, Caesar was sent to Spain as a Propraetor – a governor and military commander. There he expanded Roman rule against local tribes, to the peninsula's Atlantic coast. He gained more prestige, and like other governors he gained personal wealth. In the year 60, when his term as governor ended, he returned to Rome with enough wealth to pay his enormous debts.

Meanwhile, the Senate refused to grant lands to Pompey's veterans – despite the wealth Pompey had added to Rome's treasury by his recent conquests – and Pompey saw this as preventing him from keeping faith with his men. In 59, Pompey accepted Caesar's invitation to form an alliance as a counter to their opponents in the Senate. Crassus was annoyed with the Senate for the position it took against bribery and his business interests, and, although he disliked Pompey personally, he joined Caesar and Pompey, creating a force to be known as the First Triumvirate: Pompey with his soldiers, Crassus with his money, and Caesar with his popularity.

Benefiting from this alliance, Caesar was elected consul in 58. And as consul he proposed to the Senate a land bill for Pompey's veterans. The Senate did not respond, and, while attempting to remain affable with senators, Caesar took his proposed bill to a Plebeian Assembly, which passed the bill with a clause that senators would be required to take an oath to uphold the new law. But three tribunes vetoed the bill. Pompey lent his veterans to Caesar, and the veterans created a dominant force in Rome. The Senate acquiesced and passed the bill. Pompey's veterans got the lands they wanted. And Caesar, remaining as affable as before, took other legislation that he wanted directly to the Plebeian Assemblies. He rewarded Crassus by supporting legislation that Crassus sought, and his alliance with Pompey was reinforced by Pompey marrying his daughter, Julia.

Caesar Goes to Gaul

Forbidden by law to run for a second term as consul, Caesar won a five-year appointment as governor of Cisalpine and Transalpine Gaul. As governor there he began to quell disturbances in Transalpine Gaul, and he launched a war to extend Roman rule over the unconquered areas of Gaul – lands occupied by about fifty tribes. These tribes had been fighting among themselves, and some of them, respecting the power of Rome, allied themselves with Caesar. Caesar conquered Gaul piecemeal, his successes the result of good military tactics, well-disciplined troops and use of the kind of terror that the Romans considered necessary and appropriate to frighten an enemy. Caesar was not a bloodthirsty man, but popularity was important to him, and to maintain the support of his soldiers he submitted to their passion for blood. And with his generosity and his brilliance as a commander he won their devotion.

East of the Rhine River, Caesar came into contact with a Germanic people he described as tall and blond, warlike and utterly savage, people with wagons who had come from Scandinavia – what is now

Denmark, southern Norway and Sweden. They were running from population growth, shortages of food and wars between tribes. Already some of these Germans had settled on the western side of the Rhine River. Caesar fought them. He made slaves of those his army captured. And he made the Rhine River the empire's frontier.

Caesar against the Senate

Romans welcomed Caesar's victories against their ancient enemy the Gauls, and they welcomed extension of their empire. News of each of Caesar's victories inspired a celebration, while some senators remained unimpressed. The more glory that Caesar won the more conservative senators feared him as another Marius, and they described his victories as cheap aggressions against inoffensive peoples.

Caesar knew that he needed support against the will of the Senate. In Gaul he acquired more wealth with which to buy political support in Rome. But his position in Rome suffered with the death of his daughter Julia, which ended an important tie between him and Pompey. And Crassus was jealous of Caesar's successes in Gaul.

With Caesar agreeing, Crassus won appointment as governor of Syria. This put Crassus in charge of Rome's relations with the Parthians, and it gave Crassus his opportunity to win the glory than Caesar had been winning. In the spring of 53, Crassus took an army of around forty thousand – mainly infantry – from Syria and moved them into northeastern Mesopotamia. He had not taken the time to learn much about the local geography and local people as Caesar had. With Crassus, ignorance and impatience led to disaster. The old fireman and victor over Spartacus was forced to capitulate. Much of his army was taken into captivity while around ten thousand of his men managed to escape and return to Syria. And while a captive he died in a scuffle with a Parthian officer.

In Rome, meanwhile, the most popular gang was led by Clodius, a supporter of Caesar and a fighter for legislation that would give more free food to Rome's poor. His gang clashed with a gang led by Milos, a friend of Pompey. A clash between these two gangs in the year 57 left some dead. Another clash in 52 left Clodius dead, killed by order of Milos. Irate supporters of Clodius carried his body into the Senate, where they made a funeral pyre from Senate benches and burned his corpse and the Senate building.

The Senate turned to Pompey to establish law and order – perhaps some Senators also seeing an opportunity to split Pompey from his alliance with Caesar. The Senate decided to make Pompey the sole consul for 52 and to allow Pompey to raise an army to restore order and to suppress the gangs that roamed the streets. Pompey was delighted by the opportunity to do something heroic.

The Senate established special courts to prosecute those responsible for the recent disorders. Milos was convicted and given lenient punishment: exile to the port city of Massilia (now Marseilles) in Roman controlled southern Gaul. Pompey restored order. Then despite the illegality of second terms, Pompey won another term as consul, leading one Senator to quip that any government was better than no government.

The Senate passed a bill that called for Caesar to be replaced as governor of Gaul. A tribune ally of Caesar's vetoed the bill. The Senate ignored the veto and demanded that Caesar disband his army and resign unconditionally. Caesar refused, and the Senate appealed to Pompey for military support and voted in martial law. Rather than accept an end to his career and perhaps death, Caesar chose to attack. On his way to Rome, some Italians and other soldiers rushed to join his forces. Faced with a popular rising and the might of Caesar's army, most of the Senate fled the city in panic, leaving behind their wives and children. Pompey believed his force too meager to combat Caesar and his supporters, and, comparing himself to Sulla, he fled with his army to the east – his place of recent victories and power – in hope of gathering to his side the troops stationed there.

Caesar Triumphs against Pompey

Caesar entered Rome triumphant. People throughout Italy cheered his success. Rather than attempt to crush those in Rome opposed to him, as had Sulla and others, Caesar sought reconciliation – while in Pompey's camp in the East they damned Caesar and talked of revenge, killing and confiscating of properties. For the security of his regime, Caesar had to defeat those armies loyal to Pompey. He and his army went to Spain, and in forty days triumphed against an army allied with Pompey. They returned to Rome for eleven days while on their way to Greece to confront Pompey, and Caesar found that he had been declared dictator. Caesar presided over elections in which he was also made consul, and he passed a law creating relief for debtors.

Caesar and his army confronted Pompey in Greece, Pompey having twice as many infantrymen as Caesar, and seven thousand cavalry to Caesar's one thousand. But Caesar was brighter and his troops more experienced, and his army crushed Pompey's army. Pompey fled toward Egypt. Continuing his policy of reconciliation, Caesar offered a pardon to those whom Pompey left behind, and many of them joined Caesar's armies, while others fled.

The young Egyptian king, Ptolemy XII, saw Pompey as a loser and a danger. He had Pompey stabbed to death when Pompey stepped ashore on a sandy beach. Three days later Caesar arrived with his army, and Ptolemy offered Caesar Pompey's embalmed head as a trophy.

Caesar was annoyed and dismayed. But in Jerusalem, Pompey's death was interpreted as punishment for his having entered that city's sacred temple – the House of the Lord – and there was rejoicing.

Caesar found Egypt in political disarray, and he began asserting authority there that many Egyptians believed was not his. He would have preferred reconciliation with Pompey, and he had two Egyptians who had taken part in Pompey's murder executed. He tried to arbitrate a dispute within the Ptolemy family and finally sided with the king's daughter, Cleopatra. In the streets and harbor at Alexandria war erupted between Ptolemy XII and Caesar and his small force, with Caesar fighting Roman naval forces that had remained loyal to Pompey. Reinforcements for Caesar arrived from Palestine, and Caesar won. Ptolemy XII died in the conflict, and Caesar and his army remained in Egypt for a couple of months.

Caesar married Cleopatra to her younger brother, as was the Egyptian custom, and he set the couple upon Egypt's throne. Caesar and Cleopatra vacationed together on a ship on the Nile, which would lead to a son by the two. Then on his return to Rome, through Palestine and Syria, he stopped in Asia Minor and defeated an army of the son of Mithridates, who had attempted expansion as had his father. And Caesar described this conflict with his famous phrase "I came, I saw, I conquered."

In the autumn of 47, Caesar arrived in Rome with a great torchlight parade that included forty elephants and delirious crowds. Many Romans must have thought that their troubles were over, that at last a champion of the people had secured power. Some saw his good fortune as having been granted by the gods for the sake of his fulfilling grand aims. Some elevated Caesar to godliness. A rumor spread that the storm that Caesar had recently experienced when crossing the Adriatic he had stilled by the power of his will, just as it was believed that Alexander had imposed his will on the waters of the gulf of Pamphylia when he first journeyed to Asia Minor, or as Jews believed that Moses had parted the Red Sea.

Caesar and Reform

Opposition from abroad still concerned Caesar. Troops who had been with Pompey gathered in North Africa a little east of where Carthage had been, and there they wiped out whole communities they saw as supporting Caesar. In the spring of 46, Caesar took an army to North Africa and defeated the forces hostile to him there. From North Africa he went to Spain to battle some who had fled there, and there Caesar narrowly escaped death while winning his final victory against his opposition abroad.

Returning to Rome, Caesar turned his attention to creating a stable government and solving economic and social problems. He gave land in Gaul and Spain to his veterans. Seeking order, he announced that the revolution was over. He began to create a politics of consensus and a government of laws – but not democracy, which was commonly believed to be an unruly form of government. He banned the clubs that had created turmoil in Rome's streets. He restored the Senate, which now consisted of many new members and fewer aristocrats. And he accepted the title of "Dictator for Life."

Caesar outlined a program for the reorganization of the courts, and for the sake of order he increased the penalties for crimes committed by the rich and the poor. He passed laws against extravagance. He upheld property rights and took steps toward the restoration of Rome's system of finances and the creation of economic stability. To prevent the kind of profiteering that had taken place under Sulla and to ease the burden of debt, he put restrictions on lending and borrowing. He gave Romans temporary relief from rents and began a program of improving housing for the poor. He began welfare reform, reducing the number of those on the dole in Rome from 320,000 to 150,000 (the latter roughly fifteen percent of Rome's population). He ruled that to go onto welfare in Rome one had to wait for someone else to leave the program – a move designed to discourage people from coming to Rome to take advantage of welfare there. And the roughly eighty thousand whom he disqualified from welfare he sent to new, overseas colonies.

Caesar laid plans for economic improvements across the empire. Marshes south of Rome were drained, business districts of various cities were improved, and new theaters and temples were built. He proposed construction projects for improving trade by sea and for improving harbors. He laid plans for a new canal for the city of Corinth. Caesar began enlisting men of talent into public service, and he saw the need for improvement in the organization of municipal governments throughout Italy. He started standardizing and streamlining cumbersome local governmental operations. He sought to bind citizens in the provinces closer to Rome by doing away with laws that made distinctions between them and the citizens of Rome. He gave Roman citizenship to Gauls who had fought alongside him when he was governor there. He created better government in territories governed by Rome, including Judaea. He gave Jews there a greater autonomy, reduced their taxes, exempted them from having to serve in Rome's armies, and he allowed them freedom again to worship their god Yahweh.

Caesar placed a learned man in charge of Rome's library, and he laid plans for an increase in government involvement in Rome's public education. He gave Roman citizenship to Greek teachers in hope of encouraging them to come to Rome. Caesar also had the calendar revised. The old calendar was a hodgepodge of contributions by various priests. Caesar was an Epicurean and closer to its materialism than he was to traditional religion. He wanted a calendar that was organized around considerations not colored by religion. He drew from the expertise of astronomers and mathematicians, the result being the basic calendar of today.

Assassination

Some among Rome's privileged saw Caesar as responsible for an end to the republic, and rather than patience, argument and compromise, they opted for a return to the politics of violence: assassination. They did not understand that political improvements would need widespread consensus and respect for law and that assassinating Caesar would bring neither. Like most assassins they had little grasp of what would follow their deed.

Some of the conspirators were former supporters of Caesar who hoped to advance their careers. Some were from families as distinguished as Caesar's who resented his condescending air of superiority. Toward them and others, Caesar had been acting like a parent: chiding, urging them to get along, caring about them all and seldom asking for their opinions.

The conspiracy to assassinate Caesar was led by a former first commander under Pompey, Gaius Cassius, whom Caesar had pardoned and made a legate. Another conspirator, Marcus Brutus, was a senator and a former follower of Pompey whom Caesar had pardoned. He was also a Stoic and had a reputation as an idealist, and when he joined the conspiracy his prestige inspired twelve other senators to join. Another Stoic and senator, the great, voluble Cicero, was aware of the plot to murder Caesar. He continued to pretend friendship with Caesar while seeing the conspiracy as patriotism that would rid Rome of despotism.

Caesar was preparing to go east to do battle against the Parthians, who were creating trouble for Rome on the border if its empire, and those plotting Caesar's assassination wanted to strike before he left. Caesar had heard rumors of a plot, but he had not surrounded himself with spies, and he knew nothing of who the plotters were or when they might strike.

On the morning of March 15, 44 BC, Caesar went to a meeting at the Forum to ratify his using the title of king when outside Italy – a title for dealing with foreign peoples, who understood authority mainly by that name. As he often did, he went without his bodyguards, but he was accompanied by a rugged companion: one of his former generals and Rome's other consul, Marcus Antonius, a name to be anglicized to Mark Antony.

Brutus believed that killing Antony would be an injustice, so another conspirator detained Antony in conversation as Caesar made his way to his seat. It appeared that people were approaching Caesar, as usual, to exchange words and ask for favors. Alongside a statue of Pompey, someone pulled at Caesar's cloak. Someone else stabbed him from behind in the neck. Caesar turned and wrestled with the assailant. As many as sixty others joined in the attack, wounding one another in the fray. Nearby senators looked on, some of them stunned. Caesar saw Brutus with his knife raised and asked him: "You too my son?" Brutus plunged his knife into Caesar and shouted congratulations to the Senate's leader: Cicero. Stabbed twenty-three times, Caesar fell to the floor and died.

News of Caesar's assassination spread fast in Rome and struck terror into Caesar's close associates, who believed that they too might be targeted for death. With some others, the commander of Caesar's military guard, Lepidus, had a failure of nerve, and he failed to mobilize his troops against the assassins. Two days after the assassination, Mark Antony, seeing no reign of terror, emerged in public with a personal guard that he had organized. Still afraid, he was ready and willing to compromise with the Senate, and he made his now famous speech about burying rather than praising Caesar – his ability as a speaker to be exaggerated by Shakespeare. As the surviving consul he accepted power and spoke favorably of the powers of the Senate.

The Senate was glad to be rid of Caesar but wished to avoid civil war, and in a show of conciliation it voted for a public funeral for Caesar. The funeral was spectacular, with frenzied people packing surrounding streets. Into the funeral pyre women threw their jewelry, some threw their robes, and soldiers their weapons. Foreigners in the crowd, including Jews, joined the mourning. Some believed that Caesar's death was the signal of the end of the world. And some believed that Caesar's assassins should be punished. From the crowd of mourners came the retaliation that had failed to come from Caesar's top lieutenants. Packs of outraged people rushed to the vacated homes of those rumored to be the assassins.

THE ASCENT OF CAESAR'S NEPHEW, OCTAVIAN

A month after Caesar's death, his eighteen-year-old grand-nephew, Gaius Octavianus, to be known as Octavian, arrived in Italy from the East, where he had been waiting to serve Caesar in the war that was planned against the Parthians. Octavian had served with Caesar in Spain, and Caesar had adopted him and made him his heir. Against the advice of his stepfather and others, Octavian decided to use his inheritance politically. Like many who have inherited wealth or position from a brilliant man, Octavian would prove less capable, but he was determined, and he would prove able enough in his coming competition with Mark Antony. Antony considered himself Caesar's political heir. He controlled Caesar's private fortune, which he had quickly spent. When Octavian went to Antony to claim his share of Caesar's estate, Antony rebuffed him in a public display of contempt. With what money Octavian had, and help from friends, family and supporters, Octavian was able to make himself a public figure. He paid the gift of money that Caesar had promised citizens in his will – which Antony was refusing to pay. He paid for athletic games in honor of Caesar, and at these games a comet streaked across the sky. The crowd thought it was Caesar's star, a sign of Caesar's immortality, a sign of Caesar having risen, and a sign of heavenly favor bestowed upon Octavian. News of Caesar's star spread rapidly across the empire. And Octavian inherited the affection of soldiers and civilians who had worshiped Caesar. Many of Caesar's veterans gathered around Octavian and proclaimed their devotion to him, and war between Octavian and Antony appeared imminent.

Antony against the Senate

The accord between Antony and the Senate fell apart. As consul, Antony canceled the Senate's appointment of one of Caesar's assassins, Decimus Brutus (no relation to Marcus Brutus), to the governorship of Cisalpine Gaul. With his position as consul soon to expire, Antony appointed himself to the position. Still conciliatory, the Senate approved. But Cicero feared Antony's influence. He made a speech with an undertone of criticism against Antony. Antony took offense and attacked Cicero verbally. And before the year ended a war of words was on between the two. Antony and Cicero disliked each other personally. Antony was affable but thought good manners were hypocritical and stuffy, and stuffy was what he though of Cicero. Antony saw himself as in tune with traditional male directness and simplicity. In manner and dress he was intentionally casual, and he had a coarseness and boyishness that appealed to soldiers. Some complained that he was sloppy in eating and noisy in drinking. Cicero described him as vulgar and as a drunken, lusting debaucher, and Cicero spoke of Antony's speeches as little more than bombast.

Cicero saw Antony's choosing to go to Cisalpine Gaul as governor as an attempt to follow in the footsteps of Caesar, and he accused Antony of preparing to create a military dictatorship. Cicero decided that it best to keep Antony and Octavian divided, to exploit their differences and to help Octavian against Antony. The Senate refused Antony's attempt to have it declare Octavian a public enemy. Instead, the Senate made Octavian a senator, annulled its appointment of Antony as governor of Cisalpine Gaul and declared Antony an outlaw.

Antony did now what he could have done just after the assassination: he rallied an army against Caesar's assassins. The first of his targets was his rival in Cisalpine Gaul: Decimus Brutus. Cicero called on the governors in Spain, Transalpine Gaul and Narbonensis Gaul, to side with the Senate. But these commanders chose instead to side with Antony. The commander in Narbonensis Gaul – Lepidus – had Caesar's best troops, and Antony agreed to recognize him as equal in rank.

Octavian, Antony and Lepidus End the Republic

Octavian was uncomfortable allied with the Senate, and he saw opportunity in overthrowing those responsible for his uncle's assassination. He signaled Antony that he was willing to create an alliance against those they both opposed. Some were to claim that Octavian and Antony agreed that they had better hang together or they might eventually hang separately.

While Antony was winning his war against Decimus Brutus, Octavian and his troops marched on Rome, entering the city unopposed. There, Octavian took charge and in effect annulled the powers of the Senate. He instituted elections for the two consulships, winning one seat for himself and one for a second cousin, and he abolished the law that had made Antony an outlaw. A victorious Antony returned to Rome with his army. Lepidus, Antony and Octavian formed a ruling triumvirate. The triumvirate enlarged the Senate with their supporters. The Plebeian Assembly passed a law giving the triumvirate dictatorial powers for five years.

Octavian and Antony chose not to repeat Caesar's attempt at reconciliation. Against those who had conspired against Caesar they launched a massacre as terrible as Sulla's. Three hundred former senators and two thousand equites were killed, destroying much of what had been Rome's old governing elite. Cicero was among those assassinated – his severed head and hands presented to Antony. Caesar was declared a god of the Roman state. The two most prominent of Caesar's assassins, Cassius and Marcus Brutus, had fled east and taken command of armies there, and, in the year 42, armies under the combined command of Antony and Octavian waged war against them in Macedonia, Antony performing well as a general and Octavian, who lacked such skills, remaining in his tent. Brutus and Cassius committed suicide. An enemy navy, led by the son of Pompey, Sextus Pompeius, remained undefeated.

OCTAVIAN VERSUS ANTONY AND CLEOPATRA

Antony was considered the senior member of Rome's ruling triumvirate, and he was named authority over most of Gaul and over all of Rome's eastern empire. Octavian ruled in Rome, Italy and Cisalpine Gaul. Lepidus was left with only the promise of rule in northern Africa west of Egypt. Touring in the eastern part of the empire, Antony exacted indemnities from those provinces that had given support to Brutus and Cassius – despite this support having been forced upon them. Some of this money he put aside for a war he planned against the Parthians. He ordered Egypt's ruler, Cleopatra, to journey north and appear before him in Cilicia to explain her having aided Cassius. She arrived in her gilded ship with purple sails and silver-lined oars, and her many attendants, and to Antony she exonerated herself. She invited him to pass the winter in Alexandria, and there (in the winter of 41-40 BC) the two spent much time feasting together, playing dice and fishing on the Nile.

In the year 41, Antony's brother, who commanded an army, attempted to grab power from Octavian. He was encouraged by Antony's wife. Octavian defeated Antony's brother, and Antony arrived from the east with an army and had a standoff with armed forces loyal to Octavian. Antony backed down, blaming his brother and wife for having made war without consulting him. To patch up their differences, Octavian and Antony created a new accord in which Octavian would have authority over Spain and all of Gaul. Antony's wife had died, and Octavian and Antony reinforced their tie by Antony marrying Octavian's widowed half-sister, Octavia – a woman of high repute among the Romans.

Meanwhile, the Parthian king, Orodes, was expecting war with Rome, and he sent an army into Syria. The Parthians won a few towns in Syria and then pushed into Asia Minor and Palestine. And, in the years 39 and 38, Antony's generals drove the invaders back, out of Asia Minor, Syria and Judaea.

Octavian and Antony Renew Their Hostilities

The law that had granted the Triumvirate five years of dictatorial power expired in 38, and the Plebeian Assembly extended the dictatorship another five years. Also that year, Antony returned to the east, and Octavius married into the aristocratic Drusus family, taking Livia Dursilla as his wife. In 38, Octavius sent naval forces against Sextus Pompeius that Pompeius destroyed. Octavius needed another navy to combat Pompeius, and Antony gave him 120 warships in exchange for 20,000 Italian troops.

In the east, Antony renewed his contacts with Cleopatra. The two apparently hoped to gain from each other: Antony needing Cleopatra's wealth to pursue his conflict with Parthia, and Cleopatra wanting to revive boundaries of the old Ptolemy kingdom of her forefathers. Within a year, Antony sent his pregnant wife, Octavia, back to Rome. Antony lived in opulence with Cleopatra. He acknowledged publicly that he had fathered twins by Cleopatra – a boy and girl – while in Rome Antony's wife (Octavian's sister) presided with dignity over Antony' household, caring for Antony's children by a previous marriage and her own.

The Romans still associated marriage with morality, and many looked upon Anthony's association with Cleopatra with disgust and saw Octavia as a mistreated heroine. Octavius was outraged by what he saw as Antony's mistreatment of his sister. But conflict between them was delayed while Octavian made war against Pompeius and Antony was preoccupied with a renewed war against the Parthians.

Against Sextus Pompeius, Octavian's commander, Agrippa, won a foothold on the eastern coast of Sicily. Lepidus joined Agrippa against Pompeius and landed a detachment in Sicily. With three hundred ships on each side, the largest sea battle that had taken place in western waters followed, and Agrippa triumphed, with Pompeius escaping to Asia Minor, where he was executed by subordinates of Antony.

Octavian emerged with a military force greater than that of Antony: five to six hundred warships and forty-five legions. Italians were impressed by Octavian's victory. An encouraged Octavian began to care more about support from the people of Italy, and he promised everyone that eventually he would restore the Republic. Lepidus claimed Sicily, but he lacked support among his troops, who deserted him. Octavian took away Lepidus' triumviral powers, but he allowed Lepidus to retain his position as Pontifex Maximus and he made Lepidus a tribune. Octavian then began to clear the Adriatic Sea of pirates and to send troops into the Balkans in a successful move to advance the interests of Rome there.

In 36 BC – the same year that Octavius defeated Pompeius – Antony attacked the Parthians, through Armenia. He and his troops arrived at what is now Azerbaijan, and for months he laid siege to its major city: Phraaspa. Parthian attacks on Antony's supply lines left him facing a winter without shelter or adequate provisions. Antony fell back, through Armenia again, returning with most of his troops but losing some twenty-two thousand men in the retreat. Cleopatra met him in Syria, bringing him money and supplies. It took until 34 for his forces to regain strength for an assault against the king of Armenia, who had helped the Parthians, and in 34, Antony and his army dethroned him.

In the autumn of 34, Antony returned to Egypt, and in Alexandria he celebrated his victory in Armenia with a grand pageant, which many Romans visualized as an impious parody of their traditional celebrations of triumph. Antony's funds were now depleted, and he was more dependent on the wealth of Cleopatra. To please her, he staged a ceremony at which he pronounced her "Queen of Kings" and distributed to her children the titles that were traditionally given to children of royalty. Antony declared Cleopatra's thirteen-year-old son by Caesar, Caesarion, as Julius Caesar's legitimate son and as heir to the rule of Egypt, Cyprus and a part of Syria. Antony declared Cleopatra's six-year old boy as king of Armenia and its neighbor, Media. He gave the boy's twin sister titles to Cyrenaica and Libya. And he declared Cleopatra's two-year-old son as king of Cilicia and Phoenicia.

Making Caesar's son by Cleopatra Caesar's legitimate son was equivalent to putting the boy ahead of Octavian, who was merely Caesar's nephew and adopted son. This increased Octavian's displeasure with Antony. Antony, in turn, remained upset with Octavius for not having given him a share of Sicily. Antony gave word that he wanted Octavia and her children out of his house. This severed the final bond between Octavius and Antony. A war of words erupted between the two, with Antony trying to discredit Octavian for what he described as Octavian's past acts of disloyalty.

Octavian Triumphs

Toward the end of 33, the second five-year rule of Octavian and Antony expired, and it was not renewed. Octavian professed legal rectitude by disclaiming that he still had the powers given by the expired law. He remained a consul. But Antony continued as if he were still Rome's designated ruler in the East. In the summer of 32 Antony's divorce from Octavia was announced along with Antony's will, which included his wish to be buried alongside Cleopatra, and Antony's will reaffirmed his claim that, Caesarion – Caesar's son by Cleopatra – was Caesar's legitimate son. To many Romans, Antony, without formal office, seemed in the employ of a foreign queen. Rumor spread in Italy that Antony wanted to make Cleopatra queen of Rome and to transfer Rome's government to Egypt. By now many Romans saw him as a renegade from Roman tradition, and they disliked him for his wearing the royal clothing of the Ptolemies and for what they heard of his fondness for luxuries.

Backed by opinion across Italy and much of Rome's western provinces, Octavian, as consul, obtained a declaration of war against Cleopatra – but not against Antony. It was to be a war against a foreigner, putting Antony in a position of treason. Antony's troops also disliked Cleopatra. Their morale was low, and some high ranking officers among them deserted to Octavian.

Antony, with Cleopatra at his side, moved with his army to a strong point in western Greece. There, near the town of Actium, Octavian's talented commander, Agrippa, defeated Antony in a great sea battle, and Antony and Cleopatra fled back to Egypt. Nine months later, Octavius and his forces arrived in Egypt. Antony committed suicide. Cleopatra became Octavian's prisoner, and fearing that Octavian would take her back as display for his triumphant entry to Rome, she killed herself. Octavian saw both Caesarion and Cleopatra's eldest son by Antony as dangerous rivals and had them executed, but he adopted into his own family the other children of Cleopatra and Antony, including the daughters of Antony and Octavia.

In the summer of 29, Octavian returned to Rome. He was thirty-four and in command of all of Rome's sixty legions, and respected by the legions' rank and file. He brought with him from Egypt a wealth of treasure and two annexations: Egypt and Illyricum. His fellow Romans believed they had seen the end of war and strife, and they hailed him as the Prince of Peace and benefactor of mankind. Celebrations lasted for days. Animals were sacrificed to Rome's gods. The Senate gave Octavian the permanent title "Commander Imperitor" – from which the English word *emperor* is derived.

OCTAVIAN BECOMES AUGUSTUS CAESAR

Immediately after returning to Rome in 29 BC, Octavian fortified support for himself by giving some of the wealth from Egypt to the troops who had fought for him. He gave them land in Italy and abroad, and some of Egypt's treasure he gave as prizes to the people of Rome. Thirty years had passed since Rome's republican government had functioned normally, and Octavian considered what the nature of his rule was to be. He theorized that a republic was better than a monarchy, that the sons of kings often became incompetent rulers. He believed that Rome's republican government had helped make Rome great, but he also believed that it had produced chaos. He decided that although the republic was suited to Rome when Rome was small, it was inadequate in meeting Rome's task as the leader of the world's greatest empire. He believed that democracy could not achieve the political stability that the Senate had failed to achieve, and therefore he remained opposed to giving more power to the Plebeian Assembly. He decided also that clinging to absolute power would appear evil. He did not wish to appear to be the autocrat that Caesar had appeared to be, and he recalled that after having won against Sextus Pompeius in 36 he had promised that he would restore the republic.

Octavian and his trusted aide, Agrippa, were the two consuls, and Octavian used his powers as a consul to make the Senate more to his liking. Building on the purge of 43, in which about three hundred senators had been eliminated, Octavian purged two hundred more, and in their place he added some whom he had elevated to the rank of nobility, and the Senate became a body of eight hundred.

In 27 BC, Octavian began his seventh term as consul, and on the first day of that year he renounced his consulship and declared that he was surrendering all powers to the Senate and other bodies, including control of the army. It was a bogus withdrawal from power. As Octavian expected, the Senate, packed with his supporters, responded by returning much of his powers, claiming that it was doing so for the sake of unity and relief from factionalism and civil strife. The Senate granted Octavian a ten-year governorship over those areas where the bulk of Rome's armies were stationed: Spain, Gaul and Syria. This gave Octavian control over foreign policy, and it left him with authority over Rome's military.

The Senate voted that Octavian be given the crown of oak leaves that signified service to Rome, and it made him consul again. Octavian still held the title of Princips from the period of the Second Triumvirate – equivalent to being called first citizen or leader, or, in German, *Führer*. In keeping with his great prestige, the Senate gave him a title that had the ring of his being divinely chosen, *Augustus Caesar*, and the Senate made it law that he be included in the prayers of Rome's priests. In appearances the Republic had been restored, but in fact ultimate power still lay with Octavian – Augustus Caesar.

Augustus and Pax Romana

From the years 27 through 24 BC, Augustus continued as consul, and he spent those years outside Rome, administering and organizing, first in Gaul and then in Spain. In 26 BC, to protect commerce, he allowed a military expedition to be sent against southern Arabs who were trying to maintain a monopoly of trade with India and the coast of Somalia. While Augustus toured Gaul and Spain, Romans were enthusiastic over rumors that he was planning an invasion of Britain. But Augustus had had his fill of war. He decided to leave Britain alone. Most of Britain's tribal chieftains were friendly toward Rome and wished to maintain and develop trade with the continent. Augustus saw them as no threat to Gaul, and he saw great and ambitious military undertakings as economically harmful.

The wars against Gallic tribes that had begun with Caesar were over. Gallic tribes had come down from their fortified towns in the hills and settled onto more fertile soil in the plains, where they established new towns. What Gaul needed was administration. But in Spain between the years 26 and 19 BC, Augustus' commander, Agrippa, waged what was called pacification – a bitter but successful war in Spain's mountainous north. The warfare ended with defeated peoples being transferred to Spain's central plains and with colonies of Rome's veterans being established at what are now the cities of Merida in the southwest and Zaragoza in the northeast.

Meanwhile, Rome's main rival continued to be the Parthian Empire, on Rome's eastern frontier. Romans continued to hunger for revenge against the Parthian Empire. Instead, Augustus made a treaty with Parthia. He promised that Rome had no more ambition against any area under Parthia control, and the Parthians in turn recognized Armenia as a Roman protectorate and returned to the Romans the banners that had been captured from Cassius' army more than thirty years before.

Augustus' policy of conciliation was the mainstay of the relatively stable peace called Pax Romana. Only minor disturbances would continue, as in 17 BC, when a Roman legion was overrun by Sugambri Germans. Rome countered with an invasion of Germany in order to keep Gaul secure from German attacks and to create a new frontier along the Elbe River. Peace was disturbed again when Gauls from Noricum, Pannonia and the Alps made raids into Roman territory. Rome responded, securing Italy's northern plain by extending its authority into Noricum, Pannonia and Raetia.

More Power to Augustus

In Spain in the mid-20s Augustus became ill and returned to Rome, and in 24 BC he became ill again and close to death. When recovering the following year, he resigned again as consul, which relieved him of the routine duties that had been wearing him down. In compensation for this loss of power, the Senate revised the constitution and made Augustus Tribune-for-Life, which gave him power in domestic affairs. And, he was made Proconsul for life, giving him authority to override governors and the power to conclude treaties with foreign powers without submitting the treaties to the Senate for ratification. Technically Augustus remained an elected official and subject to the laws of the land. Officially his positions were a gift of the Senate and the Roman people.

Augustus still had the power to convene the Senate, to present legislation and to have his motions discussed in the Senate prior to any other business. He favored free discussion in the Senate, and he gave into the Senate on minor points, but most senators viewed arguments against the major thrust of his proposals as a waste of time, and the Senate merely stamped its approval on measures that Augustus proposed. Then in 18 BC the Senate was again purged of two hundred members – to a body of six hundred. Seeing themselves as having no real power, many senators would come late or not show up. And by 11 BC so many senators would be absent that a new rule was passed permitting business to be conducted with less than four hundred members present.

Not only was the Senate officially a legislative body, it became for the first time in its history a court of law and was authorized to try cases of both political and ordinary crimes, including those in which senators were involved. But with many Roman citizens looking to Augustus for help – as was traditional with kings – Augustus acquired recognition as having the power to judge appeals, a power he accepted without enthusiasm.

Augustus Patronizes and Builds

Augustus believed that each class should have its own ideals and duties. He believed that his class, the aristocracy, gave to Rome skills in leadership. He had men of business – the equites – declared a hereditary class and second in rank to the aristocracy. The equites could serve as officers in the army, as governors of certain provinces, as financial agents for the government and as agents of the courts of law. As for common people, by now their assemblies had vanished. Advocating democracy remained a crime of treason. The only labor organizations that Augustus allowed were those that appeared harmless to the state – fraternal groups of men who met merely to socialize. But Augustus allowed common people to run for minor civic posts and to advance to a higher position if they proved themselves of exceptional ability.

Waging only minor wars allowed Augustus to reduce his legions from sixty to twenty-eight, leaving more money for public works. He had begun building soon after his return from his war against Cleopatra, his first project that of repairing dilapidated temples. In the years that followed he gave Romans bread, games and magnificent shows, paying for these with both public and his own money. He began to complete buildings that had been left unfinished after Caesar's death, and he encouraged Agrippa and Rome's highest ranking military officers to spend for public works and public parks some of the wealth they had received as war booty. In 19 BC, the construction of a new aqueduct was completed. Splendid new public baths were built. A ministry of transport was begun that built and maintained roads. From a city of sun dried brick, Rome under Augustus was to become a city of marble.

The new roads improved communications and helped trade. Mail service improved, and under Augustus, improvements were made in civil administration. Augustus upgraded the qualifications for civil service jobs. He created a degree of self-government for cities and provinces and curbed the rapacity of Rome's governors. He created urban fire departments. He created urban police forces to suppress disorders, petty crime and to preserve urban tranquility, and he created police for the countryside to protect people against brigandage.

At first, Augustus planned to check the influx of people into Rome from the countryside by cutting people off Rome's welfare, but he abandoned this and instead introduced a new system of control and distribution of food, and by around 5 BC the dole increased to 200,000, roughly twenty percent of Rome's population. But while maintaining Rome's proletariat, Augustus moved to restore the small farmer, believing that the small farmer had contributed to making Rome the power that it was. Small family farms still flourished in the Po valley, in Campania, and in the southern part of Italy inhabited by those of Greek ancestry, and, to extend small-scale farming, Augustus purchased land and paid gratuities out of his own vast wealth.

A Bible for Religious Study, and Protecting the Race

As was traditional among the Romans, Augustus associated morality with the well-being of the state and pleasing the gods. To stay on the good side of the gods he began a crusade to revive temperance and morality. He tried setting an example by dressing without extravagance and by living in a modest house. He emphasized the worship of those gods he thought had given him victory in battle, among them the god Apollo. He claimed that Rome's gods had given him victory over Cleopatra and what he saw as the monstrous gods of Egypt. He forbade the worship of Isis, and he forbade Druidism and fortune telling. He collected the oracles of Sibyl – the woman believed to have prophetic power by way of Apollo – and he had her writings stored in a newly built temple for Apollo on the Palatine Hill.

Augustus tried to persuade one of the foremost writers of his time, the poet Horace, to create a work comparable to Homer's *Iliad*, that would inspire Romans to the worship of the state's traditional gods and give the Romans pride in their history and their race. Horace was not interested, but the poet Virgil was. Virgil wrote the *Aeneid,* a story about the gods and the founding of the Roman race, a myth about the Romans having descended from Trojans who had fled the flames of Troy. Aeneas was described as the son of the goddess Venus and the Trojan Anchises. According to Virgil, among the descendants of Aeneas was Rhea Silva, who married Mars and gave birth to Romulus and Remus. And Virgil described Julius Caesar as a more distant descendant of Aeneas.

Augustus decided to protect the Roman race. Between 2 BC and AD 4 he had laws passed that he hoped would reduce inter-breeding between Romans and non-Romans. These laws prohibited an indiscriminate emancipation of slaves, prohibited freed slaves from marrying Latins, and prohibited Senators from marrying freed women.

Family Values
    The Romans believed in the family, and they agreed that adultery should be against the law. They believed that the virtue of their women helped win their city favor from their gods, and they continued to be disgusted by criminality. Many Romans found pleasure in seeing criminals punished, which was done in the arena, Rome's entertainment center, where convicted criminals were forced to fight against each other or against ferocious animals. Occasionally convicted criminals ran, and men held red hot branding irons around the edge of the arena to force the unwilling participant back to the contest, while the crowd expressed its disgust with the criminal's cowardice.

    With wars having reduced Rome's population to a level lower than pleased him, Augustus saw having children as moral. He used his powers as Tribune-for-Life to initiate legislation that he hoped would encourage marriage. Infanticide remained legal and at a husband's discretion, but people who remained single or married without children after they were twenty were to be penalized through taxation. To further what he saw as morality, Augustus had prostitution taxed, and he made homosexuality a punishable offense. Adultery remained a crime, but it was no longer commonly punished by death. An adulterous wife and her lover could now be banished to different islands, with the woman obliged to wear the kind of short tunic worn by prostitutes.

    Augustus' crusade for moral regeneration satisfied those who feared that evil would come with abandoned religious traditions. Many females continued to grow up patriotically and dutifully moral, and virginity before marriage continued to be seen as highly desirable and moral. But his moral crusade was hardly a success in changing behavior. Married men continued to look other than to their wives for sexual passion. With unmarried women endeavoring to remain virgins and married women constrained by the tough laws against adultery, males, married and otherwise, continued to seek sexual gratification and to some extent affection from prostitutes, and some from each other.

    Augustus had his own daughter, Julia, punished for adultery. After Julia's two previous husbands had died – each of whom had been designated as heir to Augustus' power – Augustus arranged a marriage between Julia and his adopted son and heir apparent, Tiberius. This involved Tiberius leaving a happy marriage. The marriage between Tiberius and Julia turned out to be an unhappy match. Tiberius was often away, and Julia searched for love and sexual gratification outside her marriage. Augustus heard of her infidelities, and he threatened her with death. Instead, he sent her to an island prison from which she was never to return, and he spoke of her as a disease of his flesh.

CHAPTER 19

JEWS AND CHRISTIANS
IN ROME'S GOLDEN AGE

ESSENES, DEAD SEA SCROLLS AND THE HERODS

After Judaea lost its independence in 63 BC, some Jews there turned from hope in a great new Israel ruled by a king such as David and began to look toward individual salvation. Among them were the Essenes. They were offended by the acceptance of foreign ways by their fellow Jews and by the collaboration with Roman rule by aristocrats and priestly leaders, and they were offended by strife among the Jews. They saw Satan at work, and they denounced the Jewish majority as apostate and temple worship in Jerusalem as polluted. In likeness to Zoroastrian thought, they described the majority of Jews as the "sons of darkness" and themselves as "the sons of light." They spoke of their hatred for "the sons of darkness," and their love for "the sons of light." They saw themselves as following a strict discipline and rigid observance of Jewish law, especially kosher laws and the Sabbath – so rigid that they might let a man drown on the Sabbath rather than make an effort to save him. Disappointed over their expectations about the coming of the Messiah, and wishing to separate themselves from the unholy, the Essenes moved to desert caves that overlooked the Dead Sea. There they set up a community that avoided what they saw as impure food and what they thought were impure thoughts and acts, including sexual intercourse. The Essenes held their property in common, practiced magic, believed everything was in the hands of God and looked forward to what they believed was the approach of Armageddon: God's Day of judgment.

The Dead Sea Scrolls

In caves overlooking the Dead Sea, where the Essenes are said to have dwelled, scrolls were stored that were to be found in the twentieth century. Thirty-three of the scrolls were in Hebrew, which, in the times of the Essenes, was considered the holy language of Moses. And seventeen of the scrolls were in Aramaic, the language common among the Jews of Judaea.

The scrolls expressed a Judaic expectation of a king, a "messiah," and "a son of god" – the latter a designation for heroes and kings in numerous ancient societies. The scrolls described the Messiah as having the powers of magic, as intending to "uphold the fallen, heal the sick, release the captives" and to resurrect "those asleep in the dust." The Messiah described in the scrolls was to appear in an apocalypse in which there would be a "swallowing of all the uncircumcised." In other words, only God's chosen people, the Jews, were to survive.

Jews under the Herods

Rome reduced Judaea's territory and installed the Arab chieftain, Antipater, as its vassal over the whole of Palestine. In 43 BC, Antipater's son, Herod, succeeded him. Herod became a good friend of Marcus Agrippa, the closest companion of Rome's emperor, Augustus Caesar, and this friendship helped Herod expand his rule. Herod oversaw and profited from copper mines in Cyprus. He built great fortresses and cities. And he was called Herod the Great.

A practicing Jew, Herod observed Jewish laws, and he tried to mollify his many unhappy Jewish subjects. In 20 BC he began rebuilding Jerusalem's temple. But the bigger landowners continued to prosper more than did small farmers, and some small farmers became impoverished and fell to beggary or brigandage. Common Jews, especially those from rural areas, continued to detest Herod for being a foreigner and for his extravagant palaces and luxurious entertainments, paid for by heavy taxation and bribes. On the other hand, upper class Jews, including the Sadducees, feared disorders by the poor and accepted Herod and the presence of Roman soldiers.

Among those opposed to Herod and to foreign rule were devout Jews called Zealots. The Zealots saw Roman occupiers as greedy and lustful, and they looked forward to the day when God would rescue his people and send them the Messiah. From positions in the wilderness the Zealots resorted to small-scale guerrilla warfare against Herod and the Romans, and the Romans increased the number of their troops in Judaea and watched more closely for subversion.

Late in his life, Herod found in his family the scheming and deception that was common among royalty concerned with succession. He executed family members who had plotted against him. He executed Jewish priests who had criticized his lapses from Jewish law, and this turned the Sadducees against him.

Herod died in 4 BC, twenty-six years into the rule of Augustus Caesar. His death raised the hopes of Jews wishing independence, and, believing they could prevail with the help of Yahweh against the power of Rome, they revolted. Rome was able to restore order, and Augustus divided what had been Herod's domains among three of Herod's sons.

Then in AD 6, after hearing complaints from Jews about the son of Herod who ruled from Jerusalem, Augustus ruled him incompetent and sent in his place a Roman governor named Pontius Pilate.

JOHN THE BAPTIST AND JESUS OF NAZARETH

John the Baptist may have lived among the Essenes. The New Testament describes him as calling Pharisees and Sadducees a "brood of vipers," a view shared by the Essenes. The New Testament describes John the Baptist as living in the desert, wearing a garment of camel's hair and a leather belt and eating locusts and wild honey (Matthew 3:4-7). Like the Essenes he saw perversity in society, and he envisioned the coming of an armageddon that would bring a new Israel under God. But rather than stay separated from others as did the Essenes, John traveled about Galilee preaching – as were some other Jews.

Some of Jerusalem's sophisticates looked down upon Galilee as populated by bumpkins given to erroneous ideas. The people of Galilee, on the other hand, looked down upon outsiders. Recently, two thousand in Galilee had been crucified for rebelling against the Romans. But John had a message other than rebellion for the people of Galilee: he called on them to give up their sinful ways and to repent. All Jews, he claimed, could be forgiven their sins. Using an old religious ritual that held that water washed away one's sins, John the Baptist submerged people into the Jordan River, and he made the ritual a solemn act of conversion that signified membership in his cult.

Among the poor and dissatisfied, John acquired a following and a brotherhood of disciples. Like the Essenes they held their property in common, and they had as their central ritual the eating of a community meal at which they believed the Messiah was spiritually present. John's demise came with his criticism of Herod Antipas, the son of Herod the Great and Rome's appointed ruler in Galilee. Like the Essenes, John was given to denunciations for any deviation from what he saw as orthodoxy. He denounced the king's marriage to the former wife of the king's half-brother – a marriage technically illegal under Judaic law but of little concern to a Hellenized king such as Herod. Such criticism made John appear to Herod as a troublemaker and a subversive, and Herod had John jailed. John's criticism of Herod's marriage angered Herod's new wife, who, according to the New Testament, had her daughter, Salome, ask Herod for John's death in exchange for dancing at Herod's birthday feast. And Herod had John taken from prison and executed.

The Early Life and Historical Record of Jesus

Among the followers of John the Baptist was a young man named Joshua, a name translated into Greek as Jesus. Jesus left no writings, and known written descriptions of his life and what he said came decades after his death. These were to become known as the *Gospels* – a part of Christianity's New Testament – written by Matthew, Mark, Luke and John. The Gospels of Matthew, Mark and Luke are believed by recent scholars to have been written between the years 70 and 100 AD, the Gospel of John between 90 and AD 110.

Matthew describes Jesus as having been born before the death of Herod the Great, which came in 4 BC. Luke's account has Jesus born during or after AD 6. According to the Gospels, Jesus was born in Bethlehem – a village ten miles south of Jerusalem – a claim that might have been made to match Jesus with a prophesy in the book of Micah (5:2), where it was said that from Bethlehem one would go forth to become a ruler of Israel. Instead, Jesus may have been born in Galilee, in a village called Nazareth, where Jesus is said to have lived as a youth.

Jesus appears to have been born into humble circumstances. As a young man he worked at what was then considered a humble occupation: carpentry. The educated around him spoke Greek, while Jesus spoke Aramaic. The Gospel of John, describes Jesus as beginning his own ministry before the imprisonment of John the Baptist. The Gospels of Matthew, Mark and Luke describe Jesus as beginning his ministry after John the Baptist's imprisonment. According to the Gospels, the neighbors of Jesus and his brother John saw Jesus' attempt to fill in for the loss of John the Baptist as presumptuous, and they rejected him. But from among John the Baptist's followers Jesus was able to attract a following of his own. And according to the Book of Matthew, rather than seeing himself as the predestined leader of John's movement – as later believed by Christians – Jesus denied that he was equal to John. He said that "among those born of women there has not yet arisen anyone greater than John the Baptist." (Matthew 11:11)

According to the Gospels, Jesus felt at home in the company of common people. He surrounded himself with sinners and the poor. He welcomed women to gather around him – a treatment of women not common among the Pharisees or other Jews. And according to the Gospels, unlike the Pharisees, Jesus mixed with non-Jews, and those called Samaritans who were seen by many Jews as hateful religious rivals.

The Gospels describe Jesus as preaching in rural towns and villages for three years, and they describe the core of his message as close to that of the Essenes: the spiritual corruption of existing society and the need to repent. Jesus' message about corruption had an appeal among the poor of Galilee. Like John the Baptist, Jesus had acquired a dislike for the ways of the well-to-do and the aristocratic priesthood. The Gospels describe him as having preached against the wearing of soft clothing, for these, he said, were worn in the palaces of kings. He complained of the worship of gold and of man's indulgences, and he warned his listeners not to worship two masters: God and mammon. He called on his disciples to follow an ascetic life, to refrain from acquiring gold and silver for their money belts or a bag for their journey, or sandals, or a staff. "Woe to you who are rich," he said, "for you are receiving your comfort in full. Woe to you who are well fed, for you shall be hungry." Like the Essenes and John the Baptist, Jesus favored a way of life opposed to the prevailing economic life of his day: the accumulation of private property. Like the Essenes and John the Baptist, he appeared to favor sharing possessions. If a man asks for one's shirt, he is reported to have said, give your shirt and your coat too.

Like the Essenes and John the Baptist, Jesus was a devout Jew. He claimed that he had come to fulfill Judaic law and the word of the prophets, and he preached in Synagogues. Like the Essenes and John the Baptist, he spoke of a kingdom of heaven that was at hand. And like the Essenes he described his generation as evil and adulterous. He admonished his listeners to refrain from divorce and said that for a man to marry a divorced woman was to make that woman commit adultery. He commanded his listeners to follow the commandments of God. And, like the old prophets, he preached that foreign ways were evil, and he warned his listeners not to go the way of the gentiles.

Judaic laws were complex, and some of Judaism's rituals were expensive, and, being bold enough to condemn the rest of society as corrupt, Jesus was also bold enough to ignore those laws that he thought impractical. According to the Gospels – written when Christians were themselves diverging from some Judaic laws and were in conflict with the Pharisees – Jesus criticized the Pharisees for their impractical attempt at exactitude. Jesus, according to the Book of Matthew, saw absurdity in their selecting to refrain from certain works on the Sabbath and not other works. Of those who criticized him for healing on the Sabbath he asked, "Does not each of you on the Sabbath untie his ox or his donkey from the stall and lead him away to water him?" (Matthew 13:15)

According to the Gospels, Jesus defended the common Jew's belief in resurrection – in contrast to the Sadducees, who rejected resurrection. A Sadducee pointed out to Jesus that under Judaic law widows married their late husband's brother and that with resurrection would come confusion when the husband returned from the dead. Jesus replied that after resurrection there would be no marriage because people would be like angels in heaven. (Matthew 22:30)

The Gospels describe Jesus as claiming that his mission empowered him to forgive sins, a claim the Pharisees would have seen as a blasphemous usurpation of God's divine authority and an infringement upon monotheism. The Gospels also describe Jesus as healing people by casting out demons from within them and turning five loaves of bread into enough bread to feed and satisfy five thousand – a miracle that should have convinced any Pharisee of Jesus' divine powers and that should have brought multitudes flocking to Galilee for confirmation.

Jesus Goes to Jerusalem

According to the Gospels, when Jesus heard the news that John the Baptist had been executed he became angered. This came with the approach of the annual pilgrimage to Judaism's holy city, Jerusalem. The focus of the pilgrimage was Jerusalem's temple, the "House of the Lord." It was a pilgrimage that celebrated the Passover holiday commemorating liberation of Jews from Egyptian slavery. Jesus and his followers joined perhaps as many as a hundred thousand pilgrims who poured into Jerusalem from nearby and from outside Judaea – doubling the number of people in the city. Jesus may or may not have gone to Jerusalem with confrontation on his mind, but in Jerusalem he created a disturbance. Jesus found that at the "House of the Lord," merchants had moved into an area usually forbidden to such activity but allowed on this occasion. Perhaps his Essene-like intolerance of laxity angered him. The merchants sold the animals and birds that were accepted as suitable for temple sacrifices – Jerusalem's temple being the only place where sacrifices were allowed. And among the merchants were money changers who made it possible for people from the different areas to acquire the necessary coins to buy these creatures. Jesus, according to the Book of Matthew (21:13), accused the merchants and money changers as having turned the temple from a "House of Prayer" into a "robber's den." The Gospels describe Jesus as making a whip out of cords he had gathered and driving the merchants and money changers from the temple grounds. Perhaps the merchants and money changers failed to stand against Jesus because Jesus had the backing of others – what some would call a mob.

The Death of Jesus

The gathering crowds in Jerusalem for the Passover always heightened the spirit of nationalism there. On such occasions, joy was in the air, as was an increase in tension, and those who made street corner speeches found audiences for their passionate denunciations, including denunciations of Jerusalem's priestly city fathers, the Sadducees, who were seen as having compromised with Roman rule. The rebellious outbursts upset the Sadducees, and they must have been offended by the disturbance that Jesus created.

After his revolt at the temple, Jesus sensed that he was in danger, but rather than go into hiding he let himself be arrested, and the Gospels describe him as being arrested like a *lestes*, a Greek word meaning common criminal or undesirable troublemaker. His followers, however, were less brazen: they deserted Jesus, including one called Peter who denied to authorities that he knew Jesus.

Jesus was taken before a political council called the Sanhedrin, presided over by Jerusalem's High Priest, Caiaphas. Some historians speculate that this was a trial, others that it was merely a hearing. It is doubtful that it was a trial in the modern, American sense of that word or that it was given the importance that was later to be associated with the person of Jesus. The punishment for intending to foment rebellion or for committing blasphemy could be death, and executions for these offenses were routine in Judaea. Some argue that the charge against Jesus and his execution were Roman in character and that Jesus was executed on political rather than religious grounds. Supporting this view, some argue that the writers of the Gospels, living under Roman rule and hostile to orthodox Jews, downplayed the role of the Romans and emphasized the role of the Jews in the execution of Jesus. At any rate, each of the four Gospels describes the Sanhedrin as having accused Jesus of claiming to be the "king of the Jews." John (4:26) describes Jesus as claiming that he was the Messiah. This would have been grounds for the charge of blasphemy. The usual method of execution for blasphemy was stoning, and the usual method of execution for treason or insurrection was crucifixion. According to the Gospels, crucifixion was chosen for Jesus, which fits with Jesus not having claimed to be a god or the Messiah. It was also a sentence that would be better than stoning for artistic depictions of martyrdom.

The Gospels describe Jesus as having been placed on a cross between two thieves who tossed insults at him. A crowd mocked Jesus while he was on the cross, and a priest joked that Jesus had claimed to save others but apparently could not save himself. Among the followers of Jesus who were present no one dared expose himself as such. And, according to Matthew, Jesus did not yet understand the reason for his death, for, while dying in the dark, Jesus asked aloud the same cry that appears in Psalm 22:1 of the Old Testament: "My god, my God, why hast Thou forsaken me?"

The Resurrection

For Christians today the Resurrection of Jesus is at the heart of their faith. For some, piecing together a chronology of events is unimportant, or a diversion. They see Jesus Christ as transcending history.

As for the followers of Jesus at the time of his death, their Judaism included a belief in resurrection. Moreover, the belief in resurrection was common in the whole of West Asia. Aside from material evidence of Jesus' resurrection, it is fitting that followers of Jesus would conclude that Jesus had been resurrected. And according to the Gospels, a few days after his crucifixion, Jesus' body disappeared from his tomb. This created no shock to the world-at-large. Apparently, awareness of the resurrection was limited mainly to Jesus' followers. Others, as stated in Acts, hearing but never understanding, seeing but never perceiving.

According to Matthew (28:2) Jesus descended from heaven – as had Romulus. Jesus appeared before only a select few of his followers. Only a few days before he had asked why God had forsaken him. Now, according to Matthew, he understood the reason for his death, and he asked the following: "Was it not necessary for the Messiah to suffer these things and to enter into his glory?"

According to the Gospels, Jesus was the son of God and a part of God's plan. Rather than simply absolving humanity's sins Himself, God had staged the execution of Jesus for this purpose. Sacrifices had been a part of religion for millennia and had survived in Judaism, and Yahweh, according to the Gospels, sacrificed His son to absolve the sins of humankind.

EARLY CHRISTIANITY AND ITS APOSTLES

When Jesus was arrested and executed, his followers scattered to their homes, but soon they gathered again in Jerusalem. As Jews they continued to worship at Jerusalem's temple, "the House of the Lord," and they began living quietly and at peace with Jerusalem's authorities. They saw themselves as a group favored by Yahweh within Judaism. According to the New Testament they called themselves "The Poor" and "The Saints." They looked forward to a second coming of Jesus since his resurrection and to his bringing with him the new order that Jews had been expecting with the coming of the Messiah.

The Saints grew slowly in number, and among the new converts were Jews from outside Judaea – people referred to in Acts 6 of the New Testament as "Hellenists" perhaps because they spoke Greek. Coming from outside Judaea, they were not as attuned to local attitudes as others, and they were more inclined to offend when discussing their views with other Jews.

One among those from outside Judaea was a man called Stephen, whom the New Testament describes as "full of grace and power" and "performing great wonders and signs among the people." In his preaching, Stephen offended some who, according to the New

Testament, "were unable to cope with the wisdom and the Spirit with which he was speaking." Stephen was reported to the authorities for having spoken "blasphemous words against Moses and against God." (Acts 6:8-11) Stephen was hauled before the Sanhedrim and convicted of blasphemy, and in keeping with that charge he was stoned to death. Others who belonged to Stephen's group, including Jesus' former disciple Peter, were driven from the city, while the rest of Jerusalem's Christians continued their lives in that city.

Exiling the "Hellenist" followers of Jesus from Jerusalem was to have a great impact on the development of Christianity, for Peter and his group traveled from one Jewish community to another in cities along the coast of the eastern Mediterranean Sea. They proselytized with greater zeal than did other Jews. They experienced hostility from their fellow Jews, and occasionally violence, but in the Jewish communities of these cities the number of believers in Jesus as the Messiah began to grow.

One of these cities was Damascus, a cosmopolitan city where a few non-Jews in search of spiritual sustenance heard the story of Jesus and were allowed to join the followers of Jesus without first converting to Judaism. It was in Damascus that the followers of Jesus were first called "Christians," a term spoken with contempt and not to be used by the followers of Jesus until the next century. Meanwhile, among those followers of Jesus who spoke Greek, Jesus was becoming known as "Christ," which is Greek for *King* – kingship remaining the accepted form of supreme leadership.

The Apostle Paul and Early Christian Evangelism

Judaic authorities in Jerusalem were concerned about the obedience of Jews everywhere, and they saw the followers of Jesus outside of Palestine as a threat to Judaism. They sent agents to check on the movement. One of their agents was a man named Saul, the son of a Jewish Roman citizen from the city of Tarsus, on the coast of Cilicia, a man to be known by his Christian name: Paul. Paul had studied Judaic law in Jerusalem. He had become a Pharisee and devoted to the pharisaic belief in a Jewish nation being made holy by its people's strict observance of God's laws. The Pharisees sent Paul from Jerusalem to Damascus to observe the followers of Jesus there. According to the New Testament (Acts 9:3-4), on his way he was blinded by light and had a vision of Jesus asking him "Why persecutest thou me?" Paul arrived in Damascus still blinded. A follower of Jesus found him, converted him, and Paul's eyesight returned.* Then Paul

---

* In none of his own writings selected for the New Testament does Paul mention his blinding on the road to Damascus.

spent thirteen years studying the teachings of Jesus, and some of these years he spent in a desert retreat with other followers.

In AD 47, Paul joined others in spreading their good news about Jesus Christ – that Armageddon and the Second Coming of Christ was approaching. By now more than two-thirds of the roughly seven million Jews in the Roman empire lived outside of Judaea, and it was to Jews in cities outside of Judaea that Paul and his fellow evangelists went, where Jews spoke their language – Greek – and could understand them. In the coming thirteen years they traveled to Cyprus, Palestine and Syria; they traveled to the great cities of western Asia Minor, along the coast of the Aegean Sea, through Macedonia, south to Corinth in Peloponnesia, to the city of Syracuse on the island of Sicily; and they traveled to a community of Greek speaking Jews in Rome – where Jews had settled as early as 150 BC. The peace and security for travel that had been created by Augustus Caesar added to the ability of Paul and the other Hellenized evangelists to spread their word about Jesus. And as a Roman citizen, Paul was protected by Roman law from attacks by outraged Jews.

Circumcision and Conflict among the Followers of Jesus

Among the Jews in various cities around the Mediterranean were gentiles who were attracted to the unique Jewish meeting places -- the synagogue. Those spreading the news about Jesus were gathering followers not only among their fellow Jews but also among these gentiles, and this presented a problem for the followers of Jesus. The gentiles were uncircumcised, and they did not follow Judaism's dietary laws. The question arose among the followers of Jesus whether they ought to share meals with the gentiles and whether uncircumcised men could become followers of Jesus.

In letters Paul wrote (which would appear as a part of the New Testament) there were no references to the Gospels of Matthew, Mark, Luke and John. Paul and his fellow evangelists did not have the Gospels of Matthew, Mark, Luke and John to appeal to for authority. And, as with any group of people, the early followers of Jesus had their disagreements – as when followers of Jesus from Jerusalem visited brethren in Antioch. Those from Jerusalem insisted that unless a follower of Jesus were circumcised according to the custom of Moses – as practiced in Jerusalem – he could not be "saved." In the year 50, concerned followers of Jesus met again, this time in Jerusalem, to promote a greater unity, and at this meeting they addressed the question whether non-Jews should be required to be circumcised when accepting Jesus as their savior. Paul was among those invited to the meeting, and there he joined the pragmatists who wanted it easier to admit gentiles to their number. Paul argued that the core of their beliefs was not Judaic law but the sacrifice of Jesus and their faith in Jesus. The conference reached a compromise: circumcision would not be required for membership in their communities, but all those who wished to be recognized as followers would be required to follow other Judaic laws.

Predictably, there were those among the followers of Jesus who rejected compromise, complaining that compromise was not an appropriate basis for religious belief. For years this faction would badger their fellow Christians, trying to make them see their error in abandoning absolute obedience to all Judaic law. And like others who resist compromise or change, they would fade away, while Christianity grew. Compromising had strengthened their movement. Paul and like-minded followers had taken the first step in preventing Christianity from remaining a Jewish sect, which might have doomed it to extinction.

Early Christian Appeal

Those who had sided with compromise continued to proclaim that Jesus was the Messiah, a caring martyr, that he would return either in their lifetime or soon after, and that with his next appearance would come everlasting life, relieving them of their hardships and sufferings. It was a joyful message of love, hope and equality for the poor, and it had more appeal than asking one to worship the distant gods of Greek or Roman mythology or the bull god of Mithraism.

It was mainly among the urban poor that the evangelists found their recruits. The movement's evangelists told the poor that they did not need what they did not have: riches and education. "Do not love the world nor the thing of the world" wrote the apostle John. Great possessions, he said were obstacles to entry into heaven. Paul, in a letter to the evangelist Timothy, supported this view, claiming that love of money was the root of all evil. (Timothy 6:10) Paul proclaimed that the wisdom of the world was made foolish by God. He told his listeners merely to feel, to have faith, to surrender themselves to Jesus.

In keeping with what was believed to be the teachings of Jesus, converts were asked to surrender their property to a common fund and to live communally. The congregations of various communities took care of followers arriving from other areas, and they were instructed to look after the widows, orphans, sick and disabled among them. "We who are strong" said Paul, "ought to be bear the weaknesses of those without strength and not just please ourselves."

Stoicism, Discipline and God's Roman Law

Paul's message was compatible with Stoic concepts of asceticism, harmony, the brotherhood of man and humility, ideas he had grown up with in his hometown of Tarsus. In keeping with Stoic values, Paul proclaimed that the followers of Jesus should be honest, free of double dealing and falsehood. In keeping with Judaic law, Paul and his colleagues proclaimed that sex outside of marriage was forbidden. There had been criticism and rumors of wanton behavior of the Christians, and Paul said "By doing right you silence the ignorance of foolish men." He said, "Let us behave properly as in the day, not in carousing and drunkenness, not in sexual promiscuity and sensuality, not in strife and jealousy." (Romans 13:13)

Paul advised his fellow Christians to obey state law, and, despite its bloody origins and oppressions, he spoke of the Roman Empire as having been the work of God. "Let every person," he wrote, "be in subjection to the governing authorities, for there is no authority except from God, and those which exist are established by God." (Romans 13:1) In this he was supported by the apostle Peter, who wrote: "Submit yourself to every institution."

The Obedience of Slaves and Women

Paul and his fellow Christians believed that with the approach of the second coming of Jesus and a new world there was no need to change the institutions of the present world, and their accommodation with these institutions included an accommodation with slavery. The Christians saw recourse for slaves in Jesus and impending Armageddon. They saw slaves as equal to freemen. And Paul said, "Slaves, in all things obey those who are your masters on earth, with sincerity of heart, fearing the Lord." According to Paul, a slave who accepted Jesus became "the Lord's freedman" and a free man who accepted Christ became "the Lord's slave."

Just as slaves were to obey their masters, women were to obey their husbands. "Wives," said Paul, "be subject to your husbands as is fitting in the Lord." (Ephesians 5:22) To the apostle Timothy, Paul wrote: "I do not allow a woman to teach or exercise authority over a man, but to remain quiet." (Timothy 2:12)

Celibacy

During Paul's time, some Christians argued that Jesus advocated celibacy. Why else, they asked, would Jesus have praised women whose wombs never bore, or men who made themselves eunuchs for the sake of the Kingdom of Heaven? Paul and his colleagues opposed self-castration, but, believing that Jesus was coming soon, Paul did advocate celibacy for some Christians. To his brothers in Corinth he wrote, "the time has been shortened, so that from now on those who have wives live as they had none," (1 Corinthians 7:29). On the other hand, he also promoted sex in marriage – in order to avoid the sexual frustration that he thought might lead to Satan's temptations. He warned married Christians to stop depriving each other: "The wife," he wrote, "does not have authority over her own body, but the husband does; and likewise, the husband does not have authority over his own body, but the wife does." (1 Corinthians 7:4)

Satan the Devil

The early followers of Jesus saw Satan not as not as an instrument of Yahweh as had early worshipers of Yahweh. Their view of Satan was that of the Jews who saw Satan as an independent and evil force. According to the apostle John, Jesus described the devil as a murderer, a liar (John 8:44) and as the "ruler of the world." (John 14:30) Paul wrote of the "schemes of the devil" and of "the spiritual forces of wickedness in the heavenly places." (Ephesians 6:11-12) He described the devil as "the God of this world." He blamed the devil for the failure of people to accept Jesus. The devil, he stated, "blinded the minds of the unbelieving, that they might not see the light of the gospel of the glory of Christ..." (2 Corinthians 4:4) Peter joined Paul and warned people to "Be of sober spirit, be on the alert. Your adversary, the devil, prowls about like a roaring lion, seeking someone to devour." (1 Peter 3:8)

JEWS AGAINST CHRISTIANS AND ROMAN AUTHORITIES

Roman authorities viewed the spread of Judaism as a threat to Rome. Jewish businessmen aroused the resentment of their non-Jewish competitors. Jews were scorned for refusing to burn incense before the emperor's statue – worse than Americans refusing to salute their flag. Jews, including the followers of Jesus, aroused suspicion by their inclination to keep to themselves. They appeared to others as haters of the world outside their own circle. They were disliked for their quarrelsome denunciations of gods other than Yahweh, and they were often the targets of mockery and violence. The emperor Claudius (who ruled from AD 41 to 54) moved to curtail the spread of Judaism in Rome. He denied Jews there the right to meet outside of their synagogues. And in 49, following a disturbance involving Jews, Claudius (as described in Acts 18:2 in the New Testament) expelled Jews from the city. But elsewhere in the empire, Claudius defended the rights and privileges that had been conferred upon Jews and other minorities, except for Druids, who were viewed as subversives, performers of human sacrifices and a threat to the empire's well-being. Druidism had also been spreading, despite its having been declared a crime, and it was being punished by death.

Persecution of followers of Jesus came with a great fire in Rome in the year 64, a fire that raged for many days, that almost destroyed the entire city and was horrendous enough to seem like Armageddon had arrived. Perhaps some Christians in Rome saw the fire as the beginning of the fulfillment of their expectations that the world would be destroyed by fire. Reports of joyous dancing, looks of glee and shouts of hallelujahs would have attracted suspicion, and Christians were an easy target because they were still thought of as Jews. An official investigation concluded that the fire had been started by Jewish fanatics. This put the Jewish community in Rome in danger, and Jewish leaders in Rome may have tried to avert this danger by describing to authorities the difference between themselves and the Christians. The leaders of Jews in Rome could reach the emperor, Nero, through his new wife, Sabina Poppaea. Nero learned of the separate identity of those Jews who were followers of Jesus, and he put blame on them for the fire.

Nero had some Christians executed in the usual way of executing criminals: putting them in the arena against gladiators or wild animals, or as was commonly done to those convicted of arson, having them burned to death. It was around this time that the apostles Peter and Paul vanished. According to the historian Tacitus, who wrote decades later, many Romans remained suspicious of Nero. Many believed the rumor that Nero had started the fire to make space for his new great mansion, and they pitied the Christians, believing that instead of being sacrificed for the welfare of the state, the Christians were being sacrificed as Nero's scapegoats.

Masada: an End to the Jewish Homeland

Toward the end of Nero's reign, rioting and killing broke out between Jews and non-Jews in the port city of Caesarea, about eighty-five kilometers north of Jerusalem. Fighting between Jews and non-Jews spread from Caesarea to cities outside of Palestine, including Alexandria, where the Jewish section was left in ruins. And, in AD 66, rebellion spread to Jerusalem, which had been receiving impoverished migrants from elsewhere in Judaea, where peasants had been experiencing grinding poverty and hunger. This was the rebellion that Judaea's aristocracy had feared, with good reason: the rebels burned their homes and murdered those aristocrats they could get their hands on. And with whatever weapons the Judaeans could find they attacked the Romans. Roman troops in Judaea were hopelessly outnumbered, and the Jewish rebels killed many of them.

The opinion of Jewish aristocrats was expressed by one of their number, a man named Josephus, who would become an historian and describe the war. Josephus had been around and knew of Rome's might compared to that of the rebels. He would describe the revolt as sedition and an insanity by desperate men. Indeed, Rome crushed the rebellion. It sent to Judaea an army that was allowed to plunder, massacre and burn. A Roman blockade of Jerusalem created famine among its inhabitants. Calls for help from Yahweh went unanswered. Roman soldiers poured into the city, and, according to Josephus, they raped and massacred thousands. They left the inner city destroyed and Yahweh's temple burned ruins. The Roman army swept through the rest of Judaea. Remnants of the rebel force retreated, and it took months for the Roman army to eradicate pockets of resistance. The last of these was on a mountaintop plateau in the desert above the Dead Sea – a place called Masada. According to Josephus, as the Romans closed in on the plateau all but two women and five children chose suicide.

The Romans executed some Jews they had taken prisoner. Some they sent to Rome for punishment in the arena, and some they sold into slavery, condemned to work in mines. Rome stationed an army permanently in Jerusalem and forbade the Jews to rebuild their temple. Rome abolished Jerusalem's High Priesthood and Council of Elders. It forbade the Jews from proselytizing anywhere in the empire. According to Rome there was no longer a Jewish nation. Several million Jews remained in and around Judaea, but Rome allowed non-Jews to settle in place of the Jews who had died or had been taken away as slaves. Followers of Jesus saw the defeat of the Jews in the tradition of Yahwism: as God's punishment. Orthodox Jews responded to this by putting into their synagogue liturgy an anathema against the followers of Jesus.

More Revolts by Jewish Communities

In 115, the emperor Trajan moved against the Parthians and overran Mesopotamia. Jews in Mesopotamia preferred Parthian rule to Roman rule, and military plans by the Parthian Empire against Rome included busying Rome with another revolt by Jews. Parthia sent discontented Jews from Mesopotamia to encourage revolt by Jewish communities within the Roman Empire. And it worked: numerous Jewish communities rose against the Romans. In Cyprus and Cyrene, Jews massacred gentiles in great numbers. Trajan ended his war against Parthia and brought the great weight of Rome's military might down upon the rebellions, and Rome let local majorities have their revenge, which resulted in great massacres against the Jews. In Cyprus every known Jew was killed and a law was passed forbidding any Jew, even from a shipwreck, to set foot on the island.

Fourteen years later, Trajan's successor, Hadrian, visited Judaea, and he ordered Jerusalem rebuilt as a Roman city, to be called Aelia Capitolina. And while he was in the East, Jews planned yet another rebellion. The revolt's leader was Simeon ben Kosiba, also known as Bar Kokhba (Son of a Star). The foremost rabbi and Judaic scholar,

Akiva, hailed Simeon as another king David the conqueror, sent by God – in other words, the Messiah.

After Hadrian had returned to Rome, the revolt began. The Roman legion on the outskirts of Jerusalem was caught by surprise and was driven from its encampments. All fighting was directed against the Romans, and Simeon ben Kosiba was able to establish a government in Jerusalem. He laid plans for rebuilding Solomon's temple, and a new coin was issued describing Simeon ben Kosiba as the president of a redeemed Israel. But Rome could not maintain its empire if it did not demonstrate to others that it could hold on to a province such as Judaea, and Hadrian sent new armies into Palestine. Lacking allies, or not being part of a greater war against Rome, this latest rebellion proved as hopeless as those before it. In two years the rebellion was crushed. Perhaps as many as 580,000 Jews died fighting, including Simeon ben Kosiba. It was the last of the Jewish rebellions. The Romans again glutted the slave markets with Jewish captives. Jerusalem was rebuilt as Aelia Capitolina and colonized with non-Jews, and the penalty for Jews entering the city was death. Judaea was removed from the map. The prohibition against circumcision was renewed and celebration of the Jewish festivals, observance of the Sabbath, study of the Torah and possession of a scroll of Jewish Law became punishable by death. Judaism was outlawed in the hope that it would cause Jewish survivors elsewhere in the empire to fall away from what Hadrian saw as a troublesome creed.

Soon these laws would be rescinded, including prohibition of circumcision for Jews. Missionary activity to spread Judaism did not revive, but intellectual work did. Babylon, rather than Jerusalem, became the center for the preservation of Jewish tradition. The Talmud produced there was more detailed than previous versions, and regarded as authoritative, and in the coming centuries it became the main source of instruction for Jews outside of Palestine.

CHRISTIANITY ORGANIZES
AND STRUGGLES WITH IDEAS

During the first century, the followers of Jesus saw themselves as righteous members of God's chosen people of Israel. The gentile who authored the Gospels of Luke was among these followers, declaring that the followers of Jesus had inherited Israel's legacy as God's chosen people. But it was mostly among gentiles that Christianity was winning its converts, and by the end of the first century most followers of Jesus were gentiles, and they were struggling with their identity as the people of Israel while abandoning Jewish practices such as circumcision, the kosher diet and laws about the Sabbath. With the second revolt of the

Jews against Rome (AD 132-35) led by Simeon ben Kosiba, the break by Christians with Judaism became more pronounced. The followers of Jesus, seen as Jews, were asked by the followers of ben Kosiba to join the revolt. The followers of Jesus could not accept the claim that Kosiba was the Messiah. The followers of Jesus saw Jesus as the Messiah. They were looking forward to God's kingdom, but, unlike Rabbi Akiva and others, they did not believe that Kosiba's uprising was God's kingdom. The followers of Jesus refused to join the revolt. Bitter verbal attacks between the two groups ensued. And the Christians went their own way.

To Roman authorities, Christianity remained an outlaw faith, and being a Christian remained an offense punishable by death, but it was a law largely ignored. Ordinary Romans continued to view the Christians with suspicion. The Christians were conducting their meetings at night, which convinced their non-Christian neighbors that they had something to hide. Rumors had spread that Christian rituals included the eating of flesh and the drinking of blood – a distortion of the ritual of eating bread and drinking wine as representations of Jesus' body and blood. Christians were seen as odd too for denying themselves enjoyment, for refusing to wear perfume or adorn their heads with flowers. And Romans asked what would happen if everyone refused their civic duty to appeal to Rome's gods. The emperor Trajan (99-117) received reports about Christians from local authorities, and he held that the Christians could believe whatever god or gods they wished so long as they obeyed the law by showing reverence for Roman deities, including the deified Caesars. Trajan was aware that Christianity was growing, but he was concerned about harassment and false accusations. He wrote that anonymous accusations created "the worst sort of precedent," and he decreed that local authorities were to make no search for Christians and that Christians were to be arrested only if complaints or disturbances brought them to the attention of authorities. He declared that the accused were to receive a proper trial in which they were able to face their accusers. He declared that those charged with being Christian should have the opportunity to renounce their belief or to prove they were not Christian by their offering prayers to Rome's gods. Then, if found guilty of being Christians, they were to be executed.

The Development of Hierarchy

Christians had been organizing themselves in the manner of synagogues: a leader presiding over a group of elders. They called their local leaders *bishops*, a Greek work meaning overseer. They called their elders *presbyters,* and assistants to their bishops they called *deacons*. Bishops of different Christian congregations tried to keep in contact with each other, and they tried to coordinate their beliefs. With this contact, bishops from the greater cities – like Antioch, Alexandria and Rome – had greater prestige than did those from lesser cities. Worldly vanities were intruding into Christian thought, the bishop of Rome benefiting from the prestige of heading the Christian community in the empire's capital. The Christian community in Rome attracted Christians from around the empire. Having more wealth than other congregations in the west, it was able to give assistance to other congregations in that part of the empire. And eventually, along with its contributions to other congregations, Rome's bishop began sending pronouncements of authority.

The first Bishop of Rome, Clement, who lived to around the year 97, supported his authority by linking God with Rome. In his first letter to the Corinthians, Clement described a hierarchy of authority that began with God, then went to Jesus, then to the apostles, and finally to bishops such as he, and he added that God had granted Rome "the authority of empire," glory, and honor.

The authority of the bishops was challenged by various Christians, adding to the diversity among the Christians. Among those who struggled with this diversity was the bishop of the Antioch's congregation of Christians, Ignatius, who wrote letters championing the belief in the virgin birth of Jesus and the Trinity: God as the father, God as Jesus, and God as the spirit in all things. Ignatius is the first Christian known to have referred to Christian congregations as *catholic*, a Greek word meaning universal. In a letter to the Christians of Smyrna he supported the authority of the bishops, declaring that baptisms were not permitted without the bishop and that "he who does anything without the knowledge of the bishop is serving the devil."

Bishops against Gnosticism

Among the diversity within Christianity was a view of the world known as Gnosticism, a belief that reality was divided between spirit and matter, with spirit being good and matter being evil – similar to Zoroastrianism. Seeing matter as evil led these Christians to reject the Judaic story of the creation of the universe: that God had created matter and then called it good. Gnostic Christians rejected Jewish scripture in general, and, seeing matter as evil, they saw Jesus as having lived but not as a physical being. They believed that one acquired salvation by rejecting everything material, including one's own body. Although food is matter, some Gnostics divided foods between those that were good and those that were evil, and they attempted to avoid what they saw as evil food. The Gnostics saw light not as a part of the material world but as good, and darkness they saw as evil.

Like many others, Gnostic Christians believed that they acquired knowledge through revelations from God – not from sense experience coupled with mental processing and not from the interpretations of priests. They believed that God was egalitarian in distributing his revelations and that bishops might be among those who had been denied revelations. Some bishops saw this view of revelation as a threat to their authority. And to address this issue, bishops met in AD 172 and together denounced Gnosticism.

Bishop Irenaeus

The fight against Gnosticism was led by the Bishop of Leon, Irenaeus – who became bishop of Rome after Bishop Clement was executed by Roman authorities. Irenaeus wished to consolidate Christianity under the authority of the bishops. He argued that God had created everything, including soul and the material body. He added that with this common origin, soul and body could not be separated into good and evil. He argued that evil was not a substance but a result of human choice and that salvation was not a triumph over matter but the fulfillment of God's creation. Irenaeus argued for belief that conformed to the teachings of the Apostles. He claimed that knowledge was "a gift of love" from God, and he denounced Gnosticism as having come from "evil self-will," "vainglory" and "blindness."

In combating Gnosticism, Irenaeus had done much to outline Christian doctrine, and he addressed the variety of opinions among the Christians. There were in his time a variety of gospels circulating among Christians across the empire, with various anecdotes and sayings and various descriptions of the life of Jesus and his teachings. These were conflicting messages, including calls to seek direct access to God without the benefit of priests and opposition to any form of authority within the church. Among these gospels was that of Mary Magdalene, which described her as one of Jesus' most beloved disciples. The gospel of Mary Magdalene described her as having defended the description of her exchanges with Jesus against the doubts of Peter, with Mary asking Peter if he really thought that she would be "lying about the Lord." Among the gospels was also that of Thomas, who described Jesus as advocating finding the Kingdom of God within oneself. And there was the gospel of Philip, with the same message. Here were calls to self-discovery and becoming an authority unto oneself in conflict with the gospels of Matthew, Mark, Luke and John, which describe Christians receiving salvation by accepting baptism and the forgiveness of their sins.

Irenaeus denounced as heretics those who had more gospels than he said there really were. He described these other gospels as blasphemous and madness and proclaimed that there were only four gospels just as there were only four winds, four corners of the universe and four pillars holding up the sky. Irenaeus supported the authenticity of the four gospels by describing Matthew and John as Jesus' own disciples, Mark as a disciple of Peter and John and Luke as disciples of Paul. It was during the last twenty or so years of Irenaeus' life – around AD 180 to 200 – that the collection of books called the New Testament were formed. Other gospels were destroyed. Some were buried, to be discovered on papyrus fragments preserved by the dry climate in southern Egypt.

The Marcionites

In attempting to define Christianity, Bishop Irenaeus found heresy in the beliefs of a Christian named Marcion. Marcion was from West Asia and had become affiliated with the Christian congregation in Rome. He found conflict between putting one's faith in Jesus as described by the apostle Paul and following laws described in Judaism's sacred writings. He described the Jews as having believed in a barbarian god and Judaism as the work of the devil. Marcion believed that God had sent Jesus to humanity. Like the Gnostics he believed that Jesus had always been spirit and never a material human. He believed that Jesus had sprung from the mind of God, and he reasoned that Jesus' death had been symbolic, that Jesus had not suffered and had not died because a spirit could not suffer or die.

Marcion believed in the literal truth of what was spoken by Jesus and the apostles. He drew from Luke 20:35, which states that "those who are considered worthy to attain to that age and the resurrection of the dead, neither marry, nor are given in marriage." And so Marcion and his followers endeavored to practice complete sexual abstinence. Marcion inspired a following across numerous Christian communities. Then the bishops excommunicated him, and his movement survived into the fifth century, despite its devotion to sexual abstinence.

The Montanists and End of the Age of the Prophets

Another group of Christians, who encouraged celibacy and a literal interpretation of the gospels but who remained within the Church, was the Montanists, led by a Christian named Montanus. The Montanists believed as had Paul that procreation unnecessary because the Second Coming of Jesus was near. They found no support in the scriptures for a systematic order and hierarchy in the worship of Jesus Christ, and they saw the rise of authority and hierarchy within the Church as incompatible with Christianity and as a drift into worldliness. And not believing in authority within the Church, they believed that any one of them could acquire a special knowledge or inspiration from God.

The bishops chose to keep the Montanists within the Church, and they countered Montanist arguments with the claim that revealed truth no longer came to Christians who did not hold positions of authority within the Church. And the bishops announced that the age of the prophets had ended.

Tertullian, the Hellenized anti-Hellenist

A man named Tertullian, born in Carthage and trained in rhetoric and law, lost his respect for education and fled from a world of rival ideas into Christian certainty, converting to Christianity around the year 190. Tertullian agreed with Paul that the wisdom of "this world" was foolish. He went further and described the worldly wisdom of the educated as gloss and the creation of demons. That this was so, he argued, was obvious in the fact that as a group the so-called educated held a multitude of conflicting ideas.

Tertullian was well read in philosophy, but he had come to see philosophy as the enemy of religion. In his comment that Athens had nothing to do with Jerusalem he meant that philosophy and religion should remain disconnected. In describing an agreement he had with the Stoics, he stated that his belief in reason was the Reason of God, a reason that manifested itself in an interconnectedness of things. Tertullian was an acrobatic thinker who did not accept the foundation of Aristotle's logic: the rejection of contradiction. Like the early Taoists he enjoyed what he saw as paradoxes, believing for example that the "incarnation of Jesus Christ" was certain because it was impossible.

Tertullian opposed any association between the Christian Church and the Roman state, because Rome was pagan and therefore demonic. Christians, he stated, should not serve in the army or any other state institution. But he approved of Christians praying for emperors and the well being of their empire. "We pray," he wrote, "that they may have a long life and quiet government, that their palaces be peaceful, their armies strong, their advisors loyal, and their subjects true." (*Apologeticus*, c. 30:4.)

Tertullian was the first Christian of note to write in Latin, and he gave the Church its Latin vocabulary in theology, and some say its first theology. He was a supporter of the Trinity, which he described as one divine substance in three distinct persons: the Father, the Son, and the Holy Ghost.

Having fled from the diversity of belief in the pagan world, Tertullian found himself amid a diversity of belief within Christianity. He complained that the Christian Church was seeking peaceful coexistence with the pagan world around it at the expense of Christian values. Like the Montanist Christians, he believed that the Church was becoming too much of a political organization, and like the Montanists he thought that ordinary, or lay, Christians did not need a priest to intercede between them and God. He wrote that wherever three

Christians gathered there was a church. Each man, he wrote, lives by his own faith.

Tertullian joined the Montanists, and he described the orthodoxy of the bishops as morally lax. He wrote works entitled *On Women's Apparel, on the Veiling of Virgins, On Monogamy, On the Exhortation to Chastity,* and *On Fasting.* And the bishops declared him a heretic.

Clement of Alexandria Broadens the Church

The earliest leaders of Christianity had asked the followers of Jesus to avoid reading pagan books, but the Christians, like Hebrews and others before them, became influenced by the culture around them. They were influenced by discussing their views with non-Christians, by creating a reasoned defense of their views and a reasoned refutation of opposing ideas. An increase in devotion to reason among Christians drew them closer to Hellenism, and conversions brought into Christianity some, like Tertullian, who were already Hellenized.

Among the Hellenized who converted to Christianity was a Greek student and scholar of philosophy named Clement, who lived in Alexandria. He was one of a few men of wealth and property who joined the Christians. Unlike Tertullian, Clement maintained a respect for scholarship. He was an admirer of Plato's philosophy, and he was the first to attempt to synthesize Christianity and Plato. He accepted Plato's description of God as infinite and eternal, transcendent and independent. He saw the universe as God's perfection, and he saw Jesus as God's ultimate revelation and as humanity's guide and instructor.

Clement became an intellectual leader of Alexandria's Christian community and the head of a school for Christians. He advised his fellow Christians to seek other than a literal interpretation of scriptures, suggesting that they interpret some scriptures symbolically and as messages for the heart. This allowed Christians to bend scripture to support a new attitude toward property. To Clement, the message in Matthew about a camel passing through the eye of a needle more easily than the rich entering the kingdom of heaven was obviously a message of symbolism, and he interpreted it not as a command to give up one's possessions but as inspiration to banish from one's mind excess desires for property or worries about property that interfered with spirituality. Clement claimed that poverty was not in itself worthwhile. Having property, he said, frees one from the effort and distress of acquisition and enables one to practice charity. We must not renounce the wealth which "benefits our neighbors... as well as ourselves," he wrote. Wealth, he added, "is furnished by God for the welfare of man."

Clement also spoke against the belief that sex was sinful and that Adam and Eve had sinned by engaging in it. He described sex as necessary in procreation and a part of god's creation. But he claimed that it had to be regulated by obedience to what was good and decent.

Clement's views remained acceptable to the bishops, fitting as it did with the successful growth of the Church, with the Church's hierarchical order and with its belief in charity and acceptance of donations. Clement would come to be considered one of the early "fathers" of the Church and one of the leaders in forming early Christian theology.

Origen

One of the teachers at the Christian school headed by Clement was a young Greek named Origen. In AD 203, Origen succeeded Clement as the leader of the school in Alexandria. Then Origen moved to the provincial capital of Palestine, Caesarea, where he translated and wrote until his death in 255.

Origen's writings filled around six thousand rolls, which kept busy a staff of seven slave secretaries, provided by a wealthy Christian named Ambrose. Origen wrote a huge work on St. John in order to refute a Gnostic named Heracleon. In a related debate within the Church he rebuked those Christians who saw humanity as helpless against Satan. Origen argued that those touched by the devil had the power to choose repentance, that even the devil, who had chosen to become a fallen angel, could apply his will and repent. In Origen's greatest work, called Hexapla (which took him fifteen years to complete) he attempted to interpret the Greek translation of the Old Testament, the Septuagint.

Origen joined other Christian thinkers in describing the Romans as not responsible for the crucifixion of Jesus. Instead, he described the crucifixion as the work of God for the benefit of Christianity. Origen was another of those who saw God in the creation of the Roman Empire. He wrote that the birth of Jesus was timed in accord with the unity that Rome had brought to the world, that otherwise a divided world, "a plurality of kingdoms," would have been an obstacle to the spread of Christianity.

Origen wrote eight books in response to the published criticisms of Christianity by a scholar named Celsus. Believing in both faith and reason, he attempted to improve upon previous efforts to combine Greek philosophy and the wisdom of the Old Testament. He followed Clement in supporting Plato's view of God, and he accepted Plato's belief that the stars were rational beings with God-given souls.

Origen also followed Clement in accepting Christians choosing which scriptures to take literally and which to take allegorically. He attempted a plausible explanation of the Old Testament's story of The Creation, and he tried to explain the contradiction between God having ordained everything in advance and his answering the wishes that humans made through prayers. Trying to make faith, belief in miracles, and reason compatible he claimed that with the tools of reason that were a part of Greek philosophy one could arrive at truths found in scripture, that reason could lead one to truths demonstrated by miracles and the coming to pass of prophesies. As to why God had not made it all easier to understand, Origen claimed that the apostles had left some matters untouched and that God had created obstacles so that people would use their minds in attaining faith.

During his life, Origen was often attacked by fellow Christians who believed he was altering the gospels with pagan philosophy, but he acquired a reputation among Christians as a wise and learned man and was in great demand as a preacher. He would become recognized as one of the most remarkable Christian scholars, and after he died much of his writings would be freely plagiarized.

CHAPTER 20

RULE BY THE JULIO-CLAUDIANS

TIBERIUS, AN UNPOPULAR BUT ABLE RULER

No Roman law gave Augustus the right to pass his powers to anyone, and Augustus apparently failed to see that by passing his offices to his adopted son, Tiberius, he was creating the kind of monarchical rule that he had thought often created incompetent rulers. The public was also without qualms about Augustus' transfer of power. There were examples enough about the weakness of rule by family, and these were times when history was read more than were novels. But the Romans ignored the lesson that could have been drawn from rule by dynasty. Instead, they believed that for a continued peace and prosperity someone should rule as Augustus had ruled.

When Augustus died in AD 14 – just before he was seventy-seven – Tiberius, at the age of 56, took the title of *emperor*, and he also became a consul. Like many dynastic successions to supreme power, Tiberius' succession was accompanied by murder. The victim was Agrippa Postumus, Julia's son by her previous marriage to Augustus' commander and companion, Agrippa. Augustus had adopted him as his son and had made him co-heir with Tiberius, but the boy seemed unruly and slow in thought, and Augustus disinherited him. After the death of Augustus, the boy, as a person of royal blood, was thought a possible rallying point for disaffected persons, and he was eliminated quickly and quietly.

Tiberius was bright, and he had a long history of service to Rome, including ably leading troops in Rome's frontier skirmishes. As emperor he was a capable administrator and had genuine concern for the empire's well-being. He let the Senate know that it was he who ruled, but he left some duties to the Senate, saving himself from being overburdened with work. He told the Senate to stop bothering him about every question that came up and to take initiative, but, to his disgust, senators cringed before him.

The Senate began responding to crises that routinely appeared – one of which was the collapse of the poorly constructed amphitheater at Fidenae, which killed thousands. Regulating private businesses was recognized as in society's interest, and the Senate took action against frauds of various contractors, including the slackness of authorities that resulted in some roads becoming impassible.

The Senate was concerned about what it saw as a new freedom among women, about extravagant living and the rise in prices of food on the black market. But Tiberius saw all this as a part of the times, and he believed it was difficult to move people into the past, at least without making them unhappy and creating new opponents to his rule. But he did suggest to the Senate that it expel from Rome dancers who had come to Rome to put on obscene shows.

Tiberius did well in appointing competent people to administrative positions, although preferences were given to candidates from "better" families. He kept Rome along a path of economic stability, and the military remained disciplined. But the glory that had belonged to Augustus – now considered a god – was not his. Tiberius disliked crowds and did not appear at the gladiator contests as had Augustus. Rather than a loving father figure, Tiberius was seen as unfriendly. For the masses, which enjoyed attaching themselves to greatness, Tiberius was a disappointment.

Intrigues and Terror

Tiberius' adopted son, Germanicus, was the husband of Augustus' granddaughter, Agrippina – and unlike Tiberius he was popular. Germanicus was handsome, charming and a man of dash and informality. Tiberius sent him as military leader against a rebellion by German tribes, and he sent him about the empire as a troubleshooter. On a visit to Syria in AD 17, Germanicus fell ill and died, which shocked the Romans. The Roman governor of Syria, a man named Piso, was tried by the Senate for having poisoned Germanicus. The charge was not proven, but Piso died anyway. He was found with his throat cut – possibly a suicide.

Then in AD 23 came the death of Tiberius' son and designated heir, Drusus, after a long illness. Later Drusus' death would be attributed to the emperor's ambitious aide, Sejanus, who headed the Praetorian Guard. Sejanus was ambitious. He wished to marry Drusus' widow – which would have made him a member of the royal family. But Sejanus was a commoner, and Germanicus' widow, Agrippina, was instrumental in Tiberius' decision against the marriage. As Rome's top policeman, Sejanus created a reign of terror in Rome. Opportunists went about looking for crimes such as adultery and words of treason against the emperor, knowing they would be rewarded with the property of those they helped convict. And among those charged with treason and adultery were friends of Agrippina.

It had been Sejanus' job to control visitations to Tiberius, and Tiberius called Sejanus his "partner in labors." In the year 26, Tiberius, at the age of sixty-eight, left Rome for the island of Capri, where he would spend the rest of his life, ruling, relaxing and bathing with boys he called his minnows. Sejanus began plotting against Agrippina's sons, whom he apparently saw as rivals. In the year 31, Tiberius came to believe that Sejanus had arranged the death of Drusus by having a servant administer occasional doses of poison to him. Against Sejanus, Tiberius launched a purge, led by a high ranking Praetorian guard named Macro, whom Tiberius elevated to leader of the guard. Sejanus and his allies were overpowered and executed. One of Agrippina's sons was condemned as an ally of Sejanus, and he was starved to death in a cell. And soon after, in the year 33, Agrippina also died, supposedly by suicide.

THE EMPEROR CALIGULA

The heir-designate was now the twenty-one year-old son of Germanicus and Agrippina: Gaius, whose nickname was Caligula. Caligula was the choice of the head of the Praetorian Guard, Macro, who now had much influence in Rome. When Caligula was twenty-six, Tiberius was around seventy-nine and slowly dying, and it was to be rumored that Tiberius was finally smothered when being looked after by Caligula or one of his aides.

As expected, the Senate rubber-stamped its recognition of Caligula as Tiberius' successor. And being the son of the well remembered and popular Germanicus, the Romans welcomed Caligula as their new emperor. Caligula wanted to be popular, and he attempted to demonstrate his affection for his subjects by providing them with elaborate shows at the Circus Maximus and the Colosseum. Unlike Tiberius, he attended the circus, gladiator shows and chariot races. And, to the amusement and delight of his subjects, he participated in the races himself.

Caligula wanted to rule well. He returned to the courts the power to make independent decisions in sentencing people, and he increased the number of jurors in order to speed proceedings. He began publishing a budget, and he began more building. But along with good intentions, Caligula suffered from vanity. The godliness that was attributed to his great-grandfather Augustus and Julius Caesar may have led him to believe not that he was a god but that he should be worshiped as a god. He planned for the distribution of statues of himself for worship, including an image of himself placed at the temple in Jerusalem. This was before almost thirty years before Masada and the end of Judaea. And Jews came from Jerusalem and asked that they, the Jews be excused from having to worship him. But the request was refused.

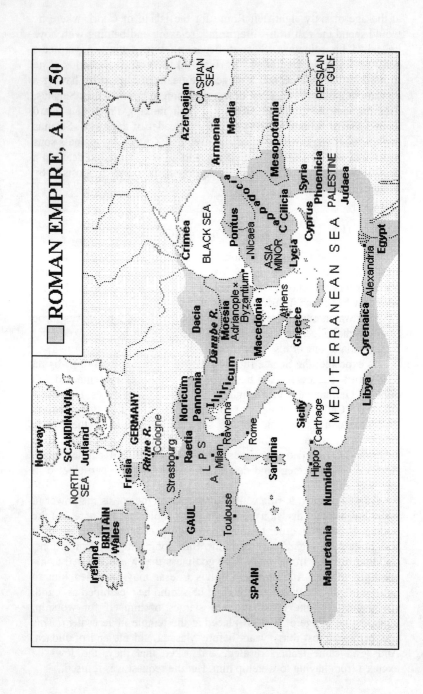

ROMAN EMPIRE, A.D. 150

Caligula believed that Jews disrespected the office of emperor. He ordered the new governor of Syria and Palestine, Petronius, to put in Jerusalem's temple statues of himself as God incarnate, and he sent two legions, with Petronius, into Judaea to meet Jewish resistance. According to the Jewish historian Josephus, "many tens of thousands of Jews" including women and children, went to Petronius and told him they were ready to die rather than submit to Caligula's statues profaning Jerusalem's temple. They were unarmed and announced that they would not fight, and they lay on the ground baring their throats for cutting. Jews left their fields, ready for harvest, unattended. The crops of the Jews were important to Rome, as Rome drew a portion of these crops as taxes. Petronius returned to Antioch and wrote to Caligula. Caligula ordered him to commit suicide for disobeying an imperial command, but events were in motion that would save Petronius.

If power corrupts, it does so with mediocrities who by chance acquire power, as had Caligula. Caligula was one of those sons of privilege who had failed to acquire the moral strengths needed in a ruler. He was self-indulgent, and indulging his appetite for food, he grew fat. In appearance he was ugly, which might have contributed to his becoming mean. Being a man of little emotional discipline or control, he allowed himself to hate and to express his hate with sadistic revenge. He behaved as if he believed he had license. He followed his sexual impulses with little restraint. Homosexuality was still frowned upon and ridiculed by most Romans, but Caligula had become familiar with it, including the bi-sexuality of Tiberius. Caligula had many homosexual and heterosexual affairs, including using his authority to obtain sexual pleasures from other men's wives. And, it is rumored, he had sexual intercourse with his three sisters.

It was not Caligula's sexual activities that resulted in his demise, it was the fear that he put into people around him who had considerable power of their own. Caligula made enemies, and he used the power that he believed was justly his to have those he saw as enemies executed. That the power of no one man was absolute was again to be demonstrated. A conspiracy against him arose among those who felt their lives endangered, including officers in the Praetorian Guard. And in AD 41, at the age of twenty-nine and in power only three years and ten months, he was assassinated.

CLAUDIUS

With the death of Caligula and the bad experience of his rule behind them, many senators considered exchanging rule by dynasty for the return to a republic. While the Senate discussed this possibility, the Praetorian Guard searched for a its own believable successor to

Caligula – in order to maintain its standing and influence. It found him in Caligula's uncle, Claudius, the brother of Germanicus and a familiar figure within Augustus' family. Claudius, in turn, rewarded the Guard with money for their support. Discussions in the Senate about the problems of succession and a republic came to an end, and monarchy was to remain the dominant form of government in Europe – into modern times.

In appearance Claudius was very unlike his heroic brother, Germanicus. He stammered and suffered a disability that made him clumsy. He had been an embarrassment to the imperial family and had spent much of his life secluded, writing books on Roman, Etruscan and Carthaginian history. Not taken seriously as a possible heir, he had survived while others around him had died in the intrigues that plagued the royal family.

If Caligula's behavior could be considered the product of his experiences as a member of the royal family, or as a man having absolute power, so too could the behavior of Claudius. But the two men were very different. It was another instance of the more capable leader being the person who read good books. Claudius was a decent, intelligent man, genuinely affable, and like Germanicus he was informal. He too cared about the empire. During his thirteen years of reign, he continued public works, he gave Rome a new aqueduct. He built a new harbor at Ostia (near Rome), and he improved the judiciary. Also he extended citizenship in the provinces and created numerous new colonies – one of which, Colonia Agrippina, was to become the city of Cologne in Germany. An edict by Claudius held that a master who murdered his slave because the slave was no longer of use to him could be tried for murder, and Claudius extended freedom to any slave who had been abandoned by his or her master.

As described in Chapter 19, Claudius tried to expel the Jews from Rome, but like other polytheists, Claudius was generally tolerant of the worship of gods other than those he worshiped – but not toward Druidism. Druids were known to perform human sacrifices, which the Romans viewed with abhorrence, and Claudius saw Druidism as a threat to the empire's well being, for around Druidism rallied Gauls who wished to be free of Roman rule. Although Druidism had been declared a crime against the state, it had spread to some non-Gauls, and Claudius had a Roman executed after noticing a Druidic talisman on his breast.

Claudius was no angel. He believed in the Roman Empire, and he desired glory and popularity enough to lead an invasion into Britain. During his reign, Britain was made a part of the Roman Empire. And Claudius expanded the empire's frontiers in Gaul. He annexed Mauritania in North Africa. He absorbed Lycia in Asia Minor and

Thrace in eastern Europe. He made Judaea a Roman province. But he avoided major wars with the Germans, and he accepted the collapse of the pro-Roman government in Armenia rather than go to war with Parthia. Claudius was attracted only to women, and he married four times. His third wife was flagrantly unfaithful. And his last marriage was to his niece, Caligula's sister, Agrippina's daughter, whose name was also Agrippina. Before she married Claudius, Agrippina poisoned her second husband – or so it is rumored. Claudius adopted Agrippina's son by a former marriage, a boy to become known as Nero, and Agrippina succeeded in getting Claudius to favor Nero as his heir-designate over his own son Britannicus.

In an attempt to make Nero eloquent, Agrippina had him schooled in mythology, the classical writers, and rhetoric. Nero was schooled also in philosophy, which was still considered by many Romans to be a Greek pastime inappropriate for well-bred Romans. While a boy, Nero developed a liking for art, drama and music, especially singing, and he liked horses. And when Nero was sixteen, Agrippina had him marry Claudius' daughter by a previous marriage: Octavia.

Agrippina used her power to destroy people she saw as a threat or who had crossed her, and the Roman historian Tacitus was to write that in the year 53 she goaded Claudius "into acts of savagery" against her imagined enemies. The following year Claudius died, some believe by Agrippina having poisoned him after he had expressed second thoughts about Nero as his successor. Nero, at the age of seventeen, became emperor. Agrippina arranged a funeral for Claudius that equaled in grandeur that of Augustus Caesar, and, perhaps at Agrippina's urging, Nero had Claudius deified, the only member of Augustus' family besides Augustus to be so honored.

NERO RULES

The Senate, having returned to being cowed, responded routinely and gave its assent to Nero's succession. And, taking his great, great-grandfather Augustus as his model, Nero began his rule adhering to what he perceived to be ideals. He made his old tutor, the Stoic philosopher and orator Seneca, his advisor, and Seneca became a power behind the throne. Like Caligula, Nero wanted public adoration, and the obvious way to acquire it was as a benevolent ruler. He delivered a speech to the Senate that inspired widespread praise, and claims arose that a new Golden Age had begun.

Nero disliked having to sign death sentences against criminals. Often, instead, he gave them clemency. Then he banned capital punishment. While attending gladiator contests he turned his head rather than watch the blow to the head that assured that a fallen man was dead, and for a while he banned contests that involved bloodshed, and in their place he organized poetry competitions.

In his first five years of rule, while under the influence of Seneca, he gave slaves the right to file complaints against their masters. He pardoned people who had written unflattering descriptions of him. He left the charge of treason unused. He gave assistance to cities that had suffered from disasters. And, he won the hearts of many of his subjects by lowering taxes.

Like some other youths with artistic pretensions, Nero believed he had sensitivity and genius. He wished to be accepted not just for the political power that he had inherited but also for this genius, and he read his poems in public, played the lyre and acted in plays. But like Caligula, Nero was a mediocrity, and as a mediocrity he lacked the elegance of restraint. He became bored with his young wife, the noble born and virtuous Octavia, and he became involved with a former slave woman. Nero's mother, Agrippina, got along well with Octavia, whom she could control, but now Nero began seeing less of his mother, and she resented seeing her influence over him slip away. Her resentment and then outrage drove Nero further away. He grew hostile toward her, saw less of her, and he took away the honor guard that had accompanied her wherever she went.

Agrippina began talking of replacing Nero with his half-brother Britannicus. Nero resented and feared this to such an extent that he resorted to family tradition and had Britannicus poisoned. And maybe having murdered one person made it easier for him to resort to more murders. He wanted to rid himself of the annoyance of his mother, and in the year 59 – when he was twenty-one – he had her murdered, presenting her death to the world as a suicide. Most of the Senate thanked Nero for having escaped from such a dangerous woman, and this encouraged Nero to rid himself of one more nuisance: his troublesome aunt, whom he also had murdered.

Apparently Nero was burdened by his having had his mother killed. He became more defensive. By the year 61, he had re-instituted treason trials. In 62, Nero feared that his wife, Octavia, was spreading dislike of him in his household and at court. He had a handyman confess to adultery with Octavia. He banished her, and soon he had her put to death. He may have been encouraged in this by his love interest at the time, Sabina Poppaea – one of many attractive women across history who sought association with men of wealth or fame. And Nero married her shortly thereafter.

In 62, Nero's minister, Burrus, died, and Nero's aged Stoic advisor, Seneca, felt alienated from those who remained in Nero's inner circle.

Seneca retired, and Burrus was replaced by Ofonius Tigellinus, who amused Nero with his callousness. Tigellinus described Stoics, including Seneca, as hypocrites for proclaiming preference for living simply, and he began exerting influence on Nero.

Nero continued to indulge his appetite for company and for food. His dinner parties might last from noon to midnight. Like Caligula he grew fat. And he continued to pursue his artistic ambitions. He entered singing contests, and needing approval he took along a group trained to clap for him. Taking his dignity very seriously – he was after all emperor – he let singers who out sang him know of his resentment, and at one contest he forbade other contestants to perform.

And Nero indulged in the pleasures of religious ecstasy. He was attracted to evangelists of various religious cults: to Zoroastrians, to a cult of a virgin-mother goddess named Arargatis, and to the cult of another virgin-mother goddess named Juno-Canathos. He spoke with Jews about Judaism. He met with a Gnostic magician named Simon Magus. And it is said by some that he interviewed the apostle Paul.

The Great Fire

In the year 64, while Nero was at his villa at Antium thirty-five miles away, a great fire broke out in Rome – as described in Chapter 19. Fanned by winds, the fire raged for five days. Then it flared up again and burned for four more days. It burned wooden tenement houses – which were as high as six stories. And it burned the homes of the wealthy, including Nero's palace.

The fire might have been started by the overturning of one of the barbecue-like stoves (a brazier) that people used inside their homes, or by an oil lamp. But suspicions of arson arose, not because evidence of arson had been found but because people were inclined to believe that disaster was the work of some kind of malevolence. And with Christians still seen as Jews, and Jews seen as haters of society, suspicions were caste in their direction.

Nero instituted relief for those made homeless by the fire. He launched a program to rebuild Rome. Streets in the burned out area were to be widened. Tenements were to be reduced in height. There was to be open space between tenements and other buildings. There was to be more firefighting equipment and an extended distribution of water. Nero had his own home to replace, and in a burned out area that had been most crowded, Nero took three hundred acres for himself and started rebuilding a palace, to be called "The Golden House." This was unpopular with the upper classes, who saw it as a waste of money, and it was unpopular with the poor who had lived in the area. Among the poor a rumor arose that Nero had started the fire to make space for his great mansion, and graffiti appeared ridiculing Nero for building his palace at the expense of others.

Countering the rumor that blamed Nero for the fire, an official investigation concluded that the fire had been started by Jewish fanatics. Nero now learned of the difference between Christians as Jews and other Jews, and he put blame for the fire on the Christians. As punishment, Nero sent some Christians to their death in the Arena. But, according to the historian Tacitus, many Romans remained suspicious of Nero and they pitied the Christians, believing that instead of being sacrificed for the welfare of the state, the Christians were being sacrificed as Nero's scapegoats.

Nero's Demise

In conformity with the notion that power corrupts, Nero was not inclined to bear frustrations with the same patience that was required of common people. He let his emotions get the best of him and flew into rages, killing his pregnant wife, Sabina Poppaea, by kicking her in the stomach. In places outside Rome, Nero remained popular, but not in Rome. There, many thought he was unfit to be emperor, and in Rome a conspiracy was hatched against him that included numerous Romans with prestige. Nero learned of the conspiracy. Executions followed, and some people were ordered to commit suicide, including Nero's old advisor, Seneca.

Nero might have thought that he could successfully counter opposition with his retaliations, but in fact, like Caligula, his power depended upon what others thought of him, and he was losing the support of too many people. Most significantly – in a society where people could not vote someone out of office – he was losing the support of those who commanded armies. Military commanders outside Rome were aware of Nero's unpopularity in Rome. Nero ordered the execution of Rome's commander in Spain, Servius Galba, and, with nothing to lose, Galba openly declared himself a subject of the Senate and the Roman people rather than of Nero. Troops in Gaul had also withdrawn their support from Nero, and in a trip there Nero failed to win back their loyalty. Nero found himself abandoned except for a few servants, and perhaps realizing that this meant death for him, he ran through the palace screaming hysterically.

Sensing Nero's lack of power, the Senate roused itself and declared Nero a public enemy and ordered his execution. Soldiers closed in on Nero at his villa four miles south of Rome. Nero blamed everybody for his demise but himself. With the help of a servant he killed himself, bringing an end to the dynasty begun by Augustus: the Julio-Claudians.

CHAPTER 21

ROME, FROM GOLDEN AGE TO POLITICAL CHAOS

THE SEARCH FOR STABILITY IN A GOLDEN AGE

A critical time had arisen in Rome's history: who or what was to replace Nero? It would not be another member of the family of Augustus. Nor would the Senate assume power in an effort to bring back the republic. Instead, power was allowed to remain with military men. This began with the army of Servius Galba. Encouraged by their success in overthrowing Nero, soldiers under Galba arrogated to themselves the power to declare their commander emperor, and the Senate cooperated, formally conferring imperial powers on Galba.

Servius Galba, aged seventy-one, had a distinguished record as a military commander, but he did not know how to maintain political power. He began his reign viewed by many as a savior. Then he narrowed his support. He punished those who did not support his taking power, and he surrounded himself with advisors who managed to alienate more people. Galba tried to correct the misrule of Nero by restoring Rome's finances and restoring discipline to the military. His frugality alienated more Romans and military men, and he responded to their displeasure by complaining that he was the kind who levied troops, not bribed them for their support. Galba turned the Praetorian Guard against him by announcing that he had adopted someone as his heir-apparent and failing to pay the Praetorian Guard the donation that it had come to expect for supporting a new emperor. A thirty-seven year-old senator, Otho, conspired to replace Galba, and Otho offered the Praetorian Guard the donation that it expected. Otho won the guard's support and the support of others. On January 15, 69, Galba was cut down in the street by guardsmen on horseback. His close associates were murdered soon after. And the Senate proclaimed Otho emperor.

Otho's rule went unrecognized among soldiers in Germany, who followed the precedent laid down by Galba's troops and hailed as emperor their own commander: Vitellius. Vitellius had become popular with his troops by having allowed them to bully civilians and to take anything they could get their hands on. Vitellius and his army marched toward Rome, and along the way they battled troops from Rome that supported Otho. Vitellius won. Otho committed suicide after only three months in office, and Vitellius marched into Rome as conqueror and as Rome's new emperor.

Vitellius did not know how to hold on to political power. He was unpopular with everyone but his troops. He executed everyone he believed had wronged him. His bloodbath disgusted the Romans, and noticing Vitellius' unpopularity, another army selected its military commander to put things straight in Rome. The commander was Titus Flavius Vespasian, aged sixty, who had led Rome's recent campaign against the uprising in Judaea that had ended at Masada. Vespasian and his army marched on Rome. They found Vitellius hiding in the palace. Vitellius was taken to the Forum, and there the crowds ridiculed him before someone stabbed him to death.

The Emperor Vespasian

By hard work, Vespasian had risen from small-town, middleclass origins. He was a tough, coarse-talking commander with an earthy humor and wit. He was impatient with incompetence but generally good natured. Vespasian offered Rome political stability. Whereas Nero had lowered taxes to win favor from the masses, Vespasian raised taxes. He spent little on himself and restored Rome's treasury. He improved management of the courts, and court cases began to be handled more quickly. He invested in public works and started the empire on a course of economic prosperity. He built new temples, ostensibly to please the gods, and he began work on a new colosseum, the ruins of which are still in Rome, on the site where Nero had begun building his great mansion.

Vespasian worked long hours. He had lost his wife and daughter early in his military career, and now he lived quietly with his mistress. He was not easily provoked into taking harsh actions against others, and he never used his power for selfish or petty purposes. If Tiberius had been smothered to death and Claudius poisoned, Vespasian was the first emperor since Augustus to have died of natural causes. After nine years as emperor, at the age of sixty-nine, he came down with the flu and died, and rule passed to his son, Titus.

The Emperor Titus and Mount Vesuvius

Titus, had been his father's aide, and he had won the admiration of the Romans for his devotion to his father. Like his father, Titus was bright and good natured, and he became one of Rome's more popular emperors. But his rule was plagued by disasters not of his making. For years geologic pressure had been increasing under Mount Vesuvius, pressure had caused the great earthquake that had shaken Pompeii and adjacent Italian cities during the latter part of Nero's reign. On August 24, 79, Vesuvius erupted, the pressure blowing off the top of the mountain. Some Christians saw the eruption as God's vengeance against recent persecutions. Some Romans believed that the gods had begun the doomsday that they had long been expecting.

The eruption buried towns at the base of Vesuvius. Titus provided relief and rehabilitation programs for survivors, and he paid for much of it with his own money. Then came another great fire that burned Rome, followed by an epidemic of disease. Titus made great efforts to find a remedy for the epidemic and to comfort his subjects. Then, after having been in power only two years, Titus himself died of fever, and the Romans responded with more genuine grief than they had with the death of any previous emperor, including Augustus.

The Emperor Domitian

Titus was succeeded by his thirty year-old brother, Domitian, younger than Titus by eleven years. Domitian was a good administrator who skillfully managed the state's finances and contributed more to public construction. He insisted on each individual being protected by law, and he was concerned with morality. He wanted senators and their families and the equites (families of wealth from commerce) to behave according to accepted moral standards and to avoid scandals. He severely punished Vestal Virgins who had given into the temptation of sexual intercourse. He drove prostitutes from Rome's streets and enforced a law against what was considered unnatural sexual practices, including homosexuality. In the interest of children he outlawed their castration, which had been the practice of some religious cults. And he sought to end the buying and selling of eunuchs.

Domitian became impatient with criticism and dissent and fearful of opposition, which started him down the same path as the failed emperors. His brother Titus had acted against subversion, banning anarchists and cynic-philosophers from Rome, but he had done so with confidence about Rome's security. Domitian, on the other hand, drew the wrong lessons from Rome's history of plots, intrigues and political turmoil. He feared that subversion was about to get out of hand. He banned philosophers from Italy, and he overreacted when some soldiers stationed on the Rhine River revolted against his rule. The revolt was easily crushed, but he began a reign of terror against imagined traitors, including the burning books and listening more to informers.

With the public, Domitian remained popular, as most people were not the target of his campaign against treason. But his zeal in weeding out enemies created fear among those who were close to power, and after seven years of rule, palace officials who felt threatened by his terror joined a conspiracy that led to his assassination – now a familiar way of recalling an emperor.

The Emperor Nerva

A new emperor had to be found, and Senators and palace officials, including those who had conspired against Domitian, hoped for consensus rather than civil war. They joined in selecting an interim ruler: a sixty-six year-old senior senator named Nerva, who had not taken part in the conspiracy against Domitian but had probably been aware of it.

Nerva began his rule by seeking a return of calm and confidence. He allowed philosophers and other critics to return to Italy and Rome. He assured senators that only with their concurrence would one of them be tried and executed. But quarrels erupted between Nerva and the Senate. Praetorian Guards threatened to punish Domitian's assassins, and, to hold onto power, Nerva sought allies in army generals. Under the shelter of these generals, Nerva was able to stay in power. And as these generals wished, Nerva adopted one of their own as his son and successor, a forty-four year-old commander named Trajan. Two years later, Nerva died, and Trajan became emperor.

Trajan's Early Successes

Like Vespasian, Trajan was a good soldier and a man of talent. He was also a man of tolerance and courtesy, and he had a balanced mind. His first love was the army, and after two years as emperor he pursued his soldiering by launching a campaign of expansion north across the Danube River into the hills and forests of Dacia. The Romans equated Trajan's daring as self-confidence with that of Julius Caesar, and four years after he entered Dacia the Romans gave Trajan a victory celebration that was the longest and most expensive that Rome would ever have.

Soon Trajan expanded Roman authority into the Arabian Desert, which included an important trade route. Then came conflict with the Parthian Empire on the Roman Empire's eastern frontier. The Parthian king, Osroes, deposed an Armenian king and put a king of his choosing in his place. Trajan interpreted this as breaking an agreement with Rome, and he made the incident a cause for war. He drove the puppet king of the Parthians from Armenia, and in 114 he made that area part of the Roman Empire. Then in 115 he took advantage of a dynastic struggle among the Parthians and sent his forces into northern Mesopotamia. The Parthian king, Osroes, was facing a rival from Persia and was too busy to counter Trajan's move. Then Trajan captured Osroes' capital, Ctesiphon, his troops taking the Parthian throne of gold and making a prisoner of a daughter of Osroes. Osroes escaped east, and

Trajan conquered to the Persian Gulf, where he saw ships setting sail to India and must have thought of Alexander's great empire.

Trajan hoped that division among the Parthians would help his position, but instead his invasion united most Parthian princes with Osroes. The Parthians counterattacked against the Romans in Mesopotamia. Suffering losses, Trajan began to withdraw, leaving Rome in control of only a finger of land protruding into Mesopotamia.

As described in Chapter 20, Trajan put down the uprising by Jews that had been encouraged by the Parthians, and he persecuted Christians. But Trajan favored applying the law against only those Christians about whom people complained, or Christians who had created disturbances, and he declared that the accused were to receive a proper trial in which they were able to face their accusers.

More significant from his point of view, during his nineteen years of rule he improved the empire's roads and harbors, he beautified Rome and he provided support for the children of Rome's poor. And although the Senate continued to have little real power, Trajan consulted it and maintained its good will. The historian Tacitus – who lived during Trajan's reign – praised Trajan for restoring Rome's "old spirit," including the feeling that one could express oneself freely.

Trajan Succeeded by Hadrian

While returning from the East to Rome in 117, Trajan, at the age of sixty-five, became ill and died. He had chosen as his successor a soldier-intellectual and Rome's military governor to Syria: Hadrian. Hadrian traveled across the empire, stabilizing local governments, patronizing the arts and adding to the beautification of cities. He continued Trajan's policy regarding law and the treatment of Christians. He penalized those who mistreated their slaves. He kept the army at peak efficiency through constant training and unannounced inspections. He was an able military man and did not shrink from taking action in defense of the empire, but he saw Trajan's abandoning Augustus' opposition to expansion as a mistake. He withdrew Roman control from the territory that extended into Mesopotamia, letting the Parthians retake it. He sent Osroes' daughter back to her family and began a peace with the Parthians that was to last forty years. He strengthened the empire's frontiers by building walls: a continuous wooden wall along the Danube frontier, a wall along the Rhine River in northern Germany, and stone walls in Numidia and northern Britain. Four generals were disappointed with Hadrian's retreat from military aggres-sion, and they plotted to overthrow him. But Hadrian learned of their conspiracy before they attacked, and he had the generals executed.

PROSPERITY, RACE, PLUTARCH AND THE CYNICS

The Roman Empire was the largest area in the world without internal customs barriers. Its roads had improved. Private industry was regulated but government did not interfere much in the economy, and the empire had prospered from internal trade in agriculture and in crafted goods. From one end of the empire to the other were bountiful farms. Improvements had been made in medicine and public health, and across the empire were good hospitals. Trade from the empire reached as far east as China, the caravan route from Parthia to China having opened in the year 115. The empire's trade reached eastern Africa, and it passed out through the Strait of Gibraltar (between Mauretania and Spain) to as far north as Norway. Gaul and Western Germany had become the workshop of Europe. Gaul was busy with metal working. The city of Cologne had a glass blowing industry. The eastern provinces of the empire, including Greece, exercised age-old skills in technology and trade, and Greek businessmen had become the wealthiest in the empire.

Rome's common people were still illiterate. They were still unequal before the law. Those whom the police detained as suspects might be tortured as the police attempted to attain the truth. Despite the prosperity of the empire many still lived on narrow streets, amid overcrowding, noise, dirt, and in tiny quarters, but their tenement houses were now likely to be of concrete faced with brick. Some of Rome's common people grumbled, while government welfare allowed them to survive in the city. But to most Romans the world seemed a better place and more civilized than before. Rome had a good water supply, domestic sanitation and sewage disposal. The city of Rome now matched some cities of the east in grandeur, and the Romans were proud of it.

Roman aristocrats were proud, but this was not the same aristocracy that Polybius and Livy had thought superior. Genetically that aristocracy had had disappeared through intermarriage and out-of-wedlock births. And Rome's common people had also changed genetically. About four-fifths of Rome's plebeians carried some genes of former slaves. Augustus' attempt at racial purity had failed.

Plutarch – Writer and Moralist

Plutarch was a Greek. He was a Delphi priest, a popular writer and a moralist whose popularity allowed him to become the acquaintance of the emperors Trajan and Hadrian. And he would influence Christians, who liked his opinions. He wrote 227 works, most of it historical biography, including sixty essays on religion, morality, physical matters and literature. It would be through Plutarch that people in the Middle Ages would learn about antiquity. Reading him would help stimulate the Renaissance. Shakespeare would draw from his biographies. He would be read by Michelangelo and Martin Luther, Rousseau, Montesquieu, Montaigne and other contributors to the Enlightenment, and by George Washington and Abraham Lincoln.

In his historical biographies, Plutarch attempted to describe noble deeds and characters to provide models of behavior. He wrote believing that men were responsible for their acts and that they should be brave, decisive, courageous, bene-volent, creative, flexible and have a manly dignity. He thought Alexander had been a great man who had lowered himself by lack of moderation and self-discipline. Others whose lives he described were: Romulus, Solon, Pericles, the Gracchi brothers, Marius, Sulla, Pompey, Julius Caesar and Cicero. Writing about both Greeks and Romans he hoped to encourage respect between them.

Plutarch was a Platonist who believed in the "Creator's magnanimity and solicitude." He believed that evil was the work of demons and that demons had damaged God's perfect plan. The force of goodness, he believed, was greater than the force of evil. He believed that atheism led to vice and that sex should be for procreation only. Like Plato and Aristotle he believed that with death the soul separated from one's body and became purified. He found grounds for such a belief in the Dionysian mysteries, which were widely accepted in his time. As his wife faced death he consoled her by referring to these mysteries.

Plutarch believed that truth in religion was the product of the Greek and Roman traditions and that religions outside of these traditions were superstitions, that they were the product of people not using their intelligence in thinking about the gods. He saw as superstitious those who attributed to the gods a power that overrode their own will and responsibility, and he saw as superstitious those who believed in the traditional Greek gods opposed by Plato: gods who treated people capriciously. The superstitious person, Plutarch wrote, believed in gods because he was afraid not to.

Plutarch's belief in tradition included a tolerance for slavery and an acceptance of monarchy as the best form of government. Philosophically, he sided with the Stoics, but foreshadowing developments within Christianity he forgave human frailty more than did the Stoics. And as would many Christians, he described Epicureanism as pernicious.

The Cynics

Cynics were numerous during Rome's Golden Age and prosperity. One of the more widely known of them was Peregrinus, an excommunicated Christian from a wealthy family. Peregrinus studied in

Egypt under the philosopher Agathobulus. To enhance his contempt for the world he submitted to various humiliations including public floggings. Peregrinus arrived in Rome and began criticizing everything and everybody. Soon, Rome's prefect told Peregrinus to leave the city, and Peregrinus went to Greece, where he called on Greeks to rebel against Rome. He lived in a hut and claimed that for the sake of honesty and justice one should avoid sin, that avoiding sin should be made easier by remembering that eventually everything is revealed.

Peregrinus decided to make a show of his inner strength and defiance by announcing to a crowd outside the Olympic games in Greece that at the next games he would burn himself to death. With the approach of the games, the prospect of Peregrinus killing himself added to the excitement. In a solemn procession followed by a large crowd, the 65 year-old Peregrinus marched to his chosen execution site. Stripped to his dirty undershirt, Peregrinus cried out "Be gracious to me, gods of my father and my mother." Then he jumped into the flames.

Peregrinus' followers were deeply moved. Some claimed that they saw a vulture fly from his flames to Olympus. Some of his followers claimed that they saw Peregrinus after death, dressed in white, walking happily with a crown of ivy on his head. Peregrinus became a new Cynic saint around which a cult developed. Some others responded to Peregrinus' death with disgust, saying he was a lunatic driven by hunger for publicity and that he deserved to die.

In response to Peregrinus, a Greek writer named Lucian stated that a man should not run away from life and that if someone had to die they should do it quietly and with dignity. Lucian complained of cities being filled with Cynics. In a satirical play called the *Runaways* he described all Cynics as people who were running from life and as people who went from house to house begging for food and money while merely pretending to be philosophers. He described the Cynics as responding with verbal abuse when questioned on any philosophical point. A character in the *Runaways* asked what would become of the world if all working men left their jobs to live off others like the Cynics, and in the play Lucian described Zeus as sending Hercules to wipe out the disease of Cynicism.

FINALLY A PHILOSOPHER KING

The emperor Hadrian, ailing and childless, adopted as his son and heir, Titus Aurelius Fulvus, a competent, intelligent, fifty year-old who had been a consul, a governor and was Hadrian's personal advisor. Fulvus became the emperor Antoninus Pius, and he reigned during twenty-three years of peace and prosperity. He, in turn, adopted his nephew, Marcus Aurelius, as his son and made him heir. Aurelius admired his adoptive father for his thoughtfulness, his lack of vanity, his dedication and love of work and his open mind, and the Roman public admired Aurelius for his devotion to his adoptive father. Aurelius tried his own hand at reason and studied philosophy, religion and morality. He became a Stoic. The thoughts he wrote down from time to time in Greek were to be collected into a book called *Meditations* and considered a good account of Stoic belief.

Marcus Aurelius became emperor in 161, and he ruled for nineteen years. As a Stoic he believed in the brotherhood of man and he exercised power with a strong sense of duty and tried to avoid letting himself be ruled by passion. He realized that he was not the most clever of men, but he believed that he could reason well enough and that he was guided by God's "divine reason." Here was the philosopher-king of whom Plato and Aristotle might have approved, and Confucius too – Aurelius being an intelligent man who wanted to do right. Here was a man who would not be corrupted by power.

Aurelius against Circumstance

Within a year after Marcus Aurelius became emperor, Parthia began military offensives into Rome's empire: into Armenia and across the Euphrates River into Syria, where Parthian troops had not been seen for two centuries. Aurelius fought the Parthians from 162 to 166, his troops retaking Armenia and marching into Mesopotamia to Ctesiphon. The Roman army came in contact with an epidemic – perhaps smallpox – that had been raging for a decade among the Kushans east of Parthia. The disease had spread along trade routes to China, southern Arabia and into Mesopotamia, where the Romans had contacted it. Racked by illness, the Roman army was obliged to retreat. Returning soldiers spread the disease through the Roman Empire. The epidemic became known as the Great Pestilence and lasted fifteen years, killing as many 25 percent in some population centers, reducing the empire's manpower while Germanic peoples on the empire's borders were growing in number.

German tribes, attracted by the pleasant climate of the Mediterranean region and by the empire's higher standard of living, pushed across the empire's border into the Danube region and into Italy. Aurelius saw it as his duty to control the empire's borders, and he dashed about with his armies from one area to another and successfully contained the invasions. Without booty or conquered people to tax, these were wars that had to be paid for by taxing Romans, with Marcus Aurelius making his contribution by auctioning off the crown jewels.

The harder times brought more fear, which in turn brought more denunciations of Christians, and more executions of Christians as

Aurelius continued the policies of Trajan and Hadrian. Aurelius still wanted to improve the world, but in his later years he saw that the power to make the world right was collective. He blamed people in general for failing to reform themselves, and he become pessimistic, believing that humanity would repeat the sordid follies of the past. But Aurelius committed a folly of his own. He made his sixteen year-old son Commodus his heir-apparent. Two years later – in 180 – while at the front taking the offensive against Germans, he died, and Commodus became emperor. Beginning with Trajan, emperors had fathered no sons and had passed rule to men of proven quality, but with Marcus Aurelius choosing his son as his heir the string of those called *good emperors* came to an end.

The Emperor Commodus

Commodus was a mediocrity, or worse, whose faults were magnified by the power he inherited. As a boy he was good-natured. He wished to emulate his father's devotion to virtue, but he had none of his father's intellectual drive or self-discipline, and he was less inclined to endure hardship. He became emperor while serving in the army along the Danube, but soon he gave a donation to the troops there, turned over the campaign against the Germans to his generals and returned to Rome, where the weather was better, where life for him would be easier and he would be able to enjoy the grandeur and pleasures that were available to an emperor.

When Commodus arrived in Rome, the public greeted their new emperor, assuming that the handsome, blond and well-built Commodus would be a good emperor like his father. Soon, the commander of the Praetorian Guard, Perennis, found that he could guide Commodus into sensual pursuits, and Commodus took advantage of the availability of numerous concubines and pretty boys. And Commodus began mismanaging governmental affairs, including the selling of government offices to highest bidders in order to acquire money for himself.

Commodus was pacifistic and liberal in his response to another incursion of German tribes into the empire. He approved of paying them to live peacefully within the empire. Then more Germanic tribes pushed into the empire, and, rather than endure the hardships of making war, Commodus made peace with them too. Senators and the upper classes saw this as treason and turned against him. Drawing perhaps on the precedence from previous assassinations, a conspiracy to assassinate Commodus developed that involved leading members of the Senate and Commodus' sister, Lucilla. Their attempt failed as the young senator who was assigned the task of killing Commodus felt compelled to make a long speech while his knife was in his hand, giving Commodus' bodyguards a good opportunity to apprehend him.

The conspirators, including Commodus' sister, were executed. And the Senate was afraid and terrorized.

Commodus disliked anyone who reminded him of his failure to live up to his father's moral standards or that in his youth he had tried to pursue virtue. Like Nero, he sought recognition in personal performances: he took pride in his physical strength, and he entered the arena, wearing animal skins or elaborate costumes that many thought too feminine. There he stabbed or clubbed animals to death to the applause of the crowd, while many who were not applauding thought that he was demeaning his position as emperor.

Insensitive about the feelings of common people, Commodus allowed his Guard in Rome and soldiers elsewhere to be abusive toward civilians. And concerned about opposition from military governors, he had their children cared for under his custody, in effect taking the children as hostages to ensure the good behavior of those commanding the armies.

Soon Commodus had a list of those he believed were opposed to his rule, whom he planned to execute. Those on his list learned they were marked for death, and with nothing to lose they conspired to assassinate Commodus, a conspiracy that included members of the Praetorian Guard. The conspirators found that for a sizeable sum of money Commodus' bath attendant would become their agent. When Commodus most needed superior strength it eluded him: the only weapon the bath attendant had was his hands, and he strangled Commodus to death. The public was told that Commodus had died of apoplexy, and the public rejoiced.

THE SEVERANS AND MORE DECAY

With the death of Commodus and no one else claiming the throne, the Senate chose one of its own as emperor: Pertinax, a sixty-five year-old former aide to Marcus Aurelius and a senator with an excellent reputation. Pertinax was the son of a freed slave. He was cautious, modest and lived without extravagance. He tried to restore the kind of good government that had existed under Marcus Aurelius, and he issued orders against abuses by soldiers against civilians.

A group within the Praetorian Guard that had enjoyed favor under Commodus remained upset over Commodus' death. Again assassination was the means chosen to remove someone from office. On the eighty-seventh day of Pertinax's rule they confronted him at his palace, and a few among them lunged forward and killed him.

The assassination of Pertinax disturbed the Senate and much of Rome, but before any move was made against the assassins, the Praetorian Guard offered its support to the highest bidder. The ambi-tious daughter and wife of a senator named Julianus urged him to take advantage of the opportunity to acquire the glory of being emperor. And, with his great wealth, Julianus bought the support he needed.

Whenever the emperor Julianus appeared in public the Romans jeered him, and when news of what was happening in Rome reached the military-governors in the provinces a number of them became interested in replacing Julianus. The governor of Syria, Pescennius, was hailed emperor by his troops. Pescennius lost time in celebrations while Septimius Severus, the governor of Pannonia (much closer to Rome than Syria) made his bid for power by starting a march toward Rome. The Senate, realizing that Julianus' days as emperor were numbered, threw its support to Septimius Severus. Julianus tried to resign. The Senate ordered his death, and after having ruled for only two months, Julianus' executioners found him alone and cringing in fear in his palace.

Severus Takes Power

Like Trajan and Hadrian, Severus had been born outside of Italy – in what is now Libya. And he had spent most of his career in the provinces, including serving as military governor in Sicily before holding the same position in Pannonia. Severus arrived in Rome, claiming that he was avenging the death of Pertinax and restoring Augustan government. In reality he was re-establishing the primacy of the military in Roman politics. Severus bolstered his support in the Senate by posing as another *good emperor* and by appealing to what interested them most: their own security. He promised them he would use no informers or summary executions against them.

To enhance his legitimacy, Severus adopted himself into the family of the emperors Antoninus and Marcus Aurelius. He arranged a funeral for Pertinax and for Pertinax's deification. He punished Pertinax's assassins and he reorganized the Praetorian Guard. He took from the guard its role as Rome's police and reduced it to the nominal duty of guarding the emperor. He gave military power in Rome to his troops, whose support he reinforced by giving them a bonus in money.

Then Severus launched a campaign to secure his rule against competition from outside of Rome. As had Commodus, he took into custody the children of military-governors. He appeased the ambitions of the commander in England, Albinus, by giving him the title *Caesar*, and he made Albinus his heir apparent. Then he moved against the governor of Syria, Pescennius, who still believed in his troop's proclamation that he was the emperor. Percennius requested help from Parthia and the independent Mesopotamian city of Hatra, and they sent him some soldiers. But most of Percennius' troops were inexperienced recruits from Damascus, and Severus' veterans won a series of battles against them in Asia Minor. Severus drove toward Syria and Perscennius fled to the city of Antioch, where he was found and beheaded.

With Pescennius eliminated as a rival, Severus felt secure enough to turn against Albinus. He took away Albinus' title as *Caesar* and dropped him as his heir apparent. Instead, Severus made his eight year-old son, known by his nickname, Caracalla, as his heir. Albinus retaliated by declaring himself emperor, and he and his army met Severus and his army in a battle at Lyon, in Gaul. Severus won a difficult but decisive victory, and he had Albinus' head displayed in Rome as a warning to would be rivals.

Severus had captured Albinus' personal papers, and unlike Julius Caesar, who for the sake of conciliation burned such papers, Severus used them for a list of enemies – those who had favored Albinus. Then, after his return to Rome and his victory celebration there, Severus launched a campaign in Rome to exterminate these enemies and also those who had supported Pescennius. His promise to the Senate proved false: twenty-nine Senators were condemned to death, and their property was confiscated and used to pay for the wars against Percennius and Albinus and as rewards to his soldiers. And with this, some senators decided that it would be prudent to remain on their estates in the provinces rather than concern themselves with matters in Rome.

To advance his own security and support, Severus removed aristocrats he distrusted from their commands in the army and from their positions as governors. Severus made the promotion of commoners to military officers routine, and he abolished distinctions within the army between those from the provinces and those from Italy. And in increasing numbers, soldiers were being recruited from the frontier provinces where people were only superficially Romanized.

Severus made it possible for a military officer to become a civil servant and for military men to rise in the government's bureaucracy. During his rule, the office of Tribune disappeared. The duties of those who had been in charge of public works – the *aediles* – were absorbed by officials under the emperor. And as court functions passed to Severus and his underlings, Rome's jury system came to an end.

It was the support of his soldiers that had given Severus his power, and he favored his military above all else, advising his sons to "reward the army and scorn the rest." He increased the pay of his soldiers substantially – paid for by taxes from civilians, especially the middle class. To bolster the morale of troops on the Rhine and Danube frontiers, he allowed them to marry and to raise a family on land near their camps. And concerned with the morale of his soldiers, like Commodus he let them bully civilians.

The Emperor Caracalla

Severus punished Parthia and Hatra with war for their support of Pescennius. Two years later – in 208 – he went to England to quell a revolt, and he took his two grown sons with him, hoping that their experience as soldiers would strengthen their character and tie them more closely with his troops.

In 211, while still in England, Severus, now sixty-five, fell ill. Caracalla – short, husky and twenty-three – asked the emperor's doctor to hasten his father's death, and the doctor refused. Severus finally died, and his two sons jointly succeeded him. Caracalla had the reluctant doctor executed. Within a year, Caracalla stabbed his brother to death in the presence of their mother, Julia Domna. Caracalla then told his army that he had been the target of a plot by his brother but had managed to save himself. To mollify the soldiers, he raised their pay – despite a lack of money in the empire's treasury. In a speech to what was left of the Senate he reported his version of events. Then he began a bloodbath in which he purged the army of his brother's supporters and executed others associated with his brother, including Senators and his brother's servants. And he had his wife executed.

Caracalla enjoyed the company of his soldiers, and following his father's advice he scorned the rest, letting his mother, Julia Domna rule in Rome and letting the army abuse civilians. He made bodyguards of German soldiers from his army, and admiring the Germans he sometimes wore a blond wig and a German cloak. Like Commodus he enjoyed showing off his strength – to the delight of his soldiers. He wished to be as admired a military leader as Alexander the Great. And to match Alexander's belief in unity among peoples and to increase revenues, Caracalla extended citizenship to all free persons within the empire. The Roman Empire was no longer Roman. The empire, dominated by men from outside of Rome, had swallowed Rome.

In sophisticated Alexandria, news of Caracalla comparing himself to Alexander the Great was treated as a joke. Making jokes about powerful people was common in Alexandria – a carryover from the old Greek comedies in which no public figure was safe from ridicule. But in hearing of his ridicule, Caracalla was not amused, and he developed a grudge against the city. During a visit to Alexandria in 215, at an outdoor assembly in his honor, Caracalla had a contingent of his troops make a surprise assault on a formation of the city's leading youths, butchering them – an act that only a autocrat would dare commit.

Caracalla traveled to the shrine of a moon goddess at Carrhae in northern Mesopotamia, accompanied by his German body guards and the praetorian prefect, Macrinus. Macrinus was from Numidia, and a seer in Numidia prophesied that Macrinus and his son were to be emperors. A dispatch from Rome was sent to warn Caracalla that

Macrinus was a danger to him, but the letter went to Caracalla's mother, Julia Domna, instead. Macrinus received a letter from a friend in Rome warning him of the new danger to him, and Macrinus believed that he either had to engineer a coup against the emperor or he would be killed. He enlisted the services of a naive, disgruntled aide to Caracalla. When Caracalla dismounted to urinate, the aide began his job of helping Caracalla remount, and he stabbed Caracalla in the back. Immediately Caracalla's bodyguards killed the aide, and Caracalla died soon after.

Caracalla's ashes were sent to Julia Domna, and she starved herself to death. The Senate was glad to be rid of Caracalla and it exercised its nominal duty of selecting the next emperor. Macrinus' praetorian army hailed him as emperor, and the Senate accepted Macrinus – fulfilling the African seer's prophecy.

The Boy Emperor Varius Avitus (Elagabalus)

Caracalla's ambitious maternal aunt, Julia Maesa, from Syria like her sister Julia Domna, had become accustomed to wealth and influence in Rome. She claimed that Caracalla had been the father of her fourteen year-old grandson, Varius Avitus – as if Caracalla had fathered the boy when he was fourteen or fifteen. The emperor, Macrinus, fought a battle against the Parthians, was unsuccessful and settled with the Parthians to the disadvantage of Rome. This cost Macrinus the loyalty of his troops. Julia Maesa took advantage of this. She championed Varius Avitus as the legitimate heir to the throne, and she bribed military officers and some Senators. Macrinus was captured and executed, and the Senate proclaimed Varius Avitus as emperor.

With her grandson emperor, Julia Maesa began ruling the city of Rome as Julia Domna had before her. She sat in on Senate meetings. And Varius Avitus, perhaps already spoiled by favor, indulged his whims. This included dressing as a female, painting his eyes, wearing rouge and squandering public funds on effeminate boys and extravagant luxuries.

Julia Maesa was from a Syrian family of high-priests that worshiped a Syrian sun god named Heliogabal, also known as Sol Invictus, and the Varius Avitus followed the family tradition and became a priest in the worship of Sol Invictus. He made Sol Invictus the official god of the empire, and he built a magnificent temple in Rome to the god. He replaced the office of Pontifex Maxiumus with a fellow priest of Sol Invictus, and he named himself Elagabalus after the god.

Many of the new emperor's soldiers worshiped the deities of eastern cults and were not offended by these moves, but many in the army saw Varius Avitus as ridiculous for other reasons. Two years into his rule, Julia Maesa feared that her grandson would not be able to hold the army's loyalty, and she had him adopt his eleven year-old cousin, Severus Alexander, which made Severus Alexander the heir apparent. The Senate accepted the arrangement and made it formal. Varius Avitus grew jealous of the attentions heaped upon his adopted son, and he ordered the executions of the boy's teachers. He began making outrageous appointments to high offices, including actors, dancers, and charioteers. Meanwhile, Severus Alexander's mother (Julia Maesa's daughter) was winning soldiers to Alexander's side through bribery. The army needed little encouragement to move against Elagabalus, and it murdered both him and his mother (Julia Maesa's other daughter). The army turned the two bodies over to a mob that mutilated them, dragged them through the streets and threw them into the sewer, from which the bodies washed into the Tiber River and perhaps out to sea.

The Rule of Severus Alexander

Severus Alexander, at the age of thirteen, became emperor. Alexander's mother and the grandmother, Julia Maesa, began ruling in his name. But they sensed that their support in the army was weak, and the two women courted the Senate, hoping it could provide them with adequate support. They replaced Varius Avitus' foolish appointments with able men, and they re-established Rome's traditional gods. They ruled with discretion and strict adherence to Roman law, while Alexander developed into a kind and considerate young man dominated by his mother.

After coming of age, Alexander still had his mother as his mentor, while he led an army against a new ruler in the east, a Persian named Ardashir, who had replaced the rule of Parthians. Ardashir wished to restore the great Persian Empire of centuries before, and he sent his armies into Armenia and Syria. Ardashir's army in Armenia was successful, but Alexander's armies threw the Persians back from Syria. Despite the success of this campaign, the Romans suffered heavy losses, some from illness and starvation, and the army experienced mutinies. Alexander's timidity had enraged some military leaders, and, rather than fight again under Alexander, many soldiers looked forward to a new emperor.

Meanwhile, Germans just outside of the empire's frontiers had begun taking advantage of what they perceived as Rome's weakness. German tribes crossed the Danube, and German tribes east of the Rhine broke through the defense line along the Rhine River and moved deep into Gaul. These Germans had become accustomed to farming and were searching for land, and they ravaged towns as they moved toward Italy. Frightened by the prospect of frontier wars along the Rhine and Danube rivers, Alexander attempted to pacify the Germans through bribery. This failed, and he went into the field again as military commander, accompanied by his mother. One of his leading officers, Maximinus, in conspiracy with other officers, led a coup against Alexander. The army backed Maximinus as emperor, and Alexander, twenty-six, was assassinated in his tent while cringing and crying in his mother's arms. His mother was also killed. Severan rule, originating from within the army, had been ended by the army. The military – Roman in name only – still ruled.

Like other recent emperors, the new soldier-emperor, Maximinus, was not from Rome. He was the son of Thracian peasants – a German and an Alan.* He had worked his way up in the military, and he had little respect for Rome's institutions. He was the first emperor who did not win or seek Senate confirmation of his rule. He did not enter Rome, but the senators, still afraid for their safety, remained subdued and only silently antagonistic toward him.

Maximinus doubled the pay of his soldiers, and he upset Rome's civilians by giving money to the army that had been slated for welfare. Farmers in North Africa grew disturbed over Maximinus' high taxes, and they began creating disturbances. Romans in various parts of the empire saw him as a barbarian pretending to be an emperor. In Rome, angry packs of men hunted down and murdered his supporters. An army of North Africans, members of the Praetorian Guard, some senators, and some who saw themselves as the Romans of Old, went north from Rome to battle against Maximinus. They managed to isolate him and a section of his army. To buy their safety, these soldiers killed Maximinus and his son.

Maximinus had ruled only three years – to the year 238. In the coming decades the rule of others would also be short. Soldiers would continue to choose their commanders as emperors, and some army commanders would become emperors only reluctantly, sensing the danger in it. Some of these emperors would attempt to bribe soldiers with gifts to ensure their continued loyalty, and the loyalty of some soldiers would depend on their being allowed to satisfy their appetite for booty at the expense of civilians. These new emperors would govern by decree, and they attempted to reinforce their rule with spies, informers and secret agents. In the coming five decades, only one emperor was to die a natural death, and only one was to die in battle. The rest were to be murdered by soldiers.

---

* The Alans were from Asia's steppe lands.

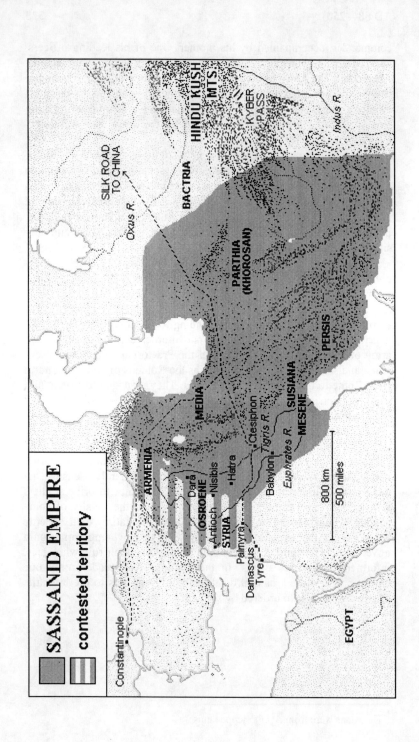

CHAPTER 22

PERSIA AND ITS RELIGIOUS MIX

A NEW PERSIAN EMPIRE AND RELIGIOUS TURMOIL

During the war between Marcus Aurelius and the Parthians, the Great Pestilence not only devastated the Romans, it threw the economy of the Parthian Empire into decline. While the Roman Empire was busy with German intrusions, plague and a rapid turnover in emperors, the Parthian Empire disintegrated. The Parthians no longer ruled in Persia. They now ruled only in Mesopotamia. And, in Persia, nobles and villagers sought protection from roaming bands of brigands and the small armies of local despots.

In the mountainous desert province of Persis, in southwestern Persia, a military leader named Ardashir saw opportunity, ventured out with his army and overran several neighboring cities. He overran the lands of other Persian lords in Persis. He either defeated them or let them join him. And, in AD 208, he was crowned king of Persis. Then in the coming years he moved against Parthian rule in Mesopotamia. He met the Parthian army in a great battle in 224, and defeated it, ending the Arsacid dynasty's four hundred years of rule.

Ardashir claimed that his family was linked to the old Persian royal family of Cyrus the Great – the Achaemenids. He took the title of King of Kings and spoke of his revitalizing the Achaemenid Empire. Ardashir began what would be called the Sassanid dynasty, named after his grandfather, Sasan. He established his rule in the old Parthian capital at Ctesiphon, on the Tigris River. He moved troops northward into Roman ruled Syria and into Armenia – which led to the war against the Roman Empire that came during the rule of Severus Alexander.

Ardashir Encourages the Zoroastrian Priesthood

In Persia, the Zoroastrian priesthood had endured rule by the foreign Parthians, and they had suffered from a prevalence of religions that were not Persian in origin. Now, the Zoroastrian priesthood was pleased under the rule of Ardashir, for Ardashir wished to ally himself with Zorastrianism. Ardashir announced that religion and kingship were brothers, and he said that his rule was the will of God. The Zoroastrian priesthood felt empowered, and they looked forward to converting non-Zoroastrians who lived within Ardashir's empire.

Ardashir had a Zoroastrian priest, Tansar, collect sacred texts of the *Avesta* – the Zoroastrian Bible – some of which is said to have been destroyed during the conquest of Alexander the Great. In the Avesta were songs, hymns, legends, prayers, prescriptions for rituals, and formulas for cleansing one's body and soul. And Tansar put Zoroastrian law into the Avesta, from which Ardashir drew his laws.

Zoroastrian priests inherited their positions – their special skills and learning passed from father to son. They operated Persia's courts, and they controlled Persia's schools. The priesthood performed the rituals that were a frequent part of the lives of the common people, including ceremonies of purification at the births of children, rituals at weddings, deaths and many other occasions. They received fees for every service performed, at the home of a believer or in their temple. And from those who confessed their sins they received payment in the form of fines – as a substitute for corporal punishment – the fines fixed according to the sin.

The Zoroastrian priesthood believed that their religion embodied the most advanced learning, and they tried to control the empire's intellectual life. They tried to frighten people with talk of hell. They claimed that only their rituals and prayers and a life of virtue and ritual cleanliness could save one's soul from the devil and make it possible for one to pass final judgment and enjoy paradise in the hereafter. They preached that for the sake of goodness and public health all putrefying matter had to be buried.

One priest, Kartir, led a crusade to purify Zoroastrianism, to obliterate what he saw as heresies. During the rule of Ardashir he succeeded in having Zurvanist myths purged from the Avesta. And Kartir had Zoroastrian doctrines inscribed on the face of cliffs, the inscriptions to number over seven hundred in the decades to come.

Various religions remained in Ardashir's empire, adhered to by people who had, under previous rulers, acquired the habit of worshiping as they pleased and the habit of running their affairs in accordance with their religious laws, so long as they paid their taxes. Ardashir had no experience ruling over a diversity of cultures, and he denied these people of different faiths the right to govern their own affairs. He forced Jews in his empire to live under his law, which for the Jews was a revocation of Judaic law. The Zoroastrian priesthood tried to extend their authority over the Jews. And, believing fire sacred, they limited the use of fire by Jews, including flames used in lamps. And attempting to dominate education among the Jews, they destroyed synagogues.

The Zoroastrian Persians

Most Persians, like the civilized elsewhere, were peasants, while a few Persians were wealthy tradesmen or the owners of estates. People within the Roman Empire tended to believe that Persians were barbarians, while the Persians saw themselves as highly civilized. And Persia's aristocracy had a proud bearing and easy grace.

The Persians mixed music with their Zoroastrian religion, using such instruments as the lyre, guitar, horn and drum. In court, they swore by their Zoroastrian faith to tell the truth, and violations of oaths were severely punished. They believed that violations of an oath would be punished after death, and they were known as a people whose word was good.

The Persians gave much respect and ritual to marriage, celebrating it with elaborate Zoroastrian rites. Parents generally arranged the marriage of their children, with females marrying only those approved by their parents, and if it appeared that a first wife could not give birth, a husband was allowed another wife. The birth of a child was seen as strengthening God in his conflict with Satan, and heavy penalties were given to those found guilty of infanticide or abortion.

Persian law allowed men to have concubines – who were usually free to come and go, while wives stayed at home. According to a Roman observer named Ammeanus Marcellinus, prostitution and pederasty was less prevalent among the Persians than among the Greeks. The Persians punished pederasty by death. But, according to Marcellinus, there was much adultery among the Persians, and while a Persian husband could divorce his wife for infidelity, a wife could not win a divorce from her husband on the same grounds. But she could divorce him for desertion or cruelty. A wife found guilty of adultery could have her nose and ears cut off. And men caught with someone else's wife could be banished.

MANI STARTS A UNIVERSALIST FAITH

Mani is believed to have been the son of Parthian royalty, born in a village near Ctesiphon and a boy when Ardashir overthrew Parthian rule. As a young boy, Mani might have been taken by his father into a cult called the "Practitioners of Ablutions" – a cult that believed in washing away sins in baptisms. Or the group may have been the Elkesaites, a Jewish-Christian sect that arose around AD 100, a group believed to have celebrated the Sabbath, practiced vegetarianism, believed in circumcision, condemned the apostle Paul and criticized what it called falsehoods in Christian scripture and Mosaic law – a sect that died out around AD 400.

In 228, when Mani was about thirteen-years-old, a Parthian prince in the city of Seleucia (a few miles from Ctesiphon) attempted but failed to restore Parthian rule. It was said that just after this failure, Mani had a revelation from God, a command to leave the religious community to which he belonged. God, it was said, told him that he did not belong in that community. God told him to keep aloof from impurity, and God told him that because of his youth he should avoid proclaiming his revelation publicly.

Mani's father had acquired a variety of religious ideas, and beliefs from the variety of religious cults were to appear in the new creed that Mani developed. By the time Mani grew into adulthood he saw commonality in various religions, and he saw himself as having a universal message. When he was around twenty-five, he claimed that he was obeying an order from heaven to abandon passions and spread the truth. He consciously imitated the apostle Paul and began traveling about in Ardashir's empire preaching his new creed. He claimed that God called on him to preach as God had called on others before him. Mani claimed that he was the successor to prophets such as Zarathustra and Jesus, and he claimed that he was the helper promised by Jesus – as described in John 14:16. He claimed that he was the final prophet and that other religions were limited in their effectiveness because they were local and taught in one language to one people. Mani hoped that his message would be heard in all languages and in all countries.

Mani traveled to Parthia – a part of Ardashir's empire – to become a stronghold of his faith and a base for missionary expeditions into Central Asia. He attracted followers whom he called upon to do missionary work in order to convert the entire world. Mani went to northwestern India, where Ardashir's son was leading an army and extending Ardashir's rule. And while there, Mani strengthened the Buddhist element in his faith. He learned Buddhist organization and propaganda techniques and proclaimed that he was successor to the Buddha. Mani sent disciples to Egypt, and he traveled as far west as the border of the Roman Empire to strongholds of Mithra worship, where he tried to associate himself with Mithraism. Mithraism – believed to have originated among the Hindus – had been popular among the Parthians and had grown in Mesopotamia, Armenia and northwestern Persia during the first centuries BC and AD. Mani had heated discussions with Mithraic priests, and he strengthened the Mithraism in his doctrine. Mani argued also with Zoroastrians, and he compared his beliefs with theirs. In Media, where Zurvanite Zoroastrians were strongest, Mani attempted to reform their movement.

Manichaean Doctrine and Organization
Mani believed that his views were the most advanced and the sum and perfection of all religious wisdom. With worldly knowledge having become a greater part of religious thought, this included Mani's positions on the origins of the universe, anthropology, history, botany, zoology and geography. Like the Zoroastrians and Zurvanites his movement had an encyclopedia. He proclaimed belief in the Buddha and acknowledged the god of the Zoroastrians. He proclaimed belief in Jesus Christ and that he had taken the best of the New Testament and cleansed it of accretions and falsifications. And, like the Christian Marcion, he rejected Judaism's Old Testament.

Mani saw himself in agreement with the Zoroastrian belief that the universe was in a battle between the forces of good and the forces of evil. But where Zoroastrians saw their god Mazda as stronger than the force of evil, Mani held that the forces of evil dominated the world and that redemption – the triumph of good – would come only with a determined struggle by a select group of devotees. Mani saw the eating of flesh as the first great sin of Adam and Eve (Gehmurd and Murdiyanag). And he believed that redemption for humanity would come by abstaining from eating meat and by fasting. He taught that someday a final purification would occur, that the earth would be destroyed, that the damned would collect into a cosmic clod of dirty matter and that the kingdom of goodness and light would separate from the kingdom of evil and darkness. This, he claimed, would come as the result of people rejecting evil.

Mani organized his followers into three groups. The first group was called The Elect. The Elect lived ascetically and devoted themselves to redemption: to separating the kingdoms of light and darkness by living as purely as possible, living ascetically, and by fasting on Sundays and Mondays. They ate mainly fruit and drank fruit juice, believing that fruit contained many light particles, that water was not heavenly like fruit juice because it was simply matter. In the pursuit of redemption, the Elect was forbidden to eat or to uproot plants, to cut down any tree or kill any animal, and, like Buddhist monks, the Elect was obliged to follow complete sexual abstinence and marriage.

Mani's second group was an accommodation with worldly realities. This group was called the Hearers. They followed Mani's teachings but they also did what was forbidden for the Elect: they worked in the making of food, and they had sex and created children. They furnished the elect with food and drink, led a normal life, even eating meat, but they were obliged to fast on Sunday, and like the Elect they observed an entire month of fasting prior to the principle feast of the year: the Bema festival.

The third group of Mani's followers was necessary in making Manichaeanism a popular religion. This third group was not obliged to adhere to any religious practices. They merely had to believe.

THE RELIGIOUS MIX UNDER SHAPUR I

Ardashir died in 241 or 242, and he was succeeded by his son, Shapur I. Shapur invited Mani to his coronation. He invited Mani to speak to him in person, and he granted that Manichaeanism could be taught freely through the empire, Shapur hoping, perhaps, that his support of Manichaeanism might contribute to a wider spectrum of loyalty.

Shortly after Shapur succeeded his father, the Romans finally retaliated against Persian aggressions against their empire. Off and on into the next decade Shapur fought the Romans in Mesopotamia, Syria and Asia Minor. Shapur took Mani and Zoroastrian priests with him on his expeditions, with the Zoroastrians more favored, wearing their conical hats and white cotton robes, the white representing light and purity. With their rituals, the Zoroastrian priests cleansed the conquered lands of demons, and in the conquered lands they established their fire temples to commemorate Shapur's victories. In seeing indigenous religions as competitors, they spoke of smashing idols and destroying the dens of demons. As advocates of good, they saw no evil in war itself or in Sassanid imperialism. Mani, on the other hand, perhaps because of his broader view of culture, developed an opposition to war.

Shapur shared Mani's appreciation of different cultures. He enjoyed talks with Greek philosophers and decreed that all people, including Manichaeans, Jews, and Christians should be left free in their worship, and he persuaded the Zoroastrian priesthood to include in the Avesta works on metaphysics, astronomy and medicine borrowed from the Greeks and Indians. He created an accommodation with the Jewish leader in Mesopotamia – Samuel. Samuel accepted that Sassanian law would be respected in Jewish courts and that taxes to the Sassanid government would be paid.

The Christians under Shapur were also tolerated. By the time of Shapur, Christians had become a noticeable minority in Mesopotamia. Christian evangelists had arrived as early as the first century, mainly in Jewish communities. More Christians arrived during Shapur's rule, with his invasion of Syria. Shapur deported the populations of Damascus and other cities that he had conquered, sending large groups of Greek speaking Christians from Syria to the provinces of Persis, Parthia, Susiana and the city of Babylon, where they were allowed to organize their own communities and follow their own leaders.

With the spread of their communities, the Christians attempted to unite and describe diocese boundaries. Disputes arose between Christian communities that spoke Syriac and those that spoke Greek. A Christian bishop, Papa bar Aggai, at the capital, Ctesiphon, claimed patriarchal rights – as had the Bishop of Rome – and the bishop of Ctesiphon remained in rivalry for influence with the Christian leadership in Nisibis.

The Zoroastrians, meanwhile, were offended by Christian beliefs, foremost by the belief in a god that was the creator of all rather than the creator just of goodness. The Zoroastrians were offended also by the Christian belief that Jesus was both a god and born of an impure, earthly woman, and they were offended by the idea that a god could be crucified and die. The Christians on the other hand, drawing from their Jewish tradition and the law of Moses, were offended by the Zoroastrians not condemning marriages between close relatives.

SASSANID PERSECUTIONS AND THE EXECUTION OF MANI

Shapur I died sometime between 270 and 273, and he was succeeded by his son, Hormizd. Mani received from Hormizd the same permission to teach that Shapur had granted him. But after only a year in power, Hormizd died, and he was succeeded by another of Shapur's sons, Bahram. With practicing a religion being a privilege granted by the king rather than a right, Manichaeanism, Christianity and Judaism were threatened by the whims of any succeeding monarch. Mani was probably aware of the danger that came with Bahram's accession to power, for he decided to leave for the east, to the Kushans around Bactria, where he could count on protection. But Bahram prohibited Mani's travel.

The zealous Zoroastrian priest, Kartir, had been elevated to chief priest. And, with Bahram's support, Kartir launched an attack on the Manichaeans. Manichaeanism was criticized for not identifying itself with the Sassanid Empire, and Persia's landed elite saw Manichaeanism as a threat because its power base was people of the cities and merchants. A bill was presented to Bahram with accusations against Mani, and Mani was ordered to present himself to Bahram at the royal residence. Mani's arrival there created a great sensation. The King spoke to Mani with hostility, and Mani asked whether he had done anything evil. The king responded with rage and reproached Mani for various ethical transgressions. The king was most displeased by Mani's dislike of war. Mani, in turn, spoke of his services as an exorcist. The king stopped Mani's attempt to defend himself and ordered Mani and three of his followers chained and sent to prison. There, Mani died in less than a month and became a martyr to his followers.

Persecution of Mani's followers followed his execution, and many of them scattered. Manichaeanism had already reached Syria, Palestine and Egypt, and now it was to spread farther into the Roman Empire. It spread into Armenia, and it spread into Sinkiang, where it would become the state religion of the Uigur Turks.

The Rulers Bahram II and Narseh

Bahram died the same year as Mani – in 276 – and he was succeeded by his son Bahram II. The priest Kartir remained a dominant figure under Bahram II, and the persecution of the Manichaeans was followed by the persecution of Christians, Jews and Buddhists. Then, sometime during the reign of Bahram II, Kartir died, and religious tolerance began to reassert itself. Bahram II was relatively tolerant. He had been influenced by his grandfather, Shapur I and had become acquainted with advanced Hellenistic culture, and he was offended by the zealotry of the Zoroastrians.

Bahram II died in 293, and he was succeeded by Narseh, who ruled to 303. Narseh claimed to restore the rule of Ardashir, which he claimed was unequaled. Power over spiritual matters remained with Narseh rather than with the Zoroastrian priesthood. And ruling over peoples of various religions, Narseh claimed that he was king in the name of Mazda and all the gods, and he claimed to be a disciple of Mani. In the Roman Empire, however, which was often at war with the Sassanids, the Manichaeans continued to be seen as representatives of a foreign power and as dangerous aliens. In the Roman Empire the Manichaeans suffered persecutions – as did the Christians. But without acquiring the backing of the brute power of a major state, by modern times Manichaeanism would all but disappear.

CHAPTER 23

ROME'S DECLINE AND CHRISTIANITY'S ASCENT

ECONOMIC DECLINE

Authority needed respect in order to rule effectively, but respect for authority was falling among Roman citizens, including among the empire's aristocracy and its tradesmen. This decline in respect was caused in part by armies on the move within the empire, armies plundering towns and farms, and it was caused by military-emperors sending tax collectors about the empire squeezing more taxes from people.

Disrespect for authority had developed also within the military. During the chaotic decades in the first half of the third century, discipline within the army continued to decline. The experienced soldiers who trained the army, the centurions, were often the victims of mutinies, and centurions began to disappear.

Meanwhile, the empire's economy had not been benefiting from advances in technology. A steam engine had been invented by a Greek named Hero of Alexandria during the rule of Augustus, but there had been no interest in saving labor. Producers had no vision of technological progress. They had been increasing production by hiring more hands. They could draw from a supply of slave labor. So, by AD 250, work was still being done by the sweat and muscle of animals and humans. And the steam engine – which would lead an industrial revolution in the eighteenth century – remained unused.

During the first half of the century, economic activity in the empire declined, especially in the empire's western half, where roads deteriorated despite programs to restore them. Economics was little understood by what there was of government under the military-emperors, and governmental policies added to the decline, as did the continued imbalance in trade and the flight of the empire's bullion east. During the first half of the century taxation encouraged men of commerce to hoard their money rather than invest it. To pay soldiers, emperors debased money, and government began paying its debts in money that it would not accept as payment from its citizens as taxes.

Prices skyrocketed. The middle class was bankrupt. More people had become beggars, and many others feared that they too would soon be impoverished. In Rome and other big cities, proletarians remained disinclined to organize themselves against authority, but here and there in the countryside desperate peasants did revolt during the first half of the century. Their uprisings were not coordinated and not widespread enough to challenge the empire militarily, while in various parts of the empire, bands of desperate people wandered the countryside, surviving by theft. In 235 – the year that Maximinus became emperor – bands of brigands swept through Italy. In Gaul, hordes of people roamed about, pillaging as they went. Piracy grew on the Aegean Sea, and tribal people from the Sahara attacked Roman cities along the coast of North Africa.

Disorders sometimes cut off trade routes. By 250, Rome's trade with China and India had ended. Agricultural lands in the empire were going unused. With the declining economy, people moved from cities and towns to rural areas in search of food. Cities began shrinking to a fraction of their former size, some to remain occupied only by administrators.

Where there was a threat of tribal invasion, estates fortified their holdings against both the invaders and Roman authorities. Their neighbors surrendered their holdings to them in exchange for protection. The enlarged estates were developing self-sufficiency. They consumed their own food, made their own clothes and provided their own services, and only occasionally did they buy luxury items. Responding to the migrations of Romans and to the deteriorating economy, emperors decreed that tenant farmers were to remain on the lands they tilled and that no one was to leave any land until they paid their back taxes. It was the beginning of what would become Europe's Middle Ages.

CHRISTIANITY AND PUNISHMENTS

Having lost their faith in government, more people sought refuge in religions that promised them well-being. For some people the austere morality of the Christians – viewed as strange during prosperous times – became an attraction. Christianity's strict moral code appealed to moralistic Romans, as did Christianity's description of existing society as evil. Christianity offered saintly abnegation, a positive attitude toward humanity, a belief in the sacredness of human life, and communal love. And Christians could point to the absurdities in traditional religion, the same absurdities that Plato and Socrates denounced, a worship of gods whose antics made them no guide for morality.

Christianity benefited from its worship of someone with a human face – easier to worship than a god that was vague, unseen, unspeaking or a creature other than human. Christianity benefited by Jesus having been a common man and a martyr with a message. Christians could see their own suffering in the suffering of Jesus. Some people were attracted by Jesus' words, by descriptions of his deeds, his belief in justice and his love for all people, and they were attracted by the promise of a new world that would offer them refuge from pain and suffering.

Christianity had an advantage in being organized and unified, and it benefited from its being open to people ignored or excluded by other religions: to women, non-citizens and slaves. In appealing to slaves, Christians claimed that although one would remain a slave in the material world, in God's eyes a good person was never a slave.

Christianity appealed to the poor, an appeal aided by the claim that poverty was an advantage in attaining salvation after death. And becoming a Christian was less expensive than entering some other faiths. To be initiated into Great Mother Worship – a major rival to Christianity – one had to bear the great expense of a bull that had to be slaughtered. Conversion to Christianity, on the other hand, was a free immersion in water.

All were welcome to join the Christians, and Christianity appealed to some among the upper classes. Many more upper class women converted to Christianity than did upper class men, so unmarried upper class women had to look for Christian husbands among the poor, or even among slaves. The bishop of Rome, Callistus, permitted such marriages, while these marriages remained illegitimate under Roman civil law.

To become a Christian to join a community that looked after the welfare of its members. Christians shared their meals. They offered health care – as it was. They shared their wealth. They took care of the indigent, including widows, whom they called "Virgins of the Church."

Christian Martyrdom

Up to the middle 200s, the persecution of Christians in the Roman Empire had been infrequent, the persecutions usually coming after a calamity, such as an earthquake, with people blaming the Christians for the anger of the gods. With the growth in Christianity, the Christians became more visible, and some Romans saw the Christian belief in an approaching Armageddon as support for an end to civilization. They continued to see the Christians as disloyal for not respecting Rome's gods. Rome continued to hold Christianity as illegal, and leading Christians complained publicly that authorities were justified in prosecuting Christians for real crimes but that Christians generally did nothing criminal.

The emperor from 244, Philippus, a man of Arabian ancestry, looked with some sympathy upon the pleading for justice by the Christian writer Origen. Philippus had been a military leader who had plotted against the previous emperor, and, unfortunately for the Christians, in 249 it was his turn to be overthrown. Troops of an able general, Gaius Decius, encouraged Decius to rebel against Philippus. Decius moved his army from Pannonia into Italy, defeated Philippus at Verona and became the eighth emperor since the death of Alexander Severus fourteen years before.

Decius wished to restore order and to lift the empire from economic ruin. As part of a thousand-year anniversary of Rome's founding, he ordered Romans to perform rituals to Rome's gods, hoping to put the empire in good stead with the gods and perhaps add to his legitimacy as emperor. The Jews, as before, were exempted from such rituals, but not the Christians, and Christian opposition to participation in the rituals drew new attention to them.

Decius acted against the Christians in a way he thought would please the gods most: he hoped for Christian conversions to the state religion. He ordered those suspected of being Christians to prove their loyalty by making sacrifices or libations to Rome's gods in the presence of official witnesses. Those Christians who did so were to receive and carry on their person a paper document certifying that they had performed the required ritual. To escape persecution, thousands of Christians renounced their faith and performed the required ritual, and there arose a flurry of business in writing the special documents that they were required to carry. Some Christians of wealth gave bribes in exchange for anonymity and safety, and some, including bishops, went into hiding.

The government arrested some prominent Christians, among them the bishops of Rome, Jerusalem and Antioch, and they were executed, going to their deaths, it was said, zealously savoring their righteousness. The belief that catastrophe was a creation of Yahweh was alive among the Christians as it had been among the Jews, and the bishop of Carthage, Cyprian, saw the persecutions as God's punishment. In hiding, he wrote of Christians delighting the Lord with their martyrdom, and he wrote of the flow of blood as a "glorious flood to quiet the flames and fires of hell." The Christians were being persecuted he claimed because Christians had "not been doing the will of god" and had been "striving for property and profit." Each person, he wrote, had been "pleasing himself alone and displeasing everyone else." "And so," he added, "we are being given the thrashing which we deserve."

The executions brought still more attention to the Christians, and people were impressed by Christians willing to suffer and die for what they believed in. Some people saw the state as more of an enemy than they did the Christians. They preferred Christians in their communities to the usual abuses that came with the arrival of soldiers. And rather than the number of Christians diminishing with the persecutions, Christianity appears to have grown.

All the appeals to the gods which Decius had demanded appeared to produce no positive results for him or for the empire, for the Germanic Goths had begun storming southward across the Danube River – the Goths being pushed upon by the nomadic Alans. Decius went to do battle against the Goths, and in June, 251, the Goths lured him and his army into a swamp, destroyed his army and killed him and his son. And this to some was an indication that God was more angry with Decius than he was with the Christians.

Church Controversy over Readmission

Decius' aide, a military commander named Gaius Gallus, succeeded Decius, and he abandoned Decius' edict against the Christians. The threat to Christians subsided. Many who had left the Church wished to re-enter, and a debate arose within the Church whether this should be allowed. Those against re-entry argued that the baptism that made one a Christian cleansed one of all sins except for original sin and that once dirtied after having been baptized one stayed dirtied. The debate broadened into an argument over whether the Church was a gathering of sinners struggling for redemption or a society of the redeemed. Purity again lost to practicality, tolerance and compromise. A council of bishops met in North Africa in the late summer of 251 and decided that one could re-enter the Church so long as he had not actually offered a sacrifice to a pagan god, in which case he would be excluded from the Church until he was on his death bed.

The deathbed for many came the following year with a plague that ran across North Africa. To many Christians, including Cyprian, this indicated that Yahweh was still angry with his fellow Christians. And to those loyal to Rome's gods it appeared that the gods were still insufficiently appeased.

In the spring of 252, while some pagans were again blaming Christians for the anger of the gods, a second Council of Bishops met, and to strengthen the Church in the face of the renewed threat they granted full re-admission to all who had lapsed under pressure of the recent persecutions – which left restless and displeased those who favored the Church as a society of the redeemed.

MORE INVASIONS, MORE PERSECUTIONS, AND AN EDICT OF TOLERATION

In 253, Emperor Gallus was murdered by his own troops, and soldiers chose another military commander as emperor: Valerian. Valerian won support from the Senate, and he managed to restore some discipline to Rome's military. He made his son, Gallienus, co-emperor and in charge of Europe. Then Valerian and Gallienus addressed the problem of the empire's frontiers. Border peoples had noticed that the borders could be easily crossed, and they were crossing again in great numbers. From 254 to 256, Gallienus pushed back Germanic tribes called Alamanni. In 256 a newly formed and powerful coalition of Germanic tribes called the Franks stormed across the southern Rhine into Gaul. And those called Saxons crossed the English Channel in pirate cutters and invaded Roman Britain. It was now that Shapur I swept into Syria and Asia Minor, believing that the Roman Empire was weakened by these invasions. And by now the plague that had ravaged North Africa had moved north into Europe, and it was killing as many as five thousand a day in Rome. Valerian sought help from the gods and ordered Roman citizens throughout the empire to perform the requisite religious rituals. Having learned more about Christianity's hierarchy in the last persecutions, this time the emperor's edict took aim specifically against Church bishops and elders. In 257 and 258, leading Christians were rounded up, executed and their property confiscated. Among those martyred was Cyprian, his execution witnessed by thousands, some climbing trees for a better view, those near Cyprian throwing pieces of cloth to catch his blood.

Again the Alamanni pushed into the empire, and into Italy, and Gallienus defeated them near Milan. In Syria, Valerian's plague-ridden army drove Shapur's army back, but then Valerian lost a battle at Edessa, in Osroene. Valerian was captured, tortured and soon died. Franks obtained a permanent hold at spots in eastern and central Gaul and northeastern Spain. The empire's long-standing political instability made matters worse as the governor of Pannonia rose against Gallienus in an attempt to make himself emperor. Gallienus defeated him, and, in 260, Gallienus had to move against a second pretender.

The persecution of Christians had again failed to make any apparent difference in Rome's struggle to protect itself, and again Romans were impressed by the integrity of Christians willing to go to their death in behalf of their beliefs. Gallienus – now sole emperor – saw the persecutions of the Christians as a failure, and in need of peace and a greater unity within the empire he issued an Edict of Toleration, making Christianity legal and giving the Christians respite from what had been the terrible years of persecution.

Eight More Emperors in Fifteen Years
Despite the Edict of Toleration, God remained unkind to Gallienus. A general in Syria, Macrianus, revolted against Gallienus, proclaiming his area independent of Rome. In Gaul, a general named Postumus rebelled and proclaimed himself emperor, and from Gaul he took control of Britain and Spain. From Syria, Macrianus invaded Europe, but Gallienus defeated him. Then in 267, Goths in large numbers again crossed the Danube and attacked Greece by sea and by land. By the year 268 Athens was overrun. As the Goths were moving to another target of opportunity, Gallienus and his legions attacked and defeated them. But while Gallienus was in Greece, another general revolted against him – in northern Italy. Gallienus rushed back to Italy, and, while besieging the rebel general at the city of Milan, he was murdered by a group of generals who believed that they could rule better than he. The leader of these generals, Marcus Claudius, became emperor and took the name Claudius II.

Claudius rallied what forces he could against the Goths. With skill he managed to defeat them and to pacify areas within the empire south of the Danube, a pacification that included allowing Goths to settle permanently on available land in Thrace and Macedonia. The upstart emperor who ruled over Britain, Spain and Gaul, Postumus, had been cut down by his own soldiers, and contenders fought for control of what had been his realm. Claudius continued to reign only in the central part of the empire, including Moesia, where he defeated another invasion of Goths. Then in 270, while preparing to move against an invasion by a Germanic people called Vandals, bad luck caught up with him: he died of the plague.

Claudius' chosen successor was a tough-minded soldier, Aurelianus – one of those who had conspired with Claudius against Gallienus. Aurelianus became the emperor known as Aurelian. He ruled energetically and enforced army discipline. An outstanding general, he reestablished Roman rule in the east, and, with the eastern front secured, he was able to regain the provinces of Britain, Spain and Gaul, the upstart who had ruled these areas submitting peacefully to Aurelian's authority.

Aurelian earned the title "Restorer of the World." He increased the amount of food distributed to the people of Rome. He tried to reform Rome's coins, and he tried to subordinate the worship of Rome's gods to the worship of the sun-god Sol Invictus. Then in 275, while on his way to another war against Persia, Aurelian was murdered by a group of officers whom his secretary had misled into believing he had marked for death.

During the next nine years Rome had six more emperors. Alamanni again pushed into Gaul. More Franks came in boats along the channel coast and penetrated the heart of Gaul by way of its rivers. The Franks sacked northern Spain, and they sailed into the Mediterranean and to North Africa, where they established a pirate base.

NEO-PLATONISM

Stoicism influenced Christianity, and so too did the neo-Platonism of Plotinus. Plotinus had studied philosophy at Alexandria. During a stint in the military in 243 and 244, he failed to meet eastern thinkers and to learn Persian and Indian philosophy, as he had hoped, and he returned from military service to Rome, where he spent much of the rest of his life teaching philosophy. He saw himself as a reformer of Plato's philosophy. It was the last significant development in philosophy before the triumph of Christianity, his views gaining a wide following among Romans. And it spread to influential Christians such as Basil the Great (330–379) and his contemporary Gregory of Nyssa in the east, and to Augustine (354–430) in the west. Had Christianity remained another Jewish sect rather than having spread to gentiles, neo-Platonism might have become the dominant faith in the western world – without any one church in authority worshipping a jealous god.

Like Christianity, neo-Platonism had appeal as an alternative to the Roman Empire's chaos and decadence. Whereas Plato wanted to put people into a perfect society, Plotinus called on people to withdraw from politics and from the world of the senses and to seek instead an awareness *of* and solidarity *with* God. It was withdrawal to the extent that it had no sense of belonging to the disreputable Roman state. Plotinus' religion was personal – without a sense of belonging to a community as did Christianity.

In the year 245, at age forty, Plotinus settled in Rome, and there he founded a school. He conducted friendly and informal discussions on commentaries that had been written on Plato and Aristotle, defending Plato against Aristotle's criticisms while making some concessions to Aristotle. Plotinus encouraged the discussions to continue until his students believed that the philosophical problems they had raised were solved.

As would Christian philosophers in the Middle Ages, Plotinus pondered what he saw as "the ordered universe," and he concluded that its "material mass" had existed forever and would "forever endure." He saw God as soul, as a supreme spirit, and soul as primary in existence. He believed that all nature had been created by this supreme spirit. He saw soul not as intellect, as did Aristotle, nor as thought, pointing out that thought requires a subject, which would make soul a duality rather than primary. Nor, claimed Plotinus, is soul a plurality of things – as it is believed by those who see God as everything. Soul, believed Plotinus, is the *source* of plurality. But Plotinus saw himself as not having answers to everything. He confessed to not having an answer as to why God created the cosmos. Some questions, he believed, could not be answered.

Like the Manichaeans, Gnostics, Zoroastrians and others, Plotinus found evil in materiality. This was a time when there was widespread disgust with the human body, and Plotinus saw the body as a prison or tomb in which one's soul was trapped. He did not believe that salvation from this prison would come from outside oneself, as a struggle between Good and Evil or God and Satan. He saw salvation, or grace, in finding one's own pure spirit, one's own godly soul, by avoiding vain preoccupations with one's body and by avoiding exaggerated worries. Like the Stoics, he believed that suffering had no effect on one who had found grace. He believed in an inner freedom through indifference toward external circumstances.

Plotinus disagreed with the Gnostics that an evil power had created materiality. And, contrary to the Gnostics, he defended the notion of God creating all (including evil) by claiming that evil had a rightful place in the universe. Most or all forms of evil, he wrote, "serve the universe." Vice, he wrote, "stirs us to thoughtful living, not allowing us to drowse in security."

Like Plato, Plotinus believed that to find truth one had to look beyond materiality (the world known through the senses). Like Plato, he believed that through reason and knowledge one could work his way to a union with and an awareness of God. He believed in an ecstatic union with God that could not be adequately expressed with words. Plotinus described his own salvation in a way that is similar to ideas in India centuries before: contact with God through repose, meditation and renunciation. He believed in fleeing alone "toward the Solitary One."

Plotinus combined his search for salvation with acts of virtue. He wrote that "Without virtue, God is only a word." He believed that a part of the self, as soul, resides in the heavens, and, ascending to that level, one rests with the Divine and experiences a love of gentle Goodness. The Good, he believed, was always gentle. He claimed that the experience of being at this higher level could remain with one as one pursued his earthly living, looking after himself and others.

It was at this higher level, according to Plotinus, that one found love, which he saw as a part of any pursuit of virtue and unity with God. On love he was close to Plato, but different from Plato in that Plato believed that love is an achievement that begins with experience at the lowly, material level. Plotinus denied that love had any such lowly origins. Plotinus believed that love was an ingredient that added to the objects or person loved, making that object something that it was not before, love being superior to the object it is placed upon. Beyond this, Plotinus saw the question *what is love* as similar to questions why is there Soul and why does the Creator create: unanswerable.

The Neo-Platonist Porphyry, Christianity's Foremost Critic

Porphyry was born of Syrian parents in the city of Tyre. He studied philosophy in Athens. In 263, he went to Rome and studied there under Plotinus, and after Plotinus' death, in 270, he took charge of the school. He arranged Plotinus' lectures for publication, and he made it possible for neo-Platonism to spread throughout the Roman Empire.

Concerned about the growth of Christianity, Porphyry joined other pagan intellectuals in criticizing it. It was a criticism similar to what would eventually arise among Christians themselves. Porphyry studied both the Old and New Testaments, and he decided that the Book of Daniel had not been written when claimed but during the time of the Maccabaean revolts. He decided that rather than prophesying the future, including the coming of Jesus and the destruction of Jerusalem's temple, the Book of Daniel described times and events that for its writer had already occurred.

Porphyry found that the genealogies of Matthew and Luke conflicted with each other, and he pointed to their conflicting descriptions of Jesus' infancy. Against the claim that the apostles were infallible, Porphyry asked why then did Peter and Paul quarrel. Believing in a God who was the author of good, Porphyry thought the idea of God's eternal punishment was nonsense. He believed that good came to people through their connecting themselves with God. He believed that people could see only a part of the whole but that it was their duty to wed their minds to God as best they could. Evil, he believed, came from people deviating from an awareness of God.

PRELUDE TO A CHRISTIANIZED ROMAN EMPIRE: DIOCLETIAN RESTORES ORDER

In the early 280s, commanders of rival Roman armies again fought for power, and a commander of humble birth from Illyricum emerged as the emperor. This was Diocletian, originally named Diocles. Diocletian went to Egypt and quelled a rebellion there. He restored Roman control in Britain. And invasions by the Goths subsided, enabling him to devote attention to reconstruction. He saw uncontrolled activity as godlessness, and he moved to create order.

With the danger of more disturbances, Diocletian judged the empire too vast for any one emperor to rule effectively, and he divided the empire among four vice-emperors, who were military men like him, and he set himself up as the exalted supreme ruler of the empire. He dressed with the grandeur of an eastern emperor, and he proclaimed himself the earthly representative of Rome's supreme god, Jupiter. He claimed that he was responsible only to Jupiter. He surrounded himself with bureaucrats and a small army of bodyguards. And his court grew in size and did its business with elaborate ceremonies and fanfare.

Diocletian ran his government as a general runs an army, giving orders and expecting them to be carried out. He attempted to maintain what was left of Roman law and customs and tried to create order in the realm of ideas. He outlawed astrologers and the alchemists of Egypt and had their writings burned. He viewed Manichaeanism as a Persian religion, and he ordered its writings and the authors of those writings burned, and he ordered death for the followers of Manichaeanism.

Diocletian tried to restore order in the ruined economy – by governmental directives. He created a national budget that aimed at balancing expenses and revenues. In 301 he responded to rising prices by an edict that fixed prices on thousands of commodities and services. In response to soaring interest rates, he fixed these to between six and twelve percent, depending upon the amount of risk involved in the loan.

Diocletian brought peace and a greater degree of order to the empire. Impressed, some people looked to him with hope. But Diocletian's economic policies failed. Despite the death penalty for violations of his laws on prices, violations became so widespread that his government stopped trying to enforce these laws. Diocletian's increased taxation resulted in the great landowners producing less for the open market and more for their own estates, and these estates continued to expand and absorb poor peasants as laborers.

For the sake of law and order and collecting taxes, Diocletian renewed an attempt made earlier in the century to prohibit people from moving off the lands they worked. Everyone was ordered to remain at his present occupation and location. Tenant farmers were to inherit the obligations of their fathers and were becoming serfs, to be sold as property when the landowner sold his land.

Renewed Persecutions of Christians and rise of Constantine the Great

By the beginning of the 300s, Christians in the eastern half of the empire had expanded to twenty or more percent of its Greek speaking population. North Africa had become largely Christian, the result of Christian evangelists having learned the Coptic and Berber languages. And Christians had also learned Syrian, Thracian and Celtic. Across the empire, Christians were around ten percent of the population – their number having doubled in about fifty years. Two kings had been converted: the king of Osroene in northeastern Mesopotamia and the king of Armenia. Christians were serving in Rome's armies, and they were working as civil servants in local government or in lowly positions on the imperial staff.

Trouble arose involving Christians during a religious ritual performed in the presence of Diocletian. One or more of Diocletian's Christian courtiers made a sign of the cross to ward off what they thought to be the demonic influences of the ritual. Afterward, the priests complained to Diocletian, and Diocletian ordered everyone in the palace to worship the gods or be beaten. Diocletian's vice-emperor in the east, Galerius, pursued the attack against Christians, demanding that the army there purge itself of all Christian officers. Galerius' palace was set ablaze, and Christians were accused of having set the fire. Galerius persuaded Diocletian to launch a drive to crush Christianity, believing that he and Diocletian could succeed where Decius and Valerius had failed. Again Christians were ordered to sacrifice to the gods of the state or face execution.

Christian assemblies were forbidden. Bibles were confiscated and burned, and churches were destroyed. But by now Christians had become to numerous to be wiped out. Unlike Germany during World War II – the Roman state had not developed an efficient method for rounding people up and executing them. Moreover, because Christians could read and write – in an effort to study scripture – they had become an indispensable part of government. The purges slowly and intermittently dragged on into the year 305, when Diocletian retired because of ill-health.

The vice-emperor in the east, Galerius, began a joint rule of the empire with the vice-emperor in Rome and the west: Constantius. The following year, 306, Constantius was in Britain commanding a force against incursions into Roman territory by the Scots, and there he died. His troops then chose his eighteen-year-old son, Constantine, to succeed him – a youth who had served briefly in the army under Diocletian in Egypt and under Galerius. Constantine was to change the world by becoming the first Christian emperor.

CHAPTER 24

CHRISTIAN EMPERORS, PERSIA, AND FALL OF ROME

CONSTANTINE, THE FIRST CHRISTIAN EMPEROR

Roman soldiers in Britain chose Constantine as ruler of the western half of the empire. The emperor of the eastern half, Galerius, refused to recognize this choice. Instead, he chose his drinking companion, Licinius. Rome revolted rather than accept such a decision from the east, and the leader of this revolt, Maxentius, the son of a former vice-emperor under Diocletian, claimed himself emperor in the west. From Britain, Constantine challenged Maxentius and extended his rule to Gaul. Maxentius extended his rule to Spain and to North Africa. And where Maxentius ruled he ended the persecution of Christians.

War erupted between Maxentius and the emperor of the east, Galerius, while Constantine marked time. In 310, Galerius contacted a disease, which he believed to be the retribution of the god of the Christians. In the east, as Galerius lay dying he issued an edict ending his persecution of the Christians, and he asked Christians to pray for him so that he might live. He died anyway, in 311, and he was succeeded by his drinking companion, Licinius.

Constantine was impressed by what he believed was the victory of Christianity's god over Galerius. Then, in an effort to assert his authority in the West, Constantine advanced from Gaul across the Alps and into Italy. The city of Milan surrendered to his forces, and Constantine won control over northern Italy. Maxentius and his army moved north from Rome to confront Constantine, and in October the two forces met and fought at the Tiber River. Like Caesar against Pompey, Constantine faced an army that greatly outnumbered his. But Constantine had trained his troops well, and his tactics were superior. His cavalry swept the left-wing of Maxentius' foot soldiers into the river. Maxentius lost many men and his own life when the pontoon bridge they were on collapsed. Surviving troops crossed over to Constantine's side, and a victorious Constantine rode into Rome with his army. There, at around the age of twenty-four, Constantine was hailed as emperor of the West, as a man of boldness, and as a man favored and guided by the gods.

Constantine Maintains His Ties with Paganism

In addition to having become emperor of the western half of the empire, Constantine took office as Supreme Pontiff. And, as Supreme Pontiff, he gave recognition to the god that had been his father's favorite: Sol Invictus, the Syrian sun god that had been brought to Rome by emperor Heliogabalus some sixty years before. Constantine's half of the empire was five or more percent Christian. His mother, Helena, was among the Christians. Constantine, open to belief in a variety of gods, had become sympathetic with the god of the Christians. And perhaps he gave Jesus at least part of the credit for his victory over Maxentius – perceiving Jesus to be another god of war.

At Milan in 313, Constantine came to an understanding with the emperor of the east, Licinius. The two recognized each other's rule, and they agreed that Christianity was to have full equality with other religions and that the property taken from Christians during the persecutions was to be returned to them. Constantine was becoming Christianity's champion and patron, Christianity having taken about the same length of time, about three centuries, that it took Buddhism to acquire the same kind of imperial support – under Asoka.

Constantine gave the bishop of Rome imperial property where a new cathedral, the Lateran Basilica, would rise, and he provided for the building of other Christian churches across his part of the empire. Constantine granted the Christian clergy special privileges: he allowed people to will their property to the Church. He exempted the clergy from taxation, from military service and forced labor – as had been granted to the priests of other recognized religions. The tax exemptions for the Christian clergy were followed by a number of wealthy men rushing to join the clergy, and in 320 Constantine would correct this by making it illegal for rich pagans to claim tax exemptions as Christian priests.

The Church was experiencing numerous ideological conflicts, and the bishops sought help from Constantine in their effort to preserve what they called true Christianity. Constantine wished Christianity to end its internal bickering and responded willingly to the bishops' requests. Like emperors before him, he saw it as his duty to suppress impiety. He put himself at the head of the Church's effort against heresy, and the bishops accepted Constantine as an authority on godly matters. The leader of the empire that had been instrumental in crucifying Jesus would now be in a position to make decisions for the church of Jesus.

Constantine's half of the empire remained from five to ten percent Christian, and the city of Rome remained largely pagan, especially the Senate, and so too did the high command of Constantine's army. Constantine had made no break with paganism. The arch dedicated to

Constantine's victory over Maxentius, erected in 315 or 316, described that victory as an "instigation of divinity" without crediting Jesus or Yahweh. Constantine by now obviously favored Christianity, but as the emperor of the west he made an effort at neutrality in what Christians saw as their conflict with demonic paganism. He appointed pagan aristocrats to high offices in Rome while tolerating from his army the greeting "Constantine, may the immortal gods preserve you for us!" Then, in 321, in a move to spite Jews and accommodate Christianity with prevailing pagan ways, Constantine made the day of Sol Invictus a holy day and a day of rest for the Christians – Sunday.

Constantine Takes Control of the Eastern Half of the Empire

The emperor in the east, Licinius, grew fearful of the respect that Christians in his realm had for Constantine. He expelled Christians from his household and executed a few bishops. In 323, Constantine and his army entered Greece. Then he drove another wave of Goth invaders north and back across the Danube River. Although Constantine was still in what was officially the western half of the empire he was close enough to the east to concern Licinius. Licinius attempted negotiations with Constantine, which failed, and war erupted between the two. In late 324, Constantine's forces defeated those under Licinius, and Constantine became emperor of the entire empire. He had publicly promised to spare the life of Licinius, but he changed his mind, and the following year he had Licinius executed by strangulation.

That same year, 324, Constantine founded a new capital city in the eastern half of the empire, at Byzantium. He called the city "New Rome." Later it would be called the City of Constantine, or Constantinople. Eventually it would be called Istanbul.

Constantine had not been baptized, but he appears to have become increasingly devoted to Christianity. He wrote of his successes as an indication of favor from Christianity's god. He attributed the failures of those recent emperors who had persecuted the Christians as an indication of the Christian god's power. He began a new series in the construction of Christian churches much grander than the Christians had before his time. He granted more lands to the Church. He gave Christian bishops the authority of judges – against whom there would be no appeal.

Constantine attempted to increase his appeal as a Christian by writing that his father, Constantius – a vice-emperor under Diocletian – had honored the "one supreme god," and that God had given his father "manifestations and signs" of His assistance. It was a claim that overlooked that his father had worshiped Sol Invictus, had supported, however half-heartedly, Diocletian's persecutions of the Christians, and had died a pagan.

Church Unity and the Nature of Jesus

Much to Constantine's annoyance, God's harmony continued to elude the Christian Church – as churchmen disagreed over the exact nature of Jesus. In 325, he called for the Church's first ecumenical (general) council, which was to meet in the city of Nicaea for the purpose of deciding by committee the nature of Jesus Christ and other issues.

Of Christianity's 1,800 or so bishops, 318 attended the conference – most of them from the eastern half of the empire. Constantine presided over the meeting. One group of bishops, led by the bishop Arius, claimed that God and Jesus were separate beings, that because Jesus was God's son there must have been a time when Jesus did not exist. Another group of bishops could not accept the notion that Jesus had been created from nothing and insisted that he had to be divine and therefore a part of God.

It was the kind of muddle that came with applying imagination to empirically unverifiable matters, and a great rift was developing that would split Christianity. Constantine decided against Arius. But, for the sake of unity, he decided that Bishop Arius and his supporters would be allowed to remain within the Church and would not be forced to recant. Constantine held that those bishops who refused to sign the settlement at Nicaea were to be exiled, and to those Christian sects that the Church considered heretical he sent a letter proclaiming that their places of meeting would be confiscated.

With the power of the state behind them, the bishops decided to make their authority law. Cutting off the possibility of common Christians choosing their own bishop, the bishops ruled that in no province of the empire was anyone to be made bishop except by other bishops within that province. The bishops granted to the bishop of Alexandria papal authority over the eastern half of the empire, and to the bishop of Rome they granted papal authority over the western portion of the empire.

Constantine's Harsh Rule

In 330, Constantine took up residence in his new capital at Byzantium: New Rome. Three years later he returned to Rome to celebrate the twentieth anniversary of his taking power there. He still held the office of Pontifex Maximus, and as Pontifex Maximus he was still the leader of the empire's pagans, but he refused to take part in the city's pagan rituals. Rome's pagan majority was offended, and Constantine returned to New Rome annoyed.

Wishing that his pagan subjects would give up their religious rites, Constantine kept the pagans fearful and cowed as he confiscated from their priests much of the wealth the pagan religions had accumulated, including their sacred icons. This brought to Constantine much wealth in the form of precious metal, which he gave to the Christian Church.

It was around this time that Constantine was experiencing domestic tensions. The source of the conflict remains unknown. His wife, Fausta, was stepmother to his eldest son, Crispus. Crispus had helped him defeat Licinius, but, for reasons unknown, Constantine ordered the execution of Crispus and forced Fausta to commit suicide.

Meanwhile, Constantine created severe penalties against adultery, concubinage and prostitution. For a variety of other crimes, people were to have their eyes gouged out or their legs maimed. Influenced by Christianity, he ended crucifixion as a form of execution. He ended branding criminals and slaves on their face – the face according to Christians having been formed in the image of divine beauty. And in keeping with Christianity's devotion to the family, he forbade the separation of a family of slaves.

But, under Constantine the old world of slavery continued. Constantine passed a law allowing masters to beat their slaves to death. Unlike Diocletian, he allowed infants born to slaves to be sold. Constantine allowed slaves who were caught seeking refuge among "barbarians" to have a foot amputated. Slaves in the public services caught attempting to leave town were to be beaten. Anyone caught sheltering a runaway slave was to be fined. With the agreement of bishops, slaves who sought refuge in Christian churches were to be returned to their masters.

And under Constantine, politics remained unchanged or was changing for the worse. In the place of the spies that Diocletian had relied on for information, Constantine revived the secret police, which was notorious for its corruption. Under Constantine taxes remained oppressive, the great landowners often paying bribes to avoid taxes or passing the burden onto their tenants. As under Diocletian, everyone was forced to follow their parent's occupation, including the sons of soldiers. The state tried to keep people working in crafts where there was a shortage of such workers. Some city officials in some cities in North Africa continued to be elected by its citizenry, but during Constantine's rule municipal government continued to decline as few people wished to serve. Local government was becoming a hereditary duty rather than inspired by any kind of civic pride.

There were still those called *consul*, but it was a title no longer with executive powers, and no office. In Rome, Senate seats continued to pass from father to son, but the Senate remained without powers: a prestigious club for conversation. Only a few senators, mainly those who happened to live in Rome, attended Senate meetings.

Power, Prestige and Popularity Transform the Church
The Church had left behind its original communal sharing and its sense of equality among members. The bishops were growing in wealth and in the splendor of their dress. Having moved from simple buildings to those that were grand and imposing, the Church also made its rituals more splendid. In place of a simple table for the rite of Holy Communion – the Eucharist – the Church now used a massive and ornate altar of marble studded with gems.

But the bishops devoted themselves to the humble through charity – much of this made possible by wealth from Constantine and gifts from wealthy Christians. The Church built orphanages, hospitals, inns for travelers, and it founded old age homes, all of which helped increase Christianity's prestige and popularity.

Christianity was supposed to be a matter of the heart, of conviction, and commitment to Jesus, but it was the increase in its grandeur, including the prestige gained from Constantine's support that helped the Church make great new gains in converts. Some conversions were accommodations to the belief that the emperor was a Christian – an accommodation to state power.

Pagan habits were modified to fit Christianity. Some evangelists, Gregory the Wonder worker among them, facilitated conversions by encouraging Christians to have the feasts of their old gods celebrated as feasts of Christian martyrs. In the western half of the empire, the popular pagan feast day celebrated as the birthday of Sol Invictus and the winter solstice, December 25th, began being celebrated as the day of birth of Jesus Christ. Christians in the eastern half of the empire disagreed with this and chose instead January 6th – the day of another great pagan festival – as the day of Jesus' birth. This difference between western and eastern Christianity was to continue into modern times.

Among the pagan practices adopted by Christians in bringing pagans into the fold were a devotion to relics, the kissing of holy objects as an act of reverence, genuflection, and the use of candles and incense. But the object of Christianity remained the same: the worship of Jesus Christ and obedience to God's laws. The acquisition of paganism's feast dates made no real change in the substance of Christian worship. What mattered from the Christian point of view was to whom people prayed. Those who had prayed to pagan gods for rain and for bestowing fertility upon women would now be praying to Christian saints. Many peasants who had venerated a pagan female guardian of grain would transfer that veneration to a new guardian and creator of their grain: Mary, the mother of Jesus.

BISHOP EUSEBIUS

In his early fifties and near death, Constantine finally chose to be baptized a Christian, to prepare himself for the hereafter. Performing the baptism was the elderly bishop and a Church historian: Eusebius. Eusebius was to claim that just before his death Constantine told him that the day before his battle against Maxentius, at the Tiber River, he and his entire army saw a flaming cross against the sun and the words "conquer with this." And Eusebius claimed that Constantine told him that the night before his battle against Maxentius he had dreamed of Christ.

Eusebius' claim accompanied his opinion that Constantine was the chosen agent of God, that Constantine had been "crowned with the virtues which are inherent in God." and that Constantine "received in his soul the emanations that come from God." (*The Tricennial Oration*, c. 5:1.)

Eusebius was a scholar of history and theology. He wrote many books, wrestled with Porphyry's criticisms of Christianity and was the creator of a history that would serve as political ideology for the Church for generations. He tried to develop a detailed history of the world that fit with his Christianity. History, he concluded, was a struggle between divine authority and a multiplicity of demonic influences that had taken the form of paganism. Seeing paganism as a deviation from devotion to the "One True God," he claimed that in reality paganism was atheism. Believing in the authority of One True God, Eusebius saw the existence of many states and rulers as the work of the devil. This multiplicity of rule he called "polyarchy." He described history as moving with divine purpose from polyarchy to an era in which all political authority united into a singular authority emanating from God: the authority of the Roman Emperor, Constantine.

According to Eusebius, Jewish religion, Greek philosophy and Roman law had come together to enable the Christian revelation to take root and to grow to maturity. He wrote that if Christ had been born into the world at any other time, the world would not have been able to receive him. Before Jesus, according to Eusebius, cities were at war against cities, nations at war against nations, and life was "being wasted and spent in all manner of confusion." Eusebius wrote (in *Praeparatio Evangelica, I, c, 4*) that "in the days when the demons tyrannized over all the nations," humanity had "rushed madly into mutual slaughter," enslaving one another and "wasting one another's cities with sieges."

Then, according to Eusebius, came the disappearance of the Jewish state and the coming of the Roman Empire, as prophesied in the Bible. According to Eusebius, Rome's rise as an empire was a part of a divine plan, as was the coming to power of Augustus Caesar, who, he wrote, brought "mastery over the nations." With Caesar, wrote Eusebius, the multitude of rulers for the most part disappeared and peace covered all of the earth, again as prophesied in the Bible. Then, according to Eusebius, Augustus prepared the way for the birth of Jesus Christ. This, he wrote (in *Praeparatio Evangelica*, I, c. 4) was when "the fortunes of Rome reached their zenith."

Eusebius wrote that, with Constantine, nations "found rest and respite from their ancient miseries." He wrote that government as practiced by Constantine was "a system and method of government for all states." He described equality of status and democracy as polyarchy and as "anarchy and dissension rather than a form of government." Supporting a singular political authority, he wrote that there is "one God – not two or three or more." *(Tricennial Oration*, c. I:6)

Eusebius wrote approvingly of Constantine schooling his sons "into harmony with the reins of inspired unison and concord." Constantine had passed his rule to his three sons. The empire was to be divided among them, and the harmony about which Eusebius wrote would soon be tested by events.

CONSTANTINE'S SONS AND GRANDSON JULIAN

Each of Constantine's three sons – Constantius II, Constantine II, and Constans – acquired the title *Augustus.* Constantius II ruled the eastern portion of the empire. Constantine II ruled in Spain, Britain and Gaul, but he wanted more, and, in 340, he invaded Italy, where Constans ruled. Constantine II and Constans warred, brother against brother, Christian against Christian – a sign of things to come.

Constans won the war and Constantine II was killed. Meanwhile, Constantius II had been occupied by a series of bloody wars against the Sassanid emperor Shapur II, who had seen Constantine's sons fighting among themselves and, in 337, had decided to push northwest into Mesopotamia and Armenia, which his predecessors had lost to the Romans. The war between Constantius and Shapur lasted twelve years and was fought mainly in Mesopotamia. In 350, Constantius left the front against Persia to confront an attempted coup by a military commander. He defeated the upstart, but his brother Constans, in the west, was not so lucky: in 350 he was defeated and executed by an upstart military commander. Constantius II crushed that uprising also, and he acquired rule over the entire empire. And, apparently to consolidate his rule, he had members of his army murder possible rivals within his family, Constantius' half-brothers and others.

Constantius attempted to extend his victories into the realm of religion. Unlike his deceased brothers and some others in his family, Constantius was an Arian Christian. Believing that he was advancing the cause of Christianity, he exiled numerous trinity-believing bishops. And, to advance the cause of Christianity, he also banned the ritual sacrifices of pagans, making participation in such rituals a capital offense. Mobs of zealous Christians followed Constantius' lead by invading pagan temples and overturning alters. And pagans across the empire responded with bitterness and rioting.

Julian the Apostate

Among those family members exterminated by Constantius were the father and elder brother of a five-year-old boy named Julian. Julian's mother had died soon after his birth, and the emperor Constantius took Julian and reared him in his household. Here Julian felt oppressed by Christian strictness and the earnestness with which his guardians espoused Christianity. Secretly Julian rebelled against Christianity. An intelligent boy, he became bookish and acquired a love for Hellenistic culture. By now, Christian bishops were proud of their Greek culture, and Julian was allowed to further his education, first in Italy, then at Pergamum and Athens. Secretly he became a neo-Platonist, while continuing an outward appearance of Christian devotion.

When Julian was twenty-three, Constantius sent him to Gaul at the head of an army against the Franks and Alamanni who were invading Gaul. There Julian proved himself an able leader, winning a great victory in 357 on the Rhine River at Strasbourg and expelling the Franks and Alamanni from the empire. Constantius became jealous of the glory won by Julian, and he was concerned about him as a rival. He kept Julian and his army short of funds and kept him under surveillance.

The Sassanid king, Shapur II, had just contained a threat from the east by Huns* and Shapur II was now ready for another confrontation with Rome. Like his great grandfather, Ardashir, he considered himself heir to the great empire of the Achaemenids, and he asked Constantius for territory that he thought rightly his. Constantius refused. Shapur moved his troops into Armenia, defeated its pro-Roman king and tried to force the Armenians to convert to Zoroastrianism. He moved troops into Roman territory in northern Mesopotamia, taking Diyarbakr in 359

---

* Huns were nomads from the steppes of Central Asia, descendants perhaps of those the Chinese called the Hsiung-nu.

and other towns. While Julian and his army were spending the winter in Gaul, Constantius sent an order that Julian's best troops were to be transferred east to counter the move by Shapur. Julian's troops mutinied against Constantius' order and proclaimed Julian emperor, and Constantius died of fever on his way to combat the rebellion.

Julian became emperor and began his rule with a policy of toleration toward all religions. Lacking the hostility felt by Christians toward the Jews, he rescinded a law that forbade marriage between Jews and Christians. He rescinded the law that banned Jews from entering Jerusalem, and he allowed Jews in Jerusalem to rebuild their temple.

While maintaining the rights of Christians as citizens, including their right to worship, Julian moved to abolish privileges that had been bestowed upon the Christian clergy, including their positions as teachers. Christian hostility toward Julian grew. In 363, Julian led a military campaign against Shapur II, pushing Shapur's forces back to his capital, Ctesiphon, as the Persians scorched the earth in retreat. Julian's army captured many, including women and youths, and he allowed no one to molest them. Again he went into battle against the Persians, and he died of wounds from an arrow or spear. Christians rejoiced at news of his death, and they expressed their belief that Julian's death was the work of God.

SHAPUR II ATTEMPTS TO EXTERMINATE HIS CHRISTIAN SUBJECTS

The wars between Rome and the Sassanid Empire were destroying caravan cities in Mesopotamia and Syria – one of which was Palmyra. This was bringing a decline in trade in the direction of the Roman Empire. But the Sassanid Empire continued to thrive economically as it benefited from its control of travel over land between it and China.

According to legend, Shapur II was a brave warrior and haughty. He expected and demanded the greatest respect from his subjects, and many of his subjects looked upon his accomplishments and believed he was a god. Shapur organized frontier cities into a defensive system. He maintained and extended irrigation systems in many areas of his empire. And, under his rule, cultivation was increasing. Food production was on the rise, and with it came a rise in population and the creation of new towns.

The gods seemed to favor the Sassanids over the Roman Empire, while the success of Christianity in wedding itself to power in the Roman Empire made Christianity in the Sassanid Empire appear to be an enemy religion. Shapur detested the Christians and favored the Zoroastrian priesthood. Needing money for his war against the Roman

Empire he doubled the taxes against Christians, and the Christians objected. Fearful of Christianity as a source of wartime treason, Shapur ordered a massacre of all Christians in his empire. Entire villages of Christians were slaughtered. Then he restricted the attacks against Christians to priests, monks and nuns. The persecutions were to last forty years, with Christians going to their deaths with what some reported was a fanatical longing for martyrdom. The survival of Christianity under the Sassanids appeared threatened, but Christianity in the Sassanid Empire was saved by the same slowness and inefficiency that had taken place in Rome's attempted extermination.

ROME'S CHRISTIAN EMPERORS CHALLENGED BY IMAGES OF THE DEVIL AND GERMAN MIGRATIONS

With Julian's death, his army's leaders chose one among them as their commander: Jovian, a trinity-believing Christian. In becoming commander of what had been Julian's army, Jovian became emperor, and Christians in the Roman Empire celebrated the return of a Christian as head of state. The war against Shapur was still in progress, and as a military commander Jovian was outmaneuvered by Shapur's forces. God apparently not on his side and his army demoralized, Jovian felt obliged to withdraw from middle Mesopotamia, and he ended the war against Shapur by ceding to him provinces along the Tigris River and all of Armenia, all that Diocletian had gained seventy years before.

Turning his attention to domestic affairs, Jovian transferred state support from pagan temples to Christian churches, but he decreed religious toleration for pagans and for Arian Christians. Then, after only months in power, he died from the fumes of his freshly plastered and unventilated bedroom.

The army declared as emperor another Christian, a general to become known as Valentinian I, a capable commander from Illyricum. Valentinian believed that defense of the empire required at least two emperors, and he appointed his brother Valens as Emperor of the East. Valentinian continued religious toleration, declaring that no religion was to be declared criminal. He created schools throughout his realm. And to protect the poor he created offices called Defenders of the People.

Meanwhile, the world of harmony that Eusebius thought God and Constantine had created for the world proved elusive even within the Church: in the year 366, rival factions in Rome supported different men for Bishop of Rome, and the factions and their supporters clashed in the streets and churches, and hundreds died in a single day.

The German Challenge to the Roman Empire

For two centuries, Germanic peoples had been moving into the empire and settling along its frontiers, and a Germanic, Arian Christian named Ulfilas had gone outside the empire, among fellow Germans called Visigoths* to spread Christianity. Ulfilas had succeeded in converting German kings, which led to mass conversions among German common folk. As a result of these conversions, many German clans or tribes that entered the empire were Christians. These German immigrants had been adopting Roman ways while maintaining a sense of worth about common people, including women, that was greater than that of most Roman citizens.

Germans inside the empire's frontiers were still only a small percentage of the empire's fifty to seventy million inhabitants. The Roman Empire might have been able to absorb more Germans, but German tribes continued to cross the Rhine River into the empire in great numbers. Rome's ability to control its borders was a problem addressed in a tract called *On Matters of Warfare,* written anonymously for the imperial bureaucracy. The author advocated an increase in defense spending by cutting the bonuses that the state paid to soldiers and civil servants and by increasing the taxes of those landowners in areas threatened by invasion. And the tract addressed the issue of hearts and minds: it claimed that official corruption and the rich oppressing the poor were causing disorder, and it called for increasing patriotism through social reform.

The tract was ignored. The imperial bureaucracy remained corrupt. Government positions were hereditary, honest government officials were rare, and the public continued to detest officials as they did soldiers. As for buying bigger and better equipped armies through increased taxation, already common people were over-taxed, and taxes were often taken with force, and at times with torture. Continual demands of the army and the empire's enormous bureaucracy were exhausting the empire's economy and helping to alienate its subjects, while tax evasions by the rich remained common, and the bigger landowners continued to pass their share of taxes onto their tenants. In the provinces suffering from invasions, hardly any loyalty to Rome remained, and, rather than contributing to their defense against the invaders, the people there were forbidden to bear arms. The empire remained as weak as it was against the Germans because circumstances limited the eagerness and ability of its subjects to fight to defend it.

---

* Visigoths are a Germanic people believed to have come from what is now Sweden.

Emperor Valentinian against German Invasions
Valentinian I, the emperor of the western half of the empire, was an effective military leader. He conscripted as best he could every year, but the wars among Constantine's sons had reduced the source of manpower for the military. Exemptions from military service were numerous, including exemptions for bureaucrats and the clergy. Farm workers remained in short supply, and landlords wished to exempt peasants whom they needed to work their lands. Great landlords could pay money, 25 gold coins, in place of each recruit they were obliged to send to the government. The landlords were supposed to send a number of recruits in proportion to the size of their land, but often they were uncooperative and would send only those men whom they wished to be rid of. Young men added to the shortage by trying to avoid military service, which offered them very low pay and hardship. Facing these shortages, the government had been recruiting Germans, who, with their warrior traditions were more willing to serve in the military than most Roman young men, especially city dwellers.

Valentinian and his army defeated German invasions three times, and he remained at the Rhine frontier for seven years, building fortifications. During this time, Rome's British province was again invaded. The invaders were Saxons, Angles and Jutes, collectively known as Anglo-Saxons. The Jutes and Angles were from Jutland, and the Saxons were from Germany. And Roman Britain was attacked by men from Frisia. These peoples journeyed a hundred miles in their boats along the northern coastline of Gaul to Britain's eastern coast. In Britain they destroyed many villages, allowing many slaves there to escape. Tribes from Scotland, called Picts, took advantage of the invasions and pushed south across Hadrian's wall, and tribes from Ireland began a series of destructive raids against Britain's western coast. Valentinian sent his best commander to rescue Britain, and by 369 the Roman army succeeded in re-establishing Roman authority there, protecting a network of councils that had been established by Britain's Celts.

In 374, German tribes crossed the Danube River into Pannonia. Some tribes of Samatians also crossed into the empire. Valentinian went to the frontier to meet the challenge. There, in 375, he died of a stroke, and his sixteen-year-old son, Gratian, succeeded him as emperor of the western half of the empire.

Defeat of Valens at Adrianople – a Turning Point
Visigoths were being driven toward and into the empire by the Huns, who were moving westward after having been diverted by

Shapur II. A confederation of about 100,000 Visigoths asked for and received permission from the emperor of the eastern half of the empire, Valens, to settle within the empire – in Moesia – in exchange for their providing him military services. The Visigoths, who were Arian Christians, might have been peacefully integrated into the empire, but Valen's agents failed to provide food for the Visigoths as had been agreed upon, and some Romans tried to buy Visigoth women and children for the slave market. This outraged the Visigoths. Visigoth warriors revolted, and discontented miners in the area joined the Visigoths as guides for their warriors.

Valens responded to the uprising by deciding to drive the Visigoths back across the border. The emperor of the western half of the empire, Gratian (Valens' nephew), had recently won victories against invading Germans along the Rhine, and he asked Valens to wait for help from him and his armies before attacking. With Galen's armies, Valens might have easily defeated the Visigoths, but Valens was jealous of the glory that Gratian had already won, and he wanted all the glory from the coming war to himself. In 378, before Gratin and his troops arrived, he attacked the Visigoths in Thrace, in what became known as the Battle of Adrianople – a hundred miles northwest of Constantinople. The empire's infantry was no match for Visigoth cavalry units. It was a revelation for the Romans about cavalry and would lead to downgrading the use of foot soldiers for centuries to come. The Visigoths destroyed two-thirds of Valens' troops and his best generals, and Valens was killed. News of the Roman defeat signaled to the world that the Roman Empire was weak and vulnerable.

Emperor Gratian against Paganism

While the empire continued to be in need of healing and unity, Gratian, moved in the direction of division. A devout Christian, Gratian resented the empire's continued support of paganism. The emperor's bureaucracy still supported a pagan college of pontiffs. It supported keepers of the Sibylline books; three priests who served the gods Jupiter, Mars and Quirinus; and the six Vestal Virgins who guarded the sacred fire. Statues of the pagan gods were still available to the public, and over four hundred pagan temples still stood. In the Senate (where Christians remained a minority) was a pagan altar – the Statue of Victory – where Senators had long sworn to observe the laws of the empire and the emperor.

Gratian's plans to remove the Statue of Victory outraged pagans and provoked three years of debate. An aristocratic senator named Symmachus pleaded for tolerance from Christians. He argued for the right of pagans to pass on Rome's great traditions to their children. He appealed to Christians by saying that heaven was common to all. He said that, whatever god one adored, all looked up to the same stars, all sought whatever truths were above the stars and that such truths were not necessarily arrived at by a single path.

Symmachus' main adversary, Ambrose, the Bishop of Milan, would have none of this tolerance and diverse approach to worship. He advised the emperor, Gratian, for the sake of his own salvation, to carry on with his plan. Ambrose favored forcing Christian domination on all of society, for the good of all. He denounced paganism as the path or error, suggesting that Christians were the only adherents of truth. Like the Hebrew priests who returned to Jerusalem from exile, Ambrose spoke against marriages between pagans and Christians. And regarding the Statue of Victory, Ambrose's view prevailed: Gratian had the statue removed from the Senate.

EMPEROR THEODOSIUS AND SONS

After the death of Valens, Gratian had chosen as the new emperor of the east a devout, trinity believing Christian like himself, a thirty-two year-old general named Theodosius, the son of a landowner from Spain. Theodosius vacillated between great energy and indolence, between asceticism and his attraction for splendor, and between cruel punishments and merciful pardons. He tried increasing taxes. He attempted wider military recruitment, but exemptions remained numerous. He ordered the army to accept more German recruits. He made it law that anyone mutilating himself to avoid military service had to serve anyway and that in the place of anyone who mutilated himself landlords had to supply the military with two other recruits.

Theodosius believed that the Visigoths could no longer be expelled from the empire by force. He entertained Visigoth chiefs at his palace, and in 382 he signed a treaty with them allowing them to settle in the empire as a nation and to live under their own laws. Whole tribes of Visigoths became a part of Theodosius' army, under the command of their own chieftains, who were paid by the empire.

Theodosius made the same move against rival faiths in the eastern half of the empire that Gratian had in the west. Arianism was thriving in Constantinople, and, while ignoring the Arianism of the Visigoths, Theodosius decreed that the doctrine of the Trinity was to be the official state religion and that all his subjects should adhere to it. Theodosius labeled Arianism, Manichaeanism and some other views that had been adopted by Christians as heresies. He announced that all heretics were "demented and insane," and he proclaimed that where these heretics met would not be recognized as churches. The Church hierarchy believed all this was a good idea and supported the ruling across the empire, and in Spain a bishop named Priscillian, who taught that matter was evil and took other unorthodox positions, became the first Christian executed by Christians for his religious beliefs.

Theodosius granted Christianity's clergy immunity from trial except by ecclesiastical courts. He revised laws to fit what he saw as Christian principles. He banned public and private activities of a non-religious nature on Sundays. And he made Easter and Christmas legal holidays.

Theodosius faced challenges from the Sassanid Empire and from a usurper who had taken power in the west. Troops in Britain had declared their commander – a Christian named Magnus Maximus – emperor. The rebels had expanded into Gaul, and many in Gaul had joyfully rallied behind them. The emperor in the west, Gratian, had gone to Gaul with an army and had been captured and beheaded. Theodosius had to deal with the Sassanid Empire first. After four years of war against the Sassanid Empire, Theodosius signed a peace treaty with its king. Then he sent an army into Italy and defeated Maximus in two battles. Theodosius had Maximus beheaded, and Bishop Ambrose saw Maximus' demise as the result of God punishing Maximus for having had a synagogue in Rome reconstructed after it had been destroyed by fire. And now with Maximus out of the way, Theodosius proclaimed Gratian's half-brother, another son of Valentinian I, as the emperor of the western half of the empire, the son becoming Valentinian II.

Theodosius, Ambrose and other Christians against the Jews

By now, Christians saw Judaism and Christianity as absolutely separate, and Christians viewed Judaism as the work of the devil as much as it did paganism. Moreover, they saw Judaism as a special competitor. The Jews were burdened by an odium that pagans were spared: the Jews had rejected Jesus, and Christians saw them as responsible for His murder. With Jews uninfluenced by the asceticism and asexuality of Jesus, and not seeing sexuality as tainted by lust and filth as Christians did, Christians were beginning to describe Jews as carnal. At Christian torchlight meetings, among the angry slogans shouted were those against Jews and Jew lovers.

As Roman citizens, Jews were protected from attack by law, and when Christians burned a synagogue, Theodosius ordered it rebuilt, the cost to be paid by the Church. Then Bishop Ambrose intervened. Outraged, he told Theodosius that he, Theodosius, was threatening the Church's prestige, and he convinced Theodosius to withdraw his move and let the destruction of the synagogue stand. Here and there across the Roman Empire, the burning of synagogues continued. In Judaea, entire villages of Jews were set ablaze. Jews living in the empire had their privileges withdrawn. They were to be excluded from holding any state office, from the army, and they were not to proselytize Christians or intermarry with them.

Theodosius and Ambrose Persecute Pagans

In the city of Salonika, in northern Greece, a local military commander of German descent imprisoned a popular chariot driver for homosexuality. A crowd of outraged fans, anti-German in sentiment, lynched the military commander. Theodosius retaliated by ordering a massacre of seven thousand or so of the city's inhabitants, and the influential bishop Ambrose refused sacraments to Theodosius until he accepted penance for this deed.

Theodosius did his penance, and in gratitude for his reconciliation with Ambrose he acted on Ambrose's views as to what should be done about paganism. Theodosius banned the Olympic games – which were considered pagan. He prohibited visits to pagan temples and forbade all pagan worship. Ordinary Christians were delighted at this move, and mobs of Christians joined the anti-pagan program by robbing pagan temples of their treasures and looting temple libraries, causing the disappearance of many writings. In the repression some of the most splendid buildings of Grecian architecture– were destroyed.

Pagans in the east tried to defend their freedom to worship, and in the west some pagans rallied in an attempt to overthrow Valentinian II. Valentinian II was assassinated. A military commander in the west, being a German and not eligible to be emperor, created an anti-Christian puppet named Eugenius, who announced that the hour of deliverance from Christianity was at hand.

In response, Theodosius cracked down harder on pagans in the eastern half of the empire. He made pagan worship punishable by death. In 394, he led an army of Visigoth cavalry and others against the reign of Eugenius, defeating Eugenius' forces at the Frigidus River, in the extreme northeast of Italy, a victory the Church was later to interpret as the work of God triumphing over paganism.

With his victory against Eugenius, Theodosius moved against paganism in the western half of the empire as he had in the east, wiping out freedom of worship across the whole of the empire. Then in 395, perhaps because of the strain of his recent military campaign against Eugenius, Theodosius died, at the age of fifty, believing that the empire had been unified by his wisdom and had become secure under the guidance of God.

Rule Passes to Honorius and Arcadius

The guidance of God included rule by Theodosius' two sons: an eleven-year-old, Honorius, who inherited the position of emperor in the west, and Arcadius, eighteen, who inherited rule in the eastern half of the empire. Honorius was moronic and would eventually spend much of his time raising chickens. Arcadius was pious and gentle, but he was also incompetent and ill-tempered. Theodosius left as regent for Honorius his talented and energetic aide and military commander-in-chief, Stilicho, who was half-Roman and half-Vandal and married to Theodosius' favorite niece. Stilicho claimed that Theodosius left him in charge of both sons, but in the east a powerful aide and authority in Constantinople named Rufinus claimed responsibility for the eighteen year-old, Arcadius.

The empire's Visigoths distrusted Honorius, Arcadius and their advisors. The leader of the Visigoths, Alaric, had bargained for pensions and for a post in the high command of the Roman army, and he had become disappointed over promises made by Theodosius that had not been fulfilled. The Visigoths wished to better themselves economically, and before Theodosius had been dead one year, Alaric and the Visigoths started marching toward Constantinople, devastating territory into Thrace. Rufinus, in Constantinople, requested help from Stilicho. Stilicho sent troops to Constantinople as requested, and members of his army murdered Rufinus. So hated had Rufinus been by the common people of Constantinople that upon hearing of his death they came running from every quarter of the city to trample upon his corpse. Someone put the head of Rufinus on the end of a lance, and the crowd followed it in a great parade through the city.

Sensing the weakness of the new rulers and taking advantage of the disunity between the western and eastern halves of the empire, the Visigoths marched into Greece where they sacked Corinth, Argos and Sparta. Athens was spared by paying the Visigoths a ransom. In 397, Stilicho led troops against the Visigoths and drove them north into Illyricum, which the Visigoths also plundered. There the Visigoths settled with permission from the eastern emperor, Arcadius. And Arcadius made the leader of the Visigoths, Alaric, prefect of the province.

ARCADIUS VERSUS BISHOP CHRYSOSTOM

In the eastern half of the empire, Arcadius and his wife Eudoxia came into conflict with John Chrysostom, who had been drafted as Bishop of Constantinople – holy father of the eastern half of the empire. Born of noble parents, Chrysostom had been a Church deacon and a presbyter. He had been tutored by Libanius, the last of the sophists. And he had developed into a talented and popular orator.

Chrysostom was as hostile toward Jews as were other Christians. He lectured Christian crowds that wherever Jews gathered "there the cross was ridiculed," Jesus was insulted and "the grace of the spirit rejected." He called the impiety of Jews "madness," and he attacked Jews for what he called their "extravagance and gluttony." But Chrysostom also attacked slavery. "God," he said, "has given us hands and feet that we might not stand in need of slaves." He attacked the slavery of children and the training of child slaves in sexual specialties for sale as prostitutes. And against the commonly held notion that work was degrading he told his listeners that when they see a man who fells trees, or is grimy with soot from labor, or who works with his hammer they should admire rather than despise him.

Chrysostom touched upon another major ill of the age: autocracy. He declared that the right of government belongs not to emperors alone but to the human race. "In the beginning God honored our race with sovereignty," he claimed. He saw the link between free will and self-government, and he spoke of humans as being able to choose from existing circumstances.

Chrysostom spoke against pagan tradition of public entertainments that featured prostitutes and against what he called the senseless excitement of the bloody spectator sports that involved contests between men and wild animals. And he criticized the double standard in morality between husbands and wives, including laws that allowed a married man to have intercourse with a slave, prostitute or an unmarried woman.

Chrysostom annoyed many within the Christian clergy, which had grown lax under the previous bishop of Constantinople. He annoyed the bishop of Alexandria, Theophilus, who was jealous of the greater power and influence that had been accorded Chrysostom as bishop of Constantinople. Chrysostom annoyed churches in Asia Minor by asserting his authority there, deposing some bishops who had bought their positions with money. He annoyed the emperor Arcadius by not acting merely as a court chaplain as had Constantinople's previous bishop. He annoyed Arcadius also by his attacks against greed and his talk of injustices. Chrysostom especially annoyed Arcadius' wife, the empress Eudoxia, who was violent in her likes and dislikes and who liked to flaunt her piety.

Chrysostom became involved in the controversy over the views of Origen, whose writings the Church had outlawed. He received four of Origen's supporters who had been exiled from Egypt. The Bishop of Alexandria, Cyril, retaliated by organizing a regional Church council (synod) composed mostly of Chrysostom's enemies. (Cyril was in later years to lead in the murder of Hypatia,* a popular woman mathemati-

---

* Hypatia was a woman with rare accomplishments for her time. She was a mathematician and a teacher of philosophy at Alexandria, where Cyril was bishop. She was a neo-Platonist, in other words a pagan, and in the eyes of people like Cyril influenced by the devil. Her popularity and accomplishments

cian and neo-Platonist). The council deposed Chrysostom as Bishop of Constantinople. Arcadius' imperial court in Constantinople confirmed the decision. An earthquake and public discontent led the empress to reinstate him, but when Chrysostom continued his criticism of the imperial family he was exiled to Armenia, where he was to die in 407.

THE FALL OF ROME

Around 395, bands of Huns invaded Armenia, and they moved into Syria and Cappadocia, where they plundered and killed. The Huns pushed against eastern Germans: Vandals, Suevi and Burgundians. These Germans crossed the Danube River in great numbers, into the Roman province of Pannonia, and the Roman population there fled westward. The empire was further challenged in 399 when Alaric and his army of Visigoth warriors and civilians moved across the Alps and into Italy. Rome military leader, Stilicho strengthened his army in Italy by withdrawing troops from the Rhine frontier and from Britain, and, in 402 and 403, Stilicho confronted Alaric and defeated him. Alaric and the Visigoths returned to Illyricum, and Stilicho and his army went north to battle invaders at the empire's frontier. .

In 405, Vandals, Suevi and Burgundians united under a leader named Radagaisus. He and about a third of his force moved from Pannonia into northern Italy, destroying cities and pillaging. The western emperor, Honorius, fled from the city of Ravenna and found refuge behind the walls of Florence, forty miles southwest of Ravenna. From behind these walls the call went out for volunteers to help combat the invaders, but no force of volunteers came. Instead, Stilicho left his battle with invaders on the frontier and arrived just in time to rescue the emperor and the city of Florence. He had Radagaisus beheaded and those of Radagaisus' army who had survived sold into slavery.

Stilicho then moved against the greater part of what had been Radagaisus' army, now between the Alps and the Danube River. He forced them northward into what is now Germany. There he arranged an alliance with the Franks, and he won the neutrality of Alamanni Germans, and with the Franks he defeated the remainder of Radagaisus' army. And for this Stilicho received the title "Deliverer of Italy."

Stilicho began to prepare for an offensive against invasions into the eastern half of the empire, and he planned to put Illyricum under the jurisdiction of the western emperor, Honorius. Stilicho made an agree-

---

made her more of a target of hatred, and in 415 a Christian mob pulled her from her chariot. And, reportedly, with sharpened abalone shells they stripped flesh from her bones and threw her body into a fire.

ment with Alaric against the eastern emperor, Arcadius. Then, in the winter of 406-07 came the greatest of invasions, interrupting Stilicho's plans: Vandals, Suevi, Burgundians and Alans, with their farm animals and children, crossed the frozen Rhine River into Gaul. The frontier there had been undermanned and weakened by desertions, and soldiers in populated areas behind the frontier had been hanging around wine shops and spending their time in debauchery. The German invaders found only feeble opposition. They spread out, ravaged, burned and raped, some of them making it all the way to the Pyrenees Mountains between Gaul and Spain, while only a few towns, among them Toulouse, attempted a significant resistance.

In response to the overrunning of Gaul, Roman troops in Britain revolted and named their commander, Flavius Constantine, emperor. Constantine and his troops left Britain and arrived in eastern Gaul, where he was joined by troops from Spain. The withdrawal of Roman troops from Britain left its defense to local efforts, which were weak and divided. Irish pirates sacked the towns of Chester and Caernavon, and some of the raiders seized territory in Wales and were able to settle there.

Stilicho and His Supporters are Murdered

Flavius Constantine would hold out in eastern Gaul for a few years. Meanwhile, Alaric marched into Noricum and asked Stilicho for 4,000 pounds of gold for helping him in the eastern half of the empire. An unenthusiastic Senate voted Stilicho the gold with which to pay Alaric, with many senators and others believing it disgraceful for Rome to buy a truce with an old enemy like Alaric.

In 408, Arcadius suddenly died, at the age of thirty-one, and, after a bloody conflict over who would replace him, the seven-year-old son of Arcadius, Theodosius II, was named emperor of the east. In the west, an aide to Honorius who was hostile to Stilicho warned Honorius that Stilicho was preparing to put his own son on the eastern throne and was usurping powers that belonged to him, Honorius. The moronic Honorius believed the aide. The aide organized a coup against Stilicho's and his supporters, who included the best military officers in the empire. These officers were largely Germans, like Stilicho. Inspired in part by hostility against Germans, Stilicho's supporters were massacred, as were the families of German soldiers serving as auxiliaries to the Roman army in the western empire. Those still alive and attached to Stilicho called on him to rally his supporters and fight back. Instead, Stilicho went to the emperor's court at Ravenna without his bodyguard to meet Honorius. Stilicho was taken prisoner, charged with treason, and without a trial he and his son were executed. The last of the great

Roman military commanders was dead, and thirty thousand or so German soldiers fled from Rome's army and joined Alaric and the Visigoths.

In Gaul, Flavius Constantine was encouraged by the death of Stilicho. He invaded Italy but was defeated by the rival force sent by Honorius. Alaric and the Visigoths were also encouraged by the death of Stilicho and by the additional troops. In the autumn of 408, Alaric and the Visigoths crossed the Alps and poured into Italy, to Ravenna. After failing to break through Ravenna's walls, Alaric decided to push on to North Africa, believing that grain grew there in great abundance, and he decided that on his way he would attack Rome to gain what he could.

Rome Besieged and Overrun

Romans had been keenly interested in horoscopes, but in their horoscopes they had not found advice to leave Rome. The consequence was dire. The city shut its gates as Alaric and his army approached. The Visigoths surrounded the city, cutting Rome off from outside help. As Alaric and his army continued to surround the city, the city's inhabitants grew hungry. Plague appeared within Rome, and corpses appeared in its streets. Rome's Senate decided to negotiate with Alaric and suggested it was not afraid of a fight. Alaric laughed and demanded gold, silver, moveable property and some three thousand pounds of Indian pepper in exchange for sparing the city and its inhabitants.

Alaric gave Germans and slaves in the city safe passage out, some of whom joined his ranks, increasing Alaric's forces to about 40,000. For more than a year Alaric kept Rome surrounded while waiting for his ransom. Then in August, 410, with assistance from within, his troops slipped into the city. For three days they looted and destroyed the houses of the rich. They killed some people, but being Christians they spared the Christian churches. Then Alaric and the Visigoths left for southern Italy, hoping to cross the Mediterranean Sea to North Africa.

Rome had not been overrun since the Gauls had done so seven centuries before – before Rome had been a great empire. News of the event left many across the empire believing that the end of civilization was at hand. In Palestine, the Christian scholar Jerome lamented that in the ruins of Rome the whole world had perished. Many Christians had believed that Rome would last until Armageddon, and when no Armageddon came they were bewildered.

In Rome, pagan survivors saw the sack of their city as the work of Rome's old gods – those gods whose power had made Rome the most powerful of cities. They blamed the Christians for angering these gods. Hoping to appease their gods, some pagans called for performance of the sacred rites of the past, and the Christian authorities in Rome, wishing help from any source, approved such rites. But, distrusting the Christian authorities, none of the pagans had the courage to attempt their rites in public, where it was thought they had to be performed if they were to be effective.

CHAPTER 25

AUGUSTINE INFLUENCES CHRISTIANITY

AUGUSTINE AND THE FALL OF ROME

Aurelius Augustinus, known to the modern world as Saint Augustine, was in his fifties and the bishop of Hippo, in Numidia, when the Visigoths overran Italy and sacked Rome – the news of which exaggerated the extent of Visigoth violence. Augustine saw the refugees pouring into North Africa, including noble families from Rome, and he heard accusations that Rome's destruction was the result of neglect to worship the city's traditional gods.

Christians were responding with uncertainty to these allegations. They believed that their god protected people, and obviously Rome had not been protected. They believed, as had Eusebius, that God had linked Rome and Christianity. And, with disaster befalling Rome, they needed a new view on God's ties with Rome and with Christians. Augustine supplied it, drawing from the old association of evil with the present world and on the habit to put things into the form of allegory.

In a series of sermons, Augustine told his demoralized flock not to worry, that they were not citizens of Rome or denizens of earth but a special and distinct, high born race and that they were citizens of the heavenly city of Jerusalem. Since the fall of Adam, said Augustine, the loyalties of the human race had been divided between two great symbolic cities. One city, the heavenly city of Jerusalem, served God along with his loyal angels. The other city, Babylon, symbolically representing Rome, served the rebel angels: the devil and his demons. He said that although Jerusalem and Babylon appeared mixed they would be separated at the Last Judgement: Jerusalem on the left, the worldly city of Babylon on the right. The righteous, he said, would return to the heavenly city of Jerusalem just as the prophets had foretold of the return of Jews to their homeland.

Augustine's first response in writing to the charge that Christianity was to blame for the fall of Rome appeared in 413 – a work entitled *The City of God*. In this work he expressed his view of history, arguing that although Rome had suffered a great demise, God was actively at work in human history, that Rome was not eternal as some people had thought, that rather than Rome being the great peace-maker as claimed by Bishop Eusebius it had been destined to decay. Augustine claimed that Rome had been influenced both by God and by demons, that worldliness, a lust for material goods, and violence rooted in impulse had made Rome wicked. Rome, he wrote, was based on self-love, robbery, violence and fraud. The Romans, he claimed, were the most successful brigands in history. Augustine described slavery and private property not as the creations of God but of sin. (Augustine thought slavery evil but accepted it as law, and he believed that after a slave's death, or after Armageddon, he or she might win a special reward.) Christianity could not save Rome, he wrote, because those with power, including Christian emperors, could not erase the taint of humanity's sin. Rome, he wrote, had to perish as had the wicked cities of the Old Testament.

Augustine described history as changing the world visually, like a kaleidoscope, but that history was linked, as claimed by the Hebrew prophets, with the wisdom of God – a process that humanity could not understand because it could not see the whole, as could God. God, he claimed, ordered all events. Augustine claimed that without the coming of Jesus Christ history would have been meaningless. He described pagans such as Platonists as having failed to understand the sequence of history or its appointed end: Armageddon.

Augustine's *City of God*, became five volumes which dealt with those who worshiped God for happiness on earth, another five volumes that dealt with those who worshiped God for eternal happiness, and twelve volumes concerning the origin and ultimate destinies of his symbolic cities, Babylon and Jerusalem. It was an elaborate work that made him the Aristotle of his times, an Aristotle of allusions and metaphysics without Aristotle's observation and cataloging.

AUGUSTINE THE THEOLOGIAN

While a youth, Augustine had been an avid seeker of truth and certainty. He had rejected Christianity after having found Luke and Matthew contradicting each other. While a student at Carthage, he accepted the Manichaean explanation to the much-asked question evil – whence evil? Goodness, he believed, was passive, like the suffering Jesus. Evil, on the other hand, was aggressive, like passion and rage. Augustine accepted the Manichaean view that evil resided in materiality: in the human body, in sexuality, in procreation and in the rest of material nature. He agreed with the Manichaeans that materiality was apart from God and that evil therefore came from outside God. He concluded that evil came from outside of God and outside of humanity – that it was an invasion. In Carthage, Augustine had worked as a freelance teacher of rhetoric. Then he went to Rome in search of better pupils. He became a professor in Milan, and there he met and fell under the influence of the famous Bishop Ambrose, who had been influenced by neo-Platonism. With other Christians in Milan, Augustine had studied the writings of Plotinus, and he found in him a great mind that drew out what he thought was the hidden meaning of Plato. Augustine accepted Plato's view that idea, God and spirit were combined, and he accepted Plotinus' view that the power of God touched everything, molding and giving meaning to passive matter. From Plotinus, Augustine believed he had gained an understanding of a permanence that was God. He now saw God as utterly transcendent, as the creator of all, all-knowing and the source of human knowledge. He had come to believe that materiality was not evil, that the universe was a continuous active whole and that evil was merely the turning away from God. And under the influence of Bishop Ambrose, and perhaps his Christian mother, Monica, Augustine, in his mid-thirties, converted to Christianity.

As a Christian, Augustine wrote of Plato's followers being right about God but wrong about gods. Augustine drew from the Judaic-Christian view of creation and criticized the neo-Platonists for seeing creation as idea manifesting itself rather than God creating things as they should be. Here he was in agreement with, if not having borrowed from, Ambrose, who had stated that creation had not just happened and that God had not created the universe with a compass and a level but instead had commanded it.

Augustine claimed that one finds truth through revelation, a sort of flash of insight emanating from God's messenger, Jesus Christ – rather than the weighing of generalizations. Truth he thought could be found in scripture, which he saw as the word of God. But he believed that to find it there, one had to search for it with a yearning for fulfillment – an attempt to find what one was looking for rather than an attempt to find whatever was there. Having come to see all of creation as God's, Augustine fought against the notion that humanity was helpless before the forces of evil. People chose to be evil or not to be evil, he believed, as in Adam choosing to sin. Despair, Augustine believed, was unnecessary and an unforgivable sin. People, he believed, had the freedom to call on God to save them. A Christian's worst enemy, he believed, was inside himself: his sins, his doubts.

Although Augustine saw God as the creator of all, he believed with other Christians that the world was also influenced by devils. Pagan gods, he believed, were devils. He described devils as vile beings, as the evil spirits of which the apostles had spoken. Augustine turned the struggle against devils inward – as had Plotinus. Men, he believed, got the demons they deserved. For Augustine there were times when humans were their own devil. He saw victory over evil as depending upon an inner strength, the source of which was an inner attachment to Jesus Christ.

Augustine railed against the remnant paganism among his parishioners, including astrology. He attacked the notion that humanity's course of action could be determined by the stars while animals such as dogs remained free to chose between doing something and not doing it. He spoke of people born in the same month – even the same hour – as not having necessarily the same destiny over the period of a day or a lifetime.

Like Origen before him, Augustine interpreted scripture allegorically. The Bible, he believed, had been veiled by God in order to exercise those seeking Him. He believed that the Bible's ambiguities provided people with ever-new facets of truth to be discovered. He saw human consciousness as the psychoanalyst Freud would see messages in dreams: truth not as simple and direct but diffracted into obscure and intricate symbols needing interpretation. Freud would believe that dreams were images rising from thoughts that had been repressed; Augustine believed that people had a repressed awareness, a loss of direct knowledge, resulting from humanity's fall at the Garden of Eden, which had left Adam and Eve able to communicate with each another only by the clumsy artifice of language and gestures. Believing that God was the source of all knowledge, Augustine believed that direct awareness was a gift of God and that the gap between direct awareness and human consciousness was mercifully bridged by the Bible and its marvelous proliferation of imagery – a direct awareness that humans could acquire only in flashes of insight. Thus it was that Augustine saw Rome as Babylon and saw Jerusalem as the heavenly city: imagery rather than seeing and analyzing phenomena in direct specifics. Augustine advocated a path to truth that was traditional in the long history of religion: imagination.

AUGUSTINE AGAINST PANTHEISTS, DONATISTS AND PELAGIANS

Augustine believed that a complete uniformity of opinion existed only among angels, but he believed that the Church needed to exclude ideas that were contrary to what he saw as fundamental to Christianity. Early in his career as a bishop he combated the view among Christians that God was everywhere and everything, that God was nature rather than a unifying force at the apex of reality. Augustine came into conflict with those Christians who believed that the Church should be restricted to those who had maintained the purity they had acquired at baptism, that the Church was a source of holiness and that no sinner should have a part in it, that the Church should expel those who were guilty of mortal sins. These were the Donatists, the descendants of those North Africans who had been for a stricter standard of readmission to the Church following the great persecutions of Christians a century before. Donatists had their own congregations and churches, and in many places in North Africa they outnumbered other Christians.

Augustine believed that sin was not just a matter of choice, that sin was inherited, that the Church should embrace all of humanity, saints and sinners alike, that the good and bad would be together until Armageddon, when they would be separated. Augustine claimed that the good Christian must try to become holy but must also coexist with sinners in the same community and be prepared to rebuke and correct them. His neo-Platonic education led him to see Christians as part of a world of development, as imperfection struggling toward the ideal as manifested in God. Augustine saw the Church not as a body of purists defying society but a body that should master society, a body capable of bringing truth to the masses.

The Donatists and Augustine differed in their view of how the sacraments of the Church should be administered. The Donatists argued that for sacraments to work they had to be administered by clergymen undefiled by serious sin. They feared that any deviation from proper ritual might alienate God from the Church, as they believed the Jews of ancient Israel had angered God by their sins. Augustine argued that churchmen who received and administered sacraments merely strove imperfectly to realize the holiness in these sacraments and that these sacraments worked by the power of Christ alone unaffected by the clergyman administering them. He saw the sacraments of the Church as holy because the Church was itself holy, participating in Christ.

Believing in authority, Augustine wished to have Donatist beliefs suppressed. Like others of his time, he believed that people lacked the will and wisdom to govern themselves. He saw Adam and Eve as having too much pride and their pride having led them to attempt to govern themselves. He believed that people had to be governed by God through his representatives: officers of the Church. Augustine led the drive against the Donatists. In 405, the Church had convinced the emperor of the west, Honorius, to outlaw the Donatists, and the Church deprived the Donatists of bishops and funds. Their meeting together for religious purposes was declared punishable by death. Donatists could not hold public office, protect their property in the courts, nor pass their property to their heirs. Under such duress, the purity of some Donatists cracked, as had many Christians during the persecutions a century before. Donatist support among people with property declined as such people found it in their interest to conform to the accepted orthodoxy of the Church.

While the Visigoths were marching up and down Italy in the years of 409 and 410, Rome's campaign to repress Donatism foundered, and a Donatist resurgence followed, with armed bands of Donatists seeking revenge by attacking rival Christians. Augustine was forced to go into hiding. But by 412, after the disruptions by the Visigoths had ended, Donatism was again repressed. Many who had fought for the Donatists committed suicide. Augustine expressed support for the repression as long as it was accompanied by instruction. He favored uprooting the Donatist heresy with arguments and opposed hunting for heretics with spies and *agent-provocateurs*.

Within the next ten years, some Donatists in North Africa continued to resist. They terrorized the countryside, plundering villages and rich farms, forcing non-Donatist Christian landowners to trade places with their slaves and enjoying the sight of the landowner's humiliations. They were engaging in the terrorism of the defeated, and eventually they would disappear.

The Pelagians

A Christian monk and theologian from Britain named Pelagius was among those who fled from Rome to North Africa after the Visigoths sacked Rome, and in the city of Carthage he joined in discussions and debates with Christian intellectuals whose confidence in Roman society had been shattered. Pelagius had been disturbed by the moral laxity he had found among Christians in Rome when arriving there some thirty years before, and now, in Carthage, he advocated a stricter morality for all Christians.

Pelagius and those who agreed with him believed that people could make choices, that they could apply themselves to their surroundings, that they were responsible for their actions and could exercise self-control, that God had made people free to chose between good and evil, that God helped those who helped themselves, that rather than being born sinful, people had no excuse for sinful behavior, that every sin was a deliberate act of contempt for God. After a year, Pelagius left Carthage for Palestine, but a follower remained in Carthage and continued to influence those who wished to reform the Church. Pelagius' ideas spread to those provinces where life had been dislocated by invasions: Britain, southern Italy and Gaul. Augustine was disturbed by the spread of Pelagian ideas, and he led the attack against them. Once again his argument involved inner feelings and patience, a belief that people should merely try to do right while convalescing within the Church. Augustine reiterated his belief in humanity's power to choose, and he added that freedom of choice was limited and, in having only a limited power to choose, people could not live flawlessly. Augustine supported his belief in the limits of will by holding up the apostle Paul as an authority on the subject and quoting Paul from Romans 7:15-18, which indicated that even Paul was incapable of doing what he willed.

Augustine on Limitations, Sex and Original Sin
    Augustine saw humanity's limits of will as the result of the original sins of Adam and Eve. Wrong choices, he believed, added to one's miseries, but right choices would never alleviate the results of Adam's fall. Augustine believed that sin made people not just limited but inherently corrupt, even dirty – born, he said, between urine and feces. People, he believed, could not overcome their faults through will and education, that if they could choose righteousness through their own ability to choose rather than through God and his agents they would not need the Church's rituals. He viewed the Pelagian interpretation of freedom as making virtue possible outside of Christianity, and such a virtue he associated with pagan virtue, which he believed was influenc-ed by obscenity and filthy devils. Unlike the Stoics, Augustine saw virtue only in religious passion – Christian religious passion. He claimed that God gave salvation to someone not from that person's outward obedience but from his or her responding to God's love with a love of their own for God.
    Augustine viewed humanity's inner world as more complex than did his rivals, or as had Socrates. There was in Augustine none of Socrates' naïveté about people doing wrong only because of not knowing truth. Augustine saw the great size of one's inner world was a source of anxiety as well as strength. Augustine believed that one's inner-self was so complex and mysterious that no one could ever know his whole personality and that no one could be certain that all of oneself would live up to the standards that he or she had adopted. He wrote of people committing sins through pride, with outcomes that did not always produce pride. He wrote of sins that happened through ignorance and weakness, and people weeping and groaning in distress.
    Although Augustine saw the world that God had created as overwhelmingly good, he believed that humanity was destined to envy and to lust for power. Though he had been extraordinarily active sexually in his younger days, now in his old age he saw humanity as gluttonous. Augustine described infants at the breast as filled with lust, jealousy and other vices. Adam and Eve could have had sex without lust, he wrote, but they chose instead to have it with lust. A carpenter moved his hands without lust, he added, and so too could people in sexual intercourse. Virtue, claimed Augustine, demanded complete control over one's body, but absolute control was impossible, he claimed, because of Adam' fall.

Pelagius Is Decreed a Heretic

Some Christian intellectuals complained that Augustine made it seem as if the devil were the maker of humanity. They found it absurd to claim that infants were already cursed by guilt in the wombs of their mothers, and they believed that this contradicted God's love of justice. Some saw a Manichaean influence in Augustine's view of evil and the body. Pelagius argued that sin was something of the soul and not the body, and they asked how sin could be passed from the soul of parents to the body of an infant. Augustine answered that sin was passed down from Adam and Eve and from generation to generation through semen, with Jesus having escaped sin by having been born of a virgin.

The Pelagians, as greater advocates of virtue, clashed with Augustine over wealth and sharing, asserting that a rich man was surely damned. Augustine replied that the Church had to find room both for its higher civil servants and its taxpayers, including the rich landowners on whose endowments and influence the monks and clergy had come to depend. Augustine preached against rich men ruining themselves by distributing their land among the poor. Instead, he called upon them to leave their land to Catholic monasteries.

Opinion within the Church went more to agreement with Augustine than the Pelagians. Bishops who had spent years upholding the necessity of baptizing infants were inclined to reject the Pelagian argument about the innocence of infants, and many Christians were inclined to believe more in human frailty than humanity's ability to perfect itself. Many believed that people should be humble rather than righteous about their virtues and rather than dare to attempt to improve themselves by their own strengths.

Defending and pushing their beliefs, Pelagians demonstrated and fought in the streets of Rome. They were viewed as disturbers of the Catholic faith and were accused of considering themselves above the rest of the Christian community. In 416, largely in response to Augustine and his followers, an African Church council met and condemned Pelagius, and the following year Pope Innocent I concurred with the condemnation and ex-communicated Pelagius. Pelagius responded with a book entitled *A Brief Statement of Faith.* Innocent I died, and his successor, Pope Zozimus, who hated muddles, pronounced Pelagius innocent of heresy. Augustine and his supporters then sought support for their crusade against Pelagius from the thirty-two year-old emperor of the western half of the empire: Honorius. To help their case they presented Honorius with eighty stallions. Honorius issued an edict banishing intransigent Pelagians. Pope Zozimus fell into line and declared Pelagius a heretic and had him exiled back to Britain.

CHAPTER 26

REMNANTS OF THE ROMAN EMPIRE

INVADERS AND THE DIMINISHING ROMAN POWER

After the Visigoths besieged and departed from Rome, a storm frustrated their plans to cross from southern Italy into North Africa. The Visigoth leader, Alaric, died, and instead of trying to cross the Mediterranean the Visigoths journeyed north into southwestern Gaul, spreading what to some appeared to be God's punishment of Rome. From his palace in Ravenna, the Roman emperor in the west, Honorius, felt obliged to make peace with the Visigoths. His sister, Placidia, married their new leader, Atauf. And, in 418, the Visigoths were granted a legal domain in southwestern Gaul. The Visigoths made Toulouse their capital, and they established themselves as protectors of those who were there when they arrived. In accord with Roman tradition, as protectors the Visigoths had the right to possess from one-third to two-thirds of the land or the produce from those lands. Local people who owned large tracts of land lost much of it to the Visigoths, while most who came under Visigoth rule had little land to lose.

The Visigoths were awed by Roman civilization. They adopted local methods of agriculture. For the time being, they held on to their Arian Christianity, which was offensive heresy to local Christians. But the Visigoths began to learn Latin, and they administered their territory as the Romans had, using local Roman bureaucrats. Those who had been there before the Visigoths (the Gallo-Romans) began adopting Germanic ways. They wanted to belong. Some of them began wearing Visigoth trousers instead of the Roman toga. Some wore the jewelry worn by Visigoths, and they imitated the rougher manners of the Visigoths.

Other Germans

The Visigoths shared Gaul with other Germans: the Franks, who occupied Gaul's extreme northeast, and the Alemanni, who moved through central Gaul to the extreme south, along the Mediterranean coast near Spain. Much of the rest of Gaul, especially in the northwest, remained Roman. And the Visigoths expanded through southern Gaul

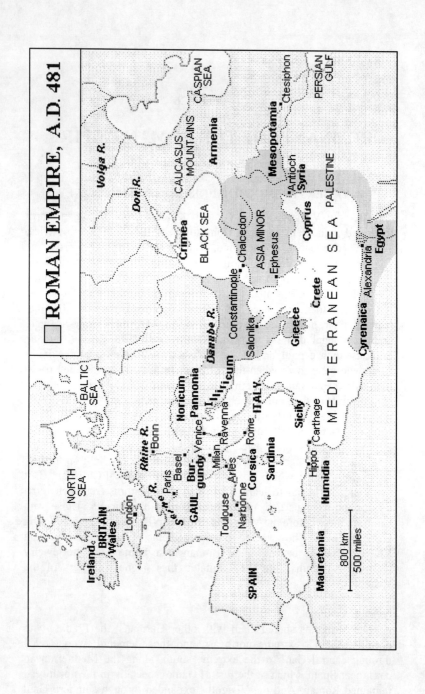

ROMAN EMPIRE, A.D. 481

and into Spain, where they found the Vandals – Germans who had advanced into Spain in 409.

With the Vandals were some local people who had joined their ranks. Pushed on by the Visigoths, they decided to move across the strait of Gibraltar to North Africa, known for its rich farmlands of wheat. And in 429, about 80,000 of them made the crossing.

The Vandals were Arian Christians like the Visigoths, and they saw God as on their side. The Christians of North Africa thought otherwise, but God did not appear to be on their side either. Their opposition to the Vandal invasion was weak. North Africa was politically and socially fragmented. Military units in North Africa were few, scattered and unpopular. Another miracle was needed, but none was forthcoming. The Vandals easily overran the coast of Mauritania and began moving eastward along the coast of Numidia. The Vandals banished the Trinity worshiping clergy and converted churches to Arian worship. Where the Vandals found resistance and suffered dead they responded by looting, sacking and destroying the offending cities or razing country villas to the ground.

Many fled from the Vandals to Augustine's city: Hippo. The Vandals came upon Hippo and surrounded it, their fleet of ships dominating waters off Hippo's coast. Hippo was fortified, and for months the Vandals remained outside the city's walls. Augustine's church became packed with the demoralized remnants of Roman society. Men who had lived in great affluence now mingled with the beggars who had envied them. They were distressed at what to them appeared to be the collapse of the empire. Believing that death might be near, despite their belief in life after death many realized their love for life.

In the third month of the Vandal's siege, Augustine's health failed, and he became bedridden. He believed in miracles, but no miracle came to rescue his people. He died on August 24, 430. Months later the Vandals overran and burned Hippo. In the happenstance of the burning and looting, Augustine's writings remained untouched by the flames, which for some was the miracle that they wished to see.

The Vandals then settled down in North Africa and consolidated their rule. Within twenty years they built up their navy and began terrorizing shipping in the Western Mediterranean. And they would soon extend their rule to Sicily, Sardinia and Corsica.

Roman Power

Honorius died of dropsy in 423. Rule in the west passed to the six year-old son of his sister Placidia, who took title Valentinian III. Placidia put her armies under the command one of the few remaining Roman military leaders: Aetius. Aetius lacked money for recruiting a greater army, but against the invaders he used diplomacy. He hoped to keep the invaders divided. He knew the Huns and the Visigoths, having on different occasions been their hostage. According to Gibbon's *Decline and Fall of the Roman Empire,* Aetius soothed the passions, consulted the prejudices and balanced the interests of those "barbarians" who occupied the Western provinces.

From the Visigoths in Gaul, Aetius recovered Arles and Narbonne. He defended northern Gaul against the Salian Franks. In 437 he defeated an attempt by more Burgundian Germans to push into Gaul around the Rhine River, and in 443 Aetius settled the Burgundians into a federated state southwest of Basel, in Switzerland.

Meanwhile, disorders continued among local peoples in Gaul and Spain. Roman citizens in Gaul and Spain did not identify with Rome to the extent that Romanized Italians did, and many preferred poverty among the invaders to rule by Roman governors. A Christian priest from Gaul named Salvian wrote a work called *On the Government of God,* a work describing the poor of Gaul as being robbed and widows groaning, "so that even persons of good birth, who had enjoyed a liberal education" were seeking refuge with the Germans. Salvian praised the virtues of the Germans and wrote that Roman citizenship was now shunned and thought "almost abhorrent." In Gaul, the homeless and others joined gangs of brigands. Rural discontent merged with Christian radicalism. Celtic nationalism re-surfaced. In Spain and Gaul serious risings occurred against Roman rule. And, with an army of Germanic mercenaries and Huns, Aetius suppressed them.

Attila the Hun

A Hun chieftain named Roua had helped Aetius against the Burgundians. Roua had created a unity of sorts among the Hun tribes. He ruled over an empire in Eastern Europe that extended from the Volga River to the Danube and as for north as the Baltic Sea. When Roua died in 435 his rule passed to his two nephews, who began ruling jointly. The stronger of these two would be known as Attila the Hun.

With the Roman Empire as weak as it was, Attila and his brother were the most powerful men in Europe. A peace treaty between the Huns and the emperor of the east, Theodosius II, included a payment of subsidies to the Huns of seven hundred pounds of gold each year. In 441, Theodosius stopped these payments. The Huns retaliated by launching an assault across the Danube River into Illyricum, razing a number of cities, including Belgrade and Sophia. Attila devastated the entire region between the Black Sea and the Mediterranean, conquering numerous Germans called Ostrogoths (formerly occupying the Crimea) and forcing them to join his army. The Huns attacked Constantinople, but they were unable to break through its great walls. They continued their attacks in neighboring areas, until Theodosius II agreed to renew his payments to them, including back payments: 2,100 pounds of gold annually.

Joint military rule with one's brother was not always a good arrangement – as Caracalla's brother had discovered – and this proved to be the case for Attila's brother. In 445, Attila murdered him and began ruling alone. A couple of years later Attila pushed into Greece, but the empire's army stopped him at Thermopylae. Attila renegotiated a peace treaty with Theodosius II.

In 450, Theodosius II died and a soldier named Marcian became emperor of the east. Marcian was married to Theodosius' sister, which did not impress the emperor in the west, Valentinian III (now thirty-two). Valentinian refused to recognize Marcian, and the lack of co-operation between the two emperors further weakened the empire. Marcian wished to avoid costly military ventures, and when the western empire asked him for help against an invasion into Italy by the Vandals, Marcian refused. Marcian, moreover, stopped paying Attila his annual subsidy, hoping this would drive Attila to the west.

In the west, Valentinian denied his strong-willed sister, Honoria, the marriage she wished, and she plotted with her lover to overthrow Valentinian. The plot was discovered, Honoria's lover was executed, and Honoria faced being forced to marry someone who could control her. She appealed to a power greater than Valentinian: Attila. She sent him her ring. Attila took it as a proposal of marriage. He claimed Honoria as his, and he claimed half of the Western Empire as her dowry.

Attila allied himself with the Franks and Vandals, and in 451 he crossed the Rhine into Gaul with his army. He sacked cities and de-vastated lands along the channel coast. Aetius and the Visigoths joined forces against Attila, and in one of history's greatest battles (at an unknown location in Gaul) they served Attila his first defeat. Attila suffered great losses – an estimated 175,000 to 300,000 of his warriors killed – and he retreated east of the Rhine.

The following year, after partially recovering from his defeat, Attila invaded Italy – where there were no Visigoths, Franks or Burgundians to combat him. He overran Milan and other cities and drove an Italian people called Veneti to seek refuge on a group of islands that were to become the city of Venice. Valentinian fled from his palace in Ravenna to Rome, and he sent the Bishop of Rome (Pope Leo I) and two Roman senators to meet with Attila. Christian legend has it that the Pope's presence awed Attila and that the ghosts of Peter and Paul appeared to Attila and terrified him. A more likely reason for Attila's withdrawal was that plague had broken out among his men, that his supply of food was running out, and that military help for Valentinian was arriving from the eastern half of the empire. Attila returned to what is now

Hungary, and the following year he died there, reportedly as the result of a burst artery. And without Attila's leadership, the collection of peoples that had made up his empire became disunited.

RIVALRY BETWEEN THE BISHOPS
OF ROME AND CONSTANTINOPLE

While the western half of the Roman Empire was being overrun, Christian bishops continued their dispute over a controversy about the nature of Jesus Christ. The Gospels described Jesus as human insofar as he had wept, hungered, thirsted and demonstrated a lack of omniscience – characteristics considered contrary to godliness. The bishop of Constantinople, Nestorius, thought it his duty as Church leader to resolve the issue. He concluded that Jesus had a dual nature, that he had a divine nature and a human nature, which were separate but loosely connected. And he believed that Mary, the mother of Jesus, had given birth to the human Jesus and therefore could not be called "The Mother of God."

The question of Jesus' nature was combined with rivalries over prestige and power between the bishops of Rome, Alexandria, Antioch and Constantinople. The bishop of Rome, Leo I, claimed he was chairman over the entire Church, and he supported his claim with a geographical argument: that Rome was where Peter had worshiped and died. Leo claimed that Peter was the highest of the apostles, that he was the rock on which God had built his church and that the bishops of Rome were Peter's successors as supreme rulers and teachers within the Church.

The bishop of Alexandria, Cyril, was jealous of the power of the bishop of Constantinople, and he attacked Nestorius not only for his views about Jesus and Mary but also for extending hospitality to Pelagians. Cyril cemented local alliances and appealed to the emperors in the East and West. This resulted in the Third Ecumenical Council at Ephesus in 431. The Council voted to depose Nestorius from his position as Patriarch of Constantinople. Nestorius retired to his monastery near Antioch, and he was soon banished to Upper Egypt.

To settle the debate over the nature of Jesus, a Fourth Ecumenical Council met at Chalcedon in the autumn of 451. The bishop of Rome, Leo I, claimed that Jesus Christ had two natures, divine and human, but was one distinct substance. The Council upheld his view, defeating those who still believed in Nestorius version, and defeating those Christians called Monophysites, who believed that Jesus Christ had but one composite nature. Leo's supporters at the meeting were jubilant and are said to have announced that it had been Peter who had spoken through Leo. But Leo also lost at the Council: the Council recognized the bishop of Constantinople as having equal authority with the bishop of Rome on the grounds that Constantinople was the New Rome as had been proclaimed by Constantine.

INDEPENDENCE AND A CELTIC REVIVAL IN BRITAIN

Roman military legions evacuated Britain in the late 300s and early 400s. In Roman-ruled Britain many had favored everything Roman. Townspeople spoke Latin, drank wine, wore the Roman toga and enjoyed Roman baths and dinner parties. But around two-thirds of the people lived outside of the towns, spoke no Latin and worshiped Celtic gods – in a country that was still half forest, shrub and marshy wasteland. And with the withdrawal of the Roman military, Celtic nationalism arose. Power passed to local, Celtic military leaders and Celtic aristocrats. These aristocrats supported a Celtic warrior named Vortigern – a Christian of Pelagian persuasion. Around the year 425 Vortigern began extending his influence, and he became the strongest force in Britain, ruling from Wales to the channel coast in the south. Pelagian Christians spread their influence, while orthodox Catholics in Britain held their ground and remained in contact with church leadership on the continent.

Vortigern defeated those Scots who attacked England from enclaves in Wales, and he battled the Picts, who attacked England from Scotland. For help against the Picts, Vortigern turned to Anglo-Saxons who had settled along England's east coast. He gave the Anglo-Saxons more land and a treaty, and for eight years the Anglo-Saxons fought the Picts according to their treaty obligations, and the Anglo-Saxons defeated the Pict invaders. Then negotiations over Vortigern's payment to the Anglo-Saxons broke down, and in 442 the Anglo-Saxons attacked Vortigern's army. The result was a terrible but indecisive battle at Aylesbury, about forty miles northwest of London, and after this battle the Anglo-Saxons continued a campaign of pillage and slaughter against the Celts.

Then came the greatest series of Anglo-Saxon invasions of Britain to date, as Angles, Jutes and Saxons on Europe's continent were running from the Huns. Vortigern's power evaporated. But unlike the people in Gaul and Spain (who were passive or accepted the presence of German authority) local Britons felt they had much at stake and vigorously resisted invasion. War between the Britons and the invaders continued with the passing of years. Trade and markets broke down. Slaves escaped, and estates were left in ruin. Those towns that were too well-fortified for the invaders and had water became places of refuge, while other towns declined with their supply of food. With England weakened by war, the Picts renewed their invasions southward across

Hadrian's wall. And the Anglo-Saxons continued their forays westward, massacring and pillaging their way to the sea that separates Britain from Ireland, while the Celtic Britons fled into the hills, or into Spain, or across the channel to Gaul.

ROMAN RULE ENDS IN THE WEST

Becoming powerful short of absolute power could be dangerous, and it was for Aetius – as it had been for Stilicho. Aetius' son was to marry the emperor's daughter, and, like Stilicho before him, Aetius became the victim of rumors and palace intrigue. Valentinian III was told that if he did not strike at Aetius first, Aetius would destroy him. When Aetius appeared before Valentinian to claim the emperor's daughter for his son, Valentinian accused him of treason, jumped from his throne and killed the defenseless man with his sword.

Six months later, two men who had been Aetius' retainers retaliated by assassinating Valentinian. Valentinian had fathered no son, and a scheming aristocrat seized the throne. Within a few months, as invading Vandals were again in Italy and approaching Rome, a mob in Rome killed the upstart. The emperor in the east, Marcian, refused to help defend Rome from the Vandals. Rome was plundered for a second time in the century, and after nineteen days the Vandals sailed away with thousands of prisoners, including Valentinian's widow and his two daughters.

Power in the western half of the empire fell to the commander of what was left of west's armies. This was Ricimer, a German and an Aryan Christian, who, according to Roman law, could not become emperor. But Ricimer was able to appoint emperors to rule under him. In 457, he appointed Majorian emperor. Majorian moved to stop abuses in tax collecting and oppression in the provinces, but he lost 300 ships to the Vandals off the coast of Spain, and after four years in office Ricimer removed him as emperor and had him executed. Ricimer appointed as emperor a member of the royal family from the east: Anthemius. After a campaign led by Ricimer against the Vandals failed, Ricimer and Anthemius quarreled, and, like Majorian, Anthemius was put to death.

Ricimer then died of a disease. The emperor of the eastern half of the empire, Leo I (not to be confused with the Bishop of Rome), appointed an emperor for the west, Nepos, and sent him with an army into the west. A military commander in the west, Orestes – a Roman from Pannonia – drove Nepos into exile. And Orestes appointed his son, Romulus, as emperor.

In 476, an Ostrogoth commander in the Roman military, Odoacer, whose troops were mostly Ostrogoths, demanded grants of land for his troops and demanded the same federal status for Ostrogoths that others Germans had won. When his demands were rejected, he and his army seized Orestes and Romulus. He had Orestes executed, but he took pity on Romulus, whose beauty he admired, and he sent Romulus into retirement with a pension. And Romulus was the last of the Roman emperors in the west.

The emperor in the east, Zeno, refused to recognize Odoacer, and he sent an Ostrogoth army against him. The army, led by an Ostrogoth tribal chief, Theodoric, crossed the Alps in the year 480 and arrived in northern Italy in late August the following year. Theodoric's army confronted Odoacer's army – Ostrogoths against Ostrogoths, Arian Christians against Arian Christians. Tribal cohesion was stronger among Theodoric's people than among Odoacer's, and during four years of fighting Theodoric wore down Odoacer's forces. While Theodoric was besieging Odoacer's capital, Ravenna, a truce was called and the two leaders met. Odoacer and Theodoric agreed to divide the rule of Italy between them. It was another sharing of power that was not to succeed. At a banquet at the emperor's palace, Theodoric killed Odoacer, and Theodoric's troops killed all of Odoacer's relatives and cut down Odoacer's troops wherever they could find them.

Theodoric assumed the title of king of Italy, and, to the relief of the other Germanic tribes within the western half of the empire, he appeared content to conquer no territory in their direction. Theodoric left administrative posts in the hands of experienced Roman aristocrats, and he respected Italy's aristocracy in general. He promoted agriculture and commerce. He tolerated various differences among Christians. Uninterested in metaphysics, he saw himself as the protector of the Trinity believing Christians as well as Arian Christians. He recognized the dignity and position of the Bishop of Rome. And the Church of Rome allied itself with Theodoric's rule. Like Constantine the Great, Theodoric intervened in disputes within the Church, and he was recognized by the Church of Rome as having this authority despite his being an Arian Christian.

THE FRANKS CONVERT TO CATHOLICISM

The Franks occupied an area north of Paris, around the Rhine River, and like the Visigoths and the Burgundians they had been federated into the Roman Empire. The Franks enjoyed singing about their past heroes, and they had many gods and were ruled by a royal family that claimed descent from the gods. When their king died in 481, he was succeeded by his fifteen-year-old son: Clovis. When Clovis was twenty he moved with his army southward and west against other Franks, believing in himself and that he had the help of the gods. He won

battles and extended his rule all the way to the river Seine. Then, intermittently, he fought more wars and enlarged his territory, assassinating, and plundering when he could, including Catholic churches.

Clovis' gains made him feared in neighboring kingdoms. An envoy
that Clovis sent to the king of Burgundy told Clovis of the king's
exceptionally attractive and graceful granddaughter – Clotilda. Clovis
sent a representative to the king asking to marry Clotilda, and the king
was afraid to refuse.

Clotilda was Catholic. A hundred years later, a Catholic historian,
Gregory of Tours, would write that three years after Clovis and Clotilda
married, Frankish people fought a major battle near what is now Bonn,
Germany, against invading Alemanni Germans. According to some
modern historians, the Franks who fought the Alemanni Germans were
led not by Clovis but by a king called Siegebert. At any rate, Gregory
of Tours described Clovis' forces as suffering during the battle against
the Alemanni and Clovis as calling on his gods for help. But no help
was forthcoming. Then, according to Gregory, Clovis "lifted his eyes
up to heaven" and, "moved to tears," said:

> Jesus Christ, Clotilda proclaims you the living God.
> You are said to give aid to those in need and to grant
> victory to those who have hope in You.*

According to Gregory, Clovis told Christ that if He helped him he
would have himself baptized in His name, and the battle then turned in
Clovis' favor and Clovis defeated the Alemanni. Jesus had apparently
taken an interest in Clovis' expansions and had seen in Clovis an agent
in his cause. Jesus, according to Gregory, had become a god of war – as
with the pagan Constantine almost two hundred years before.

Clovis continued to war for more territory and extended his rule as
far south as Switzerland, to what is now the city of Basel, on the Rhine
River just inside Switzerland. Italy's king, Theodoric, who was the
elder statesman among the German kings in western, continental Europe, warned Clovis to expand no farther toward Italy and no closer to
the kingdoms of those Germans to whom he, Theodoric, was patron.

Meanwhile, Christian evangelists had been finding converts among
Clovis' Franks. The Franks had been impressed by Christianity's
association with Roman civilization, and they had no theology that
rivaled that of the Christians. But despite the victory that Gregory
claimed Jesus gave him, Clovis remained unconvinced in his choice of
faiths. Clovis' family was divided in religion: Clotilda's uncle (the new
king of Burgundy) was an Aryan Christian; one of Clovis' sisters was
an Arian Christian and married to the Arian king Theodoric; a second
sister was also Arian; and a third was pagan. Clovis, the story goes,
consulted those closest to him: his warriors. Then, on Christmas day –
more than two years after his purported victory near Bonn – Clovis and

several of his warriors were baptized Catholics. And the conversion of Clovis' subjects was soon to follow.

ROMAN RULE IN THE EAST

The emperors at Constantinople still ruled over Greece, Asia Minor, Syria, Palestine and Egypt – areas tied together by trade as well as the imperial authority at Constantinople. The emperors at Constantinople saw themselves as the rightful heirs of a rule that dated back to Augustus Caesar. They saw themselves as the sole and legitimate ruler of the Roman Empire. These emperors believed that their rule was handed down to them by God and that they ruled by divine right. And they described themselves as God's Vicar on Earth.

After the disintegration of the western half of the Roman Empire, Constantinople continued to trade with the coast of Gaul, the Iberian Peninsula, Africa, India and China. Constantinople remained a prosperous city, populated by Romans, Greeks, Armenians, Syrians, Arabs, Asians and some Germans, all of them united by a common Roman citizenship and belief in Christ and the Trinity. Intermarriage among the different ethnicities was common, and by the 500s most people in Constantinople spoke Greek. A few spoke Latin, but Latin was declining and used chiefly on formal or official occasions. Prejudice was common only against those who could not speak Greek or who were not Catholic – the essentials, according to some in Constantinople, for civilization.

Germans made up the majority of those in Constantinople's army, and some soldiers were Huns. Many Germans labored on lands just outside the city, and some worked in Constantinople at menial jobs or as slaves in rich households. At first their blond hair, blue eyes and pink skins had been an unpleasant sight to others of the city, but by the year 500 people had become accustomed to them.

As a Christian city, Constantinople had many churches, monasteries and convents. It had free hospitals for the sick, staffed by monks and nuns. It had almshouses for the needy and the old. It had free accommodations for the homeless and city-subsidized orphanages. And in times of need, rationing was often introduced to help the poor.

Many in Constantinople saw the world as did Augustine of Hippo: as a vale of tears in which one should not place trust or hope. But the people of Constantinople were generally enthusiastic about chariot racing. From early in the morning, young and old people and priests from all over Constantinople would begin to converge on the city's circus to view and gamble on the chariot races.

CHAPTER 27

PERSIA, INDIA, AND A COMMON ENEMY

SASSANID REVERSES AND A COMMUNIST UPRISING

Across history, religious zealots would be disappointed with the failures of zeal among others of the same faith. And so it was with the Zoroastrian priesthood when the successors of Shapur II failed to continue his persecutions of Christians. Shapur III freed Christian prisoners, believing they would be of greater value to him pursuing their crafts and paying taxes. Under the rule of Yazdegerd, who began his rule in AD 399, the Christians enjoyed peace and reconstruction. Yazdegerd respected diversity, and he helped Christians rebuild their churches. He wanted peace among the religions of his realm, and he wanted peace among the Christians. He sponsored a council meeting of bishops and other Christian ecclesiastics of the empire to mend their quarrels, and the Council created rules and an organizational structure to unite Christians within the empire.

Zoroastrian priests tried to convince Yazdegerd that Christianity was a threat. They tried to pressure him into renewing repression against the Christians. And Christian intolerance toward the Zoroastrians might have helped convince Yazdegerd that he had made a mistake. Emboldened by their freedom, hating paganism as the work of the devil, Christians went so far as to destroy Zoroastrian fire temples and to attack Zoroastrian priests.

After Yazdegerd's death in 420, nobles exercised their prerogative of supporting one faction or another within the royal family, and they tried to prevent any of Yazdegerd's sons from succeeding him. But one did: Bahram V, who became known for his prowess in hunting game and women. Hostility toward Christianity intensified with an increase in influence of Bahram's Prime Minister, Mihr-Narseh – who was much honored by the Persians for his charity and his building for public benefit. Bahram V attempted to win and maintain good will for himself among the Zoroastrians, and, in 421, the persecution of Christians was resumed. Many Christians fled to the eastern half of the Roman Empire, and Bahram sought their extradition. But the Roman emperor at Constantinople, Theodosius II, refused Bahram's request.

Bahram V allowed Mihr-Narseh to seek resolution through war against Constantinople. A council of Persian Christian bishops met and sought to protect Christianity in Persia by proclaiming their independence from the Christianity of Constantinople. Constantinople overpowered Persia's forces in a series of skirmishes. Then Bahram made a hundred-year peace with Constantinople in which he agreed to grant freedom of worship for Christians in the Sassanid Empire in exchange for Constantinople granting freedom of worship for Zoroastrians under its rule. In 424, a third Synod of Bishops was held in the Sassanid Empire, and the bishops proclaimed the autonomy of their Christianity from the Christianity of the Roman Empire. They claimed they were responsible only to Jesus Christ, and with their declared independence they offered fellowship with the Church in the Roman Empire.

Meanwhile, the rights of religious minorities remained the whim of the Sassanid king. Under the influence of the now elderly prime minister, Mihr-Narseh, the new king, Yazdegerd II (438-457) attempted to force the Armenians to give up their Christianity. Zoroastrian missionaries were sent to Armenia in great numbers, and there a systematic persecution of Christians and Jews began.

More Problems

Attempts at forcing religious conformity was of little help to the Sassanid kings, and like most kings they needed help. Trouble came to them not from sin or the failures of proper worship. It came as it had for the Romans: migrating foreigners. The invaders were called Hephthalites, or White Huns, descendants perhaps of those the Chinese called Hsiung-nu. From the desert in central Asia, during the rule of Bahram V, they had penetrated Sassanian territory to the Oxus River. Bahram V had repelled the invasions, but in the second half of the 400s the Hephthalite invasions continued. In 484 the Hephthalites feigned a retreat and lured the Sassanian king, Firuz (457-484), and his cavalry and much of the Sassanid nobility into a concealed pit, and the Hephthalites slaughtered them all. The Hephthalites captured the king's family and treasury, and they forced the new Sassanid king, Balash – the brother of Firuz – to pay them tribute.

After military defeat came drought and famine, and with this came political unrest. In 488, Balash, who had been elected by nobles, was deposed by nobles and blinded. He was replaced by Kavad, a son of Firuz. Unrest among the Persians grew into rebellion, which was joined by the country's major workers' guilds – a movement led by a Zoroastrian priest called Mazdak. Mazdak's movement was a religious sect that had been founded by his father. His father had directed his followers to enjoy life and to satisfy their appetites in food and drink but to do so in a spirit of friendship and equality. He had directed them to aim also at good deeds, to extend hospitality to others, to avoid dominating others or inflicting any kind of harm on others, and especially to avoid shedding blood. Following his father as leader, Mazdak proclaimed that he had been sent by God to preach that all men are born equal. He proclaimed that no one had a right to possess more than did another. He claimed that he was reforming and purifying Zoroastrianism. He quoted from the Avesta, claiming that God had placed the means of subsistence on earth so that people could divide them equally. He claimed that people had strayed from this as some had sought domination over others, as the strong had defeated the weak and had taken exclusive possession over property and the means of production. He described the world as having been turned from righteousness by five demons: Envy, Wrath, Vengeance, Need and Greed.

Mazdak called for distributing to the community the contents of the granaries belonging to the nobles. He proclaimed that it was necessary to take from the rich and give to the poor so that all would be equal in wealth. He proclaimed that whoever has an excess of property or women has no right to them. Believing that other people's property was equally theirs, Mazdak's followers began plundering the homes and harems of the rich. Mazdak's uprising appeared strong enough that the new Sassanid king, Kavad I, feared it, and for the sake of staying in power he sided with the uprising.

Kavad approved Mazdak's call for ending the custom of intermarriage among the aristocracy and, instead, for marriage between aristocratic women and peasant men. The Nobles, outraged over Kavad's siding with the revolution, captured and imprisoned him. They put his brother upon the throne, and, after three years in captivity, Kavad escaped and fled east to the Hephthalites. The Hephthalites were eager to have a ruler in Persia dependent upon them, and they provided Kavad with an army. In 499, Kavad marched to the Sassanid capital, Ctesiphon, and re-established his rule. The nobles fled to their estates, and the century ended with rebellion still triumphant. But communism at the end of antiquity in Persia was not to remain in power as long as it would in the 20th century. The revolution failed to crush the Zoroastrian priesthood and the nobles, and eventually Khavad and his son turned against the revolution. In 528, leading followers of Mazdak were massacred, and in following years other followers were persecuted and driven underground.

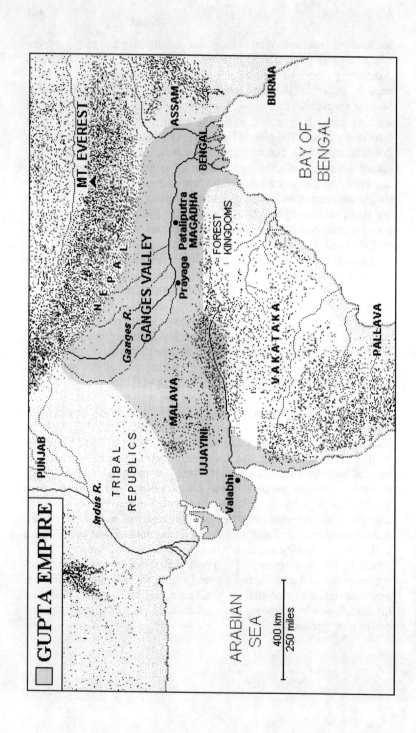

INDIA: A GOLDEN AGE COMES AND GOES

India's so-called Dark Age – from 185 BC to AD 300 – had not been hardly dark regarding trade. Disintegration of the Mauryan Empire and the invasions had been mitigated by a continued trade in which the Indians sold more to the Roman Empire than it bought, with Roman coins piling up in India. The Kushan invaders had been absorbed by India, Kushan kings adopting the manners and language of the Indians and intermarrying with Indian royal families. The southern kingdom of Andhra had extended its rule over Magadha and the Ganges Valley in the north, creating a new bridge between the north and the south, but this came to an end as Andhra and two other southern kingdoms weakened themselves by warring against one another. By the early 300s, power was returning to the Magadha region, and India was entering what would be called its classical age.

A Magadha raja named Chandra Gupta – who was unrelated to the Chandragupta who had ruled six centuries before – controlled rich veins of iron from the nearby Barabara Hills. He married a princess from the neighboring kingdom of Licchavi, and with this marriage he gained a hold over the flow of northern India's commerce on the Ganges – the major flow of north Indian commerce. Chandra Gupta extended his rule westward to Prayaga in north-central India.

Ten years into his rule, Chandra Gupta lay dying, and he told his son, Samudra, to rule the whole world. Samudra Gupta tried. His forty years of rule would be described as a vast military campaign. Samudra Gupta waged war along the Ganges plain, overwhelming nine kings and incorporating their subjects and lands into the Gupta Empire. He absorbed Bengal, and kingdoms in Nepal and Assam paid him tribute. He expanded his empire westward, conquering Malava and the Saka kingdom of Ujjayini. He gave various tribal states that he overran autonomy under his protection. He raided Pallava and humbled eleven kings in southern India. He made a vassal of the king of the island of Lanka at the southern tip of the sub-continent, and he compelled five kings on the outskirts of his empire to pay him tribute. The powerful kingdom of Vakataka in central India, however, he preferred to leave independent and friendly.

Around 380, Samudra Gupta was succeeded by his son Chandra Gupta II, and Chandra Gupta II extended Gupta rule to India's west coast, where new ports were helping India's trade with countries farther west. And his rule influenced local powers beyond the Indus River and north to Kashmir. While Rome was being overrun and the western half of the Roman Empire was disintegrating, Gupta rule was at the apex of its grandeur, prospering in agriculture, crafts and trade. Unlike the

Mauryas, who controlled trade and industry, the Guptas let people free to pursue wealth and business, and the Gupta era was more prosperous than was the Maurya era.

Like the Cynics during Rome's golden age, a few ascetics entertained pessimistic views of life, and they maintained the view that asceticism would benefit all of humanity. But many Indians were pursuing pleasure and enjoying life. In the cities were wealthy and middle class people who enjoyed their gardens, music, dancing, plays and various other entertainments. They enjoyed a daily bath, artistic and social activities and a variety of food, including rice, bread, fish, milk, a large number of fruits and juices. And despite religious prohibitions, the Indians – especially the aristocrats – drank wine and stronger alcoholic beverages.

Greater wealth accrued to those who already had wealth, and the middle class prospered. Big estates grew with the help of dependent labor and slave labor. The poor stayed poor, but apparently there was little dire want. The caste system still existed. So too did the inferior status of women. But charities abounded. The Gupta kings were autocrats who liked to think of themselves as servants to all their subjects. Hospitals offered care free of charge to everyone, rich and poor. There were rest houses for travelers along India's highways, and the capital possessed an excellent, free hospital created by the charity of its wealthier citizenry.

Although the Guptas were more organized in their administrations, with the increase in prosperity had come a greater liberality. The cruel punishments of Mauryan times had been abolished. People no longer had to register with government authorities or carry a passport when traveling within the empire. Government operated without the system of espionage often practiced by Roman emperors and by the Mauryan rulers. Law breaking was punished without death sentences – mainly by fines. Punishments such as having one's hand cut off were applied only against obstinate, professional criminals.

Among civilians, the avoidance of killing that had been a part of Buddhism and Jainism was widely observed. Across India most people had become vegetarians, except for fish which was widely consumed in Bengal and places to its south. And unlike parts of the Roman Empire, a traveler in India had little reason to fear robbery. A visitor from China, Fa-hien, traveled about in India for eleven years, and he recorded that in India he was never molested or robbed.

Hinduism Celebrates the Good Life and Prevails against Its Rivals
   With the good times came an intellectual revival. Literature flourished, and Indians exercised their proficiency in art, architecture and

mathematics. It was now that India's greatest poet and dramatist, Kalidasa, lived. He and other writers acquired fame expressing the values of the rich and powerful. Hinduism also benefited. For seven centuries before the Guptas, Buddhism had been the dominant religion in India. But helped by the support of the Guptas, including royal subsidies, Hinduism regained its supremacy. This came too with the popularity of works such as the Ramayana and the Mahabarata. And the popularity of Hinduism was aided by Hindu writers who had begun making their faith more appealing by presenting the contents of their Vedic literature with concise statements of principle.

While Christianity was becoming concerned with heresy and morosely concerned with sin, Hinduism was tolerant and happy. It had acquired more rituals. It drew more from astronomy. It appealed to common people by offering them a program of reactions to various conditions in life. Rather than see suffering as endemic to life on earth, many Hindus had come to believe suffering was the result of one's own foolishness and mistakes, or the misdeeds of others.

The good Hindu tried to live by good deeds, which was thought to help the believer achieve the higher reincarnations, with nirvana as the ultimate goal. Hindus believed that the best way to advance one's soul up the ladder of higher status was to accept and not complain about one's caste status. What mattered for a good Hindu was to eat and drink correctly, marry the right person and otherwise act in accordance with the law of one's position in life. A good father was seen as obliged to keep himself and his wife happy, to have as many children as possible, and to accumulate what wealth he could. He was seen as obliged to give an appropriate fraction of his wealth to the priests during each of the many rituals and religious holidays that he was supposed to celebrate.

Hinduism absorbed some aspects of Buddhism and Jainism that had appeal. In Hinduism, the Buddha became one of the ten incarnations of Vishnu. And Buddhism and Jainism, born from concern over human suffering, were losing their previous fervor. Hinduism was more suited to living well, without the restraints demanded from Buddhism and Jainism. Hinduism offered colorful deities, rites and sacred formulas for birth, death, marriage and illness that Buddhism did not, and Buddhist holy places began to suffer from neglect.

Some Hindus practiced yoga. Many bathed happily in sacred rivers and made joyful pilgrimages to sacred places that they believed were the sanctuaries of gods. They sought out ascetics who performed feats that demonstrated what was believed to be inordinate spiritual accomplishment. And many Hindus fasted to help unite their soul with the supreme soul of the god Brahma, a unity that they believed helped one achieve nirvana in some future existence.

Amid Hinduism's diverse trends, some gods of the Vedas continued to fade. The gods Vishnu, Brahma and Shiva remained dominant, each with its own devotees. Brahma was seen as The Creator, and He was regarded by some as superior to the others, but worship of Brahma was also on the decline. Brahma was more of an abstraction, more of a force rather than the kind of personal god that Vishnu and Shiva were.

Misfortune in Worldly Matters

Chandra Gupta II died in 415 and was succeeded by his son, Kumara Gupta, who maintained India's peace and prosperity. During Kumara Gupta's forty-year reign, the Gupta Empire did not grow in size, but it also remained undiminished. Then, as was the Roman Empire around the same time, India suffered more invasions. The same Hephthalites who were to plague the Persians crossed the Hindu Kush and occupied a portion of western India, and their power threatened the ability of the Gupta empire to hold together. Kumara Gupta's son, the crown prince, Skanda Gupta, was able to drive the invaders back: into the Sassanian Empire, where the Hephthalites were to bring disaster and death of the Sassanid king, Firuz, and his army.

In India, women and children sang praises to Skanda Gupta. Skanda Gupta succeeded his father in 455. Then the Hephthalites returned, and he spent much of his reign of twenty-five years combating them, which drained his treasury and weakened his empire. After Skanda Gupta's death in 467, India enjoyed peace and some prosperity, but, after a century and a half, the cycle of rise and disintegration of empire turned again to disintegration. Contributing to this was another common source of trouble: dissention within the royal family. Benefiting from this dissention, governors of provinces and feudal chieftains revolted against Gupta rule. For awhile, the Gupta Empire had two centers: at Valabhi on the western coast and at Pataliputra. Seeing weakness, the Hephthalites invaded India again – in greater number. Just before AD 500, the Hephthalites took control of the Punjab. After 515, they absorbed the Kashmir, and they advanced into the Ganges Valley, the heart of India, raping, burning, massacring, blotting out entire cities and reducing fine buildings to rubble. Provinces and feudal territories declared their independence, and the whole of north India became divided into numerous independent states, and divided again into numerous, independent, petty kingdoms. And, with this disintegration and rise in power of petty kingdoms, India was again torn by numerous small wars between local rulers.

CHAPTER 28

CHINA AND BUDDHISM,
KOREA AND JAPAN

CHINA, CONFUCIANISM, TAOISM
AND THE ARRIVAL OF BUDDHISM

With the breakup of Han rule around AD 200, power in China again passed to local warlords, and, as they did centuries before, local lords warred against each other. The Hsiung-nu took advantage of the division and weakness and made continuous hit and run forays into China's heavily populated northern regions. As had been happening in Europe, the breakdown of government encouraged peasants to give up their independence and gather for protection into great estates that had armed men, or armies. Here the peasants became serfs but were free from government taxation, government labor drafts and deportations.

The chaos was accompanied by a decline in Confucianism and a rise in rival worldviews. Confucianism had been the ideology of China's gentry and aristocracy. It had dominated education and the administration of the empire, but many of China's elite had begun to view Confucianism, with its advocacy of virtue by rulers and loyalty to rulers of virtue, as irrelevant, as failing to meet the challenges of a disorganized world. New rulers were looking for an ideology to replace Confucianism as support for their attempt at order. Schools of thought that had been banned were revived. And just as Christianity was offering relief to Romans, two of Confucianism's rivals, Taoism and a new arrival to China – Buddhism – offered relief to the Chinese.

According to legend, Buddhism entered China in a dream by emperor Ming-ti in AD 65. A rival theory holds that Buddhism had joined Hinduism in spreading eastward with trade from India, Buddhism arriving across the inland trade route through central Asia during the first century AD. The royal court welcomed Buddhism to China, but before the chaos that came at the end of Han rule, Buddhism in China remained isolated, adhered to only by Indian merchants – men who gave money and land for Buddhist temples and who used Buddhist monasteries as banks and warehouses.

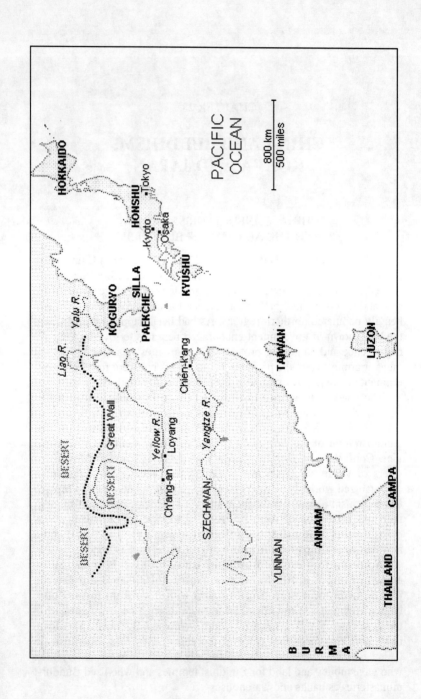

Buddhism's temples and elaborate rituals were impressive, and the first Chinese to convert were those who had become tenants on Buddhist temple lands. Buddhist teachings were translated into Chinese. Then, with the breakdown of order, conversions to Buddhism spread among Chinese masses. They had little understanding of the details of Buddhist doctrine, but they found consolation in what Buddhism offered. Buddhism was a warmer message than Confucianism: a message of salvation through moderation or abstinence and a message of pity for all creatures. Both the Hinayana and the Mahayana schools arrived in China, but it was the Mahayana branch of Buddhism, with its easier salvation and helpful gods, that would dominate.

Romance of the Three Kingdoms

Warlords absorbed various territories, reducing the warlord kingdoms to three. Wei in the north, Shu in the southeast (around Szechwan and Yunnan), and Wu in the southwest (from the Yangtze River to Annam). A famous fourteenth century novel, The Romance of the Three Kingdoms, described the times that followed as a period of romance, heroism and chivalry. But it was hardly romantic for those who lived it. The wars continued. Wei was the strongest militarily, a strength bolstered by the kingdom's economy and water transport. Shu was a more sparsely populated region, an area of mostly forest, and with many people who were non-Chinese, and, in 263, Wei overwhelmed and absorbed Shu. Then Wei was disturbed from within: one of its generals overthrew Wei's ruling family. He began a dynasty of his own, and thirty-six years later, in 280, his offspring, Chin Wu-ti, overpowered and annexed the kingdom of Wu. China was now nominally united, and Chin Wu-ti extended his power northward to central Korea and southward into Annam. The cycle between unity and disintegration now swung to unity.

Forays against China by the Hsiung-nu and other tribal people had for the time being ended, and the policy of settling tribal people within China was resumed. There was hope for peace, unity and prosperity, and, as early as 280, Chin Wu-ti began a program of disarmament. Troops were discharged, and metal weapons of value were melted down for coin. But Chin Wu-ti's disarmament proved of little benefit to China. Some discharged soldiers kept their weapons. Soldiers traded their weapons to the Hsiung-nu in exchange for land. And Princes in outlying areas did not disarm or disband their militias.

Chin Wu-ti was attempting a return to the greatest period of Han rule, when peace brought China prosperity and when there was strong central authority. He initiated reforms aimed at curbing the power of great families. But these failed. At his death in 290, China's great landlords were still powers with private armies.

With Chin Wu-ti's death came the weakness that occasionally besets monarchies: Chin Wu-ti's son and successor, Chin Hui-ti, was mentally deficient, and Chin Hui-ti's wife, Queen Chia, ruled in his place. She too lacked intelligence, and she was fearful. She began arresting and executing anyone she suspected of being a threat. This included a rival faction within the royal family. Open warfare erupted. Several dukes and thousands of others were murdered. Queen Chia failed to kill all her opponents, and in AD 300, a prince named Lun led a coup that left the Emperor, Chin Hui-ti, Empress Chia and many others dead. Lun made himself emperor, and he, in turn, was killed by another prince, Lu'i, who in 302 was killed by another prince, Ch'ang-sha, who in 303, was killed by a prince called Tung-hai. In 306, two more princes were to fall. Then came something more terrible: drought and famine. The central government had grown weak. The cycle of unity and disintegration swung back to disintegration. Military power again became divided among local rulers in the provinces, and tribal peoples on the periphery of China saw opportunity in China's weakness.

Hsiung-nu in the North, and a Migration and New Order in the South

In 308, Hsiung-nu nobles along China's northern border had a meeting, and they chose one among them as their leader: Liu Yüan. He had acquired Chinese culture and claimed to be related to China's Han royalty through marriage. And Liu Yüan claimed the heritage of his ancestors: Han family rule. But it was Liu Yüan's son, Liu Ts'ung, who acted on his father's claim. Liu Ts'ung had been brought up at the royal court in Loyang. He had become a scholar, but he still had the vigor and strength of a Hsiung-nu warrior. In 311, his army, supported by Chinese rebels, arrived at Loyang without warning. Liu Ts'ung's army sacked the city and murdered more than thirty thousand people, including the Chin crown prince. Loyang's royal palace was burned. Imperial tombs were looted. The Chin emperor was carried off and forced to become a cupbearer, until Liu Ts'ung had him executed.

In 316, Hsiung-nu cavalry passed through the city of Ch'ang-an, and amid the ruins that they left in Ch'ang-an another prince of the Chin family declared himself emperor. But his rule cut was short. Before the year was over, the Hsiung-nu returned, and the city surrendered. The newly declared Chin emperor was made to serve Liu Ts'ung as had his predecessor, by rinsing cups during feasts, until he too was executed.

The remainder of the royal Chin family sought refuge south of the Yangtze River. There, in 317, in the city of Chien-k'ang (modern Nanking), a military commander who was a member of the royal family proclaimed the renewal of Chin rule and declared himself emperor, calling himself Chin Yüan-ti. Meanwhile, the Hsiung-nu invasions into northern China inspired millions of people to migrate to the south. Most of the north's Confucian scholars were among them. With them were Taoist communities under the leadership of Taoist masters. Entire clans of northern Chinese migrated south, as did sixty or seventy percent of northern China's gentry. They brought with them what wealth they could, and they believed that their stay in the south would be temporary.

The arrival of great numbers from the north created resentment among the southerners, and southerners refused to cooperate with the new government at Chien-k'ang. But Chin Yüan-ti was patient. His regime avoided interfering with the privileges of the south's elite families, and eventually Chin Yüan-ti's regime persuaded this elite to co-operate with it. The regime at Chien-k'ang also benefited from the wealth, experience and technical skills of the refugees. It set up administrative provinces for their settlement. And in the south, one of China's most advanced periods of culture began – in art, literature, philosophy and religion.

The government at Chien-k'ang did not interfere with commerce, and in the south an unprecedented prosperity arose. For wealthy aristocrats an easily life emerged. Gentlemen remained elegantly inactive – and are said to have grown weak in their limbs unlike the warrior aristocrats before them. With Confucianism having been discredited, some of them acquired an interest in Mo-tzu. Some were interested in Legalist ideas, with its belief in tough policies for establishing law and order. And some among them became interested in the legendary founders of Taoism: Lao-tzu and Chuang-tzu.

Buddhism and Chaos in the North

The so-called barbarian rulers in the north were destined to adopt civilized ways. Some Hsiung-nu chieftains realized that it was more profitable to tax farmers than to kill them. Lacking traditions in governing agricultural regions, they needed the advice and help of their Chinese subjects. They were suspicious of the Confucianist scholars who remained, seeing them as likely supporters of previous Chinese rulers. The Hsiung-nu chieftains found trustworthy men among Buddhist and Taoist intellectuals, and they were inclined to trust Buddhist monks because they were unmarried, without loyalty to a family or clan and, therefore, more dependent upon the chieftain for favors. Buddhism became the favored religion among the chieftains, and Buddhism was becoming the dominant faith in the north.

The dominant Hsiung-nu chieftain in northern China, Liu Ts'ung, died, and his family was overthrown by one of his former lieutenants, Shih Liu Shi – who was illiterate but enjoyed having Chinese classics explained to him. Shih Liu Shi was succeeded by a nephew, Shih Hu, called Shih the Tiger, who ruled from 334 to 349. Shih Hu was unrestrained by scruples and delighted in what he could acquire. He drafted 260,000 farmers to build a palace for himself, and he is reported to have kept a harem of around 50,000 women. According to legend he served beautiful women for cannibalistic dinners. His son tried to assassinate him, and he had his son executed. Then, like some others who filled themselves with licentiousness, Shih Hu had a religious conversion. A Buddhist saint is said to have reformed him. But Shih Hu was remembered with revulsion. When he died, one of his generals ordered all gates of the royal city closed, and he had all those related to Shih Hu slaughtered.

After Shih Hu came Hsiung-nu rulers more benevolent than he, such as Fu-chien, a pious Buddhist and humane administrator, who ruled the entire north from 357 to 385. The good works of Fu-chien were undone as parts of the north were overrun by other tribes. In the first hundred years of non-Chinese rule in northern China, five tribes established sixteen different kingdoms, with conquering chieftains killing and burning, sometimes for the fun of it. Chieftains established their own feudal estates, and whole tribes of non-Chinese were installed in areas that had been depopulated.

Buddhist Influences and Adaptations

Buddhism spread though all classes of Chinese, influencing art, thought and daily customs – an impact that compares with that of Christianity in the Roman Empire. Tea, which had been used mostly by Buddhists, became China's national drink, and Buddhists introduced the Chinese to the wearing of cotton. Buddhism's great temples influenced Chinese architecture – a counter to Confucianism's condemnation of complex buildings as an extravagance. Buddhism introduced logic into Chinese essay writing – sound logic and good organization having been absent in Chinese writings. And in the place of the contempt with which Confucianists had held for the writing of stories and novels, Buddhism gave this kind of writing a new prestige.

Buddhism in the north remained closely connected to Central Asia and India across the Silk Road. Buddhism was a conduit for Hellenistic culture passing through Central Asia. From Buddhism, many Chinese gathered that China was not the only civilized country in the world. They learned respect for India and felt compelled to re-examine the theory that the Chinese emperor was the son of heaven and enthroned at the center of the world.

Buddhism in China was, in turn, influenced by pre-Buddhist Chinese culture. The Chinese interpreted Buddhist doctrine in terms familiar to them. In translating Buddhism into Chinese, Taoist words were used. And through mistranslation, Chinese Buddhism acquired a belief that was foreign to Buddhism elsewhere: belief in a soul that was as an imperishable part of one's humanity. And Buddhist art in China depicted the life of the Buddha in a Chinese context, just as Italian painters were to paint Christian saints in the dress of renaissance Italy.

Buddhism in China emphasized charity and good works, including working for one's own salvation by helping others – which contrasted with Taoism's egocentricities. And Buddhism was unique in China in linking ethics in this world with the bliss of the next world. Buddhism offered the Chinese more than did the ancestor worship of the aristocracy – which failed those who were going to die without a son to look after their spirit. For those Chinese lacking a family, Buddhism provided a substitute family. It offered community and egalitarianism. Some Chinese were attracted by the doctrine that those who exploited or treated people unjustly would in their next reincarnation be born into poor circumstances or into an inferior rank and suffer punishment for their misdeeds. And some Chinese found comfort in the doctrine that in their next life they might be born into a higher rank and a happier life.

Buddhism's moral teachings attracted some from the upper classes who had been Confucian – some of whom found a different meaning in Buddhism's reincarnation than did the poor: they believed that those who suffered from a low station in life did so because of misdeeds in their former life. Buddhism's monasteries were in conflict with Confucian ideals of the family, but the monasteries fit with the old Chinese ideal of the retired scholar, and the monasteries attracted gentry who had been unable to acquire government positions. Buddhist monasteries offered Chinese writers a refuge. And monasteries grew as centers of learning and culture.

In metaphysics, Buddhist ideas intermingled with old Chinese ideas. From Buddhist thinkers in China, ideas went westward to India. And from India to China went a new school of thought, the Three Treatise school of Buddhism, introduced by a half-Indian missionary monk named Kumarajiva, who worked and taught in Ch'ang-an in 401-02. The sect that adhered to this new school of Buddhist thought was called the Emptiness sect, holding as it did that ultimately people should interpret the world as basically empty, that the world of sight and sound changes but that the world of emptiness never does. Like the scholastic theologians in the West during the early Middle Ages, the

Emptiness sect tried to reason in absolutes and to split metaphysical hairs. And they split into more sects, which became known as the "Six Schools and Seven Sects," each with a different interpretation of emptiness.

Buddhism's splitting into sects was facilitated by the absence of a religious council or papacy. Each Buddhist master could interpret writings as he wished. And during the 300s, from within China's Mahayana Buddhism came what was called the *Pure Land* movement. Its leader was a Buddhist scholar named Hui-yuan, who meditated on *Amitabha*: the Buddha of Infinite Light. Pure Land Buddhism described life as torment, and it claimed that to escape this torment one did not need bookish learning or the grasp of obtuse doctrine or knowledge: one only had to avoid bad deeds and prove one's devotion by chanting Amitabha's name sincerely – the more often the better the chance of achieving nirvana. It claimed that at death one would be reborn into paradise. The "Pure Land," it held, was where Amitabha dwelled and where immortals lived in an atmosphere of eternal bliss, and there rivers were pure and scented.

Another branch of Buddhism developed in China called Ch'uan – to be called Zen in Japan. Like the devotional movements in India and Pure Land Buddhism, Ch'uan Buddhism offered people an attachment to divinity without years of arduous intellectual exercise: it offered sudden enlightenment. Ch'uan Buddhism saw reality as nothing more than the immediate present. Ch'uan monks sought salvation through mystical inspirations rather than reading and meditation. And Ch'uan monks believed in supporting themselves by humble, menial work.

Changes in Taoism and Confucianism

Taoists were devoted to nature while Buddhists believed in withdrawal from nature. Despite their belief in serene unconcern, the Taoists felt challenged by Buddhism, and they scurried for more doctrine to compliment what had become a religion. Both Buddhists and Taoists were denying value in the world of appearances, and both were appealing to the interest in the mystical among the Chinese. Both advocated personal salvation and protection from powerful gods.

While Buddhism was offering nirvana or eternal happiness in a western paradise, Taoism began promising the achievement of immortality through magic potions. Some Taoists created Buddhist-like monasteries, and some adopted Buddhism's burning of incense. Buddhism and Taoism acquired common communal festivals. Local Taoist saints blended with Buddhist saints. Books by Taoists revealed Buddhist influence, such as dialogues between a teacher and his disciples, not known in China before Buddhism's arrival.

Taoists saw Buddhism as an inferior version of their philosophy, while others believed the rumor that Buddhism had been created by Taoism's founder, Lao-tzu. This story held that after disappearing on a long journey into India, Lao-tzu had taught Taoism to the Buddha – a story disliked by Taoists who objected to Buddhism and feared that Buddhism might obscure Taoism's identity.

Some Confucianists repudiated loyalty to family and state, and some were attracted by Taoist spirituality. Some adopted the Taoist belief in permanence behind the visible world of change – believed also by Plato. Some Confucianists adopted the view that the world of change was sustained by one impersonal, unlimited and undiversified force. They saw Confucius as having recognized this permanence and as having kept silent about it because he held to the Taoist belief that such mysteries could not be expressed in words.

Taoism mixed with Buddhism and Confucianism in what was called Dark Learning (Hsuan Hsueh). Dark Learning involved "pure conversation" – philosophical discussions that had become a pastime for gentlemen in southern China. Rather than revelation through argumentation, the goal of these conversations was the maintenance of Taoism's serenity, with pleasant voices and poetic flashes of insight.

Purified conversations and their participants aside, Taoists continued to believe that various gods dwelled here and there – on mountains and in rivers – and they still believed that these gods had to be appeased with a proper sacrifice. Taoist priests held that they alone knew the appropriate rituals. But Taoism still had no fixed, elaborate theology as did Christianity. There was talk among the Taoists of the world having been created by an interaction of two opposites, Yin and Yang, and talk that through observation of Yin and Yang they could foretell the future. Taoism still favored being "natural," in other words behaving on impulse, the Taoists seeing impulse as the expression of one's true feelings. Taoism still advocated honesty and being true to oneself as cardinal principles. It still held that everything would be done when nothing was done. Taoists still sought a blissful detachment and peace and quiet, which they believed would be achieved when everyone gave up worldly endeavors and trying to control others. The Taoists focused on their well being: on being healed spiritually and physically. Taoism paralleled Epicureanism in its belief in pleasure and the avoidance of pain. The Taoists saw life as short, "like the morning dew," soon to disappear and to be enjoyed before it evaporated.

By now, Taoists spoke of Lao-tzu as never having died, of his having disappeared into the mountainous west. And like Christianity, Taoism offered personal immortality, personal comfort, and a refuge from fear of death. Taoist priests performed services that gave assurances to their followers that one who had died had acquired a place in the heavenly kingdom of spiritual bliss.

China in the 400s

In 417, an army from the south, led by a former cobbler named Liu Yü, went north and conquered Loyang, Ch'ang-an and surrounding territory. But after Liu Yü returned to the south, the subordinates he left behind in the north quarreled among themselves, and Hsiung-nu chieftains again overran the area. In the south, meanwhile, Liu Yü was able to force the Chin emperor to abdicate in his favor, and Liu Yü began what was to be known as the Liu Sung dynasty.

Liu Yü's successor, the emperor Wen (424-53) adopted Buddhism, believing that it would help his subjects become content, help them acquire good manners and discourage rebellion. In the North, meanwhile, Buddhist monasteries had become economically powerful landowning enterprises with hereditary serfs, and these monasteries were winning tax exemptions. This annoyed many in the north and caused some people to turn against Buddhism. And a few remaining orthodox Confucianists continued to find fault with Buddhists for leaving their families for the monastery and for a lack of sense of duty to society.

Conflict arose too between Buddhism and traditional Chinese attitudes toward sex. The Chinese had accepted sexuality as a natural part of life and necessary in preserving the family, while Buddhism's attitude toward sexuality was more negative. Buddhist men and women were segregated at their meetings, and the Buddhists saw licentiousness in the Taoist meetings of men and women together and accused them of having orgies.

In 444, Taoists in the north inspired a movement against Buddhism on the grounds that Buddhism was an alien creed. In 446, a ruler in the north issued an edict against the Buddhists. A few monks were forced to return to family life, and some monasteries were attacked and destroyed. Then in the early 450s the ruler in the north gave favor again to Buddhism.

Buddhism in the south was enjoying the patronage of its Buddhist emperor: Liang Wu-ti. But Buddhism proved no deterrent to strife and chaos. In 453, the third emperor in the line of the Liu Sung dynasty was assassinated by one of his sons, who, in 455, was murdered by his brother. This brother became emperor, and he guarded against his own assassination by massacring other princes in his extended family. He ruled until 465, when he was succeeded by a sixteen-year-old, who was assassinated six month later. The murdered boy was succeeded by his uncle, who ruled from 465 to 472 and became known as "the Pig" because of his weight. The "Pig" had all his brothers and nephews executed. He bequeathed his rule to his favorite son, who took power at the age of ten, and the boy, in the family's tradition, began taking lives. And his murdering led to his own assassination when he was fifteen, in the year of 477.

The royal Liu family was both decimated and discredited, and in 479 a state official deposed the Liu family and founded a new dynasty, called Ch'i, which occupied the throne at Chien-k'ang until 502. Then the Ch'i dynasty also became corrupted by power, and it engaged in more family assassinations.

In the north, meanwhile, war among Hsiung-nu chieftains was spreading devastation. Ch'ang-an had only about a hundred households left and was said to be the haunt of wolves and tigers. Finally, in 471, one among the chieftains emerged as ruler of all the north. He called himself Wei Hsiao-wen-ti. Under his rule taxes remained light, land was equitably distributed, disputes were mediated, people were punished for petty offenses and the sick, orphaned and destitute were taken care of. Wei Hsiao-wen-ti encouraged the integration of his people with the local Chinese, including the taking of Chinese wives. The new ruler also ordered the wearing of Chinese clothes. He made Chinese the official language, and he made it mandatory that everyone under the age of thirty learn it. He ordered all whose family names were not Chinese to adopt a Chinese family name, and he adopted the Chinese name Yüan. And because Confucianism had been the philosophy of China's elite and had been used as a system of court ritual, he made the study of Confucius a requirement for the educated.

The policy initiated by the new ruler in the north was followed by those who ruled after him. Interracial marriages were common. The offspring of these marriages were inclined to identify themselves as Chinese, and, after a few generations, those with nomadic forefathers would become undistinguishable from others, adding to the Chinese as a mix of peoples.

CONFUCIANISM AND BUDDHISM TO KOREA

Various kingdoms in Korea had warred with each other and had consolidated through conquest to three: Koguryo, in the northern half of Korea, extending north of the Yalu River; Paekche in the southwestern quarter of the Korean peninsula; and Silla in the southeastern quarter. These three remained aristocratic states. Writing had developed in Korea that used Chinese characters for Korean words. Each of the three kingdoms had a Chinese bureaucratic system of government, and with China's bureaucratic system had come Confucianism. All three kingdoms referred to Confucian values in helping to order and dominance by the aristocracy. Koguryo had a National Confucian Academy that made reading and speaking Chinese and citing the Confucian classics a part of an upper class education.

Alongside the new Confucianism, many in Korea maintained their old faith. Like others, the Koreans had been animists: seeing nature as working by the magic of a variety of spirits, one for each aspect of nature, and seeing all things as animate. They too believed in asking the gods for protection for their family or community. The Koreans saw the sun as the most awesome and powerful of spirits. They believed too in a mountain spirit. And they had shamans – priests who were thought to have a greater communication than others with spirits.

Confucianism and animism were joined by Buddhism. In 372, a monk brought Mahayana Buddhism to Koguryo, and the king of Koguryo welcomed Buddhism and patronized it. In 384, another Buddhist monk arrived in Paekche, and the royal family there welcomed Buddhism. Korea's kings adopted Buddhism as a state religion, as a vehicle for praying for the well-being of their kingdom, and Korea's aristocrats welcomed it and left the shamans to those they considered unsophisticated. Buddhists in Korea prayed for their own well-being, including or asking for recovery from illness and asking for the conception of children. And wars between the Korean states would now be fought not only for their kings but also for the *Way of the Buddha*, with monks and other soldiers, under the banner of Buddhism, exhorted to fight bravely for their kingdom.

CIVILIZATION DEVELOPS IN JAPAN

The islands of Japan are farther from the continent of Asia than England is from the continent of Europe, which gave people on the islands of Japan a little more protection from invasion than had the Britons around the time of the collapse of the western half of the Roman Empire. Being islands made a difference for Japan, but Japan was also very much affected by its nearness to the Asian mainland.

Living in Japan for millennia before 300 BC were people whom archaeologists call Jomon, named after their culture. They had stone tools, baskets, cups, bowls, vases and decorated pottery. They survived by hunting deer and boar, gathering nuts and, using dugout canoes, by fishing for porpoises, trout or salmon, and they engaged in a light cultivation of plants. Apparently they were a diverse people, and sparse in population, located across Japan in small family groups or clans, And they lived in small pit-houses with thatch roofs supported by timber – houses on slightly elevated ground and clustered into small, communal villages.

Archeologists have uncovered evidence of a sudden growth of a new culture in Japan's major southern island, Kyushu, sometime in the 200s BC – a culture with iron and bronze, tool making and a new wet-rice agriculture. Some have speculated that this developed among Jomon people. Others propose that the new culture – called Yayoi – came with migrants and that the migrants and Jomon people probably blended. A naval expedition sent in 213 BC by the founding emperor of China, Shih Huang-ti, to search for the isles of the immortals, has been mentioned as possibly bringing the new culture to Japan – the leader of this expedition having returned after nine years and having described what can pass for Japan. But this is widely dismissed by anthropologists. More likely, it is believed, the rise of a new culture in Japan came with a migration of people from Korea to the island of Kyushu – the shortest distance between the Asian mainland and Japan.

The Yayoi-Japanese raised horses and cows, hunted and fished, and grew rice where it was possible. Japan's first agricultural communities arose, with homes closely grouped, with dirt floors and wooden posts holding up thatched roofs. The Yayoi-Japanese expanded against native people, and around the time of Jesus they reached the Kanto plain, where Tokyo would one day be. From their contacts with the Asian mainland, the Yayoi-Japanese acquired the potter's wheel, and they improved their kiln techniques. From China and Korea they imported coins, bronze mirrors, bracelets and beads, iron and bronze knives and swords. The Yayoi-Japanese began smelting their own iron, making swords, saws, nails and clamps.

With a greater supply of food, the population of the Yayoi-Japanese grew rapidly. They were perhaps healthier than other peoples in Japan, and they continued to spread and to displace native peoples. By AD 100, the Yayoi-Japanese had pushed into northeastern Honshu. They pushed against and absorbed those called Ainu – a people of Jomon culture – who are believed to have lived more in the northern half of what is now Japan, a people with blue eyes and lighter skins, and with more hair than most Asians, perhaps accounting for the greater hairiness of today's Japanese.

Soon a highway system facilitated movement of people and goods, and those of Yayoi-Japanese decent developed a fleet of ships that moved goods up and down Japan's coast and between Japan and the Asian continent. Closer ties between Japan and Korea developed. Literate Koreans and Koreans with other skills were in great demand in Japan, and such Koreans who came to Japan were given noble rank. Nearing AD 300, Japanese were using iron imported from Korea, the as far north at the Kanto plain they were using iron plows, hoes, sickles, axes, adzes and chisels.

A Chinese report called the *Wei chih* (Wei records), dated AD 297, described the Japanese as divided into numerous states, or kingdoms, and as having class divisions. The Chinese described Japanese men who were most wealthy as having four or five wives, and they described some Japanese households as having slaves. They described people of lower rank as getting off a road and kneeling to show respect to people of higher rank, and people paying taxes to their local lords. The Chinese described some common folk as having become vassals, and a new class of warriors as having appeared, with horses and military technology imported from the continent. According to the Chinese, the Japanese had no theft. Members of families were described as responsible for one another, and the violations of law or custom by one member of a family brought retribution against the entire family – similar to other peoples organized by clan. In other than light violations of law, the entire household of the offender and his relatives were exterminated – a strong incentive to refrain from crime. And according to the Chinese, the Japanese treated women equally at community meetings, and clans were sometimes headed by a woman.

One such clan leader was an unmarried woman called Queen Himiko, who according to the Chinese, controlled of a large part of Kyushu between AD 183 and 248. *Himiko* meant Sun Daughter, reflecting the belief among the Japanese that their chiefs were descendant from a sun god.

The Legends of Jimmu, Queen Jingo and Hachiman

Like others, the Japanese had legends about their ancestral rulers. They believed their earliest ruler was Jimmu, who was supposed to have reigned from 660 to 582 BC and was believed to be descendant of a sun goddess. Japanese legend describes a ruling regent in the third century AD as Queen Jingo, and it describes Queen Jingo as a direct descendant of Jimmu and the Sun Goddess. It describes Queen Jingo and her son, Ojin, sending a military expedition to Korea. Gentle winds and god-like fish are said to have helped their armada cross the sea to Korea, so that no oars had to be used. Then, according to legend, a vast tidal wave carried the fleet inland, into the kingdom of Silla. The surprised and terrified Koreans are said to have surrendered at once and to have promised to pay homage and tribute to Queen Jingo until the sun rose in the west, rivers flowed backwards and stones turned into stars.

After Queen Jingo's death, Ojin is said to have ruled alone until the year 310, when he was 110 years-old. After his death he was deified as

Hachiman, the God of War. In Tokyo, Kyoto and Kamakura (just south of Tokyo), beautiful temples were built in Ojin's honor, and Japan's warriors into modern times would pray to Ojin as they embarked upon battle.

Shinto and the Creation

Not having been oppressed by others, the religion of the Japanese had no martyrs. Nor did it have proselytizing teachers or reason for proselytizing teachers. Like others, they had been animists, seeing the same magic and variety of spirits in nature as other peoples. They too believed that their supplications to the gods provided and protected them as a community. Like others, they believed they were a chosen people. They believed that their society was the first that had been created and that it was the fairest of all societies in the world.

The Japanese looked to guidance in fortune telling techniques that had been used by the Chinese, such as following the cracks in heated bones. Their rituals became known as *Shinto*, meaning *Way of Life*, or *Way of the Gods*. Like the gods of others, these gods were forces of nature: gods of mountain and valley, field and stream, fire and water, wind and rain, floods and earthquakes – all that was beautiful and terrible in nature. That which seemed to contain a superior godly power, the Japanese called *kami*, similar to the Polynesian word *mana*.

Like others, the Japanese perceived as gods those great warriors and scholars who had died after having made a special contribution to their society. Everyone believed his family had an ancestor who had become a god. Everyone saw him or herself as descendant of gods. It was believed that every Japanese was descended from the Sun Goddess, the common people more distantly than ruling families and aristocrats.

Like others, before the Japanese had writing they had professional reciters, and they passed stories from generation to generation. Among these stories was that of the Creation. According to the Japanese version of the Creation, matter and spirit were not in the beginning separate and distinct. In the beginning heaven and earth were joined in a chaotic mass. The purest and clear elements of the mass rose and became the sky and heaven, and the more gross and heavy elements of the mass sank and became earth. In heaven, of course, were the gods, and from the gross and heavy elements of earth came humanity. One of the gods was banished to earth and became a god of the ocean. Here began humanity's ancestral tie with the gods. The god of the ocean married a farmer's daughter. The son from this union, with a retinue of attendant gods, appeared on Mount Takachiho in southern Kyushu. This was the god Ninigi, grandfather of the legendary first ruler, Jimmu. Ninigi built a palace at the foot of the mountain, and then he

married a younger daughter of the local ruler. The eldest daughter of
the local ruler was outraged at being bypassed in favor of her younger
sister, and she cursed humankind. And here was the Japanese version of
the fall of humanity: the outraged daughter announced that if she had
been chosen instead of her sister, children fathered by Ninigi would
have lived forever, but now she was putting a curse on his offspring,
and humans forever after would grow and die like the flowers.

The Rise of the Yamato Family

Being basically similar to other peoples, territorial conflicts among
the Japanese arose between their local rulers – sometime before the
300s. Some rulers gained in territory and some lost. Greater territory
among the winners meant more wealth, more available manpower,
bigger armies and more military strength. Competition among the kingdoms created insecurity, which inspired the belief in growth for the
sake of power. A ruler had to keep growing or he would be swallowed
by one who did. So among the rulers were attempts to expand, which
produced more war.

One of the successful of the ruling families was the Yamato. The
Yamato family dominated the agriculturally productive plain near what
are now the cities of Osaka and Kyoto. Those rulers whom the Yamato
conquered remained as local lords and paid tribute to the Yamato ruler.
The local lords were watched by Yamato subordinates – territorial
administrators, technical experts and scribes. A hierarchy of authority
had developed, with the local lords remaining proud of their family and
conscious of their own powers and potential powers – as had local
nobles elsewhere.

The Yamato rulers called themselves *Tenno*, or heavenly ruler, and
the Yamato family believed that they were directly descended from
Jimmu and the gods and that they ruled by divine right. The Yamato
spread their rule northward onto the Kanto plain, including Tokyo, and
to most other areas populated by Japanese.

In the early years of Yamato glory, China was falling apart, with
Hsiung-nu chieftains taking over in northern China and southern China
remaining split from the north. Colonies of Chinese in Korea were
dispersed, and some of them fled to Japan, as did some from northern
China. And among them were people of education, increasing Yamato
contact with Chinese culture.

In the late 300s, Paekche's army overran Koguryo, and on the
southern coast of Korea a new kingdom emerged: Silla. The Yamato
spread their rule to the southern coast of Korea, to an enclave they
called Mimana. Soon the Korean kingdoms of Paekche and Silla were
paying the Yamato tribute. Now, more Koreans moved to Japan:

weavers, smiths, irrigation experts, and teachers of Chinese writing and Chinese arts. And from the Asian continent came more ideas: on Chinese law, medicine, science and social and political organization.

In the 400s, Japan built more complex irrigation systems. By the 500s, Yamato emperors had raised various families to a position of responsibility over specific matters, such as the military, supervision of religion, technological projects and over territorial administration. Yamato rule was moving toward a Chinese-style bureaucratic state. And in the mid-500s would come the Buddhism that had recently been adopted by Koguryo and Paekche.

CHAPTER 29

THE AMERICAS, AFRICA, SOUTHEAST ASIA AND OCEANIA

THE AMERICAS

Studies of people of the Americas indicate that hunting and gathering as a way of life was at times more healthful and pleasant than farming. With hunting and gathering there might be occasional leisure. But with the ups and downs in the availability of game there was also occasional hunger. Births keeping up with the availability of food also kept people on the verge of hunger. It was likely hunger that motivated people to take up the additional work of growing food. Births probably kept up with this additional food, until communities were absolutely dependent on farming. And this dependence left them more vulnerable than hunters and gatherers had been – hunters and gatherers never having been threatened by drought or insect infestations. By increasing their numbers during their transition from hunters and gatherers to farmers, people had defeated the purpose of growing more food. Examination of the skeletal bones of early farmers in the Americas indicate episodes of malnutrition during childhood, and the average height of early farming populations have been estimated to be shorter than that of hunters and gatherers, probably because of worsening nutrition and a reduction of protein in the diet. And with the denser populations of agricultural communities came unsanitary conditions and the spread of diseases rare among hunters and gatherers.

The Olmecs and Teotihuacán

From before 5000 BC, people living in the Tehuacán Valley around what is now Mexico City, were collecting wild plants such as beans and amaranth, which they ate with chili peppers. They lived out-of-doors except during the rainy season, when they lived in caves. They ground seeds for food, and they grew squash. Between the years 5000 and 3500 BC, these people grew beans and an early variety of corn, which, with their squash, amounted to about ten percent of their food, the rest of their food having been acquired through hunting, fishing and gathering plants. In this span of 1500 years, their population increased ten times. After 3000 BC, they began to grow around thirty percent of what they ate, roughly half of this corn from a larger cob, and they began to raise turkeys. And by around 2500 they were growing much of what they ate, and they built villages next to their fields, with small pit houses similar to those of Shang civilization.

People in the Tehuacán Valley and elsewhere in Mexico did not have goats, sheep or cattle to domesticate. The bison, antelope and mountain sheep of North America had not migrated south into Mexico. They had no animal to pull a plow, so people farming in central Mexico continued using the digging stick. They planted in the spring and harvested in the fall. Their beans and corn did not provide enough protein for young children or lactating women, and, needing game to supplement their diets, in the summer they hunted jackrabbits and in the winter they hunted the deer that descended then from the hills.

The beginnings of civilization in the Americas came around 1200 BC – a mere three or four hundred years after the beginnings of Shang civilization. It came in the lowlands in what is now southern Mexico, along the humid coast of the Gulf of Mexico, centered at a site now called San Lorenzo. There a people belonging to a culture called Olmec had a well-developed agriculture and a denser population than other societies in the Americas. They had monumental architecture. They lived in villages. The Olmecs commanded a trading network to other peoples, and they dominated peoples as far south as Tazumal, in what is now El Salvador, and as far northwest as Chalcatzingo. San Lorenzo was destroyed around 900 BC, and the center of the Olmecs shifted fifty miles northeast to La Venta. The Olmecs worshiped a variety of gods, among them a god of fire, god of corn, god of rain, and a god in the form of a feathered serpent. Their major god took the form of a jaguar and a human infant. Traces of Olmec culture survived into modern times in the form of their monumental sculpture, small jade carvings and complex pottery. And they left behind evidence of mathematics and writing – created without influence from European or Asian civilizations.

Eventually, like other civilizations the Olmecs weakened themselves with civil war. And sometime around AD 100 they were overwhelmed by people from the Tehuacán Valley. The center of this expanding power was the city of Teotihuacán, about thirty miles northeast of the center of what is now Mexico City – a place that had transformed itself from villages to city. By AD 500, Teotihuacan would be the most populous city in the world, a city with a population of more than 125,000.

Teotihuacán's power was trade, mainly control of obsidian, a dark green volcanic glass found on mountains – a material that could be cut and pierced. And Teotihuacán produced and traded highly polished ceramic figures. With no horses or wheeled transport, it took traders months of walking to cross Teotihuacán's area of influence, and Teotihuacán tied together its trading region with relay points and regional distributors. These settlements became cities, and Teotihuacán's culture spread with its goods, north into what is now the United States and south into what is now Guatemala.

In becoming a state power, Teotihuacán formalized its religion. It had numerous temples, and two pyramids faced with stone dedicated to the sun and moon. Its main god was Quetzalcoatl, a feathered snake god of fertility. Amid its religious monuments it had stone carvings depicting people in song and at play amid gardens, streams and fountains – an imagined paradise.

The Maya

The Maya lived in and around the tropical rain forests of what are now Guatemala and Belize, in small villages of one or two room houses. They worked plots of land, taking food from trees and other wild plants. They hunted and trapped small animals. They made pots from clay, and they made string, cloth, ropes and nets. It is estimated that around 900 BC they migrated into the lowlands on what is now called the Yucatán Peninsula. And there they grew beans, maize, chili peppers and squash.

Trade linked the villages of the Maya. And by the first century AD, their settlements grew larger and more complex. Becoming more developed in their agriculture and denser in population, villages grew into a few cities. Commerce advanced with networks of trade and communication stretching across the Mayan world and to Teotihuacan. Mayan cities emerged as political, economic and social focal points for surrounding villages and farmsteads. By the mid-200s AD, Mayan cities were more numerous, with temples on tall platforms and their buildings of limestone or coral with plaster interiors. One of the cities, Tikal, was twenty-five miles wide, and its population grew to around 10,000, with numerous temples and shrines, ceremonial centers, residences, ball courts and plazas.

Private property, a division of wealth and class differences had arisen. The Maya cities – like the cities of Greece before Philip V – never united. The rulers of cities lived in elaborately decorated palaces, and they were buried in grand tombs. And like rulers in Eurasia and Japan, Mayan rulers spoke of themselves as having ties with the divine, derived through their ancestry.

In their time and until the arrival of the Europeans, the Maya were the only people in the Americas with a system of writing. With their

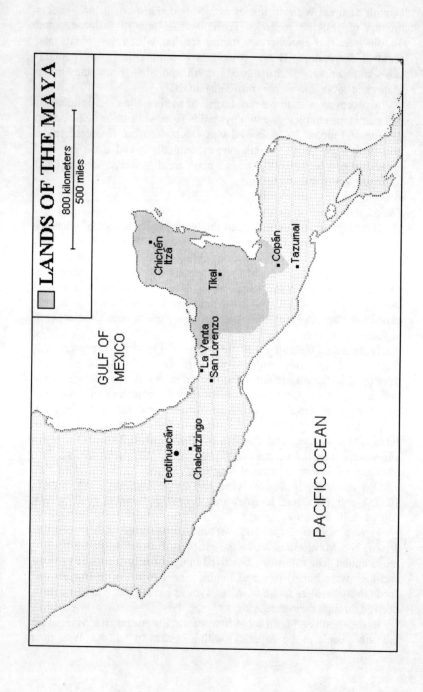

LANDS OF THE MAYA

800 kilometers
500 miles

GULF OF
MEXICO

Chichén
Itzá

Tikal

Copán

Tazumal

La Venta
San Lorenzo

Teotihuacán

Chalcatzingo

PACIFIC OCEAN

writing they had a coherent set of beliefs about the nature of the universe. Their writing was pictorial representation and abstract symbols, without an alphabet. And, as in other early civilizations, writing was limited to their elite, some of whom wrote poetry. But mainly their writing was about religious matters.

Their religion was astrology, and Mayan astrologist-astronomers created a sophisticated calendar system, improving their astronomy with detailed observations and an extensive use of mathematics. The Maya counted in the same manner as the Olmecs: a dot for one and a bar for five. And the Maya had a zero as a mathematical symbol. With naked-eye astronomy, the Maya plotted the movement of the moon and the planet Mercury. The Maya saw the universe as turning in cycles, and from these cycles and the positions of stars they interpreted the past and made prophesies. They believed that in the distant past, cycles had brought cataclysms and rebirths and that eventually cycles would bring another cataclysm in which all the world's inhabitants would perish.

They believed, as do astrologers today, that the date of one's birth determines one's fate and is a guide to what actions one should take – not mindful that fate and willful action were incompatible. They believed in omens, that omens were of crucial importance in determin-ing the suitability and probable outcome of a proposed action.

These cycles of time were, of course, controlled by the gods, and the Maya saw gods in great variety. They saw the sun, moon and the planet Venus as deities, each with its own place in the cyclical calendar of life. Each of their gods was a patron of a unit of time. Each of these gods came into prominence and power over life as its unit of time reappeared.

The Maya believed that a great tree supported each quarter of the heavens, that the earth was flat and the heavens layered, with specific deities and celestial bodies occupying each of heaven's thirteen tiers. The place where the spirits of the dead mingled – the underworld – had nine levels, each with its own lord of darkness. The Maya saw most of their deities as having four pairs of opposing attributes: male and female, old and young, good and evil, celestial and underworld.

To demonstrate piety, appease their gods and guarantee fertility and cosmic order, priests performed an elaborate cycle of rituals and ceremonies, including torture and human sacrifice. Human blood was thought to nourish the gods and thought necessary to achieve contact with the gods. The Maya thought the blood of kings especially in demand by the gods. And Maya rulers, as the intermediaries between their people and the gods, had to undergo a ritual bloodletting and self-torture.

North of Mexico

The earliest known people in North America belonged to a stone-age culture called Clovis, which dates back to around 9500 BC. These people lived on the plains and gathered food, fished and hunted with a flexible wooden spear, with a stone tip, which they threw with a lever for increased speed, similar to that used in modern times by Australian aborigines and Eskimos. They hunted ice-age mammals such as the now extinct mammoth, mastodon and specie of bison.

Soon, in what are now Illinois, Alabama and Missouri, people lived in caves and foraged for food. West of the Rocky Mountains, people gathered wild seeds and plants. And those in the west who lived in oak forests learned how to take the acid out of acorns and turn it into flour. Where they found fish in rivers they invented traps and nets for catching the fish, and they made smoking equipment for preserving their catch. And gradually these people learned to assist plants in their growth. They began burning undesirable vegetation to make more room for the growth of that which they could eat and to create meadows for herds of deer.

As early as 2500 BC, some people in what is now the United States were cultivating plants that most likely came from Mexico: gourds and squash. By around 800 BC, small-scale farming was taking place in the Ohio River valley. In the southwest, corn was grown as early as 500 BC. By 300 BC, people in what is now called British Columbia were living a settled life in villages and houses built of wood, and they were moving about in dugout canoes, living off of fish, shellfish and game. Also from around 300 BC, in Ohio and Illinois a people who came to be known as the Hopewell were living in towns and growing corn, beans and squash – plants that apparently came from Mexico. Hopewell trade extended across great portions of the continent. Hopewell culture spread as far west as the Rocky Mountains. One town of Hopewell culture was built where the Missouri and Mississippi rivers meet. Another was built at what is now Macon, Georgia.

By AD 100, the Anasazi people – the ancestors of the Navaho – moved into Arizona and began farming. And by the 400s AD in the plains of what is now the United States, the bow and arrow were replacing the spear, the bow and arrow giving hunters and warriors a greater striking distance. People were content with their animistic religion. The horse, which would give tribes a greater mobility, had not yet arrived – as it would with the Europeans. And with plenty of game to hunt and rivers to fish, larger-scale farming and its corresponding rise in population had not developed.

South America

On the continent of South America, people were hunting game and gathering wild foods as early as 9000 BC. The population density was very sparse, but it grew denser in the Andes mountains, where, in what is now Peru, people were growing plants many centuries before 3200 BC. It was around 3200 BC that corn is believed to have reached the northern Andes, in what is now Ecuador. By 2500 BC, people in the central Andes were also growing potatoes and raising llamas. Also by 2500 BC, people in a narrow strip of lowland along the coast of Peru were weaving cotton into textiles and eating fish, shellfish, sea mammals, beans and squash. As many as a hundred village communities existed along this coast, each with a few hundred people, and between 2500 and 1750 BC the population along this coast increased substantially. Then, for some unknown reason, these coastal towns were abandoned, people migrating inland and to higher elevations alongside rivers.

By around 1200 BC, the population increased around Lake Titicaca in the Andes to the extent that towns had appeared. Here people herded llamas, grew potatoes and fished. After 500 BC, complex societies occupied the southern coast of Ecuador and southern highlands in Colombia. In the 200s AD a civilization in Peru arose called Mochica that had armies ruled by warrior-priests. It would be a thousand years or more before the Inca civilization and empire would rise. Meanwhile, sometime between AD 220 and 250, with more wars, the Saladoid peoples along the coast of what is now Venezuela were driven by others to Caribbean islands, where their descendants would meet Columbus, who mistook them for people of India and called them Indians.

DEVELOPMENTS IN AFRICA

By 1000 BC, people in western Africa were clearing portions of tropical forest with stone axes and planting yams, harvesting fruits and palm nuts and keeping goats. And east of central Africa's equatorial rain forest, cattle raising was being extended, with cattle raising favored in the drier areas free of the tsetse fly. Tribes that herded more than they farmed were neighbors to those who farmed more than they herded, each tribe believing that their way of life superior to the other.

Around 800 BC, the Nubians invaded and occupied upper Egypt, continuing the back and forth between the Nubians and Egyptians that had begun as early as 2100 BC. In 730 BC, the Nubians again invaded northern Egypt, and the Nubian king, Piankhi, moved his capital to Memphis and started Egypt's 25th dynasty. An Egyptianization of

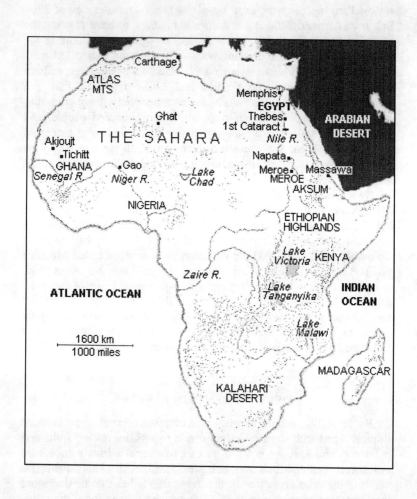

Nubian culture had begun, including the use of Egyptian writing. Egyptian became the official language of Nubian government, and gods among the Nubians acquired Egyptian names.

The Assyrians came, drove out the Nubian king, and they brought with them to Egypt the knowledge of iron making and iron tools and weapons. Iron making became common in Egypt, and it spread south along the Nile to Nubia. Soon after the Nubian kingdom acquired iron, it expanded southward, beyond desert into the wooded, rainy lands of a region called Meroe. Perhaps they were escaping from the forays of the Egyptian army, which in 593 BC sacked the city of Napata.

The region of Meroe had advantages for the Nubians: they had the Nile and Atbara rivers as barriers against the Egyptians; Meroe had an abundance of iron ore; and it had the hardwood from which charcoal could be made for smelting iron. The Nubians made iron weapons and iron tipped spears and arrows for hunting. They made iron axes, which helped them cut timber and clear land for farming, and they made iron hoes for tilling the soil.

Unlike the desert region to the north, around Meroe there were summer rains, which allowed the Nubians to extend their farming away from the rivers. They grew sorghum and millet, and away from the rivers they were able to graze cattle on wild grasses. Presumably, the increase in food production brought an increase in population, which probably helped them in conquering their neighbors. And, drawing from their expanded territory, a few Nubians grew rich trading in ivory, ebony, animal skins, ostrich feathers, perhaps gold, and slaves.

Meroe was in a good position for trade: trade passing north to Egypt stopped at Meroe, Meroe had a route to and from the Red Sea, and, on the Red Sea, trade was increasing to and from India and East Asia. Meroe became a center of iron smelting and manufacturing, and in the centuries to come it sent its iron products far and wide, including to India. And some people in India began migrating to port cities on Africa's eastern coast.

Among the Nubians, a local language replaced Egyptian, and the Nubians developed their own distinctive writing – which has never been successfully deciphered. Nubian priests saw kings and queens as having the approval of the gods, and to their pantheon of gods the Nubians added a lion god: Apedemek. Most Nubians were still farmers and fishermen and lived in mud and reed houses clustered in small rural villages, where they were ruled by minor chiefs and heads of family clans. Nubian craftsmen lived in towns, worked full time at their craft and were under less control than their counterparts in Egypt. And some Nubians wore silk from China and cotton from India.

Iron Reaches Western Africa

From about 1000 BC, iron-using Phoenicians traded along the coast of North Africa. By 800 BC they had colonies on this coast, alongside the Berbers. The Berbers had been farming, and they sold their products to the Phoenician towns, and the Phoenicians introduced the Berbers to iron. By 600 BC the Phoenician town of Carthage had grown into a formidable city-state, in part from its trade across the Sahara, with Berbers and others acting as trade intermediaries. Their means of transportation across the Sahara was the horse drawn chariot, camels not being introduced until centuries later.

By 400 BC, Carthage had established a trading settlement at Cerne on the west coast of Africa, and by now iron had traveled south to tropical areas across trade routes through small Saharan trading towns such as Akjoujt and than Tichitt. And iron was passing south across the Sahara to Ghat, Gao and perhaps to the Lake Chad region. Iron smelting appeared in what is now Nigeria, and the use of iron there improved hunting and forest farming, which may have helped to build population pressures of the Bantu speaking people there. Bantu people began migrating from this area eastward through savanna and forests.

The Soninke of Ancient Ghana

A thousand miles west of the Bantu community, just inland from the western coast and just south of the Saharan desert, an iron using state arose called Ghana – unrelated to modern Ghana. Its people were the Soninke, who might have grouped together into a state for strength against their exposure to attacks from Berber nomads to their north. With iron tools, their hunting efficiency had increased, and farmers there were able to form larger settlements. They were illiterate, but they had horses they had obtained from Saharan nomads, and they had iron swords and lances, and they seized farming and grazing land from their weaker, less organized neighbors. From about AD 200, Ghana grew as a trading power. The importation of camels to the Sahara boosted trade, and the demand for gold increased. The Soninke were midway between the source of salt in the Sahara and gold fields to their south along the Upper Senegal River, and the Soninke of Ghana acted as middlemen, passing salt to the gold producers and gold to the north.

Aksum and the Fall of Meroe

Hunters and traders from southern Arabia had crossed the Red Sea and established settlements on the coast near the Ethiopian highlands, and by 500 BC they had mixed and intermarried with the people who had been there before them. Their languages mixed, producing a language called Ge'ez. Ge'ez speakers were settled at the port town of

Massawa, through which passed trade to and from the Indian Ocean. And Ge'ez speaking traders and farmers were forming a new state, Aksum, which was taking trade away from the state of Meroe. Meroe's wealth rested on its iron industry, its agriculture and its trade. But its kings wanted more territory northward along the Nile, and they expanded to the Nile's first cataract. In 23 BC, Meroe's army raided farther north, and the Romans, who then ruled Egypt, retaliated and pushed them back as far as Napata, destroying along the way and capturing several thousand Meroeans, whom they sold as slaves. The Meroean nation continued to thrive, and it acted as a middleman for Roman trade through the Red Sea and into the Indian Ocean, but between AD 200 and 300 Meroe's trade and iron industry declined. The charcoal needed to make iron consumed trees that had been cut down faster than growth. Some scholars believe that topsoil had eroded, that lands had lost fertility and that agriculture had declined because of over-exploitation. Also, with the economic decline of the Roman Empire had come less demand for goods from Meroe, and much of what trade there was with the Roman Empire was acquired by Aksum.

By AD 300, Aksum had craftsmen who were making crystal, brass and copper luxury goods, which were being exported to Egypt and the eastern half of the Roman Empire. It was also exporting frankincense, a highly valued product used in burials and as a medicine, and myrrh, also used as medicine – products taken as sap from trees that grew in Aksum's higher elevations. By now, Aksum had irrigation and terraces for its agriculture, and Christian missionaries had come from Egypt.

As for the nation of Meroe, between AD 300 and 350 it stopped giving its kings royal burials, and the city of Meroe was abandoned. A pastoral people moved into the abandoned city. Then Aksum's king Ezana – now or soon to be a convert to Christianity – invaded. And the nation of Meroe vanished.

The Bantu and Other Developments in Eastern Africa
Around AD 200, Indonesians arrived by boat and settled in Madagascar. They brought with them a banana plant that had a higher yield than any African banana. The Asian banana was transplanted on the eastern coast of Africa, and it spread inland, improving the food supply. By now, Bantu speaking people had moved alongside hunters and gatherers in eastern Africa. They were spreading past Lake Victoria, northeast to the Indian Ocean on the coast of what is now Kenya. By AD 300, they spread to areas around Lake Tanganyika and Lake Malawi. And by AD 400 they arrived at the southern tip of the continent.

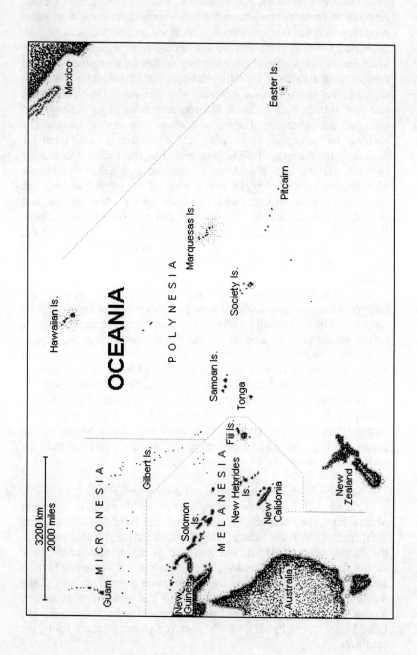

Mexico

Easter Is.

Pitcairn

Marquesas Is.

Society Is.

OCEANIA

Hawaiian Is.

P O L Y N E S I A

Samoan Is.

Tonga

Fiji Is.

Gilbert Is.

M I C R O N E S I A

New Hebrides
Is.

New
Caledonia

New
Zealand

3200 km
2000 miles

Guam

Solomon
Is.

M E L A N E S I A

New
Guinea

Australia

The Bantu mixed with local hunters and gatherers. And working with iron created a greater productivity in agriculture. More people cut into forests and settled down into villages. New, primarily agricultural communities of Bantu speaking people developed, with women working in the fields and the men hunting for meat. And the Bantu speakers traded with neighboring hunters and gatherers, the Bantu giving iron tips for their weapons in exchange for killed game, medicinal plants or as payment for herding livestock.

SOUTHEAST ASIA AND OCEANIA

Hunters and gatherers had been in Southeast Asia at least since 8000 BC, some of them the ancestors of today's Australian aborigines. Mixing with these people were newcomers, and some of them, in addition to hunting and gathering, using tools of stone and wood, began growing crops to supplement their supply of food. Perhaps like others who began growing food they were responding to increases in their numbers. At least some among them responded to this growth in numbers by choosing to migrate in their dugout canoes to nearby uninhabited islands.

People in small boats had sailed from China to Taiwan as early as 4000 BC. In the 2000s, people in small boats had begun populating islands in the Philippines. It was around 2000 BC, give or take a century or two, that people who were ancestral to today's Malays began migrating across the ocean from the Asian mainland to what are called Indonesian islands, bringing with them the cultivation of rice and domesticated animals. Around this time a people called Mon migrated across land, from central Asia over mountain passes, to the southern tip of Burma, where they began growing rice. And it was around 2000 BC that people left the Mulucca Islands (now a part of Indonesia) and migrated to uninhabited islands farther east, north of Australia.

Across generations, a chain of migrations of people with chickens, dogs and pigs occurred from islands north of Australia eastward, the seafaring made easier by predictable monsoon and trade winds. Around the year 1800, dark-skinned migrants in magnificent little boats reached islands of Micronesia, some 1500 miles south of Japan and west of the Philippines. By around 1300 BC, people from Micronesia had sailed southeast into Melanesia, including the Solomon and the Fiji islands. From around 1200 BC, brown skinned people began migrating into Polynesia: to the Tonga and Samoan islands. These people were a mix of black and Asian, and perhaps the proto-white that made up the Ainu of Japan. They were animists like other pre-civilized peoples. And by

1200 BC they and the Micronesians and Melanesians had pottery, breadfruit, the coconut, sugar cane and taro, all originally from Asia. It was around 100 BC in what is now southern Burma that urbanization began in Southeast Asia. Beginning around AD 200 a kingdom or kingdoms that the Chinese called Funan arose in what is now southern Cambodia – kingdoms that were influenced by India and where Hinduism and Buddhism coexisted peacefully.

Around AD 300, Samoans ventured across 2000 miles (3200 km) of ocean to the Marquesas Islands, on twin-hulled sailing craft sixty feet in length. And in such boats the Polynesians migrated from the Marquesas to the Society Islands, including Tahiti, and to Easter Island (Rapa Nui) farther east. By AD 500 they had not yet arrived in New Zealand or the Hawaiian Islands, places blessed by isolation from the passing imperial armies such as the Hebrews and other peoples of West Asia had to suffer. But the Polynesians spoiled their paradise by warring against each other. Hawaiians would be among those who did so, as did the Maori who moved into New Zealand. The people of Easter Island divided into two opposing camps and decimated each other in a bloody civil war. And eventually the isolation of the Pacific islanders was disturbed by the coming of Europeans and new diseases against which they had weak or no immunity.

CHAPTER 30

POST-ANTIQUITY CONTINUITIES

HISTORICAL TRENDS IN JAPAN

Buddhism arrived in Japan in the 500s, imported by a noble family, the Soga, and opposed by the noble family in charge of Shinto: the Nakatomi. A newly arrived Buddhist statue was blamed for an epidemic of disease, but the panic and hostility toward Buddhism was short lived, and Buddhism survived and spread. It spread also to the royal Yamato family, into which the Soga family was marrying its daughters. And for the Yamato emperors, the Buddha became a god called upon to protect the Japanese nation – as had happened in some other lands. Like other major religions, Buddhism had developed associations with state power.

Whatever the religion, historical trends in earthly matters continued. In the 500s, Japanese grew economically, the Japanese using better tools and fertilizer and more draft animals in agriculture, and they used better tools in the crafts. And Japan grew in population, to two or three million. Better roads and a fleet of ships facilitated trade. Horses and fighting equipment continued to pour into Japan from the Asian continent. And with the increase in population and power came efforts at expansion. The Japanese expanded against indigenous people, including the Ainu, who were overrun and pushed farther north. And the horses and new equipment were used in wars that erupted between ruling Yamato family factions struggling over succession for power.

The Nakatomi family rose in power to become Japan's second most influential family, its family head serving as Prime Minister and occasionally as a regent, and its daughters married into the most influential family: the royal Yamato family. The Nakatomi still supplied the state with Shinto's high priest, but the Nakatomi family followed the worldwide trend toward integration: it had acquired a tolerance of Buddhism. Buddhist doctrine and Japan's native Shinto religion were influencing each other, while Shinto continued to be practiced for official state functions.

In Japan, the wealthy continued to gain while prosperity for the majority of Japanese declined. Land reforms were circumvented or postponed. Aristocratic officials, the nobility and Buddhist monasteries continued to absorb lands, making less and less land available to common people – repeating what had occurred in China – while land reclamation favored the wealthy, including Buddhist monasteries, who could afford the costs involved.

Buddhists continued to see the material world as illusory, holding that reality was one's own consciousness and the cosmological harmony under the Universal Buddha. Nevertheless, Buddhism in Japan continued its accommodation with the material world. The Buddhists founded charity hospitals, free clinics, orphanages, old people's homes and free lodging houses. And appreciating the disturbing realities of the material world, Buddhist monasteries had their own armies, and they were unscrupulous in making alliances. As readers of Chinese, some Buddhist monks became expert in administration and technical matters, such as engineering, and these monks served Japan much as the Latin reading clergy would serve Medieval Europe.

While a succession of emperors became more interested in Buddhist study than in ruling and some emperors withdrew to monasteries, the power of the Yamato family declined, which meant a rise in power of the Nakatomi – who had changed their name to Fujiwara. They continued to run the ministries and the daily court ceremonies and to exercise power as regents, and they had come to own much land. Nakatomi tolerance of the growth of the big estates allowed Japan to continue a drift into feudalism similar to developments in Europe. On the lands of the Buddhist monasteries and the court nobles, hierarchies had formed. At the top were the landlords or Buddhist proprietors. Under them were the managers. Under the managers were those who did the actual farming. Those who did the farming often hired seasonal help. And, on these estates, ties to the landlord became stronger than were ties to the central government.

Conflicts arose between the Fujiwara and clans distantly related to the royal Yamato family. These clans expanded their estates, recruited disenchanted peasants, workers and soldiers and defied central authority, much as the great lords of the estates in France defied the authority of its monarchs. In Japan, private armies, obligations and rewards for service to powerful families accompanied a weakened central government. With a weakened central government, clans warred against each other for territory. And the great estates, Buddhist and otherwise, continued to employ men who went about with weapons as a private police or private army to exercise local control – men called Samurai.

CHINA, ITS BUDDHISTS, TAOISTS AND CONFUCIANS

In the 500s, Hsiung-nu chieftains ruled in northern China, and in keeping with one of the oldest trends in civilization, in AD 577 one of the chieftains unified the area. Then in 580, the new ruler of the north died, under suspicious circumstances, and his son-in-law, Yang Chien, or the Duke of Sui, came to the fore. Yang Chien was a tough Buddhist soldier from an aristocratic Chinese family that had inter-married with Hsiung-nu rulers. He proclaimed that heavenly and earthly signs indicated that those who had been ruling in the north had lost the mandate of heaven and that he, Yang Chien, being virtuous and wise, had been designated by heaven as the rightful successor. However virtuous, Yang Chien managed to have fifty-nine members of the ruling family murdered. And he adopted the royal name of Wen-ti – the first of a dynasty whose family name was Sui.

Wen-ti united all of China, and his dynasty began the greatest public works in China's history, including the building of its Grand Canal system, which brought the north and south closer together and made the north and south more interdependent. Prosperity returned during the Sui dynasty. But after little more than two decades, Sui rule came crashing down. Hostility to the Sui had arisen from those the Sui had worked too hard on public works projects. The Sui dynasty had ruined itself economically and militarily with its wars against Korea. And finally with flooding and famine came rebellion. It was more of the same rise and fall of dynasties that had passed before.

In 618, a new family came to power. This was the T'ang dynasty, which united China once again. Like the sons of David, the sons of the founding emperor, Kao-tzu, fought each other over who would succeed their father. Under the winner, T'ai-tsung (627-49), China reached a height in power equal to what it was during the Han dynasty. Under T'ai-tsung came what is called the T'ang renaissance and an "era of good government." The T'ang family had the family name of Li and they took pride in claiming descent from Lao-tzu, who had the same family name. Tang emperors, including Tai-tsung, expressed a bond with Taoism. The melding that was much a part of development in the world was alive in China. Tai-tsung was eclectic, showing favor to Buddhism and also Confucianism. However ugly the conflict with his brothers that brought him to power, he tried to model his rule after the Confucian ideal of strong, able, energetic, and moral leadership. He surrounded himself with an able team of Confucian advisors, and he tried to develop and refine the policies begun by his father.

Tai-tsung tried to spread his authority evenly across China so that no one region gained dominance. He instituted a scholarship system to encourage learning. He extended the examination system for government service, which in theory were open to all. But most who entered the bureaucracy were the sons of upper level officials or those promoted from clerical service or the military guard. The poor had little hope of entry into governmental service other than in the military. Tai-tsung had begun what would become a highly educated court elite, while authority delegated by the emperor remained almost exclusively among those of aristocratic birth.

Like his father, Tai-tsung kept the bureaucracy at a minimum to control expenses. Prosperity allowed him to provide tax relief for areas that suffered natural disasters. He maintained reserves of grain to combat famines, and the abundance of reserve grain allowed low prices. Under Tai-tsung, prosperity increased, as did trade with Central Asia and India. China's contacts extended to Persia and Constantinople – powers that traded embassies with his regime. The capital city filled with many foreign merchants and a variety of foreign communities. Ethnic variety spread to various Chinese cities, which had – in addition to Buddhist monasteries – Zoroastrian, Manichaean and Christian* temples. And China reached a new height in prestige and the arts.

Tai-tsung strengthened his military, building it with peasant recruits who were encouraged to enlist for a lifetime military service. He put them into garrison communities scattered about the country and especially near the northern frontier, each garrison with land that the soldiers worked on, making them self-supporting. He rotated the units between duty along the Great Wall, duty as imperial guards in the capital, and duty on active campaigns. And he supplemented the militia forces with an elite corps of old-line Tang supporters and their heirs, whose job was to defend the capital.

Wars against the peoples on China's frontiers were still considered worthwhile or necessary, and Tai-tsung took advantage of a split among the leadership of Turkish peoples in Mongolia that occurred in 630. That year he defeated them, becoming recognized by them as their sovereign, the Heavenly Khan. In 639, he launched a drive westward – against the wishes of his Confucian advisor. And in 647-48, his armies subjugated what is now called Turkestan, parts of Afghanistan and Tibet. He had extended Chinese power farther west than it had been in the great days of the Han Dynasty. And, in 648, an expedition of Chinese crossed the Himalayan Mountains into northeastern India. But he was unable to subdue the Koreans, who inflicted heavy losses upon his armies.

At the age of forty-nine Tai-tsung died, and the weakness of dynastic rule manifested itself as Tai-tsung was succeeded by an ineffective son, Kao-tsung. The civil disorder common with dynastic

---

* These Christians were believers in the christology of Nestorius, the Patriarch of Constantinople deposed in the fifth century.

rule returned. Advisors to Kao-tsung brought a concubine, Wu-huo, out of retirement in a Buddhist monastery, and in 655 Wu-huo managed to have Kao-tsung's wife deposed and herself elevated to her place. She ruled as Empress Wu. She had the deposed empress and another rival murder-ed. From 657 to 659 she exiled, murdered and drove to suicide elder ministers remaining from Tai-tsung's reign, and in the coming decades she continued to purge real or imagined enemies. In 659 a new genealogy and family ranking was written, which placed Wu-huo's family on top. She continued to draw her most solid support from people from the lower level of the bureaucracy, mainly those who benefited from her power, while others in high places feared her whims.

Despite all this brutality, Empress Wu was inclined toward Buddhism. She surrounded herself with a succession of holy men or monks. Empress Wu changed state rituals to serve her religious views and her concern with symbolism. She had a temple erected that was described as the Supreme Shrine to Heaven and called the "Hall of Light." She ordered a Buddhist temple set up in every prefecture, where monks were obliged to claim that she was an incarnation of Buddha. All significant members of the family into which she had married – the T'angs – were either executed or banished, eliminating rival claims to the throne.

As can be seen in looking at antiquity, authoritarian rule by family dynasty was in the long run unstable, and it had its short runs of stability. Expressing the stability side of the equation, Empress Wu ruled for fifty years. But in old age, she lost control of events at court. Court bureaucrats had grown tired of the incompetence of those with whom she had surrounded herself, and in 705 they forced her to resign in favor of an acceptable surviving member of the T'ang royal family: Chung-tsung.

Chung-tsung had a domineering wife, Empress Wei, and perhaps encouraged by the example of Empress Wu, she tried to rule. Chung-tsung died in 710, perhaps murdered by the empress. It was a time of natural disasters and economic strain. Empress Wei sold public offices and neglected civic affairs. The court, including the palace army, re-belled, overthrew Empress Wei and elevated to the throne the brother of Chung-tsung: Jui-tsung. The sister of Jui-tsung tried to dominate her brother. Then in 713 another coup brought to power Hsüan-tsung, who allowed Jui-tsung to retire, and the sister committed suicide. Conflicts at court would continue, making good material for historical novelists and playwrights, but Shakespeare was to stay focused on the bloody intrigues of European royalty.

Demise for the T'angs and China's Buddhists

In the early 700s, the prosperity and grandeur of the T'ang period peaked. Generals and eunuchs were involved in court politics, and China descended into another of its ruinous civil wars, with plunder, destruction and the abandoning of farms. Buddhism had already begun to lose intellectual momentum, and now it declined as the T'ang emperor, Wu-tsung, a Taoist, closed forty thousand Buddhist shrines and temples. Two hundred and sixty thousand monks and nuns returned to lay life. Vast acreage of Buddhism's monastic lands were confiscated and sold and their slaves freed. And Buddhism's rival, Confucianism, backed by state officials, enjoyed a renewed intellectual life.

Taoism had adopted alchemy and magical applications of potions as a means of achieving immortality, or, short of that, improving one's health. Confucianists viewed Taoism as a popular religion, and despised it. They associated chemistry and medicine with Taoism and the work of charlatans. Confucianists and other intellectuals viewed the study of chemistry and medicine as Taoist nonsense, and this discouraged science in China. The Confucianists and other intellectuals in China advocated devotion only to literature and history. Despite their reputation for wisdom and their devotion to the interest of society as a whole, the Confucianists were contributing to what would become China's backwardness vis-à-vis the West. And another major contribution in this direction was on the way.

In 907, after more rebellions, invasions and a decimated population, the T'ang dynasty went the way of previous dynasties, and it was followed by a succession of short-lived dynasties. In 960, came the Sung dynasty, and more invasions. China had coats of mail and steel weapons, and it had gunpowder, but these were used mainly as a part of popular religion, influenced by Taoism – gunpowder being used in firecrackers to scare away evil spirits. And the T'ang rulers were weak in determination. Its military was under the command of its Confucian bureaucracy, which tended toward pacifism. Confucians saw soldiers as the lowest of all groups of people. The Ju-chen – the ancestors of China's future rulers, the Manchus – took control of northeastern China. In 1215, Genghis Khan and his Mongol army made it over the Great Wall to plunder and kill. And China's population fell precipitously.

Eventually, the Mongols learned that more could be gained from conquest than plunder. They learned there was benefit in settling down and taxing the conquered. In 1276, Genghis Khan's grandson, Kublai Khan extended Mongol rule into southern China. And like those who invaded India, the conquerors of China, including Kublai Khan, adopted the ways of those they had conquered. Kublai Khan not only conquered the whole of China; he won the hearts of the people as he established law and order. And there was mixing between Chinese and the Mongols, mainly Mongol soldiers taking Chinese wives.

By 1360, the population of China had grown back to 80 million – still short of the 100 million from before the Mongol invasion. The Mongol military had grown soft in peacetime, and, by 1368, the Mongol princes were driven from China, an effort led at first by a poor peasant who had risen as a warlord. This peasant founded a new dynasty: the Ming. Prosperity returned, and the population of China soon doubled to around 160 million.

The Ming rulers tried to establish a political rule modeled after the Han and T'ang dynasties, but they also maintained some features of Mongol rule. They were concerned about Mongol resurgence, and they made an effort to maintain their military strength. They established Chinese garrisons at strategic points and created a hereditary military caste of soldiers who sustained themselves by farming. Exports grew, and Chinese merchants prospered. And in the early 1400s the Chinese again had a superior navy. This included an estimated 317 ships, some 440 feet long and 180 feet wide, ships with four to nine masts up to 90 feet high, with as many as fifty cabins and crews as large as five hundred – ships that traveled to India, the Persian Gulf and the east coast of Africa. In the great age of sail that was dawning around the globe, Ming China was in the lead, but China did not press its advantage. Influential Confucian scholar-officials saw trade and profit as ignoble. China chose instead to concentrate on maintaining power at home. Shipbuilding became restricted to small vessels, and trade abroad was restricted. Trade – the key to prosperity – would decline in China as trade in Europe was increasing, along with technology and science.

CONSTANTINOPLE, PERSIA AND ISLAM

The spread of religion continued to be influenced by military power. Islam was to spread from Arabia because of a weakened Persia and a weakened eastern half of the Roman Empire.

Despite their unity with Jehovah, Christian emperors continued to preside over decline, and Christianity's intolerance continued to contribute to that weakness. The Christian emperor at Constantinople, Justinian, began his reign, in 527, outlawing paganism, including academies in Athens, among them Plato's old academy (which had been teaching a mixture of Christian mysticism and neo-Platonism). Justinian drove philosophers into exile. Fearing that God might bring famine against his sinful subjects, he outlawed blasphemy, sacrilege and homosexuality. He persecuted the Samaritans. And he put restrictions on the religious and civil freedoms of Jews, including outlawing the Talmud, which he described as puerile fabrications, insulting and blasphemous.

Justinian wished to do God's work, and to prepare for the Second Coming of Christ he wanted to unify what he saw as God's empire under the Catholic creed. He wanted to liberate the western half of the empire and North Africa from the Arian Christians.

In North Africa, the Vandals had grown soft in the one hundred years since they had conquered that area. And the Vandals were weaker vis-à-vis the power of Constantinople for not having allying themselves with their fellow Arian Christians, the Ostrogoths of Italy. And they were weaker too for not having absorbed or integrated more with of the local populations of North Africa, including the Catholics, towards whom they remained hostile. In December 533, Justinian's general, Belisarius, invaded North Africa and expelled the Vandals from their power base around Numidia. And despite the Christianity of the Vandals, Belisarius, made slaves of the defeated Vandal warriors.

Continuing his drive to reunite the Roman Empire and to defeat Arianism, Justinian moved next against the Ostrogoths in Italy, Belisarius' troops landing at Naples in 536. A war had begun for the West that was to last the rest of the century. Food production and distribution in Italy diminished and many died of hunger. Belisarius captured Rome. The Ostrogoths besieged Rome. Amid the devastation there, Cannibalism appeared. Taking advantage of Italy's vulnerability, the Christianized Franks, Catholic like Justinian, invaded Italy in search of plunder, slaughtering along the way. Naval superiority helped Justinian win control over much of Italy by 540, but his generals took advantage of their power to plunder the Italians, which turned many Italians against Justinian's rule. The Ostrogoth army advanced, besieging Rome again, leaving the city in ruins. In 551, Justinian's navy allowed his forces to obtain the upper hand again. The following year, Justinian's forces also seized two strongholds on the southern coast of Spain. And in 554 his armies finally defeated the Ostrogoths. The costly and painful enterprise was over, but Italy was in utter ruin. Violence again had settled a question of worship. The Pope and Catholicism now reigned supreme in Rome and central Italy – which they saw as the work of God. The Trinity version of Christianity had won, as Arianism in Italy had come to an end – until after the Reformation centuries later. Change, which had been a part of religion since the Sumerians, would eventually bring back Arianism and the variety that was a part of civilization.

Justinian against the Persians

Justinian's conquest of Italy did not leave Constantinople stronger. Before Justinian's victory in Italy, he remained troubled by renewed hostilities with the Persians. Justinian sent armies against the attempts at expansion by the Sassanid king, Khosro, who had been rebuilding his empire while Constantinople was busy at war in Italy. While warring against Khosro, Constantinople was cursed by bubonic plague, a plague as devastating if not worse than Europe's Black Death during the fourteenth century. At its peak, Constantinople lost up to ten thousand a day to the disease. The plague ravaged Constantinople's empire, with no one understanding why God would punish his servant Justinian, or how to control such plagues.

While fighting elsewhere, Justinian had been unable to defend his empire's northern frontier along the Danube River. After the war in Italy ended, a worn-out Constantinople remained vulnerable to assaults, from both the north and east. From the north came Slavic tribes. From the steppes just west of the Don River came Bulgarians, who ravaged towns and farms north of Constantinople. Then came an Asiatic people called Avars. The Avars had dominated the Gobi desert and Outer Mongolia, including the Turkish peoples there. The Turks revolted and drove the Avars out of Mongolia and westward, and the Avars invaded Constantinople's empire and settled in the Danube region, leaving a portion of their people between the Caspian and Black Seas and the Caucasus Mountains.

By the time of Justinian's death in 565, much of the wealth of the Eastern Empire had been spent. Justinian's successor, Justin II, was unable to prevent a Germanic people called Lombards from moving in and taking power in Italy. All that Justinian had fought for there was lost. The Lombards took control of territory between Ravenna and Rome and taxed those in Italy whom they had conquered. Catholics led by the Bishop of Rome were able to keep control of Rome and some surrounding territory, the Pope remaining the political leader of this area and the symbol of Roman tradition. Soon the usual assimilation between invaders and Romans took place, the Lombards adopting Latin as their language and Catholicism as their religion. And in Spain the Arian Visigoths also converted to Catholicism.

Persia and Constantinople Grow Weaker

While Justin II was losing Italy to the Lombards, that portion of Armenia governed by Persia revolted and requested help from Constantinople. This and other events led Justin II to invade the Sassanian Empire, opening another expensive and wasteful war between Constantinople and Persia and that engendered hatred and atrocities on both sides. The Persians repelled Justin's forces and invaded Constantinople's empire, capturing numerous cities, including Dara in November 573, the fall of which is said to have caused Justin to lose his sanity.

Ascending the throne in Constantinople was Maurice, a former soldier who had risen to the rank of commander and had displayed valor in warfare. As emperor, he waged war against advancing Avars. He was in desperate need of soldiers, but he received little support from his Christian subjects, thousands of whom entered monasteries to escape from the danger posed by the Avars. Maurice forbade the monasteries to receive new members until the danger from the Avars was over, and monks reacted by clamoring for Maurice's fall. And Maurice increased dislike for himself by persecuting Monophysite (non-trinity) Christians, including exiling Monophysite bishops, some of whom had been popular in their diocese.

The Avar advance was defeated, but Maurice's frugality angered his soldiers, whose pay he had reduced and who were obliged to pay for their own arms and clothing. Maurice's frugality also angered his civilian subjects, who had enjoyed the benefits of government spending and had no use for the asceticism in Maurice that they admired in Jesus Christ. In 602, Maurice's army mutinied in response to his order to winter beyond the Danube River. The rebellious army marched on Constantinople and seized the city. Civilians joined the revolt, aiming their hostilities against the wealthy as well as Maurice. The rebel army's leader, Phocas, sided with the civilians against the wealthy, and he became emperor. Maurice's five sons were butchered, one at a time in front of him, while Maurice prayed. Then Maurice was beheaded. The six heads were hung up as a spectacle for the people of Constantinople, and the bodies of Maurice and his sons were cast into the sea. The empress, Constantina, and her three daughters, and many of the aristocracy, were also slain, some of them after being tortured. In Rome, Pope Gregory joyfully applauded Maurice's demise, and he described the coming to power of Phocas as the work of Providence. He asked his Catholics to pray that Phocas might be strengthened against all his enemies.

Instead, Phocas was a disaster for Constantinople. Maurice had befriended the Sassanian king, Khosro II. Both had been committed to peace between the two empires. But now Khosro went to war against Phocas, claiming he was avenging the death of Maurice. The Avars were advancing toward Noricum, seizing agricultural lands without resistance, and they were joined by the Slavs. Phocas agreed to an attempt to buy-off the Avars with an increase in tribute payments, and he allowed Khosro's forces to advance into Constantinople's empire. In 610, Phocas was deposed by Heraclius, who had arrived with an army from North Africa. Phocas put up no struggle, and he died on the scaffold.

In 614, Khosro's forces invaded Constantinople's empire and sacked Jerusalem, massacring 90,000 Christians, burning to the ground many Christian churches and carrying Christian relics back to Persia, and that year the Avars sacked cities in Greece. Khosro's forces invaded and occupied Egypt in 616, meeting little resistance. The following year, the Avars reached the suburbs of Constantinople, while the Slavs continued spreading southward, large numbers of them settling in Greece. In 623, Slavs ravaged the island of Crete. In 626, Avars, supported by Slavs, attacked the walls of Constantinople. The Persians also attacked Constantinople. The Patriarch of Constantinople, Sergius, led a courageous defense of the city and defeated the Avars. The Avars withdrew to Pannonia and never again threatened Constantinople. And Khosro withdrew his forces from around the city.

Emperor Heraclius then organized a counterattack against the Persians. With his superior navy, he sailed into the Black Sea and around the Persian army, the elite of which was luxuriating in Asia Minor and Egypt. Behind Persia's armies, Heraclius' troops disembark-ed and began marching toward Persia's capital, Ctesiphon, destroying what they could along the way, while the Persians fled before them, breaking dikes to create floods in order to slow their progress. It was the end of the great canal works in Mesopotamia. The neglected canals would fill with silt, and the dikes would remain difficult and expensive to repair.

Khosro II fled Ctesiphon. His armies remained undefeated and angry in their humiliation, and his generals, who had often smarted from his insults, joined with the old rivals of the monarchy, the nobles, and they imprisoned Khosro, fed him bread and water and killed eighteen of his sons before his eyes. Then the generals, encouraged by Khosro's remaining son, Sheroye – who sided with the generals – executed Khosro.

Sheroye was crowned king, and he took the name Kavad II. In 630, Kavad signed a peace treaty with Constantinople that returned Egypt, Palestine, Asia Minor and western Mesopotamia to Constantinople. Meanwhile, a plague was now killing thousands in Persia, and Kavad did not survive. His seven-year-old son, Ardashir III, was proclaimed ruler. A general killed the boy and usurped the throne. In turn, the general's own soldiers killed him and dragged his dead body through the streets of Ctesiphon.

While the Persian Empire was already exhausted by twenty-six years of war, anarchy swept the land. And in the coming four years, nine men tried to gain Persia's throne, and all disappeared. Cities and provinces declared their independence. A weakened Persia was now more vulnerable to the growing power of the Arabs, who were strengthened by their new unity under a faith called Islam.

The Rise of Islam

The biggest development in politics and religion after AD 500 was the rise of Islam. Islam spread across Arabia, and because of the weakness of the Roman and Persian empires, it spread across North Africa and into Spain and it spread through West Asia, including Persia and what is now Afghanistan. It also spread southward into Africa. And with India weakened by divisions, Muslim armies spread Islam there with their conquests. Islam spread into Southeast Asia. And Islamic armies extended Islam into the Balkan states, including what is now called Bosnia.

All this, including the rise of Islam, according to Islamic scholars, was an act of God rather than a development rising out of historical and geographical circumstances. But this is the same as Jews and Christians seeing divine intervention as fundamental to their faith. Islamic scholars are consistent, for the belief in divine intervention is incompatible with the vision of new religions rising from social change, however much some wish to believe both.

One of the earlier worldly developments that some may wish to associate with the rise of Islam is the contact between Arabia and the Roman and Persian empires. By AD 500 Arab tribes had moved to the borders of these empires. Also, in Arabia were the descendants of Jewish refugees from centuries before. And by AD 500 Christian missionaries had arrived in Arabia. Before the rise of Islam, the entire Arabian province of Najran had been Christian, and Christianity was established superficially in various other centers of trade. The founder of Islam, Muhammad, had been familiar with Christianity through his wife's cousin, who was a Christian. Muhammad was familiar with the New Testament of the Christians and the Old Testament of the Jews, and with Zoroastrianism. And in his travels as a merchant he had become familiar with Arabia's monotheistic Hanif movement, which was neither Jewish nor Christian but had discarded polytheism and rejected worshipping objects called idols.

Muhammad acquired the habit of some Christian ascetics in Syria and occasionally withdrew to meditate in a cave outside of his hometown, Mecca. And there, the Muslim's believe, at around forty years of age, he began hearing messages from God, via the angel Gabriel. The messages told Muhammad that God (Allah in Arabic) had chosen him to preach the truth, that he was to be God's final and foremost messenger, superseding the message proclaimed by Jesus. Muhammad decided that the great god he knew as Allah was also Jehovah. He claimed to foresee the end of the world, when the dead would be awakened and all would be judged according to their deeds and sent to either paradise or eternal flames. The core of his belief became the coming of this day of judgement, which he claimed to fear.

Muhammad saw his faith as monotheistic, like the Hanes and the Jews. And like the Christians he saw the world between God and humanity as occupied by angels and demons. He saw the future as in the hands of God, and he felt it was his duty to convert people to what he called "submission to the will of God" and to warn his fellow Meccans of God's Final Judgment.

Around 613, Muhammad began preaching publicly in Mecca – where tribal ties were weakening, where the old values of simplicity and sharing were diminishing and some were turning to the new vices of gambling and drunkenness. Muhammad failed to win but a few adherents among the inhabitants of Mecca, and his tribe's elders thought him insane. But Mecca was a holy city visited by pilgrims, and pilgrims from the town of Yathrib – soon to be called Medina – were more favorably impressed by Muhammad, and Muhammad made converts among them and followed them back to Yathrib.

Muhammad found Yathrib without any stable authority among its Arabs, and he became a respected authority in town. Yathrib had a large Jewish community, and Muhammad approached its leaders, claiming to be a leader of Judaism. These Jews saw his knowledge of Judaism as an absurd muddle, and they rejected him. Until then, Muhammad and his followers had been bowing toward Jerusalem. Now, an angered Muhammad and his movement began bowing toward Mecca.

Muhammad's followers suffered from poverty, and some of them resorted to their tradition of raiding the caravans that traveled from Mecca to Syria. Muhammad began leading these raids, excusing them on the injustice of poverty and describing the raids as part of a holy war (Jihad) against the ruler of Mecca for their having rejected his teaching. Energized by religious fervor, a sense of unity and the prospect of booty, his men fought well. His success in warfare bred more success and more converts in Yathrib. Once again, success in violence was influencing faith.

Muhammad's troops slaughtered Jews in Yathrib, drove the survivors out and took over their property. They waged war against Muhammad's major rival, Mecca, and eventually Muhammad conquered the city. The holy shrine in Mecca, called the Kaaba, was turned from a place of worship for the traditional polytheist religion of the Arabs into a holy place of worship for Islam. Mecca's rich were obliged to donate to the well being of its poor. Muhammad added Mecca's army to his own and conquered the rest of Arabia. And, as in other parts of the world, with conquest went conversion.

Muhammad spoke of his followers as a chosen people with special access to heaven. He demanded taxes from those who had not converted to Islam, and, in exchange, he offered them protection – as rulers had for millennia before him. He proclaimed that Jews and Christians were "people of the book" and were to be tolerated, to be guaranteed the right to practice their religion and to have security in their goods and property.

Muhammad wanted none of the pomp and display that had been adopted by potentates of some other religions. He asked no service from a slave that he had time and strength to do for himself. He saw himself as fallible. He proclaimed no power to perform miracles and no power to foretell the future. He was, he claimed, just a messenger that had received truth from God.

Neither an ascetic nor a celibate, Muhammad lived his last two years without harsh words about life. He and his most devout followers remained married and had children. He continued the custom of polygamy – which had helped compensate for the high death rate among Arabs and a diminished ability to conceive because of Arabia's hot climate. But perhaps as a move against the rich, he limited the number of wives a man could have to four, except for himself, allowing himself thirteen.

In his final two years of life, Muhammad worked at governing his political and religious order. All he is known to have said about succession was his pronouncements that after him would be no other prophets. Instead of creating a new political structure, he focused on what he wished to be the character of his followers. Muhammad called on them to have courage, to practice charity and hospitality and to be modest in their bearing. Now in power, he was discomforted by quarrelsome speech. "Subdue thy voice," he is said to have written. "The harshest of all voices is that of an ass."

Arabic Imperialism

After Muhammad's death in 632, Islam became imperialistic. This began with raids across the border into Persia – an alternative to raiding "the faithful" in Arabia. In Egypt and Palestine, Islamic warriors were victorious against Constantinople's mercenary armies, and their conquests were made easier if not possible because local peoples hated Constantinople for its oppressions and religious intolerance. And they found they the Arabs more tolerant. In Egypt and Palestine, Islam allowed local autonomy. In Mesopotamia, Islamic armies conquered without much difficulty.

Conquests were a source of wealth. And motivated by gain in wealth, the Arabs invaded Persia. But the conquest of Persia was hard – the fighting there against people not conquered by empire and willing to fight to defend their homeland.

Muhammad had been born into an authoritarian age. His rule had been authoritarian, as was rule that followed him. And, as had occurred

with other authoritarian rule, there were problems of succession. First
was the squabble over who was to succeed Muhammad. The new
rulers, called caliphs (a short form of Commander of the Faithful) were
from a clan called the Ummayads. The first two caliphs, Abu Bakr and
Umar I, were frugal and modest leaders, but their clan began enriching
themselves. Opposition to the Ummayads developed. Islam fell to that
which had plagued other societies, assassination and civil war. And
with civil war, Islam split into two factions: Sunni and Shi'ite. The
winners were the Ummayads, who were Sunni.

Ummayad rule had shifted its rule from Medina to Damascus. The
Syrian army helped hold the Islamic empire together. And helping to
hold the empire together was the Ummayads making alliances and
pleasing tribes through the offerings of autonomy. And with an end to
civil war, Islamic armies were able to conquer North Africa to the Strait
of Gibraltar and then Spain.

The spread of Islam did not bring security for the Ummayads. Its
Syrian army was tired of war, and dissatisfaction in Persia led to an
uprising and civil war. The Ummayads were overthrown, butchered and
replaced by the Abbasids, and the capital shifted again, to what had
been a small Christian village on the west bank of the Tigris river:
Baghdad.

Persians had helped overthrow the Ummayads, and their culture
acquired great influence if not dominance in Islamic rule. Among the
conquered Persians many had converted to Islam, and there had been
extensive integration between the conquering Arabs and the converted
Persians – despite efforts by the caliphs to prevent it. Islam was governed by the trends extant during antiquity. Diffusion ruled. And Arabic
Islam had been swallowed by its empire much as had Rome by its
empire.

The Empire's Golden Age
Like Rome's empire, Islam's empire had its golden age with a rise
in trade. Islam had no scorn for the merchant as did Christians and
Confucians – Muhammad himself having been a merchant. From
Alexandria in Egypt, goods were transported by sea, with the commerce of Islam's followers – Moslems – dominating the Mediterranean
Sea. Caravans connected Baghdad to India, the Chinese frontier, Aden,
Syria and Egypt. At Baghdad, the river was 750 feet wide, with docks,
wharves and hundred of ships: warships, trading vessels including
Chinese junks, and pleasure boats. It was the time fictionalized in the
adventures of Sinbad the Sailor in *A Thousand and One Nights*, drawn
from reports of actual voyages made by Muslim merchants. In the holy
cities of Medina and Mecca asceticism remained an ideal, but luxury
and the pursuit of pleasure were fact.

Islam had no ecclesiastical councils or hierarchy of priests as did Christianity, and in Islam diversity developed. From 750 to 900 works on science and theoretical mechanics were translated into Arabic. New universities arose in Basra, Kufa, Cairo, Toledo and Cordoba. The Muslims were interested in Aristotle's systematic biological observations. Medical doctors drew from classical Greek medical texts, and they expanded medical research. Works on astronomy from India were translated into Arabic. For West Asia and Europe, Arabic became the language of science. Arabic texts on astronomy, chemistry and mathematics remained influential until the rise of science centuries later in Europe.

Contact with the works of Plato, Aristotle and the neo-Platonists stimulated thinking and influenced religious belief among Muslims. Muslims who were exposed to Hellenistic ideas wished for reconciliation between the reason in these works and the writing of the Koran, and they called for an interpretation of the Koran that was allegorical. In lectures at colleges and in mosques the new rationalism won a voice. Study of the Koran included studying its symbolism and ambiguities, which gave rise to applications of grammar and definitions (lexicography) and the creation of an Islamic theology.

Among the variation that developed within Islam was the same kind of mysticism and religious ecstasy that had risen elsewhere. This was the Sufist movement, whose followers believed in a divine love through an immediate and direct personal union with God – without need of interpretation or intellectuality. Sufism spread among the Shi'ites, and it took a variety of forms. Some Sufists became pantheists. Some denounced the luxury of the caliphs and merchants, and they proposed a return to the simplicity of the first caliphs: Abu Bakr and Umar I. Sufists wanted no intermediaries between themselves and God. And some of them saw ritual at the mosques as an obstacle to losing earthly awareness and to achieving a blissful unity with God.

The tradition of passing stories orally from generation to generation had continued among the Arabs, and oral teachings called *Hadith* emerged. These carried tales of Muhammad having performed miracles, including his feeding a multitude from food hardly adequate for one man, of Muhammad touching the udders of dry goats and the goats then giving milk, of Muhammad healing the sick with his touch, and his exorcising demons. And there was the story of Muhammad loving his enemies. At first, these tales appeared absurd to other Muslims, but with time, Hadith became accepted by orthodox Muslims, Islam changing much as had Buddhism and other religions.

The Empire Disintegrates
The Islamic Empire was too vast for control from any one center. Rule by force alone was too much of a burden for the caliph at Baghdad. Disrespect for centralized authority grew. There were various rebel-lions, including another rebellion by Shi'ites. This began with some among the Shi'ites believing that the world and all its injustices were about to end and that a great religious leader, Ubayd Allah, the *Mahdi*, would soon appear and rule. The Shi'ites in Arabia, with the help of Bedouins, established an independent state, and from there the rebellion spread through Palestine and into Syria. The great Islamic Empire was, like empires before, disintegrating.

In Baghdad, power fell into the hands of the Turkish generals who had been hired by the Caliph, much as Germans had been hired by Rome. After the year 908, palace intrigues developed, followed by a quick succession of turnovers in power. In 909, a Shi'ite rebellion spread from Mauritania eastward to Numidia. In Numidia, the *Mahdi*, Ubayd Allah, was freed from prison and declared caliph. From his base in North Africa, Ubayd Allah extended his rule to Sicily and then to Egypt, where the Abbasids had never been popular, and Cairo became his new capital. There were now three caliphs: one in Cairo, one in Cordoba Spain, and one at Baghdad. Ubayd Allah began a dynasty called the Fatimids, claiming descent from Muhammad's daughter Fatima. During the first half of the 900s, the Fatimids expanded their empire into Palestine and southern Syria and into that part of Arabia known as the Hijaz, which included Medina and Mecca.

The Turkish generals in Baghdad lost power, not to an Abbasid resurgence but to a Shi'ite family called the Buwayhids from just south of the Caspian Sea. The Buwayhids occupied Baghdad in 945. They kept the Abbasids as figureheads, and the Abbasids clung to what prestige they could as the nominal successors of Muhammad – until 1258, when the Mongols arrived.

CHANGE IN INDIA AND THE DEMISE OF BUDDHISM

India proved that empire was not a requisite for prosperity. After the fall of the empire of the Guptas, prosperity continued there – unlike Western Europe after the fall of Rome. In India, village, town and regional governments performed the duties that had been performed by imperial bureaucrats. Local governments controlled taxation, kept the peace and settled disputes. Some villages were perhaps ruled by oligarchies, but some were democratic, divided into electoral units and with rules for governing debate at public assemblies. Local governing included communal organizations, and included worker's guilds, which regulated working hours and wages and had the power to enforce their decisions with fines – organizations that were to last into the nineteenth century. .

Hinduism remained a religion with much variety. It remained less organized and less concerned with heresy than Christianity, and it developed new trends. As early as the 500s a movement called *Bhakti* – meaning devotion – took hold among some of the poor of southern India. Bhakti worshipers rejected Brahmin scholarship and ritual Brahmin sacrifices – in which the poor, for lack of time as well as money, could not participate. The Bhakti movement was more of the move away from religion by aristocrats that had taken place during antiquity. Being of lower caste, the Bhakti movement rejected, or at least minimized, caste. And the followers of Bhakti followed the same impulse of humility and devotion to God as the Christians. They sang of their adoration and love for a generous, merciful, supreme God. And in the centuries to come, the Bhakti movement would grow and sweep through northern India, attracting many away from Buddhism and Jainism. As in Christianity, Bhakti had some upper class devotees. About sixty outstanding followers and evangelists within the Bhakti movement were made saints: one woman, and fifty-nine men who had been peasants, washers, potters, fishers and hunters.

In the early 600s came a revival of empire, as a ruler named Harsha expanded across much of northern India. In his later years, Harsha favored Buddhism, and he tried to emulate the Buddhist monarch Asoka. He made the killing of any creature or the eating of any flesh within his empire a capital offense – with possibility of a pardon. But his efforts came to naught when his empire fell apart after his death. And after Harsha's rule, Buddhism declined further. In places, Buddhism diffused with Hinduism and lost its identity – similar to paganism in Christianized Europe. And where Buddhism was absorbed into the worship of Vishnu, Buddha became an incarnation of Vishnu.

Meanwhile, the Hindu god Krishna had become a god apart from Vishnu, and rivalry between Vishnu worship and Shiva worship became a wider division within Hinduism. The worshipers of Shiva tended to be more rural and more extreme in their devotion. They were seen by worshippers of Vishnu as country folk, and the worshippers of Shiva were more concerned with sin – similar to the rural prophets who disliked what they found in Israel. The worshippers of Shiva were especially concerned with what they saw as the sin of carnality. They were awed and afraid of Shiva and saw Shiva as a god of asceticism, death and destruction. The worshipers of Vishnu, on the other hand, tended to be more urbane and moderate. Some of them derided the followers of Shiva as phallus worshipers – Shiva worshippers being closer to fertility worship. The priests of Vishnu worship tended to be Brahmins and saw their god Vishnu as both a god of love and a protector of order. They thought themselves more dignified than the priests of Shiva, and they saw themselves as maintaining Hinduism's noble tradition.

In the 600s, twelve worshipers of Vishnu began wandering about in southern India singing songs in praise of Vishnu. They too were uninterested in intellectual arguments. They believed that worldly enjoyments were ultimately unprofitable and that only a loving surrender to Vishnu was durably satisfying. They sang in temples, villages and markets. The number of singers grew to hundreds or more. A book of four thousand of their songs was to be compiled in the 900s and would become the prayer book called the Tamil Veda.

Also in the 600s, some Hindus, including worshipers of Vinshu, became involved in secret rituals called Tantrism. While acknowledging the supreme authority of the Vedas, the Tantrists brought offerings of fruit and sweets to the icons of their gods. Their rituals celebrated the power of motherhood. They saw birth as the highest form of divine strength. The emotionalism and worship of birth of some Tantrist groups led them to group sexual intercourse, traditionally opposed by the Brahmins. Tantrists believed that sexual intercourse was a route to inner peace and harmony. They believed in liberated bodies in contrast to the asceticism and rigidities of those who practiced yoga. And some Tantrists ate meat and drank alcohol – also opposed by Brahmin tradition.

The biggest change in India came with the arrival of Islamic warriors. A land that was very much divided, India was vulnerable to attack from outside. From Afghanistan, in the late 900s, Muslim warriors began making raids into northwestern India. In the century that followed, Islamic rulers held territory in India's northwest, and by the 1300s their rule stretched across the whole of India. What was left of Buddhist worship in India suffered a final blow, the Muslims seeing Buddhism as debased idol worship. But Hinduism was too widespread for the Muslims to exterminate. Islam moved in alongside Hinduism, melding with it in places but creating a conflict that was to last into modern times.

AFRICA

After AD 500, Aksum expanded into Nubia and across the Red Sea to the Arabian Peninsula and what is now Yemen. That same century, Monophysite Christian monks reached Aksum and began a monastic tradition there. While Aksum was enjoying its glory it was denuding its lands by cutting down trees and over-exploiting its soil. Its trade declined as trade across the Indian Ocean was diverted from the Red Sea. Aksum was driven out of Yemen and the Arabian Peninsula, and by the 700s it was a diminished power. In the 800s, its capital was moved inland, into the Ethiopian Highlands, and Aksum became an isolated outpost of Christianity, largely agricultural and controlled by a landed aristocracy.

By the 700s, the whole of North Africa was conquered by Islam, and the Muslims increased their trade into sub-Saharan Africa. The Soninke kings of ancient Ghana had been receiving their wealth from taxing the trade in gold as it passed through their territory, and when they lost their hold on the gold trade their power declined. The Soninke of Ghana had no writing and records of their own, and it would be from the Arabs that the modern world would learn of ancient Ghana and the Soninke. Also, Ghana's agricultural land had become worn and less able to support as many people as before. By AD 1050, a Muslim empire extended from the Strait of Gibraltar south to ancient Ghana. Ghana's kings converted to Islam. Berber Muslims moved into the area with their herds and overgrazed its lands. And in small groups, the Soninke moved away and settled elsewhere.

With the demise of Ghana, another empire arose nearby in western Africa: Mali. This empire stretched from the Atlantic coast around the Senegal and Gambia rivers eastward over 1300 miles to Timbuktu and Gao. Mali was literate insofar as it employed Muslim scribes at the court of its kings. Like empires in Europe and Asia, Mali kings kept local kings in place as their agents. The gold of western Africa, at Bure, was a source of wealth for Mali, but trade in food was a source of greater wealth, Mali growing sorghum, millet and rice. Mali reached its peak in international fame and in fortune in the 1300s. Thereafter Mali went the way of empires before it: eventually weak and incompetent kings inherited power, dynastic struggles occurred, and incursions were made by armies against Mali's weakened center of power.

In the 1500s, Muslim conquests of the remains of the empire of Mali created a Muslim empire called Songhay – from the Senegal and Niger rivers northward and stretching over a thousand miles east and west. To the south of the Songhay Empire, the kingdom of the Congo had arisen in the 1400s, near where the Zaire River emptied into the Atlantic. Here prosperous farming communities were united under a single king. They had craftsmen in metals and weaving and a developed trade.

Meanwhile, Muslim traders looking for opportunity had moved south along Africa's eastern coast. The Somali coast became an important Muslim settlement with trade contacts from across the Indian Ocean. Muslim merchants also made themselves dominant in what is now the Sudan. Where Muslims went in eastern Africa, intermarriages occurred between them and local blacks. Also in eastern Africa, cattle raising and cereal farming spread. And many societies of hunters and gatherers integrated with the cattle raising and agricultural societies around them.

Traders on the eastern coast of Africa, many of them blacks, profited from a rise in trade with Asia. Coastal African towns exported gold and ivory – the ivory of the African elephant more in demand than the harder ivory of the Indian elephant. And from India they imported silks, cottons and glassware.

In the 1300s, communities in what is now the Katanga region of Zaire were united into a kingdom of farmers, fishermen and crafts people. They traded in dry fish and products of metal, including iron. To the southeast – about 180 miles from the eastern coast – was Zimbabwe, the center of the state of Shona. Here, cattle raising was important, and so too was trade, largely in gold and ivory. Between 1300 and 1450, this trade made Zimbabwe the richest state on Africa's eastern coast. But Zimbabwe was abandoned around 1450, after timber, grazing areas and farmlands had become exhausted and trade had shifted northward.

In the late 1400s the Portuguese began colonizing points along Africa's Atlantic coastline – and in the early 1500s on the east coast, in what would be called Mozambique. The Portuguese exiled about 2,000 Jewish children to island of São Tomé. They sent missionaries to what is now Angola, and there they converted to Christianity an heir to local rule, who in 1506 became King Afonso I. To no avail the king protested the slave trade in which Christians were participating, in collusion with black slave traders. Afonso acquiesced and, dependent on Portuguese soldiers and guns, he launched wars of conquest inland that included taking whomever could be captured for sale.

ENGLAND, FROM PAGAN, ANGLO-SAXON CHIEFTAINS TO THE CENTER OF WORLD TRADE

In the 500s, more Anglo-Saxons invaded England. They warred their way westward up the Themes River, looking for more land to cultivate, taking lowlands and leaving less desirable lands in the hills to the native, Celtic Britons. The Anglo-Saxons moved inland also at England's narrow neck in the north, along the Humbler River and its tributaries. The Britons suffered heavy losses. Entire communities were massacred. Britons again fled into the hills, and they fled to Wales and to Ireland. Some Britons were sold into slavery – Pope Gregory finding English boys on the slave market in Rome.

In eastern England, the native Celts disappeared along with Roman institutions. The Celts survived in the west of England, where the names of rivers remained Celtic. They survived around Cornwall in southwestern England, in Wales, and Celts remained in the hilly lands

of Scotland, where they had driven out those few Anglo-Saxons who
had invaded there. Ireland remained Celtic, and divided among
numerous petty kingdoms. And where the Celts survived so too did
Christianity, especially in Ireland, where Catholic scholarship continued to flourish.

Trade resumed between these kingdoms and the continent, and with
this communication, the king of Kent, Ethelbert, married a Catholic
princess from Paris, a descendant of Clovis. Ethelbert allowed her to
bring with her to Kent a Catholic bishop – while Pope Gregory in
Rome was hoping to begin a drive to make England Christian once
again. Ethelbert was converted, which gave Christianity a prestige
among his subjects. Pope Gregory urged Ethelbert to destroy the
temples of rival religions. Then Gregory had second thoughts. He
advised that the pagan temples be left standing if they were well built,
that the idols in the temples be destroyed but that the temples be
converted to Christian churches, leaving the local people with their
customary places of worship. Gregory thought that local people could
be more easily converted if they were left with their customary sacrifices of oxen and their festivals. Thus in England the Saxon's spring
festival of the goddess Eostre would become the Christian Easter, and
the Christian missionaries would take the Saxon mid-winter festival of
Yule and identify it with the celebration of Jesus Christ's birth.

In the 600s, missionaries from Ireland evangelized across England.
Some Anglo-Saxons exposed to the Christian evangelists accepted
Jehovah as another god to be included into their pantheon of gods, but
getting Anglo-Saxons to adopt Christianity's intolerance and to
abandon and smash the images of their other gods was more difficult.
The missionaries were helped by scriptural support of monarchy and
Christianity's monotheism. Monotheism was better suited to monarchy
than a religion with many gods and numerous local shrines, and some
of England's Anglo-Saxon kings were attracted by the power of one
god supporting the king.

Catholicism spread across England, but the power rivalry between
kings remained, and it put England on the same course toward
unification that had been common among earlier civilizations. Christians again fought against Christians, as well as against pagans, until
one kingdom, Mercia, emerged as the dominant power in England.

The English language was developing out of German. And an
Anglo-Saxon named Bede, born in 673, became the foremost scholar of
his time. He was educated in monasteries and ordained as a priest in
703. He devoted his life to teaching theology, Hebrew, Greek and Latin
and to writing. He wrote forty works, in Latin: Biblical commentaries,
homilies, treatises on grammar, math, science and theology. The most
important of these was the *Ecclesiastical History of the English Nation*,

completed in 731. He specified his sources, sought first hand evidence, and he quoted pertinent and available documents. "I would not," he wrote, "that my children should read a lie." It was Bede who started dating from Jesus rather than from the times that kings ruled. Wars, meanwhile, remained incessant in England, through Bede's century, and the next. And, in the late 700s, Vikings began raiding England. The Vikings were responding to an increase in their population. They ventured out with swords and battle-axes as pirates, and they found little or no resistance to their assaults, which encouraged more and bigger invasions. In England their raids eventually extended to conquest at points. They struck in Scotland, and they overran Ireland.

The Viking attacks subsided and came to an end. Anglo-Saxon kings remained in power in England, but in government they were weak and poorly organized, and their political backwardness contributed to military weakness. The Anglo-Saxons had not yet learned to fight on horseback. Then in the eleventh century, at Hastings, came the invasion of England by the Normans – offspring of Vikings who had settled in France. The battle of Hastings had little affect on the majority of the Anglo-Saxons, who were peasants, but it resulted in the demise of the Anglo-Saxon nobility, who either died in battle or were deposed from their lands and made serfs. Clergy from Gaul replaced Anglo-Saxon bishops and abbots. And for four decades the Normans treated everything Anglo-Saxon with contempt. Anglo-Saxon art was destroyed, and the Anglo-Saxon language became a peasant dialect.

Eventually, trade picked up between England and the European continent. Then English tradesmen benefited from the advances made in sailing technology. And with the discovery of the Americas and the rise in trade across the Atlantic Ocean, England became a great maritime power.

A large part of this trade was in slaves. Why had slavery survived through antiquity into modern times? Because people benefited from slave labor and imagined that they were superior to the slaves. It did not matter whether the sellers or owners of slaves worshipped Zeus, Jehovah or some other god. Into the 1800s religious faith would be part of the struggle against slavery, but for the time being religion was more of an accommodation to worldly matters and an effort at a state's salvation, or an effort a one's own salvation, than it was an engine of social change.

CONTINENTAL WESTERN EUROPE

Learning, literature and art suffered during the Germanic invasions that destroyed the western half of the Roman Empire. Literature suffered also from many Christians and ecclesiastics seeing books other than their Bible as heathen, pernicious or dangerous works of the devil. The only reading that the Church encouraged was the Bible – in keeping with Augustine's insistence that only the scriptures contained an authoritative account of the world and its phenomena. Under Church influence, many books were burned or not copied. The empire's great libraries were ruined. Of the works at the greatest of libraries, at Alexandria, only a small fraction survived. But works by the pagan historian Zosimus survived. And so too did the encyclopedic work by Martianus Capella, *The Seven Liberal Arts,* which was to play a role in the reawakening that came during the Middle Ages.

The advances in medicine that had come with Hippocrates and then Galen in the second century waned. Among Christians, disease was still regarded as punishment for sin, which demanded prayer and repentance. Christian hospitals remained, but vivisection was forbidden because the Church held the human body as sacred.

Roman populations in areas that were part German or who remained under the Roman nobles, continued to live under what remained of Roman law, which in Italy included a prohibition against marriage with Germans. But local people and the Germans eventually mixed, as different peoples had been doing for millennia.

The bishop of Rome, remained as head of the Church in the west, still split with the bishop of Constantinople over the issue of who had authority. In Gaul, meanwhile, Clovis left his kingdom divided among his four sons – in keeping with Frankish custom. Rather than receive revenues from taxes, the sons of Clovis continued the tradition of plunder. As had their father, they assaulted their neighbors, extending their power over Provence and Marseilles and ending what had been the kingdom of Burgundy. For the Franks, fighting remained the business of good weather, and carousing was the business of bad weather. Each spring the king's warriors set out on hunts for game or raids against some distant lord or king. Then they would go to the shrines of Christian saints, such as St. Martin, and offer their thanks for their victories and newly won treasures. For generations, the kings who were descendent from Clovis did little except pursue their pleasures, enrich themselves and their dependents and lead an occasional military expedition. They made little effort to maintain a Roman administrative system. Eventually they began collecting taxes, but taxes were so detested that if a king wished to rid himself of an official that he disliked he could send him out to collect taxes, never to hear from him again.

Gaul became divided into a number of petty kingdoms, with local aristocrats assuming as much power as they could. These aristocrats accumulated wealth and left little for the kings, and Gaul's kings became mere figureheads. The aristocratic landowners, like some of the kings, were crude, violent and unprincipled men, removed from the old tribal culture that had helped control individuals. They exercised authority as suited their passions, taking and discarding wives and concubines as they pleased and believing that they had the right to deflower a commoner's bride before he was allowed to consummate his marriage.

In Gaul, large, self-sufficient estates that had survived Roman times dominated agriculture. These estates were populated by servile workers – ninety percent of Gaul's population – and a few craftsmen. These people wore clothing of hides and rough cloth and lived in huts, rising at dawn and bedding down with the setting of the sun. They heated their homes with gathered wood or grass and cow's dung. And rarely did they have candles to light their homes.

Continuing the habit of the pagan Romans, people looked for the supernatural everywhere. In stormy skies they saw the coming and going of armies or dead or demons. They saw wars, epidemics of disease and all other ills as the work of demons. In an attempt to acquire the powers of the supernatural, they worshiped relics. For relics, people began breaking up the bodies of early saints and martyrs. And relics were widely traded – a new commerce that was a step in a restoration of trade.

The distinction between Roman and German courts was disappearing. Trials were often judged by two or three commoners under a nobleman or his representative. Eyewitnesses testified, but attempts to determine a person's innocence or guilt was made through ordeals in which God was thought to assert his powers. This involved combat between two who had come to court as parties in conflict, the court adhering to the age-old belief that God would favor the one who was in the right. Some who were on trial were thrown into water in the belief that floating to the surface was a sign of guilt (the purity of water rejecting the guilty) and that sinking was a sign of innocence. Attempts were made to prove innocence or guilt also by having the accused walk on hot coals, or by the accused putting his hand into boiling water, the court believing that if the hand healed properly it was a sign of God's favor and therefore innocence. Punishments were often less severe than they had been during the Roman republic when ties among people were stronger and violations against others were considered more horrendous.

Disintegration in Western Europe contributed to the spread of eccentricities among Christians. Some engaged in self-torture as a substitute for martyrdom. Some, including a man named Benedict, rolled naked in thorny bushes. Some joined a new monastery movement that had appeared in Italy and Gaul. These monasteries attracted Christian conservatives who tended to oppose the worldliness of the Church and the luxury with which some of the clergy lived. But in some places monasticism took on a worldly character, as people, including some who were wealthy, joined merely for a retreat and a place of quiet.

Monasteries for women – convents – appeared, which, in addition to spirituality offered women an escape from male domination and from the polygamy that was still being practiced by some nobles and German kings. The convents offered some women positions such as abbess or prioress and provided the possibility for intellectual development or training in the arts.

Thirteen monasteries were established by Benedict – who had moderated his asceticism. His monasteries had three cardinal rules: poverty, chastity and obedience. Residents were to renounce their personal possessions, commit themselves to living their entire life in his community and to obey the monastery's leader: the abbot. The monastery was to be a family based on love, and the abbot was to consult all the brethren in matters of grave concern. Members were to spend their days at labor and prayer – Benedict believing that idleness was the enemy of the soul. The Benedictine monks reclaimed drained swamps, improved soil, carved woods, worked with metal, made glass, weaved, and brewed beverages. And they wrote books and reproduced manuscripts by hand.

In the chaos and continuing wars that plagued western Europe, a few monasteries were pillaged and burned. The Benedictine monastery at Monte Casino was sacked within sixty years of its founding in 529, and twice more within the next five hundred years. But, for the most part, the Christian monasteries were havens of peace and were to become a significant cultural force through the Middle Ages.

In western Europe, trade returned slowly – as it had among the Greeks during their Dark Age. Religious festivals became medieval fairs. Northern merchants with their furs and wool came from England and Scandinavia to barter with the southern Europeans who brought wine and honey.

And there were improvements in technology: the horseshoe, stirrups, and the rigid horse collar. The horse collar permitted a horse to pull a load three or four times as great as it had with a line around its neck. A tandem harness was invented, which allowed an indefinite number of animals to be combined in pulling. And a wheeled plow was introduced.

During the reign of the Frankish king Charlemagne (771-814) agriculture production improved with the invention of the three-field system. From the middle of the 800s, trade between western Europe and the Islamic countries increased. Slaves, furs, metal products and timber went to the Islamic countries and luxury goods returned, which made the harsh life of the nobility a little more comfortable. By the

900s, Venetian and other Italian merchants had become the middlemen of this commerce. Italian towns such as Milan, Venice, Genoa and Pisa were recovering from the demise that had come to Roman cities. And north of the Alps, some German and French towns were also on the rise – among them towns such as Cologne, Mainz, Verdun and Lyons. Raiding by Vikings, Magyars and Muslims terrorized people in the 800s and 900s, but these subsided.

The use of the water wheel and windmill was imported from Islamic lands, and the works of the ancient Greeks, preserved by Muslims, crept back into Italy and France, along with universities. Christianity benefited from the growing trade and contact with Islamic lands. In the early 1100s, a devout French monk and university lecturer, Peter Abelard, claimed that doubting led to inquiry and inquiry led to wisdom. He claimed that by choosing the best among rival arguments people came to perceive truth. Influenced by Europe's recent exposure to Aristotle, he believed in dialogue as the basis of logic.

After Abelard, medieval knights were still throwing a metal tipped wooden lance in the manner of Comanche warriors. These were the times of the Crusades. But towns were growing in number and in size. In the towns, people were free from the landed lords, and freedom was taking Europe on a course leading to the Renaissance. With the Renaissance Christianity would grow, some of its adherents absorbing the developments in science. Eventually the Catholic Church would give up its support of monarchy and rule by divine right and would embrace democracy, and Christians would be a part of the increase in toleration that came with the Enlightenment. Christianity continued to be based on its devotion to Jesus Christ, but it was changing in other respects in response to historical developments.

DEVELOPMENTS IN THE AMERICAS

Maya civilization reached its peak around AD 700. As had others, the Maya grew in number – dependent, as always, on an increase in the availability of food. Maya ceremonial centers became more numerous. The Maya also expanded culturally. They developed the most extensive literature and the greatest art in the Americans to that time. The entire area as far northeast as Teotihuacan had become prosperous. But 100 to 150 years later in the southern half of Maya country, including Tikal, much of the population disappeared. Exactly why is unknown.

One suggested cause is the same kind of population pressures that disturbed the Greeks in Solon's time. A decline in food production may have appeared with the Maya rather than the increase needed to meet the growth in population. The Maya had a slash and burn agriculture, and after two to five years of cultivation, their land had to be left fallow for five to fifteen years. With agricultural fields replacing natural forest and an increase in water runoff there may have been soil erosion.

Another source of trouble for the Maya may have been an increase in mosquitos and disease, or their water ponds. Unlike the northern half of Maya country, the southern half had water ponds that were used as a source of drinking water and aquatic food, such as frogs, and there are indications that these ponds had become silted.

As indicated by skeletal remains, the southern Maya had thinner bones and were shorter in stature after their decline began – a sign of malnutrition. And these bones have more signs of diseases and dental enamel problems – another sign of insufficient nutrition.

With the diminishing supply of food came social upheaval. Trade was disrupted. Sculpture, architecture and ceramic production decayed. Perhaps the growing scarcity of good land stimulated the wars that occurred at this time. In these wars, the winners of battles captured, tortured, mutilated and sacrificed to their gods those they had defeated, creating massive killing fields, with piles of skulls. Whether the great city in central Mexico, Teotihuacan, became involved in these wars or suffered from internal strife in unknown, but around the year 750, Teotihuacan was among those cities destroyed and left in ruins. Soon Maya lands were abandoned. Abandoned cities, where the gods had been thought to dwell, became overgrown with jungle and filled with the chatter of monkeys and birds.

Around AD 1000, the northern half of Maya lands were overrun by Toltec people from Mexico. At Chichén Itzá these people built their own monuments, a great pyramid and ball court. Chichén Itzá acquired control over the northern half of what had been Maya country. Then around AD 1400 came a decline of Toltec power, and Chichén Itzá was abandoned.

Soon Vikings came to North America. They had no guns, and indigenous Americans annihilated them. Then around 1500, the Portuguese and Spaniards came with guns, and horses, and behind their guns came Christian churchmen concerned with humanity and saving souls.

Soon European colonists would land on the eastern coast of what is now the United States, and at first the so-called Indians there failed to see these migrants as a danger to their way of life. Europe had a greater density in population than did North America, similar to the greater density in population in West Asia had compared to Europe when Europe was first becoming civilized. Like the Greeks and just about everyone else, the peoples of North America had been fighting among themselves and were divided, and these divisions made them vulnerable.

The Portuguese conquered points on the eastern coast of South America. A Spaniard named Cortez confronted a tribal people called Aztecs, who had migrated into the region around Teotihuacan and had dominated neighboring, hostile peoples. As had others during antiquity, Cortez strengthened his position through alliances: he allied himself with those tribes that were hostile to the Aztecs. Then after defeating the Aztecs he defeated his allies.

The Spaniards came upon Inca civilization in Peru and seized the Inca rulers. The Spanish overran Mexico. They overran what was left of the Maya. And because of the religious nature of Mayan writings, Spanish priests burned all of it that they could find – and only four such books are known to have survived. Military power had again influenced religion.

In what is now the United States, by the time that indigenous American societies united to defend themselves and their territory it was too late. Like the Sumerians and the people of ancient Israel, they were overwhelmed – by migrations from the densely populated eastern coast and by imperial armies.

Similar to the blending that took place between the slave and the free in ancient Rome, soon the people in the Americas began to blend. And into the twenty-first century migration continued its gradual work, as it had on the Eurasian continent across ancient millennia. The days of tribal migrations were, however, over. Migration had destroyed tribes.

INDEX